NICOLAS SLONIMSKY: THE FIRST HUNDRED YEARS

Edited,
with an Introduction,
by
Richard
Kostelanetz

Joseph Darby
Assistant Editor

SCHIRMER BOOKS
An Imprint of Macmillan Publishing Company
NEW YORK

Maxwell Macmillan Canada
TORONTO

Maxwell Macmillan International
NEW YORK OXFORD SINGAPORE SYDNEY

Introduction Copyright © 1994 by Richard Kostelanetz
Text Copyright © 1994 by Schirmer Books
An Imprint of Macmillan Publishing Company

Page 393 constitutes an extension of this copyright page.

Schirmer Books
An Imprint of Macmillan Publishing Company
866 Third Avenue
New York, NY 10022

Maxwell Macmillan Canada, Inc.
1200 Eglinton Avenue East
Suite 200
Don Mills, Ontario M3C 3N1

Library of Congress Catalog Card Number: 93–26110

Printed in the United States of America

printing number
1 2 3 4 5 6 7 8 9 10

Library of Congress Cataloging-in-Publication Data
Slonimsky, Nicolas
    [Selections]
    Nicolas Slonimsky: the first hundred years/edited, with an introduction, by Richard Kostelanetz; assistant editor, Joseph Darby.
        p.   cm.
    "Biographical notes": p.
    Includes bibliographical references.
    ISBN 0–02–871845–3
    1. Music—History and criticism.   I. Kostelanetz, Richard.
II. Title.
    ML60.S645   1993
    780—dc20

                    93–26110
                       CIP
                       MN

The paper used in this publication meets the minimum requirements of American National Standard for Information Sciences—Permanence of Paper for Printed Library Materials. ANSI Z39.48–1984. ∞™

Especially for Electra

CONTENTS

Epigraphs vii

Preface ix

Biographical Notes on the Editors xi

Introduction xiii

AUTOBIOGRAPHIES

Self-Entry from Eighth Edition of *Baker's* 3

Entry from *Music Since 1900* 5

Translator's Foreword, de Schloezer's *Scriabin* 7

Preface to *51 Minitudes for Piano* 9

Paris, from *Perfect Pitch* 14

Preface to the Sixth Edition of *Baker's* 19

Entry from *Music Since 1900* 42

Charles Ives, from *Perfect Pitch* 43

Preface to the Seventh Edition of *Baker's* 45

Grossmutterakkord, from *Perfect Pitch* 54

Entry from *Music Since 1900* 58

The Age of Absurdity, from *Perfect Pitch* 59

Introduction to *Thesaurus of Scales and Melodic Patterns* 61

Self-Review of *Perfect Pitch*, from *Notes* 66

Conclusion of *Perfect Pitch* 68

HISTORIES

"Non-Acceptance of the Unfamiliar," from *Lexicon of Musical Invective* 71

"Incidental Music" from *A Thing or Two About Music* 90

Sex and the Music Librarian 95

"A Formula for Musical Eligibility," from *Music in Latin America* 99

"Electronic, Concrete and Aleatoric Music," from *The Road to Music* 101

"The Beautiful Noises," from *A Thing or Two About Music* 105

Twentieth-Century Opera Summaries (Excerpts from *Music Since 1900*) 107

"Conductorless Orchestras," from *A Thing or Two About Music*   151
Hidden History of Modern Music (Excerpts from *Music Since 1900*)   153
"Star-Spangled Stravinsky," from *A Thing or Two About Music*   168
"Songs of World War II," from *A Thing or Two About Music*   169

BIOGRAPHIES
Entries (mostly without documentation) from *Baker's*   175

CONCEPTS
Definitions (mostly from *Music Since 1900*)   307

TRANSLATIONS
Down with the Tango and Parsifal!   389
Futurist Manifesto of Aeromusic   391

EPIGRAPHS

In a recent attempt at definition, I commented to another librarian that "reference books are not meant to be read, but to be dipped into." "Except for Slonimsky," he replied.

—Ann P. Basart,
Notes (December 1986)

When Slonimsky writes about musicians, the people themselves emerge, not just what they wrote but who they were. His writing is informed by a charm and warmth and individual personality you don't find in most other contemporary dictionaries, and yet it's objective. His analysis of musical forms is invariably exact, and his critical judgment absolutely pristine. And this is true of all his subjects, whether they arrived on the scene four hundred years ago or just the day before yesterday.

—Abram Chasins,
in an interview (1986)

He has this strange pattern: he sleeps, he gets up, he sleeps some more, gets up again—all night long. At one point, around three in the morning, I woke up and came out of my room, and there he was, pacing in the living room, with a sheaf of papers in one hand and a pen in the other. "I'm writing the Bach entry," he told me. "Rewriting it entirely." And he did the same with Mozart and all the other major entries.

—Charles Amirkhanian,
in an interview (1986)

PREFACE

Not unlike other readers seriously interested in music, I have more than once consulted the indispensable compendia of Nicolas Slonimsky, and before long I began to admire them as much for style as for information. So often is the reader of Slonimsky struck by audacious vocabulary, appropriate metaphors, and witty phrases that one is persuaded to say, as one would of any major writer—he or she wouldn't write a common sentence if they could help it. Since a recent book of mine, *A Dictionary of the Avant-Gardes* (1993), is dedicated to Slonimsky as "cher maître," and, as he is reaching 100, it seemed appropriate to collect favorite *writings* into a single volume representing him at his literary best.

All of these writings are in English, which is not Slonimsky's first language but his second or third or fourth, depending upon what or how you count; because I think of him as perhaps the greatest writer on music this country has ever harbored, I did not include anything initially written in other tongues. I have excerpted from his books as well as his articles, knowing full well that I barely scraped the cream. All appear as they were. Nothing has been updated, not even to acknowledge death. I would be remiss if I did not add that, because Slonimsky has been a distinguished American writer for over a half-century, I once nominated him for a senior fellowship from the "literature" department of the National Endowment for the Arts, the grant purportedly reserved for those with over twenty-five years of commendable professional service. Reasonable though this seems, the NEA administrator replied with a request for a 100-word introduction to his work! (My nomination was not approved.)

No matter how many copies a book sells upon publication, no matter how large an advance an author receives, the only sure measure of a classic is survival; and not only has Nicolas survived, but so have his books. The fourth edition of *Music Since 1900* has recently appeared, some fifty-six years after its first publication, along with Slonimsky's fifth update of *Baker's Biographical Dictionary of Musicians*. Both have the classic's virtues of being not only indispensable but unique, mostly because no one else could do them. Though I selected and sometimes prefaced the writings in this compilation, may the same be said about all of this book's contents—no one other than Nicolas Slonimsky could have written them.

Every effort has been made to trace the ownership of all copyrighted material and to make full acknowledgment of its use. If any error or omission has occurred, it will be corrected in all future editions, provided that appropriate notification is submitted in writing to the Publisher. I am grateful to the editors of

The World & I and *Musical America*, where portions of the introduction previously appeared, to Philip Friedman of Schirmer Books for commissioning and titling this reader, to various other publishers for reprint permission, to Timothy Virkkala and Michael Ochs for delivering selections I would have otherwise missed, to Electra Yourke for her cooperation, and to cher maître for his inspiration at the beginning and best prose at the end.

R.K.
New York, 14 November 1993

BIOGRAPHICAL NOTES
ON THE EDITORS

RICHARD KOSTELANETZ has published many books of poetry, fiction, criticism, and cultural history, in addition to editing over two dozen anthologies of art, literature, criticism, and social thought. His articles on music have appeared in several sections of the *New York Times, Rolling Stone, Look, Esquire, Musical America, Musical Quarterly, Perspectives of New Music*, and other magazines. His book *On Innovative Music(ian)s* (Limelight, 1989) collects his earlier essays, mostly on the classical avant-garde tradition. Kostelanetz has produced several books devoted to John Cage and several more about avant-garde theater. As a composer, Kostelanetz has received grants from ASCAP and the National Endowment for the Arts. Three extended works of his are currently available on discs—*Invocations* (Folkways/Smithsonian, 1983), *The Gospels Abridged* (Norton Foundation/Archae, 1990), and *Americas' Game* (Curious Music, 1993). Other audiotape compositions have been commissioned and aired by radio stations around the world. He has recently been making cameraless videotapes based on his audio art and completing a second book of essays on music.

JOSEPH DARBY, assistant editor, is a doctoral candidate in musicology at the City University of New York. At the University of Illinois he did his M.M. thesis on Charles Ives's string quartets. He is also a violist and performs in the New York City area.

INTRODUCTION

It takes approximately twenty years to make an artistic curiosity out of a modernistic monstrosity; and another twenty to elevate it to a masterpiece.

—Nicolas Slonimsky,
Lexicon of Musical Invective (1953)

At a music conference in Sweden in the late 1980s, the distinguished Argentine-German composer Mauricio Kagel, in the midst of a conversation about something else, asked me, "Have you seen Nicolas Slonimsky recently? I saw him in Leningrad in May. He's ninety-four, and he travels!" Colleagues tell stories about Slonimsky's prodigious feats, and they always have; and now that he's approaching his centennial, most of the stories concern how he has recently been journeying (say to his birthplace, St. Petersburg, Russia, for his 98th birthday) and, yes, *working*.

He was born in St. Petersburg, Russia on April 27, 1894, three years to the day after Sergei Prokofiev. As Slonimsky wrote of himself, with characteristically extravagant irony, "Possessed of inordinate ambition, aggravated by the endemic intellectuality of his family of both maternal and paternal branches (novelists, revolutionary poets, literary critics, university professors, translators, chessmasters, economists, mathematicians, inventors of useless artificial languages, Hebrew scholars, speculative philosophers), he became determined to excel beyond common decency at all these doctrines."

Taking his first piano lesson in 1900, Slonimsky studied harmony and orchestration at the St. Petersburg Conservatory. After the Revolution, he became a rehearsal pianist at the Kiev Opera; from there he traveled successively to Yalta, Turkey, Bulgaria, and, eventually, Paris, where he worked as a secretary to his compatriot, the conductor Serge Koussevitzky. Finally coming to America in 1923, he held miscellaneous musical jobs, first in Rochester, then in Boston. Learning to write English, he contributed articles to Boston newspapers. He also conducted concerts of avant-garde American music, not only in the United States but in Europe. Historians credit him with presenting the world premieres of Edgard Varèse's *Ionisation* (1931) and Charles Ives's *Three Places in New England* (also in 1931, though written decades before), which rank as two of the most pioneering works in the high modernist canon. For such competence, however, there were few remunerative opportunities.

Temperamentally an unemployable free spirit, Slonimsky freelanced and house-husbanded around Boston until teaching for five semesters at Harvard, in the mid-1940s, a part-time position teaching Slavonic languages and literatures. In 1962–63, he traveled through Eastern Europe, Greece, and Israel, as he wrote, "as a lecturer in native Russian, ersatz Polish, synthetic Serbo-Croatian, Russianized Bulgarian, Latinized Rumanian, archaic Greek, passable French, and tolerable German." For the next three years, he taught music at UCLA, until put out to pasture at 73. Little did he (or anyone else) imagine that twenty years later he would receive his first Guggenheim fellowship.

The turning point of his professional career came in 1937 with the publication of his first big book, *Music Since 1900*, a tome that must be seen and held in one's hands to be believed, because there is nothing quite like it in the historiography of any art. Essentially it is a day-by-day chronology of the most important events in modern music, from 1 January 1900 to the present. There was a second edition in 1938, a third edition in 1966, a fourth in 1971, and a fifth late in 1993. In 1986 appeared a 390-page *Supplement to Music Since 1900* that continued the 1971 story in addition to correcting prior errors; it likewise reveals Slonimsky's superlative talents for stunning vocabulary and encompassing summary, usually within a single sentence:

17 February 1970. Alfred NEWMAN, native American film composer, one of the few successful writers of cinematic music who was not born in Vienna, author of nearly 300 motion picture scores which transmogrified the most marketable elements found in the symphonies of Tchaikovsky, in the piano works of Rachmaninoff, and in the operas of Wagner, dies in Hollywood at the age of sixty-eight.

That's style, at once informative and playful, allusive and opinionated, high and low prompting me to suggest that no one else ever wrote as stylishly (really, style-fully) about music, at least in English.

Given such displays of lexicographical competence, Slonimsky was by 1946 hired to edit the next five editions of Thompson's *International Cyclopedia of Music and Musicians*; in 1958, he switched to edit the more prestigious *Baker's Biographical Dictionary of Musicians*, producing a 1,855-page Fifth Edition in 1958, a 1,955-page Sixth Edition in 1978, a 2,577-page Seventh Edition in 1984, and a 2,115-page Eighth Edition in 1991, all typically done almost all by himself. No other name appears on the title page, though helpers are acknowledged in the preface. My own opinion is that no one else, in any field known to me, has writ-ten biographical entries as witty, concise, and yet full of surprising asides and obscure words, with scarce stylistic repetition, as Slonimsky.

In between, Slonimsky wrote several other books, including *Music of Latin America* (1945) and *The Road to Music* (1947)—the first a pioneering history, the second a charming introduction to basic principles—both of which are still in print. He also compiled a characteristically prodigious *Thesaurus of Scales and Melodic Patterns* (1947), a notation encyclopedia that likewise must be seen to be believed, and a *Lexicon of Musical Invective* (1952), which collects from several languages (with all translations typically by himself) "Critical Assaults on Composers Since Beethoven's Time," to quote its subtitle. Perhaps the strongest testimony to the continuing relevance of Slonimsky's books is that, including the latest editions of the encyclopedias, all but one are currently in print.

What distinguishes *Music Since 1900*, which I take to be his single most extraor-dinary book, is not only the accuracy of his prodigious research (Lord knows how he did it) but the quality of the writing, which is straightforward and yet complicated, ironic (especially in the concise plot summaries of new operas now forgotten), continually spikey (so that you come to trust his judgments) and clear (even when using arcane vocabulary), always realized within the heroic constraint of a single sentence. Its entries are, as a result, no less accessible to layman than to music professionals. One of my favorite passages portrays himself on 15 February 1938:

> While listening to the radio broadcast of Tchaikovsky's *Fourth Symphony* by the New York Philharmonic, Nicolas SLONIMSKY suddenly discovers, at 4:30 P.M., the formula for the "Grossmutterakkord," containing all twelve tones (C, B, D-flat, B-flat, D, A, E-flat, A-flat, E, G, F and G-flat, in this order) and eleven different intervals, the equidistant intervals from the central interval being inversions of one another, and the central interval, the tritone, being the inversion of itself, with even-numbered intervals forming an increasing arithmetical progression, and the odd-numbered intervals forming a decreasing arithmetical progression, with a semitone as a unit.

Were that not extravagant enough, he adds, in smaller type, these conflicting testimonials:

> I wish great prosperity and more progeny to the "Grossmutterakkord." (Paul Hindemith in a guest album of Nicolas Slonimsky, 1938)

> To the devil with the Grandmother! Let us write real music! (Sergei Prokofiev, *ibid.*)

Music Since 1900 ranks among the few compendia that can be read from beginning to end, simply for the pleasure of its prose—I know, because I've done it, more than once; in its pages is also a wealth of facts unavailable elsewhere (e.g., *23 June 1939* "By the order of the War Department in Washington, the marching cadence of the United States Army is reduced from 128 to 120 steps per minute, effective as of September 1939").

Since this (and the other encyclopedias) has gone through several editions, he's had ample opportunity to fine-tune the instrument by which the musical world knows him best. For *Since 1900* he began not with previous reference books, which he finds riddled with errors (and thus refuses to keep in his own house), but with magazines and newspapers housed in the Boston Public Library. Collecting information on 4 by 6 cards, he also wrote to composers for their scores. Dogged in his research, he wrote archivists for birth certificates and autopsy records. Thus, he has the soprano Lily Pons born in 1898, instead of the 1904 found in previous books. (He never queries journalists or musicologists, because, he says, they can be expected to consult the standard references that he has already dismissed.) As he believes in the integrity of verifiable facts and the epistemology of chronology, Slonimsky is essentially a historian, if not one of the most prodigious historians of any art. Just consider that nothing intrinsic has kept others from writing similarly chronological, comparably international histories of painting, architecture, literature, or dance. (One can imagine a publisher handing a cocky arts historian *Music Since 1900* and inviting him or her to write something comparable about another art, only to watch the prospective author's confidence melt away!)

One sideline of Slonimsky's temperament has been debunking historical myths, such as the snow that reportedly fell at W. A. Mozart's funeral. Writing to Austrian meteorological bureaus, he gained proof that the weather that day, 7 December 1791, was free of precipitation. "When I read books on music," he told me, "I became extremely irritated by the number of errors that could be easily corrected and statements that are perfectly ridiculous, such as Johannes Brahms proposing to Clara Schumann, which he never did. All you had to do was read their correspondence to see there could have never been any intimacy. Tchaikovsky never committed suicide; he died of cholera. There were physicians in Russia in 1893 who could see the baccili."

Establishing the birth of a famous musician is less problematic than noticing his or her death, especially after fame has passed. As a result, the first thing he and his secretary do each morning is compile the daily "stiff list," as he calls it. When I asked him recently about another St. Petersburg-born musician, now in his early nineties, Slonimsky replied, authoritatively, that the figure in question "was not yet a stiff." The publisher Ken Stuart, once Slonimsky's editor for *Baker's*, remembers him working around the clock to correct proofs. "He'd get really mad when people died out of alphabetical order. While working in the letter R, he'd have to go back into C." Out of such petty problems are lexicographers's nightmares made.

> *Anybody can write a good symphony—and it takes a better man to conduct it. But only you and Sam Johnson can write a good encyclopedia.*
>
> *—Charles Ives, in a letter to Slonimsky, regarding the first edition of* Music Since 1900

When we first talked at length, in 1988, the nonagenarian had come to New York to visit his daughter and adult grandchildren. The man himself has gray eyes and gray hair, neatly parted; his skin has not yet gained that waxy luminosity that affects almost everyone else his age. Of medium height, gloriously pot-bellied, he has evidently ignored his doctor's advice about dieting. At leisure, dressed in blue jeans and a shirt open at the neck, he was prepared to talk, speaking easily and relevantly, with great animation, without any pause for refreshment, for three full hours. When he glanced at a text, he did not use the glasses stuffed into his shirt pocket. He looked and sounded, at most, seventy-five. Only when he got up to walk did he reveal his real age.

Back home in Los Angeles, Slonimsky, a widower, lives in a small detached cottage with his cat (named "Grody to the Max" after an epithet in a Moon Unit Zappa song). He typically eats orange juice, two eggs and toast or a bagel for breakfast, having apparently ignored familiar warnings about cholesterol. A secretary comes about 10:30 to help with his voluminous correspondence and prepare his manuscripts on her personal computer. For dinner, he takes friends to a French-speaking café in his neighborhood; otherwise, he prefers barbecued chicken or pork chops. He acknowledges that he has been told to "stop eating bread, sugar and any kind of meat that has fat. What am I going to do? I ignored it; so my doctor said, 'What's the use?'" The only concession he has made to dietary caution is adding a lot more milk to his coffee. As the state took away his driving licence in his early eighties, he is usually at his West Los Angeles home or at the nearby U.C.L.A. library.

Later in 1988, Slonimsky published an autobiography, marvelously titled *Perfect Pitch* (1988), which opens: "When I was six years old my mother told me I was a genius." Credible though that be, given what he has done since, the book itself is less about his genius than a conventional narrative about an independent activist who did various kinds of musical work, with varying worldly success, until he found a niche as our foremost "musical lexicographer," as he calls it. While filled with marvelous stories, among them with his amusing relationship with the rock musician Frank Zappa, *Perfect Pitch*, with its long quotations from letters, etc., is the sort of book that someone else could have written about him. As such, it is less reflective of his genius than, say, *Music Since 1900* which, as it is a book that no one else could do, is essentially about his genius.

My own sense is that Slonimsky is an egomaniac who thankfully got interested in investigating the rest of the world. Having devoted his life to pursuing his genuine enthusiasm for other people and their works, he paradoxically demonstrates his genius precisely by knowing more about everyone else than anyone else, and in the size and range of his cultural appetite. Nothing in music is unacceptable to him. What Slonimsky displays is know-it-all-ism raised to its highest professional pitch. His books are the sort that lesser minds would cull from a variety of sources into a compendious "Oxford Companion"; but as Slonimsky is Slonimsky, it is not surprising that this very fat tome should be wholly written out of a single head. Were his most ambitious books to be done from scratch today, the publisher or a funding organization would insist upon having a committee which, sure as sure could be, would succumb to all the vices of collective work.

I first saw Slonimsky perform at a Continuum concert at Alice Tully Hall in New York late in 1987. On an evening wholly devoted to honoring him "at 93," a chamber group played not only his own compositions (*Suite for Violoncello and Piano*, 1951; *Gravestones at Hancock, N.H.*, 1945; *Five Advertising Songs*, 1925; *Piccolo Divertimento*, 1928/1941/1983) but works whose premieres he had conducted (a Henry Cowell composition from 1928, a 1925 piece by Carlos Chavez). Slonimsky's music compositions resemble his prose writing, involving as they do audacious wit and intellectual gymnastics in short forms.

His compositions are best understood in relation to two composers whose works they most resemble: Erik Satie, who likewise specialized in miniatures, and "P.D.Q. Bach (1807–1742?)," the alter ego of Peter Schickele, forty-one years Slonimsky's junior, who likewise exploits a sophisticated mixing of musical styles. The differences are that Slonimsky's inventions are more various than Satie's and more extreme and audacious than Schickele's, which is to say, in sum, more innovative. "My own pieces are written in a language that has never been used—consonant intervals only," he told me, his voice exuding contagious enthusiasm, "twelve-tone techniques in tonality, which Schoenberg specifically proscribed—four different triads that are mutually exclusive, and so forth. Practically every piece is based upon a stylistic device taken from my *Thesaurus*."

To put it simply, Slonimsky the composer is essentially a master miniaturist, with nearly a hundred pieces, none more than six minutes long. However, in the bulk of his compositions is a wealth of uniquely constructivist experiments that, in my analysis, synthesize the intelligence of J. S. Bach with the inventiveness of his friend Charles Ives—an opportune synthesis that no one has else has realized as well before or since. Some of these Slonimsky scores have been released through Cambria, a music publisher in Lomita, CA. What is just as necessary now is discs that would make all his innovative music conveniently available.

Now I have reached the Age of Absurdity. I refuse to believe I am 93. Have I really outlived Tolstoy and Goethe? I don't even have a white beard or bushy eyebrows to attest my age. My eyes still see, my ears still ring with sounds, and my jaws (yes, especially my jaws) are still sufficiently lubricated on their maxillary supports to sustain a steady flow of garrulity.

　　　　　　　　　　　　　　　　　　　　　—*Nicolas Slonimsky,*
　　　　　　　　　　　　　　　　　　　　　Perfect Pitch *(1988)*

The best part of the 1987 Alice Tully evening was Slonimsky's "Post-Intermission Talk," which was essentially a display of verbal and musical virtuosity that would be quite extraordinary for a man of any age. At the piano, he played different keys and different rhythms in his two hands; he played the ivories with his back turned to the keys. He used an orange to depress the black keys of Chopin's *Etude in F♯ Major*. Standing up, apart from any instrument, he confessed to "logorrhea, not to be confused with any other rrheas—an inability to stop talking." He recited limericks previously unfamiliar to me, perhaps of his own invention: "There was a young woman named Hatch, who was fond of the music of Batch. It isn't as fussy as that of Debussy. Sit down, and I'll play you a snatch." This became the cue for him to play music, of his own authorship I assumed, that mixed the stylistic mannerisms of major composers born two centuries apart. It was a winning performance. After offering "to exchange autographs—I will autograph whatever you have; you will autograph whatever I have"—he sat in the lobby greeting well-wishers until the last one went home. Had Continuum announced a return engagement for the following week, I would have gone again. Having been a modernistic monstrosity for much of his professional life, Slonimsky outlived his contemporaneous critics, thereby taking upon them the ultimate revenge, and had indeed become a masterpiece.

To meet him recently is to be reminded of your previous meeting, if not to hear him identify something of yours that only you remember; it would seem that his cranial retention has only improved with age. (He speaks of needing to discipline himself to block out the telephone numbers in television ads; otherwise, he'd remember them.) Nearly everyone involved in modern music has a Slonimsky story. Francis Schwartz, a composer teaching at the University of Puerto Rico during Slonimsky's visit in 1966, tells of meeting him two decades later, in another place, and finding that Slonimsky remembered not only the visit but Schwartz's own work. I was reminded of the sportscaster Howard Cosell, likewise a cranially retentive egomaniac, beginning an interview with a retired athlete by asking about a mistake the athlete had made back in 1953. Not even "research" or "research assistants" can instill such displays of concern for others.

The music publisher, Lance Bowling, recently wrote me, "In the early 1970s, when Nicolas was putting together a recording of his works for Orion Records, he did not have a copy of his *Five Advertising Songs*. He therefore had to reconstruct from memory the entire work. In 1974, my teacher, Joseph Wagner, a close friend of Slonimsky's dating way back, died. When I cleaned out Wagner's musical materials, a copy of the score surfaced. (Nicolas had given the score to him in the 1930s.) Comparing the recording with the score, I found it most amazing that after fifty years Slonimsky was able to reconstruct the work with no visible changes."

Lawrence Weschler, in a *New Yorker* profile (1986), tells this awesome story:

> While he was briefly in another room, I meandered over to the piano and mindlessly klimpered [sic] out a fairly complex and utterly inchoate sequence of nonsense chords— about ten seconds' worth. He came back in, I returned to my chair, and he went over to the piano and reproduced my sequence exactly, concluding with an elegant harmonizing flourish.

Another story told by Weschler has a doctor recently testing Slonimsky's hearing with two tones over earphones. Which sounds higher, the doctor asked? " 'Well,' I told him, 'the first one was 3,520 cycles per second and the second was 3,680 cycles per second. Is that what you mean?' He rechecked his dials and then looked over at me, dumbfounded."

I would be remiss if I did not tell my own Slonimsky anecdote. Meeting him for the first time after that 1987 Alice Tully concert, the man nearly twice my age said, "So finally we meet. I feel as though I've been reading you all my life." He then cited an article published in a literary magazine a decade before in which I had mentioned another composer's work based upon a fragment of Slonimsky's speaking voice. No one else in the world, absolutely no one, could have risked either unforgettable stunt—that audacious gag or that obscure reference.

AUTOBIOGRAPHIES

Though Slonimsky has written a fairly conventional autobiography, *Perfect Pitch* (1987), much of his best autobiographical writing appears in other places, beginning with his own entry to *Baker's*, reprinted first, and then including his prefaces to the sixth and seventh editions to his monumental compendia. These prefaces typically reveal how the book was done, which is to say problems he encountered, amid his personal situation. Indeed, it is hard to think of any lexicographer since Dr. Samuel Johnson whose prefaces are better written. The section includes Slonimsky's own audacious review of his *Perfect Pitch*.

SELF-ENTRY FROM EIGHTH EDITION OF *BAKER'S*

Slonimsky, Nicolas (actually, **Nikolai Leonidovich**), legendary Russian-born American musicologist of manifold endeavors, uncle of **Sergei (Mikhailovich) Slonimsky**; b. St. Petersburg, April 27, 1894. A self-described failed wunderkind, he was given his 1st piano lesson by his illustrious maternal aunt **Isabelle Vengerova**, on Nov. 6, 1900, according to the old Russian calendar. Possessed by inordinate ambition, aggravated by the endemic intellectuality of his family of both maternal and paternal branches (novelists, revolutionary poets, literary critics, university professors, translators, chessmasters, economists, mathematicians, inventors of useless artificial languages, Hebrew scholars, speculative philosophers), he became determined to excel beyond common decency in all these doctrines; as an adolescent, wrote out his future biography accordingly, setting down his death date as 1967, but survived. He enrolled in the St. Petersburg Cons. and studied harmony and orchestration with 2 pupils of Rimsky-Korsakov, Kalafati and Maximilian Steinberg; also tried unsuccessfully to engage in Russian journalism. After the Revolution he made his way south; was a rehearsal pianist at the Kiev Opera, where he took some composition lessons with Glière (1919); then was in Yalta (1920), where he earned his living as a piano accompanist to displaced Russian singers, and as an instructor at a dilapidated Yalta Cons.; thence proceeded to Turkey, Bulgaria, and Paris, where he became secretary and piano-pounder to Serge Koussevitzky. In 1923 he went to the U.S.; became coach in the opera dept. of the Eastman School of Music in Rochester, N.Y., where he took an opportunity to study some more composition with the visiting prof. Selim Palmgren, and conducting with Albert Coates; in 1925 he was again with Koussevitzky in Paris and Boston, but was fired for insubordination in 1927. He learned to speak polysyllabic English and began writing music articles for the *Boston Evening Transcript* and the *Christian Science Monitor*; ran a monthly column of musical anecdotes of questionable authenticity in *Etude* magazine; taught theory at the Malkin Cons. in Boston and at the Boston Cons.; conducted the Pierian Sodality at Harvard Univ. (1927–29) and the Apollo Chorus (1928–30). In 1927 he organized the Chamber Orch. of Boston with the purpose of presenting modern works; with it he gave 1st performances of works by Charles Ives, Edgar Varèse, Henry Cowell, and others. He became a naturalized U.S. citizen in 1931. In 1931–32 he conducted special concerts of modern American, Cuban, and Mexican music in Paris, Berlin, and Budapest under the auspices of the Pan-American Assoc. of Composers, producing a ripple of excitement; he repeated these programs at his engagements with the Los Angeles Phil. (1932) and at the Hollywood Bowl (1933), which created such consternation that his conducting career came to a jarring halt. From 1945 to 1947 he was, by accident (the head of the dept. had died of a heart attack), lecturer in Slavonic languages and literatures at Harvard Univ. In 1962–63 he traveled in Russia, Poland, Yugoslavia, Bulgaria, Rumania, Greece, and Israel under the auspices of the Office of Cultural Exchange at the U.S. State Dept., as a lecturer in native Russian, ersatz Polish, synthetic Serbo-Croatian, Russianized Bulgarian, Latinized Rumanian, archaic Greek, passable French, and tolerable German. Returning from his multinational travels, he taught variegated musical subjects at the Univ. of Calif., Los Angeles; was irretrievably retired after a triennial service (1964–67), ostensibly owing to irreversible obsolescence and recessive infantiloquy; but, disdaining the inexorable statistics of the actuarial tables, continued to agitate and even gave long-winded lecture-recitals in institutions of dubious learning. As a composer, he cultivated miniature forms, usually with a gimmick, e.g., *Studies in Black and White* for Piano (1928) in "mutually exclusive consonant counterpoint," a song cycle, *Gravestones*, to texts from tombstones in an old cemetery in Hancock, N.H. (1945), and *Minitudes*, a collection of 50 quaquaversal piano pieces (1971–77). His only decent orch. work is *My Toy Balloon* (1942), a set of variations on a Brazilian song, which includes in the score 100 colored balloons to be exploded *f f f* at the climax. He also conjured up a *Möbius Strip-Tease*, a perpetual vocal canon notated on a Möbius band to be revolved around the singer's head; it had its 1st and last performance at the Arrière-Garde Coffee Concert at UCLA, on May 5, 1965, with the composer officiating at the piano non-obbligato. A priority must be conceded to him for writing the earliest singing commercials to authentic texts from the *Saturday Evening Post* advertisements, among them *Make This a Day of Pepsodent, No More Shiny Nose*, and *Children Cry for Castoria* (1925). More "scholarly," though no less defiant of academic conventions, is his *Thesaurus of Scales and Melodic Patterns* (1947), an inventory of all conceivable and inconceivable tonal combinations, culminating in a mind-boggling "Grandmother Chord" containing 12 different tones and 11 different intervals. Beset by a chronic itch for novelty, he coined the term "pandiatonicism" (1937), which, *mirabile dictu*, took root and even got into reputable reference works, including the 15th ed. of the *Encyclopædia Britannica*. In his quest for trivial but not readily accessible information, he blundered into the muddy field of musical lexicography; publ. *Music Since 1900*, a chronology of musical events, which actually contains some beguiling serendipities (N.Y., 1937; 4th ed., 1971; supplement, 1986); took over the vacated editorship (because of the predecessor's sudden death during sleep) of Thompson's *International Cyclopedia of Music and Musicians* (4th to 8th eds., 1946–58) and accepted the editorship of the 5th, 6th, 7th, and 8th eds. of the prestigious *Baker's Biographical Dictionary of Musicians* (N.Y., 1958, 1978, 1984, 1991). He also abridged this venerable vol. into *The Concise Baker's Biographical Dictionary of Musicians* (N.Y., 1988). In 1978 he mobilized his powers of retrospection in preparing an autobiography, *Failed Wunderkind*, subtitled *Rueful Autopsy* (in the sense of self-observation, not dissection of the body); the publishers, deeming these titles too lugubrious, renamed it *Perfect Pitch* (N.Y., 1988). He also translated Boris de Schloezer's biography of Scriabin from the original Russian (Berkeley and Los Angeles, 1987), which was followed by his *Lectionary of Music*, a compendium of articles on music (N.Y., 1988). His other writings include *Music of Latin America* (N.Y., 1945; several reprints; also in Spanish, Buenos Aires, 1947); *The Road to Music*, ostensibly for children (N.Y., 1947); *A Thing or Two about Music* (N.Y., 1948; inconsequential; also lacking an index); *Lexicon of Musical Invective*, a random collection of pejorative reviews of musical masterpieces (N.Y., 1952); numerous articles for encyclopedias; also a learned paper, *Sex and the Music Librarian*, valuable for its painstaking research; the paper was delivered by proxy, to tumultuous cachinnations, at a symposium of the Music Library Assoc., at Chapel Hill, N.C., Feb. 2, 1968.

ENTRY FROM
MUSIC SINCE 1900

It is not surprising that something autobiographical appears, thinly or ironically disguised, in his Music Since 1900.

27 APRIL 1905

On his eleventh birthday Sol MYSNIK stages, in the recreation hall of High School No. 11 in St. Petersburg, in which he is a student, the world première of his politico-revolutionary opera in eleven scenes, *The X-Ray Vindicator*, scored for three countertenors, basso profundo, piano, balalaika, toy pistol and a static electricity generator, the action dealing with a young scientist confined in the dreaded Peter-and-Paul Fortress for advocating the extermination of the Tsar and the termination of the Russo-Japanese war, who escapes by directing a stream of Röntgen rays at himself from a hidden cathode tube as a Secret Police officer enters his cell to question him, putting him to flight in superstitious horror by appearing as a skeleton, and then calmly walking through the open gate to resume his terroristic propaganda, with petty-bourgeoisie characterized by insipid arpeggios on the balalaika and the playing of the waltz *On the Dunes of Manchuria* on the phonograph, revolutionary fervor by the songs "The Sun Goes Up, the Sun Goes Down, I Wish the Tsar Would Lose his Crown" and "We Fell as Martyrs to Our Cause Because We Scorned the Tsarist Laws," the X-rays by chromatically advancing sequences of diminished seventh-chords, and Freedom through Terror by blazingly incandescent C major.

This memoir of his wife appears in his intentional autobiography, Perfect Pitch *(1986).*

An event took place in Paris that overshadowed all my artistic achievements. On 30 July 1931 I was married by the Mayor of the 16th arrondissement to Dorothy Adlow, who had joined me in Paris to hear my concerts in June. Varèse was our best man. After a brief ceremony, I was handed a marriage booklet, with space provided for twelve children, including an appendix detailing instructions for proper 'allaitement', wet nursing.

Dorothy was seven years younger than I, but an eternity wiser. I was a bundle of nerves when she took me under her protective wing; patiently did she listen to my litanies, and with infinite tact taught me social amenities. Where I was ungovernable, she provided guidance, and where I was suspicious of others, she calmed me by rational argument.

Dorothy's parents were Jewish immigrants from Russia. Her father, who started out as a pushcart peddler, built a flourishing furniture business in Roxbury, a suburb of Boston. His name was Orlow, but to immigration officials the name sounded like Adlow and was thus transcribed. He spoke English with an Irish lilt, since most of his customers were from Ireland, but he never learned to write properly. Dorothy's mother could hardly speak English at all. Uneducated as the parents were, however, they knew the importance of education and sent their three daughters to Radcliffe and their son to Harvard. Dorothy studied art at Radcliffe College. Shortly after graduation, she became an art critic for the *Christian Science Monitor*; later she was appointed head of its art department, the only member of the editorial staff who was not a Christian Scientist.

Translator's Foreword,
de Schloezer's *Scriabin*

This autobiographical memoir comes from the preface to a book translated by Slonimsky, Scriabin: Artist and Mystic *(University of California Press, 1987).*

I feel particularly close to both the author and the subject of this book. I met Boris de Schloezer in Kiev, in 1918, as we converged in the capital of the Ukrainian Republic among the multitudes fleeing the famine and cold of Petrograd and Moscow. Schloezer, his widowed sister Tatiana Schloezer-Scriabin (Scriabin died in 1915), and her children Ariadna, Marina, and Julian were guests of the Kiev industrialist Balachowsky, who was a friend and champion of Scriabin. I stayed at the same house, which was the only "skyscraper" in Kiev (it rose six stories and dominated the broad expanse of the Dnieper River). Such a conspicuous building was an obvious target for requisition by various military forces active in the area during the Civil War. (Kiev had changed hands seventeen times in three years.) To protect ourselves against intrusion, we organized a Scriabin Society, and, amazingly enough, the Red Army and some Ukrainian revolutionary groups actually respected our Society as a legitimate shield. At one point an aggressive raiding party of the Soviet military attempted to dislodge us. I remember the intruders as a curiously mixed group led by an officer who carried a tennis racket. During the peculiary internecine struggle, I developed a certain expertise in handling various feuding factions and was particularly adept in confronting the Bolsheviks, with whom I even used the technique of dialectical materialism. However, my efforts did not avail with the tennis-playing Bolshevik officer, who gave us twenty-four hours to clear out of the "skyscraper." In desperation, I sent off a telegram to Lenin, asking for his intercession as head of the Council of People's Commissars at the Kremlin. "While Moscow is erecting a monument in honor of the great Russian composer Scriabin," my telegram read, "a squad of the Red Army is trying to evict his widow and her children from the apartment they occupy in Kiev. Please intercede for the sake of Russian culture." I knew that Tatiana Schloezer-Scriabin was not legally married to Scriabin because his first wife refused a divorce, but such legalistic niceties would be no obstacle to action for a revolutionary regime. I never found out whether Lenin actually made a ruling on my appeal, but we were left alone, and the tennis-playing officer never bothered us again.

A tragedy darkened our lives when the eleven-year-old Julian Scriabin, who seemed to inherit his father's genius and wrote remarkable piano pieces in the style of Scriabin's last opus numbers (even his physical appearance bore close resemblance to his father's), drowned during an excursion on the Dnieper River. Until this day, nearly seventy years after the event, I shudder at the memory. It was already getting dark when we found him in the island bay, where he had apparently waded and miscalculated the depth of the water; he could not swim. A fisherman in our search party attached his pathetic, slender body to the boat and rowed ashore. His mother was in Moscow and communications were difficult, so Julian was buried in her absence. A Russian Orthodox service was held for the peace of his young soul; his teacher Reinhold Glière, then head of the Kiev Conservatory, made a heartfelt speech, and a school chorus sang the Russian requiem "Let him sleep with the saints." His mother arrived several days later, and Schloezer had to break the news to her; they spoke in French. "Mais non, mais non . . .," he kept repeating, trying to defer the dreadful news. Some years later Julian's compositions were published in Moscow, and thus he entered the children's paradise of unformed talent.

PREFACE TO *51 MINITUDES*
FOR *PIANO*

These prefaces to Slonimsky's composition, 51 Minitudes for Piano *(1972–76), become autobiography by talking about his music so clearly and wittily.*

1. $\sqrt{B^5}$
   The square root of Beethoven's Fifth Symphony, the intervals of which are cut in half. The Fate Motive of a major third becomes a major second; octaves become tritones. The ratio of vibrations for a major third is 5/4; its square root approximates the ratio of vibrations of a major second which is 9/8. To verify this, square 9/8; you will get 81/64, very close to 80/64 = 5/4. Q.E.D. Play it over several times; then play the Fate Motive, etc. as per Van B. After a while you will like the square root better; it is more salty, and acrid.

2. **Borborygmus**
   This is the medical term for a rumble in the stomach. The piece sounds like it.

3. **Felinity**
   A kittenish impression of a cat striding quietly in whole tones.

4. **Lambent Flames**
   The piece intends to project a flickering, soft radiance.

5. **Schoenwagnerberg Boustrophedon**
   The garbled concatenation of syllables becomes clear when broken into its components: Schoen-Wagner-Berg. Schoenberg's Opus 33a is turned inside out and reharmonized in a Tristanesque arrangement. In fact, the initial three notes in the Schoenberg original are identical with the initial three notes in the prelude to Tristan. Then it is played backward, *Tristantissimo*, and forward again. This operation is described by the word "Boustrophedon", which means in Greek to turn like oxen in ploughing right, left, and right again: Bous=Ox; Strophein=to turn.

6. 7. 8. **Palindromes**
   Palindromes are palindromes: "Able was I ere I saw Elba." "Madam, I'm Adam." Any more?

9. **Omphaloskepsis**
   Webster defines this as: "Meditation while gazing at the navel." Safer it is than Valium or other tranquilizers. The music is appropriately soothing.

10. Dodecaphilia
The love of 12, the number cultivated by composers of dodecaphonic music.

11. Triskaidecaphobia
Fear of 13. A very common aberration of hotel owners who skip the 13th floor and of many nonowners of hotels, among them Schoenberg, who suffered from acute triskaidecaphobia. When he reached the age of 76, some foolish person pointed out to him that the sum of the digits of his age was 13. Schoenberg was quite upset by it. He died at 76, on July 13, 1951. The title of his opera *MOSES UND ARON*, lacks the second *A* in Aaron in order to avoid 13 letters. Rossini was another triskaidecaphobiac among composers. In addition, he was also afraid of Fridays. He died on Friday, November 13, 1868.

12. Casanova in Casa Nueva, Hollywood, California
A deliberately gooey, tonal mucilage imitative of movie music, reeking with maundering, maudlin miasma.

13. Ach du lieber Augustin!
Not the lovely Augustin of yore, but a dodecaphonic rendition thereof. The accompaniment carries its own tone row, and there is not a consonant interval in a carload. One sensitive auditor complained upon hearing the piece that it made him seasick.

14. Dummkopfmarsch in His/Deses/Dur
The tempo is *Stupido ma non troppo*. His is B sharp, enharmonically equal to C; Deses is D double flat, enharmonically equal to C; Dur is major. So this piece is in plain C major, and all that barbed wire of sharps, double sharps, flats and double flats are there just to annoy and stultify. It's a dumbhead march all right.

15. Blitzpartie
This is a quick chess game. The opening is a regular Luis Lopez beloved by international grandmasters; then it becomes confused as any tournament game is apt to do.

16. Meditazione Transcendentale
This is transcendental meditation to end all transcendental meditations.

17. Pièce Enfantine
As the title says, it is infantile.

18. Elan
An attempt at lofty expression.

19. Fragment from an Unwritten Piano Concerto
Usable for the middle of a cadenza. On second thought, it is just as well that the concerto remained unwritten. Caution: the right hand is dodecaphonic, but the harmonies are according to Hoyle.

20. La Tromperie ensourdinée
Muted trumpeting, doing no harm.

21. Marche Ridicule
Sure is.

22. Three Blind Mice
They march blindily following the descending chromatic scale in the bass.

23. Anabolism
This is constructive metabolism.

24. Catabolism
This is destructive metabolism.

25. Pervicacious Dodecaphilia
Pervicacious means stubborn, and most dodecaphiliacs are very stubborn.

26. Oligophrenia
Olin means little, and *phrenia* has to do with skull and brains. So this is brainless music; but is the brain necessary for musical enjoyment?

27. Intertonal Interplay
Tonalities clash but come out in the clear.

28. A$\leftrightarrow$c'''' = 88
This takes in the entire range of the grand piano keyboard.

29. Exercise Hanonique
Next to Czerny, Hanon was the most industrious purveyor of piano exercises. He never got out of the key of C, but in this *Minitude* Hanon is forced to move up and down into other keys on a chromatic ladder. Inexcusable brutality.

30. Czerny, Shmerny
Czerny never married and he wrote all those schools of velocity, dexterity, agility, etc., because he hated children, or so his haters claimed. This *Minitude* takes dire revenge on Czerny, making a Shmerny of him.

31. Fugato Innocuo
This fugato is not so innocuous as it seems. The right hand plays on white keys and the left hand plays on black keys. The theme is transposed a semitone down, a most unorthodox procedure. But there is not a single dissonance in the entire piece, so it cannot be very noxious.

32. Pandiatonic Melodies
These are tunes using the seven notes of the diatonic scale and avoiding repetition. The term was excogitated by the composer in 1937, and has since been adopted widely in music dictionaries.

33. Pandiatonic and Panpentatatonic Clusters
These are the grapes of notes played pandiatonically on the white keys and panpentatonically on the black keys.

34. Quaquaversal Quarks
Quaquaversal means going every which way, askew and athwart. Quarks are subliminal particles that no scientist has ever seen, smelled or touched. But conceptually they are important. The word "quark" is found in James Joyce's unintelligible classic *Finnegans Wake*.

35. Déjà Vu
A Biedermeier tunery, remembered from Russian childhood.

36. Déjà Entendu
A sentimental tune, probably from an old German salon piece; a snatch from an Argentine tango is inserted for relief.

37. Danse du faux Orient
The dance is meretricious, the rhythms are synthetic, and the whole thing is obnoxious.

38. Old Russian Song
A sweet lullaby from an old collection of Russian folksongs, harmonized according to the best recipes of the composition class at the St. Petersburg Conservatory.

39. A Bad Egg Polka
Something is rotten here, but the egg has to be bad if it is to be made into a musical theme. Good is no good, because there is no "o" in the scale. The scheme is obvious: A/BAD/EGG and backwards, G, G, E, D, A, B, A. In polka time, it is quite edible.

40. Cabbage Waltz
Cabbage is the only vegetable that can be expressed in music: C, A, B, B, A, G, E. It is also melodious when spelled backwards and it is quite cachinogenic (generating loud laughter) when played in waltz time.

41. Quodlibet (La Putaine)
This is a contrapuntal blend of the Matchiche and *La petite tonquinoise*, the latter being a putative putaine. A putaine is a lady of the evening.

42. Marcia Bitonale
Right hand is on white keys, the left hand on black.

43. Valse trop Sentimentale
The humidity exuded by this waltz is positively perspirational.

44. Obsolescent Foxtrot
This is an understatement. The present foxtrot was obsolescent long before it was composed.

45. Modinha Russo-Brasileira
Modinha is a Portuguese ballad also indigenous to Brazil. The melodic outline of this Minitude suggests a Russian folksong pattern. To Russians it sounds Russian, to Brazilians, Brazilian.

46. A National Anthem in Search of a Country
There are so many new and emergent nations without a national anthem that this particular anthem has a fair chance of finding a home somewhere in the interior of New Guinea, or in a newly emancipated Arctic island.

47. Bach in Fluid Tonality
In this bit of musical cannibalism, Bach's wonderful c-minor fugue from the first book of the Well-tempered Clavier is subjected to Procrustean tortures up and down the chromatic scale.

48. Bach x 2 = Debussy
Now the intervals of the Bach c-minor fugue are multiplied by 2. Result: all minor seconds become major, and it all begins to sound like something written by Debussy in the whole-tone scale.

49. Happy Birthday
A dodecaphonic birthday greeting, calculated to make the celebrant miserable. But is not misery essential to art?

50. Implosion
This is a nerve-wracking intervallic grind strong enough to compress the medulla oblongata into a spaghetti stick. But, wonder of wonders, the contrapuntal structure is totally consonant.

51. Orion
This piece of melodically derived from the Grandmother Chord consisting of 12 different notes and 11 different intervals. The eponymous Grandmother is then stretched out horizontally to the bursting point.

PARIS, FROM *PERFECT PITCH*

I reached Paris in late 1921. By then the invasion of the city by Russian *émigrés* had assumed astronomical proportions. Ideologically, the Russian colony in Paris was a detritus composed of derelicts of all political factions, from the defeated generals of the White Army to bandits of the Green Army, interspersed with some genuine members of aristocracy and royalty. There were also writers of varied political colours. All these factions conducted continuous feuds among themselves. Comical scenes were enacted at Paris cafés. A Jewish journalist would engage in loud debate with another Jewish journalist about the equitable borders between autonomous parts of the future Russian Democratic Republic. The most vociferous of them, Boris Gourevitch, drew up a plan for a world government of which he himself was to be installed as a supreme spiritual mentor without portfolio. After his death in New York, he left behind a huge manuscript in Russian which expounded his ideas.

Boris Gourevitch had a brother Gregory, a talented, though erratic, pianist, who specialized in works of Liszt and Skriabin, which he played in a state of dreamy alienation, focusing his gaze on the ceiling and letting the wisps of his greying hair fall listlessly on the back of his balding head. Fond of sensational exploits, he made headlines by flying to America on the first passenger dirigible that crossed the ocean in 1922. He induced the captain of the airship to install a lightweight piano on board, and played Liszt and Skriabin on it, looking upwards towards the richly ornamented candelabras while muttering incantations.

But the general mass of Russian *émigrés* in Paris were not concerned with high politics or mystical insights. Their problem, and my own, was physical survival. Those capable of manual labour hired themselves out as bricklayers or doormen. I knew a Russian literary critic who stood in line all night to get a factory job, and had to cope with a mob of husky hungry men when the gates opened. Those who rushed in first got the few jobs available, while the others were chased away by armed guards. I was, of course, in the fortunate position of having a marketable skill as a pianist. Once I was offered a well-paying job at a reception for the Shah of Persia who was visiting in Paris, but the occasion demanded a tuxedo, which I did not own.

I also lost my chance of being hired by Chaliapin as an accompanist. I had an audition with him in a private house. He came in, looked around and said, 'I need a woman'. This was a strange introduction, but Chaliapin was known for his rough ways. At my audition Chaliapin asked me whether I could play the *Songs of Death* by Mussorgsky. I could. Chaliapin sang in his velvety bass; I played. Without finishing one song, he tried another. Then he stopped paying any attention to me and asked for a drink of vodka. I was not hired. Perhaps it was just as well, for Chaliapin was beastly to accompanists. In America his favorite pianist was Max Rabinovich, who attuned himself wonderfully to the vagaries of Chaliapin's free rhythm. Whenever Chaliapin was not in full command of his voice, however, or forgot the words, he would point his forefinger accusingly at Rabinovich as if to suggest that something was wrong with the pianist and not with himself. After a few exhibitions of this nature, Max Rabinovich quit. Chaliapin was unhappy about losing his pianist, and hired a British accompanist, very tall and very blond, who played the piano quite well but was unable to re-create the peculiarly Russian mood of the songs. After one particularly unsatisfactory concert, Chaliapin flew into a rage. 'Take these goddamn Jews away from me!' he screamed. 'Give me Rabinovich!'

Chaliapin was also notorious for his brutal behaviour towards his colleagues on the opera stage. Even the great Koussevitzky stood in awe of him. During a rehearsal of *Boris Godunov* at the Paris Opera conducted by Koussevitzky, Chaliapin suddenly stopped singing and said to him in Russian, 'Can't you count?' Thereupon he proceeded to beat time with his foot to set the right tempo. Koussevitzky became so flustered that he could not go on with the rehearsal, and after the intermission notified the management that he would not conduct the opera. Chaliapin feigned disbelief when he was told the news. 'I only asked this haemorrhoidal Jew to keep time,' he observed.

One of my most striking memories of Paris comes from a mixed Russian–French party I attended. Among those present was a very tall, middle-aged woman with a rather small head which looked like an extension of a long slender neck, continued in an elongated torso, with the whole upper body reposing rather incongruously on a disproportionately large pelvis and fat legs. I asked the hostess who the woman was. 'Why, she is Mademoiselle Eiffel,' was the reply, 'the daughter of the builder of the Eiffel Tower.' I was amazed at the genetic resemblance between the woman and the tower, but I withheld comment.

In Paris I renewed my acquaintance with the Russian bass singer Alexander Mozzhuhin, whom I had accompanied in Kiev, and whose interpretations of Mussorgsky's songs were musically superior to Chaliapin's, if not as dramatically effective. Mozzhuhin asked me to play for him again at his Paris recital. At the intermission, an artistic-looking man with a shock of greying hair approached me. It was Serge Koussevitzky. He asked me whether I would be interested in playing for him while he practised conducting. I certainly would. He gave me his address which was in a fashionable Paris suburb, and asked me to come to lunch the following day.

At lunch I met Koussevitzky's wife Natalie. She was an imperious-looking woman who rarely spoke, and when she compressed her taciturn lips, she reminded one of an owl at her silent watch. The famous Koussevitzky publishing house, Éditions Russes, listed her as partner. In fact, this important publishing enterprise was financed by her family fortune derived from a large lumber company. It was her money that had enabled Koussevitzky to start his career as conductor in Moscow. He used to hire an entire orchestra to come to his palatial mansion for weekly rehearsals, and he practised conducting until he was ready to appear before an audience. At first he lacked the purely technical skills of conducting, but he was a superb 'animateur', as the French put it.

Koussevitzky gave me a piano arrangement of Rimsky-Korsakov's *Scheherazade* and asked me to play it. I banged out the familiar opening unisons. Koussevitzky sat down, with the full orchestral score in front of him, and proceeded to conduct, giving cues to imaginary instruments in the room. I followed his beat with

great curiosity and not a little trepidation. So this was the way conductors practised. Still, I had never known a conductor who used a pianist for practising;
Koussevitzky was apparently unique in this respect. But whatever he did, the very
fact that he could beat time, now with the right hand, now with the left, then
with both hands, turning his head towards the imagined orchestra, was to me a
revelation.

While working for Koussevitzky I had plenty of time to fill other engagements,
among them a stint with the Diaghilev ballet company. Despite his fame, Diaghilev
was in constant financial straits. One morning before a rehearsal he came in and
announced the bad news to his company: he had no money to pay either his
dancers or the pianist. Would we continue to rehearse on credit? There was no
choice, not for me anyway. I had plenty of time on my hands, and very little
money. Eventually, Diaghilev found a new sponsor with money and paid us off.

Koussevitzky was apparently satisfied with my playing and asked me if I would
care to join him for a summer in Biarritz. He planned to conduct *Le Sacre du
printemps* by Stravinsky, and had to practise to master the tricky rhythms of the
score. I was but vaguely aware of the tremendous impact that the work had produced on the audience during its first performance in Paris in 1913, and accepted
Koussevitzky's offer without a moment's hesitation. Koussevitzky gave me money
for the train fare to Biarritz where I was to join him a few days after his own
arrival. In Biarritz I rented an inexpensive furnished room, which included breakfast consisting of *café au lait* and a delicious croissant. I telephoned Koussevitzky as
soon as I arrived and he told me to come to lunch. Both he and Mrs Koussevitzky
were extremely cordial, and I no longer had a fear of failing the test. He gave me a
four-hand piano arrangement of Stravinsky's score, and I quickly adapted myself to
combining the four staves of the arrangement so as to preserve the essential harmonic and rhythmic elements of the music. It was my first experience in tackling a
real modern work. What discords! A simple tune in C major was set against the
same tune in C-sharp major. A B major triad was combined with a B minor triad.
No wonder a French critic suggested that the title should be changed to *Le Massacre
du printemps*. But I was determined to do my best to give a fair account of the
music. As usual during a particularly intense challenge, I projected myself in my
imagination into a higher dimension. Stravinsky's asymmetrical metres were not
entirely new to me. I was familiar with compound time signatures such as 11/4 in
Rimsky-Korsakov's opera *Sadko*, which constituted a stumbling block to the chorus,
and sometimes to the conductor. Indeed, conservatory students devised a jingle of
eleven syllables to practise this particular section of the score, with the words,
most disrespectful of the great master of Russian music, 'Rimsky-Korsakov sovsyem
sumasoshol' ('Rimsky-Korsakov is altogether mad'). But the changing metres of
Le Sacre du printemps compounded the difficulties far beyond such simple arithmetical arrangements; they ran in fast rhythmic units, so that one had to follow the
music not bar by bar, but beat by beat.

To my dismay, I realized that Koussevitzky was incapable of coping with these
complications. When precise metrical changes occurred, as from 3/16 to 2/8, he
kept slowing down the sixteenth-notes and accelerating the eighth-notes so that
the distinct binary ratios dissolved into formless neutral triplets. It occurred to me
that the situation could be remedied by combining adjacent bars so as to reduce
the basic beat to an eighth-note; for instance, the succession of bars of 3/16, 2/8,
1/16, 4/8 could be integrated into a single bar of 4/4. To be sure, the downbeats
would be dislocated at several points, but Stravinsky had numerous syncopated
accents anyway, so that the basic rhythm would be preserved. In the very beginning of the most difficult segment in the score, *La Danse sacrale*, there was a sixteenth-note rest followed by a full orchestral chord on an eighth-note, with a fer-

mata over it. The conductor was supposed to give a powerful downbeat for the sixteenth rest and expect the orchestra to come in together on the following chord. But, since that chord had an indefinite duration created by the fermata, the effect would be no different if this bar were to be written without the initial rest. The joke went around that when Stravinsky himself conducted this bar he made an audible burp on the downbeat which justified the syncopation that followed. But Koussevitzky was too delicate a person to make animal sounds to emphasize the rhythm, so a different expedient was required.

I showed Koussevitzky how all those metrical fractions could be connected up without sacrificing a single beat, but he dismissed the idea out of hand. 'We can't change Stravinsky's rhythm!' he said. Koussevitzky also had trouble in passages of 5/8 in a relatively moderate time, particularly when 5/8 was changed to 6/8, or to 9/8 as happens in Stravinsky's score. He had a tendency to stretch out the last beat in 5/8, counting 'one, two, three, four, five, uh'. This 'uh' constituted the 6th beat, reducing Stravinsky's spasmodic rhythms to the regular heartbeat. When I pointed it out to Koussevitzky, he became quite upset. It was just a 'luftpause' he said. The insertion of an 'airpause' reduced the passage to a nice waltz time, making it very comfortable to play for the violin section which bore the brunt of the syncopation, but wrecking Stravinsky's asymmetric rhythms.

Stravinsky also spent much of the summer of 1921 in Biarritz, and he came to Koussevitzky's house practically every day. At evenings we played poker for nominal stakes, but I was never allowed to lose a single sou. I took the opportunity of these leisurely evenings to talk about composers with whom I had become friendly. In particular, I tried to boost the career of a young Polish composer, Alexandre Tansman, whose manuscript scores I brought with me to Biarritz. Koussevitzky amiably agreed to consider a piece by Tansman for performance, but Stravinsky, with his usual gross humour, said, 'A person named Danceman should dance, not compose'. (In Russian, or for that matter in German, the pun comes out better: 'Tanzmann muss tanzen.') Who could foresee that Tansman would become one of Koussevitzky's favourite composers and a worshipful friend and biographer of Stravinsky? Tansman appreciated my efforts in his behalf by inscribing one of his scores to me, 'A mon accoucheur'.

The Biarritz interlude over, Koussevitzky and I returned to Paris. Rehearsals of *Le Sacre* went badly. Koussevitzky made the expected mistakes, and kept adding those obnoxious 'luftpausen'. He was sullen as we drove back to his suburban villa in a chauffered limousine. After lunch he suddenly said: 'Show me that arrangement you made in the score.' I eagerly explained to him my idea of summation of adjacent bars. He looked at the music with glazed eyes. 'I can't understand a thing you say,' he remarked. 'Sit down and put the barlines in blue pencil in the score.' I withdrew to the workroom and at the end of the afternoon had the tricky metre all nicely rebarred in long lines in blue traced from top to bottom of the huge score. 'You have a genius for mathematics,' Koussevitzky said to me after he looked over my handiwork. The mathematical genius involved required no more than the ability to add fractions, but to Koussevitzky it was high science. The parts of *Le Sacre du printemps* which Koussevitzky used in Paris and later in Boston were rebarred according to my arrangement, and Koussevitzky used it at all his performances of the work. Interestingly enough, some twenty years later Stravinsky himself published a simplified arrangement of *Danse sacrale*. Not being constrained to follow his original metrical divisions, he freely altered his syncopated textures.

In the natural course of musical events, Leonard Bernstein, the instantaneous magician of the art of conducting, was engaged as guest conductor with the Boston Symphony Orchestra, with *Le Sacre* on the programme. No sooner did he begin the *Danse sacrale* than he was confronted with my metrical rearrangement. He quickly collated the score with orchestral parts and proceeded to beat time according to my simplified Koussevitzkian version. In a note he sent me in April 1984, on the occasion of my ninetieth birthday, he recalled the occasion.

'Dear Nicolas,' he wrote. 'Every time I conduct *Le Sacre*, as I did most recently two weeks ago (and always from Koussy's own score, with your rebarring), I admire and revere and honor you as I did the very first time. Bless you, and more power to you. Lenny B.'

PREFACE TO THE SIXTH EDITION OF *BAKER'S*

If I were to write an autobiography (which God forbid!) I would call it *I am a footnote*, or *I am a parenthesis*. I am a footnote in the entry on Carl Maria von Weber in the Fifth Edition of *Grove's Dictionary* and a parenthesis in the article on Lully in *Die Musik in Geschichte und Gegenwart*. And I am a paragraph in the Fifteenth Edition of the *Encyclopedia Britannica* under Pandiatonicism, which is my polysyllabic brainchild.

Dr. Samuel Johnson defines a lexicographer in his famous dictionary as "a harmless drudge." Harmless? Not necessarily. In fact, lexicography, when practiced in excess, may well be harmful to the lexicographer's psyche. Consider the melancholy case of John Wall Callcott (1766–1821) as related in *Baker's Biographical Dictionary of Musicians*: "His mind gave way from overwork on a projected biographical dictionary of musicians, . . . He recovered, but not sufficiently to continue his work." Callcott reached the letter Q, associated with such disturbing images as queer, quaquaversal, and quagmire, and then quit.

One of my predecessors in editing *Baker's* jotted down these words in the margin of the galley proofs: "I will go mad if I have to continue this for a long time." Another music editor, working on another dictionary, deliberately rented a room on the ground floor lest he should be tempted to jump out the window in despair over the contents of the book.

Although most of my friends regard me as an eccentric, I am not given to suicidal impulses while working on a dictionary. But I am rather paranoiac in my suspicions about melodrama, except in opera librettos. I never believed that Salieri poisoned Mozart, even though I memorized, as part of my school assignments in St. Petersburg, Salieri's monologue in Pushkin's play *Mozart and Salieri*, in which Salieri explains his reason for poisoning Mozart lest his blazing genius should eclipse the work of such humble votaries in the divine art of harmony as himself. In another tale of Mozart, I became suspicious of the reports in practically every reference work and every biography that a fierce snowstorm was raging in Vienna on the day of his funeral in December 1791, which made it impossible for his friends to follow his body to the cemetery (the snowballs were as large as tennis balls, the top Vienna Mozartologist, Erich Schenk, asserts). Why wasn't this meteorological phenomenon as much as mentioned in early Mozart biographies? It would have at least explained why Mozart's widow did not attend the funeral, if not her failure to pay dues for keeping Mozart's grave in perpetuity, which was the reason why he was eventually moved to the place of common burial. The snowstorm episode appears for the first time in Otto Jahn's monumental biography of Mozart, and the only source to substantiate it was an anonymous article published in a Vienna newspaper on the occasion of Mozart's centennial in 1856. Some Mozartologists identified the writer (who signed his report as "a man of the people") as the bartender of Mozart's favorite Vienna tavern, although by the time of Mozart's centennial he himself, if still living, would have been about a hundred years old. To resolve my puzzlement, I wrote to the Vienna Weather Bureau for a report on the climatic conditions on that December day in 1791. Great was my malicious sense of gratification when I received a report that the temperature on that day was well above freezing and that a gentle Zephyr wind blew from the West. No snowballs. No frigid weather which frightened away Mozart's friends. No melodrama, except the tragedy of Mozart's death so young. Encouraged by the prompt response of the Vienna Weather Bureau (which had kept records for more than two centuries), I inquired about another melodramatic episode: an electric storm on the afternoon of Beethoven's death. Yes, there was an electric storm, even though it was hardly likely that Beethoven in his debilitated physical condition could have lifted his clenched fist toward heaven in a gesture of defiance of *Jupiter tonans*.

Not every melodramatic report is necessarily a pabulum for the gullible. I became incredulous of the tale told in *Baker's* about the French singer Alexandre Taskin, who reportedly displayed an untenorlike bravery during a conflagration at the Opéra-Comique in Paris on the night of May 25, 1887, when he sang in *Mignon*. The lives of hundreds of panic-stricken opera-goers were supposedly saved thanks to his *sang-froid*. Well, it turns out that there was a rather horrendous fire at the Opéra-Comique on that night, and that "le beau Taskin," as he was known to his admirers, did display courage in calming down the audience, and was commended for it by the French government.

I was smugly confident of the accuracy of the report that the Italian conductor Gino Marinuzzi was assassinated by the anti-Fascist partisans in Milan on August 17, 1945, as duly noted in *Baker's*, and also in *Grove*, in Riemann's *Musik-Lexikon* ("ermordet") and in the Italian encyclopedia *La Musica* ("mori assassinato"). But why did the anti-Fascist partisans wait so long after the end of the Mussolini regime to shoot him? True, he was the author of a triumphal ode on the occasion of the historic meeting between Hitler and Mussolini in an Alpine tunnel, but many other Italian composers expressed a similar lack of precognition in glorifying the Fascist regime. I received many letters from Italian composers during the fascist years, dated E.F. XV, E.F. XVIII, etc, i.e., Era Fascista followed by the year, in Roman numerals, since Mussolini's march on Rome ("tough on Jesus Christ," a witty Bostonian remarked when I showed him these letters), and they remained unscathed. However that might be, the publishers of *Baker's* received an irate letter from a Milan lawyer, acting on behalf of the Marinuzzi family, protesting that the account of the assassination was false and demanding an immediate rectification. Gino Marinuzzi, the letter said, died peacefully in a Milan hospital on the date correctly given in *Baker's*, succumbing not to a bullet wound but to hepatic anemia. Fortunately, *Baker's* VI was still in a fluid state, and the publishers were able to pacify the Marinuzzi family lawyer, promising to make a correction. But why did the Marinuzzis wait all these years to fire their salvo, and why zero in on *Baker's* rather than on their own Italian dictionaries? And where did the original report of assassination come from? The *Corriere della Sera*, Milan's major newspaper, carried an *R.I.P.* notice of Marinuzzi's death, with no mention of the cause. The case was clinched eventually by the Servizio Mortuario of the city of Milan, stating that Marinuzzi had indeed died of acute atrophy of the liver. No bullets, no assassination, no melodrama.

Beware of false suspicions! Could two musicians with identical last names (except for a nobiliary particle), Victor Alessandro of Texas and Raffaele d'Alessandro of Switzerland, have died on their respective, albeit mutually different, birthdays? They could, and they did. Could Raselius have written a book on Roselius? He could, and he did. Could Gabriel Faure (no accent) have written a monograph on Gabriel Fauré (accent)? He could and he did. Was Schubart really the author of the words of *Die Forelle* by Schubert? Yes, he was. Could two composers, each named Victor Young, have been active in the movies in Hollywood during the same period? They were. Could I myself have had a classmate, in a St. Petersburg high school, called Nicolas Slonimsky? I had, and since I joined the class after him, my name was registered as Nicolas II, which was the official name of the then reigning Czar of all the Russians.

Among the many persistent errors plaguing musical biography is the belief that Wagner originated the term *Leitmotiv*. He did not; it was first proposed by Friedrich Wilhelm Jähns in the preface to his book on Weber published in 1871. Bizet did not write the famous *Habanera* in *Carmen*. He took it from a collection of Spanish songs by Sebastián Yradier, without any alteration of key, harmonization, tempo, rhythm, and dynamics.

The Russians have a marvelously expressive word for a story unsupported by evidence—"nyebylitsa," an "un-was-ity." Famous last words by historic personages are almost all such un-was-ities. Madame Roland's exclamation on her way to the guillotine, "Liberty, how many crimes are committed in thy name!" first appeared in print in Lamartine's *Histoire de la Révolution française*, or so it is cited in *Bartlett's Familiar Quotations*. But browsing through the 1793 volume of *The Annual Register* of London, I came upon a Paris dispatch quoting the famous phrase. Is one to suppose then the British Paris correspondent actually followed the tumbril taking Madame Roland to the place of execution and actually heard her utter the famous apostrophe? Not bloody likely.

"Lexicographis secundus post Herculem labor" was the judgment pronounced by Joseph Justus Scaliger (1540–1609), himself a lexicographer of stature. The mythological reference is, of course, to the labor performed by Hercules in cleaning up the manure-filled stables of King Augeus, son of the sun god Helius. Hercules did the job in twenty-four hours; to clean up a clogged music dictionary takes a little longer. But sanitation must be done with circumspection; one never knows what shining gems, what bits of fascinating tektite, are embedded in rejected debris. Take the story of the Italian singer Giulio Rossi as related by *Baker's*. He started out as a tenor, but unintentionally plunged into the Tiber on a cold day and as a consequence became a *basso profondo*. Incredible? Yes, incredible, but what lexicographer would have the heart to throw it into the pile of refuse? I couldn't. So—*stet!*

There should be no such spirit of acceptance for the purple prose that some editors indulged in while describing the life and works of admired persons. I had to deflate somewhat the verbal effusions in the original *Baker's* entry on A.W. Thayer, biographer of Beethoven. Here is a sample: "Unhappily, his wonderful capacity for work was overtaxed, and volume IV of his nobly conceived Beethoven biography, executed with a painstaking thoroughness and scrupulous fidelity beyond praise, was left unfinished. Though he lived for years in straitened circumstances, he resolutely refused offers from firms like Novello & Co. and G. Schirmer, Inc., hoping to recast entirely the English version of his *Beethoven*." Suffocating! Give us air to breathe!

A biographical dictionary ought to be a democratic assembly of factual information. Great masters are by right to be given preferential treatment, but opaque
luminaries, e.g., Bibl, Kittl, Lickl, or Titl, ought to be tendered hospitality, if not
lavish accommodations. Ay, there's the rub! Proportionate representation is the
ideal desideratum, but availability of information and productivity of work determine the space allowance. One would fain wish that there were more biographical information on Shakespeare than on Pepys, on Josquin Des Prez than on a
whole gallery of later madrigalists, on Bach than on Reger. As it is, an unhappy
editor must gather every bit of information on the great masters of the past and
make a judicious selection of biographical data and a list of works of *dii minores*
in the arts.

One must also beware of lexicographical zombies, typographical clones and
monsters. The great Eitner, who spent a lifetime tabulating manuscripts in
European libraries, was also a progenitor of such teratological creatures. Working
on a pile of anonymous French songs, he apparently mistook the nouns in their
titles for names of composers. Thus we learn from Eitner that "La Chanson d'un
gai Berger" was a song by Ungay Berger, and that "La Chanson de l'Auberge
Isolée" was composed by Mlle. Isolée L'Auberge. There must be a number of desperate music researchers trying to find out who Mr. Gay Shepherd and Miss
Isolated Tavern were in life. *Cobbett's Cyclopedia of Chamber Music* is responsible for spawning D. Michaud (a misprint for D. Milhaud), Marcel Babey (for
Marcel Labey), and, most intriguing, a famous violinist, Heinrich Wehtan, generated through the transliteration of the Russian spelling in Cyrillic letters of the
name of Henri Vieuxtemps via a German translation of an article originally written in Russian by a contributor to *Cobbett*.

To exorcise such vampires and to drive a stake through their hideous hearts I
myself decided to create a monster as the last entry of the 1958 edition of *Baker's*.
Never fear: I killed it in page proofs. But here it is *à titre documentaire*:

Zyžik, Krsto, Czech composer; b. Pressburg, Feb. 29, 1900. [1900 was not a
leap year in the West.] He traveled widely to Pozsony and Bratislava [Pozsony and
Bratislava are respectively the Hungarian and Slovak names of Pressburg], and
back to Pressburg. He attracted attention with his oratorio *Dieta Wormsová*, written for the quadricentennial of the Diet of Worms in a vermicular counterpart
[the Diet of Worms was an actual historic assembly, held in the city of Worms in
1521; it condemned Luther as a heretic]; then brought out a bel canto work, *Strč
prst skrz krk* (a Czech tongue twister, meaning *put your finger on your throat*),
using only consonants in consonant harmony. His works include *Pinč mj šuga*
(*Pinch me, Sugar*, or *Pinch Meshuga* in phonetical transcription) for chorus and
pinched strings; *Smyccový Kvartet* (string quartet) for woodwind quintet; *Sappho
LXIX* for 2 female participants (Lesbos Festival, 1955): *Macho* for large secular
organ (male player), etc. In 1979, after many years of aggravated floccillation and
severe dyscrasia, he was committed to a dissident asylum. See Sol Mysnik [rather
obvious anagram of Slonimsky], *A Czech Checkmate: The Story of Krsto Zyžik*
(Los Angeles, 1979).

The most authentic sources of information ought to be diaries and autobiographies, correspondence, and reminiscences of friends and relatives. But much too
frequently, at least in musical biography, accounts by musicians themselves are
tainted by a desire for self-glorification hidden behind a mask of assumed mod-
esty. "Look at me," they seem to tell the reader, "and marvel at my accomplishments; starting out in poverty, privations, and need, and by dint of faith in my

destiny and hard work, rising to the top of the pyramid of fame, recognition, and even wealth." Wagner's autobiography abounds in trivia, including some tedious pages about his pet dogs, but he never mentions the episode of his incarceration at the Clichy prison in Paris from October 28 to November 17, 1840, for non-payment of debt. True, it was one of those permissive jailings, with easy family furloughs, but still the episode is a legitimate part of Wagner's biography. Naturally, Wagner never gave an account in his autobiography of his cavalier treatment of the women in his life, nor did he make clear the circumstances of the birth of his natural daughter Isolde, born to Cosima on April 10, 1865, while she was still married to Hans von Bülow. In 1914 Isolde petitioned the Bavarian Civil Court to grant her a share in Wagner's royalties; her claim was rejected on the ground that there was no evidence that Cosima had ceased all communication with her legitimate husband, Hans von Bülow, within the period of ten months before Isolde's birth, a legal maximum for the length of gestation. The court also overruled the evidence submitted by Isolde's lawyer husband, based on the phrenological and hemological similarities between Wagner and Isolde.

It was fashionable among artists of the nineteenth century to claim paternity from celebrated or titled persons. Was the French cellist François Servais actually a bastard child of Liszt, as was claimed for him in various sources, including *Baker's*? He was born in St. Petersburg, or so the dictionaries said, in 1846, a date that fits the chronology of Liszt's liaison with Princess Sayn-Wittgenstein. But nothing in the voluminous correspondence between her and Liszt during that period indicated that she was a prospective mother. My earnest inquiries in Russia brought no results. The verdict in this case, therefore, must remain unproven.

A more involved claim of desirable paternity concerns the once famous pianist Sigismond Thalberg, who apparently authorized the report that he was the son of a Prince Dietrichstein and a baroness. Further inquiries were discouraged by a footnote in the 1954 edition of *Grove's Dictionary* stating that Thalberg's birth certificate (he was born in Geneva) was unobtainable. Distrustful of this notice, I wrote to Geneva and obtained a copy of the certificate by airmail within a matter of days. I discovered later that the document had been previously published in a Belgian magazine on the occasion of Thalberg's centenary in 1912. The certificate stated that Thalberg was a legitimate son of Joseph Thalberg and Fortunee Stein, both of Frankfurt am Main, and that he was born in Geneva on January 8, 1812. The case was further complicated by the publication in various sources of a letter allegedly written by Thalberg's natural mother to Prince Dietrichstein at the time of Thalberg's birth, suggesting that he should be given the name Thalberg, so that he would grow as peacefully as a Thal (valley) and would tower over humanity as high as a Berg (mountain). Just who fabricated this letter and for what purpose remains unclear. The Supplement to Riemann's *Musik-Lexikon*, published in 1975, adds the intriguing bit of information that Thalberg was indeed adopted by Prince Dietrichstein later in life.

The strange lure of aristocratic birth seems to be undiminished even in our own century. An English singer who was active in recital and on the light-opera stage in the early 1900s under the name Louis Graveure declared in an interview published in the *New York Times* in 1947 that he was of royal or possibly imperial birth, and that it would be worth a fortune to him to find out who he really was. Well, for the modest sum of two shillings and sixpence I obtained from London a copy of his birth certificate which dispelled the mystery. His real name was Wilfrid Douthitt, and he used it in his early appearances in England as a baritone; later he changed to tenor and gave concerts as Louis Graveure, which was his mother's maiden name.

Much more honest was the search for true paternity undertaken by the American folk songster and poet Rod McKuen. He knew he was illegitimate, and his mother never told him who his father was. He undertook a long quest, almost epic in its simple grandeur, and in the end established the identity of his father, a backwoods lumberjack.

The desire to recreate one's life according to one's fancy is universal, and artists are particularly apt to imagine, and at times consciously to contrive, the tales of might-have-been. Was Liszt actually kissed on the brow by Beethoven at the concert he played in Vienna as a child? There is a charming lithograph of the supposed event, which is reproduced in several Liszt biographies. But the evidence of Beethoven's archives suggests that Beethoven was annoyed by Liszt's father's bringing the child Liszt to Beethoven's quarters, and that he never went to the concert, despite Schindler's efforts to persuade him to attend. Liszt did play for Beethoven in private, but whether he was kissed on the brow or not remains uncertain.

Working on a biographical dictionary of musicians, I have found myself in the uncomfortable position of private detective. Some years back I received a letter from a Russian woman living in Rome. She asked my help to find out whether her father, the Russian violinist Bezekirsky, who emigrated to America when she was a child, was still alive. Since Bezekirsky was in *Baker's*, I had to search for him anyway to bring him up to date, dead or alive. Tracking him down through several music schools where he taught violin, I finally reached him in a small locality in upstate New York. Delighted that I could restore a missing father to an anxious daughter, I wrote to both, giving their mutual addresses. Frankly, I expected letters full of emotional gratitude for my humanitarian endeavor, but I got none from either father or daughter. I do not relish unfinished human symphonies, so I wrote to Bezckirsky again, asking him to let me know whether he had established contact with his long-lost offspring. Great was my shock when I received from him a postcard scribbled in English in a senile hand, saying as follows: "Your mission was successful, if you call several unpleasant and demanding letters from my daughter a success. I am in no position to help her in any way." I never heard from the daughter.

One of the sharpest rebukes I ever received for trying to obtain information was administered by the remarkable English composer Kaikhosru Sorabji. I made the terrible *faux pas* of describing him as an Indian composer. "Do not dare to call me an Indian," he thundered in reply. "We are Parsi, followers of Zarathustra." He flatly refused to supply biographical data about himself, but he sent me a signed copy of his formidable *Opus Clavicembalisticum*, and pointed out for my information that it is the greatest polyphonic work since Bach's *Kunst der Fuge*. For all I know, it may be exactly that, at least in the grandeur of conception and extraordinary skill of its structure. But his rebuke to me was mild in comparison with the eruption of invective he poured on Percy Scholes for what he deemed to be an undignified and inadequate entry on himself in the *Oxford Companion to Music*. Scholes sent the letter to me with the inscription "For your delectation." It is worth reproducing *in toto*:

Corfe Castle, Dorset, XXII.II.MCMLII A.D.

My Good Sir:

A valued friend draws my attention to a lucubration of yours under the entry of my name in a recently published book of reference. One is hard put to it at which to marvel the more, the exiguity of your sense of proportion or the poverty of your taste in devoting double the amount of space to cheap impertinences regarding the place and date of my birth (which is as little business of yours as of any other prying nosey busybody) to that which is devoted to my work, which is all that concerns anyone and which carefully conveys inaccurate and false information by leaving our material facts. Formerly I used to consider it enough when dealing with these stupid and impudent enquiries from lexicographical persons, deliberately to mislead them as to dates and places. This is a mistake: their enquiries should either be ignored or refused. And the sooner folk of their kidney grasp the fact that one is under no moral obligation to provide them with accurate, or indeed any information at all just because they choose to ask for it, the very much better for all concerned.

I have the honor to be, Sir, Yours very faithfully,
Kaikhosru Shapurji Sorabji

Sorabji is a unique figure in music, and his full biography would be fascinating. Erik Chisholm, who knew him personally, told me that the gate of Sorabji's castle in Dorset bears this legend: "Visitors Unwelcome. Roman Catholic Nuns in Full Habit May Enter Without An Appointment." In reckless disregard of Sorabji's demurrer at biographical information about himself, I wrote to the London registry of birth to find out at least when and where he was born. To my surprise the document stated that his real name was Leon Dudley Sorabji; Kaikhosru was apparently his Parsi name assumed later in life. I informed Eric Bloom, who was then working on the Fifth Edition of *Grove*, of my findings. His response was prompt. "I knew right along," he wrote, "that Sorabji's name was Leon Dudley, but if you value your life I would not advise you to put it in print, for I fear that if you do he would take the next plane to America and assassinate you personally." And Samuel Johnson said that a lexicographer is a "harmless drudge"!

Once in a while in a beleaguered lexicographer's life the subject of an entry in a biographical dictionary voices his gratitude for the honor. A letter I received from Walter Stockhoff, an American composer whose music was praised by Busoni as "a fresh voice from the New World that could revitalize the tired art of Europe," certainly warmed the cockles of my heart. "As pure, cool, crystal-clear water," he wrote me, "revives one thirsting in the desert, so intelligence, understanding, sympathy and sense of values come to brighten one's pathway. There is a noble generosity in your giving thought to my work. Through the greatness of your nature you strengthen others."

Chronological memory is treacherous. Casals owned the manuscript of the B-flat major string quartet, op. 67, of Brahms, given to him by a Vienna collector. It was, he told me, mysteriously connected with his life, for he was conceived when Brahms began the composition of the quartet, and was born when Brahms completed it. Leaving aside the problem of knowing the date of one's conception, the chronology does not support this fancy. Brahms wrote the work during the summer and fall of 1875, and it was first performed in Berlin on October 30, 1876. Casals was born two months after its performance and could not have been conceived fourteen or fifteen months previously.

Lexicographical cross-pollination of inaccurate information in similar wording is a hazard. Philip Hale used to say that when several mutually independent reference works vouchsafe identical data, he deems the information reliable. Not necessarily so. If we consider the case of Mascagni, one comes upon a curious iteration of idiom that arouses suspicion. The 1906 edition of *Grove's* states that Mascagni was compelled to study music "by stealth" because his father, a baker, wanted him to be a lawyer. The *Oxford Companion to Music* paraphrases *Grove's*: "Mascagni was the son of a baker who took music lessons by stealth." The 1940 edition of *Baker's* echoes: "Mascagni's father (a baker) wished him to study jurisprudence, but he learned piano-playing by stealth." What is this obsession with the quaint locution "by stealth" in all these reference works? In point of fact, Mascagni's father was quite proud of his son's achievement as a musician and eagerly supported his studies at the conservatory of Milan, as attested by their published correspondence.

If autobiographies are inevitably images of one's life as refracted through a prism resulting in an attractive and colorful spectrum, it is nevertheless strange that a composer would alter the history of the creation of a particular work. Berlioz did so paraleptically in his most famous score, *Symphonie fantastique*, by leaving out of its program the fact that one of the movements was taken from his early school work and that he implanted the unifying *idée fixe* surgically in a vacant measure containing a fermata, in order to justify its inclusion. And yet this manipulation creates the false impression of coherence. Of course, composers need not apologize to their biographers and analysts for revising their works in the light of later wisdom. Mahler denied the programmatic intent of several of his symphonies even though the descriptive titles appeared in the manuscripts. Beethoven carefully disavowed the pictorial nature of his *Pastoral Symphony* by stating that the music represented an impression rather than a description of a day in the country, and this despite the birdcalls and the electric storm in the score. Schoenberg, who was opposed to representational music, nevertheless yielded to the importunities of his publishers in authorising romantic titles for the individual movements of his *Five Orchestral Pieces*.

On the other hand, Stravinsky's latter-day denial that his early *Scherzo fantastique* was inspired by his reading of Maeterlinck's *La Vie des Abeilles* is puzzling. In Robert Craft's *Conversations with Igor Stravinsky*, in reply to the question about the subject matter of the work, Stravinsky replies unequivocally: "I wrote the *Scherzo* as a piece of pure symphonic music. The bees were a choreographer's idea . . . Some bad literature about bees was published on the fly-leaf of the score to satisfy my publisher who thought a 'story' would help to sell the music." This declaration was most unfair to the publisher and to the choreographer. In his own letters to Rimsky-Korsakov at the time of composition of the score (1907), published in Moscow in 1973, Stravinsky writes: "I intended to write a scherzo already in St. Petersburg, but I lacked subject matter. It so happens that I have been reading *La Vie des Abeilles* by Maeterlinck, a half-philosophical, half-poetic work, which captivated me completely. At first, I intended to use direct quotations so as to make the program of my piece quite clear, but then I realized that it would not do because in the book the scientific and poetic elements are closely interwoven. I decided therefore to guide myself by a definite programmatic design without actual quotations, and to entitle the work simply *The Bees*, after Maeterlinck, a fantastic scherzo."

In the nineteenth century America was, to all practical purposes, a German colony in instrumental music and an Italian colony in opera. Lillian Norton would never have made a singing career had she not changed her name to Nordica. Conductors had to be German or Austrian (Damrosch, Muck, Henschel, Nikisch, Mahler). Pianists prospered when their last names ended with "sky" or "ski." Paderewski was a shining example of grandeur and glory. (I myself profited peripherally when I entered the United States in 1923 exempt from the rigid quota imposed by the Immigration Office on Slavs and such, exception being made for "artists," particularly those whose names looked and sounded artistic.) Ethel Liggins, an Englishwoman intent on making an American career, was advised to change her name to Leginska ("ska" being the feminine counterpart of "ski"). She told me interesting stories about herself; among her many memories, she said that as a child she was bounced by Winston Churchill on his knee after his return as a hero from the Boer War. She volunteered her own date of birth, April 13, 1886, and I checked on it by securing her birth certificate; it was correct. Now, Churchill came home in glory in 1899, and since it is unlikely that he proceeded right away to bounce Liggins (not yet Leginska) on his knee, she must have reached a nubile adolescence at the time, and the whole episode assumed a totally different complexion. "Botheration!" she exclaimed when I pointed out the embarrassing chronology to her. "How do you know when Churchill returned to England from South Africa? You are not British!"

No greater splendor among contemporary orchestral conductors surrounded the career of Leopold Stokowski, who lived to be 95, working in music to the last days of his life. And his name ended in "ski"! Invidious rumors had it that his real name was Stokes, and that he polonized it as many other artists did. False! He was born in London, the son of a Polish cabinetmaker named Kopernik Joseph Boleslaw Stokowski and an Irishwoman, Annie Marion Moore-Stokowski, on April 18, 1882. Not satisfied with his true half-Polish origin, he for some reason chose to maintain that he was totally Polish, born in Cracow in 1887 (rather than 1882), and that his name was Leopold Boleslawowicz Stokowski. This bit of fantasy appears in the main volume of Riemann's *Musik-Lexikon*. When I sounded the alarm, pointing out that the patronymic ending on "which" or "wicz" or "witch" is possible in Russian, but not in Polish, the Riemann's editors sent me a photostat copy of the original questionnaire in Stokowski's own hand embodying all this fanciful information. By way of rebuttal, I forwarded to the Riemann's people a copy of Stokowski's birth certificate which I had obtained from London. The 1975 supplement to Riemann's carries a corresponding correction.

Among many fantastic tales that accompany musical biographies there is one concerning Werner Egk. The name sounded like a manufactured logogriph, or an acronym for "ein guter Künstler," and even more self-anointed, "ein genialer Künstler." I wrote to the director of the archives of the city of Augsburg where Egk was born, and elicited the information that his real name was Mayer. If so, whence Egk? The composer himself came forward with an explanation that was more puzzling than the original riddle: he changed his name from Mayer to Egk after his marriage to Elisabeth Karl; the initials of her first and last name formed the outer letters of Egk, and the middle "g" was added "for euphony." Guttural euphony?

No experience in my "harmless drudgery" equaled the Case of Walter Dahms, an obscure German author of musical biographies. According to musical lexica that listed his name, including *Baker's*, he went to Rome in 1922, and promptly vanished. I did not care to leave him dangling like an unshriven ghost, an elusive zombie. I used to mention Dahms to every musicologist I met as a disappearing act, and one of them told me that there was nothing mysterious about Dahms, that he went to Lisbon, adopted a Portuguese-sounding pseudonym, and continued publishing books on music. I inserted this seemingly innocuous bit of information in my 1965 Supplement to *Baker's*, but unbeknownst to myself it unleashed a fantastic chain of events. The editors of the Supplement to Riemann's *Musik-Lexikon*, who were also interested to bring Dahms up to date, seized upon my addendum and inquired through Santiago Kastner, a London-born German-educated music scholar resident in Lisbon, to find out facts about Dahms. But no one in the rather flourishing German colony in Lisbon, not even anyone at the German embassy, knew anything about Dahms. The Riemann editors would not be pacified. "Baker (really Slonimsky)," they wrote Kastner again, "is greatly valued here because of its reliability. Behind the bland statement that Dahms was still in Lisbon in 1960 must lie a lot of painstaking research." Kastner volunteered a guess that Dahms might be a German-speaking Portuguese citizen named

Gualterio Armando, Gualterio being a Portuguese form of Walter, and Armando containing three letters of the name Dahms. He addressed the question directly to Dahms, whether he was or was not Dahms. All hell broke loose thereafter. "I am not identical with anyone but myself," replied Gualterio Armando. "I have absolutely nothing to say about Herr W. D. mentioned in your letter because I know nothing about him. I hope that this will put an end to this whole business once and for all." Kastner reported his failure to the Riemann's editors, and announced that he was through with his investigation, but voiced his conviction that Dahms "must be identical with that asshole Gualterio Armando after all." Why was he so vehement in denying his real identity? He died on October 5, 1973, carrying the secret to his grave.

Among the unburied musical ghosts that haunted me through the years was Alois Minkus, an Austrian composer of operas and ballets who spent most of his career in Russia. For a hundred years, first under the Czars, then under the Soviets, his ballets never ceased to be the favorite numbers in the Russian ballet repertory. Not a year passed without my receiving an insistent inquiry from Russia and abroad as to the fate of Minkus after he left Russia in 1891. Some reference works have him dead in that year; others prolong his life until 1907, with the date accompanied by a parenthetical question mark. I must have written a dozen letters to various registries of vital statistics in Vienna on the supposition that Minkus returned to Vienna, where he was born, and died there. I did obtain his birth certificate ascertaining that he was born on March 23, 1826, rather than 1827 as most Russian and other music reference sources have it, but the Vienna archivists could tell me nothing as to his date of death. Then in the summer of 1976 I made one more half-hearted inquiry in Vienna. To my astonishment I got a clue that all death notices before 1939 were moved from the Stadtarchiv, the Landesarchiv, and the Vienna Rathaus and its numerous subdivisions to the corresponding parochial registries. Hot on the scent, I wrote the proper Lutheran parish, and to my absolute joy of discovery I received a document certifying that Alois Minkus died at Gentzgasse 92 in Vienna, on December 7, 1917, in the 92nd year of his life, from pneumonia, and that his mortal remains were deposed at the cemetery of Döbling. I immediately rushed this information and the pertinent documentation to the editors of the big Russian musical encyclopedia, which had just reached the letter M, and the date got in at the last moment before going to press, with an appropriate proud parenthetical clause testifying to its authenticity.

One of the most fantastic episodes in my hunt for missing musical persons was the search for Heinrich Hammer, a German conductor and composer who emigrated to the United States about the turn of the century, and then vanished from the musical scene. I appealed for help to William Lichtenwanger, who combines profound erudition with a detective flair that would have made him a rich man had he dedicated himself to the search for missing heirs and holders of unused bank accounts. Quick as a panther, he produced a clipping from the *Los Angeles Times* of October 25, 1953, which carried on its society page a photograph of Heinrich Hammer, 91, and his young bride Arlene, 22. Their address was given in the story, but when I wrote to him my letter came back with the notation "Deceased." But when and where? Lichtenwanger got on the telephone, and after a few inquiries got hold of Hammer's son, a repair worker of the California telephone company. Unbelievably, contact was established with him atop a telephone pole, and he gave Lichtenwanger the needed information. Hammer had moved to Phoenix, Arizona, where he died on October 28, 1954, just a year after his marriage.

How much of personal life ought to be reported in a dignified biographical dictionary? Volumes have been written speculating about the identity of

Beethoven's "Immortal Beloved," even though the famous letter addressed to her was never sent off. Should a biographer be so bold as to doubt a great man's own confession of love? A conscientious biographer took exception to Goethe's declaration that he had never loved anyone as much as Lili Schönemann. "Here the great Goethe errs," he commented: "His greatest love was Frederike Brion." From the sublime to contemporary love lore. The formidable Hungarian pianist Nyiregyházi was married nine times, and admitted to 65 extramarital liaisons. Is this proper information in a biographical dictionary? The marriages, perhaps; the liaisons, only famous ones, like Liszt's and Chopin's.

It was only recently that the known homosexuality of Tchaikovsky became a matter of open discussion in his biographies; the first inkling of it appeared in the preface to the 1934 edition of Tchaikovsky's correspondence with his benefactress Madame von Meck. In 1940 a collection of his letters to the family, including those to his brother and biographer Modest, who was also a homosexual, was published in Russia, but it was soon withdrawn from publication and became a sort of bibliographical phantom; an expurgated edition was published later. In subsequent books on Tchaikovsky published in Russia the matter is unmentioned. But a strange mass of unfounded rumors began circulating both in Russia and abroad shortly after Tchaikovsky's death that he committed "suicide by cholera," that he deliberately drank unboiled water during a raging cholera epidemic in St. Petersburg, and this despite his fear of cholera, which had been the cause of his mother's death. The stories that I heard during my visit to Russia in 1962 were right out of Gothic horror tales. It seems that Tchaikovsky became involved in a homosexual affair with a young member of the Russian Imperial family, and that when Czar Alexander III got wind of it, he served the Tchaikovsky family an ultimatum: either have Tchaikovsky take poison, or have him tried for sodomy and sent to Siberia. Tchaikovsky accepted the verdict, and with the connivance of his personal physician, Dr. Bertenson, was given a poison that produced symptoms similar to those of cholera. As additional evidence that Tchaikovsky did not die of cholera, the proponents of this theory argue, is the fact that his body was allowed to lie in state and that several of his intimates kissed him on the mouth, as the Russian death ritual allows, whereas cholera victims were buried in zinc-lined sealed coffins to prevent contagion.

Dramatic deaths should rightly be noted in biographies, but grisly details had better be left out. It is not advisable to follow the type of reporting exemplified in an obituary of Sir Armine Woodhouse in *The Annual Register of London* for the year 1777, noting that his death "was occasioned by a fishbone in his throat."

Percy Scholes took credit for sending the British writer on music, Arthur Eaglefield Hull, to his death under the wheels of a train. He wrote me: "Hull's suicide was the result of my exposure of his thefts in his book *Music, Classical, Romantic and Modern*. He threw himself under a train."

A suicide directly connected with a musical composition was that of Rezsö Seress, Hungarian author of the sad, sad song "Gloomy Sunday." At one time the playing of the tune was forbidden in Central Europe because it drove several impressionable people to suicide. Seress himself jumped out the window, on a Monday, not a gloomy Sunday.

Musical murders are surprisingly few; singers are occasionally murdered out of jealousy, but not famous singers. The most spectacular murder, never conclusively solved, was that of the French eighteenth-century musician Jean Marie Leclair, stabbed to death in his own house. Since nothing was taken, it could not have been a burglary. I proposed a theory that he was done to death by his estranged wife, who was a professional engraver and publisher of some of Leclair's music, and had sharp tools at her disposal, but my painstaking argumentation in favor of this theory was pooh-poohed by the foremost French music historian Marc Pincherle and others.

Dementia, insanity, and bodily disintegration are scourges that hit many composers, and in most cases they were caused by syphilis. Undoubtedly, the tragic illnesses of Schumann, Smetana, Hugo Wolf, and MacDowell were all caused by the lues, the *morbus gallicus*, as it was usually described in the past centuries. In his book on Delius, Sir Thomas Beecham remarks ruefully that the goddess Aphrodite Pandemos repaid Delius cruelly for his lifelong worship at her altar. Delius died blind and paralyzed.

In light of recent disclosures, free from displaced piety for a great man, it appears that Beethoven, too, was a victim of syphilis. His deafness was only a symptom (as in the case of Smetana) which does not necessarily indicate a venereal infection. But there are too many other circumstances that lead to this sad conclusion, recounted in the recent study by Dieter Kerner, *Krankheiten grosser Musiker*.

Even the worshipful speculation as to psychological causes of physical decline and death, so cherished in old-fashioned biography, has no place in a book of reference. I brushed aside such probings into a person's psyche as were found in an old entry on the eighteenth-century French composer Isouard, to the effect that he was so deeply "mortified" by his failure to be elected to the French Academy that "although a married man" he abandoned work, "plunged into dissipation, and died."

Triskaidecaphobia, an irrational fear of the number 13, demonstrably affected the state of mind of two great composers, Rossini and Schoenberg. In addition to his superstition about the malevolent character of 13, Rossini was also fearful of Friday. He died on November 13, 1868, which was a Friday. Numerologists could cite his case to prove predestination. Schoenberg's case is remarkable because there is so much recent evidence that his triskaidecaphobia was not a whimsical pose. He was born on the 13th of the month of September in 1874, and he regarded this as ominous in his personal destiny. He sometimes avoided using 13 in numbering the bars of his works. When he realized that the title of his work *Moses und Aaron* contained 13 letters, he crossed out the second "a" in Aaron, even though the spelling Aron cannot be substantiated either in German or in English. When someone thoughtlessly remarked to him on his 76th birthday that $7 + 6 = 13$, he seemed genuinely upset; he died at the age of 76. On his last day of life, July 13, 1951, he remarked to his wife that he would be all right if he would survive the ominous day, but he did not, and died.

Going over my list of *morituri*, centenarians or near-centenarians, I came upon the name of Victor Küzdö, a Hungarian-American violinist born, or so the old edition of *Baker's* said, in 1869. I wrote to Küzdö at his last known address, which I found in an old musical directory, in effect asking him whether he was living or dead. A few days later I received from him a dictated postcard saying that, although practically blind, he was still alive and well, in Glendale, California. Furthermore, he took the opportunity to correct his date of birth: he was born in 1863, not in 1869, and had shortly before celebrated his 100th anniversary! But this was not the end of the story; soon afterwards I got a letter from a real-estate man in Glendale notifying me that Küzdö was in the habit of diminishing his age, and that he was actually 103, not 100! How could he be sure? Simple: he was a numerologist. When the inevitable end came to Küzdö on February 24, 1966, his death certificate gave his age as 106. He was born in 1859, not in 1863, not in 1869.

The most remarkable woman centenarian on my list was Margaret Ruthven Lang, of the Boston musical dynasty of Lang, who died at the age of 104 in 1972. She was a regular symphony-goer since the early days of the Boston Symphony.

On her 100th birthday the orchestra played the hymn *Old Hundred* in her honor. The Russian-French singer Marie Olénine d'Alheim lived to be 100. Among other recent centenarians was the French conductor and composer Henri-Paul Busser, who died in 1973 at the age of 101.

It would be most interesting to compile actuarial tables of the life expectancy of musicians according to their specialties. One thing appears certain: great musicians die young; consider Mozart, Schubert, Chopin, Mendelssohn, Scriabin. It is a fascinating speculation to project Mozart's life from 1756 into 1840, and Schubert's life to an even later date! One may indulge in a revery that very great musicians are summoned to Heaven because they would be more at home there.

Statistically speaking, organists live the longest lives, perhaps because their sedentary occupation keeps them from wasting their energy on idle pastimes. Scholars and pedagogues come next in longevity; conductors are fairly durable, too; among instrumentalists, those handling big instruments, like the double bass or trombone, live longer than violinists, who in turn live longer than flutists and oboe players, who are apt to be frail in physique. Among singers, tenors dissipate their vitality faster than bass singers. In all musical categories mediocrities outlive great artists by a large margin.

In addition to all the troubles involved in the compilation of a biographical dictionary, there are people who concoct sinister plots to further bamboozle the proverbial "harmless drudge." Mikhail Goldstein, a respectable Russian violinist, annoyed by his unfair treatment by the Soviet Music Publishing House in systematically rejecting his compositions, decided to take revenge on them. He invented a Russian composer named Ovsianiko-Kulikovsky, furnished him with a plausible biography, obtained a quantity of old manuscript paper, and composed a symphony in his name, pretending that he had found the score in the archives of the Odessa Conservatory, where he was librarian at the time. The Soviets swallowed the bait and published the score, proclaiming it to be a major discovery; it was also recorded, and greeted with enthusiastic reviews, not only in Russia but elsewhere. (Shall I confess, blushingly? I reviewed the recording for the *Musical Quarterly*, and announced with some reservations that if the work were genuine it would be the first Russian symphony ever written.) A doctoral dissertation was published on the work. When Goldstein admitted the hoax, he was accused of trying to appropriate an important piece of the national legacy. The situation degenerated into a farce, and Goldstein got out of Russia as soon as he could get an exit visa. But, as in Prokofiev's *Lieutenant Kije*, it was too late to kill off Ovsianiko-Kulikovsky, and his symphony is still listed in some record catalogues and is kept on the shelves of music libraries.

An even more dangerous mystification was perpetrated by the eminent Italian music scholar Alberto Cametti, who claimed discovery of an important biographical notebook of Palestrina, which established the elusive exact date of Palestrina's birth. He said he had purchased the document from one Telemaco Bratti, and even went to the trouble of reproducing, or rather forging, part of the manuscript in an article he wrote on the subject. Another Italian music scholar, Raffaele Casimiri, embraced the "discovery" as a gift of God to all true Palestrinologists. Then Alberto Cametti let it pass through various channels that the name of the alleged discoverer of the document, Telemaco Bratti, was an anagram of Alberto Cametti. A great inner storm ensued in the confined company of Italian music scholars, but in the meantime the hoax found its way into reputable bibliographies. (It was thanks to a knowledgeable friend that I myself did not fall into the trap in giving the exact date of Palestrina's birth in my edition of *Baker's*; this date remains unknown to this day.)

It is amazing that grown men and women would deliberately falsify their vital statistics, particularly their dates of birth, in order to appear younger in a reference work. The gambit is understandable among actresses and prima donnas; and it has been said that a woman has the privilege of improvising her age. It would also be understandable for men in their dotage who marry girls in their nonage, but both men and women of music rejuvenate themselves lexicographically even when they are not stage performers.

The Spanish composer Oscar Esplá produced his passport to prove to me that he was born in 1888 and not in 1886 as I had it in *Baker's*. But I had obtained a copy of his birth certificate which confirmed the accuracy of the earlier date.

Mabel Daniels, the Boston composer, once included in a piece a C-sharp against C, explaining that she "had to use a dissonance," since she was living in the same town with me. She petulantly accused me of being "no gentleman" in putting her down as born in 1878 rather than 1879, her own chosen year. She was born in November 1878, just a few weeks away from 1879, so why should I not accept the later year, she pleaded. Poor Mabel! She lived a full life until well into her tenth decade, dying in 1971.

A desire to appear young, if only on paper, is not a modern phenomenon. Since time immemorial, musicians, poets, painters, actors, even politicians, have exercised their unquestionable prerogative to fib about their age. Johann Jakob Froberger gave the date of May 18, 1620, as that of his birth to his physician, but his certificate of baptism reveals that he was baptized on May 19, 1616. It is a reasonable assumption that the day and the month of his birth, as given by himself, were correct, and that he was baptized on the next day, in 1616, not 1620.

In his handwritten autobiographical note for Mattheson's *Grundlage einer Ehrenpforte*, Telemann stated that he was born in 1682, whereas he was born a year earlier; as in many such cases, the day and the month of his birth, March 14, were given correctly.

The Italian composer and conductor Angelo Mariani, who was born on October 11, 1821, insisted in his communications to Francesco Regli, editor of an Italian biographical dictionary, that he was born on October 11, 1824. Mariani's birth certificate proves that he was born in 1821.

It was common practice in Catholic families to give identical Christian names to infants born after the death of a previous son, or a daughter, so as to perpetuate the memory of the lost child. This has led to a number of mistaken identities. The bicentennial of Giovanni Battista Viotti was widely celebrated in 1953, commemorating the birth in Fontanetto, Italy, of an infant of that name born on May 23, 1753, who died in the following year, on July 10, 1754. On May 12, 1755, another child was born to the Viottis and was given the names Giovanni Battista Guglielmo Domenico, retaining the first two names from those of their deceased son. This second similarly named child was the composer, whose bicentennial was celebrated two years early.

Biographical notices for Giacomo Insanguine found in old music dictionaries list his year of birth variously between 1712 and 1742. I applied for a copy of his birth certificate from the registries of his native town of Monopoli, and received a document purporting to show that he was born in 1712, a date that did not seem to agree with the known facts of his education and career. I pressed for a further search, which revealed that a Giacomo Insanguine who was born in 1712 died in 1726 at the age of 14. On March 22, 1728, a boy was born to the bereaved parents, and was given the names Giacomo Antonio Francesco Paolo Michele. This was the composer Insanguine.

Beethoven was eager to prove that he was born in 1772, not in 1770, and that he had an older brother who was born in 1770. It was discovered that a Ludwig Maria van Beethoven was born on April 1, 1769, but he died a few days later. The great Beethoven was born in the following year.

Next to birth certificates, the best sources of information are family Bibles, marriage certificates, and school registries. The date of birth of Kaspar Othmayr—March 12, 1515—is verified by his astrological chart, and one can be sure that in those remote times no one would hoodwink one's own astrologer. Even in modern times there are practicing astrologers among composers; of these, Dane Rudhyar is professionally the most successful.

In one famous event the correct age of the protagonist became a matter of life or death. On June 28, 1914, Gavrilo Princip, a young Serbian patriot, assassinated Crown Prince Franz Ferdinand of Austria. His act precipitated World War I, which precipitated the Russian Revolution, which precipitated the rise of Hitler, which precipitated World War II, etc., etc., etc. According to the Austrian law of the time no person less than twenty years of age could be executed for a capital crime. Gavrilo Princip was born on July 25, 1894, according to the Gregorian calendar, and was not quite twenty when he turned the world upside down. This saved him from execution, and he died in prison of tuberculosis of the bone marrow on April 28, 1918.

Oscar Wilde was not so lucky in his own chronology. He had whittled two years off his true age, claiming that he was born in 1856, whereas his real year of birth was 1854. Owing to a peculiar twist of English law, persons under forty indicted for immorality were granted leniency. Oscar Wilde was arrested for sodomy in 1895, and would have benefited by the law had it not been for the prying investigation of the court clerk, who secured Wilde's birth certificate proving that he was over forty at the time of his offense. This precluded leniency, and Wilde got a severe sentence. Despite the availability of the correct date, the *Encyclopaedia Britannica* carried the 1856 date in its article on Oscar Wilde right through its thirteenth edition. The *Century Cyclopedia* still gives the wrong date.

Much confusion is created in musical biography by the discrepancy in dating past events according to the Russian and Western calendars. The Greek Orthodox Church refused to accept the Gregorian calendar, and continued to use the Julian calendar until 1918. The Julian calendar was also in force in Bulgaria and Rumania during the same period. As a result, the dating of Russian births and deaths lagged behind the Western calendar, by 11 days in the 18th century, 12 days in the 19th century and 13 days in the 20th century. (The increase in discrepancy was caused by the fact that the years 1800 and 1900 were leap years in Russia but not in the West.) Stravinsky was born on June 5, 1882, according to the Julian calendar, which corresponded to June 17 of the Western calendar. But after 1900, when the difference between the two calendars increased by a day, he began celebrating his birthday on June 18. As his 80th anniversary approached in June 1962, he let it be known that he was going to celebrate it on June 18, which gave occasion to the *New York Times* to say that the faces of some lexicographers would be red on June 18, Stravinsky's preferred date for his birth, seeing that most dictionaries, including two edited by me, gave this date as June 17. I sent a rebuttal explaining my reasons for sticking to the June 17 date, and the *New York Times* published it under the caption, "It Is All Clear Now." This aroused Stravinsky's anger, and he shot off a wire to the paper reasserting his prerogative to celebrate his birthday on any date he wished. He declared his intention to mark the date in the twenty-first century on June 19, assuming that the difference between the two calendars would continue to increase a day each century, but he overlooked the fact that the year 2000 will be a leap year according to both the Gregorian and Julian calendars, because Pope Gregory ruled, on the advice of learned astronomers, that a year divisible by 400 must be reckoned as a leap year.

Are trivia worth mentioning in a biographical dictionary? It all depends. If such trivia have significant bearing on the subject's life and career, they should be given consideration. The unique case of the male castrato Tenducci, who eloped with a young girl and subsequently married her, deserves comment to dispel incredulity. He was a triorchis, and was therefore capable of marriage even after he was two-thirds castrated. His wife wrote a book of memoirs on the affair.

There remain a few categories that ought to be dealt with in separate rubrics.

INCLUSION AND EXCLUSION. *Baker's Biographical Dictionary of Musicians* must necessarily include men and women active in music who were not professional musicians, such as aristocratic patrons and patronesses, wealthy promoters of musical events, impresarios, music publishers, ballet masters who played important roles in commissioning and performing works from composers, and of course music critics. A practical criterion for including names of little-known composers, performers, and pedagogues should be the degree of likelihood that a music student, or a concertgoer, or a person who wants to know who is who in music would look it up in a dictionary. Thousands of names hover in the periphery of the music world and many more populate the index pages of biographies of famous composers. Still more are modest members of world orchestras who have distinguished themselves in various ways. Hugo Leichtentritt told me that Riemann, with whom he studied, used to play chamber music with amateurs and professionals at his home in Leipzig, and after each session, would ask them to fill out questionnaires for inclusion in his *Musik-Lexikon*. Theodore Baker, the compiler of the original edition of the present dictionary, collected biographical data from his friends who played in the Boston Symphony Orchestra. As a result, the early editions of both lexica became overpopulated with individuals who were perfectly honorable practitioners of their art, but who failed to leave an indelible, or even delible, mark on the sands of music. Most of these long-dead servants of music, whether borrowed by Baker from Riemann and other collectors of musical flesh, or installed anew by Baker and his successors out of personal friendship, have been allowed in the present edition to remain under their individual lexicographical tombstones for humanitarian reasons, rather than relegated to the common graves of crumbling newspaper clippings in public libraries; still, the paragraphs devoted to them originally have been mercifully cut down to commensurate size. No more will the impatient user of the dictionary be offered long lines of printed matter dealing with this or that obscure orchestral player, church organist, or provincial music teacher, relating in stultifying detail the advancement of their dull careers. But musical, or even unmusical, figures that multidentally smile on us from huge posters or gold-rimmed record albums, the glamorized purveyors of popular subculture of whatever degree of vulgarity, the Beatles and other singing coleoptera, are welcomed to this edition of *Baker's* even more liberally than they were to the 1958 edition and to the 1965 and 1971 Supplements. When, overcoming a natural revulsion, I dictated to my California secretary a paragraph on Humperdinck, the pop singer whose manager had the supreme *chutzpah* to appropriate the honored name of the composer of *Hänsel und Gretel* because it sounded "funny" and would attract attention, she was genuinely surprised at my liberality, but revealed her complete ignorance as to the existence of an earlier musician of the same name as the glorified rock singer.

DATES OF PERFORMANCE. A determined effort has been made in the present edition to list as many exact dates as possible of first performances of major works, especially operas and symphonies, not only by celebrated masters but also by modern composers. Care had to be taken to avoid duplication, for many composers are, and have been, in the habit of changing the titles of their works and then presenting them as new compositions. For instance, Don Emilio Arrieta y Corera wrote an opera, *La Conquista de Granada*, which was produced in Madrid in 1850 and revived under the title *Isabel la Católica* in 1855. The opera got a double billing in the valuable compilation *Cronica de la Opera italiana en Madrid*, published in 1878, the index of which correctly lists the two titles interchangeably, but this precaution has failed to deter other publications from duplicating the work. Quite often, composers append an optional descriptive title to an earlier work, which is apt to be duplicated in the catalogue.

SPELLING OF NAMES. Variants of spelling of celebrated musical names cause uncertainty, and choice had to be made in the present edition of *Baker's* guided by common usage; alternative spellings are then cross-referenced. Spanish, Portuguese, and Latin American names commonly include both the paternal and maternal surname; a selection has to be made according to the preferred usage. Thus, Alejandro García Caturla is listed under Caturla, the name he used in his published works; Oscar Lorenzo Fernandez is listed under Fernandez. In some instances, a musician changes the form of his name in the middle of his career. In the earlier editions of this dictionary the main entry on Edmund Rubbra appeared under Duncan-Rubbra; Duncan was the name of his first wife, which he adopted in some of his works; later he reverted to the legal name Rubbra, which is therefore used in the present edition of *Baker's*. Philip Heseltine published most of his music under the witching surname Peter Warlock, but Heseltine would seem preferable for a biographical dictionary. Americanization had produced several changes in the spelling of names; Arnold Schoenberg changed the spelling of his last name from Schönberg to Schoenberg when he emigrated to the United States. Carlos Salzedo dropped the acute accent that marked the antepenultimate letter of his original name. Eugen Zádor dropped the accent and changed his first name to Eugene when he came to America. Aladár Szendrei made his career in Europe under his original Hungarian name and surname, but changed it phonetically to Sendrey when he emigrated to the United States; a cross-reference has been made in the present edition under Sendrey to his original name. Edgar Varèse was baptized as Edgard Varèse, but most of his works were published with the first name spelled Edgar; in 1940 or thereabouts he changed it back to his legal name, Edgard. However, the present edition of *Baker's* keeps the familiar form Edgar. The existence of the alternate spellings Carl and Karl in many German names creates considerable confusion. The 1958 edition of *Baker's* modernized virtually all Carls to Karls, with some curious results, such as the spelling Karl Philipp Emanuel Bach instead of the standard Carl; the traditional spelling has been restored in the present edition. A curious case is that of Carl Ruggles, the American composer, whose real first name was Charles. He changed it to Carl as a youth when he decided to devote himself to music; he hoped that the Germanic form of the name would give him a better chance to succeed in the highly German-minded musical world of early twentieth-century America.

NOBILIARY PARTICLES. Early in this century it was common in American and British usage to put the nobiliary particle "von" in front of German names, such as "von Bülow" and the like. In the wake of World War I the "von" became unpopular among the Allied nations. The original full name of the English composer Gustav Holst, who was of Swedish ancestry, was von Holst. During the war, at the suggestion of Percy Scholes, he dropped the objectionable "von" from his name. Anton von Webern eliminated the "von" after the fall of the Austro-Hungarian Empire in 1918; the present edition lists his name under Webern, Anton von, in appreciation of the fact that he used the full name in the titles of many of his early works. A more difficult problem is encountered in the Dutch and Flemish nobiliary particle "van." Beethoven was very proprietary about his own "van" and regarded it as a proof of his noble origin, an important claim at the time when he tried to assure the guardianship of his nephew. The French and Spanish "de" and the Italian "di" often become coalesced with the last name. Debussy was Bussy to friends in his youth; Madame von Meck, the patroness of Tchaikovsky, who employed Debussy as a house musician and teacher in Moscow, referred to him as Bussy. No book of reference would list Bussy as an alternative for Debussy, but in some other names, not necessarily French, this nobiliary particle retains its independent existence. De Koven is an example. But De Falla is improper; his name should be listed under Falla, Manuel de.

RUSSIAN NAMES. The Russian alphabet has two intractable letters: one is represented by the Cyrillic symbol "ЫI," the other by a fence of three sticks with a line underneath it, and a wriggle, or a cedilla, on the right of the protracted horizontal line. Only Turkish has the phonetic equivalent of "ЫI," represented by an undotted "i" in the new Turkish alphabet. As for the second Cyrillic symbol aforementioned, it can be very adequately represented by the coalescence of the sounds "sh" and "ch" in a compound word such as fish-chips. The Russian sound for "e" is palatalized into "yeh" as in the new accepted English spelling of Dostoyevsky. English and American music dictionaries have inherited the spelling of Russian names of composers and performers from German, which has no "ch" sound, and in which the Russian (and English) "v" sound is represented by "w." As a result, we had Tschaikowsky for at least half a century. British and American librarians, realizing that Tsch = Ch, began spelling Tchaikovsky as Chaikovsky. But if we follow phonetics, then why do we need the diphthong "ai"? Why not plain "i" as in China? Here we come to the antinomy of sound, sight, and audiovisual association: Chikovsky has an impossible look. A compromise is necessary: hence, Tchaikovsky in *Baker's*. "Ch" in Rachmaninoff has a guttural German sound that English does not possess. The spelling Rachmaninoff is part-German ("ch") and part-French ("ff"), but this is the way he signed his name, familiar from printed music and concert programs. Most British sources prefer Rakhmaninov.

Once we start on the road to phonetics we will be bound for disaster. The name of the poet Evtushenko is pronounced Yevtushenko, but the eye rebels against its aspect. Besides, an unpalatalized "e" in such an initial sound is not necessarily un-Russian; some people from the northern provinces or from Siberia would say Evtushenko, just as if it were written in English. Another thing: the final diphthong "iy," as it is often represented phonetically in names like Tchaikovsky (or for that matter in Slonimsky), is nearest to the French "ille" in "volaille," but it is not as emphatically articulated. There is no reason to add ugliness to a name like Tchaikovsky by spelling it Tchaikovskiy. Then there is the vexing problem of transliterating Russian names of French or German origin back into their original languages. Some music dictionaries transliterate Cui as Kyue, a visual monstrosity. Cui was the son of a Napoleonic soldier who remained in Russia after the campaign of 1812 and married a Russian woman. His French name Cui ought to stay. The Soviet composer Shnitke (spelled phonetically in English) was of German origin, and his father signed his name in German as Schnittke; this spelling ought to remain even in an English reference work. The same consideration holds for names like Schneerson (Jewish-German) or Steinpress (pronounced Shteinpress in Russian) and Steinberg (for Shteinberg). If we try to transliterate foreign names in Russian back and forth, we will arrive at mutations such as Betkhoven and (yes, unbelievable but true) Poochcheenee, used for a time in the bibliography of *Notes*. I am proud to say that I opened such a vigorous letter-writing campaign against this practice that it was stopped. To conclude, the transliteration of Russian names and Russian titles of works should be guided by ear and by sight. There are seasonal changes and fashions for some Russian names. It used to be Sergey, Bolshoy Theater, etc. Now it is Sergei, Bolshoi, etc. Both visually and phonetically, these altered spellings are fine. In this edition of *Baker's* the paternal names have been omitted in listings of Russian composers, except in that of Piotr Ilyich Tchaikovsky, which has become traditional. The pronunciation of Russian names has been indicated only when mispronunciation is common, as for instance in Balakirev (stress on the second syllable, not the third), Borodin (stress on the last syllable). The pronunciation of Khachaturian's name with the accent on the third syllable has become so common that it would be idle to try to change it to the proper pronunciation, with the accent on the last syllable; equally futile would it be to persuade people to compress the last two vowels into one: "yan." The doubling of "s" between vowels in Russian names such as Mussorgsky is admittedly Germanic in origin; but in seeking to avoid the vocalization of the middle "s" in Mussorgsky the doubling of "s" becomes essential. Thus it is Mussorgsky rather than Musorgsky; but in less familiar names like Stasov, a single "s" is postulated. Illogical? So is the language itself.

GEOGRAPHIC NAMES. Place names have been playing musical chairs during the wars and revolutions of the first half of the present century. I was born in St. Petersburg, left Petrograd in 1918, and revisited Leningrad in 1962. One can travel from Pressburg to Bratislava to Pozsony without budging an inch. A person born in Klausenburg finds himself nominally transferred to Kolozsvàr and then to Cluj without moving from one's house. Sometimes a town renamed to honor a current revolutionary figure resumes its original name when the eponymous hero falls into disfavor. Perm was renamed Molotov after the Soviet Revolution, but became Perm once more when Molotov faded out in 1956. In Poland, Katowice was named Stalinogorod in 1953 but became Katowice once more in 1956 when Stalin was posthumously disfranchised. Then there is Liège. For over a century it bore an unnatural acute accent over its middle letter. In 1946 its Municipal Council resolved that the accent should be changed to the grave one. A Belgian musician born in a town with an acute accent may die there with a grave.

ABBREVIATIONS. All abbreviations except the obvious ones, like vol., prof., symph. orch., etc., and the names of the months (except March and April, which remain unabbreviated), have been eliminated from this edition. No more the impenetrable jungle of Ztsch., Vsch., vcs., mvt., or Kgl.

BIBLIOGRAPHY. In listing sources of information pertaining to the subject of an entry, a conscientious bibliographer ought to use common sense. It would serve no rational purpose to cite general histories of music for references to Bach, Mozart, or Beethoven in the bibliographical section; obviously each of such books will have extended chapters on great masters of music. But in bibliographies on modern composers, it is worthwhile to mention collections of articles containing informative material relating to such composers. The same consideration would apply to books on great conductors, great instrumentalists, or great singers; they ought to be listed if they contain useful biographical information. Magazine articles of extensive length are also proper bibliographical material. Title pages are sometimes deceptive. A brochure on Louis-Gilbert Duprez by A. A. Elwart bears the claim on its title page "avec une biographie authentique de son maître A. Choron." Upon examination, it turns out that it contains only a couple of pages on Choron. On the other hand, there are books modestly titled that provide a wealth of biographical information not available in special monographs on the subject. Since it is patently impractical to append an evaluation of each bibliographical item in a book of general reference, a reader's attention can be called to a particularly valuable publication by a word or two, such as "important," "of fundamental value," etc. Conversely, a warning should be given against worthless publications of a biographical nature that for some reason have become widely read. A famous, or infamous, example is a purported book of memoirs attributed to the nineteenth-century German prima donna Wilhelmina Schröder-Devrient and duly listed under her name in the bibliography of a number of respectable music dictionaries. It is a mildly pornographic (as pornography went at the time of its publication a hundred years ago) volume recounting her amours with famous people. It was made available in German and French; there is even a French edition in existence illustrated with erotic drawings. Less obvious in intent, but much more harmful in its effect, is the notorious correspondence between Chopin and Potocka manufactured by a Polish woman in 1945 and broadcast over Warsaw Radio during the first months after the liberation of Poland from Nazi occupation. Respectable music scholars and Chopinologists eagerly accepted these letters, which portrayed Chopin as a sex maniac given to verbal obscenities, as genuine. In one of Chopin's alleged letters he is made to use a sexual pun on a vulgar Polish word that was not in use until 1900; and there were other indecencies. The poor woman who concocted these letters committed suicide, but even then some people refused to give up their faith in the authenticity of this clumsy forgery.

Archaic spelling of the titles of old books is preserved in the present edition of *Baker's*. Martin Agricola's work *Ein kurtz deudsche Musica* retains its ancient title. Varieties of spelling in different editions of old English books are indicated, as in Christopher Simpson's *Practicall Musick*. Inordinately long book titles are abbreviated unless they contain some specific limiting clauses. For instance, Karl Grunsky's volume *Die Technik des Klavierauszuges entwickelt am dritten Akt von Wagners Tristan und Isolde* treats the problem of piano reduction only of the third act of *Tristan*, and it would be misleading to list it as *Die Technik des Klavierauszuges* plain and simple. In all such cases, practical sense rather than pedantic considerations should guide the compiler.

POLTERGEIST. Typographical errors are not just human failures of perception. They are acts of a malevolent mischievous spirit that lays its eggs in the linotype ribbon. Or else how are we to account for alterations that are obviously intended as mockery? Such fanciful conceits as "scared music," "public rectal," or "anals of music" cannot be accidents endemic to the typesetter. Avaunt! Avaunt! (Memo to proofreader: typos intentional to illustrate the dreadful dangers in writing books; do not change to "sacred music," "public recital" and "annals of music.")

I have a recurrent dream: I am in the dock facing a trio of stern judges vaguely resembling my schoolteachers of long ago, about to hear a sentence pronounced upon me for incompetence, negligence, dereliction of duty, fraudulent pretense at lexicographical expertise. The judges exhibit grotesquely enlarged entries from my edition of Baker's, engraved on huge slabs of granite, as evidence against me. In my anguish I plead extenuating circumstances. Yes, I was guilty of procrastination, sloth, accidie, pigritude (a lovely old word for laziness), stupidity perhaps, but did I not try? Did I not get from Naples the birth certificates of thirteen Enrico Carusos before giving up? Did I not locate Edward Maryon in England after his publisher told me he had been dead for years? Maryon bequeathed to me his manuscripts and other memorabilia, going back to the seventeenth century (he was of the nobility; his full name was Maryon d'Aulby), which were sent to me in a huge trunk by his executors after his death. I donated the materials to the Boston Public Library.

At least one living composer showed kindness to me in appreciation of my efforts to get his biography right (and failing), Ezra Sims of Massachusetts. I got his string quartets all mixed up in my 1971 Supplement to *Baker's*, and created a nonexistent String Quartet No. 2, composed, according to my mistaken impression, in 1962. In an unparalleled act of forgiveness, Sims composed a piece scored for a quintet of winds and strings, called it String Quartet No. 2, dated it 1962, although he wrote it in 1974, and dedicated it to me so that I "may be now less in error."

De minimis non curat lex, says an old legal maxim. But still there are minutiae that ought to be attended to in a reference work. The title of Leoncavallo's most famous opera is *Pagliacci*, without the definite article, not *I Pagliacci*. The original manuscript score is in the Library of Congress in Washington, D.C., and the title page can be examined by any doubting person. But the bronze plaque underneath the precious relic bears the wrong title *I Pagliacci*! Aaron Copland's best-known work, *Lincoln Portrait*, was listed in *Baker's* 1958 as *A Lincoln Portrait*, and Copland specifically pointed out to me that the score has no such indefinite article in its title. And yet the program of its very first performance carried an intrusive "A," and many symphony programs repeated the error.

My medulla oblongata, or whatever part of the brain controls lexicographical reflexes, overflows with gratitude to many unselfish people who have helped me in putting together the 1958 edition of *Baker's*, its two Supplements, of 1965 and 1971, and, most importantly, the present swollen edition. First to be thanked are the multitudinous registrars, clerks, and keepers of city or state archives all over the habitable world who have provided me with copies of birth and death certificates that have made it possible to establish correct chronology in the lives of thousands of musicians represented in *Baker's*. The editors of the Riemann *Musik-Lexikon* have most generously let me have hundreds of documents pertaining to musical biography and copies of a number of birth and death certificates which I had not had in my possession—a most extraordinary example of scholarly cooperation. Boris Steinpress, editor of the Soviet musical encyclopedia, patiently collected for me dates of first performances of Russian operas and symphonies and corrected numerous errors encountered in the articles on Russian composers in the previous editions of *Baker's*. Grigori Schneerson of Moscow was a great lexicographical and personal friend during the many years of our correspondence. And there were many others in Russia and in other countries in Europe.

How can I thank William Lichtenwanger, that magus of musical, and not only musical, encyclopedias, the polynomial scholar who possesses in his head a cross-reference to all subjects biographical, historical, and lexicographical? A polymath, a polyglot at home in all European languages, an enlightened opsimath in Russian and a philological connoisseur of Turkish and Japanese, he was willing to read and to critically annotate the galley proofs of the entire bulk of the present edition of *Baker's*; he got for me precious biographical data on *Baker* inmates who dwelt in the lexicographical nirvana for decades. To quote from James Joyce's passage in *Finnegans Wake*, written in bird language, "Nobirdy aviar soar anywing to eagle it." Lichtenwanger is unique.

Much as I welcome people volunteering corrections in *Baker's* and other lexicographical publications of which I have been in charge, I admit that I was somewhat startled when in August 1972 I received a letter from Stephen W. Ellis of Glenview, Illinois, in which he tore to pieces my 1971 Supplement to *Baker's*, sideswiping also at the basic 1958 volume. "Grossly incomplete," "flagrantly inaccurate," "absurd," "shockingly out of date," "sadly inadequate," "ridiculous," "disgraceful," and even "criminal," were some of his expletives. The 1971 Supplement must have been a "one-man job," he correctly surmised. But who *was* Stephen W. Ellis? I had never heard of him, and I could not find his name in any index of articles on music. Yet the man exhibited such precise knowledge of many obscure items of music history and musical biography that he could not have been just an amateur. My first impulse was to respond with lofty indignation: "Sirrah! Do you realize that you are addressing one whom the *Penguin Dictionary of Music* called 'a modern prince of musical lexicography,' and for whom Percy A. Scholes invoked, in a personal letter (*rubesco referens*), the famous lines of Goldsmith, 'and still the wonder grew that one small head could carry all he knew'? One, who . . ." But I quickly cooled down, realizing how valuable Ellis could be for the completely new edition of *Baker's*. I wrote him with genuine curiosity, asking how on earth he could have collected such a mountain of information on music and musicians, which he dispensed with such certainty of his sources. I was sure he was not an academic person, I wrote him, but I guessed that he was a record collector, that he was about 42 years old, married, and had two children. I was right, as it turned out, that he was not a professional musicologist (no professional musicologist would possess such a variety of knowledge), that he was an ardent collector of records, and subscribed to bulletins issued by unions of composers all over the world. He was not 42, but only 30 years old at the time; yes, he was married, but had only one child (a second child came along soon). By profession, he was a copy reader for a small publishing house. A fortunate publishing house it was indeed! It did not take me long to persuade Ellis to help me in putting together the present edition of *Baker's*; in fact he was eager to help. His proofreading ability, I soon found out, was prodigious, but what was most remarkable, and what still astounds me, is his uncanny knack for digging up information about contemporary composers, in precise detail, and his perseverance in getting these data for *Baker's* from reluctant, recalcitrant, and unwilling musicians. The wealth of information about modern Finns, Swedes, Norwegians, and Danes which he was able to gather for me was truly comprehensive; he was comparably "teeming with the news," to borrow a phrase from Gilbert and Sullivan, about composers of Iceland, Japan, Belgium, Holland, Spain, and Portugal; he seemed to be able to get more information about the musicians of Rumania than I could after my trip to Rumania in 1963; he was equally successful with Poles, Yugoslavs, Czechs, and Bulgarians, not to mention Americans. His special contribution was information on hard-to-get Australians. All told, he sent me about 1,250 biographies, each having a very complete list of works. I could not use all this material, and I had to cut down drastically on some catalogues of works. Inevitably, I had to use my own verbiage for the introductory paragraphs of each entry, but the hard core of information on hundreds of these contemporary composers from all lands under the lexicographical sun was furnished by Ellis.

My effusive thanks are owed to Samuel Sprince of Boston, Massachusetts. Like the Canadian Royal Mounties, he never failed to get his man; in this context, the man (or the woman) was some obscure musician whose opaque name made an insignificant blur on a page in an old edition of *Baker's* and who somehow remained unnoticed by subsequent editors. Still, such unfortunates had to be taken care of, dead or alive, to preserve the continuity of the *Baker's* heritage. Sprince tracked down for me quite a number of such personages, most of them hovering between uncertain life and certain death in some wretched nursing home. Several of them met their Maker without the benefit of an obituary, and were lost until some relative could be found to supply the missing obit. It is unfortunate that so many musicians die out of alphabetical order, so that when a dictionary is already half-printed, a *revenant* from the early part of the alphabet is apt to make a belated appearance. The entries under the early letters of the alphabet in the present edition of *Baker's* already constitute a sizable mortuary.

I conclude this rather inflated preface, as I did in my 1971 Supplement to *Baker's*, with a cherished quotation from a letter I received from Alfred Einstein shortly before his death. In his characteristic mood of gentle humor, he wondered "ob wir, und natürlich vor allem Sie, im Himmel einmal dafür belohnt werden, dass wir einige Ungenauigkeiten aus der Welt geschafft haben. . . ." Onward to a heavenly reward!

Nicolas Slonimsky
Los Angeles, California
September 1978

Entry from *Music Since 1900*

The absolute world première is given in New York by Nicolas Slonimsky, conducting his Chamber Orchestra of Boston, of *Three Places in New England* by the prophetic genius of American music Charles E. Ives, limning three tonal images of historic American sites, landscapes and monuments, written between 1906 and 1914 but never performed heretofore, anticipating by many years such novel usages as emancipated harmony, atonal extensions of essentially triadic structures, asymmetrical rhythms and polymetrical superpositions, and palimpsests of folksongs, creating a sense of pantechnical freedom in an individual style of national expression:

(1) *Colonel Shaw and his Colored Regiment*, evoked by the famous basrelief on Boston Common, opening with a lyric recollection of the Civil War victory song, *Marching Through Georgia* with its refrain, "Hurrah! Hurrah! We Bring the Jubilee!" in a polyharmonic setting, gradually growing into a rousing march, then subsiding into a memory and an echo (2) *Putnam's Camp*, suggested by martial relics of the American Revolution, making ingenious use of old songs and march tunes refracted into angular atonal configurations in a polymetric arrangement making it imperative for the conductor to beat four bars in *alla breve* time with his left hand against three bars in 4/4 time in the right hand to illustrate the episode in which two marching bands meet in a village square while playing tunes at two different tempi (3) *The Housatonic at Stockbridge*, painting the majestic flow of the great New England river in polymetric designs of great complexity, mathematically precise as to rhythmic values and yet spacious and free in its poetic progress, with the main motto formed by Zeuner's *Missionary Chant* and the "Fate motive" of Beethoven's Fifth Symphony, annexing in its course a number of old American tunes, expanding into a fantastic panoply of simultaneous melodies and polytriadic harmonies, and after a thunderous climax ending suddenly in a residual hymnal chorale, a unique effect of colorful sonority.

14 July 1942

My Toy Balloon, a set of symphonic variations of a Brazilian folk song by Nicolas Slonimsky, scored for a regular orchestra supplemented by one hundred multicolored toy balloons to be perforated with hatpins at the final *sforzando*, is performed for the first time by the Boston Pops Orchestra, Arthur Fiedler conducting.

CHARLES IVES,
FROM *PERFECT PITCH*

It was through Henry Cowell that I met Charles Ives. In 1928 Ives invited Cowell and me to his brownstone on East 74th Street in New York, and Mrs Ives, providentially named Harmony, graciously served us lunch. They had adopted a girl named Edith. At the time I met him Ives was only 54 years but looked frail, suffering from a variety of ailments, as a result of a massive heart attack in 1918, and he had practically ceased composing. I learned to admire the nobility of his thought, his total lack of selfishness and his faith in the inherent goodness of mankind. There was something endearingly old-fashioned in his way of life; he spoke in trenchant aphorisms, akin to the language of Thoreau and Emerson, and he wrote in a similarly forceful manner. He possessed a natural wisdom combined with an eloquent simplicity of utterance. Amazingly enough, he started his career as a successful insurance man. His achievements in business were postulated, so he explained, on his respect for people at large. Yet Ives was capable of great wrath. He inveighed mightily against self-inflated mediocrity, in politics and art alike. The most disparaging word in his vocabulary was 'nice'. To him it signified smugness, self-satisfaction, lack of imagination. He removed himself from the ephemeral concerns of the world at large. He never read newspapers. He did not own a radio or a phonograph, and he rarely, if ever, attended concerts. The only piece of modern music he ever heard was Stravinsky's *Firebird*; reports differ whether he also heard *La Mer* of Debussy.

Ives was extremely biased in his opinions. Toscanini was a 'nice old lady' and Koussevitzky a 'soft seat'. Some of his aphoristic utterances are fit for an anthology. 'Dissonance is like a man . . .' 'Music is the art of speaking extravagantly . . .' 'A song has a few rights, the same as other ordinary citizens . . .' 'What has sound got to do with music? . . .' 'Beauty in music is too often confused with something that lets the ears lie back in an easy chair . . .' And he urged people to 'stretch their ears'. He was impatient with copyists who questioned rough spots in his manuscript. 'Please don't try to make things nice!' he would admonish. 'All the wrong notes are right!'

Ives was a transcendental rebel in politics. He once circulated a proposal to amend the Constitution of the United States and establish a system of direct vote for President. When Harding was elected President in 1920, Ives gave vent to his indignation in a song damning politicians who betrayed the ideals of the nation. He never participated in active political campaigns; his politics were those of mind and soul. So far removed was he from the reality of the world that he was not aware of the rise of the Nazis. When I told him what evil things Hitler was doing in Germany, Ives rose from his chair to the full height of his stature and exclaimed with rhetorical emphasis: 'Then why does not someone *do* something about this man!'

I told Ives about my chamber orchestra and asked if he could give me one of his works. He suggested *Three Places in New England*. As I looked over the score, I experienced a strange, but unmistakable, feeling that I was looking at a work of genius. I cannot tell precisely why this music produced such an impression on me. The score possessed elements that seemed to be mutually incompatible and even incongruous: a freely flowing melody derived from American folk-songs, set in harmonies that were dense and highly dissonant, but soon resolving into clearances of serene, cerulean beauty in triadic formations that created a spiritual catharsis. In contrast, there were rhythmic patterns of extreme complexity; some asymmetries in the score evoked in my mind by a strange association of ideas the elegant and yet irrational equations connecting the base of natural logarithms and the ratio of the circumference of a circle to its diameter with the so-called imaginary number, a square root of a negative quantity. The polytonalities and polyrhythms in the Ives score seemed incoherent when examined vertically, but simple and logical when viewed horizontally.

The more I absorbed the idiom of *Three Places in New England* the more I became possessed by its power. After conducting the score numerous times in public I felt total identification with the music, so much so that years later, when it became extremely popular, I would turn it off when I heard it on the radio, mumbling, 'It is mine, it is mine.'

The original scoring of *Three Places in New England* exceeded the dimensions of my chamber orchestra, but fortunately most orchestral music of Ives was scored for a 'theatre orchestra', capable of different arrangements. In fact, Ives called *Three Places in New England* an 'orchestral set', implying optional instrumentation. I asked if he could possibly arrange the score to accommodate my chamber orchestra. Yes, he could, and would. In fact, the resulting arrangement became the last orchestral score that Ives wrote out, at least in part, in his own handwriting; later he was unable to handle a pen.

I gave the world première of *Three Places in New England* at the Town Hall in New York on 10 January 1931. Ives was present; it was one of the few occasions that he came to a concert. By that time my conducting had improved considerably so that I was no longer preoccupied with its technical aspect. And I was also able to control my nerves. I was not disturbed by the whispered refrain of the leader, 'So far, so good,' after each movement. The rest of the programme included Henry Cowell's *Sinfonietta*, *Men and Mountains* by Carl Ruggles, and a couple of simpler pieces intended to mollify sensitive ears. The final number was Mozart's *Ein musikalischer Spass*, the 'joke' of the title being a polytonal coda. I put it on as if to say, 'Look, listen, Mozart did it too.'

There were a few boos and hisses after the Ruggles piece. I was told that Ives stood up and said to a person who grumbled against Ruggles: 'You sissie, you don't realize that this is a piece of real strong masculine music.' This report found its way into the Ives literature, but I cannot very well believe it. It would have been utterly out of character for him to make such a public display of himself.

PREFACE TO THE SEVENTH EDITION OF *BAKER'S*

This is the third time I preside over the changing fates of *Baker's Biographical Dictionary of Musicians*: the number would be five if I were to count the 1965 and 1971 Supplements between the regular 1958 and 1978 editions. Every time I approach my task I make a solemn vow to myself that this time over there will be no avoidable errors generated by a mysterious amblyopia, the cause of which may be hysteria, poisoning with ethyl or methyl alcohol, lead, arsenic, thallium, quinine, ergot, male fern, carbon disulfide, or *Cannabis indica* (the plant from which marijuana and hashish are derived). Green cucumbers! The cow jumped over the moon! I swore to myself in the paragraph on the Poltergeist in the preface to the 1978 edition of *Baker's* that I would exercise strict control over common dyslexia leading to the transposition of adjacent letters, such as occurs when "sacred music" is converted into "scared music." But lo and behold, there was "scared music" again on page 1866 in the 1978 edition on which I worked with such desperate dedication. Dyslexia is treacherous and elusive. I asked a couple of professional writers to read the sentence containing "scared music" and they sailed right through it, asking irrelevantly, "What's wrong? He did not compose any sacred music?"

In this edition I have determined to include a number of rock-'n'-roll musicians, crooners, songstresses, movie stars who occasionally sang, in fact, everyone with an operative larynx short of singing whales.

The most delicate part of my lexicographical pursuits is to determine who is alive and who has crossed the bar, to use Tennyson's poetic euphemism. I have in my possession a list of all the inmates of *Baker's Biographical Dictionary of Musicians* who were born in the nineteenth century (myself included) and who, according to actuarial tables, ought to be among the "stiffs," as I inelegantly call them. More than two hundred of them have already died on me since the 1978 publication of *Baker's*. The champion among the living as of the summer of 1984 is Paul Le Flem, who celebrated his 103rd anniversary on March 18, 1984.* I hold my breath for his continued health out of grateful remembrance for his front-page write-ups in the Paris journal *Comoedia* of the concerts of American music I conducted in Paris in the summer of 1931. The trouble about the unknown dead is that not all of them rate an obituary in the public press. The only way the newspapers can be apprised of the demise of a notable musician (or artist, or writer, or actor) is for a relative or friend of the departed to inform a

*Alas, Paul Le Flem died at his summer estate in Trégastel, Côtes-du-Nord, on July 31, 1984.

newspaper. The death of Hugo Leichtentritt, an estimable German-American scholar, is a case in point. He lectured at Harvard, and after his mandatory retirement lived in Cambridge with his nonagenarian mother. She kept a vigilant eye on his whereabouts. Once he ventured forth with a middle-aged woman student, who induced him to have dinner with her. His mother anxiously waited for him to return, and reprimanded him severely for going out unescorted. She soon died. One day Leichtentritt's sister, who also lived in Cambridge, phoned me and asked what to do with his manuscripts; I could not understand what she meant. "But Hugo is dead," she said. "I buried him on Tuesday. I have to get his belongings out of the apartment to avoid paying his rent next month." I said I would come right over. When I arrived at his place, his sister had already piled up his pitiful music manuscripts for further disposition. I noticed the score of his cello concerto, in which he had written, in German, "Herr Piatigorsky said he might perform it upon occasion." This *Gelegenheit* never came. Leichtentritt's sister grumbled something to the effect that he was not a composer but only a writer about other composers, and that his own compositions were of no importance. I said all manuscripts by scholarly musicians were of value, and volunteered to send them to the Library of Congress for safekeeping in perpetuity. They were gratefully accepted by Harold Spivacke, chairman of the Library's Music Division, who had studied with Leichtentritt in Berlin, and were deposited in a special collection in the Music Division, to be kept until the unlikely eventuality that some music historian would "discover" them. I notified the *Boston Herald* of Leichtentritt's death, and a belated obituary appeared under the caption "Noted Music Scholar Dies in Obscurity." I also sent a telegram to Olin Downes, the music editor of the *New York Times*, who knew and admired Leichtentritt. According to the rules of the obituary department of the *New York Times*, I had to submit some kind of official certification of his death or a statement from a member of the family, to avoid a possible error. (It had happened once that the *New York Times* published an obit of a living person.) In due time a compassionate notice appeared on the obituary page.

It is annoying to miss a ghost, but it is terrifying to bury someone who is still alive. The strangest case of such a premature burial is found in the 1928 edition of a memoir by Amy Fay, entitled *Music-Study in Germany*. In his preface to this edition, the eminent Oscar Sonneck remarked that almost all the people mentioned therein were dead, including the author herself. But Amy Fay was not dead at the time; she had only moved to a small town in Massachusetts, a locality that seemed to be the equivalent of a cemetery to people living in larger communities. She died on Feb. 28, 1928, and Sonneck himself died later that year, on Oct. 30, 1928. I inquired at the publisher whether she had collected any royalties in her incorporeal state, but was told that the information was restricted.

Shall I confess? In rushing into print my 1971 Supplement to *Baker's*, and eager to bring up to date the latest entombments, I caught sight of an obit in the *New York Times* of William John Mitchell, an American music pedagogue; he died in Binghamton, N.Y., on Aug. 17, 1971. I received the last page proofs of the 1971 Supplement in September of that year, and in haste jotted down the date under the entry on Donald Mitchell, a British musicologist who was just then transacting business with G. Schirmer, the publisher of *Baker's Dictionary*, and was commuting between London and New York. I could not believe my eyes when I received the published copy of the Supplement and saw that the date of death of W.J. Mitchell had got into the entry on Donald Mitchell. Trembling in fear, I tried to calm myself with the thought that it would be unlikely that Donald Mitchell himself would come across this item and discover himself dead. No balm in Gilead! Only days after the publication of the tainted little book, I received an anguished letter from Hans Heinsheimer, director of publications at G. Schirmer, bristling with despairing question marks and exclamation points, addressed, "Not so dear Nicolas," and telling me that Donald Mitchell had just stormed into his office brandishing the dreadful book. He had never even been to Binghamton, he protested, so how could he have died there? This is one of those situations in which the more you try to explain the reasons for your predicament the deeper you sink into the ill-smelling mud of inconsistency. In desperation I wrote to the managing director of the firm telling him of what I had wrought, and begging him to eliminate the entire entry containing the hideous death notice, or else to blacken and cover utterly the single horripilating line. If the printer could not do it, would he hire a couple of menial helpers to ink out the mortuary reference manually? Only a couple of thousand copies of the 1971 Supplement were printed, and I volunteered to cover the expenses of the reparations. No, it could not be done; the books had already been sent out to retailers and music stores and could no longer be retrieved. Just as I was slowly recovering from my distress, a letter came from Donald Mitchell containing some up-to-date information about his newest publications, and mentioning ever so casually that he did not die in Binghamton, or any other place. A sense of gnawing guilt was instantly washed off the atrium and ventriculum of my heart, and I wrote Mitchell an impassioned letter hailing his spirit of Christian forgiveness. He replied that it was well worth it to endure a temporary (and, as it proved, a harmless) burial to have received such a "charming" letter from me.

The avenging Eumenides willed it that I myself became, retroactively, a victim of a premature entombment. Early in the 1960s the Philadelphia Orchestra program book quoted something I wrote on Shostakovich, prefixing my name with the adjective "late." Several of my friends were greatly alarmed and called me up to find out under what circumstances I had died. I immediately shot off a wire to the management of the Philadelphia Orchestra, protesting that I was late only in delivering my manuscripts to the publisher. In reply, I received a penitential letter from the orchestra's program book annotator, apologizing for his "stupid" mistake, but trying to deflect my discomfiture by saying that he was definitely under the impression that he had read about my demise in the papers. I wrote back, saying that he must have read about the actual decease of Lazare Saminsky, with whom I was often confused.

During recent years, a tendency has developed to add demeaning details to the lives of the great. To judge by some recently published scholia, it is essential for a composer of stature to have had syphilis. Of course, some of them did, but why should a respected music dictionary inject spirochetes and vibrions into Schubert's arteries? Even more fascinating for biographers is the discovery that a great composer was a victim of poison. The alleged murder of Mozart by Salieri still agitates playwrights and would-be Mozartologists. A variant of the Mozartocidal theories is that he was killed by the estranged husband of his alleged mistress. The tale is calculated to stir the blood of idle readers much more than a prosaic finding that Mozart had died of nephritis.

Suicides by famous musicians make equally attractive reading. In my preface to the 6th edition I covered the case of Tchaikovsky's Choleric Suicide, but now more is to be added. Rumors of Tchaikovsky's suicide sprouted in British and American journals almost immediately upon his death. Tchaikovsky was a notoriously melancholy genius, and once he really tried to end his difficult existence by walking into the cold waters of the Moskva River, but the chill was so unpleasant that he walked right back to shore. When he died of cholera in November of

1893, it was widely believed that he had deliberately drunk unboiled water in a restaurant during a raging cholera epidemic. Why would Tchaikovsky commit suicide? Imagination ran wild. Tchaikovsky had had a homosexual liaison with a member of the Romanov dynasty, it was said; Czar Alexander III found out about it and in his righteous wrath served notice on Tchaikovsky either to do away with himself or else stand trial, be disgraced, and undergo exile for life in Siberia. It is true that homosexuality was a statutory offense in old Russia, and it continued to be such under the Soviet regime. When subterranean gossip began to spread around the Moscow Conservatory, where Tchaikovsky was teaching, about some exotic sexual ways among faculty members, Tchaikovsky decided to end the nasty talk by marrying a rather stupid spinster. But on the wedding night she sat on his lap, and Tchaikovsky, repelled by such an unnatural (to him) contact, ran out of his apartment and walked the streets of Moscow in utter despair. He never faced his uncomprehending bride again, but he paid her substantial alimony from funds generously provided by his adoring but not very bright benefactress, Madame von Meck, whom Tchaikovsky was careful never to meet face to face. The first Russian mention of Tchaikovsky's pederasty appeared in the preface to the correspondence between Tchaikovsky and Madame von Meck, published in 1934; but Tchaikovsky was an idol of Russian musicians, and Soviet officials gave orders not to mention in print that he was what he was. A serial biography of Tchaikovsky that began publication in East Germany was quickly suppressed. But this Victorian prejudice did not apply to articles and books published outside Russia, and if anything, it whetted the appetite of writers in the West for more sensational stories. The most outrageous of them all, because it totally lacked any documentary evidence, was the one published in a small Russian periodical in America, authored by a Madame Orlova, who before emigration had worked in a music publishing house in Moscow. In her story, it was not a member of the Romanov dynasty who was involved with Tchaikovsky, but the nephew of a certain Russian nobleman. Outraged by the victimization of his young relative, the uncle threatened to report it to the Czar unless Tchaikovsky committed suicide. A court of honor was then set up by alumni of the law school which Tchaikovsky had attended as a youth, and he was sentenced to death by a unanimous decision of this incredible "court." A Czarist official gave Tchaikovsky some arsenic tablets, with instructions for use. Tchaikovsky's family doctor, Lev Bertenson, a highly esteemed physician, was also drawn into the conspiracy, according to the story. This was in striking contradiction to the known correspondence between Dr. Bertenson and Modest Tchaikovsky, Tchaikovsky's brother and biographer, detailing the course of Tchaikovsky's illness. But the crucial letter in which Dr. Bertenson offered his condolences to Modest Tchaikovsky had mysteriously disappeared from the archives at the Klin Museum, or so asserted one of the champions of Madame Orlova's theories. This was a surprise to me, for I had copied the letter in question during my visit at Klin in 1935, and published it, in an English translation, in Herbert Weinstock's biography of Tchaikovsky. Cholera epidemics in St. Petersburg were frequent and deadly. Tchaikovsky's mother had died of cholera. Tchaikovsky's body was allowed to lie in state, and friends reverentially kissed him on the mouth, as was the common Slavic custom. Had Tchaikovsky died of cholera, would they not have risked contamination? Not so; cholera could be transmitted only by the ingestion of contaminated food or water, not by contact with the body of one of the victims. Chekhov, the famous Russian writer who served as a medical inspector during the cholera epidemic that carried off Tchaikovsky, makes no mention in his reports of such a danger. The sources of Madame Orlova's story would hardly stand in court. A certain person told her in

1966 that he had heard it in 1913 from a woman who heard it in turn from her husband, who died in 1902. This is certainly an extraordinary way of building up the chain of evidence, without a single piece of paper to substantiate it.

Dealing with people and their inevitable frailties is often a problem of morality, compassion, and decent respect for personal privacy. But in retelling a person's life one cannot omit essential facts. So when Liberace's chauffeur and constant companion sued him for $379,000,000 for abandonment, and the story made the front page of that scrupulously informative publication, *The National Enquirer*, one could not ignore it simply because of its scabrous connotations. And what a strange sum to ask in payment for dissolution of employment! Why not a round sum, like $400,000,000? Anyway, the plaintiff lost his suit and was left to make do with just a house, a car, and some petty cash in five figures granted oh, so liberally by Liberace before the break.

A delicate problem confronted me in putting together a biographical sketch on the electronic composer Walter Carlos, who on St. Valentine's Day of 1971 had surgery performed in which his natural male organ was everted to form a respectable receptive vagina, and thereby became Wendy Carlos. He recounted his transformation in full anatomical detail in an interview with *Playboy* magazine. I listed him/her as Carlos, Wendy (née Walter). In my preface to the 6th edition of *Baker's* I had already cited other curious biological phenomena, such as the elopement of the castrato Tenducci with a young English girl who bore him a child (he was a triorchis).

Such human stories are always welcome to the prurient palate, but the fundamental duty of any self-doubting lexicographer is to make sure that hard facts are accurately reported, and this requirement applies especially to the dates of birth and death. Copying data from other dictionaries would be a case of *petitio principii*, considering that editors and publishers of supposedly immaculate lexica must know deep in their heart's ventricula and their brain's sulci, or wherever conscience resides in their mortal frames, that when these facts come ostensibly from the horse's mouth, they may in reality originate at the other end of the horse. For years, Riemann's *Musik-Lexikon* was my "freeman's music-lexicon"; I put total faith in its Supplements. When it said "nicht," canceling a date as it appeared in the basic volume, I accepted the negation absolutely. Thus, when the Riemann Supplement said "nicht" to Cherubini's date of death, March 15, 1842, and replaced it with March 13, I corrected my correct date as it appeared in *Baker 5*, and replaced it with the incorrect correction in *Baker 6*, only to be assailed by a chorus of private correctors telling me that the Riemann correction was all wet. Unbelieving, I wrote to the registry of deaths in Paris, asking for Cherubini's death certificate. Blessed be the Catholic countries and their public servants, who since Napoleonic times discharge their services free to anyone! By return airmail (they did not even charge me for the *timbres-poste*!) I got a photocopy of Cherubini's death certificate, stating that he expired on March 15, not March 13, 1842, thus confirming my *Baker 5* date, confounding my *Baker 6* date, and enabling me to restore the correct *Baker 5* date in the present *Baker 7*. Now that my faith in Riemann's Supplement has been so rudely shaken, I have begun questioning every "nichting" in it, which means more work. But, normal, intelligent people may ask, who the hell cares? Well, nobody except a small band of benighted chronologists who are determined to put things straight.

Some facts, reports, or accepted interpretations of musical events that took place, or did not take place, according to the fancy of a particular historian, are obviously impossible to verify. What was the origin of the British custom of standing up when the strains of the Hallelujah Chorus ring out at the close of Part II of

Handel's *Messiah*? Seems that George II was so moved when he heard it at the first London performance in Covent Garden Theatre on March 23, 1743, that he stood up; the audience followed suit, and by so doing established a British custom. Another interpretation, amounting to a *lèse majesté*, is that George II was seized with an irrepressible itch in his buttocks, and had to get up to put his hand inside his breeches to scratch.

Beethoven specifically denied having said "Thus fate knocks at my door" with reference to the opening notes of the Fifth Symphony, but the quotation lingers in the corridors of music history. One of my favorite stories about Rossini deals with the project of his *concitoyens* of Pesaro to erect a statue for him while he was still living. They had raised enough money to build the pedestal but they needed 10,000 francs for the statue itself, so they put it up to Rossini. "Ten thousand francs!" Rossini was supposed to have exclaimed. "For 10,000 francs I will stand on the pedestal myself." *Se non è vero è ben trovato.*

Historic facts are by necessity historians' facts, for we know about them from reports by historians. Did Caesar really exclaim "Et tu Brute" when he was stabbed by his friend? Shakespeare was right in his use of ungrammatical double superlatives, saying that it was "the most unkindest cut of all." Great men often quote themselves in their memoirs for self-aggrandizement. Did Napoleon really deliver that famous phrase, on seeing the Egyptian pyramids, that forty centuries looked down upon his soldiers? Goethe did say "mehr Licht" before he died, a phrase that has been elevated to a philosophical profundity, but some of those present thought he merely asked that the window blinds be raised to let more light into the room. The most famous words of recorded history may have never been uttered, or if they were, their meaning might have been unremarkable.

Titles of famous musical compositions are often nicknames generated by popular usage or created by publishers for the sake of promotion. *Moonlight Sonata* was merely *Sonata quasi una fantasia*. God only knows who gave the name *Emperor Concerto* to Beethoven's Piano Concerto in E-flat. *Appassionata Sonata* fits the music but Beethoven never called it so. Chopin had a batch of unwarranted sobriquets for many of his works. The *Raindrop Prelude* may have been written while rain was falling rhythmically on the roof of the monastery of Valldemosa, but Chopin denied this connection. Then there is the *Minute Waltz*, which can be played in sixty seconds only by omitting repeats. Handel never heard any blacksmith whistle the tune he incorporated in one of his harpsichord suites, but the title *The Harmonious Blacksmith*, spontaneously generated more than a hundred years after its composition, can no longer be removed from hundreds of published editions of the piece. Haydn holds the record of nicknamed compositions. The most notorious is the *Farewell Symphony*, in which one player after another departs from the scene, leaving the conductor to wield his baton before a nonexistent orchestra. According to the common accounts in music dictionaries, Haydn's intention was to indicate to his employer, Prince Esterházy, that his musicians needed a vacation, but the more plausible explanation is that the Prince planned to disband the orchestra and that Haydn tried to move his heart by his clever stage play. At least a dozen of Haydn's string quartets have acquired a nickname. Of Mendelssohn's *Songs without Words*, only a couple or so have authentic titles. And whoever thought of calling Mozart's great C major Symphony the *Jupiter Symphony*? The name apparently first emerged in England. Spurious as many of these titles may be, it is the duty of a conscientious lexicographer to list them, in quotation marks or in italics, according to typographical preference.

In my preface to the 6th edition I sang paeans, dithyrambs, hosannahs, and hallelujahs to Steve Ellis, who corrected oodles of stupid errors that infested the previous edition of my ailing dictionary. And I paid tribute to the dogged determination of Samuel Sprince in tracking down solitary deaths of *Baker's* musicians who never made it into the public press. After the publication of the 6th edition of *Baker's*, Ellis continued to supply me with up-to-date lists of works by composers of so-called third-world countries, and whenever the sad occasion required it, their dates of death. I joyfully added all this information to the present edition.

A few months after the publication of the 6th edition of *Baker's* in 1978, I received a letter from one Dennis McIntire of Indianapolis, asking my forbearance for his intrusion upon my busy time. His justification for addressing me frontally was his concern about the omission in my tome of a number of reputable contemporary singers, conductors, violinists, and pianists. Would I have time to answer his queries? I jumped from my seat at the very thought that I might not be interested, and replied in an exclamatory affirmative. During one of my transcontinental travels I stopped over in Indianapolis to meet McIntire. Age: 35; glasses. Profession: college instructor in cultural history and literature. Avocation: voracious, ferocious reading. Passion: listening to recordings from his own immense collection of phonograph albums. Knowledge about composers and performers, dead and living: unbounded. We cemented a firm intellectual and personal friendship. I invited him to visit me in Los Angeles; he stayed with me for a week, and spent most of his time examining my card file that I had collected in anticipation of the birth of the 7th edition of *Baker's*, yet in limbo, picking up errors and pointing out inadequacies, right out of his head. Ever since, we maintained a voluminous correspondence, if that is the term to describe the constant flow of information arriving from him in a steady stream on neatly typed single-spaced sheets, while I could reciprocate only by acknowledging receipt in florid terms of wonderment at his erudition and his investigative skill in finding out things. Altogether he sent me 1,425 new articles, including many rewrites of the old entries.

It has ever been my notion that people who know most about composers and performers are not professional musicians, while venerable academics whose names stand for musicological greatness know their Mozart and Beethoven, their Handel and Haydn, their Brahms and Bruckner, their Schubert and Schumann, but are utterly ignorant of the lesser breed who populate biographical dictionaries of musicians. As if to confirm my contention, I found, to my absolute astonishment and delight, that Dennis McIntire did not compose music, could not even read music, and did not play an instrument. Yet he possessed a fine discrimination as to the absolute value of musical compositions and the relative artistry of performers, and is the author of numerous articles in music journals.

I must be lucky. On top of the galactic immensities of McIntire's contribution, I received a communication from Mike Keyton, a mathematician (a specialist in advanced calculus) from Dallas, Texas, who was also a reader of *Baker's*. He, too, scrutinized it carefully, weeding out discrepancies, logical hiatuses, vacuities, and various puzzlements. He, too, was a rabid record collector, and he had access to obscure newsletters and dealers' catalogues containing information not obtainable in general reference works. He was writing a doctoral dissertation on Euler, the famous mathematician who also was a musician of sorts, and whose name I had in *Baker's*. Sure enough, he found that the date of Euler's death in *Baker's* was a month off, which was a shame, since Euler had spent many years in Russia and died in the capital city of St. Petersburg where I was born 111 years later. Knowing my interest in mathematical puzzles, Mike sent me some good ones. We exchanged comments on such abstruse subjects as the sieve of Eratosthenes, the Greek who devised an early trick of fishing out prime numbers. Mike arranged for me to give a series of lectures, some of them on nonmusical subjects, in schools where he taught. Unafraid of tackling enormous tasks, he proceeded to systematically check *Baker's* dates vs. the dates in the formidable multivolume *New Grove*. The *New Grove* had me down on some British biographies, but I had some winning points too, which filled me with justifiable pride. Some time later Mike came to visit me in Los Angeles, and we had a wonderful time together. Contrary to all expectations, he not only could read music but could actually compose some, not without a measure of modernistic fioritura.

The number of people who seemed to take a masochistic pleasure in scanning the thousands of entries in *Baker 6* in search of inconsistencies, self-contradictions, imbecilities, inanities, and plain idiocies, was augmented by an accession from England, in the person of a schoolteacher named David Cummings. True to form among musicographical volunteers, he could not read music, but by God, he knew more about musicians than most editors of special dictionaries, myself included. The wonderful thing about him was that he was willing and able to collect detailed information on contemporary British composers, including the exact dates of first performance of their major works. He seemed to be surprised that I was so glad to receive his addenda atque corrigenda, and said that most music editors regarded him as a nuisance. I assured him that such was not the case with me. So herewith I extend to David Cummings my hand in lexicographical friendship across the sea.

In handling the materials which I received first from Ellis and then in an even greater abundance from McIntire, I faced a case of conscience: to what extent should I acknowledge their contributions? There was no problem about the lists of works that I received from them; there can be no individual authorship attached to such compilations. But what about the biographical sections? Well, in practically all cases, I revised them radically, imparting to the text, for better or for worse, my inimitable touch; whether I ruined their original by such wholesale substitution is beside the point. *Le style c'est l'homme*, and I surely injected my verbiage into the text without stint. No one, I hope, can dissect the final product so as to discover stylistic, grammatical, or syntactic elements existing before my intervention. *Dixi et animam levavi.*

The help I received from these friends and correspondents is not all. In addition, Ellis, McIntire, and myself were the recipients of priceless information from countless librarians, curators, orchestral managers, opera directors, and individual musicologists from all parts of the world. Russian musicians have been amazingly cooperative. I recall with sadness and gratitude the various bits of information I received from my dear late friend Gregory Schneerson; Boris Steinpress, the author of an invaluable book on operatic premieres, helped me enormously to establish exact dates of performances of works by Soviet composers. And the Union of Soviet Composers itself sent me all kinds of informative material. In Russia they publish monographs about their composers; my nephew Sergei Slonimsky already had a rather solid book on him published in Moscow long before he reached the status of bona fide celebrity (if he has reached it now).

All those wonderful contributions from far and wide would amount to naught if they were messed up by copyists and proofreaders. During the last year of my travail I had the extraordinary luck of securing the services of the sweetest 28-year-old lady who ever belied the common belief that good-looking girls are necessarily dumb. And to add to my lucky find, she is bilingual in English and German, unafraid of Umlauts, and attacking sesquipedalian compound Teutonic nouns with hardly a blink of the eye. She claims that she actually enjoys doing lexicographical work. But she has one serious defect: unwarranted shyness. So her name will have to be noted here in the form of a Krebsgang: M.M. Elk Anid. Here M.M. may stand for Music Major, which in fact she is.

Effusive credit is to be given to the splendiferous Laura Kuhn, who lent me spiritual succor in the lamentable state of my mental exhaustion by illuminating scholiums to adorn my rather sciolistic pages. Thanks, Laura.

Last but not least. I am perilously short of laudatory participles or exalting gerunds to describe the editorial assistance I received from Sylvia Juran, charged by my publishers to exercise vigilance over the factual contents of the multitudinous entries in the present volume, to watch over grammatical and syntactical propriety, and to weed out insidious solecisms. For these tasks she is admirably equipped. She is a linguist, with expertise not only in the "usual" Roman and Teutonic languages but also in Russian and Polish, and fully versed in the bewildering variety of diacritical signs occurring in the titles of musical works and bibliographic items in such exotic idioms. She sent me hundreds of queries, couched with a compassionate regard for my sensitivity, never correcting my recurring inanities and gross incongruities with blunt remonstrances but invariably using gentle question marks even in the most obvious cases of my embarrassing delinquencies. As Shakespeare said, and Schubert sang, "Who is Sylvia? what is she . . . that she might admired be."

El Pueble de Nuestra Senora
la Reina de Los Angeles
September 1984

GROSSMUTTERAKKORD, FROM *PERFECT PITCH*

Parallel to my exploration of musical exotica, an idea began to form in my restless mind whether an entirely new taxonomy of scales and melodic patterns could not be formed outside major and minor modalities. In my usual extravagant way of thinking, I boldly compared my neo-musical elucubrations to non-Euclidean geometries, in which strange things happen in space, and the shortest distance between two points turns out to be a stereo-metrical curve. I viewed the entire evolution of musical composition before the present as a constricting course limited to the arbitrary compass of seven diatonic degrees, with occasional chromatics growing inside and outside a given mode. The antiphonal strength of modulatory processes and fugal imitation had its source in the unequal division of the octave into two parts, from the tonic to the dominant and from the dominant to the tonic, leading to non-symmetric procedures. But why not try a democratic division of the octave in two equal parts, with the tritone rather than the perfect fifth as the line of demarcation? Yet the tritone was the 'diabolus in musica' of medieval theorists, a cardinal sin for teachers of counterpoint.

What fascinated me in the division of the octave into two tritones was not the aura of diabolism, but the possibility of generating new scales. The tritone contains six semitones. Why not form a scale made up of two sections, each containing the succession of three, two and one semitones? The resulting scale is most provocative. For one thing, it is binary; for another, it contains three different intervals. Experimenting further, I discovered that it could be harmonized euphoniously by a sustained dominant seventh chord with its fifth omitted, provided the chord is made up of the tones contained in the scale itself. Either the entire scale, or any part thereof, can be harmonized by such a chord, creating beguiling sonorities of the dominant ninth with a trilling, thrilling, lowered fifth in the upper octave. The scale could be shuffled and permutated at will. It could be arranged melodically in a most attractive impressionistic manner by convergence (playing the first note, then the last note, the second note, then the penultimate note, the third note, and then the ante-penultimate note), or by divergence (playing the convergent version in reverse), or in permutations, in any order of the tones whatsoever, with the same fifthless dominant seventh chord sonorously supporting the resulting pattern. By skipping every other note of this scale beginning with the first, and repeating the same operation beginning with the second, one obtains two mutually exclusive major triads at the distance of a tritone. When struck together, these triads form the 'Parisian' bitonal complex so dearly beloved by modern composers of the first quarter of the twentieth century. When these triads are spaced in open harmony in the bass register and in close harmony in the treble, the result is positively enchanting. Under such circumstances, the medieval 'devil in music' becomes an inspiring 'daemon' in the Socratic sense.

The formula for this bitter-sweet bitonal scale, reckoned in semitones, is 3, 2, 1, 3, 2, 1. By starting on the second interval, we obtain the progression 2, 1, 3, 2, 1, 3. By starting on the third interval, we get 1, 3, 2, 1, 3, 2. Each modal displacement of this scale yields the same succulent bitonality of two major triads distanced by a tritone.

Another unexpected connection: if we arrange a series of intervals in a descending arithmetic progression, from nine semitones to three, we obtain a wonderfully euphonious bitonal chord in diminishing intervals; starting on C we have C, A, F, C, F-sharp, B, D-sharp, F-sharp.

The notes of scale 3, 2, 1 (in semitones) can be permutated in any desired order and arranged in a canon of 2, 3, 4, or 6 voices. The whole complex can then be projected against the background of the dominant seventh chord, minus a fifth, with the resulting spectrum of coruscating harmonic colours, while the canonic progression itself yields delectable melodic excrescences and acrid secundal protuberances. By manipulating the rhythmic patterns of these elements, including the device of repetition of the same note, it is possible to improvise a whole impressionistic musical landscape, using both piano pedals (since the harmonies are euphonious), assigning to it some oxymoronic title such as *Le Soleil sombre*.

The basic design of the division of an octave into two equal parts can be further variegated by multiple interpolation (as in the case of the scale 3, 2, 1, 3, 2, 1), ultrapolation (by inserting a note, or several notes, above the tritone), and infrapolation (by adding a note, or several notes, below the initial note of the basic design). An attractive example of interpolation of the tritone division is C, D, E, F, F-sharp, G-sharp, A-sharp, B, C, a truly bitonal scale combining the tetrachords of the two polar major tonalities, C major and F-sharp major. The whole scale, or any section of the scale, can be harmonized by a fifthless dominant seventh chord, such as B-flat, D, A-flat, or E, G-sharp, D, with euphonious effects.

The octave has twelve semitones. This is fortunate, for it is divisible into two, three, four and six. By dividing an octave in three parts, we produce an augmented triad, which is amenable to ornamentation by interpolation, ultrapolation and infrapolation. The next step is obvious. We divide the octave into four equal parts, resulting in an arpeggiated diminished seventh chord. Interpolation here will produce a scale of alternating whole tones and semitones, beloved by Rimsky-Korsakov. By ultrapolation of one, two, or three notes and a symmetrically arranged infrapolation we obtain melodic patterns encountered in Wagner's *Tristan und Isolde*.

Division of the octave into six equal parts produces the familiar wholetone scale. There is no sense in applying interpolation to this scale, which would result in the formation of the chromatic scale. But ultrapolation and infrapolation of the whole-tone scale will provide interesting melodic patterns evoking technical passages used by Liszt.

The division of an octave into twelve equal parts yields the chromatic scale. By using devices of ultrapolation and infrapolation, we obtain arabesques of fascinating technical brilliance. Yet even thorough exploration of scales of equal division within a single octave will not exhaust our newly discovered melodic resources. We can now proceed to divide a double octave into three parts, forming an expanded augmented triad. By inserting a pentachord on each node of this division, we will obtain a most interesting formation of a continuous scale of three different major or minor keys, with their respective pentachords flowing into one another with the utmost naturalness. Beginning with C, we obtain a most alluring triple scale, C, D, E, F, G, A-flat, B-flat, C, D-flat, E-flat, E, F-sharp, G-sharp, A, B, C.

Continuing along these lines, five octaves can be divided into six parts, resulting in a formation of consecutive minor sevenths, which can be filled in by interpolation. The division of five octaves into twelve parts will provide the cycle of perfect fourths. By filling each fourth with a tetrachord, we obtain a conjunct polytetrachord, either major or minor. The cycle of fifths results from the division of seven octaves into twelve parts, familiar from elementary theory books. By filling up the empty spaces we obtain a disjunct polytetrachord, a companion to the conjunct polytetrachord formed by a cycle of perfect fourths.

In the process of compiling a self-consistent system of scales of equal division, I came upon some fascinating phenomena. I found, for instance, that the seemingly atonal melody resulting from the triply ultrapolated tritone division of the octave, C, upper B-flat, lower A, G, F-sharp, upper E, E-flat, D-flat, C, yields, when arranged canonically in three voices, a succession of tonally unrelated major and minor triads. Stumbling upon this quite unexpected development, I felt like the bewildered stargazer of Keats when 'a new planet swam into his ken'. Even more fantastic was the curious interweaving of twelve different notes with eleven different intervals in a huge dissonant chord.

The problem of arranging twelve different notes in a column using eleven different intervals is analogous to the problem of covering the face of the clock by advancing the hour-hand 1 hour, 2 hours, 3 hours, 4 hours, etc., up to 11 hours, without stopping at the same hour twice. It is useless to try the simple arithmetical progression 1, 2, 3, 4, etc., because at number 5 we will land at 3 o'clock which has already been covered. A solution was discovered by a Hungarian-born theorist, Fritz Heinrich Klein, who made use of it in his orchestral work *Die Maschine*, which he published under the characteristic pseudonym, *Heautontimorumenos*, meaning self-tormentor in Greek. Alban Berg was amused by it; he called this column of notes 'Mutterakkord', for it had as its progeny the entire chromatic scale. Ernst Krenek referred to it in one of his articles as a unique combination which cannot be altered without repeating a note or interval.

Somehow I could not believe that the Mutterakkord was unique. I sensed that there had to be a tritone somewhere in the middle, because the tritone is the only self-inverting interval. Going to bed I imagined that the pillow was a tritone which hurt my medulla oblongata with its protruding F-sharp. Then I woke with a start and shouted, 'Eureka!' The general formula for the construction of mother chords came to me in a flash. I called Krenek who was staying in a Boston hotel nearby and told him the news. There was a pause at the other end of the phone, and Krenek said, 'Unglaublich! Ich komme sofort!' We sat together at the piano figuring out the many possibilities for forming chords of twelve different notes containing eleven different intervals, totally oblivious of the life around us. We could have passed for a couple of medieval monks debating a thorny theological problem.

With my new-found formula, there was such a proliferation of mother chords that I began weeding them out by further specifications, until I hit upon the idea of ultimate symmetry of intervallic invertibility with the self-inverting tritone in the centre. I called this chord Grossmutterakkord. Then it dawned on me how obvious the generating formula was (all great discoveries are obvious after the fact). The Grossmutterakkord could be constructed by the method of the clock. Setting the clock at 12 o'clock, you advance it 1 hour, then go back 2 hours, advance 3, go back 4, advance 5, go back 6, advance 7, go back 8, advance 9, go back 10, advance 11, in a marvellously symmetric pendulum motion: 12 o'clock,

1 o'clock, 11 o'clock, 2 o'clock, 10 o'clock, 3 o'clock, etc., covering every hour spot on the face of the clock. And the numbers can be read backwards too! In musical notation, the result would be as follows: C, B, D-flat, B-flat, D, A, E-flat, A-flat, E, G, F, F-sharp. The Grandmother could be stood on her head with equal ease! Krenek was impressed, and signalized his approbation in our guest book. Not so Prokofiev, who wrote: 'To the devil with grandmothers! Let us write music!' Hindemith opined on the same page: 'I wish great prosperity and more progeny to the Grossmutterakkord.' The Swedish composer Karl-Birger Blomdahl used the melodic version of it as the principal motto of his interplanetary opera *Aniara*, and several other composers applied it in their compositions as well.

Fascinated by the suppleness and subtlety of the apparently rigid framework of twelve tones of the chromatic scale, I investigated the possibility of tying it up with triadic structures by arranging twelve different tones in four mutually exclusive triads. I felt intuitively that the tritone was the crucial interval in this arrangement. And so it turned out to be. Two major triads in the relation of a tritone and two minor triads in the relation of the tritone would form a group of four mutually exclusive triads: C major, F-sharp major, D minor, and G-sharp minor. I also found that it is possible to arrange the chromatic scale in four different kinds of mutually exclusive triads: an augmented triad, a major triad, a minor triad, and a diminished triad. Still I had no inkling as to the underlying principle of this crystallographically symmetric division.

I then faced what was perhaps the most formidable problem, concerning the nature of triads within the matrix of the chromatic scale: Is it possible to form a chain of four mutually exclusive triads linked by major or minor thirds? In other words, is it possible to construct a chord of the 23rd? Modern composers have used chords of the 11th and the 13th, arranged in a chain of thirds; the next link would be a chord of the 15th, completing the cycle of fifths. It was by sheer luck that I was able to extend the structure to the minor 23rd, formed by the triads of C major, B-flat major, G-sharp minor, and F-sharp minor, with linkages in thirds. To avoid enharmonic imbroglios, it is expedient to start the chain on F-sharp, as follows: F-sharp major, E major, D minor, C minor. The order of tonalities is readily obtainable by running a descending whole-tone tetrachord from F-sharp to C—the ubiquitous tritone again!—and building two major and two minor thirds on these notes. I asked a friend who had access to a large computer to check whether my chord of the minor 23rd was really unique. He arranged the problem in mathematical terms and fed it into the machine. The motors whirred, the stroboscopic lights flickered, and after a few hours of mighty labour, the computer came to a halt, flashing my solution in red. The chord proved unique! The line of Horace comes to mind: 'Parturient montes, nascetur ridiculus mus.' Well, the nascent mouse may not have been so ridiculous in the computerized parturition and the mountain may not have laboured in vain. The creation had a musical meaning.

ENTRY FROM *MUSIC SINCE 1900*

24 OCTOBER 1956

At the opening of the concert series Musik der Zeit at Cologne, the world première is given of *Il Canto Sospeso (Broken Song)* for three voices, chorus and
orchestra by Luigi NONO, to the texts selected from letters written by members of
European resistance groups in Nazi-occupied countries condemned to death,
among them a 14-year-old Greek schoolboy and two young Russian girls, set to
music in the manner of a modern litany, making use of the hoquet technique, in
which words, broken into syllables, are given separately to different voices creating
an anguished effect of human discontinuity, employing as serial determinants the
row derived from the horizontalization of the *Grossmutterakkord* consisting of all
12 different tones of the chromatic scale and all 11 different intervals and the
Fibonacci series in which each number is the sum of the two preceding numbers.

THE AGE OF ABSURDITY, FROM
PERFECT PITCH

One late Saturday evening in the spring of 1981, I received a telephone call. 'Nicolas Slonimsky?' (correctly pronounced) the caller inquired. 'This is Frank Zappa. I never realized you were in Los Angeles, and I want so much to get in touch with you about your book of scales.' I was startled. Frank Zappa was the last person who, to my mind, could be interested in my theoretico-musical inventions. His name was familiar to me from a promotional record jacket showing him seated on the john with his denuded left thigh in view, and a legend in large letters: PHI KRAPPA ZAPPA.

We arranged to meet on the following Monday at 2.30 in the afternoon, and, at the appointed time on the appointed day, his assistant knocked at my door. I stepped out of my apartment and beheld something that looked like a space shuttle—a black Mercedes taking up almost half a block of Wilshire Boulevard. I could not refrain from asking the driver how much such a machine cost. 'Sixty,' he replied.

It took us nearly an hour to get to Zappa's place in the hills of Hollywood. Zappa met me at the door. He looked like a leading man in the movies—tall, slender, sporting a slight Italian moustache. For starters, I asked him the origin of his last name; he replied it meant 'the plough' in Italian.

Zappa's wife came in, an ample, young woman, and served coffee and tea. Zappa told me he did not drink alcoholic beverages; contrary to the legendary habits of most rock-and-roll musicians, he never partook of drugs. But he smoked cigarettes incessantly, tobacco being his only, and quite venial, sin. Zappa led me to his studio, which housed a huge Bösendorfer piano. I asked him how much he paid for this keyboard monster. 'Seventy,' he replied.

Zappa declared himself an admirer of Varèse and said he had been composing orchestral works according to Varèse's principles of composition, with unrelated themes following in free succession. To substantiate this claim, he brought out three scores, in manuscript and each measuring 13x20 inches, beautifully copied and handsomely bound. Indeed, the configurations of notes and contrapuntal combinations looked remarkably Varèsian. Yet he never went to a music school, and had learned the technique of composition from the study of actual editions. He had had a contract with an orchestra in Holland to play one of his works, but they had demanded a piece from his recording royalties on top of the regular fee. 'I offered them a quarter,' Zappa said, 'if they would put up a quarter.' It took me some time to figure out that the fractions he used were those in millions of dollars.

Zappa's teenage daughter flitted in, introduced by Mrs Zappa as Moon Unit. She did not seem to be embarrassed by this esoteric appellation. A year or two later she became a celebrity in her own right by making a record with her father's band in which she carried on a telephone conversation in a California language known as Valley Girl Talk. The Valley in question was the San Fernando, nestled north of Los Angeles and populated by a gaggle of young boys and girls, but mostly girls, who seemed to exude a special *joie de vivre*. Most of their lingo was incomprehensible to common terrestials. Everything they liked was not just 'great', but 'tubular' (a term derived from surfing), and something extra good was 'mega' or 'awesome'. They would say 'fer sher' when signifying assent, and express their aversion with such locutions as 'gag me with a spoon', 'I mean, like, *totally*,' and 'gross me out!' About that time, I acquired a cat, black and white and plenty mischievous, which I christened Grody to the Max, i.e. Gross to the Maximum.

Zappa invited me to try out his Bösendorfer. I sat down at the keyboard and played the coronation scene from *Boris Godunov* which required deep bass sounds. Zappa was impressed by these Russian harmonies. He asked me to play some of my own compositions, and I launched into the last piece in my *Minitudes*, based on an interplay of mutually exclusive triads and covering the entire piano keyboard. 'Why don't you play this piece at my next concert?' Zappa asked. 'When will that be?' I inquired. 'Tomorrow. We can rehearse in the afternoon.' I was somewhat taken aback at the sudden offer, but after all, I had nothing to lose. So I decided to take my chance as a soloist at a rock concert.

The next day I arrived at the large Coliseum in Santa Monica where Zappa's concert was to take place. A huge, towering man led me to Zappa's room. 'Mr Zappa is expecting you,' he said, satisfied with my identity. He was Zappa's bodyguard, hired after Zappa had been attacked during a concert by a besotted admirer and hurt his back.

On the stage I sat at the electric piano and played my piece. For better effect, I added sixteen bars to the coda, ending in repeated alternation of C major and F-sharp major chords in the highest treble and lowest bass registers. Zappa dictated to his players the principal tonalities of my piece, and they picked up the modulations with extraordinary assurance. I had never played the electric piano before, but I adjusted to it without much trouble.

The hall began to fill rapidly. Zappa's bodyguard gave me ear plugs, for, when Zappa's band went into action, the decibels were extremely high. Zappa sang and danced while conducting, with a professional verve that astounded me. A soprano soloist came out and sang a ballad about being a hooker, using a variety of obscenities. Then came my turn. Balancing a cigarette between his lips, Zappa introduced me to the audience as 'our national treasure'. I pulled out the ear plugs, and sat down at the electric piano. With demoniac energy Zappa launched us into my piece. To my surprise I sensed a growing consanguinity with my youthful audience as I played. My fortissimo ending brought out screams and whistles the like of which I had never imagined possible. Dancing Zappa, wild audience, and befuddled me—I felt like an intruder in a mad scene from *Alice in Wonderland*. I had entered my Age of Absurdity.

INTRODUCTION TO *THESAURUS OF SCALES AND MELODIC PATTERNS*

Once Slonimsky gets beyond definitions, this Thesaurus of Scales and Melodic Patterns (1947) *documents the historical development of alternative scales, which happens to be the subject of the book.*

The present Thesaurus is a reference book of scales and melodic patterns, analogous in function with phrase books and dictionaries of idiomatic expressions. But while phrase books are limited to locutions consecrated by usage, the Thesaurus includes a great number of melodically plausible patterns that are new. In fact, many compositions appearing in recent years contain thematic figures identical with those found in the THESAURUS.

From time to time musical theorists have suggested the possibility of forming entirely new scales based on the division of the octave into several equal parts. As early as 1911 the Italian musician Domenico Alaleona proposed such new scales. Alois Haba, in his *Neue Harmonielehre* (1927), classifies a great number of scales based on equal intervals and suggests harmonizations of these new scales. Joseph Schillinger in his posthumously published *Schillinger System of Musical Composition* classifies new tonal progressions in the chapter Theory of Pitch-Scales.

The scales and melodic patterns in the THESAURUS are systematized in a manner convenient to composers in search of new materials. The title THESAURUS OF SCALES AND MELODIC PATTERNS is chosen advisedly. The term scale, as here used, means a progression, either diatonic or chromatic, that proceeds uniformly in one direction, ascending or descending, until the terminal point is reached. A melodic pattern, on the other hand, may be formed by any group of notes that has melodic plausibility. There are scales of 4 notes only; and there are scales and patterns of 12 different notes. But counting repeated notes appearing in different octaves, a scale may have as many as 48 functionally different notes, as in the Disjunct Major Polytetrachord (No. 958). As to melodic patterns, there is virtually no limit to the number of such tones.

The THESAURUS is arranged in the form of piano scales and melodic studies. No fingering is given, for the pianist will readily find the type of digitation best suited to the hand. Other instrumentalists, too, will find most of the scales and melodic patterns in the THESAURUS adaptable to their instruments. The notation throughout is enharmonic, and accidentals are used according to convenience. Double sharps and double flats are avoided entirely. Precautionary natural signs are placed here and there when an unusual melodic interval occurs. All accidentals affect only the note immediately following.

The scales and patterns in the THESAURUS are arranged according to the principal interval of each particular section. In order to avoid association with a definite tonality, these basic intervals are here referred to by Latin and Greek names derived from old usage. In addition, new terms had to be coined for intervals not in the system of historic scales. In these new terms the prefix *sesqui* stands for the addition of one-half of a tone. Thus, Sesquitone is 1½ tones, or a minor third; Sesquiquadritone is 4½ tones, or a major sixth; and Sesquiquinquetone is 5½ tones, or a major seventh.

The table of intervals from the semitone to the major seventh appears as follows:

Semitone	Minor Second	*Tritone*	Augmented Fourth
Whole Tone	Major Second	*Diapente*	Perfect Fifth
Sesquitone	Minor Third	*Quadritone*	Minor Sixth
Ditone	Major Third	*Sesquiquadritone*	Major Sixth
Diatessaron	Perfect Fourth	*Quinquetone*	Minor Seventh
	Sesquiquinquetone	Major Seventh	

The interval of a major ninth is called Septitone, to indicate that it contains 7 whole tones.

These basic intervals are regarded as fractions of one or more octaves. Thus, the Tritone Progression represents the division of the octave into 2 equal parts, and it produces sequential scales and patterns. The Ditone Progression is the division of the octave into 3 equal parts, and is intervallically identical with the augmented triad. The Sesquitone Progression is the division of the octave into 4 equal parts, and is identical with the familiar diminished-seventh chord. The Whole-Tone scale represents the equal division of the octave into 6 parts. The Semitone Progression is equivalent to the chromatic scale. By the process of permutation the chromatic scale is productive of characteristic patterns of the 12-tone technique.

By dividing 2 octaves into 3 equal parts we obtain the Quadritone Progression, which is closely related to the Ditone Progression, being in fact a spread-out augmented triad. By dividing 3 octaves into 4 equal parts we obtain the interval of the major sixth. This is the Sesquiquadritone Progression, which is an unfolded Sesquitone Progression, productive of patterns related to diminished-seventh harmonies.

In the cycle of scales the interval of a perfect fifth is one-twelfth part of 7 octaves, and it is so represented in the Diapente Progression. A perfect fourth is one-twelfth part of 5 octaves, and is classified as such in the section Diatessaron Progression.

Pursuing a similar process, we find that the Sesquiquinquetone Progression, or the progression of major sevenths, is the result of the equal division of 11 octaves into 12 parts. Finally, the Septitone Progression is the equal division of 7 octaves into 6 parts, with the basic interval of a major ninth.

Scales and melodic patterns are formed by the processes of Interpolation, Infrapolation, and Ultrapolation. The word Interpolation is in common usage; here it signifies the insertion of one or several notes between the principal tones. Infrapolation and Ultrapolation are coined words. Infrapolation indicates the addition of a note below a principal tone; Ultrapolation is the addition of a note above the next principal tone. Infrapolation and Ultrapolation result in the shift of direction, with the melodic line progressing in zigzags. Infrapolation, Interpolation and Ultrapolation may be freely combined, resulting in hyphenated forms: Infra-Interpolation, Infra-Ultrapolation, and Infra-Inter-Ultrapolation.

Progressions and patterns based on unequal division of the octave are exemplified by Heptatonic scales and Pentatonic scales. Among Heptatonic scales, or 7-tone scales, are our familiar major and minor scales as well as the church modes. In the section Heptatonic Arpeggios the scales are spread out in thirds. In the section Bitonal Arpeggios the C major arpeggio is combined with arpeggios in all other 23 major and minor keys.

Busoni, who had earnestly explored new musical resources, found 113 different scales of 7 notes. Mentioning as an example the scale: C, Db, Eb, Fb, Gb, Ab, Bb, C (it is No. 1035 in the THESAURUS), he writes in his *Entwurf einer neuen Aesthetik der Tonkunst*: "There is a significant difference between the sound of this new scale when C is taken as the tonic and when it is taken as the leading tone of the scale of Db minor. By harmonizing the tonic with the customary C major triad as a fundamental chord, a novel harmonic sensation is obtained."

In his *Chronicle of My Musical Life* Rimsky-Korsakov mentions the use he made of an 8-tone scale, formed by alternating major and minor seconds. This is Scale No. 393 in the THESAURUS. Sporadic uses of the Whole-Tone scale are found in Glinka and even in Mozart (as a jest to mock the inept *Dorfmusikanten*), but it did not become a deliberate device before Debussy. In Debussy's piano piece *Voiles* the principal melodic structure is in the Whole-Tone scale, but the middle part is written exclusively on the black keys, exemplifying the Pentatonic scale.

The Whole-Tone scale has 6 notes to the octave; the Pentatonic scale has five. The Whole-Tone scale is possible in only one form on a given note, but there can be many Pentatonic scales. There are 49 Pentatonic scales in the THESAURUS.

The 12-Tone Technique of composition promulgated by Schoenberg is based on permutations of the Semitone scale. Various 12-tone patterns are found in the THESAURUS in examples No. 1214 to No. 1318. For example, it is possible to arrange the 12 chromatic tones in 2 major and 2 minor triads without repeating a note. It is also possible to form 4 mutually exclusive augmented triads using all 12 chromatic tones. The theme of Liszt's *Faust* Symphony is composed of 4 augmented triads. It is further possible to split the chromatic scale into a diminished triad, a minor triad, a major triad, and an augmented triad. These mutually exclusive triads can be arranged in the form of Quadritonal Arpeggios.

A recent development of the 12-Tone Technique is the 11-interval technique, which prescribes the formation of progressions containing 11 different intervals. The idea was first introduced by the Austrian musician Fritz Klein in 1921 in a curious composition entitled *Die Maschine*, with the sub-title *Ex-Tonal Self-Satire*. The name of the composer was concealed behind a characteristic nom de plume *Heautontimorumenus* which means Self-Torturer. In this piece Klein introduced a Mother Chord which contains not only all 11 different intervals, but 12 different notes as well.

A further elaboration on the Mother Chord is an invertible 11-interval, 12-tone chord introduced by the author and appropriately christened Grandmother Chord. It has all the intervallic properties of the Mother Chord plus an especial order of intervals so arranged that they are alternately odd-numbered and even-numbered when counted in semitones, with the row of odd-numbered intervals forming a decreasing arithmetical progression and the row of even-numbered intervals forming an increasing arithmetical progression. The order of notes in the Grandmother Chord is identical with the 12-tone Spiral Pattern No. 1232a.

All chords composed of 11 different intervals add up to the interval of 66 semitones, which is the sum of the arithmetical progression from 1 to 11. The interval of 66 semitones equals 5½ octaves, and so forms a Tritone between the lowest and the highest tones in the Pyramid Chord, Mother Chord, Grandmother Chord, and other 11-interval structures.

Scales and patterns listed in the main body of the THESAURUS readily lend themselves to new melodic possibilities. For instance, a descending scale may be played in the form of the melodic inversion of the ascending scale, as suggested in the section Mirror Interval Progressions. It is possible to form complementary scales in the range of 2 octaves, by using in the second octave the notes not used in the first. Other possibilities for the formation of new patterns are demonstrated in the section on Permutations.

A Diatonic counterpart of the 12-Tone Technique is the system of Pandiatonic composition. The term Pandiatonic, first introduced by this writer in 1937, denotes the free use of all 7 tones of the diatonic scale, both melodically and harmonically. In one-part Pandiatonic Progressions, the melody is made up of 7 different notes of the diatonic scale. Such a progression may then be melodically inverted, read backward, or both, resulting in 4 different forms. Pandiatonic Counterpoint in strict style uses progressions of 7 different notes in each voice, with no vertical duplication.

Pandiatonic Harmony is the twentieth century counterpart of classical harmony. Modern composers of such varied backgrounds and musical persuasions as Ravel, Stravinsky, Hindemith, Milhaud, Copland and Roy Harris make use of this technique, arriving at it by different creative processes. Jazz composers, too, have found, by sheer experimentation, effective application for the enriched chords of Pandiatonic formations. It is a common practice to end an orchestral arrangement of a popular song by the enriched major triad with an added sixth, seventh, or ninth.

The concluding sections of the THESAURUS demonstrate the various methods by which tonal materials may be used to best advantage. The section Double Notes shows the combinations derived from corresponding scales and patterns. Plural Scales and Arpeggios give examples of common major and minor progressions arranged consecutively in chromatic transposition. Polytonal Scales are simultaneous progressions in different keys. Polyrhythmic Scales are progressions in different rhythms. Polytonal Polyrhythmic Scales combine different rhythms in different tonalities.

A special word is to be said about Palindromic Canons. Palindromes are words or sentences that read the same forward or backward, as the sentence *Able Was I Ere I Saw Elba* (applied to Napoleon). Similarly, Palindromic Canons read the same backward or forward. The two Palindromic Canons based on Pattern No. 72 are particularly interesting. They result in a progression of enharmonic triads or their inversions, alternating in major and minor keys.

Fragments of the scales and patterns in the THESAURUS may be used as motives and themes. The rhythmical elaboration is left to the imagination of the composer. By using a portion of a pattern in forward and retrograde motion, in varied rhythms within a given meter, it is possible to form an unlimited number of melodic figures.

Two formulas are used in the harmonization of the scales and patterns: one by common triads, and one by seventh-chords. In the harmonization by common triads, only root positions of major triads in close harmony are applied. Either the root, the third, or the fifth may appear in the melody. These positions are referred to as Octave, Tertian, and Quintan, or in figures, 8, 3, and 5. When the melody ascends, diatonically or chromatically, the positions change from the Octave to the Tertian to the Quintan to the Octave. When the melody descends, the order of the positions is reversed. Furthermore, the order of positions may be reversed at the end of a cadence even in ascending motion. When the melody is stationary, the order of positions is free. The resulting harmony traverses several tonalities in an alternation of successive major chords.

The harmonization in major triads is found in the music of Debussy, Moussorgsky, and other composers of the French and Russian schools. A classical example is the scene in the monk's cell in Moussorgsky's opera *Boris Godunov*. In the second act of Puccini's opera *Tosca* the Whole-Tone scale in the bass is harmonized by a row of major triads with the positions following the Octave-Tertian-Quintan (8-3-5) formula.

The second type of harmonization is effected by means of Master Chords. These Master Chords are dominant-seventh chords with the fifth omitted. In combination with melodic elements of a given scale or pattern, these chords form harmonic structures of the type of seventh-chords, ninth-chords, or whole-tone chords. The Master Chords are indicated for ascending scales and patterns in the sections Tritone Progression, Ditone Progression and Sesquitone Progression by figures within circles, as ⑤, and are used to harmonize an entire rhythmic group in a given progression. In the Tritone and Sesquitone Progressions it is also possible to harmonize the entire octave range with a single Master Chord. Furthermore, any Master Chord suitable for harmonization of a given progression may be transposed a tritone up or down with satisfactory results.

Harmonization of both types is given in the tables on pp. 240–241. To harmonize in major triads, it is necessary to alternate the Octave, Tertian, and Quintan positions given in the table. In harmonizing by seventh-chords, ninth-chords, and whole-tone chords, any chord under a given melody note will furnish a workable harmony.

The patterns in the Diatessaron and Diapente Progressions lend themselves to harmonization characteristic of the Dominant-Tonic cycle. When harmonized in consecutive seventh-chords, such patterns acquire a Schumannesque quality.

Traditional harmonization in major and minor keys uses chords formed by the diatonic scale. Similarly, new scales may be harmonized with the aid of chords formed by the notes of the scale itself. Examples of such Autochordal Harmonization are given in a special table. There are scales that admit of only 2 different triads, as Scale No. 7, which can be harmonized with C major and F♯ major triads. The 8-tone scale No. 393 is capable of forming 8 different triads, while other scales, such as No. 5, do not yield a single triad.

All scales and patterns in the THESAURUS are centered on C as the initial and concluding tone. It goes without saying that these progressions can be transposed to any tonal center according to a composer's requirements.

John Stuart Mill once wrote: "I was seriously tormented by the thought of the exhaustibility of musical combinations. The octave consists only of five tones and two semitones, which can be put together in only a limited number of ways of which but a small proportion are beautiful: most of these, it seemed to me, must have been already discovered, and there could not be room for a long succession of Mozarts and Webers to strike out, as these have done, entirely new surpassing rich veins of musical beauty. This sort of anxiety, may, perhaps, be thought to resemble that of the philosophers of Laputa, who feared lest the sun be burnt out."

The fears of John Stuart Mill are unjustified. There are 479,001,600 possible combinations of the 12 tones of the chromatic scale. With rhythmic variety added to the unbounded universe of melodic patterns, there is no likelihood that new music will die of internal starvation in the next 1000 years.

Self-Review of *Perfect Pitch,* from *Notes*

Perfect Pitch: A Life Story. By Nicolas Slonimsky. Oxford: Oxford University Press, 1988. [viii, 263 p. ISBN 0-19-315155-3 $21.95.]

The opening sentence of Nicolas Slonimsky's preface to the sixth edition of *Baker's Biographical Dictionary of Musicians* begins with these fateful words: "If I were to write an autobiography (which God forbid). . . ." God failed to forbid, and Slonimsky went ahead and put together the present volume retailing the facts of his life (kind of gloomy). The original manuscript was titled *Failed Wunder-kind*, with a subtitle, *A Rueful Autopsy* ("autopsy" in this context was to mean self-observation, from *auto* = self and *ops* = eye), but the publishers said that the implication of failure would adversely affect sales, and that to most readers "autopsy" means the dissection of bodies. They suggested *Perfect Pitch* instead for the main title. One does not talk back to publishers, and the author had to submit, for indeed he *is* in possession of that precious sensitivity of hearing. But when a friend desirous of boosting sales asked for *Perfect Pitch* in a bookstore, he was told to go to the sports section.

If Slonimsky were a tree, his body would already have counted more than ninety annual rings on its trunk, indicating the age when he began working on his life story. But only God can make a tree, and Slonimsky was totally lacking in divine favors. In lieu thereof, he had enough of an archivist's sense to save—throughout his travels from Russia to Turkey, from Turkey to Paris, from Paris to the United States—a pile of family correspondence, official documents tracing his wanderings, and precious period photographs to make his account authentic. He was helped in this pursuit by the ingrained intellectualism of his family, in both its paternal and maternal branches, who left footprints in encyclopedias, newspapers, magazines, and even, in one case, a museum portrait of a great-grandfather who invented an early calculator.

Slonimsky begins his autobiographical narrative *ab ovo*, from his birth—an event recorded in prose and poetry by his older brother, who would later become a professional historian. Then, chapter by chapter, he recounts his efforts, most of them painful, to become a pianist, a composer, a symphonic conductor, and a lexicographer. It is in this last endeavor that he apparently made the grade, publishing books on music that were widely acclaimed and were sold in impressive quantity.

At this point let us shed a furtive tear (*una furtiva lagrima*, to borrow a line from Donizetti's opera *L'Elisir d'amore*) to commemorate the elision from the book of several episodes that in the publisher's view were not "germane" (I hate that word) to the subject. At least one such story was very germane: it told of the author's two piano pupils in St. Petersburg during World War I, children of a crooked banker, who themselves became major gangsters in New York after emigration. The younger of the two, quoted as saying that Slonimsky was a major influence on him in his life, was strangled to death in his Fifth Avenue penthouse by parties unknown.

There was also originally a section on the grammatical versatility of the Russian language that included an enormous list of verbal derivations—subjunctive, optative, imperative, pluperfect, gerundive, intermittent, future passive, infinitive—for a particular word meaning "to have sexual intercourse." The list went overboard, for "it might give offense." But after much argument, an equally offensive paragraph about the favorite palace guards of Catherine the Great who bore names that sounded mighty peculiar when spelled in English was allowed to stand.

No book is free from avoidable errors, and this one is no exception. Slonimsky tells an anecdote (which he now confesses he got secondhand) about an Italian clarinet player in the New York Philharmonic who was bored by the conductor Otto Klemperer's protracted explanations during a rehearsal about the meaning of the music and who grumbled, "Hey, Klempie, you talka too much!" Well, the player was actually an oboist, not a clarinetist. In the author's theoretical meanderings, he gives an account that according to medieval theological writings, the octave is considered "pure" because Abraham was circumcised on the eighth day (*octava die*) after his birth. Wrong. Abraham was quite old when he had his circumcision; it devolved on his progeny to be circumcised on the eighth day.

Inevitably, when a book becomes a physical entity, the author experiences an unquenchable desire to supplement it with tangential vignettes, mostly of a self-congratulatory nature. While honestly reporting the disaster he suffered at his first (and last) appearance as conductor at the Hollywood Bowl, Slonimsky could have mentioned that half a century later John Cage told him that he had attended every one of those concerts and that Slonimsky's program of modern music produced a deep impression on him. (Cage was twenty years old at the time.) Besides deploring the faulty English he employed in his talks on music at the Boston Public Library in 1926 (he called Pablo Casals "an eminent spaniel"), Slonimsky could have mentioned that Elliott Carter attended all of those talks with great interest, as he told this reviewer sixty years later. There was prophylactic balm for Slonimsky's generally depressed ego in one of Alfred Einstein's letters, in which he wrote, "I wonder if we, and above all, you, will ever be rewarded in Heaven for having removed some inaccuracies from books of reference" (in the original German it sounds much more poetic). Einstein is already there, but Slonimsky fears he might land in a hotter place. And finally, Slonimsky might have quoted *Notes* of December 1986 (review by Ann P. Basart of his *Music Since 1900: A Supplement* [New York: Scribner's, 1986], 310): "In a recent attempt at definition, I commented to another librarian that 'reference books are not meant to be read, but to be dipped into.' 'Except for Slonimsky,' he replied."

Dixi et animan levavi.

NICOLAS SLONIMSKY
Los Angeles

CONCLUSION OF *PERFECT PITCH*

Now I have reached the Age of Absurdity. I refuse to believe I am 93. Have I really outlived Tolstoy and Goethe? I don't even have a white beard or bushy eyebrows to attest my age. My eyes still see, my ears still ring with sounds, and my jaws (yes, especially my jaws) are still sufficiently lubricated on their maxillary supports to sustain a steady flow of garrulity. My arms gesticulate in rhythm with my speech, my nether limbs are ambulatory, and I can still run (well, walk) a 40-minute mile. At my latest check-up, the doctor suddenly pinched my forearm. 'Your anabolic reflex is remarkable,' he said. An average nonagenarian's skin, when pinched, stays up like a piece of cured leather for minutes. Mine doesn't. I was so amused by this bit of personal biology that I appended the title '*Anabolism*' to one of the numbers in my piano album, *51 Minitudes*.

To exorcise the ghostly digits of my age, I have now adopted a personal countdown, modulo 100. I am now 7. Next year, *diabolo volente*, I will be 6. In 1994 I will be zero. On this hopeful note, I conclude my rueful autopsy.

LOS ANGELES
SEPTEMBER 1987

HISTORIES

Though trained in music, Slonimsky has a mind of a historian, believing as he does in chronology and verifiable facts (rather than, say, textual interpretation), not to mention the scrutiny of primary sources. This opening history comes from *The Lexicon of Musical Invective* (1948), which reprints from several languages (all translated by Slonimsky) of the nastiest reviews ever accorded major composers—a true invectorium.

Though modestly titled, *Music Since 1900* remains his most extraordinary book with a concept so unique. Whereas a committee could produce biographical dictionaries of prominent individuals in any field, no one has ever done anything comparable to *Music Since 1900* in any other art (the closest semblance being a direct imitation, great scholarship always breeding derivatives, Richard Burbank's *Twentieth-Century Music* [Facts on File, 1984], which comes with Slonimsky's generous preface). *Music Since 1900* also has much of his best writing, as he forced himself to compress every entry into a single sentence. This strategy is particularly effective in introducing modern operas, each of which becomes no less ridiculous than its predecessor. Since I once suggested that a book could be compiled from operatic plot summaries alone, here is my initial draft. In chronological order, with examples drawn from throughout the world these implicitly document the development a twentieth-century art.

"NON-ACCEPTANCE OF THE UNFAMILIAR," FROM *LEXICON OF MUSICAL INVECTIVE*

The only things we really hate are unfamiliar things.
—SAMUEL BUTLER: *Life and Habit*

Prelude to a Lexicon

This is an anthology of critical assaults upon composers since the time of Beethoven. The criterion of selection here is the exact opposite to that of a press agent. Instead of picking a quotably flattering phrase out of context from an otherwise tepid review, the LEXICON OF MUSICAL INVECTIVE cites biased, unfair, ill-tempered, and singularly unprophetic judgments.

The present collection is, then, not a chrestomathy but a Schimpflexicon. Its animating purpose is to demonstrate that music is an art in progress, and that objections leveled at every musical innovator are all derived from the same psychological inhibition, which may be described as Non-Acceptance of the Unfamiliar.

The music critics whose extraordinary outpourings are detailed here are not necessarily opinionated detractors, grouching and grumbling at anything new just because it is new. Many of them are men of great culture, writers of brilliant prose, who, when the spirit moves them, excel in the art of imaginative vituperation. They are adept at effective figures of speech, and they apply metaphorical language with considerable inventiveness to demolish the musical transgressors. Their only failing is that they confuse their ingrained listening habits with the unalterable ideal of beauty and perfection.

The Phenomenon of Non-Acceptance of the Unfamiliar is revealed in every instance when custom clashes with an alien mode of living or a heterodoxal mode of thinking. The Polish language is unpronounceable to non-Slavs; words in Czech and Bulgarian, containing nothing but written consonants, are monsters to the eye.

Unfamiliar customs offend. Gestures have widely divergent social connotations in different lands. A Tibetan sticks out his tongue and hisses when he greets a friend, but such salutation is an insult to an Occidental. Lusty whistling after a theatrical number is an expression of delight among American audiences; but in Europe it is equivalent to booing, as American soldiers found out to their dismay in 1945, when they wished to show their appreciation of a Paris ballet performance. The ballerinas were in tears at what they thought was an ill-mannered expression of displeasure.

To listeners steeped in traditional music, modern works are meaningless, as alien languages are to a poor linguist. No wonder that music critics often borrow linguistic similes to express their recoiling horror of the modernists. The Chinese language, as the ultimate of incomprehensibility, serves the critics particularly well for such comparisons.

The *Musical World* of June 30, 1855 gives this account of the music of *Lohengrin*: 'It has no more real pretension to be called music than the jangling and clashing of gongs and other uneuphonious instruments with which the Chinamen, on the brow of a hill, fondly thought to scare away our English blue-jackets.'

Ninety-five years later, by an ironic turn of history, the Chinese actually played *Lohengrin* music to British and American soldiers in Korea, to scare them away! An International News Service dispatch from the northwest Korean front, dated December 5, 1950, quotes Henry Roose, twenty-year-old private from Lima, Ohio, as saying: 'I was one of five hundred men who fought their way out of a Chinese Communist trap. . . . Around 9 P.M., an eerie sound sent shivers along my spine. A lone bugler on a ridge one hundred yards away was playing Lohengrin's Funeral March.* A Chinese voice speaking English floated across the valley, saying: "That's for you, boys—you won't ever hear it again." '

H. T. Finck wrote in 1910: 'Strauss lets loose an orchestral riot that suggests a murder scene in a Chinese theater.' A Philadelphia critic said about Schoenberg's Violin Concerto that it was as comprehensible as 'a lecture on the fourth dimension delivered in Chinese.'

If to Western traditionalists modern music sounds Chinese, to some unoriented Orientals all Western music is unintelligible. One Jihei Hashiguchi spoke his mind on the subject after attending the New York première of *Madama Butterfly* in February 1907. He wrote to a New York daily: 'I can say nothing for the music of *Madama Butterfly*. Western music is too complicated for a Japanese. Even Caruso's celebrated singing does not appeal very much more than the barking of a dog in faraway woods.'

When Russian music made its incursion into Europe and America during the last quarter of the nineteenth century, the critics were fascinated and shocked at the same time. The very sound of Russian names seemed forbidding. 'Rimsky-Korsakov—what a name!' exclaims the writer in the *Musical Courier* in 1897. 'It suggests fierce whiskers stained with vodka!'

The Boston *Transcript* wrote of Tchaikovsky's B♭ minor Piano Concerto in 1875: 'This elaborate work is as difficult for popular apprehension as the name of the composer.' One wishes that the critic might have lived to see the day when the opening theme of Tchaikovsky's Concerto became a popular song under the inviting title, *Tonight We Love*!

Stravinsky and Prokofiev were greeted by a horrified chorus of music critics whose ears were still attuned to the aural comforts of nineteenth-century har-

*There is no funeral march in *Lohengrin*—presumably it was the introduction to the third act of the opera, the melody of which can be played by a single bugler.

monies. *Le Ménestrel* of June 6, 1914 suggested that *Le Sacre du Printemps* should be called 'Massacre du Printemps.' As late as December 1918 a writer in *Musical America* was profoundly shaken when he heard Prokofiev conduct and play his works: 'Those who do not believe that genius is evident in superabundance of noise, looked in vain for a new musical message in Mr. Prokofiev's work. Nor in the *Classical Symphony*, which the composer conducted, was there any cessation from the orgy of discordant sounds. As an exposition of the unhappy state of chaos from which Russia suffers, Mr. Prokofiev's music is interesting, but one hopes fervently that the future may hold better things both for Russia and listeners to Russian music.'

Incredible? Then read this by Henry Fothergill Chorley, reviewing a Chopin recital in London in 1843: 'M. Chopin increasingly affects the crudest modulations. Cunning must be the connoisseur indeed, who, while listening to his music, can form the slightest idea when wrong notes are played.'

The same Chorley wrote that Schumann's harmonies were 'so obtrusively crude that no number of wrong notes would be detected by the subtlest listener.' This species of *argumentum ad notam falsam* is stock-in-trade with reactionary music critics.

After the American première of *Salome*, an American critic echoed Chorley's argumentation: 'Thanks to the prevailing dissonance, nobody knows—or cares—whether the singers sing the right notes, that is, the notes assigned to them, or not.' When Alban Berg's opera *Wozzeck* was produced, there was more of the same: 'Whether one sings or plays wrong notes in such an insalubrious style is utterly immaterial,' wrote one newspaper reviewer.

The Russian critic Hermann Laroche wrote in the St. Petersburg *Golos* of February 11, 1874: 'The overabundance of dissonances and the incompetence in handling vocal parts in *Boris Godunov* reach the point where the listener is unable to distinguish intentional wrong notes from the wrong notes of the performers.'

Another Russian critic, Nicolas Soloviev, described *Boris Godunov* as 'Cacophony in Five Acts and Seven Scenes.'

Professional music critics rarely possess any aptitude for mathematics. Hence, they like to compare musical processes unintelligible to them with the equally darksome methods of mathematical thinking. Here is an assortment of such expressions of helplessness before a modern enigma: 'The science of Monsieur Berlioz is a sterile algebra' (P. Scudo, *Critique et Littérature Musicales*, Paris, 1852); 'The music of Wagner imposes mental tortures that only algebra has a right to inflict' (Paul de Saint-Victor, *La Presse*, Paris, March 1861); 'The Brahms C minor Symphony is mathematical music evolved with difficulty from an unimaginative brain' (Boston *Gazette*, January 22, 1878); 'Herr Bruckner realized and extended the acoustician Euler's belief that it is possible to figure out a sonata' (New York *Tribune*, November 13, 1886); 'The Russian composer Rimsky-Korsakov has evidently evolved a musical enigma which is too complex of solution now' (Boston *Globe*, March 13, 1898); 'Mathematics . . . are not music, and to non-dodecaphonists the effect of Schoenberg's works on the ear is one of unintelligible ugliness' (*Musical Opinion*, London, July 1952).

The art of musical invective flourished in the nineteenth century and the first decade of the twentieth, when music critics indulged in personal attacks on nonconformist composers. Nowadays, a critic will say that the music he doesn't like is ugly, but he will not say that the composer himself is ugly. And he will not defame the composer by comparing him with a member of an 'inferior' race. James Gibbons Huneker did both in his extraordinary description of the physical appearance of Debussy. He wrote in the New York *Sun* of July 19, 1903: 'I met Debussy at the Café Riche the other night and was struck by the unique ugliness of the man. His face is flat, the top of his head is flat, his eyes are prominent—the expression veiled and sombre—and altogether, with his long hair, unkempt beard, uncouth clothing and soft hat, he looked more like a Bohemian, a Croat, a Hun, than a Gaul. His high prominent cheek bones lend a Mongolian aspect to his face. The head is brachycephalic, the hair black. . . . The man is a wraith from the East; his music was heard long ago in the hill temples of Borneo; was made as a symphony to welcome the head-hunters with their ghastly spoils of war!'

Paul Rosenfeld, the subtle chronicler of the arts, forsakes the customary elegance of his prose to inveigh against the music and the physical features of Max Reger. In his *Musical Portraits*, Rosenfeld describes Reger as 'an ogre of composition . . . a swollen, myopic beetle with thick lips and sullen expression.'

A century ago, music critics freely mixed esthetic invective with scandal-mongering. The *Musical World* of October 28, 1841, having first dismissed Chopin's music as 'ranting hyperbole and excruciating cacophony,' plunged headlong into Chopin's liaison with George Sand: 'There is an excuse at present for Chopin's delinquencies; he is entrammelled in the enthralling bonds of that arch-enchantress, George Sand, celebrated equally for the number and excellence of her romances and her lovers; not less we wonder how she who once swayed the heart of the sublime and terrible religious democrat Lamennais, can be content to wanton away her dreamlike existence with an artistical nonentity like Chopin.'

No newspaper today would publish a piece of music criticism in which the composer is called an idiot or a madman. Yet, on April 19, 1899 the *Musical Courier* suggested that Richard Strauss is 'either a lunatic, or is rapidly approaching idiocy.' The same journal declared some years later: 'Arnold Schoenberg may be either crazy as a loon or he may be a very clever trickster.'

The *Musical World* of June 30, 1855 castigated Wagner as a 'communist,' purveying 'demagogic cacophony, the symbol of profligate libertinage.'

The German-American *Newyorker Staatszeitung*, in its issue of May 23, 1888, suggested that the proper title for *Götterdämmerung* should be 'Goddamnerung.'

There is no more scornful epithet in the vocabulary of partisan critics than impotence and its paronyms. Hugo Wolf, out of Wagnerophilic factionalism, described the music of Brahms as 'die Sprache der intensivsten musikalischen Impotenz.' Nietzsche spoke of Brahms as having 'die Melancholie des Unvermögens.' A French critic wrote of *Pelléas et Mélisande*: 'Les amoureux de M. Debussy semblent fatigués de naissance, des amants anémiés, qui ne peuvent se hausser jusqu'à la volupté et prennent leurs petits spasmes d'une seconde pour des transports d'amour et de passion.'

Music critics of the uninhibited era liked to embellish their invective with gastro-intestinal figures of speech. 'Wagner takes himself for a Dalai Lama,' wrote Heinrich Dorn, 'and his excrement for the emanation of his godlike spirit.'

In an article entitled 'On the Cult of Wrong Notes,' published in the *Musical Quarterly* of July 1915, the English writer Frederick Corder describes the music of Béla Bartók as 'mere ordure.'

After listening to a performance of *Sun-Treader* by Carl Ruggles, a Berlin critic suggested that the title should be changed to 'Latrine-Treader.' He said he had a sensation of 'bowel constrictions in an atonal Tristanesque ecstasy.'

The composers under attack have not been remiss in answering the critics in scatological language. When Gottfried Weber published an article accusing Beethoven of desecrating the high purpose of his art in writing the score of *Wellington's Victory*, Beethoven scrawled on the margin of his copy of the magazine *Cæcilia*, in which the article appeared: 'O du elender Schuft! Was ich *scheisse*, ist besser als du je gedacht!'

The most outspoken letter in its specific imagery was the one that Max Reger dispatched to the Munich critic Rudolf Louis: 'Ich sitze in dem kleinsten Zimmer in meinem Hause. Ich habe Ihre Kritik vor mir. Im nächsten Augenblick wird sie *hinter* mir sein.'*

Animal noises, particularly the meowing of amorous cats, furnish the critics with a vivid vocabulary of invective. Oscar Comettant, writing in *Le Siècle* of May 27, 1872, found cat music in Bizet as well as in Wagner. 'M. Bizet et son patron Wagner ne changeront pas la nature humaine. Ils ne feront pas que les miaulements chromatiques d'un chat amoureux ou effrayé . . . remplacent jamais, chez un auditeur sain d'esprit et d'oreille, une mélodie tonale.' The Boston *Gazette*, in its issue of February 28, 1886, described Liszt's music as 'a choice selection of the various shades of expression of which the voice of the nocturnal cat is capable.'

The atonal music of Wallingford Riegger's *Dichotomy* inspired the Berlin critic of the *Signale* to draw this surrealist animal landscape: 'It sounded as though a pack of rats were being slowly tortured to death, while, from time to time, a dying cow moaned.'

The Mozart-loving Oulibicheff heard 'odious meowing' and 'discords acute enough to split the hardiest ear' in Beethoven's Fifth Symphony! He referred specifically to the transition from the *Scherzo* to the *Finale*.

Lawrence Gilman described the music of one of the *Five Orchestral Pieces* by Anton von Webern by the striking phrase: 'The amoeba weeps.'

New musical instruments, too, have been likened to animal sounds. The London *Times* wrote of the Theremin after a demonstration of the instrument in London in April 1950: 'In the Theremin we have a machine which in the baritone register suggests a cow in dyspeptic distress.'

An anonymous cartoon printed by G. Schirmer in New York in 1869 under the title, 'The Music of the Future,' displays eight cats (labeled A, B, C, D, E, F, G, A), several donkeys, and a group of goats, as participants in a Wagnerian orchestra. The score on the conductor's stand reads: 'Liszt's Symphonic Poem.' Another score, at the conductor's feet, is marked: 'Wagner, not to be played much until 1995.'

Anti-modernists like to use the *argumentum ad tempora futura* to shoo away the immediate assault on their fossilized senses. 'If the future can relish such a chaotic piece of music,' wrote Max Kalbeck about Bruckner, 'we wish this future to be far from us.'

Fiorentino, the French anti-Wagnerian, gallantly declined the blandishments of the musicians of the future: 'J'honore infiniment la musique de l'avenir,' he wrote, 'mais souffrez que je m'en tienne à la musique du passé.'

The New York *Musical Review* of December 23, 1880 published the following aphorism about Liszt's *Faust* Symphony: 'It may be the Music of the Future, but it sounds remarkably like the Cacophony of the Present.'

When Ernest Bloch conducted a program of his works in New York in May 1917, the critic of the New York *Evening Post* bracketed him with Schoenberg as futurists trying to 'distract attention from their creative shortcomings by pelting the ears of the hearers with cacophonies.' He said that 'Mr. Bloch's ideal of the Jewish music of the future is apparently the grotesque, hideous, cackling dispute of the Seven Jews in Richard Strauss's *Salome*.' Admitting that Ernest Bloch 'got plenty of applause,' he added, venomously, that the audience was 'largely of the Oriental persuasion.'

In his attempt to justify the obdurate tradition, Richard Aldrich wrote in the New York *Times* of November 15, 1915: 'Music that has been veiled to one generation has often been revealed to the next as a clear and intelligible advance. Will

---

*'I am sitting in the smallest room of my house. I have your review before me. In a moment it will be behind me.'

our grandchildren see it and smile indulgently at the bewildered listeners of 1915? The question is not really important; bewildered listeners of 1915 can only listen for themselves.'

Eight years later Aldrich wrote: 'The liberated music-maker and listener of the farthest advanced line are strangely uncritical persons. Whatever is presented to them as acrid ugliness or rambling incoherence is eagerly accepted as emanations of greatness and originality. It never occurs to them that it may be really simple, commonplace ugliness. . . . Is it only necessary to sound bad to be really good?'

Sometimes critics are fortunate enough to catch up with the musical future during their own lifetimes, and change their minds accordingly. The astute Philip Hale wrote disdainfully about Strauss's symphonic poem, *Don Juan*, in the Boston *Post* of November 1, 1891: 'Strauss uses music as the vehicle of expressing every-thing but music; for he has little invention, and his musical thoughts are of little worth. This symphonic poem is supposed to portray in music the recollections and regrets of a jaded voluptuary. Now, granting that music is capable of doing this, what do we find in this composition? There are recollections, not of Don Juan, but of Liszt and of Wagner. There are also regrets, but the regrets come from the hearers. Besides, Don Juan was more direct in his methods. His wooing was as sudden and as violent as his descent to the lower regions. According to Strauss, he was verbose, fond of turning corners, something of a metaphysician, and a good deal of a bore. When he made love, he beat upon a triangle, and when he was dyspeptic, he confided his woes to instruments that moaned in sympathy.'

Eleven years later, Philip Hale heard *Don Juan* again. This time, the music pro-duced a vastly different impression on him—rivers of modernistic harmonies had gone over the dam in the meantime, and the perceptive ear had made the inevitable adjustments to a new mode of musical expression. Writing then in the Boston *Journal*, in its issue of November 2, 1902, Philip Hale responded enthusi-astically to *Don Juan*: 'A daring, brilliant composition; one that paints the hero as might a master's brush on canvas. How expressive the themes! How daring the treatment of them! What fascinating, irresistible insolence, glowing passion!'

When Hugo Leichtentritt, a fine and liberal-minded scholar, heard Schoenberg's *Three Piano Pieces*, op. 11, for the first time in 1911, he wrote: 'I see in them com-plete dissolution of all that was heretofore regarded as musical art. It is possible that the music of the future will be like that, but I have no understanding of its beauty. Whether the pianist played the piece well or badly, I cannot judge, because in this music the listener cannot distinguish between right and wrong.'

In his treatise *Musical Form*, published in 1951, Leichtentritt revised his earlier judgment: 'These piano pieces have often been criticized as constructions which mock the laws of reason, the demands of the ear, as in fact "non-music," to which the usual reaction has been amused laughter and sneers. The following analysis will prove that these pieces are constructed not only sensibly, but strictly, logically, and concisely.'

Ill-starred prophecies abound in the annals of music criticism. '*Rigoletto* lacks melody,' wrote the *Gazette Musicale de Paris* in 1853; 'this opera has hardly any chance to be kept in the repertoire.' A correspondent of a London newspaper wrote in 1854: '*Lohengrin* has been given a few times . . . and I scarcely think it will be able to keep the stage for any length of time.' The Boston *Daily Advertiser* declared in 1874: 'It needs no gift of prophecy to predict that Berlioz will be utterly unknown a hundred years hence to everybody but the encyclopedists and the antiquarians.'

In their horror of the latest abomination, critics are often willing to forget and to forgive the trespasses of the musical sinners of the immediate past. By dint of an *argumentum ad deteriora* they hope to confound the newest monster through mock surrender to the monster of yesteryear. Thus, Chorley, the hater of

Schumann, was willing to grant him some virtue, when confronted with the greater menace of Wagner. 'Dr. Schumann is as clear as Truth and as charming as Graces themselves,' he wrote, 'if he be measured against the opera composer who has been set up by Young Germany, at the composer's own instigation, as the coming man of the stage—I mean, of course, Richard Wagner.'

In 1893, Philip Hale described Brahms's First Symphony as 'the apotheosis of arrogance.' Thereupon, he drew a symbolic program of the score: 'The musicians are in a forest. The forest is dark. No birds are in this forest save birds that do not sing. . . . The players wander. They grope as though they were eyeless. Alarmed, they call to each other; frightened, they shout together. It seems that obscene, winged things listen and mock the lost. . . . Suddenly the players are in a clearing. They see close to them a canal. The water of the canal is green, and diseased purple and yellow plants grow on the banks of the canal. . . . A swan with filthy plumage and twisted neck bobs up and down in the green water. . . . And then a boat is dragged towards the players. The boat is crowded with queerly dressed men and women and children, who sing a tune that sounds something like the hymn in Beethoven's Ninth Symphony. . . . Darkness seizes the scene.'

The critic of the New York *Times* in the 1890's had his misgivings about Brahms, but when he was assigned to review a work by Strauss he was eager to concede that Brahms might be, relatively speaking, a charming composer. He wrote in an unsigned article of February 28, 1896: '*Till Eulenspiegel* is a horrible example of what can be done with an orchestra by a determined and deadly decadent. There was a time when Brahms was regarded as the Browning of music. Richard Strauss has made the symphonies of Brahms sound like Volkslieder.'

The Boston *Herald* wrote: '*Till Eulenspiegel* casts into the deepest shade the wildest efforts of the wildest follower of the modern school. It is a blood-curdling nightmare.'

The *Musical Courier* of January 29, 1902 said: 'Strauss's *Heldenleben* and *Thus Spake Zarathustra* are clear as crystal waters in comparison with Gustav Mahler's Fourth Symphony.'

When the Fourth Symphony of Sibelius was performed in America in 1913, the Boston *Journal* described it as 'a tangle of most dismal dissonances' which 'eclipses the saddest and sourest moments of Debussy.'

It is not clear why the mild music of Vincent d'Indy impressed some critics half a century ago as being worse than Strauss. The New York *Sun* thought so: 'Even *Ein Heldenleben* becomes as the croon of a cradle song besides d'Indy's Second Symphony.'

Then came Debussy. The New York *World* reported on March 22, 1907: 'New York heard a new composition called *The Sea*, and New York is probably still wondering why. The work is by the most modern of modern Frenchmen, Debussy. . . . Compared with this, the most abstruse compositions of Richard Strauss are as primer stories to hear and to comprehend.'

The New York *Sun*, reviewing the same performance, makes a similar concession to the relative agreeableness of Strauss vs. Debussy: 'Debussy out-Strausses Strauss. *The Sea* and all that's in that painted mud-puddle was merely funny when it fell to whistling Salome's own shrill trill.'

After listening to Varèse's symphonic work *Arcana*, Paul Schwers of the *Allgemeine Musikzeitung* was eager to welcome Schoenberg: 'Great Arnold Schoenberg, your famous *Five Orchestral Pieces* are gloriously vindicated! They are the utterances of pure classicism beside this barbarous monstrosity.' Conversely, Olin Downes invoked the gentle muse of Varèse to exorcise Schoenberg. 'How we would have been thrilled by some good red-blooded, rousing tune of Edgar Varèse!' he exclaimed upon hearing Schoenberg's *Variations for Orchestra.*

Unfamiliar music impresses a prejudiced listener as a chaos of random sounds. No wonder that to some critics the labor spent on rehearsing a modern piece appears a waste of effort. César Cui, who was a professional music critic as well as a composer, wrote after hearing a performance of *Sinfonia Domestica*: 'Put blank music sheets before the conductor and the players. Let the musicians play anything they wish and let the conductor conduct anything he wishes, giving cues and indicating the time, tempo, and the intensity of sound at random. Perhaps, the result would be even more remarkable in its genius than Strauss himself.'

The same procedure was suggested to conductors of Liszt's music by a London critic in *Era* of February 25, 1882: 'The conductor wields his baton, but the effect is not a bit more agreeable than if each performer threw down the notes and played at random with all his might and energy. . . . Let the conductor give instructions to each player to produce every discordant sound that is in the range of his particular instrument, and let the cacophony continue for half an hour under the title of *Lunacy* or *Moonstruck*.'

In all fairness to these particular prophets, it must be said that ultra-modern music of the mid-twentieth century made their nightmares come true. In 1948, a Paris radio engineer launched a 'musique concrète,' in which random sounds and noises are recorded and presented as a new method—we should call it the 'aleatory method'—of composition. The American composer John Cage later rationalized the idea by writing music according to a system of throwing Chinese dice.

Music critics often complain that modern works cause them actual physical pain. August Spanuth described Schoenberg's Chamber Symphony as a 'Chamber-of-Horrors' Symphony. Huneker wrote: 'Schoenberg mingles with his music sharp daggers at white heat, with which he pares away tiny slices of his victim's flesh.' Louis Elson suggested that a more fitting title for Debussy's *La Mer* should be 'La Mal de Mer.' The urbane Percy A. Scholes reported in the London *Observer* of May 13, 1923 that hearing Béla Bartók play his piano works made him suffer more than at any time in his life 'apart from an incident or two connected with "painless" dentistry.'

When pain becomes unendurable, music critics themselves take part in the audible protest against the offending work. At a Vienna performance of Schoenberg's Second String Quartet, Ludwig Karpath pleaded, by way of extenuation for his own breach of professional decorum, a physiological necessity of crying out for relief.

René Brancour, the Paris critic, offered no apologies for his part in a public demonstration against the brassy importunities of Milhaud's symphonic suite *Protée*. 'I was in the first rank of objectors,' he wrote in *Le Ménestrel* of October 28, 1920, 'and a zealous, but otherwise courteous police officer was prepared to deliver me to the secular arm entrusted with the expulsion of heretics.' Brancour was saved from this indignity by the intercession of a similarly minded colleague who persuaded the officer to let Brancour remain in the hall.

On the other hand, the critic of the *Berliner Morgenpost* took it upon himself to defend the right of a modern composer to compose as he pleased. When a riot broke out at the second Berlin performance of Schoenberg's *Pierrot Lunaire*, on October 7, 1922, he rose from his seat and belabored the disturbers of the peace as 'ungebildete Lausejungen.'

Just as all good people are in favor of virtue, so music critics are unanimously in favor of melody. Berlioz, Brahms and Liszt were all charged at one time or another with willful neglect of melodic writing. 'Non seulement M. Berlioz n'a pas d'idées mélodiques, mais lorsqu'une idée lui arrive, il ne sait pas la traiter,' opined the ineffable Scudo, the French writer, who ended his career in an insane asylum.

Hanslick described the Wagnerian melody as 'formlessness elevated to a principle.' The Boston *Traveler* lamented in 1882: 'Brahms might afford occasionally to put a little more melody into his work, just a little now and then for a change.' Another Bostonian wrote: 'If the fair and ingenious Scheherazade related her stories as confusedly and unmeaningly, not to say cacophonously, as Rimsky-Korsakov has related them musically, the Sultan would have ordered her to be bowstrung, or to have her head lopped off after the second or third night.' The Boston *Gazette* of January 5, 1879 said this about *Carmen*: 'Of melody, as the term is generally understood, there is but little.'

The *Gazette Musicale de Paris* declared in 1847: 'There has not yet appeared an Italian composer more incapable than Verdi of producing what is commonly known as a melody.'

In 1907 the New York *Post* dismissed Debussy in these words: 'Debussy's music is the dreariest kind of rubbish. Does anybody for a moment doubt that Debussy would write such chaotic, meaningless, cacophonous, ungrammatical stuff, if he could invent a melody?'

Arthur Pougin, who, as the editor of the supplement to the *Biographie Universelle des Musiciens*, had described the score of *Die Meistersinger* as a collection of 'absolutely indecipherable puzzles,' and who lived to witness the rise of Debussy, wrung his hands at the monstrosities of *Pelléas et Mélisande*: 'What adorable progressions of consecutive triads, with the inevitably resulting fifths and octaves! What a collection of dissonances, sevenths, and ninths, ascending even by disjunct intervals!'

Hanslick was horrified by a 'monstrous edifice of fifths—E, B, F♯, D, A, and E' in Liszt's *Mephisto Waltz*. The American critic W. F. Apthorp was racked by 'the most ear-flaying succession of chords' in *Tosca*.

George Templeton Strong, the magnificent reactionary whose diary reflecting the New York scene in the middle of the nineteenth century was published in 1952, was naturally anti-Berlioz, anti-Liszt and anti-Wagner. With an uncommon gift for an imaginative phrase, he described the introduction to *Lohengrin* as 'two squeakinesses with a brassiness between them.' He said that Wagner wrote like an 'intoxified' pig, and Berlioz like a tipsy chimpanzee. Liszt's Piano Concerto in E♭ was to him 'catarrhal or sternutatory.' He heard in it 'a graphic instrumentation of a fortissimo sneeze' and 'a protracted, agonized bravura on the pocket handkerchief.'

Anti-modern critics are, of course, aware of the historical fact that the musical classics of today were the unmelodious monsters of yesterday, and they like to disassociate themselves from their short-sighted predecessors. Raphaël Cor, the compiler of the extraordinary symposium of impatient vituperation published in 1910 under the pointed title, *Le Cas Debussy*, took cognizance of the fact that Wagner had, like Debussy, been assailed for the unmelodiousness of his music: 'Let no one interpose that the same criticism was once directed against Wagner, for the Wagnerian melody eluded his adversaries, whereas the music of Monsieur Debussy, according to his own admission, contains no trace of melody.'

In a spirit of good-humored raillery at the Debussyan rage at the Paris Conservatory, Erik Satie drew a table of 'commandements du catéchisme du Conservatoire' in which the students were enjoined: 'Thou shalt not be melodious!' And he wittily deified Debussy as *Dieu*bussy:

> *Dieu*bussy seul adoreras
> Et copieras parfaitement—
> Mélodieux point ne seras
> De fait ni de consentement.*

---

*Satie signed these verses ERIT SATIS, i.e., This Will Be Enough; they were published posthumously in *La Semaine Musicale* of November 11, 1927.

Charles Villiers Stanford, who was in his prime a Wagnerian modernist, was distracted by the novel modernism of the incipient twentieth century. In protest against the musical depredations of Debussy and Strauss, he concocted a rather heavy-footed *Ode to Discord*, stuffed it with unresolved dissonances and whole-tone scales, and presented it to the London public on June 9, 1909. Stanford described his score as a 'chimerical bombination in four bursts' (with a learned reference to the line 'Chimaera bombinans in vacuo' from Erasmus) and dedicated it to the Amalgamated Society of Boiler Makers. The orchestration included a 'hydrophone' and a 'dreadnaught drum' measuring eight feet nine inches across. There was an aria which apostrophized in mock-solemn verse:

> Hence, loathed Melody!
> Divine Cacophony, assume
> The rightful overlordship in her room,
> And with Percussion's stimulating aid,
> Expel the Heavenly but no longer youthful Maid!

New music always sounds loud to old ears. Beethoven seemed to make more noise than Mozart; Liszt was noisier than Beethoven; Strauss, noisier than Liszt; Schoenberg and Stravinsky, noisier than any of their predecessors.

Reviewing the first London performance of the Ninth Symphony, the *Musical Magazine and Review* made this philosophical observation: 'Beethoven finds from all the public accounts that noisy extravagance of execution and outrageous clamor in musical performances more frequently ensures applause than chastened elegance or refined judgment. The inference, therefore, that we may fairly make, is that he writes accordingly.'

After the first Boston performance of the Ninth Symphony, the Boston *Daily Atlas* reported that the last movement 'appeared to be an incomprehensible union of strange harmonies,' and sought explanation of Beethoven's decline in his deafness: 'the great man upon the ocean of harmony, without the compass . . . the blind painter touching the canvas at random.'

Robert Browning, who loved Rossini, was outraged by the noisiness of Verdi's operas. He wrote in wrathful verse:

> Like Verdi, when, at his worst opera's end
> (The thing they gave at Florence, what's its name),
> While the mad houseful's plaudits near out-bang
> His orchestra of salt-box, tongs, and bones,
> He looks through all the roaring and the wreaths
> Where sits Rossini patient in his stall.

The loudness of Wagner's music was lampooned in hundreds of contemporary caricatures, variously representing him as conducting a siege of Paris or driving a nail into the listener's ear. Yet, in computable quantity of decibels, Wagner's noisiest orchestral interludes fall far below a German military march.

One of the characters in Oscar Wilde's novel *The Picture of Dorian Gray* points out conversational advantages of Wagner's music: 'I like Wagner's music better than anybody's. It is so loud that one can talk the whole time without other people hearing what one says.'

A poem entitled 'Directions for Composing a Wagner Overture,' published in an American newspaper in the 1880's, ends with this quatrain:

> For harmonies, let wildest discords pass:
> Let key be blent with key in hideous hash;
> Then (for last happy thought!) bring in your Brass!
> And clang, clash, clatter—clatter, clang and clash!

In 1924 a bewildered subscriber to the Boston Symphony concerts contributed these lines upon hearing Stravinsky's *Le Sacre du Printemps*:

> Who wrote this fiendish Rite of Spring,
> What right had he to write the thing,
> Against our helpless ears to fling
> Its crash, clash, cling, clang, bing, bang, bing?

The last lines of the anti-Wagner and anti-Stravinsky poems are practically identical. It is safe to assume that the author of the anti-Stravinsky poem regarded Wagner's music as a thing of beauty.

A fairly accurate time-table could be drawn for the assimilation of unfamiliar music by the public and the critics. It takes approximately twenty years to make an artistic curiosity out of a modernistic monstrosity; and another twenty to elevate it to a masterpiece.* Not every musical monstrosity is a potential musical masterpiece, but its chances of becoming one are measurably better than those of a respectable composition of mediocre quality.

One musical curiosity that was not destined to become an immortal masterpiece was the *Network of Noises* by the Italian futurist Luigi Russolo. When he conducted it in Milan on April 21, 1914, the excitable audience actually threatened bodily harm to the futurist offenders. A skirmish followed, as a result of which eleven members of the audience had to be hospitalized, but the futurists suffered only minor bruises. Who remembers now these excitements? The Italian futurists seem to have a brilliant future behind them.

When a modern composer is not accused of noise making, he is assailed for the annoying tenuousness of his musical speech. Camille Bellaigue, a musical reactionary blessed with a gift of elegant prose, conceded that Debussy's orchestra makes little noise, but said that it is 'a nasty little noise' ('un vilain petit bruit').

The London *Times* of April 28, 1924 compared Ravel's music to the work of 'some midget or pygmy, doing clever but very small things within a limited scope' with an 'almost reptilian cold-bloodedness.'

Anti-modernist critics who prepare their reviews in advance, but fail to attend a concert, ought to make sure that the performance of the offending music has actually taken place. Leonid Sabaneyev, the Moscow critic, published in 1916 a damning review of the announced première of Prokofiev's *Scythian Suite*. He did not go to the concert and did not know that the work was taken off the program at the last moment. Sabaneyev was forced to resign from his paper as a result of this indiscretion, but he refused to make amends to the composer.

Under similar circumstances, H. E. Krehbiel of the New York *Tribune* was much more of a gentleman. In his review of a New York concert of Russian music, Krehbiel indignantly attacked Prokofiev for the 'musical bestiality' of *Hircus Nocturnus*, a composition by Sergei Vasilenko. The next day, Krehbiel published a

---

*With what precision the law of a forty-year lag in the integral acceptance of a modern masterpiece operates, was demonstrated by the wild cheers that greeted Stravinsky at the performance of *Le Sacre du Printemps* in Paris on May 8, 1952, thirty-nine years after its première. Pierre Monteux, who conducted both performances, in 1913 and in 1952, remarked: 'There was just as much noise the last time, but of a different tonality!'

note of apology, blaming the dim light in the hall for his failure to read the composer's name on the program, and good-naturedly congratulated Prokofiev for not having written the score.

Non-Acceptance of the Unfamiliar in music extends to unsymmetrical rhythms as well as atonal melodies and dissonant harmonies. The celebrated Hanslick seriously suggested, upon hearing Tchaikovsky's *Pathétique*, that the 5/4 meter of the *Allegro con grazia* might well have been arranged in 6/8, thus sparing the annoyance to both listener and player.

In *La Revue des Deux Mondes* of July 1, 1892, Camille Bellaigue gives a satirical description of the musical notation of the future. Little did he realize how prophetic was the tableau presented by him! 'Let us wait a few years,' he wrote, 'and there will be no sense to study the laws of harmony, nor those of melody, which are set down only to be violated. The key signatures will no longer carry the necessary sharps or flats, these guardians of tonality. A piece of music will be no more in 3/4 or 12/8 than in C major or D minor. Caprice will become the rule, and chance, the law. The musical speech, disarticulated, deprived of grammar and syntax, devoid of logic, without proper notation, without punctuation, will meander aimlessly, and lose itself in the chaos of infinite melopoeia and errant modulation.'

In his 'Reminiscences of a Quinquagenarian,' published in *The Proceedings of the Musical Association of London* for the year 1910, George Bernard Shaw offers some illuminating remarks on the growth of musical tolerance: 'It is not easy for a musician of today to confess that he once found Wagner's music formless, melodyless, and abominably discordant; but that many musicians, now living, did so is beyond all question. . . . The technical history of modern harmony is a history of growth of toleration by the human ear of chords that at first sounded discordant and senseless to the main body of contemporary professional musicians.'

When Varèse presented his early symphonic work *Bourgogne* in Germany, it was met with obtuse hostility by the critics. Varèse reported the event to Debussy, declaring that he was not in the least concerned about this reception. In his reply Debussy made some penetrating remarks about the public and the critics. He wrote to Varèse on February 12, 1911: 'Vous avez parfaitement raison de ne pas vous alarmer de l'hostilité du public. Un jour viendra ou vous serez les meilleurs amis du monde. Mais dépêchez-vous de perdre l'assurance que la critique de chez nous est plus clairvoyante qu'en Allemagne. Et ne perdez pas de vue qu'un critique aime rarement ce dont il a à parler. Souvent même, il apporte un soin jaloux à ne pas savoir du tout de quoi il est question! La critique pourrait être un art si on pouvait la faire dans des conditions de libre jugement nécessaires. Ça n'est plus qu'un métier. . . . Il faut dire que d'ailleurs les soi-disant artistes ont beaucoup aidé à cet état de choses.'*

In the minds of righteous reactionaries, musical modernism is often associated with criminality and moral turpitude. Operas dealing with illicit love have been consistently assailed for the immorality of their librettos. In an inflammatory editorial published in the New York *Evening Journal* of January 21, 1907, William Randolph Hearst vesuviated: 'Many crimes have been committed in the name of music. Men of genius have exhausted their ingenuity, degraded the human voice and all musical instruments by causing them to describe murders and every kind of loathsomeness. But it is left for *Salome*, this latest opera, combining the musi-

---

*'You are perfectly justified in not being alarmed by the hostility of the public. The day will come when you will be the best of friends in the world. But you had better give up your belief that our critics are more perspicacious than those in Germany. Also, do not forget that a critic seldom likes what he has to describe. Sometimes he makes a special effort not to know what he is talking about! Criticism could be an art if it were practiced under the necessary conditions of free judgment. But it is now no more than a trade. It must be said in passing that the so-called artists have contributed a great deal to this state of affairs.'

cal genius of Strauss and the vile conception of Oscar Wilde, to produce a so-called work of art and show to the people a great singer in a scene that can be best compared to a hen trying to swallow a toad. . . . In a public performance, a woman is made to declare a desire to bite the swollen lips of a severed head, "as one would bite a ripe fruit." . . . If that is art, will somebody set to music that department of Armour's packing house in which they make the sausages?'

The London *Times* devoted a special 'leader' in its issue of August 7, 1856 to the iniquities of *La Traviata*, attacking the opera as 'public representation of prostitution' in the 'brothels and abominations of modern Paris, of the Boulevards as they exist in the year 1856.' The writer issued a solemn warning to 'the ladies of England to take heed of this matter,' lest their husbands and sons should be 'inoculated with the worst type of Parisian vice.'

In another 'leader' published four days later, the *Times* renewed its 'indignant protest against this exhibition of harlotry upon the public stage.' The article continued: 'An unfortunate young person who has acted the part of a public prostitute . . . coughs her way through three acts, and finally expires on the stage in a manner which, however true to nature, ought to be revolting to the feelings of the spectators. . . . Next season we trust to hear no more such abominations.'

The *Music Trade Review* of London declared in 1878: 'If it were possible to imagine his Satanic Majesty writing an opera, *Carmen* would be the sort of work he might be expected to turn out.'

The London theatrical paper *Figaro* published this comment on *Carmen* in 1884: '*Carmen* is a *fille de joie* of the very worst type, passing from man to man without a particle of scruple. The libretto revels in immorality of the most flagrant kind. No sooner do the factory girls, smoking real cigarettes, come on the stage than the evil spirit of Carmen asserts itself. The *Habanera*, replete in sensuality, is made still more telling by the attitude and the open gestures of the shameless girl.'

Die Walküre elicited some protests on the part of London moralists in 1882. 'The thirty minutes devoted to the indecent presentation of a brother and sister's incestuous love,' ran one comment, 'is rather too much for Anglo-Saxon ideas of propriety, and that this part of the opera was not prohibited after the first performance is unaccountable to a number of highly moral journals.'

A British reviewer had this to say after the London première of Puccini's *Tosca*: 'Those who were present were little prepared for the revolting effects produced by musically illustrating the torture and murder scenes of Sardou's play. The alliance of a pure art with scenes, so essentially brutal and demoralizing, results in a contrast that produced a feeling of nausea. There may be some who will find entertainment in this sensation, but all true lovers of the gentle art must deplore with myself its being so prostituted. What has music to do with a lustful man chasing a defenseless woman, or the dying kicks of a murdered scoundrel?'

To proper Anglo-Saxons, including music critics, Paris has always been an alluring and a shocking symbol of profligacy, the navel of immorality. In reviewing the first American performance of Charpentier's opera *Louise*, H. E. Krehbiel wrote in the New York *Tribune* of January 4, 1908:

'This opera is Parisian in its immorality. Coupled with its story, which glorifies the licentiousness of Paris and makes mock of virtue, the sanctity of the family tie and the institutions upon which social stability and human welfare have ever rested and must forever rest, the music may also be set down as immoral. . . . To the intellectual and moral anarchism universally prevalent among the peoples of Western culture, which desires to have idealism outraged, sacred things ridiculed, high conceptions of beauty and duty dragged into the gutter, and ugliness, brutality and bestiality placed upon a pedestal, it makes a strong appeal.'

The erotic naturalism of Shostakovitch's opera *Lady Macbeth of Mzensk* was denounced, in a policy-making article in the Moscow *Pravda*, as a neurotic product of bourgeois decadence. It also shocked some listeners and critics at the opera's production in New York. W. J. Henderson wrote in the New York *Sun* of February 9, 1935:

'*Lady Macbeth of Mzensk* is a bed-chamber opera. We see much of the coarse embraces of the two sinners mumbling and fumbling about in bed with the side of the house removed so we shall miss nothing. For their first embraces the composer has written music which for realism and brutal animalism surpasses anything else in the world. Here indeed we can indulge in superlatives. Shostakovitch is without doubt the foremost composer of pornographic music in the history of the art. He has accomplished the feat of penning passages which, in their faithful portrayal of what is going on, become obscene. And to crown this achievement he has given to the trombone a jazz slur to express satiety, and this vulgar phrase, rendered tenfold more offensive by its unmistakable purpose, is brought back in the last scene to help us to understand how tired the lover is of his mistress. The whole scene is little better than a glorification of the sort of stuff that filthy pencils write on lavatory walls.'

The custodians of public morals were profoundly shocked by the rise of syncopated music in America at the turn of the century. The *Musical Courier*, in an editorial entitled 'Degenerate Music,' published in its issue of September 13, 1899, took note of the new peril: 'A wave of vulgar, filthy and suggestive music has inundated the land. Nothing but ragtime prevails, and the cake-walk with its obscene posturings, its lewd gestures. . . . Our children, our young men and women, are continually exposed to the contiguity, to the monotonous attrition of this vulgarizing music. It is artistically and morally depressing, and should be suppressed by press and pulpit.'

The Most Reverend Francis J. L. Beckman, Archbishop of Dubuque, told the National Council of Catholic Women at Biloxi, Mississippi, on October 25, 1938: 'A degenerated and demoralizing musical system is given a disgusting christening as "swing" and turned loose to gnaw away the moral fiber of young people. . . . Jam sessions, jitterbugs and cannibalistic rhythmic orgies are wooing our youth along the primrose path to Hell!'

In Russia, American popular music was damned as 'a rhythmically organized chaos of deliberately ugly neuro-pathological sounds.' American jazz band leaders were described in Soviet publications as 'jazz bandits.'

Maxim Gorky, to whom American dance music was a capitalist perversion, reported his impression of a jazz band concert in these words: 'An idiotic little hammer knocks drily: one, two, three, ten, twenty knocks. Then, like a clod of mud thrown into crystal-clear water, there is wild screaming, hissing, rattling, wailing, moaning, cackling. Bestial cries are heard: neighing horses, the squeal of a brass pig, crying jackasses, amorous quacks of a monstrous toad. . . . This excruciating medley of brutal sounds is subordinated to a barely perceptible rhythm. Listening to this screaming music for a minute or two, one conjures up an orchestra of madmen, sexual maniacs, led by a man-stallion beating time with an enormous phallos.'

Sir Richard R. Terry saw in jazz a challenge to the white race. He wrote in *Voodooism in Music*: 'The White races just now are submerged in a spate of negroid sentiment. Hot Jazz, Fox Trots and Black Bottoms occupy the young folk; Negro Spirituals send the adults into tears; the Crooner wails his erotic inanities every night over the Radio. We have reached the stage of a spineless acceptance of all these phenomena. . . . We may see no paganism in what we deem mere harmless amusements, but the observant onlooker cannot fail to see that in the not too far distant future the Catholic Church will be standing as the one barrier in the path of the pagan advance.'

Jazz was assailed as the work of Satan by the English composer and theosophist Cyril Scott: 'After the dissemination of jazz, which was definitely put through by the Dark Forces, a very marked decline in sexual morals became noticeable. Whereas at one time women were content with decorous flirtation, a vast number of them are now constantly preoccupied with the search for erotic adventures, and have thus turned sexual passion into a species of hobby.'

In dance, art, literature, and in politics, the psychological phenomenon of Non-Acceptance of the Unfamiliar operates as forcefully as in music. The good old Waltz was excoriated in Rees's Cyclopedia, published in London in 1805: 'Waltz is a riotous German dance of modern invention. Having seen it performed by a select party of foreigners, we could not help reflecting how uneasy an English mother would be to see her daughter so familiarly treated, and still more to witness the obliging manner in which the freedom is returned by the females.'

When the Tango invaded Europe in 1913, there were outcries of shock and consternation from the press, the pulpit, and the throne. In his message of January 1, 1914, the Archbishop of Paris threatened excommunication to Tango addicts: 'We condemn the dance of foreign origin known as the Tango, which by its lascivious nature offends morality. Christians ought not in conscience to take part in it. Confessors must in the administration of the sacrament of penance enforce these orders.' Cardinal O'Connell of Boston declared: 'If this Tango-dancing female is the new woman, then God spare us from any further development of the abnormal creature.'

To vindicate the honor of his country, the Ambassador of Argentina in Paris was compelled to state formally that the Tango was 'a dance peculiar to the houses of ill fame in Buenos Aires, and is never cultivated in respectable gatherings.'

The suggestive posturings of modern ballet roused the moralists as much as lasciviousness in opera. When Diaghilev presented Debussy's *L'Après-midi d'un faune* with Nijinsky to the Parisian public in 1912, there was an outcry in the reactionary wing of the Paris press. Calmette, the editor of *Le Figaro*, refused to publish a customary account of the production on the ground that its animal realism *à la russe* was a breach of decency. Diaghilev issued a statement in protest, and said, among other things, that Nijinsky's interpretation of the faun had received high praise from the sculptor Rodin. To this, Calmette replied that Rodin himself was guilty of exhibiting obscene sketches in a building formerly occupied by a church. Calmette's moral sense did not deter him, however, from publishing, for political purposes, the intimate correspondence between the French Minister Caillaux and Mme. Caillaux before their marriage. One day, Mme. Caillaux broke into Calmette's office and shot him dead, for which impulsive act she was duly acquitted by a sympathetic Paris jury.

When Isadora Duncan danced, barefoot, before a Boston audience, in October 1922, the then Mayor Curley forthwith issued an order barring her from further appearances. Miss Duncan figuratively shook the Boston dust off her bare feet, and declared (to a New York reporter) that 'all Puritan vulgarity centers in Boston.' She added that 'to expose one's body is art; to conceal it is vulgar.'

Modernist painters have been attacked as viciously as modern composers. The French publication *L'Artiste* declared in its issue of May 1874: 'Monsieur Cézanne is a madman afflicted with delirium tremens. . . . His weird forms are generated by hashish and inspired by a swarm of insane visions.'

Gasperini, a French anti-Wagnerite of a century ago, draws a parallel between the Music of the Future and a putative Art of the Future. How could he foresee that, a mere half-century later, his caricature of modern art would turn out to be an excellent description of the technique of distortionism and angular transposition? Here is what he wrote, as quoted in *Le Ménestrel* of August 20, 1865: 'Do you wish to know what the Music of the Future will be like? Let us suppose that a sculptor, finding nature little to his taste, would fashion a statue to suit his fancy. What would he then do? Exactly the opposite of what had been done before him. In place of a mouth parallel to the chin, he would chisel a perpendicular mouth; in place of the nose, he would put a cheek; and in place of the generally accepted two eyes, a single eye in the middle of the forehead. He would then proudly lift his head and exclaim: This is the Sculpture of the Future!'

Leo Stein reminisced dyspeptically about his sister Gertrude and their mutual friend Picasso: 'They are in my belief turning out the most Godalmighty rubbish that is to be found.'

Albert Wolff, the French art critic, wrote in 1874: 'Just try to explain to Monsieur Renoir that the torso of a woman is not a mass of decomposing flesh, its green and violent spots indicating the state of complete putrefaction of a corpse.'

The *Churchman* delivered this judgment in 1886: 'Degas is nothing but a peeping Tom, behind the coulisses, and among the dressing-rooms of the ballet dancers, noting only travesties on fallen debased womanhood, most disgusting and offensive. It demands no unusual penetration to detect on these walls that satanic and infernal art whose inspirations are verily set on fires of Hell.'

John Burroughs, the American naturalist, wrote in *Current Opinion* in 1921: 'I have just been skimming through an illustrated book called *Noa Noa* by a Frenchman, Paul Gauguin, which describes, or pretends to describe, a visit to Tahiti. Many of his figures are distorted, and all of them have a smutty look, as if they had been rubbed with lampblack or coal dust. When the Parisian becomes a degenerate, he is the worst degenerate of all—a refined, perfumed degenerate.'

The psychological drama of the *fin de siècle* outraged the moralists. William Winter, the American drama critic, wrote in the New York *Tribune* of February 6, 1900: 'There is no surer sign of mental and moral obliquity than a taste for decadent literature and art—the morbid trash of such authors as Ibsen, Pinero and Maeterlinck. No man who is in good health ever bestows attention upon stuff of that kind. He would just as soon haunt a slaughterhouse to smell the offal.'

Walt Whitman was the recipient of lashing invective. 'Walt Whitman is as unacquainted with art as a hog with mathematics,' wrote *The London Critic* in 1855. 'The chief question raised by *Leaves of Grass*,' commented the New York *Tribune* in November 1881, 'is whether anybody—even a poet—ought to take off his trousers in the market-place.'

As in the arts and literature, so in social mores there is always an attitude of shock at the new ways of the world. In his amusing history of manners, *Learning How to Behave*, Arthur Schlesinger, Sr., quotes this from an old book of etiquette: 'We think the prospects for the future happiness of that young girl are small, who will be seen in public with a gentleman who is smoking.' Worse things were in the offing. 'Ladies no longer affect to be disgusted by the odor of tobacco, even at table,' revealed an etiquette book published in 1887. And finally, in a later edition, came this shocking news: 'Women, and women in America—in certain sets—do smoke.'

The horrendous secret in Wolf-Ferrari's opera *Secret of Suzanne* is that Suzanne indulges surreptitiously in cigarette smoking. Her husband, finding an ash tray with a cigarette in it, suspects that Suzanne had been entertaining a gentleman friend. He is both appalled and relieved to find that the mysterious cigarette had been smoked by Suzanne herself. There is a happy ending.

As late as 1923, American males in some regions regarded women who smoked as creatures of evil deserving death for their transgressions. The following story appeared in the New York *Times* of November 12, 1923:

SLAYS BRIDE WHO HAD PACK OF CIGARETTES

CLARKSBURG, W. VA.—When pretty Luella Mae Hedge, a bride of five months, refused to tell how she came to have a package of cigarettes, her husband, Okey Hedge, shot her dead. Hedge said he was maddened at finding the package of cigarettes in her pocketbook and at her taunting laugh when he questioned her on the subject.

In politics, Non-Acceptance of the Unfamiliar is demonstrated every time liberal legislation is debated. Daniel Webster, John Adams and James Madison all joined hands against universal suffrage, decrying the rule by 'King Numbers,' and the political power of the 'ring-streaked and speckled population of our towns and cities.' Women's suffrage aroused even greater protests. An editorial in *Harper's Magazine* for November 1853 made use of a musical metaphor, to carry its anti-suffragist argument: 'This unblushing female socialism defies alike the Apostles and the Prophets. Nothing could be more anti-biblical than letting women vote. . . . Instead of that exquisitely harmonized instrument which comes from the right temperament of the sexual relations, it would make human life a tuneless monochord, if not, in the end, a chaos of all harsh and savage dissonance.'

The obscurantist opposition to progressive ideas in science is often made in the name of rational thinking and logic. Fromundus of Antwerp advanced what he must have deemed an unanswerable argument against the rotation of the earth: 'Buildings and the earth itself would fly off with such rapid motion that men would have to be provided with claws like cats to enable them to hold fast to the earth's surface.'

Melanchton wrote in *Elements of Physics*: 'The eyes are witnesses that the heavens revolve in the space of twenty-four hours. But certain men, either from the love of novelty, or to make a display of ingenuity, have concluded that the earth moves. It is a want of honesty and decency to assert such notions publicly, and the example is pernicious.'

Scipio Chiaramonti declared: 'Animals, which move, have limbs and muscles; the earth has no limbs or muscles; therefore, it does not move.'

Dr. John Lightfoot, Vice-Chancellor of the University of Cambridge, announced, as a result of his study of the Scriptures, that 'heaven and earth were created all together, in the same instant, on October 23, 4004 B.C. at nine o'clock in the morning.' When geological and paleontological evidence began to pile up tending to show that things existed before October 23, 4004 B.C., the fundamentalists proffered an ingenious explanation in a pamphlet, *A Brief and Complete Refutation of the Anti-Scriptural Theory of Geologists*, published in London in 1853: 'All the organisms found in the depths of the earth were made on the first of the six creative days, as models for the plants and animals to be created on the third, fifth, and sixth days.'

Cardinal Manning declared that Darwin's theory was 'a brutal philosophy,—to wit, there is no God, and the ape is our Adam.' Disraeli coined a famous phrase when he said: 'The question is this: Is man an ape or an angel? I, my Lord, am on the side of the angels.'

Dr. Nicolas Joly of Toulouse ridiculed Pasteur. 'It is absurd to think,' he declared, 'that germs causing fermentation and putrefaction came from the air; the atmosphere would have to be as thick as pea soup for that.'

Bishop Berkeley argued fervently against the rationality of differential calculus. In his paper, *The Analyst, or a Discourse Addressed to an Infidel Mathematician*, he wrote: 'The further the mind analyseth and pursueth these ideas the more it is lost and bewildered; the objects, at first fleeting and minute, soon vanishing out of sight. Certainly, in any sense, a second or third fluxion seems an obscure Mystery. The incipient celerity of an incipient celerity, the nascent augment of a nascent augment, i.e., of a thing which hath no magnitude. . . . And what are these fluxions? The velocities of evanescent increments. And what are these same evanescent increments? They are neither finite quantities, nor quantities infinitely small, nor yet nothing. May we not call them the ghosts of departed quantities?

Einstein's famous formula which underlies the release of atomic energy was ridiculed as meaningless in a book by Samuel H. Guggenheimer, *The Einstein Theory Explained and Analyzed*: 'It is well to note here an example of the danger of relying too much on mathematical abstraction, afforded by the formulation of Einstein's application of his transformations to problems of additions of energy to moving masses. He tells us that the kinetic energy of a mass, *m*, is no longer given by the expression

$$ m \, \frac{v^2}{2} $$

but, according to the Lorentz transformation, by the expression

$$ \frac{mc^2}{\sqrt{1 - \frac{v^2}{c^2}}} $$

where v is the velocity of m and c the velocity of light. In other words, the energy, for all ordinary velocities, becomes mc^2, meaning the mass multiplied by the square of the velocity of light. This is certainly a meaningless expression unless the c value be eliminated by making it unity, and is so felt to be by the Professor.'

Prospects of controlled release of atomic energy were deemed negligible as late as 1931, as appears from Frank Allen's book *The Universe*, published in that year. 'Should some method be devised,' he wrote, 'whereby the proper energy could be released, which at present cannot be done, and, indeed, seems quite beyond the range of possibility . . . the experimenter, his laboratory, and even his city would forthwith be swept to destruction.'

The forced acceptance of formerly untenable theories is illustrated by the following story. At the opening lecture on chemistry in the 1890's, the professor wrote in large letters on the extreme left corner of the wall-size blackboard: ELEMENTS ARE NOT TRANSMUTABLE. It so happened that after the lecture the janitor propped up a bookshelf against the blackboard, covering the inscription. Several years elapsed, and radium was discovered. The professor announced a special lecture on atomic transmutation. He needed the entire blackboard for his formulas, and ordered the obstructing bookshelf removed. The words, chalked down in the days of intransmutability, were revealed to the students who read with amazement: ELEMENTS ARE NOT TRANSMUTABLE.

Even the harmony of the spheres seems to have gone modern, if the classical-minded astronomers are to be believed. The New York *Times* of August 27, 1950 brought modern music into play in its account of the new radio telescope that registers the static electricity of distant galaxies: 'If this be the music of the spheres, it is more like the cacophonies of modernistic composers than the harmonies that the ancient Greeks extolled.'

The first musical Schimpflexicon, limited to anti-Wagnerian outbursts, was compiled by Wilhelm Tappert, and published in 1877 under the interminable title, *Ein Wagner-Lexicon, Wörterbuch der Unhöflichkeit, enthaltend grobe, höhnende, gehässige und verleumderische Ausdrücke welche gegen den Meister Richard Wagner, seine Werke und seine Anhänger von den Feinden und Spöttern gebraucht worden sind, zur Gemütsergötzung in müssigen Stunden gesammelt.*

The assorted entries in the *Wagner-Lexicon* give an idea of what the critics can do to a man they really hate. The virulence, the animus seething in the inflamed breast of the invective-hurling, foaming-at-the-mouth vilifier, find their culmination in the verbal implosion in a most unlikely tome—a treatise on the Spanish theater by the German historian J. L. Klein. Wrote he:

'The wild Wagnerian corybantic orgy, this din of brasses, tin pans and kettles, this Chinese or Caribbean clatter with wood sticks and ear-cutting scalping knives. . . . Heartless sterility, obliteration of all melody, all tonal charm, all music. . . . This revelling in the destruction of all tonal essence, raging satanic fury in the orchestra, this diabolic, lewd caterwauling, scandal-mongering, guntoting music, with an orchestral accompaniment slapping you in the face. . . . Hence, the secret fascination that makes this music the darling of the feeble-minded royalty, the plaything of the camarilla, of the court flunkeys covered with reptilian slime, and of the blasé hysterical female court parasites who need this galvanic stimulation by massive instrumental treatment to throw their pleasure-weary frog-legs into violent convulsions . . . the diabolical din of this pig-headed man, stuffed with brass and sawdust, inflated, in an insanely destructive self-aggrandizement, by Mephistopheles' mephitic and most venomous hellish miasma, into Beelzebub's Court Composer and General Director of Hell's Music—Wagner!'

This tirade bids fair to excel, in sheer intensity of vituperative logorrhea, the American classic of vilification, delivered by W. C. Brann of Waco, Texas, against a newspaper editor: 'I can but wonder what will become of the editor of the Los Angeles *Times* when the breath leaves his feculent body and death stops the rattling of his abortive brain. He cannot be buried in the sea lest he poison the fishes. He cannot be suspended in mid-air, like Mahomet's coffin, lest the circling worlds, in their endeavor to avoid contamination, crash together, wreck the universe and bring about the return of chaos and Old Night. The damn scoundrel is a white elephant on the hands of the Deity, and I have some curiosity to know what He will do with him.'

Why do music critics, who are in private life, most of them, the mildest of creatures, resort so often to the language of vituperation?

Philip Hale may have provided an answer to this psychological paradox, when he commented, in the Boston *Journal* of January 14, 1893, upon Hanslick's tirade against Tchaikovsky's Violin Concerto (Hanslick said the Concerto stank to the ear): 'I think that the violence of Dr. Hanslick was as much inspired by the desire to write a readable article as by any just indignation.'

"Incidental Music," from
A Thing or Two About Music

This opening chapter of A Thing or Two About Music *(1948) survives as a pronto-history of proto-electronic music.*

Broadcasting by Telephone

In March 1904, the Boston papers carried a momentous announcement. A company with a reported capital of two million dollars was incorporated in Massachusetts for the purpose of piping music into American homes and public restaurants by telephone wires. The inventor of the system of telephone broadcasting was Theodore Cahill, and his invention was called Cahill Telharmonic. The Boston *Transcript* of March 30, 1904, gave the following description of the Telharmonic:

> "The general plan is to establish a central station in every large city. The best artists only will be employed, and the music will be varied from Wagner to ragtime, to suit the tastes and whims of the public. The machine is operated by making and breaking electric circuits. When the plant is in working order, one of the dreams of Edward Bellamy will be realized. By the turning of the switch, the room or hall or hospital will be filled with the music of the great masters. There will be slumber music for the person troubled with insomnia, and there will be waking music to rouse the sleeper for the duties of the day. The service will be on the same plan as the telephone."

There was a feature article in *Harper's* Magazine showing the inventor amidst a bewildering agglomeration of funnel-shaped loud-speakers. There were stories about the new invention in music magazines. Busoni, who was eternally enthusiastic about new ways of spreading musical culture, wrote admiringly about the Telharmonic in his *Essay on New Esthetics in Music*. But despite these manifestations of interest, the whole idea was quietly dropped. Sixteen years after the incorporation of the Cahill Telharmonic, the first commercial broadcasts of musical programs were launched by wireless.

Opera by Cable

The first international opera broadcast was transmitted in 1896 over the cable connecting Calais and Dover. An opera performed at the Paris Grand Opera

House was thus heard at the Pelican House in London where an electrophone, or a loud-speaking telephone, was installed. Contemporary reports glowed with excitement about this new achievement of the nineteenth century which one of the enthusiasts described as "the century of enlightenment, electricity, and music."

Gaspipe Radio

Long before Bellamy's prophecy of a central musical station, dreamers, inventors, and visionaries thought of devising a system whereby music could be acoustically piped into homes and public halls. At an exhibition in the Polytechnic of London, experiments were made as early as 1855, with gaspipes transmitting music. *The Builder* published an account of this "Music Laid on Like Gas."

> "At the Polytechnic a band playing in a distant apartment is unheard; but connect the different instruments by means of thin rods of wood, each with the sounding board of a harp in the lecture theater, and the music is audible to all as if it were present. The experiments prove what we have often speculated on, that music might be laid onto the houses of a town from a central source, like gas or water."

Machine-made Music

The idea of mechanical music is not new. An instrument named the Componium, invented by M. Winkel of Amsterdam, was exhibited with great success in Paris in the year 1824. The inventor claimed that it could compose variations all by itself. The *Harmonicon* of 1824 reported:

> "The astonishment of the hearers was at its height when, after having executed a march with variations by Moscheles, the instrument was left to follow its own inspirations; the applause was loud and unanimous, and some exclaimed that it was altogether miraculous. Still, the more perfect the execution, the stronger the feeling of incredulity became, the result of which was a general and decided opinion that the effects of the Componium could be produced only by some highly finished automaton."

To dispel such suspicions, several scientists were invited by the manufacturers of the Componium to examine the inner mechanism and to certify that no human manipulated the levers inside. The scientists, members of the French Academy, did so and on February 2, 1824 issued a report confirming the claims of the inventor:

> "When the instrument has received a varied theme, it decomposes the variations of itself and reproduces their different parts in all the orders of possible permutations. None of the airs which it varies lasts above a minute. Yet through the principle of variability which it possesses, it might without ever resuming precisely the same combination, continue to play not only during years and ages but during so immense a series of ages that though figures might be brought to express them, common language could not."

A Musical Bicycle

A patent for a musical bicycle was deposited in 1896. A music box is attached to the front forks of a bicycle, and is operated by means of a cord that revolves around a pulley fastened to the spokes. The inventor, an Iowa man, devised the musical bicycle especially for bicycle racing, claiming that the music would encourage the rider to make greater speed.

A Musical Bed

A French inventor of the 1880's contrived a musical bed which played a varied repertoire of melodies. The beds were constructed like a chain of music boxes, wound up like a clock and running as long as twelve hours. This enabled the insomniacs to idle away their sleepless hours listening to waltzes, quadrilles, or minuets. The musical bed was a fitting predecessor of the bedside radio set.

The Cylindrichord

Player-pianos seem to be more ancient than commonly believed. In January 1825, a French inventor, one Courcell, presented to the public a contraption which he called the Cylindrichord, and which, according to a credulous contemporary, "is found to be an admirable and efficient substitute for a first-rate performer on the pianoforte." The advantages in using the newly invented instrument are further outlined:

> "In small or family parties, where dancing to the music of the pianoforte is practiced, one of the company had always been necessarily engaged at the instrument; that unpleasant necessity became obviated; for by the aid of the Cylindrichord, a person totally unacquainted with music, a child or a servant, may perform in the very best and most correct style quadrilles, waltzes, minuets, country dances, marches, songs, overtures, sonatas, choruses, or indeed any piece of music, however difficult. This instrument is extremely simple and differs altogether from the barrel or self-playing pianoforte: it can be accommodated to the height or dimensions of any pianoforte and, when not in use for that purpose, forms a piece of elegant furniture."

The Nototype

During the last years of life, Haydn was very much aware of his body's weakness. He complained in a letter (which is quoted in the article, "*Die Sonate auf der Schreibmaschine*," published in the *Hamburger Fremdenblatt* of September 13, 1936):

> "The piece on which I am now working would have been already finished if it were not that my hand gets tired of setting the notes on paper. Why doesn't some ingenious person invent a machine which would enable the afflicted composers to write the notes faster and with less fatigue?"

Many attempts to construct an efficient musical typewriter have been made, but composers still write their symphonies and sonatas the hard way, putting notes on music paper manually. Yet in the case of the aging and ailing Haydn, a musical typewriter would have been a perfect solution. Another solution is to engage a musical amanuensis. Delius, the English composer of nostalgic mood pieces, was blind and paralyzed in the last years of his life. But his mind was alert and active, and his musical invention needed an outlet. Fortunately for him, a young English musician, Eric Fenby, volunteered to act as his musical secretary. Stretched in his invalid chair, Delius dictated to Fenby his ideas, note by note, correcting and revising as the work progressed until the piece was finished. Delius even managed to dictate a complete orchestral score, entitled *A Song of Summer*. It was performed for the first time by the British Broadcasting Company

Orchestra under Sir Henry Wood on September 17, 1931, and the composer had the unique pleasure of hearing a broadcast of that performance in his room in a French village where he spent the last years of his life.

It is conceivable that even a blind man could use a musical typewriter by the touch system, and it is further conceivable that such a typewriter would play back the notes and chords with the aid of some electronic gadget, so that the composer could check on the results.

The most promising musical typewriter was put on the market in Germany in 1937. It was called Nototype. It had a standard keyboard of forty-four keys, with the carriage slightly widened. A special hand lever controlled the vertical line for typing chords. The upper row of the typewriter keys was given to clefs, numerals for time signatures, sharps, flats, and bar lines. The second row was given to notes of the musical staff below the third line, and on the third line itself. The third row carried the notes above the middle line, and the lowest row had stems from a quarter note to a sixty-fourth note. Rests, dots, and other signs were distributed among the corner keys of all four rows of the typewriter, just as punctuation, quotation marks, and the less frequent letters of the alphabet are tucked away in the corners of the regular typewriter.

Typewritten music is a convenient substitute for engraving, less costly, and more practical for the publication of non-commercial music. Musical typing need not be more difficult than handling a stenotype machine. Each key on a musical typewriter may be assigned a special sound. A musical office, with musical secretaries typing music, may not produce celestial harmony, but the typing polyphony will be both novel and impressive.

Phonographic Typewriter

Every modern music machine had its granddaddy or perhaps its grand uncle. The *Musical World* of February 25, 1871 reports the invention by a Frenchman of a machine for writing music by an electrical contact with the piano keyboard:

"The inventor passes over a metal cylinder, turning regularly by means of a clock movement and communicating with a battery, a band of paper impregnated with a solution that will decompose under the influence of an electric current. The clock movement may be put in motion or stopped at will by an electric or mechanical stop. The band of paper, being placed on the cylinder, the inventor places above it a series of metal wires or plates, isolated from each other in such a way that as they rest at one point on the paper in a parallel direction to the axis of the cylinder, they each communicate, by means of a separate metallic wire, with a contact apparatus placed under each of the keys of the keyboard of the instrument. These contact apparatuses are worked by the motion of the key, either by bringing together two wires or metallic plates, or by plunging one point in a jar of mercury communicating with the battery. The circuit is thus closed for each of the wires only when the key corresponding to it is lowered."

A Musical Petticoat

The Boston *Musical Times* of September 1860 described an extraordinary invention, a musical petticoat, credited to a Parisian couturier:

"With the aid of scientific mechanism, the crinoline is inflated like a life-preserver. The elegant wearer need only touch a spring arranged to communicate with the pocket of her dress, and the air in the skirt sets in motion a musical attachment, not unlike a bird organ, playing a variety of tunes from the gems of the operas to a nursery lullaby. The inventor declares that the ballroom orchestra may be entirely dispensed with in the future. The ladies wearing his musical petticoats can provide themselves with waltzes, quadrilles, and polkas to their hearts' content."

Modern Ballet A.D. 1883

The modern ballet with characters representing the machines of the modern age was anticipated by the "electrical ballet" presented at the Vienna Electrical Exhibition in 1883. A contemporary account reports:

"The chief features were the electromagnets, dynamo machines, telegraph apparatus, and telephones, which were dragged on the stage by fantastic goblins and handled by the graceful danseuses with as much ease as if they were especially trained in the mysteries of electricity."

The Anthropoglossos

On January 5, 1939 a machine looking like a stenographic typewriter, named Voder, was exhibited at the Franklin Institute in Philadelphia. It synthetized the primary hisses and buzzes into human song or speech, speaking with the deliberate impersonality of a robot. As often happens in the history of invention, the thing was anticipated many decades before. It was called the Anthropoglossos, and the name undoubtedly impressed the innocents who flocked to watch it perform at St. James's Hall in London during the summer of 1864. The *Musical World* reported:

"The inventor of this extraordinary piece of mechanism is M. Saguish of Constantinople. It represents the head and shoulders of a human being holding in his mouth a trumpet through which issues the sound of the human voice. This extraordinary automaton head sings a variety of songs in so perfect a manner that it is impossible to believe it is produced by mechanism alone. The words of the song are heard quite distinctly, the quality of the voice (a tenor) although somewhat nasal, is exceedingly agreeable, and the inventor altogether one of the most astonishing in this age of miracles. The program consisted of *The Dark Girl Is Dressed in Blue, Polly Perkins, Annie Lisle, A Gypsy's Life Is a Joyous Life, God Bless the Prince of Wales*, and *God Save the Queen*. The exhibition is to be varied daily. Every curious inquirer will go and hear the Anthropoglossos."

Talking Machine A.D. 1846

Miracle machines and mechanical contraptions always found an admiring public a hundred years ago. Chopin, who was inordinately gullible, was very much impressed with a "talking machine" exhibited in Europe in the 1840's. He wrote to his parents on October 11, 1846:

"Mr. Faber of London, a professor of mathematics and a mechanician, has exhibited a very ingenious automaton which he calls Euphonia, and which pronounces fairly clearly not one or two words, but whole sentences and, still more surprising, sings an air of Haydn and *God Save the Queen*. If opera directors could have many such *androids*, they could do without chorus singers who cost a lot and give a lot of trouble."

SEX AND THE MUSIC LIBRARIAN

This is Dybbuk speaking, through the invultuation of Bill Lichtenwanger. I am sorry that I am unable to be present in person, but the Philadelphia Orchestra program book some years ago referred to me as "the late Nicolas Slonimsky." (I wired them back protesting that I was late only in delivering manuscripts to my publishers, and that I was still technically alive and even capable of running a forty-minute mile.) Furthermore, according to the caption underneath a Kodak snapshot of me as a neurotic Russian boy, taken in a Finnish spa during the summer of 1910, I died in 1967. In view of these circumstances, any discussion of sex must be strictly posthumous.

Since my name appears in various respectable, though not always accurate, musical encyclopedias, I feel that I owe an explanation to the honorable members of the Music Library Association how it is that, next to highly dignified topics of the talks scheduled for the present meetings, sex was allowed to raise its exhibitionistic head. Well, I plead not guilty. As I was making my customary pre-Christmas tour of music libraries, one staff member after another greeted me with a display of prurient interest utterly incompatible with the customary image of a music librarian as a bespectacled, sandy-faced, scholarly-looking lady or gentleman, uncertain as to age or sexual classification, and covered by a layer of dust gathered in the stacks. Virtually everyone said, with a suggestive twinkle, "I can't wait to hear your talk at the MLA convention," and unaccustomed as I am to compliments, I worked my facial muscles into a responsive smile. Not until I received the mimeographed notice of the meeting did I discover what the title of my talk was to be! Some clown in the Music Library Association must have played a nasty trick on me, and I think I know who.

I was aware, of course, that sex lurks even in music libraries, and that its repression often finds an outlet in sexo-typographical fantasies. My publisher once received an order from a music library for a book of mine itemized in the order form as *Sexicon of Musical Invention by Solo Minsky*.

What is the proper place of sex in the music library? Ten years ago, sweating out the fifth edition of *Baker's Biographical Dictionary of Musicians*, I was tipped off that the autobiography of the German prima donna Wilhelmine Schröder-Devrient, retailing her nightly tours of the boudoirs of musical celebrities, which is solemnly listed as an authentic document in the bibliographies of most reference books, was a fake put together by an anonymous, and largely unimaginative, pornographer. To be sure, the volume is kid stuff by present-day standards, but it was hot enough a hundred years ago to be banned from German bookstores. Naturally I was aroused, and on my next visit in the marble halls of the Library of Congress, I filled in a request slip for the book. The librarian, an innocent-looking chap, asked me with a show of uncommon alacrity, "Do you want the French edition too? It's illustrated, you know." In no more than ninety seconds, both the German and the French editions were placed in my hands—the quickest service I had ever had in any library. I expressed my amazement at the page's expeditiousness, and the librarian remarked casually, "Oh, we all know where *those* books are."

I used to sign my letters to a friendly member of the staff of the Library of Congress, "Formicatingly yours," to express my itching eagerness in pursuit of a musicological point. He automatically misread the word and asked me, "With whom?" The same librarian figuratively raised his eyebrows when he came across an item in *Baker's* on the Neapolitan opera composer Luigi Ricci, Sr., which mentioned the fact that Ricci had a son by his wife's identical twin sister. He jotted in the margin, "Could he tell any difference?"

From yet another skeptical librarian I received a request for the clarification of my statement in *Baker's* that the French cellist François Servais was an illegitimate son of Liszt and Princess Carolyne Sayn-Wittgenstein. "Is this a presumptive, assumptive, or documented statement?" he demanded. "In other words—can you prove it, and if so, how?" That posed quite a problem. According to my dictionary and several other sources, Servais was born in darkest Russia in the 1840s, about the time when Liszt was traveling there in the company of the princess. I wrote to the Soviet author of a history of Russian-born cello players asking him to check on the registries of Russian lodginghouses where Liszt and the princess might have slept about nine months before Servais was born, but the dismaying reply came that there was no evidence at all that Servais was ever born in Russia. I then approached the problem from the other end, the reported death of Servais in Asnières near Paris. I wrote to the mayor of the town for a copy of the death certificate, and received an obliging answer from him to the effect that there was no record of Servais's death there, but pointing out there are fourteen towns in France called Asnières, and one in Switzerland, and suggesting to me to try all those towns. He also directed me to an illegitimate descendant of Liszt living in Paris on Avenue du Président Kennedy. But what could this descendant know about another illegitimate offspring of Liszt? I gave up the whole thing in disgust.

Insofar as musical bastardy is the incontinent result of overt sex, such topics are of legitimate concern to the music librarian. But what to do about celebrated musicians who claim to be bastards but are nothing of the sort? Such as the claim of the famous pianist Sigismond Thalberg. He spread the rumor that he was the illegitimate son of a petty duke and a shabby baroness. *Grove's Dictionary* [5th ed.] supported the claim and declared in a footnote that his birth certificate was lost. Well, I got that birth certificate from the archives of Geneva, where Thalberg was born, and it says in plain French that he was the son of a non-ducal Frankfurt merchant Thalberg and a non-baroness named Stein. But so attractive was the glamour of noble origin, however illegitimate, in the nineteenth century that Thalberg allowed the circulation of a fabricated letter, supposedly written by his baroness mother to his duke father, suggesting that he should be named Thalberg, since he was destined to become as deep an artist as a valley—*Thal*—and as lofty a spirit as a mountain—*Berg*!

Is it necessary to know a composer's sex syndrome in order to understand his music? Heterosexual melancholy oozes out of every note and every appoggiatura of Tchaikovsky's music, so it comes as a shock to discover that the signals are crossed and the signs point in the opposite direction. A deep Freudian would probably uncover the truth by noting the prevalence of feminine endings in most of Tchaikovsky's melodies as well as his predilection for minor effeminate-sounding keys. Before the advent of the era of candor, Tchaikovsky's biographers, including his brother (who had tastes similar to those of Tchaikovsky himself), duly reported the "fact" that Tchaikovsky was married, that his wife did not understand him, and that he poured out his soul to Madame von Meck, whom he studiously avoided in the mortal fear that she might have heterosexual designs on him.

Incidentally, all references to Tchaikovsky's homosexuality have been deleted in recent Soviet editions of the composer's diaries and letters. The ban has also been extended to East Germany, where a fictional biography of Tchaikovsky, with a frank discussion of his proclivities, has been confiscated. For a sexually alert music librarian it is of special interest to know that an early Soviet edition of Tchaikovsky's correspondence with his relatives, which contains some juicy passages (e.g. Tchaikovsky responding in full empathy to his brother Modest's ecstatic description of his excitement at watching a bevy of young seminarians filing out after classes), is an un-book whose very existence is denied by Soviet bibliographers. Inquiries from persistent Western librarians are usually referred to a new edition of the correspondence, in which such objectionable episodes are carefully removed, with or without benefit of eloquent dots of ellipsis.

A music library is by intent a depository of wisdom and information, ever ready to answer questions from perplexed music lovers. Was Wagner an illegitimate son of the actor Geyer whom Wagner's mother married after Wagner's father's death? Who cares? The Nazis cared, very deeply so, because there was something suspiciously semitic in Geyer's profile and even in Wagner's own profile. To their great relief, Nazi genealogists managed to prove that all the Geyers were hereditary Aryans. Illegitimacy never bothered them; the important point was to prove that, whether legitimate or illegitimate, Wagner was racially pure.

As all music librarians know, Wagner stole Liszt's daughter Cosima from her wedded husband Hans von Bülow, while the latter was busy rehearsing *Tristan und Isolde*. When Cosima von Bülow procreated a female child, Wagner brazenly named her Isolde. Some forty years later, Isolde sued her mother for equal rights in Wagner's estate, but the court ruled against her, pointing out that the putative time of conception—the period between eight and ten months before her birth—took place when Bülow was still lodging in direct proximity to Cosima, and therefore could have been Isolde's real father.

The Russians have a wonderful word *Nebylitza*—literally, an "unwasity" (unwas-ity). Many sexual unwasities are found in popular biographies of great composers. Take Brahms. When he had his first confrontation with females *en masse*, conducting a Hamburg girls' chorus as an unbearded youth (he matured, pogonologically speaking, only when he began writing symphonies), he fainted and had to be carried away. Some biographers try to whip up his platonic friendship with Clara Schumann into something passionate, only to fail dismally. No feminine companion could possibly be foisted on Brahms by romantic writers. An enterprising American author undertook a tour of Viennese bordelli in the 1920s and interviewed a number of ancient hags who were only too eager to tell, for a consideration, all about their servicing Brahms in an exotic way—the only way he could function, or so they said. The music librarian ought to be able to render an unbiased judgment about the value of such a biography in response to an inquiry.

Of all the wild stories found in dictionaries of musical biography the most fantastic is the story of Giusto Ferdinando Tenducci, a male soprano, who eloped with an English girl. According to his intimates, he was a triorchis. The extra cylinder enabled him to procreate.

One of the most fantastic unwasities perpetrated on the unsuspecting public was the unwarranted publication of a batch of fabricated Chopin letters purportedly addressed to one of his early lady friends, Delphina Potocka, in which Chopin reveals himelf as an ardent sensualist, an experienced Don Juan, and a gross pornographer. The letters were produced by a Polish woman, who claimed that she had copied them from originals in the palace of the descendants of the Potocka family. (The originals, she explained, were sent by messenger to Paris after the German invasion of Poland, but they were never found.) The trouble with the letters was that Chopin used in them some obscene slang expressions that were not current in Polish until about 1900. For instance, he referred to his *Polonaise in A-dur* as "A Durka," which means hole in Polish, with clear anatomical connotations. There were also chronological discrepancies. When confronted with the cumulative evidence of these incongruities, the woman who concocted the "Chopin" correspondence in the first place swallowed poison.

When a sex scandal about a musician spills into public print, it becomes proper material for the shelves of a music library. Paganini chose to defend himself when he took a sixteen-year-old English girl across the channel to France to promote her singing career. Eventually she made her way to America. The manuscript of her memoirs is in the possession of a collector in St. Louis, along with many other unique memorabilia of celebrated musicians, but he is unwilling to let his treasures be published.

An ideal sex story, from the standpoint of fact-conscious music librarians, is the courtship of Miss Smithson by Berlioz via the Fantastic Symphony: there is a unique romantic story, opium smoking, psychedelic hallucinations, and in the end actual marriage. This is sex in excelsis.

The sex question that comes up most often in the music library is this: Who was Beethoven's Immortal Beloved? The answer is: The incorporeal eternal femininity in Beethoven's loncly visions. The absence of all parameters of time, space, and locus in the letter points up the unreality of the object of Beethoven's fantasy. The letter was never dispatched and remained in Beethoven's possession. The style, the wording, the emotional pitch closely approximate the passionate expressions in Goethe's *Sorrows of Young Werther*. It would be most interesting to compare Beethoven's letter to some of Werther's appeals: "Yes, dear Charlotte! I will take care of everything as you wish. Do give me more errands to perform, etc., etc., etc." But, of course, Beethoven did not use a name in his letter.

Confronted with Beethoven's loveless life, Freudian and non-Freudian biographers have labored mightily on romantic unwasities. There is a book centered on a certain day in Beethoven's life when he visited a certain town coincidentally with a certain lady of his Vienna circle. Nine months later the lady, married, gave birth to a child. Ergo, the child was Beethoven's. One can easily imagine how many paternity claims could be made on such evidence. Another book, very deep and very dark, interprets Beethoven's relationship with his nephew as a case of latent homosexuality.

In the monastic seclusion of their windowless cubicles, music librarians often exchange succulent bits of sex gossip about composers, performers, and even their own colleagues. Yes, Virginia, sex is rampant in your music libraries.

"A FORMULA FOR MUSICAL ELIGIBILITY," FROM *MUSIC IN LATIN AMERICA*

This example of speculative (and eccentric) historiography initially appeared in Slonimsky's Music of Latin America *(1945), essentially a country-by-country history that, incidentally, has no sequel.*

Formula for Musicological Reliability

In the spirit of frivolous profundity, I drew up a formula expressing the necessary requirements for a musician to be put on a geo-musical map. I called it a "Formula for Musicological Eligibility." Quantity as well as quality are factors in my formula. Did not Dr. Samuel Johnson himself recognize the value of a purely numerical achievement? Said he to Boswell, commenting on a contemporary poetaster: "To be sure, he is a tree that cannot produce good fruit; he only bears crabs. But, sir, a tree which produces a great many crabs is better than a tree which produces only a few."

In alloting space in a music dictionary, composers of music in larger forms should naturally receive preferential treatment. Other things being equal, a symphony is a more impressive achievement than a piano sonata, and an opera merits more attention than a ballad. Let us assign an arbitrary numerical coefficient to each musical form, expressing approximately their relative values. Let us take a song with piano accompaniment as a musicological unit. Let us rate a piano piece as worth five songs (always regarding quality as a constant), a piece of chamber music equal to twenty-five songs, a symphony to fifty songs, and an opera to one hundred songs.

Popularity and mass appeal should also be taken into consideration as positive factors. Thekla Badarczewska, the Polish girl who wrote that perennial of the drawing-room, *A Maiden's Prayer*, was no female Chopin, but her name is rightfully preserved in music dictionaries. The composers of national anthems are in almost every case musical amateurs, but their names, too, are placed alongside those of real musicians.

The more primitive the cultural state, the more important looms even a mediocre talent. Therefore lexicographical eligibility ought to be measured in the inverse ratio to the state of local culture. Let P stand for popularity and Q for quality. The "Formula for Musicological Eligibility" will then appear as follows:

Eligibility = PQ (100 × Opera + 50 × Symphony + 25 × Chamber Music + 5 × Piano + 1 × Song) ÷ Musiculture

The following table gives the number of composers by country who are included in my biographical panorama. The density of composers, per area and per population, is also indicated.

COUNTRY	NUMBER OF COMPOSERS	COMPOSERS PER POPULATION	COMPOSERS PER AREA IN SQUARE MILES
Argentina	60	1/220,000	1/18,000
Brazil	41	1/1,100,000	1/80,000
Mexico	33	1/600,000	1/23,000
Peru	22	1/320,000	1/22,000
Dominican Republic	22	1/75,000	1/880
Chile	20	1/250,000	1/14,000
Cuba	15	1/280,000	1/3,000
Uruguay	12	1/180,000	1/6,000
Guatemala	12	1/275,000	1/4,000
Colombia	10	1/800,000	1/44,000
Costa Rica	7	1/90,000	1/3,300
Panama	7	1/80,000	1/5,000
Bolivia	6	1/575,000	1/70,000
Venezuela	5	1/700,000	1/70,000
El Salvador	4	1/450,000	1/3,300
Honduras	4	1/250,000	1/11,000
Ecuador	3	1/1,000,000	1/60,000
Paraguay	3	1/350,000	1/56,000
Haiti	3	1/900,000	1/3,600
Nicaragua	1	1/1,380,000	1/57,000
ALL COUNTRIES	290	1/443,000	1/15,000

"ELECTRONIC, CONCRETE AND ALEATORIC MUSIC," FROM *THE ROAD TO MUSIC*

Human music is never scientifically accurate. Even the greatest violinist would be found off pitch if scrutinized by a computer. Music lovers have to be satisfied with a fair approximation of tonal perfection. Only when a player departs too audibly from prescribed notes do they begin to notice that something has gone wrong.

Then came the electronic dawn. The Russian engineer Leon Theremin inaugurated the era of musical electricity in 1920 with his Thercminovox—"Theremin's Voice." He drew musical tones from a large box topped with an antenna by a gentle movement of his hand to and fro. This motion altered the electrical forces involved in the operation, effecting a change of pitch. Still, the Thereminovox required manipulation by a human hand in an electrical field and could not produce precise intonation. It was not until some years later that electronic instruments became truly scientific and could sound any given note with absolute accuracy. On these modern instruments one could dial a tune by pressing push buttons.

Electronic synthesizers—machines that synthesize sounds—can create new instrumental individuals by cross-breeding. A bassoon can be mated with a clarinet and produce an offspring with the paternal characteristics of the masculine bassoon and the maternal traits of the feminine clarinet. Shall we call this strange child a claribassoon? A whole zoo of such instrumental hybrids can be assembled through electronic wizardry: a violoflute, a trombocello, a drumhorn.

Dynamic shadings of subtle refinement are within the capacities of electronic machines. Theoretically, there are 18 gradations in piano playing from pianississississimo (pppp) to fortissississississimo (ffff), but no pianist can hope to produce them with any degree of accuracy. Electronic instruments, on the other hand, can conjure up at the push of a button the softest moan of a tone or the mightiest bells of decibels. Incidentally, the term decibel is made up of deci, one-tenth, and the name of Alexander Graham Bell, the inventor of the telephone. The decibel is the universally accepted standard of loudness.

In the domain of rhythm, too, electronic music is omnipotent. No human musician can play a fast rhythmic passage of even notes with scientific precision, but electronic instruments can reproduce any rhythm with absolute accuracy and combine different rhythms in a marvelously varied kaleidophonic polyrhythm. (Kaleidophonic is to the ear what kaleidoscopic is to the eye.)

The old phonographs could speed up or slow down the tempo, but such a change of speed would inevitably produce the rise or the fall of pitch. The newest electronic machines can increase the tempo without raising the pitch. A piano exercise can be accelerated to a superhuman speed that no virtuoso can approach even remotely, and yet preserve the clarity and distinction of individual notes. The effect on the ear is uncanny.

Music produced by electronic machines is abstract and scientific. Quite different is another type of ultra-modern sound production, *Musique Concrète*, invented by a Paris radio engineer in 1948. Working with magnetic tape in his broadcasting studio, he recorded all kinds of sounds at random, then cut up the tape, spliced its sections in various ways, combined and recombined them and produced a salad of instrumental and vocal bits seasoned with a spray of asymmetrical rhythms. Since all ingredients were concrete, taken from life, the name *Musique Concrète* was fittingly chosen.

Even rests can be used as material for concrete music. John Cage, the American experimenter in ultra-modern music, published a piece for silent piano entitled *4' 33"*. The pianist sits at the keyboard and waits for 4 minutes 33 seconds without playing a single note. Someone recorded the nervous coughs in the audience during the performance of such a silent composition and rearranged them electronically into an orchestral piece, appropriately entitled *Cough Overture*.

Composers of ultra-modern music like to show their scientific turn of mind by attaching mathematical titles to their works. There is a piano piece entitled $Sin^2x + Cos^2x = 1$. The author of this book has himself perpetrated a mathematical round, *Möbius Strip Tease*. It takes its name from August Ferdinand Möbius, a German mathematician who invented a remarkable geometric figure, a twisted paper strip with a one-sided surface, so that a line drawn on it comes out from inside to outside without a break. In a musical Möbius strip, the last bar of music adjoins the first, creating a perpetual melody.

An amusing example of mathematical music is the symphonic poem for 100 metronomes by the Hungarian composer György Ligeti. In it the metronomes are set at different speeds and tick away until they become completely unwound, creating a rather interesting polyrhythmic pattern, with a soft ending, as the last surviving metronome gives up the ghost.

Conventional musical notation is practically abandoned by avant-garde composers. Instead, they use lines, curves and graphs, so that their scores look more like abstract paintings than music. Loudness is represented by thick black lines, with notes perching on them like so many sparrows on a building ledge. Rests are not written out in orchestral compositions, but the staff is simply discontinued for the duration of silence in an instrumental part. Such a score presents the appearance of a jagged curtain or broken Venetian blinds. Sometimes a giant treble clef is drawn across a whole page of music to economize on the effort of writing small clefs in each part. The time signature is indicated by a huge number, and a multi-terraced flat or sharp may show up, too. The dimensions of the score itself have a tendency to grow. Some avant-garde scores are five feet high and have to be pasted on large pieces of cardboard and placed on a row of painters' easels, with the performers moving from one stand to another as the music goes on.

Classical music can be mathematically distorted to make it sound modern. An innocent Bach fugue can be modernized by doubling its intervals, thus causing semitones to become whole tones. The result will be Debussyan, for Debussy was a pioneer in the wholesale use of whole-tone scales. The Debussyization of Bach can be expressed in the following equation:

Bach × 2 = Debussy.

Another attractive way of dislocating Bach is to shift the keys up and down a semitone with every new phrase. It makes Bach sound like Prokofiev.

The 19th-century was mechanistic in science and romantic in music. In the 20th-century scientists have established that the laws of nature are not absolute but statistical, or probabilistic, working out only because of the large numbers of atoms or subatomic particles involved in each physical phenomenon. Modern composers have become fascinated by this notion of scientific indeterminacy and began experimenting with musical probabilities. What are the chances of picking up a beautiful melody by spattering ink spots on manuscript paper? Perhaps some new, unsuspected, exotic, esoteric, ethereally enchanting tone poem can be conjured up by such applications of the theory of probability to the art of music. Anyway, lots of composers today write "random music," or "chance music" or, in a more elevated scientific lingo, Aleatoric Music. This fancy term comes from the Latin word Alea—'a throw of dice.' When Caesar crossed the Rubicon River in his Roman campaign he exclaimed "Alea jacta est!"—The die is cast.

The parlor game of telephone music is a good illustration of the Aleatoric School of Composition. You ask a friend to give a phone number. Designate middle C as number one and run up a number scale, diatonically, on white keys of the piano keyboard, as follows: C = 1, D = 2, E = 3, etc. C an octave above middle C will be 8, D above will be 9. We will call next E zero. Let us take a random telephone number and see what kind of melody it will spell out: 124–3765 = C, D, F, E, B, A, G, a fairly plausible melody. The same telephone number can be spelled pentatonically on black keys, by designating C sharp as number one, D sharp as number 2, etc. The result will be more exotic than the simple diatonic telephone piece: C sharp, D sharp, G sharp, F sharp, D sharp an octave above, C sharp an octave above, A sharp. We can also write out the numbers following the chromatic scale: C = 1, C sharp = 2, D = 3, etc. Our telephone number will then sound as follows: C, C sharp, E flat, D, F sharp, F, E. Finally, we can try the whole-tone scale in which C = 1, D = 2, E = 3, F sharp = 4, G sharp = 5, etc. The result will be as follows: C, D, F sharp, E, C an octave above, A sharp, G sharp.

Two telephone numbers, those of an engaged couple, for instance, can be combined contrapuntally. Perhaps the chances for their happy marital life can be computed according to the relative harmoniousness of their mutual counterpoint.

The Italian-American composer Mario Castelnuovo-Tedesco has devised an aleatoric specialty by assigning the letters of the alphabet to the notes of the chromatic scale. The English alphabet, containing 26 letters, covers two octaves and a semitone, from A to the upper B flat. In this unique notation he has written greeting cards to friends and colleagues, based on the chromatically alphabetized letters of their names.

The musical avant-garde of the second half of the 20th-century employs various forms of serialism. Serial music owes its origin to Arnold Schoenberg, the creator of the method of composition with 12 tones, or as it became known, *dodecaphonic* method, from the Greek word *dodeca*, twelve. In it, each piece is based on a single series of 12 different notes. The series is then played backwards. Next, it is inverted, so that intervals that went up go down, and those that went down go up. Then this inversion itself is played backwards. Such a dodecaphonic series is used not only horizontally as a melody, but also vertically in chords. Practically all modern composers have in one way or another applied the dodecaphonic method in their works. Some experimented with serial composition using only ten or eleven different notes in the series. The Greek names for such methods would be *decaphonic* (from *deca*, ten) and *hendecaphonic* (from *hendeca*, eleven).

From this total serialization of melody and harmony a logical step is towards a similar treatment of intervals, durations and instrumental solos. Composers began to write music based on a series in which all different eleven intervals were used, without repeating a single interval. Next, it was the turn for rhythm to be serialized, so that each note had to have a different rhythmic value from any other note in the series. This meant that if you used a quarter-note once, you cannot use it again until you have used up an eighth-note, a dotted quarter-note, a half-note, a sixteenth-note, etc.

Finally, it was the instruments themselves that had to be serialized. In an orchestral composition with serial instrumentation, no instrument is allowed to play more than a single note of a series until all other instruments have had their chance. This is the ultimate in musical democracy—to each man one vote, to each instrument one note.

Can one learn to appreciate and love music constructed according to such arbitrary specifications? Well, classically trained listeners learn to love Bach's fugues which are pretty complicated pieces of music and quite arbitrary in structure. And there are some sharp dissonances in Bach, too.

When my daughter, to whom this little book is dedicated, was an infant, I made an experiment. When she cried for her bottle, and I happened to be baby sitting, I would play Chopin or other sweet music, but would not give her the bottle. Then I would switch abruptly to highly dissonant modern music and immediately would let her have her warm milk. I hoped that in time she would learn to associate pleasure with dissonance and frustration with sweet sounds, and so get conditioned to modern music. But the results of my experiments were disappointing. She grew up and lost all interest in music, whether sweet or sour, consonant or dissonant, and went into journalism instead.

With all this emphasis on scientific music, it was natural that computers were called upon to act as composers. The programmer feeds the computer's electronic brain with dozens of different melodic, harmonic and rhythmic patterns, specifying the form and duration of a required piece, and the computer proceeds to disgorge a prelude, a fugue, a march or a waltz, in any desired style, from classical to ultramodern, from diatonic to dodecaphonic. Even emotional content can be computerized. For instance, if we need a sentimental piece entitled *The Aching Heart*, the computer can be loaded with a lot of falling cadences in minor keys with instructions to use them in every bar. For an exotic tone poem called something like *California Lotus Eaters*, the computer's melodic resources can be programmed in the pentatonic scale to be played on the black keys of the piano keyboard, or in an artificial oriental scale with alternating minor and augmented seconds. And since the computer's brain is indefatigable, it can try again and again in case its first efforts are unsuccessful. With proper rhythmic programming a computer can produce popular songs by the hundreds. Probability would be high then that one of these would become a hit under the title *Compute 'n' Roll*.

Will computers drive out human composers? Not for a while yet, for even a poor composer's brain has more power of invention and selection than the most formidable computer in existence. But with further refinement of electronic techniques, perhaps by 2000 A.D., the art of composition may become so thoroughly computerized that college students would be required to take courses taught by electronic brains. Such peaceful coexistence between men and machines will be beneficial for both parties, and electronic musicians will become faithful and helpful assistants of the unserialized and over-individualized human makers of music.

"THE BEAUTIFUL NOISES," FROM
A THING OR TWO ABOUT MUSIC

This essay, which initially appeared in A Thing or Two About Music *(1948), became a common source for subsequent historians of the avant-garde tradition.*

In an orchestral score by Musard, a contemporary of Chopin, there is found an indication, *Chaise*, which meant that the player should seize his chair and bring it down on the floor with a loud thump. The inclusion of noises and even animal cries is not exceptional in orchestral music, and certainly not in modern music. There is a thunder machine in Strauss's *Alpine* Symphony, a factory whistle in the Second Symphony by Shostakovich, and a steel sheet in the score of *Iron Foundry* by Mossolov. Werner Janssen's score, *New Year's Eve in New York*, calls for a klaxon, a siren, and automobile horns. In the section marked New Year's Celebration, the score bears this indication: "All those not occupied with wind instruments shout, *ad libitum*, Happy New Year and cheer." In the meantime the trombones play *Auld Lang Syne*.

In a performance of Walter Piston's ballet, *The Incredible Flutist*, the recorded sound of a barking dog was included in the section which represents a circus show. In another score by a contemporary composer, toy balloons are exploded with the aid of hairpins at the climax.

Henry Cowell has achieved a modicum of percussive immortality by his invention of tone-clusters, which are played on the piano with fists and forearms. When he gave the first and last performance of his fist-and-forearm concerto in Havana, Cuba—where Latin tempers are likely to reach the boiling point at the slightest provocation—the conductor of the orchestra asked for police protection. Cowell was told to run for the nearest exit in case of a riot, but the sight of the Cuban constabulary was enough to secure tranquility. As a matter of fact, there was applause, and praise in the newspapers.

The American composer, John Cage, has put musical noises on a commercial basis by conducting concerts of percussion music, including such esoteric contrivances as tin pans, buzzers, water gongs, rice bowls, Korean dragons' mouths, Japanese temple gongs, anvils, and Indian rattles. He has also perfected the so-called "prepared" piano, which one might describe as a tampered-with clavichord. Another American, Harold G. Davidson, went Cage one better in his *Auto Accident*. In the score there is an instrumental part described as follows: "Two glass plates, each resting on a wash bowl or crock, with a hammer or mallet in readiness to smash them. On page nine, measure four, these plates are to be shattered with the hammer, one on the second count, and the other on the second half of the third count. In the next measure, the bowls containing the broken glass are to be emptied on a hard surface, table, or floor."

George Antheil, the American composer who began his career as a musical noisemaker and went to Hollywood where he blossomed forth as a columnist for the lovelorn, achieved a spectacular sensation with his *Ballet mécanique*, which was to expound "the esthetic of an automobile built for speed, yet mechanically beautiful." When it was performed in Carnegie Hall in 1927, an airplane propeller was put up in front of an orchestra of multiple pianos. The *New Yorker* said after the performance: "The notes we carefully took on our program were blown away by George Antheil's wind machine." but Antheil confessed afterward that the propeller was merely a stage prop, and that there was not enough atmospheric turbulence to agitate a feather. The skeptics said that some of the audience reactions—such as a man's hoisting a white handkerchief attached to his cane as a sign of surrender—may have been stage-managed. A pun was circulated: "Don't make a mountain out of an Antheil." To make things sound more shocking than they were, Antheil was quoted as having replied to the question, "What is your opinion of Beethoven?": "I love him but I do not respect him."

The reviewers had a field day of wit and invectives. Lawrence Gilman wrote:

"The *Ballet mécanique* is unconscionably boring, artless, and naive. Throughout its stupefying length, it never once speaks vividly, creatively. Its rhythms are infantile, its dynamic effects are unresourceful and unexpressive."

The true apostles and martyrs of noise music were the Italian futurists who flourished, if it can be called flourishing, shortly before World War I. The leader, Luigi Russolo, published a book entitled *The Art of Noises*, now a collectors' item, in which he outlined the basic theory of noise music. "We derive much greater pleasure," he wrote, "from ideally combining the noises of streetcars, internal combustion engines, automobiles, and busy crowds than from rehearing the *Eroica* or the *Pastorale*." In place of the classical orchestra, he suggested a noise ensemble with such effects as thunderclaps, crashes, splashes, roars, whistles, hisses, snorts, whispers, murmurs, mutterings, screams, screeches, rustlings, buzzes, shouts, shrieks, groans, howls, laughs, wheezes, and sobs.

Before giving a concert of futurist music in Paris, in April 1914, Russolo and his comrades-in-arms wisely took a training course in boxing, which stood them in good stead. For during the performance of a *Fourth Network of Noise*, the audience advanced menacingly on the performers. The futurists, always ready, divided their forces so that some of them continued to manipulate their thunderclaps and screechers while others repelled the attacking audience so efficaciously that eleven persons had to be hospitalized while the futurists got off with minor bruises.

TWENTIETH-CENTURY OPERA SUMMARIES (EXCERPTS FROM *MUSIC SINCE 1900*)

At the Costanzi Theater in Rome the world première is given of *Tosca*, opera in three acts by Giacomo PUCCINI, after Victorien Sardou's poignant melodrama *La Tosca* (the definite article is used in the title of the French play but not in the title of the opera); wherein a voluptuously desirable Italian songstress Floria Tosca, mistress of an artist member of a Napoleonic conspiracy of June 1800 at the time of Napoleon's surprising victory at Marengo, slays the lecherous, treacherous chief of Roman police at a private dinner as she feigns a willingness to submit to his desires as a price to save her lover, but is posthumously outwitted by him when the secret order of execution is carried out, and in despair throws herself to her death from a high parapet, the score couched in the most effective manner of Italian Verismo, containing such harmonic innovations as systematic progressions of parallel triads, parallel progressions of inverted seventh-chords, and ominously sounding whole-tone scales.

2 FEBRUARY 1900

Louise, "roman musical" in four acts by Gustave CHARPENTIER, his first opera, to his own libretto (his mistress at the time was also named Louise and, like the heroine, was employed in a dressmaking shop), portraying with sensuous melodiousness and sentimental harmoniousness the pleasures of Paris, "cité de lumière, cité d'amour," amid lovable nyctophiliacs, amorous artists, grisettes, soubrettes and midinettes, alive with city noises and precisely notated cries of vegetable vendors, is produced at the Opéra-Comique in Paris, destined to become the most popular French opera of the 1900's and the first successful example of French operatic naturalism.

17 FEBRUARY 1900

Anton, opera in three acts by the 27-year-old Italian composer Cesare GALEOTTI, wherein a young Libyan, whose pagan mistress slays his early Christian concubine known as the "Flower of the Catacombs," flees to the Egyptian desert, suppresses his sensuous memories, resists a series of diabolically contrived temptations and becomes sanctified as Saint Anthony, to a musical score gushing out crimson floods of curvilinear melos, is produced at La Scala, Milan.

11 APRIL 1900

Le Juif polonais, opera in three acts by Camille ERLANGER, after a ghostly novella from Erckmann-Chatrian's tales, detailing the murder in an Alsatian inn of a transient Jew who comes back to torment his murderer in a realistic posthumous appearance, is produced at the Opéra-Comique in Paris.

26 AUGUST 1900

Prométhée, "tragédie lyrique" in three acts by Gabriel FAURÉ, his first opera, wherein Prometheus (who has only a spoken part) deters Pandora from opening her baleful box, thus assuring a temporary tranquillity in a strife-torn world, set to an austerely economic score in neo-Grecian modalities, is performed for the first time in the ancient Roman Arena at Béziers.

17 JANUARY 1901

Le Maschere, opera in three acts by Pietro MASCAGNI (originally dedicated "to myself, with my distinguished consideration and unaltering esteem"), wherein the familiar characters of the commedia dell'arte are embroiled in conflicting emotions, culminating in a wedding feast when Arlecchino weds his Colombina, with a musical setting in a traditional Italian manner, is produced in a sextuple première on the same day in Milan, Venice, Turin, Genoa, Verona and Rome (where Mascagni himself conducted the performance).

15 FEBRUARY 1901

Astarté, opera in four acts by Xavier LEROUX, depicting in Gallically Wagnerian colors the story of the Lydian queen Omphale, the worshipper of the moon-goddess Astarte, who subjects Hercules to humiliatingly effeminate work at her spinning wheel while she struts girt in a lion-skin as lady paramount, is produced at the Paris Opéra.

3 MARCH 1901

Der polnische Jude, opera in two acts by the Bohemian composer Karel WEIS, his most successful work, to a libretto from Erckmann-Chatrian's tale of the robbery and murder of a rich Polish Jew by an Alsatian innkeeper, avenged fifteen years later on a wintry Candlemas day in 1833 when another rich Polish Jew arrives at the inn, inducing in the murderer a fatal nightmare, the curtain falling as the reincarnated Polish Jew gazes meaningfully at the dead body, is performed for the first time at the German Opera in Prague.

26 SEPTEMBER 1901

Judith, lyric drama in three acts by George Whitefield CHADWICK, after the biblical story of a heroic Hebraic widow who enters the tent of the Assyrian chieftain Holofernes laying siege on her home town of Bethulia in 656 B.C., and, after making him drunk with lust and wine, decapitates him with his own sword, returning in triumph to her people with the bearded head of the foe concealed under her mantle, to a musical score competently imitative of the best varieties of European biblical operas, is performed for the first time in concert form at the Worcester, Massachusetts, Music Festival.

23 OCTOBER 1901

Les Barbares, lyric drama in three acts with a prologue by Camille SAINT-SAËNS, dealing with the assault upon the last refuge of the vestal virgins during the siege of Orange in southern Gaul by the Cimbri and Teutones in 105 B.C., wherein the conquering chieftain takes the priestess as his wife, but is in the last act stabbed to death by the widow of the fallen Roman commander, with the musical score harmoniously arranged in a series of dramatic scenes and lyrical arias, is produced at the Paris Opéra.

29 APRIL 1901

L'Ouragan, lyric drama in four acts by Alfred BRUNEAU, to a libretto from Émile Zola's stormy tale of raging passions on a French island in the tempestuous English Channel, wherein a 40-year-old seaman, loved by his 25-year-old sister-in-law and her 35-year-old sister, sails away from them for the French West Indies with his tropical 15-year-old shipmate Lulu, the music heaving in tidal waves of Gallic recitative supported by the pillars of major ninth-chords and anchored deep in sustaining pedal points, is produced at the Opéra-Comique in Paris.

9 NOVEMBER 1901

Hans PFITZNER conducts in Elberfeld the world première of his romantic opera *Die Rose vom Liebesgarten*, a modern German fairy-tale in two acts with a prologue and an epilogue, in which the rose from the garden of love grows amid star-maidens, sunchildren, little woodwomen, giants, elves, mossmen, marshmen, minnesingers, as well as some incorporeal mystical abstractions, with a musical setting suggesting woodsy murmurings, watery drippings, aerial meanderings and cosmic maunderings in a polythematically allusive idiom of deep Wagneromantic colors.

21 NOVEMBER 1901

Richard STRAUSS conducts at the Dresden Opera the first performance of his third opera *Feuersnot* (completed on 22 May 1901), with a libretto derived from a poem by Ernst von Wolzogen dealing with a preternatural deprivation of phlogiston in medieval Munich, relieved when a virginal town belle accedes to a Tristanesque tryst with the local magus whose philosophy is that only a warm young woman's body can give light, with the promise fulfilled in a tremendous climax in an instrumental interlude building up into a single silent post-coital measure at which moment all the fires—the pyres before the doors, the lanterns of the townsfolk, the torches of the men of armor, the lamps in the house—flare up simultaneously, set to music marked by Wagneromantic fervor, with a sly intent to berate the Munich society, which disdained Richard I (Wagner) and failed to appreciate Richard II (Strauss).

11 MARCH 1902

Germania, lyric drama in two acts by the 41-year-old German-educated Italian composer Baron Alberto FRANCHETTI, wherein a German girl, seduced by a university student, marries his comrade in an atmosphere of continued seething rivalry, and in the epilogue conciliates them as they lie dying of patriotic wounds on the battleground of Leipzig on 19 October 1813, to a Wagneromantic setting strongly impregnated with a Tristanesque fluid, is produced at La Scala in Milan.

28 APRIL 1902

A public rehearsal is held at the Opéra-Comique in Paris of DEBUSSY's sublime masterpiece, *Pelléas et Mélisande*, lyric drama in five acts and twelve tableaux, portraying with translucent penetration the peripeteia of Maeterlinck's poignantly symbolic play, from the mysterious finding of Mélisande forlorn in a medieval forest to the insensate murder by the jealously deluded Golaud of his young half-brother Pelléas, and to the serene death of Mélisande in childbirth, with a musical setting of startling originality and concentrated power of latent expressiveness, the voices singing the poetic lines according to the inflections of natural speech following every nuance of sentiment in a continuously diversified declamation, the melodic curves tending towards their harmonic asymptotes in tangential proximity and forming chords of quasi-bitonal consistency, the modal intervalic progressions with their concomitant cadential plagalities imparting a nostalgically archaic sound to the music, the frequent parallel motion of triadic units, seventh-chords and ninth-chords providing instant modulatory shifts, extensive vertical edifices in fourths and fifths reposing on deeply anchored pedal-points giving stability in fluidity, while the attenuated orchestra becomes a multicellular organism in which the instrumental solos are projected with pellucid distinction echoing the text in allusive symbolism (when light is mentioned, the strings are luminously tremulous; for water, harps respond), and the psychologically adumbrative motives reflect the appearances of dramatic characters in graphically imprecise identifications. (Composition begun in August 1893; the score completed in August 1895, but revised; the second version finished in 1898, reorchestrated in December 1901; some symphonic interludes written shortly before the first performance, in 1902.)

17 AUGUST 1902

Parysatis, incidental music of operatic proportions by Camille SAINT-SAËNS, to a play taking place in Persia in 401 B.C. dealing with the Persian Queen Parysatis and the struggle between her son Artaxerxes and her grandson Darius for love of the Greek concubine of her slain son Cyrus, is performed for the first time at the Grand Roman Arena in Béziers, France, by a grandiose ensemble of 450 orchestra players plus 20 harps, 15 trumpets, 12 cornets, 250 choristers and 60 dancers.

6 NOVEMBER 1902

Adriana Lecouvreur, lyric drama in four acts by Francesco CILÈA, his most celebrated work, to a libretto dealing in a highly dramatized manner with the life and the loves of the French actress Adrienne Lecouvreur (1692–1730), who undergoes a series of misadventures including mistaken identities, misdirected letters, mislaid jewels, and misfired amourettes, and dies from the fumes of poisoned violets sent to her by a jealous rival (the real Adrienne died of an internal hemorrhage), with a musical setting luxuriating in sonorous cantilena and throbbing with melodramatic diminished seventh-chords, is produced at the Teatro Lirico in Milan.

20 FEBRUARY 1903

Bruder Straubinger, operetta in three acts by Edmund EYSLER, wherein a virginal child of nature in a sinful Teutonic town is unwittingly procured by a dissimulating panderer to satisfy the perverted lust of a licentious landgrave but is rescued from debauched perdition by a young peasant impersonating his own 114-year-old grandfather who volunteers to marry her, ostensibly to provide matrimonial cover, is produced in Vienna.

3 AUGUST 1903

Sarrona; or the Indian Slave, one-act opera by the American composer William Legrand HOWLAND to his own libretto, wherein the queen of a kingdom on the Ganges River, preparing to plunge a dagger into the dissipated flesh of her treacherous royal husband embroiled with a Greek dancer, is prevented in her design by a slave who demands carnal gratification as a price for his silence but, deterred by her reminder of his untouchability to a person of her caste, stabs himself to death, is performed for the first time on any stage in Bruges, Belgium, in an Italian version.

15 November 1903

Tiefland, lyric drama in three acts by the Scottish-born but self-Germanized composer Eugen D'ALBERT, to a libretto drawn from the play *Terra Baixa* (*Lowlands*) by the Catalan writer Angel Guimerá, wherein a young shepherd descends from his mountain pastures into the valley to marry a village maiden only to find that she is his master's mistress, a revelation that drives him to such homicidal fury that he strangles her seducer as he once strangled a prowling wolf, and carries his bride to the highlands where they can breathe the unpolluted air and enjoy unviolated love, set to music in an effective Wagneromantic style in which the contrapuntal woof is thematically enlaced with chromatic warp in the dramatically tense scenes that take place in the iniquitous lowlands while the episodes in the highlands are exalted in the spacious intervals of the natural scale, a contrast that made the opera a durable product despite the derivativeness of its eclectic idiom of composition, is produced at the German Opera House in Prague.

17 November 1903

Mam'zelle Fifi, one-act opera by César CUI, after a celebrated novelette by Maupassant in which a Prussian lieutenant, nicknamed Mam'zelle Fifi for his ephebic beardlessness, stationed with an occupational squad near Rouen in 1871, is stabbed to death by a patriotic fille de joie when he dares to speak slightingly of France, is performed for the first time in Moscow.

27 November 1903

Le donne curiose, musical comedy in three acts by Ermanno WOLF-FERRARI, whose name hyphenates that of his German father and his Italian mother, with a libretto drawn from a play by Carlo Goldoni, wherein a bevy of inquisitive Venetian wives intent upon discovering the agenda of an exclusive men's club where their husbands habitually congregate, enter it by ruse only to find that, contrary to their suspicions, the club is indeed womanless, written in a merry settecento vein with Wagneromimic simulation, is performed for the first time in Munich, in a German version under the title *Die neugierigen Frauen*.

19 December 1903

At the Teatro alla Scala in Milan, a gala première is given of *Siberia*, opera in three acts by the 36-year-old Italian composer Umberto GIORDANO, dealing with the deepest passions in darkest Tsarist Russia, wherein the lover of the mistress of a St. Petersburg nobleman nearly kills him in a duel and is dispatched to Siberia, whither she follows him and stabs herself to death after a failure to engineer his escape, the musical setting constituting a veritable anthology of Russian songs and dances wherein the doleful Volga Boatmen's song ungeographically serves as a Siberian motto and a complete rendition of the Tsarist national anthem is given by a police band during the hero's arrest, while the composer's own contribution is limited to Italianate mimicry of Russian sentimental ballads and to instrumental interludes such as a chromatic blizzard in the Siberian "Hungry Steppes."

28 December 1903

La Reine Fiammette, opera in four acts by Xavier LEROUX, French composer of Italian extraction on the maternal side, to a semidemihistorical novel of Catulle Mendès, wherein a young monk is induced by a wily secular cardinal in medieval Bologna to assassinate the local reigning queen for dynastic reasons, but upon penetrating into her chambers recognizes in her his hebdomadal inamorata of a suburban convent and falls into her passionate embrace, whereupon a more reliable hired killer slays them both at the crucial moment, with a musical setting in the lyrico-dramatic manner of Leroux's master, Jules Massenet, is produced at the Opéra-Comique in Paris.

29 JANUARY 1904

Der Kobold, opera in three acts by Siegfried WAGNER, to his own libretto dealing with sprites and fays, nymphs and sylphs, dryads and hamadryads, oreads and limoniads, kobolds, gnomes and other elfenfolk puckishly intervening in the otherwise realistic events taking place in a small German town early in the 19th century, with the paternal ghost of the composer's great father determining the shaping of musical themes and the formation of harmonies, is performed for the first time in Hamburg.

18 FEBRUARY 1904

Hélène, lyric poem in one act and four tableaux by Camille SAINT-SAËNS, to his own libretto in rhymed verse detachedly detailing the fateful flight of Helen and Paris in a boat propelled by the "double caresse des zéphires et des baisers" undeterred by the monitory and minatory vision of burning Troy conjured up by Pallas Athena, who sides with the forces of conjugal fidelity against Aphrodite's aphrodisiac proddings, the music bathed in impeccably fluid harmonies, is performed for the first time at Monte Carlo, as a commissioned work dedicated "to His Serenest Highness Prince Albert I of Monaco."

16 MARCH 1904

La Fille de Roland, "tragédie musicale" in four acts by Henri RABAUD, wherein a young warrior in Charlemagne's ranks loves the daughter of the great paladin Roland, unaware that it was his own father who betrayed his beloved's father to the infidels at the battle of Roncesvalles in 778 A.D., with a musical score set in two-dimensional heterophony to impart the feeling of the period but exploding in ample arpeggios in the scenes of passion, is performed for the first time at the Opéra-Comique in Paris. (The title page of the printed score gives the date of the first performance as 15 March 1904, but the account of the production in *Le Ménestrel* gives 16 March 1904)

18 MARCH 1904

Baba-Yaga, symphonic poem by Anatoly LIADOV, picturing in uninterrupted presto motion the flight through the air of a fabulous Russian witch Baba-Yaga in a mortar propelled by a pestle and navigated with a broom, taking off in a whirlwind of whole-tone scales and disappearing beyond the horizon in a chromatic pianissimo, is performed for the first time in St. Petersburg.

30 MARCH 1904

Koanga, opera in three acts by Frederick DELIUS, recounting the story of a royal African prince Koanga abducted from his proud equatorial domain and sold into slavery in 18th-century Louisiana under the Spanish rule, of his ardently reciprocated love for the mulatto half-sister of the planter's wife, his death in a futile uprising and the consequent suicide of his beloved, to a score brightened by authentic creole rhythms and pentatonically stylized. Negro tunes, with an ensemble of banjos integrated into the orchestra, while the harmonic setting adheres to the conventional German-Italian formula in its chromaticized idiom, is performed for the first time anywhere, in Elberfeld, to a German translation of the originally English libretto.

20 APRIL 1904

Le Fils de l'Étoile, music drama in five acts by Camille ERLANGER, to a libretto of Catulle Mendès, wherein the legendary "son of the star" leading the Hebrews in their last rebellion against the Roman rule becomes entangled with the malignantly passionate imprecatrix Lilith and loses the battle, set to a Wagneromantically luxuriant score, is produced at the Paris Opéra.

17 MAY 1904

At a concert of the Société Nationale de Musique in Paris the first performance is given of *Shéhérazade*, song cycle for voice and orchestra, by the 29-year-old Maurice RAVEL, to the texts of three exotic poems of Tristan Klingsor: (1) *Asie*, breathlessly exhaling puffs of Gallically perfumed Orientalistic vapors, apostrophizing in hypnotic glossolalia the distant "Asie, Asie, vieux pays merveilleux," enticing by its very longuinquity, tonally illustrated by rapid melismatic arabesques and delicately dissonant instrumental couplings against a deeply resonant foundation of open fifths (2) *La Flûte enchantée*, depicting a timeless girl standing immobile listening as the sounds of a flute fall on her cheek with the intangible caress of a wafted kiss (3) *L'indifférent*, a fleeting image of an effeminate youth whose lips shape the vocables of an alien language ("comme une musique fausse") intimated by a linear discord in false modality, and terminating on a pandiatonically extended triad with a major ninth. (At the same concert, Albert ROUSSEL's symphonic prelude *Résurrection*, his first orchestral work, inspired by Tolstoy's moralistic novel of that name and written in a congenially religious mood concluding with a liturgical chorale from the Catholic Easter service, is performed for the first time anywhere)

12 NOVEMBER 1904

Die lustigen Nibelungen, a gaily irreverent operetta by Oskar STRAUS, wherein the Teutonic divinities of Valhalla frolic in a most unseemly manner hurling portentous Wagnerian quotations in the brass, is produced in Vienna.

13 FEBRUARY 1905

Les Dragons de l'Impératrice, comic opera in three acts by André MESSAGER, detailing in exhilarating Offenbachian tunes the multiplex imbroglio wherein a resplendently uniformed captain of the guards of the Third Empire steals the affections of the mistress of a captain of the dragoons, and the latter avenges himself twelvefold by seducing a dozen of his rival's former mistresses, with a conciliatory ending when a chorus of seducers, adulteresses and cuckolds chant a hymn to love in perfect harmony, is performed for the first time at the Théâtre des Variétés in Paris.

3 MARCH 1905

The Mystic Trumpeter, symphonic fantasy by Frederick S. CONVERSE, inspired by Walt Whitman's poetic vision of a strange musician hovering unseen in the air, vibrating capricious tunes, incarnating haply some dead composer in whom musical oceans chaotically surge, the musical score articulated, like Whitman's poem itself, into five distinct sections—serene, amorous, warlike, sullen, joyful—with the solo trumpet carrying the mystic message, is performed for the first time by the Philadelphia Orchestra, Fritz Scheel conducting.

16 MARCH 1905

Amica, opera by Pietro MASCAGNI, in two acts separated by an orchestral intermezzo, to a French libretto recounting a torridly Mediterranean tale wherein a young married woman pursues her brutish lover through a precipitous mountain pass, stumbles and, oblivious to her loyal husband's anguished pleas, perishes in a torrent, to a musical setting in a dramatic manner of the Italian verismo foreshadowed in his famous *Cavalleria rusticana*, is performed for the first time in Monte Carlo.

28 JUNE 1905

L'Oracolo, opera in one long act by Franco LEONI, Italian composer resident in London, to a libretto based on the short story *The Cat and the Cherub* by C. B. Fernald, dealing with multiplex villainy in San Francisco's Chinatown, wherein a wily opium-den keeper kidnaps the child of the uncle of a girl he covets, kills her young lover, and is in the end strangled by the latter's father (a passing policeman mistakes his death rattle for Chinese talk), with a local astrologer delivering remarkably accurate oracles, an Italianate musical score tinkling with tiny bells, booming with deep gongs, and bubbling with orientalistic pentatonicisms, is performed for the first time at Covent Garden, London.

27 AUGUST 1905

Les Hérétiques, opera in three acts by Charles LEVADÉ, dealing with the struggle of Albigensian antisacerdotalists and Catharist anticonsubstantialists against the sanguinary crusader Monfort, set to a melodramatically exploding score, generously sprinkled with multiple drops of whole-tone scales, is produced in the open-air Arena of Béziers in southern France, the town where the action of the opera itself evolved seven centuries before.

13 OCTOBER 1905

Bruder Lustig, opera in three acts by Siegfried WAGNER, to his own libretto from a 10th-century German legend with a historical background, wherein a Frankish knight nicknamed Brother Lusty for his virile joy of life desecrates the person of King Otto by pulling his red beard, communes with witches and nixes and takes one of them for a bride, then makes peace with the King, helps him to capture an important Rhenish town, and in the last act of lustful generosity gives his soldiers the freedom of all unattached local women and maidens; with a musical setting in a ripe style of *Die Meistersinger*, from its C-major overture to its C-major ending, and 88 leading motives serving to identify the characters and concepts, is produced in Hamburg.

7 NOVEMBER 1905

Miarka, opera in four acts by Alexandre GEORGES, after Jean Richepin's novel about a nomadic girl, strangely born in a Gypsy camp in medieval Picardy without a mother but with a grandmother, who upon reaching the flower of eager nubility dreams prophetically of becoming the Queen of Rumanian Gypsies, and after repulsing the inopportune advances of a locally amorous peasant, marches eastward as her grandmother dies on the dusty roadway within sight of royal glory heralded by slightly orientalized fanfares, the score incorporating primitivistic hymns to the sun, to the clouds, to the running water, to love and to other natural things, set in unisonal or quintal harmonies (these hymns were originally published by the composer in a successful song album), is staged at the Opéra-Comique in Paris.

9 DECEMBER 1905

At the Dresden Opera, the world première is given of *Salome*, one-act opera by Richard STRAUSS (completed by him in Berlin on 20 June 1905), to a German libretto drawn from Oscar Wilde's French play, exhibiting with horrendous naturalism Salome's immund passion for the imprisoned John the Baptist who curses her variously and powerfully when she implores him to let her kiss his mouth, with murderous vengeance swiftly forthcoming as she prevails upon her stepfather Herod, the tetrarch of Judea, who covets her himself to deliver to her, as a pledged reward for dancing before him a voluptuous dance of the seven veils during which she casts off one cover after another from her body (a ballerina actually performing the dance by adroit substitution on the stage), the severed head of the prophet, which she proceeds to kiss avidly after it is brought in on a silver platter, sinking her teeth into the dead mouth "as into a ripe fruit" in an ecstasy so hideous that Herod, appalled and frustrated in his own lust, orders his soldiers to slay her, with the score embodying all the resources of the modern orchestra (a newly constructed baritone oboe, the Heckelphone, is here used for the first time), scaling the heights and plumbing the depths of vocal expression in a Wagnerogenic psycho-musical identification of characters (the prophet vociferating in piously wrathful monody, Herod raising his voice in whole-tone steps, Salome writhing in anguishedly languishing, lasciviously languorous orientalistic chromatics), with acervative polyharmony reaching its maximal embroilment in a well-nigh unresolvable tonal tangle of five unsympathetic Jews, and eventually leading, through a plethora of labyrinthine peripeteia, to a long-deferred catharsis in a magniloquently protracted cadence.

31 JANUARY 1906

The Pipe of Desire, "romantic grand opera" in one act by Frederick S. CONVERSE, to a diffusely symbolic libretto dealing with an old man with a magical pipe ruling over a forestful of sylphs, a riverful of undines and a swampful of salamanders, who wreaks dire punishment upon a defiant shepherd who seizes the pipe (corno di bassetto) and by playing tunes disastrously harmonized by inverted major seventh-chords and augmented triads, inadvertently causes his young bride to wither and die of malaria, set to an ambitiously Wagnerian score, is performed for the first time in Boston. (This was also the first opera by an American composer to be produced by the Metropolitan Opera Company, in New York, on 18 March 1910)

26 MARCH 1906

The Free Lance, comic opera by the American "March King" John Philip SOUSA, to a story wherein the Prince of Graftiana and the Princess of Braggadocia, slated for a diplomatically convenient marriage sight unseen, run away from their palaces in peasant dress to escape the forced wedding, meet accidentally and fall in love incognito, thus arranging things to universal satisfaction, is performed for the first time in Springfield, Massachusetts.

2 AUGUST 1906

Zino-Zina, ballet-pantomime in two acts by the 43-year-old French composer Paul VIDAL, written in an elegant Gallic idiom, dealing with an 18th-century Calabrian poet Zino who kills himself for the love of a socially impregnable and physically insurmountable Signora, and is avenged by his sister Zina who seduces and marries the lady's royal lover, is produced in Paris.

10 NOVEMBER 1906

The world première is given at the Leipzig Opera of a German version of the three-act opera *The Wreckers*, composed by the mannish English suffragette Ethel SMYTH, after the original French drama *Les Naufrageurs* by Henry Brewster, wherein a youth and a maid who light fires to warn off mariners on stormy nights in a Cornish seacoast village are left to die in a cave at high tide by looters of wrecked ships, with a score full of Wagnerian sound and fury. (An English version was first performed in London in concert form, on 30 May 1908, and on the stage on 22 June 1909; a revised version was produced at Sadler's Wells, London, on 19 April 1939)

12 NOVEMBER 1906

The Vicar of Wakefield, a romantic light opera by Liza LEHMANN, London-born soprano of German extraction, to Goldsmith's classical novel dealing with a commendably equanimous Dr. Primrose who unostentatiously rescues his venturesome daughter from the primrose path of dalliance with an unscrupulous squire by proving to him that he cannot escape legal marriage, and judiciously arranges his other daughter's marriage to the squire's uncle, is produced in London.

8 DECEMBER 1906

Moloch, musical tragedy in three acts by Max von SCHILLINGS, to a libretto dealing with a priest of the Moloch cult in Carthage who leaves the ruins of his city destroyed by the Romans and goes to Ultima Thule where he instructs the sub-arctic natives in agriculture, viniculture and apiculture, but, frustrated in his attempt to organize a local army against Roman rule, leaps from a cliff into the cold North Sea, with a score of viscously Wagneromantic music, is produced in Dresden.

29 DECEMBER 1906

Three weeks after his 41st birthday Jean SIBELIUS conducts in St. Petersburg, at one of the Siloti concerts, the first performance anywhere of his symphonic fantasy *Pohjola's Daughter*, based, as so many of his works are, on the Finnish epic *Kalevala*, painting in majestically modal melodies and granitically stable harmonies the rune of mighty Väinämöinen on his ride through northernmost Lapland (in smoothly gliding rhythmic passages in the strings), who is struck by the arctic beauty of the Virgin of the Air, Daughter of the North, as she spins reclining on the rainbow (in spirally involuted melismas), and asks her to come down and share his sled with him (jingling the sleighbells by instantaneous grace notes in the wind), to which she agrees on condition that he split a horsehair for her (by chromatically halving the diatonic steps), tie an egg in knots (by involuting arpeggiated augmented triads), peel a stone (by enharmonic compression of brass chords) and build a boat out of her spindle, which latter he fails to accomplish, only bruising his fingers against prickly whole-tone scales, and sadly slides away under the midnight sun foreglimpsing perhaps her hideous end when the Finnish Zeus Kullervo lets loose a pack of wolves on her, and she is devoured.

2 FEBRUARY 1907

Naïs Micoulin, opera in two acts by Alfred BRUNEAU, after Zola's novelette *La Douleur de Toine*, wherein a Marseille fisherman's daughter, infatuated with a Parisian wastrel, is unrequitedly admired by an honest toiler of the sea and embraces virtue in the end by pushing the former off a precipitous cliff and marrying the latter, set in effectively gallicized Wagneromantic harmonies, is performed for the first time at Monte Carlo.

7 FEBRUARY 1907

Thérèse, music drama in two acts by Jules MASSENET, expertly put together in his most effective style, to a libretto drawn from the events of the French Revolution, wherein the heroine's loyalty is torn between her husband, a Girondin, and her pre-nuptial lover, a royalist, both of whom are seized as the tide of terror rises in 1793, and greet her as their open cart passes under her window on the way to the guillotine whereupon she shouts "Vive le Roi!" to provoke arrest, and joins them in death, is produced at Monte Carlo.

20 FEBRUARY 1907

Legend of the Invisible City of Kitezh and of the Maiden Fevronia, opera in four acts by RIMSKY-KORSAKOV, to a libretto from ancient Russian chronicles telling the tale of a Russian city that disappears under the surface of a lake in the year 6751 after the Creation to save itself from Tatar invasion while the saintly maiden Fevronia is taken prisoner, with an apotheosis in which she joins her slain bridegroom in a transfigured eternal Kitezh, with church bells pealing majestically, the score rich in Wagnerian undertones (which caused it to be described as the Russian *Parsifal*), employing the scale of alternating tones and semitones to depict the Mongolian horde in a symphonic interlude, asymmetrically divided meters in modal chants, and a highly colorful orchestration, is produced at the Imperial Theater in St. Petersburg.

21 FEBRUARY 1907

A Village Romeo and Juliet, fourth and the most important opera by Frederick DELIUS, in three acts with a prologue, after a story (based on an actual event that occurred in Germany in 1847) dealing with two neighboring children of opposite sexes forbidden by their feuding parents to intermingle, who hold secret trysts and, upon maturity, become lovers and elope on a stolen river barge but, perturbed by the wickedness of their unsanctified bliss, scuttle it and in the last ecstatic embrace float to their chilly deaths, the score presenting a musicorama of romantic nature painting contrasted with the brooding quality of human peripeteia elaborated with the aid of para-Wagnerian thematic identifications and tesselated with artful canonic developments, is performed for the first time in a German version by Mrs. Jelka Delius (translated from a discarded English version made by a friend of Delius) under the title *Romeo und Julia auf dem Dorfe*, at the Kroll Opera House in Berlin.

2 MARCH 1907

Ein Walzertraum, operetta in three acts by Oskar STRAUS, dealing with the foundering marriage of the princess of Snobia happily salvaged after she takes a course of exotic *ars amandi* from her husband's Gypsy mistress, is produced in Vienna.

13 APRIL 1907

Les Enfants à Bethléem, Christmas oratorio by Gabriel PIERNÉ, to a poetic story of children guided by a soprano-voiced star to the manger where the Christ Child, pale and underweight, is tenderly tended by a devout ox (tenor) and a perspicacious ass (baritone) exhaling animal warmth in the December chill, the musical idiom eclectically combining quasi-Gallic folksong melos with solemn organum-like harmony, is performed for the first time in Amsterdam.

17 APRIL 1907

Circé, lyric drama in three acts by P. L. HILLEMACHER (actually two brothers, Paul and Lucien, both former Prix de Rome winners), a conventional operatic portrait of the Homeric enchantress from whose dehumanizing magic Ulysses was protected by a fabulous herb, receives its belated first production, ten years after its composition, at the Opéra-Comique in Paris on the same bill with *La Légende du point d'Argentan*, one-act opera by the 27-year-old French composer Félix FOURDRAIN, to a story about a poor lacewoman trying to win a prize for needle point such as was practiced in Argentan (hence the title) supernaturally helped by a chorus of angels who weave a divinely inspired mantle under the instructions of a Gothic Madonna descended from a Fra Angelico fresco.

2 NOVEMBER 1907

Die Dollarprinzessin, operetta by Leo FALL, exhilaratingly propounding the legend of the Plenipotential Dollar, personified by a Chicago heiress who regards European nobility as a purchasable commodity but in the end marries an untitled German for love, while her widowed father enters matrimony with a moderately voluptuous Russian songstress, is produced in Vienna.

9 NOVEMBER 1907

Marcella, opera by Umberto GIORDANO, in three episodes bearing descriptive subtitles: (1) *Trovata*, wherein a disillusioned artist's model is found in a Paris café-chantant by a young expatriate painter (2) *Amata*, wherein she is loved by him (3) *Abandonnata*, wherein she is abandoned by her lover who confesses that he is no painter but the legitimate heir to a distant Slavic throne to which he is summoned by his oppressed people to wrest the reins of the reign from the imbecilic hands of his senile father fallen under the sway of greedy and cruel ministers, with a musical setting expertly synthesizing the Parisian music of other Italian operas, from *La Traviata* to *La Bohème*, is produced at La Scala in Milan.

3 DECEMBER 1907

Tragaldabas (*Der geborgte Ehemann*), one-act opera by the Germanized Scottish-born composer Eugen D'ALBERT, wherein a professional pauper hired to pose socially as a wealthy lady's husband, is dismissed when he becomes unduly familiar with her, and is given the job to impersonate a recently deceased ape in a circus, is produced in Hamburg.

21 JANUARY 1908

Der Mann mit den drei Frauen, operetta by Franz LEHÁR, positing in gayly waltzing and polkaing rhythms the horns of the modern trilemma of de facto trigamy among philogynous men, is produced in Vienna.

21 JANUARY 1908

Sternengebot (*The Stars' Command*), opera in three acts by Siegfried WAGNER, son of Richard Wagner and grandson of Liszt, to his own libretto dealing with the power struggle among the Ripuarian Franks of the 10th century, wherein a German ruler, informed by an astrologer that the house of his chief tribal rival is to inherit his throne, orders the whole enemy clan slain but lets a youngling inadvertently escape only to discover that he is his own bastard son, the score presenting a weird simulacrum of the composer's father's music dramas and his grandfather's mystical rhapsodism, is performed for the first time in Hamburg.

25 JANUARY 1908

Leili and Medzhnun, first opera by the 23-year-old Shusha-born Azerbaijan composer Uzeir GADZHIBEKOV, to his own libretto, after an ancient Caucasian legend dealing with the tragic love of a fearless warrior for a beauteous mountain maiden, written in a homophonic style making use of native instruments in the orchestra, is produced in Baku, the heroine's part being sung by a man in deference to the Moslem customs forbidding the appearance of women on the stage, and conducted by an amateur musician ignorant of written notes.

5 APRIL 1908

Toman a lesní panna (*Toman and the Forest Nymph*), symphonic poem by the romantic Czech composer Vítězslav NOVÁK, inspired by an absorbingly horrifying folk tale of murder by massive osculation, wherein a faithless lover is kissed to death by a congregation of forest nymphs to avenge his kissing betrayal of one of their trusting sisters, set to an ingratiatingly titillating score punctuated by brady-seismic rhythms, is performed for the first time in Prague.

11 APRIL 1908

Rhea, opera in three acts by the Greek composer Spiro SAMARA, to an Italian libretto recounting the tale of multilateral passion, bilateral jealousy, intentional adultery, murder, suicide and general human turbulence, projected against the paradisiac scenery of the fabled Greek island Chio, wrested in 1346 from the infidel Saracens by an Apollo-like Greek warrior in the service of the podestà of Genoa, who is loved by the podestà's young Greek wife Rhea and is affianced to her stepdaughter, with the tragic denouement as an envious love rival stabs him to death, and Rhea, falling on his lifeless body, takes a potently poisonous potion contained in her votive ring, to a singingly Italianate score saturated with dramatic chromatics occasionally relieved by ethnically Grecian, orientally florid arabesques, is produced in Florence.

4 MAY 1908

The Garden of Death, symphonic poem by Sergei VASSILENKO, tonalizing Oscar Wilde's story of a disenchanted phantom with orientalistically twisted scales conjuring up an air of ultramundane mysteries and promises of millennial tranquility, is performed for the first time in Moscow.

10 MAY 1908

Arthur LEMBA, 22-year old Estonian graduate of the St. Petersburg Conservatory under Rimsky-Korsakov, conducts in Tartu the first performance of his Estonian opera *Lembitu Tütar* (*Lembitu's Daughter*), in which the valorous daughter of the commander of pagan but noble Estonians resists to the death the wiles of the victorious leader of the well-caparisoned crusaders of the Teutonic Order of the Knights of the Sword intent on converting her after Lembitu himself falls on the field of honor in 1217.

5 SEPTEMBER 1908

Ettore PANIZZA, Argentine-born composer of Italian extraction, conducts at the inauguration of the renovated Teatro Colón in Buenos Aires the first performance of his patriotic opera *Aurora*, in three acts, expressly commissioned for the occasion by the Argentine government and competently written in an effective Italian idiom, to a libretto wherein Aurora, daughter of the Spanish Governor of Argentina, enamored of a young rebel imprisoned by her father during the war of liberation in 1810, is fatally shot in a pre-auroral encounter and dies in her temporarily unchained lover's arms, pointing at the rubescent horizon symbolically incarnadined by her blood as the harbinger of national independence (the initial strains of the Argentine National Anthem are here sounded in the orchestra).

4 NOVEMBER 1908

Versiegelt, one-act comic opera by Leo BLECH, to a Falstaffian story of a jolly
widow who conceals a philandering burgomaster in a cupboard containing her
friend's wardrobe subject to confiscation for debts, and when the bailiffs have it
sealed (hence the title) uses his discomfiture to force his consent to the marriage
of his daughter to a disapproved swain, is produced in Hamburg.

25 NOVEMBER 1908

Kunálovy ocj (*Kunala's Eyes*), opera in three acts by the Czech composer Otakar
OSTRČIL, to a libretto from an old Indian legend dealing with the incestuous passion of a queen for her stepson whom she blinds by magic when he rejects her
overtures but who regains his eyesight through countermagic, is produced in
Prague.

25 JANUARY 1909

The world première is given at the Dresden Royal Opera House of *Elektra*, opera
in one act by Richard STRAUSS, scored for a huge orchestra including the
Heckelphone, a bass oboe specially constructed by Heckel, to a libretto by Hugo
von Hofmannsthal, marking their first collaboration, in which the terrifying story
of the daughter's vengeance for the assassination of her father through the murder, with the aid of her brother, Orestes, of their guilty mother and her lover, is
told in terms not of inexorable fate but of personal will, pervaded by unremitting
and unresolved dissonances, set in a network of identifying motives, characterizing Elektra's hatred by a venomously disfigured fanfare of royal pride, the bloody
footsteps by inspissatedly clotted chromatic progressions of hissingly discordant
bitonalities, her resolve of matricide by a stately ascent along the major scale
stumbling midway into chromatic blocks, her dance of joy by maniacally triumphant battology, and her sudden collapse by an abrupt chordal spasm;
Klytemnestra's remembered misdeed by an atonally rising syncopated figure, her
imperiousness by dark successions of unrelated triadic harmonies, her tinkling
jewelry by futile flights of flutes against incongruously broken chords, her spiritual decay by cadential dejections into exhausted minor heteroharmonies in low
register, and her fear of death by tense, prolonged and discordant suspensions;
the revelation that Orestes lives by rapid knocks along the notes of major triads,
and the virginal virtue of Elektra's sister Chrysothemis by concordantly harmonized implorations.

3 FEBRUARY 1909

Hircus Nocturnus, symphonic poem by Sergei VASSILENKO, inspired by an episode
in Dmitri Merezhkovsky's novel *The Resurrected Gods*, wherein the nocturnal
goat suddenly throws off his animal vesture and, brandishing a thyrsus and a cluster of grapes, reveals himself as Dionysius, the orgiastic god of vinous revelry, and
flies away surrounded by a nymphomaniacal swarm of witches whirling under the
full moon, to a score written in the fine tradition of Russian musical demonism
with ominously syncopated thematic pronouncements intervalically based on the
"diabolus in musica" of medieval lore, the tritone, is performed for the first time
in Moscow.

9 FEBRUARY 1909

Quo Vadis?, opera in five acts by Jean NOUGUÈS, after the celebrated historical
novel from Nero's time by Henryk Sienkiewicz, panoramically depicting with a
fine sense of dramatic theatricality and an easily accessible inventory of effective

melodies, resonant harmonies and nicely calculated vocal effusions and instrumental colorations, the immoral Roman ways, the burning of Rome while Nero sings to the accompaniment of an anachronistic lute, the martyrdom of the Christians and the salvation of a young maiden loved by a Roman patrician whom she has converted to Christianity, as her giant of a slave slays the bull to whose back she was tied as a bait for carnivorous beasts in the Coliseum, with the central episode recounted by Apostle Peter—his vision of Jesus returning to Rome to be crucified again to whom he poses the famous question of the title—all these varied scenes fittingly characterized by hymnal harmonies, ominous progressions of chromatically ascending diminished seventh-chords and reservedly orgiastic wide-ranging arpeggios, is performed for the first time anywhere in Nice.

13 FEBRUARY 1909

Le vieil Aigle, lyric drama in one act by the Rumanian-born French impresario Raoul GUNSBOURG, to his own libretto from the tumultuous history of the Tatar khanate in 14th-century Crimea, wherein the Khan throws his favorite concubine into the Black Sea when he discovers his son's infatuation for her, and as he belatedly realizes that by this impetuous act he has alienated his son's affections, he plunges into the dark waters himself, is produced at the Monte Carlo Opera under Gunsbourg's own management, in an arrangement from disparate musical materials supplied by the nominal composer, made by Léon Jehin, and with Chaliapin in the title role of the "old eagle." (Loewenberg in his *Annals of Opera*, Grove's *Dictionary of Music and Musicians*, Baker's *Biographical Dictionary of Musicians* edited by Nicolas Slonimsky, and *Die Musik in Geschichte und Gegenwart*, all incorrectly state that the libretto is taken from a story by Maxim Gorky)

16 FEBRUARY 1909

Le Cobzar, one-act lyric drama by Gabrielle FERRARI, a pupil of Gounod and one of the very few female composers of opera in France, depicting a Rumanian itinerant musician whose strumming on his four-stringed backbent-necked *cobza* fascinates a local matron so irresistibly that she kills her husband and follows the Cobzar to hard labor in the salt mines whither he has been sent for the previous murder of his Gypsy mistress, with both going blind from the reflected white light of the saline rocks while their hypersalinated bodies disintegrate into painful compounds of flesh, to a musical setting in a competently imitative style with some coloristic Rumanian dances appearing in a symphonic intermezzo, is produced in Monte Carlo.

21 FEBRUARY 1909

Enchanted Lake, "fable-tableau" by Anatoli LIADOV, a concentrically symmetric symphonic cinquefoil, in which the serene surface of the water is gently agitated by a summer wind on a starlit Russian night, calling forth a lyrical round of romantic Russian mermaids, with fleeting thematic motives following a tertian modulatory scheme shifting either by minor or major thirds in the characteristic manner of Rimsky-Korsakov's marine music, and rich harmonies of ninth-chords supported by deeply anchored pedal points, scored for an orchestra vibrant with airy harps, celesta raindrops and fluid flute figurations, is performed for the first time in St. Petersburg, Nicolas Tcherepnin conducting.

27 FEBRUARY 1909

Katharina, dramatic legend in three acts by the Belgian composer Edgar TINEL, dealing with the life and death of Saint Catherine, the Egyptian virgin of

Alexandria converted to Christianity in 307 A.D., who became so steadfast in her new faith that she confuted the court philosophers charged with her repaganization (she is the tutelary saint of philosophers) and rejected the passionate proposal of the Emperor Maximinus to be his concubine, whereupon he ordered her to be drawn and quartered on a specially constructed wheel (she is the patron saint of wheelwrights), and when the wheel was providentially split by a bolt of lightning, had to resort to decollation, and in despair took poison himself, the score being constructed in the style of a religious oratorio, with the martyred saint's ecstasy illustrated by harp arpeggios and the Emperor's anger by trumpet fanfares, the Christian spirit being reflected in noble triadic harmonies imitative of *Tannhäuser* and *Parsifal*, and paganism represented by a fugal counterpoint derivative of *Die Meistersinger*, is produced in Brussels.

8 DECEMBER 1909

Le Cœur du Moulin, "pièce lyrique" in two acts by the aristocratic French composer Déodat DE SÉVERAC (he descended from the kings of Aragon), to a libretto dealing with an 18th-century villager in Languedoc who leaves home and a fiancée in quest of better fortunes and upon return tries to win her back from his friend who in the meantime has honorably married her, but is dissuaded from his treacherous design by the miraculously audible voices emanating from the heart of the local mill (hence the title), to a musical setting in which the intrinsic operatic monotony is relieved by the intercalation of melodic refrains from old French songs, is produced at the Opéra-Comique in Paris.

12 DECEMBER 1909

Kikimora, fantastic scherzo for orchestra by Anatoly LIADOV, depicting the posthumous pranks of an unbaptized infant girl, in two sections, a poetic *Adagio* wherein the kikimora is incubated in a crystal carriage tended by a cat, in gently swinging feline cradle rhythms, and a demoniacal tritone-laden *Presto*, representing her emergence into a life of mischief, is performed for the first time in St. Petersburg, Alexander Siloti conducting.

15 JANUARY 1910

Maia, lyric drama in three acts by Ruggero LEONCAVALLO, to a melodramatic libretto by his French publisher Paul Choudens, culminating in a fatal encounter between two competitors for Maia's favors on the island of Camargue and her suicide by drowning in the delta of the Rhône River, with an undistinguished musical score palely reminiscent of his striking *Pagliacci*, is produced in Rome, with Pietro Mascagni conducting.

19 JANUARY 1910

Malbruk, comic fantasy in three acts by Ruggero LEONCAVALLO after a story from Boccaccio, dealing with a semi-legendary king of Lower Navarra who woos the Damsel of the White Goose but is diverted into a crusade and ends up as the master of a Turkish harem with 49 odalisques, is produced in Rome.

23 APRIL 1910

At the Royal Opera of Berlin the world première is given of the three-act Indian opera *Poia* (in a German version) by the 39-year-old American composer Arthur NEVIN, the first opera by an American to be staged in Berlin, and dealing with an American Blackfoot Indian who journeys to the court of the Sun God to cure himself of an evil scar which renders him ineligible for the hand of a beautiful squaw, is made clean in his sleep by the magical intercession of The Four Seasons, but loses his bride who is slain by a rival's arrow aimed at Poia himself, the score strewn with authenticated pentatonic tunes in sterilized Wagnerian harmonies.

21 AUGUST 1910

Héliogabale, lyric tragedy in three acts by Déodat DE SÉVERAC, the action taking place during the brief rule (218–222 A.D.) of the profligate Roman Emperor who assumed the name of the Syrian sun-god Elagabalus whom he worshipped and who was slain by his praetorian guard as the Christians whom he persecuted passed by singing Alleluia, with a musical score containing amid operatic banalities some interesting ballet numbers, in the oriental style, and incorporating the twelve instruments (reeds, drums, trumpets) of the Catalan cobla of deep antiquity in the orchestra, is performed for the first time at the Théâtre des Arènes, itself going back to the Roman times, in Béziers.

26 JANUARY 1911

Der Rosenkavalier, "Komödie für Musik" in three acts by Richard STRAUSS (completed on 26 September 1910; begun on 1 May 1909), full sophisticated waltzes and ironically sentimental arias, to Hugo von Hofmannsthal's tale placed in 18th-century Vienna, in which a conniving dowager designates her young lover as the bearer of a symbolic silver rose sent from her aging cousin to a young coquette in proposing marriage, with a characteristic reversal of roles as the cavalier of the rose woos and wins her after many a transvestiture (in the third act the Rosenkavalier, a mezzo-soprano, is disguised as a maid thus reverting to her natural sex), the score containing 118 identifiable leitmotivs, according to officious exegetes, is produced at the Dresden Opera, Ernst Schuch conducting.

26 APRIL 1911

La Jota, lyric opera in two acts by the 34-year-old French composer Raoul LAPARRA, a sequel to his opera *La Habanera*, to his own libretto wherein a young soldier and his fiancée, torn apart by conflicting allegiances during the Aragon-Navarre clash of 1835, are reunited in a ruined church and dance a sanguinary jota in a mortal embrace as a renegade priest monstrously lusting after the bride is nailed by the invading soldiery to a life-size crucifix from which the figure of Christ has been wrested by an explosion, is produced for the first time at the Opéra-Comique in Paris, on the same program with the first performance of *Le Voile du Bonheur*, a lyric scene in two acts by the 40-year-old Charles Pons, to a libretto from a play by the French statesman Georges Clemenceau.

19 MAY 1911

L'Heure Espagnole, one-act opera by Maurice RAVEL, after a play of Franc-Nohain of that name, wherein a vivacious Spanish señora in 18th-century Toledo conceals two of her lovers in the clock cabinets in the shop of her horologist husband, and when they are discovered by him, explains that they are customers interested in the workings of the mechanism and, while he is preoccupied with making a sale, takes a muscular muleteer to her upstairs chamber for an interlude of amours, set to music with horological precision, wherein the tiniest rhythmic wheels transmit melodic motion to the metrical cogs in nicely calculated kinetic impulses, with spacious tertian harmonies integrating in the chord of the 13th, and human voices declaiming in finely inflected prosody imparting the sense of continuous action, is produced at the Opéra-Comique in Paris.

2 JUNE 1911

Isabeau, opera in three acts by Pietro MASCAGNI, to a libretto based on a modified version of the famous horseback ride of the medieval Lady Godiva, wherein the daughter of a tyrannical feudal lord parades through town mounted on a white horse completely naked to protest against being forced into a physically and morally abhorrent marriage, and when a fervent swain who throws roses on her unclad figure from a balcony is condemned to death at the stake, leaps into the flames herself on a sudden impulse, set to music full of incandescent Italianate emotionalism, is produced at the Teatro Colón in Buenos Aires.

15 DECEMBER 1911

Bérénice, "tragedy in music" in three acts by Albéric MAGNARD, to his own libretto fashioned from Racine's play about the Jewish concubine of the Roman Emperor Titus, who, like the legendary Egyptian queen of the same name, surrenders her luxuriant tresses to Aphrodite in exchange for an aphrodisiac potion she desperately needs to lure back an errant lover, set to music, according to Magnard's own admission, "dans le style wagnérien," but containing some enticing illustrative inventions such as canons in the octave to illustrate a consummated amour, is produced at the Opéra-Comique in Paris.

23 DECEMBER 1911

I Gioielli della Madonna, tragic opera in three acts by the paternally Bavarian and maternally Venetian composer Ermanno WOLF-FERRARI, to a highly charged melodramatic story of his own invention wherein a maddened lover lays the jewels stolen from the Madonna's altar at the feet of his beloved, who thereupon surrenders herself to him, but jumps into the Bay of Naples when she realizes the enormity of the sacrilege, and her suitor stabs himself to death, is performed for the first time anywhere at the Berlin Opera, in a German version under the title *Der Schmuck der Madonna*.

6 FEBRUARY 1912

Die verschenkte Frau, comic opera in three acts by Eugen D'ALBERT, in which a susceptible 18th-century Italian innkeeper finds his wife acting a loving columbine with a harlequin in a company of visiting comedians, explodes in fury and offers her to him in perpetuity, but relents as he realizes that it was all a play, set to music in an automatized abecedarian idiom of the opera buffa, is produced in Vienna.

7 FEBRUARY 1912

La Lépreuse, opera in three acts by the Tyrol-born French composer of Italian extraction Sylvio LAZZARI, wherein a beauteous yet piteously leprous girl contaminates her vacillating lover to secure his fidelity and settles with him on an isolated mountain retreat conducted thither by a Wagneromantic chorus of monks, nuns and peasants in a triadically harmonized procession, is produced at the Opéra-Comique in Paris.

22 APRIL 1912

Mary Carr MOORE conducts in Seattle the first performance of her four-act opera *Narcissa*, to the libretto by her mother, detailing the missionary exploits of Marcus Whitman in the American Northwest culminating in his and his wife Narcissa's murder on 29 November 1847 at the hands of Oregon Indians armed with authentic-sounding pentatonic war cries when they suspect that an outbreak of measles is the result of the white man's pale-faced sorcery.

8 JUNE 1912

Daphnis et Chloë, ballet in one act and three tableaux by Maurice RAVEL, with a scenario fashioned after a Greek erotic tale of pastoral love, wherein Daphnis plays the alto flute to lure Chloë, as Pan once lured Syrinx, and leopard-skinned Bacchantes burst out in a corybantic dance in rapid quintuple meters while delicate drums and poetic harps suffuse the scene in a translucid neo-archaic gauze, suspended in an aerostatically euphonious equilibrium above deep-rooted pedal points, is produced by Diaghilev's Ballet Russe in Paris.

12 NOVEMBER 1912

Liebesketten, ninth opera by the self-Germanized English-born composer Eugen D'ALBERT, wherein the tangled chains of adulterous love among fisherfolk of Brittany are tragically resolved by the brown-skinned castaway maiden who dies of stab wounds protecting her lover from the cuckolded husband of his former mistress, is produced in Vienna.

1 APRIL 1913

La Vida breve, lyric drama in two acts by Manuel DE FALLA, dealing with the pathetically brief life of a Gypsy girl in Granada who dies of a broken heart after denouncing the perfidy of her seducer on the day of his marriage to a street vendor, to a score vibrant with Andalusian modalities, fandango rhythms and orientalistically chromaticized arabesques, against the background of strumming guitars, clapping castanets and outcries of "Olé," is performed for the first time in Nice.

3 APRIL 1913

Le Festin de l'Araignée, ballet-pantomime by Albert ROUSSEL, an arachnoid drama wherein an inhumanly voracious spider lures a multicolored butterfly into his net by deceptively ingratiating melodies wrapped in a gauze of impressionistic harmonies but, as he prepares his cannibalistic feast, is killed in turn by a vigilant praying mantis attacking in dramatically detonating dissonant chords, is performed for the first time in Paris, two days before Roussel's 44th birthday.

10 APRIL 1913

L'Amore dei tre re, opera in three acts by Italo MONTEMEZZI, set in 10th-century Italy, wherein a blind barbarian king strangles his daughter-in-law whom he rightly suspects of infidelity to his son, and puts poison on her dead lips so that when her princely lover kisses her in her crypt, he dies, as does her husband who kisses her too, leaving the old man alone with three cadavers, set to music in the style of Italian Verismo in opulent Wagneromorphic harmonies, is produced at La Scala, in Milan.

19 DECEMBER 1913

Flup!, the first and the most popular operetta in three acts by Jósef Zygmunt SZULC, 38-year-old Warsaw-born Parisianised composer of light music, with action taking place in Ceylon in May 1913, wherein a British Duke exchanges identities with a waterfront porter known under the quasi-canine appellation Flup (the exclamation point in the title indicates the vocative case suitable to Flup's profession) in order to win by proxy the hand of the British Colonial Resident's daughter, a royalty-hating militant suffragette, is produced in Brussels.

24 JANUARY 1914

Madeleine, lyric opera in one act by Victor HERBERT, dealing with a temperamental prima donna whose friends insist on spending New Year's day with their mothers, is produced at the Metropolitan Opera in New York, with considerable acclaim and 16 curtain calls.

26 MAY 1914

Le Rossignol, opera-ballet in three tableaux by Igor STRAVINSKY, after the tale of Hans Christian Andersen, in which a manically depressed Emperor of China, mortified by the metallic tintinnabulations of a mechanical nightingale made in Japan, with its Nipponese pentatonicism polluted by chromatic impurities, is restored to life by the thrilling trills and therapeutically euphonious atonal melismata of a sinologically authentic philomel brought back from the woods whither he fled from his insular rival, written in a dissonantly bitonal idiom rooted in quartal harmonies superimposed on structures of major sevenths and tritones, is produced in Paris by Diaghilev's Ballet Russe, with the orchestra under the direction of Pierre Monteux.

14 JANUARY 1916

The Critic, or an Opera Rehearsed, a comic opera in two acts by Charles Villiers STANFORD, after Sheridan's play (but Sheridan's subtitle was "a tragedy rehearsed"), wherein the author Puff and critic Sneer engage in a deep philosophical discourse on the meaning of art, with a Spanish soldier Don Whiskerandos providing exotic color, is produced in London, conducted by Eugene Goossens (who is himself included in the cast of characters, pretending that something has gone wrong with the music.)

28 JANUARY 1916

The Boatswain's Mate, two-act opera by England's most prominent woman composer Ethel SMYTH, to her own libretto dealing with an ex-boatswain who asks a friend to fake a burglary of a pub owned by a comely widow, intending to pose as her rescuer and thus impress her into marrying him, the plot miscarrying when she surprises the pretended burglar and decides to marry him instead, is performed for the first time in London.

18 MAY 1917

Serge Diaghilev's Ballet Russe presents in Paris the first performance of "ballet réaliste" *Parade* by Erik SATIE, to a surrealist scenario by Jean Cocteau, wherein three frantic American managers advertise their rival shows, featuring a Chinese prestidigitator, a girl dancing ragtime, two acrobats passing "in parade" before the public, and a battery of American-made typewriters in the orchestra pit, with a cubistic curtain by Pablo Picasso, set to music in an ostentatiously "dépouillé" style, as a reaction against both the luxuriant impressionism of Debussy and the primitivistic *fauvisme* of Stravinsky.

19 JANUARY 1918

Sylvio LAZZARI, 60-year-old French composer born in Tyrol of Italian parents, conducts the Chicago Opera in the world première of his three-act opera *Le Sauteriot*, an epic of life among lowly Lithuanians, in which an illegitimately conceived girl surnamed *sauteriot* (grasshopper) for her saltatory amours, commits suicide by poison when her desirable beau, after spending a night with her, joins his regular mistress in the morning, set to music in a Wagnerogenically Gallic vein, with some exotic supplements such as Lithuanian Bear Dance.

16 APRIL 1919

Don Ranudo de Colibrados, comic opera in four acts by the Swiss composer Othmar SCHOECK, to a libretto from a Danish play by Ludwig Holberg, dealing with a fatuous Spanish grandee who indignantly rebukes a colored aspirant for his daughter's hand, only to find that the latter is a Royal Ethiopian prince, which makes him accept his offer with supine obsequiousness, set to music in a Wagneromantic manner with a profusion of flamboyant sonorities, is produced in Zürich.

20 DECEMBER 1919

La Boîte à joujoux, "ballet pour enfants" by Claude DEBUSSY, written in 1913 in piano score and subsequently arranged for orchestra by his intimate collaborator André Caplet, to a scenario in which a wooden soldier parades to the burlesqued sounds of the military march from Gounod's *Faust*, woos and wins a handsome doll in mortal combat with the wily Polichinelle, set to music of diaphonous infantiloquy and harmonized in gently archaic open fifths and translucently fragile ninth-chords, with the application of whole-tone scales and chromatically moving consecutive major seconds to depict scenes of infantile terror, and incorporating an exotic episode based on an authentic Hindu elephant-training chant in 5/4 time, is performed posthumously for the first time in Paris, under the direction of André Caplet.

21 JANUARY 1920

Der Schatzgräber (*The Treasure Digger*), opera in four acts by Franz SCHREKER to his own libretto from the realm of German fable, in which a minstrel, guided by a sensitive lute which raises its pitch and accelerates the tempo in the vicinity of gold, locates a treasure-trove and presents it to his Queen who graciously commutes his long-standing death sentence and enables him to rejoin his bride who, however, succumbs to anemia, set to music with Wagneromantic fervor, with an inventory of seminal motives immersed in sebaceously pregnant sonorities, is produced in Frankfurt.

31 MARCH 1920

Mirra, opera in two acts by the Italian modernist Domenico ALALEONA, wherein a young woman of Cyprus, possessed by incestuous love for her young father, neglects her ardent husband causing him to wither in utter inanition in gymnosophistical naked fifths, while her father curses her in highly chromaticized dissonances, driving her to suicide by stabbing herself with the aid of perpendicularly integrated columns of whole-tone scales, making use also of non-tempered "pentafonia" dividing the octave into five equal intervals, is produced in Rome.

16 MARCH 1921

Kaddara, opera by the Danish composer Hakon BÖRRENSEN, to a libretto set in Greenland, wherein Kaddara, an intransigent Arctic housewife, locks out her whaling husband when he comes home without booty, whereupon he reembarks in his kayak, harpoons a giant whale and takes it to a local widow whose daughter bites his shoulder according to the ancient Greenlandian welcoming ritual, which fails to fascinate him, and he returns to his igloo, as his wife sings a lullaby for their child and the sun appears on the horizon after a long polar night, set to music with the application of authentic modes of Eskimo songs, is performed for the first time in Copenhagen.

16 MAY 1921

Sirocco, opera in three acts by Eugen D'ALBERT, wherein a Parisian cocotte, nicknamed after the devastating desert wind, demoralizes the stalwart soldiers of fortune in North Africa and is ultimately throttled by a member of the French Foreign Legion, set to a synthetic score, incestuously combining elements of

German romanticism and Italian Verismo, is performed for the first time any-where in Darmstadt.

10 MAY 1922

Othmar SCHOECK, foremost lyric composer of Switzerland, conducts in Zürich the first performance of his three-act opera *Venus*, after a tale of Prosper Merimée set in Paris in 1820, wherein a newly unearthed ancient statue of Venus materializes as an ectoplasmic apparition between the bridegroom and his bride on their wedding night effectively preventing the consummation of their marriage, and crushes him to death in her marmoreal embrace, set to music in a lyrico-dramatic vein of romantic opera.

13 MAY 1922

Hagith, one-act opera by the prime modernist of Poland Karol SZYMANOWSKI, to a dramatic libretto paralleling the Biblical story of David and his last untouched concubine Abishag, wherein a young country damsel, summoned to the royal palace to give the dying King the comfort of her bodily warmth, becomes enamored of the heir to the throne and lets the old King die, in consequence of which impiety she is stoned to death at the orders of the priests, set to music in turbulent modernistic harmonies and coloristic orchestration, is performed for the first time in Warsaw.

21 MAY 1922

Doktor Eisanbart (*Doctor Iron Beard*), opera in three acts by the German composer Hermann ZILCHER, dealing with a medical charlatan who guarantees the birth of a male heir to a childless ducal couple in Germany circa 1680, and is sentenced to hang when no pregnancy results from his ministrations, but is saved from the gallows when the duchess reveals that her gestation period is elephantine in duration, set to music in an infra-modern idiom containing a modicum of prophylactic dissonances, is performed in a double premiere on the same day in Leipzig and Mannheim.

3 JUNE 1922

Mavra, comic opera in one act by Igor STRAVINSKY after Pushkin's poem *A House in Colomna*, dealing with an amorous hussar who disguises himself as a *cuisinière* and is hired by his sweetheart's mother, with a catastrophic denouement when he is surprised while shaving and thus exposed as an intruding transvestite, set to music in a typical Stravinskian neo-Russian manner, marked by lyrical ariosos in compact pandiatonic harmonies with off-base basses, is produced by the Diaghilev Ballet Russe in Paris, on the same bill with *Renard*, *Pétrouchka* and *Le Sacre du Printemps*. (A private performance of *Mavra* was first presented at the Hotel Continental in Paris on 29 May 1922)

9 FEBRUARY 1923

Die gelbe Jacke, romantic operetta in three acts by Franz LEHÁR, dealing with a Viennese girl of 1912 who goes to China to marry a technically polygamous mandarin, but soon becomes disenchanted with exotic living, obtains an instant oriental divorce and weds her original Viennese suitor, lieutenant of the Imperial Hussars, set to music with pseudo-Sinological pentatonic melodic patterns lending local color to a typically Viennese score, is performed for the first time in Vienna. (The operetta was revised and produced under the title *Das Land des Lächelns* in Berlin on 10 October 1929)

18 FEBRUARY 1923

Germelshausen, fantastic opera by the 37-year-old German composer Hans GRIMM, recounting the tale of the village of Germelshausen, obliterated from the face of the earth by a vengeful deity for its unspeakable sins, with a merciful amendment allowing it to revive in its pristine hypostasis for twenty-four hours once in a hundred years, is produced in Augsburg.

14 MAY 1923

The Perfect Fool, one-act opera by Gustav HOLST, wherein a maleficently thaumaturgic wizard standing on top of a Stonehenge trilithon brews a potion to make himself irresistible to women, but is outwitted by a mentally retarded narcoleptic youth who drinks it first and marries a nubile princess, with two secondary characters, a Troubadour singing a Verdian aria and a Traveler intoning baleful Wagnerogenic incantations, is produced at Covent Garden in London.

25 JUNE 1923

In the Paris salon of the Princesse de Polignac, the first stage production is given of the marionette opera *El Retablo de Maese Pedro* by Manuel DE FALLA, after an episode in *Don Quixote* where the errant knight wrecks a little theater trying to save a noble damsel from a pack of maleficent puppet Moors, realistically including spoken parts for the director of the theater and a singing role for Don Quixote seated in the orchestra, the music palpitating with Andalusian melorhythms in a gibbous tonality astutely maintained by recurrent Phrygian cadences on a major dominant.

11 JANUARY 1924

La plus forte, in four acts by Xavier LEROUX, wherein a passionate woman of the people, married to a harried tiller of the soil, engages in an affair with a sensuously supercharged youth, who turns out to be her own stepson, whereupon she hurls herself into the sea, while father and son return to their fertile earth, the "stronger one" of the title, is produced posthumously at the Opéra-Comique in Paris, in a version completed and orchestrated by Henri Busser.

6 MARCH 1924

The White Bird, one-act opera by the American composer Ernest CARTER, wherein a forester passionately involved with his employer's wife shoots her by accident mistaking the white scarf around her bosom for a low-flying white bird, and in desperate fury strangles the husband, making use of American songs peculiar to the scene in upper New York State, arranged in abecedarian harmonies, is performed for the first time in Chicago.

16 NOVEMBER 1924

Příhody Lišky Bystroušky (*Cunning Little Vixen*), comic opera in three acts by Leoš JANÁČEK to his own libretto in the form of an animal parable, in which a schoolmaster and a parson contend for the love of a Gypsy girl while a vixen entices hens to rebellion and is finally shot by the forester who fashions from its skin a fox muff for his wife, with an epilogue in which the vixen's progeny symbolizes the renewal of the life cycle, set to music in vivid melorhythms of the Bohemian countryside, is produced for the first time in Brno.

20 DECEMBER 1924

La Cena delle Beffe (*The Feast of the Jests*), opera in four acts by Umberto GIORDANO, dealing with a tubercular poet scorned by a fishmonger's daughter in favor of a muscular army captain, with the grim operatic jest delivered in the last scene when the captain kills his own brother believing him to be the poet lurking in the bride's room, is produced at La Scala, Milan, Arturo Toscanini conducting.

11 MARCH 1925

No No Nanette, musical comedy by Vincent YOUMANS, in which a compiler of hymn anthologies with an insecure penchant for semi-pregnant young girls, finds himself enmeshed with three abandoned damsels and a jealous wife, but extricates himself thanks to a cunning lawyer, containing the famous songs *Tea for Two* and *I Want to be Happy*, is produced for the first time in London, England, before its New York opening on 16 September 1925.

21 MARCH 1925

The world première is given at Monte Carlo of *L'Enfant et les Sortilèges*, opera in two parts by Maurice RAVEL, to a tale based on a "fantaisie lyrique" by Colette, with animated characters of house furniture, in which a mischievous six-year-old boy smashes the Chinese mezzo-contralto cup, pulls the pendulum off the baritone horloge, breaks the tenor teapot, rips the bass armchair, and pulls the tail of the mezzo-soprano cat, set to music in an asymmetrically rhythmic idiom, reaching the climax when the crockery accompanied by a sofa, the ottoman and the wicker chair, joined by exercises from his torn arithmetic book, engage themselves in all kinds of baleful sortileges, aided and abetted by an amorous duo of the baritone tomcat under the window meowing in nasal glissandos in ascending intervals and the female domestic cat responding in feline glissandos in descending intervals, the whole score attaining the illustrative quality of a children's picture book in its imaginative and poetic infantiloquy.

24 NOVEMBER 1925

The Asra, one-act opera by the American composer Joseph Carl BREIL, to his own libretto after Heine's orientalistic poem *Der Asra*, wherein a low-caste musician is seized with a strangling paroxysm during an illicit embrace with a high-caste damsel and gives up the ghost, is performed for the first and last time in Los Angeles, two months before the composer's death precipitated by acute neurasthenia.

2 DECEMBER 1925

Mozart, "musical comedy" by Sacha Guitry with a Mozartian musical score by the Venezuelan-born Parisian composer Reynaldo HAHN, depicting Mozart's imaginary amourettes during his sojourn in Paris as a youth of 22, with a variety of women from the former mistress of Rousseau to a chambermaid, is performed for the first time in Paris.

14 DECEMBER 1925

After one hundred and thirty-seven rehearsals, the State Opera in Berlin presents the world première of Alban BERG's expressionistic masterpiece *Wozzeck*, opera in three acts to the libretto from a play by the early 19th-century romantic German writer Georg Büchner (his original spelling of the name of the protagonist was *Woyzeck*), focused on a private soldier whose mistress Marie has a child by him but keeps company with a swashbuckling drum major, a situation leading to a fateful dénouement when the desperate Wozzeck stabs her to death and then accidentally drowns while trying to retrieve his bloody murder weapon from a pond, with a poignant epilogue in which their uncomprehending child rocks on a hobby-horse urging it on with infantiloquent interjections, set to music in a style of emancipated melody and harmony, employing both atonal and tonal media in a free flow of the sonic liquid, unified by a conscious formal scheme of classical organization in a Baroque-like triptych, evolving in these peripeteia.

25 APRIL 1926

PUCCINI's three-act opera *Turandot*, left unfinished at his death, completed by Franco Alfano who added the last duet and the brief final scene, dealing with a cruelly beautiful Chinese princess who, to avenge the abusive treatment of her ancestress at the hands of male invaders, rules that all suitors unable to solve the three riddles of her invention ("What is it that is born at night and dies during the day?"—*Hope*; "What is it that blazes like a fever and grows cold at death?"—*Blood*; "What is the ice that sets you on fire?"—*Turandot*) are to be executed, but who is herself challenged by the heroically astute youth to guess his name after he has successfully answered the riddles, replies *"Amore"* and succumbs to his charms, to a score filled with ultra-modernistic usages, such as frank bitonalities, concatenations of unresolved discords, angularly atonal melodic deviations and asymmetric rhythms, is performed for the first time at La Scala, Milan, conducted by Arturo Toscanini, up to the last measure written by Puccini himself, omitting Alfano's ending.

26 MAY 1926

La Pastorale, ballet by Georges AURIC, to a scenario in which a messenger boy falls asleep after a swim and is caught in the camera-grinding turmoil when a cinema company moves in, with a happy ending provided by a starlet who rides off with him on his bicycle, is produced by Diaghilev's Ballet Russe in Paris.

19 JUNE 1926

Król Roger, opera in three acts by Karol SZYMANOWSKI, dealing with the 12th-century Norman king of Italy, and involving the participation of supernatural forces in the historic events, set to an expansively sonorous lyrico-dramatic score rich in dissonant content, is produced in Warsaw.

18 SEPTEMBER 1926

Deep River, "native opera with jazz" by the American composer W. Franke HARLING, in three acts focusing on a New Orleans ball in 1830, at which a lovely quadroon girl tries to bewitch a wealthy plantation owner with the aid of a voodoo amulet, set to a Puccinian score filled with pseudo-exotic effusions, is produced for the first time anywhere at Lancaster, Pennsylvania.

27 NOVEMBER 1926

The Miraculous Mandarin, pantomime by Béla BARTÓK, composed in 1918, dealing with a prostitute who lures an inexhaustible Chinese *homo libidinus* into a den of iniquity where he is set upon by her accomplices, robbed, suffocated by cushions, thrice stabbed by a rusty knife and hanged from a collapsible lamp hook, but rebounds each time with renewed chromatic inturgescence and tremulous tremolos in artfully copulated intussusceptions in dissonant double counterpoint, with the emphasis on the angst-ridden intervals of the tritone and major sevenths, in a relentlessly monistic élan, culminating in a series of monstrous orgasms *fortissimo*, followed by a labile sonic detumescence in trombones and strings glissando, is performed for the first time in Cologne.

18 DECEMBER 1926

Věc Makropulos, opera in three acts by the 72-year-old grandmaster of modern Czech music, Leoš JANÁČEK (begun 11 November 1923 and completed 12 November 1925) after a play by Čapek, *The Makropulos Affair*, centering on a litigation involving Elina Makropulos, 342 years of age, whose father, the court alchemist to the Emperor Rudolf II, gave her an elixir of indefinite longevity, and who became a famous singer in the 20th century, set to a musical score of pointed modernity in its thematic brevity, rhythmic asymmetry and dramatic precipitation, is performed for the first time in Brno.

8 JANUARY 1927

Penthesilea, one-act melodrama by Othmar SCHOECK, after Kleist's play wherein the Amazon queen captured by Achilles is engaged in a game of hostile passion with him and after Achilles is slain to the sound of an excruciatingly dissonant polychord, falls dead on his body while secundal disharmonies clash, is performed for the first time in Dresden.

10 FEBRUARY 1927

Jonny Spielt Auf, opera in two acts and eleven scenes by the 26-year-old Viennese composer Ernst KRENEK (completed 19 June 1926), to his own libretto portraying in an astutely dissonant idiom, liberally spiced with jazzified polyrhythms, the adventures of the Negro jazzband leader Jonny, indulging in miscegenating amourettes with an accessible prima donna and a Paris chambermaid, appropriating a Stradivarius from an anachronistically long-haired violin virtuoso, entering into a lucrative business relationship with a euphoric American concert manager, set against the background of mystically humanized nature, singing glaciers and other supernatural phenomena, employing the scientific marvels of radio loudspeakers, and culminating in Jonny's apotheosis as he triumphantly straddles a revolving terrestrial globe, dancing jazz on top of the world, is performed for the first time at the Leipzig Opera House.

15 APRIL 1927

Flivver 10,000,000, a Joyous Epic: Fantasy for Orchestra Inspired by the Familiar Legend *The Ten Millionth Ford Is Now Serving Its Owner* by Frederick S. CONVERSE, the main stops in the course of the music being Dawn in Detroit, The Call to Labor, Birth of the Hero (in a whole-tone trumpet fanfare), Trying His Metal, May Night by the Roadside (America's romance), The Joy Riders (America's Frolic) and The Collision (America's Tragedy), with frictional secundal harmonies illustrating the close call, concluding on an apotheosis, Phoenix Americanus, with the Hero recovering from the shock of the accident proceeding on his way "with redoubled energy, typical of the indomitable American spirit," the music set in a modestly modernistic vein, and the score including the wind machine and the Ford auto horn, is performed for the first time by the Boston Symphony Orchestra, Serge Koussevitzky conducting.

4 DECEMBER 1927

Satuala, opera in three acts by Emil von REZNIČEK, involving a fair-skinned Hawaiian girl-spy who lures a captain of the landing American forces in Sandwich Islands in 1893 in order to delay the operation but becomes enamored of him in earnest and stabs herself to death as he, realizing his delinquency, shoots himself to the strains of the *Star-Spangled Banner*, in an effective theatrical setting including a hula-hula ballet accompanied by secundal harmonies and syncopated rhythms, is produced in Leipzig.

16 January 1928

La Tour de Feu, opera in three acts by the Tyrol-born composer of Italian extraction Sylvio LAZZARI, to his own libretto wherein the passion-ridden wife of the lighthouse keeper in a small island off the coast of Brittany, whose Portuguese seaman lover is shipwrecked when her husband extinguishes the guiding beacon in a stormy night, jumps to her death in the raging waters and he sets the lighthouse afire and perishes in the "tower of fire," set to a musical score of effective melodramatic power, is produced for the first time at the Paris Opéra.

10 September 1928

Harry Lawrence FREEMAN, American Negro composer, conducts in New York the first performance, with an all-Negro cast, of his opera *Voodoo*, to the story of a Louisiana snake-cult queen who kidnaps her rival for the affections of a Creole lover, and is about to put her to death in a voodoo orgy when the lover arrives, rescues the victim and slays the prospective murderess, set to music compounded of Negro spirituals, barn dance tunes and jazz, with recitatives in southern dialect.

1 December 1928

Die schwarze Orchidee, opera-grotesque in three acts by Eugen D'ALBERT, focused on a gentleman-thief who customarily leaves a rare black orchid in apartments he robs in New York, then suddenly inherits an English estate and a title of nobility, and marries an eccentric American lady whose house, situated on Fiftieth Avenue, No. 5, he has once burglarized, the cast of characters including "Tanzgirls" dancing the "Eros Foxtrot" at the Mount Everest Bar, a reporter named Schmuckele and an ensemble of "Jazz-Neger" playing syncopated banjo music, all this immersed in a heterogeneous compost of pre-fabricated discords and whole-tone scales, is produced in Leipzig.

9 February 1929

Der Tenor, opera in three acts by Ernst DOHNÁNYI, to a libretto dealing with a provincial German tenor who captivates multiple feminine hearts but fails to achieve artistic success, is produced in German in Budapest.

13 April 1929

Maschinist Hopkins, opera in three acts with a prologue by the Austrian composer Max BRAND, to his own libretto, with the action taking place in factories and nightclubs in New York, wherein a cuckolding libertine pushes the husband of his mistress to his death in the cogs of a monstrous machine and strangles her when he finds out that she has become a promiscuous prostitute, whereupon the foreman Machinist Hopkins, dismisses him from his job ostensibly for inefficiency, set to a polytonally jazzy score, is produced in Duisburg, Germany.

27 November 1929

Fifty Million Frenchmen, musical comedy by Cole PORTER, in which an American playboy woos and wins a footloose American girl in Paris against the formidable competition of an expatriated Russian Grand Duke, is produced in New York.

8 June 1930

Der Fächer (The Fan), opera-capriccio in three acts by Ernst TOCH, to a whimsical story dealing with a Chinese widow who swears a binding oath to remain chaste as long as the earth covering her old husband's grave retains moisture, and then speeds up the drying process by ventilating it with a magically efficient fan so as to be able to yield herself to a cinemactor during a radio performance of Toch's own opera *Die Prinzessin auf der Erbse*, while China is in the throes of revolutionary disorders, with a finale in which the rebels and the dispossessed classes dance a universal foxtrot in the spirit of syncopated solidarity, to an ingeniously contrived musical setting containing quasipentatonic chinoiseries, is performed for the first time at the festival of the Allgemeiner Deutscher Musikverein in Königsberg.

26 OCTOBER 1930

The Age of Gold, ballet by the 24-year-old Soviet composer Dmitri SHOSTAKOVICH, is produced in Leningrad, to a satirical scenario picturing the capitalist way of life in the West, with the cast of characters including a racist referee discriminating against a Negro challenger in a prize fight, an immoral operatic diva, an imperialist *agent-provocateur*, and—on the virtuous side of the ledger—a young girl Communist, a downtrodden shoeshine boy, and a host of oppressed proletarians, with a discordant polka portraying the international disarmament conference in Geneva, and an optimistic finale projecting a *Solidarity Dance* of Soviet and Western workers.

11 NOVEMBER 1930

Spiel oder Ernst? by Emil von REZNIČEK, one-act comic opera with the action taking place during a rehearsal of Rossini's opera *Otello*, dealing with a dishonorable pianist-répétiteur, who, lusting after the soprano who sings the part of Desdemona and who is in private life the wife of the tenor who sings Otello, insinuates that she is cuckolding him with the bass who sings Iago, but is exposed and dismissed from his job, is produced in Dresden.

12 NOVEMBER 1931

Das Herz, music drama in three acts by Hans PFITZNER to a supernatural story of cadaverous and astral heart transplants, suggested by Pfitzner himself and elaborated by his pupil Hans Mahner-Mons, dealing with a 17th-century German doctor, who successfully transplants a healthy heart from a corpse he saw in a dream into the body of a prince with a hopelessly damaged heart, only to discover that the heart he so recklessly used was his wife's (she dies, and her heart in the prince's body dies too, precipitating his death and the doctor's political downfall), with a happy ending provided by her astral body with the heart restored, carrying him into the realm of heavenly dreamland, is produced for the first time simultaneously in Berlin and Munich.

19 NOVEMBER 1931

Jack and the Beanstalk, "a fairy opera for the childlike" by the 47-year-old Russian-born American-bred composer Louis GRUENBERG, to the book by John Erskine, with a modernistic musical setting imparting a surrealist touch to the old nursery tale, in which the cow sings tenor, and the giant counter-tenor in falsetto, while golden eggs are laid in impressionistic harmonies, is performed for the first time at the Juilliard School of Music in New York.

26 DECEMBER 1931

Of Thee I Sing, a musical comedy with book by Morris Ryskind and George Kaufman, lyrics by Ira Gershwin and music by George GERSHWIN, describing in tones of supreme persiflage the presidential campaign of Wintergreen and Throttlebottom running on the platform of Love, with embarrassing problems ensuing when the President-elect jilts his fiancée of Imperial lineage being the illegitimate granddaughter of an illegitimate nephew of Napoleon and marries a country girl who can cook, so that it devolves upon the Vice-President to marry his chief's former fiancée, is produced in New York.

4 MAY 1932

Striženo-Košeno (*Cut-Mown*), opera in three acts by the 37-year-old Croatian composer Krešimir BARANOVIĆ, dealing with a quarrelsome couple who argue interminably whether it is more proper to say that grass is cut or mown, finally bringing the philological discussion to the attention of the court, set to an appropriately humorous musical score with numerous allusions to popular songs of Serbo-Croatia, is produced in Zagreb.

29 OCTOBER 1932

Der Schmied von Gent, fairy opera in three acts by Franz SCHREKER, to his own libretto dealing with a Ghent blacksmith who sells his soul to the devil to save himself from political persecution by the Spanish authorities of the Netherlands in the late Middle Ages, but refuses to carry out his bargain and instead opens a restaurant at the heavenly gates, ingratiating himself by his culinary art with St. Peter and the Holy Family, until he is finally granted admission to Heaven, is produced in Berlin.

9 JUNE 1934

Maschinenmensch, ballet by the 39-year-old Hungarian composer Eugen ZÁDOR, dealing with a superhumanly efficient robot who, at his inventor's command, kidnaps a famous violinist's mistress, written in an ostentatiously mechanistic style in polytonal harmonies bristling with asymmetric rhythms, culminating in a grandly copulative C major chord, is performed for the first time in Braunschweig, Germany.

24 DECEMBER 1935

Nerghiz, opera in four acts by the 50-year-old Azerbaijan composer Muslim MAGOMAYEV, relating in epical tones and ethnically Caucasian accents the story of a native village girl named Nerghiz, who fights in the Bolshevik ranks against the imperialist forces operating in the Caucasus in 1919, shoots to death a lecherous landlord who tries to lure her to his capitalistic habitat and subvert her proletarian consciousness, and liberates her shepherd lover, as the Red Army batters down the last bastion of the enemy's defense, is produced in Baku.

21 JUNE 1937

Dreadnaught Potemkin, realistic opera in four acts by the Soviet composer Oles TCHISHKO, to a libretto from the historical naval mutiny during the abortive Russian revolution of 1905, containing such naturalistic lines as "Our borsht is full of vermin," set to music according to the Soviet doctrine of Socialist Realism, in broad Russian harmonies, is performed for the first time in Leningrad.

17 JULY 1937

Mekhano, mechanical ballet by the modern Argentinian composer Juan José CASTRO, featuring a dance of the hammer, a dance of seduction, and a realistic transfusion of blood to a robot (illustrated by runs of whole-tone scales), is produced at the Teatro Colón in Buenos Aires, conducted by the composer.

24 NOVEMBER 1937

Tobias Wunderlich, opera in three acts by the 58-year-old German composer Joseph HAAS, dealing with a Bavarian cobbler and town councilman who refuses to agree to the sale of a wooden church figurine of Santa Barbara to an American tourist for half a million dollars, and is rewarded for his devotion when the Gothic saint descends from her wall and offers her services to him as a *Mädchen für alles*, gets back on the wall when he incautiously reveals her identity to the council, but returns to his household to alleviate his sincere distress while the American millionaire assuages his financial troubles by an annual order of 10,000 wooden shoes, set to music in Regeromantic harmonies with an infusion of pietetic modalities and dietetic dissonances, is produced in Kassel.

7 JANUARY 1938

Oriane et le Prince d'Amour, choral ballet by the 67-year-old dean of French modernists Florent SCHMITT, dealing with a polyandrous Renaissance lady who successively seduces a poet, a Mongol merchant and a Prince of Love, but perishes when she dances at a masked ball with Death, in a musical setting saturated with polyharmonies and marked by incisive asymmetrical rhythms, is produced at the Paris Opéra.

27 JANUARY 1938

Horoscope, ballet by the urbanely mundane 32-year-old English composer Constant LAMBERT, to a scenario dealing with an astrologically incompatible love of a boy, born under the sign of Leo, for a zodiacally divergent girl born under the sign of Virgo, with a happy ending provided by their discovery of a mutual selenological congruence since both were born with the moon in Gemini, set to music in an eclectically modernistic manner, is produced in London.

16 MARCH 1938

Julietta, fantastic opera in three acts by Bohuslav MARTINU, to a libretto wherein a young man exteriorizes his three dreams about an ethereally beauteous maiden amid oneiristically fluctuating scenes involving Arabian camel riders, pawnbrokers and blind souvenir vendors, in a musical setting full of languorous polyharmonies, is performed for the first time in Prague.

2 JUNE 1938

La Femme à Barbe, pogonological musical farce by the 50-year-old French composer Claude DELVINCOURT, recounting the transsexual adventures of a bearded woman, is performed for the first time in Versailles.

20 OCTOBER 1938

The Serf, opera in three acts by the 25-year-old English composer George LLOYD, to his father's libretto, dealing with the tragic love of a Saxon vassal youth for a Saxon maiden in 11th century Britain, who discover to their incestuous horror that they are both natural children of the old Norman King, is produced in London.

15 DECEMBER 1938

Sensemayá, "indigenous incantation to kill a snake" for voice and orchestra by the great Mexican composer Silvestre REVUELTAS, to the text of the Afro-Cuban poet Nicolas Guillen, full of voodoo words (Mayombé, Bembé, Mayombé!), with a bumbling bass tuba giving the main theme, is performed for the first time in Mexico City.

5 FEBRUARY 1939

Der Mond, "theatrical macrocosm" in three acts by the 43-year-old German composer Carl ORFF, to a libretto adapted from a tale of Brothers Grimm about four village boys who capture the moon for the private illumination of their lodgings and take it underground after their deaths, waking up neighboring corpses by lunar luminosity, until St. Peter retrieves the satellite by dispatching a supersonic comet to reinstate it in the firmament to the accompaniment of a zither solo, scored for a modernistically economic instrumental ensemble vivified and rhythmically enriched by a diversified flora and fauna of exotic percussion, is produced in Munich.

10 OCTOBER 1939

During the Storm, opera in four acts by the 26-year-old Soviet composer Tikhon KHRENNIKOV, dealing with the turbulent events during the communization of agriculture in the Tambov region in 1919–1921, incorporating a romantic love story between two militant young collectivists, with the epicenter occupied, for the first time in Soviet opera, by the vigilant but benevolent figure of Lenin in his Kremlin office, couched in a socialistically realistic, melodious and harmonious idiom, is produced in Moscow.

26 OCTOBER 1940

Gherman, symphonic poem by the Bulgarian composer Filip KUTEV, a ritual prayer for rain during which a stone idol nicknamed Gherman is mourned to the refrain "Gherman died of drought, send a drop of water, o God," melorhythmically derived from orientalized Balkan motives in asymmetrical rhythms, is performed for the first time in Sofia.

20 FEBRUARY 1942

The Island God, one-act opera by the 30-year-old Italian-born American composer Gian Carlo MENOTTI, to his own libretto, dealing with a married couple marooned on a Mediterranean island during World War II and a young fisherman who seduces the wife, starting a tumult and rousing an obsolescent Greek god from his musty antiquity in a ruined temple, who hurls an Olympian thunderbolt at the offenders, but loses so much electric potential by this violent discharge that he lapses into an ontologically primordial nihility, is produced by the Metropolitan Opera Company in New York.

29 MARCH 1942

Solomon and Balkis, one-act opera by the 42-year-old American composer Randall THOMPSON, to a libretto adapted from Kipling's story *The Butterfly That Stamped*, dealing with a magical butterfly that stamped its feet with great uproar to deter Solomon's 999 wives from quarreling, set to music in a mock-heroic Handelian manner, with sinuously orientalistic arabesques characterizing Balkis, the Queen of Sheba, is performed for the first time over the radio in New York.

7 JANUARY 1943

Something for the Boys, a musical comedy by Cole PORTER, in which two nightclub songstresses and a New York street vendor unexpectedly inherit a Texas ranch, with intermingled love affairs entering their financial squabbles, further diversified by the discovery that one of the trio is a human radio receiver through the carborundum fillings in her bridgework, featuring besides the title song a popular ditty *Hey, Good Looking*, is produced in New York.

8 APRIL 1946

Adam Zero, choreographic spectacle in 16 scenes by the 54-year-old English composer Arthur BLISS, in which the life cycle of a symbolic Adam is traced, from birth to death, adding up to Zero, which God, personified by a stage director, marks on a blackboard, with the creation of Adam illustrated by agonizingly chromaticized harmonies and his illicit acquisition of the knowledge of good and evil by jazzy percolation of thematic fragments, is produced in London.

7 NOVEMBER 1947

The Young Guard, opera in four acts by the Ukrainian composer Yuli MEITUS, depicting in epic Russian modalities the heroic resistance against the brutal Nazi occupation by a group of young boys and girls in a mining locality in the Don basin in 1943, who perish with the name of Stalin on their lips as the red dawn heralds liberation, is produced in the Ukrainian language in Kiev, on the 30th anniversary of the Soviet Revolution.

9 FEBRUARY 1949

White Wings, chamber opera by the 55-year-old American composer Douglas MOORE, to a libretto concerning an incompatible romance blossoming up in 1900 in the fetid fragrance of unpaved New York streets between a sanitation department worker assigned to the removal of equine merde (the title *White Wings* refers to the antiseptic uniform of the corps), and the daughter of an automobile manufacturer whose horseless carriages threaten the abolition of his job, written in a sophisticated simplicistic idiom combining elements of mock-grand opera, ragtime rhythms, and sentimental balladry, with a patina of euphoniously pandiatonic non-odoriferous dissonant counterpoint, is performed for the first time in Hartford, Connecticut.

14 MARCH 1949

The Bronze Knight, ballet in four acts by Reinhold GLIÈRE, after Pushkin's poem centering on a St. Petersburg youth driven to despair when his beloved perishes in the catastrophic inundation of the river Neva in 1824, and who hurls imprecations at the equestrian statue of Peter the Great, the founder of the city, whereupon the bronze giant chases him down the streets to his death, is produced in Leningrad.

7 APRIL 1949

South Pacific, musical play by Richard RODGERS, with lyrics by Oscar Hammerstein II, based on James A. Michener's *Tales of the South Pacific*, wherein a French planter dwelling in paradisiac contentment on a south Pacific island sires two Polynesian children, performs other deeds of valor during World War II, and subsequently woos and wins an American girl in marriage, containing the ineffably mellifluous tropical songs *Bali Ha'i, Happy Talk, I'm in Love With a Wonderful Guy, Younger Than Springtime,* and *There is Nothing Like a Dame*, is produced in New York.

11 OCTOBER 1949

Regina, musical drama in three acts by the American composer Marc BLITZSTEIN, to his own libretto based on Lillian Hellman's play *The Little Foxes*, focused on a vulpine covey of contentious siblings of an ante-bellum Southern family torn by avarice and pride, with Regina outfoxing the other little foxes in obtaining the largest share in a lucrative contract for building a cotton mill, set to music in a diversified but distinctly vigesimosecular idiom with a lively influx of antique ragtime, is produced in Boston.

23 JUNE 1950

Philomela, opera in seven scenes by the 57-year-old Dutch composer Hendrik ANDRIESSEN, to a libretto from the Greek myth of a tyrannical king who carnally violates the chastity of his sister-in-law Philomela and cuts out her tongue to prevent her from reporting the outrage to others, but suffers grim retribution when Philomela kills his child and serves its roasted body at the royal feast, for which deed she is metamorphosed into a nightingale, is performed for the first time at the Holland Festival in Amsterdam.

4 OCTOBER 1950

Ekvinocij (Equinox), music drama in three acts by the 43-year-old Croatian composer Ivan BRKANOVIĆ, wherein a rich American immigrant returning to his native Dalmatia on June 21, 1867, is confronted by the abandoned mother of his illegitimate Dalmatian son who is in love with the ship captain's young daughter coveted by his natural father as well, with a tragic retribution meted out when the mother kills the American by a well-aimed stone so as to enable their son to marry the captain's daughter, set to music in a melodramatic idiom, modernistically titivated by polytriadic harmonies and non-corrosive dissonances, is produced in Zagreb.

16 JANUARY 1951

From the Bottom of My Heart, opera in three acts by the 37-year-old Ukrainian composer Herman ZHUKOVSKY, with action taking place on a Ukrainian collective farm, wherein an unsocialistically individualistic youth is won over to the collectivistic way of life by his proletarian bride and together they attend the unveiling of an electric power station, set to music modeled after Mussorgsky's realistic style, is produced at the Bolshoi Theater in Moscow.

30 NOVEMBER 1951

Ugrum-Reka (River Ugrum), opera in four acts by the 45-year-old Soviet composer Daniel FRENKEL, with its action set in Tsarist Siberia in 1910, wherein a mine owner strangles his bride when he finds out that she is a member of the Bolshevik party, and is driven to suicide by the outraged proletarian masses, set to music in a socialistically realistic style rooted in Russian melorhythms, is performed for the first time in Leningrad.

28 JUNE 1953

Abstrakte Oper No. 1 by the 50-year-old China-born Estonian-German Boris BLACHER, scored for three vocalists, two speakers, chorus and orchestra, to a libretto by Werner EGK set in a surrealistically unintelligible language projected in a stream of syllabic glossolalia with the component scenes identified only by their emotional content, e.g. Fear, Love No. 1, Pain, Panic, Love No. 2, to denote the abstraction from the concrete, is performed for the first time in the course of *Die Woche für Neue Musik* in Frankfurt.

25 DECEMBER 1953

Sevil, opera in three acts by the 31-year-old Azerbaijan composer Fikret AMIROV, to a libretto centered on an emancipated Soviet woman of Baku named Sevil who renounces the traditional ways of Moslem life, abandons her obsolete polygamous husband, goes to Moscow for a scientific education, publishes a book and returns home in feminine glory, set to music with a profusion of native melorhythms encased in mellifluous Russian harmonies, is performed for the first time in Baku.

17 AUGUST 1954

Penelope, "opera semiseria" in two parts by the 43-year-old Swiss-born composer Rolf LIEBERMANN, taking place the 3137th year after the end of the Trojan war, written in the style of modern antiquity, with baroque recitatives reflecting the Odyssean peripeties, contrasted with the dissonant counterpoint and stark bitonalities characterizing modern life, the score incorporating a recorded session of boogie-woogie, is performed for the first time in Salzburg.

19 OCTOBER 1954

Analfabeta, musical burlesque in one act by the 41-year-old Croatian composer Ivo LHOTKA-KALINSKI, to a libretto focused on an analphabetic municipal clerk who believes that analphabet is the name of a secret subversive political party and proceeds to take police action when he hears someone being called an analphabetic fellow, written in a satirically dissonant idiom in utilitarian modernistic harmonies marked by propulsive asymmetric rhythms, is produced in Belgrade.

4 NOVEMBER 1954

A Tale of a Mask Maker, one-act opera by the 43-year-old Japanese composer Osamu SHIMIZU, dealing with a disfranchised samurai's love for the beauteous daughter of a lowly mask-maker in 1204, and ending in the death of both, set to music derived from ancient Nipponese melorhythms, is performed for the first time in Osaka.

23 NOVEMBER 1954

Sandhog, "ballad in three acts" based on the short story *St. Columbia and the River* by Theodore Dreiser, dealing with a true adventure of an Irishman, father of twins, employed as a "sandhog" in digging the tunnel under the North River in New York City in the 1880's, and who is blown up through the muck to the surface of the river, but escapes unscathed, featuring a *Work Song* and a *Sweat Song*, is produced in New York, with a folksy musical score by Earl ROBINSON.

4 DECEMBER 1954

Double Trouble, one-act opera by the 50-year-old expatriate German composer Richard MOHAUPT, in which a pair of identical twins named Hocus and Pocus are involved in a series of amatory imbroglios, set to music in the manner of an Italian opera buffa, is performed for the first time as a commissioned work by the Louisville Orchestra, vocal soloists and chorus.

27 DECEMBER 1954

The Saint of Bleecker Street, music drama in three acts by Gian Carlo MENOTTI, to his own libretto dealing with a mystically illuminated young woman in the Italian section of Greenwich Village in New York, whose religious frenzy causes psychosomatic stigmata to appear on her hands and feet on Good Friday at the conclusion of her aria in the first act, emulating the wounds of Christ, and whose brother strangles his fiancée when she taunts him regarding his quasi-incestuous brotherly love, and the "Saint of Bleecker Street" falls lifeless to the ground as she receives the nun's veil, set to music combining elements of religious chants with mundane balladry, and including a scene in a subway station in the best tradition of Italian Verismo, is produced in New York, with Menotti himself acting in the multiple capacities of coordinator and stage director.

27 JANUARY 1955

The Midsummer Marriage, opera in three acts by the 50-year-old English composer Michael TIPPETT, to his own libretto, dealing with two pairs of lovers mating symbolically with their own antinomic selves representing the masculine element in a woman and a feminine element in a man, set to music in a capaciously diatonic idiom diversified by opulently terraced dissonances, is produced at Covent Garden in London.

24 FEBRUARY 1955

Susannah, musical drama in two acts by the 28-year-old American composer Carlisle FLOYD, to his own libretto, fashioned after the biblical story of Susannah and the elders transferred to rural Tennessee, wherein a fire-breathing Baptist preacher defiles a virginal cornfed farm girl after watching her swim innocently in the nude, whereupon her brother slays him during a baptism exhibit, set to music in a simplistically hymnal triadic idiom, with a modicum of modernistic bitonalities, is performed for the first time at Florida State University in Tallahassee. (The first New York performance of the opera was given at the New York City Center on 27 September 1956)

30 APRIL 1955

Dawn, operetta in three acts by the Albanian composer Kristo KONO, to a libretto depicting the successful discovery and condign lethal punishment of an unliquidated Albanian kulak scheming to murder a newly-wed socialistic couple, is produced in Tirana.

5 MAY 1955

Damn Yankees, musical comedy by Richard ADLER and Jerry ROSS, based on Douglass Wallop's novel *The Year the Yankees Lost the Pennant*, a modern Faust story in which an elderly baseball fan sells his soul to the devil in exchange for the career of a rejuvenated pitcher, enabling his favorite team, the Washington Senators, to win the pennant from the New York Yankees with psychosomatic assistance from a reincarnated witch Lola, and then cheats the Devil by refusing to play in the World Series, regains his soul and returns to his proper age, is produced in New York.

25 MAY 1955

The Committee, comic opera in four scenes by the 33-year-old American composer Matt DORAN, detailing an examination for a Music Doctor's degree in a Western American university, with a multiplicity of academically inane questions, including one asking which symphony ends with a timpani beat on the dominant (the correct answer is the first symphony by the chairman of the committee), is produced for the first time at the Del Mar College of Music in Corpus Christi, Texas.

31 MARCH 1956

Comoedia de Christi Resurrectione, Easter passion play by Carl ORFF, scored for soloists, mixed chorus and children's voices, 3 pianos, 2 harps, 4 double-basses and percussion, a surrealistic interlingual tale of the Resurrection, with historical planes translocated and parasynchronized, in which the Roman soldiers guarding the tomb are Bavarians, and the devil objurgates Christ in ecclesiastical Latin, is performed for the first time on the Munich Radio.

21 OCTOBER 1956

The Unicorn, the Gorgon and the Manticore, a madrigal fable for chorus, 10 dancers and nine instruments by Gian Carlo MENOTTI, subtitled *The Three Sundays of a Poet*, to his own libretto descriptive of a magically endowed poet, who thrice emerges from his seclusion on Sundays, leading successively a prome-nade with a pet unicorn, a gorgon and a manticore, and creating such a demand among local women to obtain similar pets, that the populace is driven to distrac-tion, set to music in a translucidly euphonious manner, making use of dramatic dissonances to point the surrealistic quality of the tale, is performed for the first time at the Library of Congress, in Washington, as a commissioned work by the Elizabeth Sprague Coolidge Foundation.

9 MAY 1957

Panfilo and Lauretta, opera in three acts by Carlos CHÁVEZ, dealing with a group of 14th-century aristocrats hiding in a Tuscan villa hoping to escape the raging pestilence, diverting themselves by impersonating their true natures in uninhibited play, during which a soldier gives a demonstration of carnal intercourse with a Florentine noblewoman, the socio-sexual egalitarianism reaching the climax when a pestiferous monk invades their refuge with a theatrical troupe and infects guests and hosts alike with the bubonic plague, is produced at Columbia University in New York.

15 JANUARY 1958

The Metropolitan Opera presents in New York the world première of *Vanessa*, opera in four acts by Samual BARBER, to the libretto by Gian Carlo Menotti, recounting the melodramatic tale of "a lady of great beauty" (Vanessa is a genus of butterflies to which an American variety, the "painted beauty," belongs) lan-guishing "in a northern country about 1905," and the handsome young son of her dead lover who seduces her niece Erika, nearly causing her death as she tries to abort the fruit of their liaison, and who in the end marries Vanessa herself as a symbolic redemption of his father's defection long ago, set to music of colorful opulence freely applying chromatic, atonal, polytonal, and pandiatonic devices, with aerostatic melodies reposing on long-stemmed chords rooted in deep over-tone-fertile basses, and with the vocal line varying from impassionate cantilena to ostentatiously prosaic spoken lines.

19 MARCH 1958

Gallantry, one-act "soap opera" by Douglas MOORE, in which a hospital nurse is libidinously coveted by a lascivious surgeon about to perform an appendectomy on her fiancé, set to music in mock-melodramatic tones, is performed for the first time in New York.

18 JUNE 1958

Noye's Fludde, one-act opera by Benjamin BRITTEN after a 14th-century English miracle play dealing with Noah's Ark and the Flood, and scored for a pleasingly bruitous ensemble of recorders, bugles, handbells, drums, cups hit by wooden spoons, string instruments and piano, with singing parts for the principal charac-ters, a spoken part for the Voice of God (accompanied by a wind machine), and children's voices for seven groups of seven pairs of animals—lions, oxen, swine, camels, asses, dogs, cats, polecats, etc. and birds—is performed for the first time in the church of the village of Orford, England, during the course of the annual Aldeburgh Music Festival.

3 DECEMBER 1958

Mrika, first national Albanian opera, written by the Albanian composer Prenk JAKOVA, wherein a young Albanian girl named Mrika is sabotaged in her work involving the construction of a collective hydro-electric power plant by her treacherous temporary bridegroom acting at the behest of foreign imperialists, with the socialistically realistic ending vouchsafed when she overcomes all interventionist wiles and, as the plan is completed, marries a progressive co-worker, set to music in a congenially optimistic idiom, based on proletarian Albanian tunes, is produced in Shkodra.

11 DECEMBER 1958

Ikuma DAN, Japanese composer, conducts in Tokyo the world première of his grand opera *Yang Kwei-fei*, on an ancient Chinese tale dealing with a concubine of the Chinese Emperor who falls in love with the Emperor's eunuch, featuring a Mongolian wrestling dance as a choreographic interlude.

24 JANUARY 1959

Moskva Tcheryomushki, the first operetta by Dmitri SHOSTAKOVICH, depicting the urban predicament of the newly wed Sasha and Masha, trying to obtain an apartment in the new housing development in the Moscow suburb of Tcheryomushki, with a score full of dulcet waltzes and hedonistic tunes, is produced in Moscow.

31 MAY 1959

Aniara, "revue of mankind in space-time," by the 42-year-old Swedish composer Karl-Birger BLOMDAHL, wherein an animated female electronic brain Mima guides the space ship Aniara to Mars after the atomic disintegration of the earth, with the passengers delivering themselves nostalgically to the last terrestrial pleasures (a sex orgy in a hall of mirrors, a jazz session, etc.), the music running the entire gamut of expression from a Lesbian waltz to a jazz solo in 7/16, with some weird sounds on magnetic tape creating a suitable interplanetary mood, and recordings of the voices of Hitler, Khrushchev and Eisenhower remindful of the past forces of evil, half-evil and good, the nuclear musical motif being an involuted *Grossmutterakkord*, consisting of 12 different notes and 11 different intervals spiralling out of the central C, and ever returning to it, is performed for the first time at the Royal Opera in Stockholm.

17 JUNE 1959

A Hand of Bridge, for four solo voices and chamber orchestra by Samuel BARBER, to a libretto by Gian Carlo Menotti, revealing in audible asides the wishes, anxieties and fantasies of a bridge foursome: a florid businessman conjuring up an alabaster palace at Palm Beach with "twenty naked girls and twenty naked boys tending to my pleasures," a lawyer wondering where his unstabilized blond-tressed mistress was, and their vacuous wives engaged in inconsequential chatter, set to music in a tense polyrhythmic idiom, is performed for the first time at the Festival of Two Worlds in Spoleto, Italy.

19 JUNE 1959

Salto Mortale, electronic opera by Henk BADINGS for five voices with electronic accompaniment, to the composer's libretto, in which a professor of biochemistry (lyric tenor) restores to life a recent suicide poet by using an elixir perfected by him and enabling him to vitalize dead bodies, if not too decayed, and who kills him again when the poet, whose voice suddenly changes from tenor to bass, forms a mutual attraction with the professor's favorite young laboratory assistant (a high soprano), is produced by the Dutch Television Network, as the first opera totally accompanied by an electronically recorded score.

12 JUNE 1960

Spring, opera in two acts by the Albanian composer Tish DAIJA, taking place in Albania in the spring of 1944, and centered on a heroic partisan dying "with the name of the Communist Party on his lips" before the firing squad of the Nazi occupying forces, betrayed by an Albanian Fascist who failed in love rivalry for the hand of a beautiful mountain maiden, set to music in melodramatic colors of the traditional opera, with a stimulating injection of asymmetrical Albanian rhythms, is produced in Tirana.

21 SEPTEMBER 1960

Rosamunde Floris, opera in three acts by Boris BLACHER, to a libretto wherein a promiscuous damsel premaritally impregnated by an unscrupulous galant and abandoned by him, marries an aspiring librarian, after the latter defenestrates his previous fiancée, with a polymonotonous tension created by solitonal system of repetitious effects in variable meters, is produced at the Berlin Music Festival.

25 NOVEMBER 1960

The era of soap operas, daily radio broadcasts telling stories of heartbreak, mental and physical illnesses, frustrated female amours, and teetering business enterprises (usually sponsored by manufacturers of soaps and detergents, hence also known as sudsy programs), formally comes to an end as the Columbia Broadcasting System removes from the ether the long enduring serials, *Ma Perkins*, veteran of 27 years of struggle to maintain her lumber mill (inaugurated 13 August 1933), *The Right to Happiness*, 20-year-old story of a nubile widow and perpetually adolescent son (inaugurated 22 January 1940), *Young Dr. Malone*, wise and lovable, medically and socially (inaugurated 29 April 1940) and *The Second Mrs. Burton*, a widow infatuated with a young and unscrupulous artist (inaugurated 7 January 1946), the final episodes all provided with happy or at least morally gratifying endings, to the accompaniment of saturated diminished seventh-chords on the organ, the instrument indissolubly linked to radio serials from time immemorial.

30 DECEMBER 1960

Mariuta, opera in three acts by the Soviet composer Dmitri TOLSTOY, after the story *Forty-First* by Boris Lavrenev, dealing with a Soviet girl guerrilla fighter who is left to guard a White Russian officer taken prisoner during the civil war in Central Asia, falls in love with him, but despite their intimacy, kills him unhesitantly when he tries to join the crew of an anti-Bolshevik motor boat on the Aral Sea, as she did forty previous enemies, is performed for the first time in Perm.

25 NOVEMBER 1961

Vittorio GIANNINI conducts the Chicago Lyric Opera Company in the world première of his opera *The Harvest*, dealing with a somber tale of multilateral lust on an American farm circa 1900, wherein two brothers covet the third brother's young bride, who is ultimately strangled by their blind father when she rejects his groping advances.

6 DECEMBER 1961

The Padrone, two-act opera by George Whitefield CHADWICK, in which the figure of the padrone, in the period of Italian and Irish immigration in the late nineteenth century, symbolizes human corruption in the exploitation of poor immigrants, musically based "on the union of Wagner's symphonic recitative and Italian lyricism," with its four principal characters singing in Italian and all others in English, is produced in an abridged concert version in Carnegie Hall.

5 APRIL 1962

The Communist Manifesto, oratorio by the Prague-born composer Erwin SCHULHOFF, written in 1932, to the classical text of Karl Marx, beginning with the celebrated sentence: "A ghost is walking across Europe, the ghost of Communism," set in declarative triadic harmonies, and ending with the appeal "Proletarians of all nations, unite!" in a virile Dorian mode, is performed posthumously in Prague, from a manuscript copy discovered in Russia.

27 JUNE 1962

Ausgerechnet und verspielt, "Spiel-Oper" for television by Ernst KRENEK, to his own libretto in which a mathematician loses a lot of hard-earned-money using his highly scientific theory of probability at the roulette table, but breaks the bank by playing a series of consecutive numbers taken from the intervals in semitone units in a tone-row selected at random by a humanoid computer, is performed for the first time on television in Vienna.

11 OCTOBER 1962

The Passion of Jonathan Wade, opera in three acts by Carlisle FLOYD, to his own libretto dealing with a noble-souled Yankee commander who marries a Southern belle in the post-bellum turmoil of 1866 undismayed by a rude raid of the Ku Klux Klan during their wedding, to a musical score bathed in lyrical melodiousness and set in the traditional sequences of arias, duets, and dramatic interludes in the orchestra, with some nice plantation ballads sung by a mamma named Nicey, is produced by the New York City Opera Company.

23 FEBRUARY 1963

The Darkened City, opera in three acts by the 52-year-old Americanized German-born composer Bernhard HEIDEN, dealing with the year of the plague, 1319, in East Anglia, during which a lethargic victim Lazarus rises from the mass of presumed cadavers frightening the populace and precipitating ecclesiastical hysteria, set to music in a measurably tonal, rhythmically propulsive manner, verisimilitudinarily illustrated by authentic passages of Gregorian chant, is produced by the Indiana University Opera Theater in Bloomington, Indiana.

3 MARCH 1963

Labyrinth, surrealist opera by Gian Carlo MENOTTI, to his own libretto in which a distraught bridegroom misplaces the key to his hotel room on his wedding night, gets lost in a maze of nightmarish corridors, meanders into a non-adjacent spatial continuum, is suspended weightless in an orbiting spaceship, and is measured for interment by an ultra-dimensional mortician while holding in his hand the crucial hotel room key, set to music with a somewhat atonal lilt, reverting to terrestrial tonality in non-cosmic scenes, is performed for the first time as a commissioned work by the National Broadcasting Company Television Opera Theater.

21 OCTOBER 1963

The Last Savage, opera buffa by Gian-Carlo MENOTTI, to his own libretto dealing with a whimsical American heiress who undertakes a search for the abominable snowman in the high Himalayas, locates a putative specimen, imports him to her native Chicago and when he recoils in horror from abstract impressionist art, dodecaphonic music and beatnik poetry, takes him back to his mountain habitat and eventually marries him, set to music in urbane satirical tones, with illustrative persiflage of American avant-garde pursuits, is produced at the Opéra-Comique in Paris.

16 JUNE 1964

Ernst KRENEK conducts in Hamburg the first performance of his opera *Der gold-ene Bock* (*The Golden Ram*), to his own libretto in which the Argonaut Jason inadvertently breaks the time barrier, finds himself on Route 66 in the United States, marries the termagant Medea, divorces her after she serves him a dish of human soup made of the flesh of a Greek shipping magnate and flies back in time and space to ancient Greece in a jet plane called Chrysomallos (i.e. golden fleece), which is attacked by Medea transformed into a dinosaur-sized dragon (she is thrown off the liner and perishes), with an ironic finale when Greek customs officers seize the golden fleece as contraband, the music written in a complex but logically impeccable serial idiom embellished by pre-recorded electronic sounds.

12 NOVEMBER 1964

One-Man Show, chamber opera by the 29-year-old British composer Nicholas MAW, dealing with an impecunious young art student whose back is discovered to be tattooed in a theoretically abstract pattern (actually it spells JOE upside down), and who therefore becomes the target of covetous art dealers, is performed for the first time in London.

27 MAY 1965

The Judas Tree, "musical drama of Judas Iscariot," by the 30-year-old British composer Peter DICKINSON, for speakers, singers, chorus and chamber orchestra, wherein the tree on which Judas hanged himself is mystically identified with the tree of the true cross, utilizing in the score various forms of serial devices and electronic effects and simplicistically tonal harmonies, with the tri-tone (the medieval "diabolus in musica") representing Judas, progressing through a series of excruciating (*ex cruce*) discords to a theologically immaculate unison symbolizing the sacrificial identity of Jesus and Judas, is performed for the first time in the College of St. Mark and St. John in London.

24 DECEMBER 1965

Ayikuli, Chinese opera composed collectively by a group of Communist musicians, adapted from a film entitled *Red Blossom on Tien Shan Mountains*, and dealing with a heroic Kazakh woman, a former slave, who becomes a revolutionary leader, is produced in Peking.

14 MAY 1966

The Magic Chair, one-act opera by the Hungarian-born American composer Eugene ZADOR, in which a malingering bureaucrat is seated in a magic chair that forces him to tell scandalous truths about his management of municipal affairs, is performed for the first time (with piano instead of the orchestra) at Louisiana State University in Baton Rouge.

2 JUNE 1966

17 Tage und 4 Minuten, opera buffa in three acts by Werner EGK, a fanciful version of Calderón's comedy *El mayor encanto amor*, with wandering Ulysses and nymphomaniacal Circe making love for exactly 17 days and 4 minutes surrounded by half-mythological, quarter-realistic and quarter-surrealistic creatures, is produced in Stuttgart.

12 OCTOBER 1966

Esther, opera in two acts by the German composer Robert HANELL, in which the non-Aryan animal warmth of a young Jewish girl violinist is used by the Nazi doctors to restore the life of an experimentally frozen Aryan youth, with anti-fascist love blossoming forth between the two enabling the girl to go to her death in a gas chamber with a renewed hope in the inherent decency of at least one German in a flood of Hitlerian diabolism, is produced at the German State Opera in East Berlin.

4 MARCH 1967

Kaiser Jovian, opera in four acts by the 35-year-old Swiss composer Rudolf KELTERBORN, wherein Jupiter assumes the identity of the ephemeral Roman emperor Jovian (reigned 363–364 A.D.), marries his bride, and ultimately reveals himself and returns to Mt. Olympus, opening and ending with a vociferous dodecaphonic chord, is produced in Karlsruhe.

17 APRIL 1967

The Crook, comic opera in two acts by the Israeli composer Menahem AVIDOM, the first musical satire on the government of Israel, wherein its fiscal troubles lead to the promulgation of a decree forbidding the population to breathe after the expiration of the deadline for payment of taxes, is produced in Tel Aviv.

29 APRIL 1967

Geschäftsbericht, minimal opera (duration 600 seconds) by the prime German Communist composer Paul DESSAU, a "business report" to the text of the indictment of the American aggression in Vietnam by the International Tribunal for War Crimes in Stockholm, with an epilogue in which dead American soldiers curse President Johnson for depriving them of their lives, is produced in Leipzig.

17 JUNE 1967

Heroine, opera in two acts by the Albanian composer Vangjo Novo, in which an Albanian girl guerrilla heroically refuses, despite inhuman torture, to disclose the names of the Communist-led partisans to the Nazi invaders in 1943, culminating in a total liberation of the land and the execution of local traitors, set to music according to the romantic formula of socialist opera, with tragedy and sacrifice in minor modes leading to a triumphant finale in marching major keys, is produced in Tirana.

17 OCTOBER 1967

Hair, a rollicking rock 'n' roll musical, with lyrics by several hands including William Shakespeare (in Hamlet's complaint about air pollution, smog and "a foul and pestilent congregation of vapors"), and music mostly by Galt MacDermot, a spontaneously designed far-out mass spectacle in which the audience is invited to get it on with the cast and vocally participate, featuring for the first time in the musical theater a scene of total nudity mitigated only by stroboscopically freaked-out lights, including such mind-blowing songs as *Let the Sunshine In*, the title song *Hair* and the psychedelically astrological chorus *Aquarius*, couched in the bemused plagal modalities of old English balladry with incredibly heavy raps laid on the audience by uninhibited proliferation of Anglo-Saxon profanity, opens in New York under the aegis of the Shakespeare Festival Public Theater.

24 MARCH 1968

Prometheus, opera by Carl ORFF, the third part of his trilogy of Greek tragedies, after *Prometheus Bound* of Aeschylus, set to the original ancient Greek text, in one continuous act, constituting a series of homophonic monologues, dialogues, trialogues, tetralogues and choruses in neo-Grecian diatonic modalities accoutred in rudimentary triadic harmonies and orchestrated for 4 pianos, 6 flutes, 6 oboes,

6 trumpets, 6 trombones, 4 banjos, 4 harps, 2 organs, 9 doublebasses, 5 kettle-drums and an ensemble of 70 percussion instruments, is performed for the first time in Stuttgart.

19 DECEMBER 1968

Help! Help! The Globolinks! a space opera by Gian Carlo MENOTTI, to his own libretto in English depicting the invasion of the earth by extraterrestrial globolinks (i.e. global links) who speak an electronic language of dodecaphonic provenance but who are vulnerable to the sounds of human music and are eventually routed by a school band playing a diatonic march, is produced at the Hamburg State Opera.

28 FEBRUARY 1969

Luisella, opera in four acts by the 44-year-old Italian composer Franco MANNINO, expanded from his original one-act opera, to the libretto from a short story by Thomas Mann, in which a cuckolded husband dressed up as a woman at a beer party in a German provincial town in 1897 suffers a fatal cardiac arrest while singing the song Luisella composed by his wife's lover, with a lethally dissonant polychord serving as his epitaph, is performed for the first time in Palermo, conducted by the composer.

12 MARCH 1971

The Most Important Man, opera in three acts with music and libretto by Gian Carlo MENOTTI, in which a black man in an unnamed segregated nation invents an ultimate formula to attain total dominion of the world and himself achieves a liaison with an unpigmented woman, strangles his laboratory assistant and then destroys himself and the formula in a luminous death dance, set to music with a liberal application of Africanesque percussion, is performed for the first time at the New York City Opera.

11 MAY 1972

The Four-Note Opera by the 32-year-old American composer Tom JOHNSON, to his original libretto for five voices and piano in which the characters commit mass self-immolation at the end, the entire score based on four notes, A, B, D and E, in ostentatiously tetraphonic monotony fertilized by rhythmic diversification, is performed for the first time at the ultramodern emporium the Cubiculo in New York, with a prelude for a rebellious tape recording which demands individualistic deprogramming.

9 MARCH 1973

Karlheinz STOCKHAUSEN conducts in London the first production of his multimedia pantomime *Ylem*, purporting to represent the formation of the primordial first substance (Hyle in Greek) which expands to a full-size universe and contracts to its initial atom every 80 billion years, with players instructed to wander and roam probabilistically with eyes closed carrying their instruments around and playing on them at will, finally congregating around the center of the contracted universe represented by a grand piano, electronium, three synthesizers and a closed television circuit.

29 FEBRUARY 1976

Bilby's Doll, opera composed for the United States bicentennial by the 49-year-old American composer Carlisle FLOYD, wherein Doll, a young French girl brought to America by a sea captain named Bilby, is accused of witchcraft by

Bilby's wife (who contends that Doll had caused to wither the fetus in her womb), eventually becomes herself convinced that she is a witch and prays for Satan to come to her rescue, is produced in Houston.

1 APRIL 1976

Ines de Castro, opera by the 30-year-old American composer Thomas PASATIERI, based on an apparently true historical episode involving the mistress of Pedro I of Portugal who was assassinated by a court clique in 1355, whose corpse was exhumed by her imperial lover who forced her assassins to kiss her skeletal remains during her postmortem coronation, is produced in Baltimore.

25 JULY 1976

Einstein on the Beach, phantasmagorical spectacle by the surrealistically minimalistic American composer Philip GLASS, to the scenario of a dadaistically propended dramatist Robert Wilson, in which hypnopompic events are oxymoronically juxtaposed in a deliberately antisyllogistical sequence, is produced at the Festival of Avignon, France.

12 APRIL 1978

Le Grand Macabre, eschatological anti-opera by the musical thaumaturgist Györgi LIGETI, dealing with the apocalyptic ultima hora and written in a gloriously antimusical idiom of beguiling allure, with singers shouting and whispering inarticulate vocables, to the altered text adapted from dramas by the Belgian surrealist Michel de Ghelderode, the action being set in a chimeric town of Breugelland, and centered on the thanatopherous necro-czar who sexually mutilates a local hausfrau before ordering the world's end, but shrinks himself into a death mask when the forces of life refuse to stop functioning, is produced for the first time in Stockholm.

26 OCTOBER 1988

Symphony No. 7, Hyönteissinfonia (Insect Symphony), by the 39-year-old Finnish composer Kalevi AHO, a continuation of the satirical pose adopted in his opera *Insect Life* composed the year before and based on a play by Josef and Karel Čapek in which a drunken and narcissistic vagrant is the only human character and ultimately discovers that human life is but a form of insect life, composed in an intentionally postmodern and polystylistic idiom of six episodic movements titled "The Tramp and the Parasitic Hymenopteran and Its Larva," "The Butterflies," "The Dungbeetles," "The Grasshoppers," "The Ants," and "Dayflies," with the symphony's overall form . . . "a negation of the conventional striving forwards (as) each new movement questions the preceding one, acting as its antithesis," is premiered in Helsinki.

19 DECEMBER 1991

The Ghosts of Versailles, "grand opera buffa" in two acts by the 53-year-old American composer John CORIGLIANO, to a libretto by William Hoffman based on Beaumarchais' play *La Mère coupable* written as a sequel to his *Le barbier de Séville* and *Le mariage de Figaro*, for which Hoffman was called upon by Corigliano "to create a libretto that did not set me in 1792 but in a world of smoke and haze from which I could leap in and out of the past," bringing Beaumarchais himself, Marie Antoinette, Louis XVI, and other French aristocrats of the Revolutionary era back as ghosts to the palace of Versailles where Beaumarchais stages a Figaro opera-within-an-opera meant to court the queen he has phantomly loved for 200 years and which eventually turns into an attempt by

Beaumarchais and Figaro to spare her historic fate (the orchestra plays "La Marseillaise" when her head ultimately rolls again), with the music at times teasingly quoting Rossini's and Mozart's famous Figaro treatments, is premiered with Teresa Strata, Marilyn Horne, and Håkan Hagegård at New York's Metropolitan Opera (its first premiere in twenty-five years), James Levine conducting.

26 SEPTEMBER 1991

Genesis, cantata in five movements for chorus and orchestra by the 53-year-old American composer Charles WUORINEN, extolling God the creator with traditional chants woven into modern contrapuntal ecstasy, its middle movement a Vulgate setting of the first Biblical chapter and opening verses of the second followed by an orchestral-only, big-bang fourth movement, is premiered in San Francisco as a joint commission with the Honolulu Symphony and Minnesota Orchestra, Herbert Blomstedt conducting.

"CONDUCTORLESS ORCHESTRAS," FROM *A THING OR TWO ABOUT MUSIC*

Slonimsky is a master at recalling "hidden history," which is to say important episodes commonly omitted from the standard records.

Among the most prized musical collectors' items is a recording made during one of the orchestral rehearsals under the direction of a world-famous conductor. Visitors are banned at his rehearsals but someone managed to install a hidden microphone and made this recording. The classical strains of great music superbly phrased are here frequently interrupted by outbursts of bilingual abuse and vituperation that is more fascinating than the music itself. Invocations to pagan and Christian dieties alternate with personal advice to some of the players to take up the sewing machine instead of their particular instruments. It is said that the conductor found out about the existence of this recording and tried to suppress it but found the task as impossible as the proverbial attempt of a movie star to destroy every single print of a candid film imprudently made by her in her days of struggle toward film stardom.

Most conductors are autocrats by nature, and orchestral players accept their outbursts as an inevitable evil. But once in a while a cry is heard: "Down with conductors!" Such a cry led to the formation of the first conductorless orchestra of modern times. It was the Persimfans, the abbreviation of *Pervyi Simfonicheskyi Ansambl*, i.e., First Symphonic Ensemble, which was launched in Moscow in February 1922. The idea behind the formation of this conductorless orchestra was in keeping with the revolutionary trends of the first years of the Soviet Republic. Capitalist bosses were liquidated or otherwise removed from social life; why then keep musical bosses?

The First Symphonic Ensemble presented five seasons of concerts featuring classical and modern works. The quality of performance was high. Leading political and artistic personalities of Soviet Russia praised the accomplishments of the new organization. The Chairman of the Council of People's Commissars declared:

"The principle of conductorless performance based on collective creative activity is a revolutionary step in music and is profoundly consonant with our epoch. As a pioneer of symphonic music carried to the factories and Red Army barracks, the First Symphonic Ensemble gives a vivid demonstration of excellent results attained by collective work. This is particularly important at the present stage of the reconstruction of national economy which can be successfully accomplished only with the collective participation of working masses."

The Vice-Chairman of the Council voiced a similar sentiment:

"The idea of collectivism is particularly important in our time, and its realization in the domain of Soviet music should be regarded as a significant accomplishment."

Still another representative of the Soviet government declared:

"The First Symphonic Ensemble has dispensed with the conductor and thus demonstrated that even in such a complex process as the interpretation of a musical composition, the individual will and knowledge brought by a conductor may be replaced by a collective interpretation of musical works. The First Symphonic Ensemble is particularly near and dear to every Soviet listener because in its work it has reaffirmed the power of collectivism as a guiding principle in the revolutionary transformation of the social and economic system. My wish is that the First Symphonic Ensemble should be followed by similar ensembles in Russia and abroad, and that its basic idea should embrace not only interpreters but composers of music as well. For in the final analysis, musical composition must adopt a similar principle of the collective creation."

The President of the State Academy of Fine Arts joined the official representatives of the Soviet government in endorsing the conductorless orchestra. He declared:

"The First Symphonic Ensemble is an epoch making organization. It is connected with the idea of collectivism which inspired us all in the first unforgettable days of the Revolution. The romanticism of those days is dead, but the First Symphonic Ensemble is alive, and it carries this idea into life. It has retained its principles in the revolutionary storms, and has forever established itself as a unique artistic organism."

But despite this encouragement on the part of important personalities in the Soviet Union, the First Symphonic Ensemble soon began to show inner contradictions. The first violinist of the orchestra was often referred to as the actual leader, for he gave the tempo at the beginning of the performance and often regulated instrumental balance by signaling with his head and his body. Then suddenly the First Symphonic Ensemble began to disintegrate. Conductors from abroad were invited to lead it in guest appearances. It was found that less time was lost with a competent conductor in settling the tempi and the dynamics than during the conductorless regime. By 1928, the conductorless orchestra was no more.

A conductorless orchestra was organized in New York in the 1920's and gave several concerts of competently performed music. But again there were sly references in the music press to the first violinist's being "the conductor of the conductorless orchestra." Economic insolvency soon forced the New York edition of the Persimfans to fold up. Conductors took over once more. They shouted and ranted during rehearsals. They grimaced at the players during concerts. But they delivered highly polished performances. The musicians often wished that one day the conductor would drop dead. They prayed that some other conductor would be engaged to lead the orchestra. But the necessity of having a conductor was admitted by all. The conductorless days were over.

HIDDEN HISTORY OF MODERN MUSIC
(EXCERPTS FROM *MUSIC SINCE 1900*)

Another recurring theme of Music Since 1900 *is hidden history, which is to say events that are generally forgotten. One methodological advantage that Slonimsky has over the rest of us is a love of, and faith in, newspapers.*

17 AUGUST 1902

Parysatis, incidental music of operatic proportions by Camille SAINT-SAËNS, to a play taking place in Persia in 401 B.C. dealing with the Persian Queen Parysatis and the struggle between her son Artaxerxes and her grandson Darius for love of the Greek concubine of her slain son Cyrus, is performed for the first time at the Grand Roman Arena in Béziers, France, by a grandiose ensemble of 450 orchestra players plus 20 harps, 15 trumpets, 12 cornets, 250 choristers and 60 dancers.

29 JANUARY 1904

Der Kobold, opera in three acts by Siegfried WAGNER, to his own libretto dealing with sprites and fays, nymphs and sylphs, dryads and hamadryads, oreads and limoniads, kobolds, gnomes and other elfenfolk puckishly intervening in the otherwise realistic events taking place in a small German town early in the 19th century, with the paternal ghost of the composer's great father determining the shaping of musical themes and the formation of harmonies, is performed for the first time in Hamburg.

> I am well aware that of the applause bestowed upon my *Kobold* only 20% is due me, and 80% due my father. If my name were not Siegfried Wagner, but Müller or Schulz, this distinguished assembly would not be gathered here. (Siegfried Wagner's remark at a banquet given in his honor after the production of *Der Kobold* in Graz on 3 December 1904)

1 FEBRUARY 1904

Enrico CARUSO makes his first phonograph recording in America for the Victor Company, singing the aria *Vesti la giubba* from *Pagliacci*, which he made famous by the application of the "Caruso sob," known technically as *coup de glotte*.

21 MARCH 1904

On his first visit to the United States, Richard STRAUSS conducts in New York a concert of his music with the Wetzler Symphony Orchestra, in a program including *Don Juan, Also Sprach Zarathustra*, and the world première of his enormously protracted *Symphonia Domestica* (completed by him in Charlottenburg on the last day of 1903), scored for a huge orchestra and dedicated "to my beloved wife and our young one," presenting a systematic chronological account of 24 hours of domestic felicity, the psychomusical material containing 67 distinct but tonally interrelated motives in constant mutation and mutual adaptation through inversion, augmentation, diminution, canon and fugue.

16 MAY 1904

Exactly one month before "Bloomsday" proclaimed by James JOYCE in his novel *Ulysses*, replete with musical anamneses, he enters a contest at the Dublin *Feis Ceoil*, judged by Luigi Denza, the composer of *Funiculi-Funicula*, and sings adequately in a tenorized baritone voice the two test pieces (*Come Ye Children* by Arthur Sullivan and the Irish air *A Long Farewell*), but refuses to try his unconsummate skill at sight reading, and so loses the potential gold medal, although he obtains a second prize when its original winner is in turn disqualified.

16 JUNE 1904

Leopold BLOOM, Irish-Jewish Ulysses of James Joyce's novel of that name, fulfills in a single Bloomsday the exagminations round his factification for incamination as a Dublin newspaper advertisement canvasser, in the course of which he experiences a number of musical impressions, viz. (1) hears a barmaid intone a tune from the vaudeville show *Florodora* (2) befriends a blind piano tuner (3) overhears a Jesuit priest sing Lionel's aria *M'appari* from Flotow's opera *Martha* (4) hears a bass "barreltone" render a ballad in native Doric (5) punningly recollects his wife's chamber music ("empty vessels make most noise, and the resonance . . . is equal to the law of falling water, like those rhapsodies of Liszt's Hungarian, gypsy-eyed diddle-iddle-addle"), follows "chordsdark lumpmusic" harping slower, paronomastically muses that "tenors get women by the *score*" (6) attends a gathering to bid farewell to Hungarian printers as a band of Irish pipers strikes up *Come Back to Erin* and the *Rákóczy March* (7) chants medieval Latin hymns in church (8) listens attentively to a recurrent playing of Ponchielli's *Dance of the Hours* on a pianola in a local brothel in the drunken belief that the clanking timepieces are his parcae.

14 FEBRUARY 1906

President Theodore ROOSEVELT receives at the White House a delegation of Negro students from the Industrial Institute of Manassas, Virginia, and declares, after hearing them perform some songs for him, that "gradually out of the capacity for melody that the Negro race has, America shall develop some school of national music." (President Says Negro Makes American Music—May Furnish the Foundation of the True National Music—captions in the New York *Times*, 15 February 1906)

23 NOVEMBER 1906

Enrico CARUSO is found guilty of molesting a woman in the monkey house in the Central Park Zoo in New York City by touching her left forearm with his right elbow, and is fined ten dollars in a New York City Municipal Court. (Caruso cabled his father in Italy after the verdict: "I swear upon thy white hair that I am innocent")

5 MARCH 1907

Lee DE FOREST, the American wizard of the cathode rays, succeeds in transmitting by wireless a performance of Rossini's *William Tell* overture from Telharmonic

Hall in New York to the Brooklyn Navy Yard, marking the first broadcast of a musical composition.

16 MAY 1907

Miller R. HUTCHISON files at the U.S. Patent Office the original application for his invention, a motor-driven Diaphragm Actuated Horn and Resonator, for use as a signal in automobiles, which under the trade name Klaxon became a musical instrument used in various orchestral scores of the automobile age, including Gershwin's symphonic tableau *An American in Paris*. (The patent was granted on 3 May 1910; it was subsequently acquired by F. Hallett Lovell, manufacturer and distributor, who died on 19 May 1962 at the age of ninety-four)

12 JUNE 1907

Alexander GLAZUNOV is awarded the honorary degree of Doctor in Music by the University of Cambridge, England.

> Gaudium nostrum cumulavit hodie vir in arte musica insignis, qui Russorum in imperio maximo iam per annos quinque et viginti in luce publica versatus, primum abhinc annos decem Britanniae innotuit. Argumenta magna vir magnus aggressus, popularium suorum artis musicae hodiernae in "Raymonda" praesertim documentum splendidum protulisse dicitur. Inter peritos vero constat, "nympham pulchram dormientem" illiam a Tschaikovskio, doctore olim nostro, musicis modis accommodatam, quasi statuarum elegantissimarum ordinem effingere; viri huius autem "Raymondam" figuris potius ex aere fusis immensis comparari. Iuvat nunc iterum ex imperio Russorum ad nos advectum salutare magistrorum in arte musica magnorum aemulum, qui artis suae genus pulchrum, genus severum et sobrium repraesentat, patriaeque cantus populares non minus fideliter quam feliciter exprimit. (Text of the speech delivered by the Public Orator in presenting to the Chancellor the recipient of the honorary degree of Doctor in Music)

13 JUNE 1908

BLIND TOM, American Negro slave who amazed the world as a musical child prodigy playing whole concerts of piano pieces of moderate difficulty (a brochure, *Le merveilleux prodigue musical Tom l'Aveugle*, published in Paris in 1867, adequately glorified his achievements), dies at the age of 59, in Hoboken, New Jersey, in the family home of Colonel Bethune to whom he was originally sold as a suckling.

> Tom was born in Georgia, owned by a man named Jones. He was an idiot from birth. His father and mother were offered for sale. Price: $1,500 without Tom, $1,200 with him." (Dwight's *Journal of Music*, ca. 1880)

10 DECEMBER 1908

The Russian Symphony Orchestra of New York City, under the direction of its founder Modest ALTSCHULER gives the first performance anywhere of SCRIABIN's Fourth Symphony, *Le Poème de l'Extase*, completed in Lausanne in the summer of 1907, reflecting in a solipsistically erotic and pantheistically expansive continuous movement the mystic intent to "possess the Cosmos as a man possesses a woman," the music traversing eight initially passive but progressively active states of ecstasy—languor, yearning, volitation, emergent creativeness, anxiety, volition, postulation of self, challenge—symbolized by thematic figures mutually combining in augmentation, diminution, truncation, apocopation, intervalic torsion and rhythmic contortion in an ambience of tonal obliquity yet adhering to fundamental tonality with a purposive predominance of major triads and cohering in the formal symmetry of cyclic unity.

12 FEBRUARY 1909

F. T. MARINETTI, Italian protagonist of *Futurismo*, publishes in the Paris newspaper *Le Figaro* his First Futurist Manifesto promulgating the militant ideals of futurist drama, literature, art and music—irrealistic, irrational, illogical, intuitive, improvisatory, autocephalous, synthetic, abstract, fantasmic, cerebral, unpredictably fulminating and stupefying.

9 APRIL 1909

In a historic first wireless transmission of the human voice Enrico CARUSO's singing is broadcast from the Metropolitan Opera House in New York through two microphones placed in the footlights of the stage to the home of Lee DE FOREST, inventor of the Audion, three-element vacuum tube which made radio possible.

13 JANUARY 1910

The first radio broadcast of operatic selections is made from the stage of the Metropolitan Opera House in New York, with Caruso singing arias from *Cavalleria Rusticana* and *Pagliacci*, "trapped and magnified by the dictograph directly from the stage and borne by wireless Hertzian waves."

1 MARCH 1910

The Superior Court of Boston orders the management of the Lenox Hotel to desist from using the name of the Russian prima donna Lydia Lipkovska in the chef Niccolo Sabattini's special "soufflé de fraises à la Lipkovska," charging $2 for it à la carte.

11 MARCH 1911

Francesco Balilla PRATELLA issues in Milan a "Manifesto Tecnico della Musica Futurista" in which he advocates the creation of new music that would synthesize melody and harmony in a chromaticized continuum, confidently predicting the eventual victory for an ideal enharmonic mode to be discovered by true harbingers of the future and a universal emergence of a "futurist melody" similar to an ideal line formed by the "incessant flowering of thousands of ocean waves."

4 NOVEMBER 1911

E. H. CRUMP is reelected Mayor of Memphis, Tennessee, after an arduous campaign, helped along by a song *Mr. Crump* especially composed for him by the Negro balladeer W. C. Handy, and later renamed *Memphis Blues*, which created a new style of American popular music technically distinguished by a flatted "blue" seventh and a flatted "blue" third in a major key.

(The following statement from Mr. Crump's secretary obtained by Mrs. Frances Fink at the author's request seems to contradict the story of *Memphis Blues*: "Mr. Crump did not use Handy's song in either of his elections. The song was written a couple of years after Mr. Crump was elected Mayor the first time. . . . He was elected the second time in November 1911, and again in November 1915. I do not think Handy wrote the song as a campaign song, but simply used Mr. Crump's name in the composition of same." But from Mr. W. C. Handy comes a rejoinder: "I did not write the *Memphis Blues* as a campaign song for Mr. Crump but wrote *Mr. Crump* as a campaign song for Mr. Crump and then changed the title for publication to the *Memphis Blues* and published it in

1912 myself . . . I then followed that with the *St. Louis Blues*, copyrighted on 14 September 1914")

11 NOVEMBER 1911

The AEROPHOR, a tone-sustaining instrument, consisting of a rubber bulb with a tube appliance, enabling the player on a wind instrument to hold a note indefinitely, is given its first demonstration by the inventor, Bernard Samuels, in Berlin.

6 APRIL 1912

A thousand years have elapsed since the death of NOTKER (BALBULUS), the St. Gall monk who was one of the earliest church musicians to develop the ecclesiastical sequence.

5 JULY 1912

In the presence of qualified witnesses in a photographer's studio at 42nd Street and Sixth Avenue, New York City, Professor Charles MUNTER hypnotizes an admittedly inept vocal student Marian Graham into performing a series of thrillingly Trilbyesque trills.

18 JULY 1913

Nine centuries have passed since the birth of Hermannus CONTRACTUS (nicknamed "contracted" because he was a hunchback), enlightened musical scientist and inventor of a system of intervalic notation that anticipated equal temperament.

19 OCTOBER 1913

Festliches Præludium by Richard STRAUSS (completed on 11 May 1913) for orchestra and chorus, making use of the novel device Aerophor, helping to sustain breath playing long notes in the brass instruments, is performed for the first time at the inauguration of the Konzert-Haus in Vienna, for which occasion the work was commissioned.

5 NOVEMBER 1913

Men on the Line, cantata by the 30-year-old English operetta composer Hubert BATH, containing in the score some onomatopoeic sounds descriptive of the bustle and commotion of a large railway in operation, is performed for the first time by the Great Eastern Railway Musical Society in London.

11 MARCH 1914

Hashish, symphonic poem by the Russian composer Sergei LIAPUNOV, illustrating the vividly sensual visions of lissome oriental beauties seductively disporting themselves in serpentine chromatics induced by the smoking of hashish, is performed for the first time in St. Petersburg.

21 APRIL 1914

Luigi RUSSOLO, Futurist composer, inventor of *Intonarumori* (intonators of noises), presents in Milan the first performance of his bruitistic *Networks of Noises*. (The first public demonstration of *Intonarumori* as an instrumental medium was given by Russolo in Modena on 2 June 1913) The program of the first concert of 4 *Networks of Noises* comprised the following works: (1) *The Awakening of the Capital* (2) *A Meeting of Automobiles and Airplanes* (3) *A Dinner on the Terrace of the Casino* (4) *A Skirmish in an Oasis*. Russolo conducted the orchestra composed of 19 bruiteurs:

3 bumblers	2 exploders	2 gurglers
3 thunderers	3 whistlers	2 rufflers
1 fracasseur	2 stridors	1 snorer

There was an enormous crowd. Boxes, the orchestra and balcony seats were filled to capacity. A deafening uproar of "passéistes" greeted us. They arrived with the express purpose of interrupting the concert at all costs. For an hour, the Futurists offered passive resistance. But an extraordinary thing happened just at the start of *Network of Noise No. 4*: five Futurists—Boccioni, Carra, Amando Mazza, Piatti and myself—descended from the stage, crossed the orchestra pit, and, right in the center of the hall, using their fists and canes, attacked the "passéistes," who appeared to be stultified and intoxicated with reactionary rage. The battle lasted fully half an hour. During all this time Luigi Russolo continued to conduct imperturbably the nineteen bruiteurs on the stage. It was a display of an amazing harmonic arrangement of bloody faces and dissonances, an infernal mêlée. Our previous battles took place in the streets or backstage after the performance. For the first time on this occasion the performing artists were suddenly divided into two groups: one group continued to play, while the other went down into the hall to combat the hostile and rioting audience. It is thus that an escort in the desert protects the caravan against the Touaregs. It is thus that the infantry sharpshooters provide cover for the construction of a military pontoon. Our skill in boxing and our fighting spirit enabled us to emerge from the skirmish with but a few bruises. But the "passéistes" suffered eleven wounded, who had to be taken to a first-aid station for treatment. (F. T. Marinetti, *L'Intransigeant*, Paris, 29 April 1914)

Real battles took place during my concerts. The incomprehension of the very serious principles underlying my music on the part of the public and the critics was exasperating. Only a few musicians of stature—among them Ravel and Stravinsky—understood the value of my innovations, as yet realized only in part. The financial impossibility to do my research compelled me to discontinue my work several years ago. I regret that I did not have an occasion to give a demonstration of my instruments when I had the pleasure of meeting you in Paris, at the time you conducted concerts of modern American music there. (Letter to Nicolas Slonimsky from Luigi Russolo, dated 24 August 1934)

15 MAY 1914

Erik SATIE composes (in the morning, before breakfast) his dyspeptic *Choral inappétisant,* set in regurgitating modalities with ecclesiastical borborygmuses, concluding on a cathartic C major cadence, serving as a postlude to a series of short piano pieces under the general title *Sports et Divertissements.*

19 SEPTEMBER 1914

Camille SAINT-SAËNS publishes in *L'Écho de Paris* the first of a series of articles denouncing German art and music under the title *Germanophilie*, vehemently denouncing Wagner (whom he knew in Paris and who admired Saint-Saëns) and urging a total ban on Wagner's operas in France.

8 DECEMBER 1914

Watch Your Step, "a syncopated musical show" by Irving BERLIN, in which Giuseppe Verdi appears on the stage to protest against the syncopation of his arias, but is eventually won over to the novel zip of ragtime, is produced in New York.

1 DECEMBER 1915

The American inventor Lee DE FOREST publishes an article entitled *Audion Bulbs as Producers of Pure Musical Tones* in *The Electrical Experimenter*, in which he refers for the first time to music produced by vacuum tubes.

19 JANUARY 1916

At a meeting of the Russian cult of Abstainers in Vyritza, near Petrograd, twenty phonographs and several recordings of Bach and Beethoven are solemnly burned in a bonfire as products of "German abomination." (Date and circumstances found in the weekly *Russian Musical Gazette*, St. Petersburg, No. 3, 1916, p. 78)

21 AUGUST 1916

The Happy Ending, a play with music by Eugene HAILE, wherein a girl summons at a spiritual séance the ghost of her aviator lover fallen in aerial combat and is told that he did not suffer when he was shot down because "life was instantaneous," a "spoken opera" in which words are accompanied by the orchestra, with the melodic line calculated to follow the rhythmic verbal inflections, is produced in New York City.

10 OCTOBER 1916

K-K-K-Ka—ty, Beautiful Katy, stuttering and stammering ballad by Geoffrey O'Hara, inspired by a lady named Katy Richardson, is copyrighted in Washington. (A pedicular parody on this song, dedicated to the typhoid carrier, C-C-C-Coo—tie, *Horrible Cootie, you're the only B-B-B—Bug that I Abhor*, dedicated to the typhoid carrying *parasita vestimenti*, became popular in the American Expeditionary Force in 1918)

20 JANUARY 1917

Third Symphony by Karol SZYMANOWSKI, subtitled *Song of the Night*, in three connected movements for orchestra, chorus and tenor solo, to the words of the mystical *divan* by the Persian poet Jalal al-Din Rumi (1207–1273), with an orientalistic ambience suggested by serpentine melodic arabesques, alternating with whole-tone progressions and pedal-pointed bitonalities, ultimately reaching the firmament of celestially cerulean C major, with glissandi along the overtone series in the cellos and violas leading to a sempiternal moment of vibrant silence, is performed for the first time in Petrograd, conducted by Alexander Siloti.

22 JANUARY 1917

In a historic decision, Victor Herbert vs. the Shanley Co., Justice Oliver Wendell HOLMES of the United States Supreme Court rules that "the performance in a restaurant or hotel of a copyrighted musical composition, for the entertainment of patrons without charge for admission to hear it, infringes the exclusive right of the owner of a copyright under the act of 4 March 1909, to perform the work publicly for profit."

2 FEBRUARY 1917

The first full-fledged JAZZ BAND makes its first appearance in New York City.

The Jazz Band has hit New York at last, but just how popular it will become here is a matter that is going to be entirely in the hands of certain authorities that look after the public welfare. There is one thing that is certain, and that is that the melodies as played by the Jazz organization at Reisenweber's are quite conducive to making the dancers on the floor loosen up and go the limit in their stepping. Last Saturday night the Jazz musicians furnished the bigger part of the music for dancing at the 400 Club, and the rather "mixed" crowd that was present seemed to like it, judging from the encores that were demanded, and from the manner in which the dancers roughened up their stepping. The band carries its strongest punches in the trombone and the piccolo, the latter hitting all the blues. (*Variety*, 2 February 1917)

9 FEBRUARY 1917

Walter DAMROSCH, German-born conductor of the New York Symphony Orchestra, whose acquired Americanism was the product of his sincere devotion to the cause of democracy, lectures his mostly Germanic players at a rehearsal on the necessity of being loyal to their adoptive country.

I gave the men a lecture . . . on their patriotic duties toward the country in which they made their living. The last was necessary because a few German members objected to being made to play *America* so often, "as if they were an American orchestra." I told them plainly that that was just what we were. (From Damrosch's letter to his wife, in the archives of the Library of Congress)

7 MARCH 1917

The world's first jazz recording is issued by the Victor Company, with *Livery Stable Blues* on one side and *Dixieland Jazz Band One-Step* on the other.

8 MAY 1917

The Provisional Government of Russia, headed by Alexander Kerensky, offers to Serge KOUSSEVITZKY the position of musical director and conductor of the former Imperial Court Orchestra in Petrograd, which he accepts.

7 JUNE 1917

We Are Out for the Scalp of Mister Kaiser Man, the first of a series of 88 American Kaiser-hanging war songs, is copyrighted in Washington, to be followed by such titles as *We Will Make the Kaiser Wiser* (copyrighted 25 August 1917; several other songs used the same rhyme); *We're Going to Hang the Kaiser Under the Linden Tree* (1 October 1917); *We're Going to Whip the Kaiser* (12 November 1917); *We're Truly on Our Way to Can the Kaiser* (19 December 1917); *We're Going to Show the Kaiser the Way to Cut Up Sauerkraut* (14 March 1918); *We'll Lick the Kaiser If It Takes Us Twenty Years* (2 April 1918); *Ropin' the Kaiser* (11 April 1918); *We All Want a Separate Piece of Kaiser Bill* (16 April 1918); *I'd Like to See the Kaiser with a Lily in His Hand* (8 May 1918); *We'll Give the Stars and Stripes to the Kaiser* (15 May 1918); *We're Going to Kick the Hell Out of Will-Hell-em* (15 May 1918); *I'd Kill the Kaiser for You* (15 July 1918); *If I Only Had My Razor Under the Kaiser's Chin* (20 July 1918); *We'll Take the I Out of Kaiser* (24 July 1918); *Shoot the Kaiser* (3 August 1918); *We'll Yank the Kaiser's Moustache Down* (19 August 1918); *When We've Taken the Kaiser's Scalp* (22 August 1918); *The Kaiser's Pants Afire* (14 September 1918); *We'll Swat the Kaiser for Uncle Sam* (30 September 1918); *If I Catch That Kaiser in de Chicken Coop* (16 October 1918); and—after the Armistice—*Hang the Kaiser to a Sour Apple Tree* (23 November 1918); and *Kaiser Now Is Wiser* (16 December 1918).

13 OCTOBER 1917

The Board of Education of New York City rules that operas by German composers, being products of enemy provenance, are not to be used as subjects for school and college lectures under its jurisdiction.

29 NOVEMBER 1918

Booze, Booze, Booze, the first song of the Prohibition era, is copyrighted in Washington.

18 JUNE 1921

Luigi RUSSOLO, Italian musician and painter, conducts in Paris a concert of Futurist music with a noise orchestra, consisting of Thunderclappers, Exploders, Crashers, Splashers, Bellowers, Whistlers, Hissers, Snorters, Whisperers, Murmurers, Mutterers, Bustlers, Gurglers, Screamers, Screechers, Rustlers, Buzzers, Cracklers, Shouters, Shriekers, Groaners, Howlers, Laughers, Wheezers, and Sobbers.

14 SEPTEMBER 1921

Six centuries have passed since the formation of the first musicians' union, when 29 minstrels and 8 female jugglers banded together in Paris on 14 September 1321.

23 DECEMBER 1921

Krazy Kat, an orchestral suite from the "jazz pantomime" by John Alden CARPENTER, inspired by the famous newspaper comic strip, in which the misspelled cat, "Don Quixote and Parsifal rolled into one," is driven to madness by a bouquet of catnip presented with malice aforethought by an impudently aggressive mouse, set to music replete with jazzy inflections, constituting the first such jazzification of a piece of concert music, is performed for the first time by the Chicago Symphony Orchestra, Frederick Stock conducting.

10 JANUARY 1922

Thomas WILFRED presents in New York the first demonstration of his CLAVILUX, an instrument which throws colors on a screen according to the key struck on the keyboard, thus correlating the visual and auditory sensations.

3 AUGUST 1922

The first artificially contrived sound effect on radio is introduced at Station WGY in Schenectady with the aid of two strips of wood slapped together to imitate a door slammed in anger. (Date from an article by Lucille Fletcher in *The New Yorker*, 13 April 1940)

1 NOVEMBER 1923

Hugo GERNSBACK, Luxembourg-born inventor and science fiction writer, gives a demonstration over Radio Station WJZ in New York unveiling his STACCATO-PHONE, an electronic piano with vacuum tubes instead of strings, capable of producing the pitch of all 88 notes of the keyboard.

8 MAY 1924

Angel MENCHACA, Paraguayan-born music theorist who invented a keyboard with the black keys sloping towards the white keys so as to make the playing of chromatic scales more comfortable, and who also devised a system of musical notation to make sight reading more uncomfortable, dies in Buenos Aires, where he served as an emigration officer, at the age of sixty-nine.

10 MAY 1925

All records for precocious musical wunderkindism are broken by the 2¼-year-old Spanish girl Giocasta CORMA (born in Barcelona on 4 February 1923), at her pub-

lic concert in a program of ten classical pieces in the Salle Mozart in Barcelona.
(Dates from *Diccionario de la Música Ilustrado*, Barcelona, 1930)

30 JANUARY 1926

The Perfect of Police in Paris decrees a ban on jazzing up the *Marseillaise* by dance
hall bands.

3 JUNE 1926

Préface au Livre de Vie, the initial fragment of the pantheistic *Livre de Vie* by the
Russian expatriate Nicolas OBOUHOV, scored for orchestra, two pianos and four
soloists, making use of shrieking and hissing sounds to express religious ecstasy, is
performed for the first time in public, at a Koussevitzky concert in Paris, with the
composer and Nicolas Slonimsky playing the piano parts.

1 NOVEMBER 1926

Der Krämerspiegel, a self-satirizing musical pastiche written for the amusement of
friends by Richard STRAUSS, in which themes and phrases from his symphonic and
operatic works collide and recoil in witty counterpoint, to a set of texts attacking
various music publishers for their mercenary attitude towards composers (hence
the title, *A Mirror for Merchants*), is performed for the first time at a semi-private
gathering in Berlin.

13 DECEMBER 1927

The Bromberg Jazz Orchestra in Warsaw, Poland, establishes the world's endurance
record by playing thirty-three hours and ten minutes, with only forty-five seconds'
intermission between the numbers, bettering the previous record by two hours.

10 AUGUST 1928

In a public address Mustafa KEMAL PASHA, the founder of modern Turkey, urges
the adoption of Western dances and jazz to relieve the traditional homophony
and rhythmic indeterminacy of Turkish folk music.

18 JANUARY 1929

The Path of October, the first collective symphonic work by nine Soviet composers: Victor BIELY, Henrik BRUCK, Alexander DAVIDENKO, Marian KOVAL, Zara
LEVINA, Sergei RIAUSOV, Vladimir TARNOPOLSKY, Nicolai TCHEMBERDZHI and Boris
SCHEKHTER, all members of the Production Collective (Procoll), is performed for
the first time in Moscow.

19 JANUARY 1929

Ernst KRENEK's "jazz opera" *Jonny Spielt Auf* is produced in English for the first
time at the Metropolitan Opera in New York, with the role of the miscegenating
Negro bandleader performed by a black-faced white singer in deference to the
segregationist susceptibilities of patrons from the southern states.

8 JUNE 1929

Neues vom Tage, journalistic 'Gebrauchsoper' in three acts by Paul HINDEMITH,
wherein a married couple performs a Hate Duet, the chorus sings a Divorce
March, and, in the second act, the wife takes a naked bath in her hotel room in
the presence of witnesses and a detective impersonating a lover to establish a case
of adultery, with a number of other news items, including stenographers taking
atonal dictation in dissonant counterpoint, typewriters clicking in asymmetric
rhythms, etc., is performed for the first time in Berlin.

28 JULY 1929

At the concluding concert of the *Musiktage* in Baden-Baden, a *Hörspiel* ("hearing play," i.e. a radio cantata), entitled *Lindberghflug*, with music by Kurt WEILL and Paul HINDEMITH, to the text by Bertolt Brecht, is performed for the first time, illustrating the realistic and surrealistic aspects of Lindbergh's transatlantic solo flight of 21 May 1927.

28 NOVEMBER 1929

The First Airphonic Suite by Joseph SCHILLINGER, written for the electronic instrument Thereminovox and orchestra, is performed for the first time anywhere in Cleveland, with its Russian inventor Leon Theremin, as the soloist, manipulating the instrument by the wave of the hand, to and fro, thus changing the heterodyne frequency and producing the desired tone.

1 NOVEMBER 1931

The first piece in *Klavarskribo* notation, based on the tablature principle with the position of each note indicated on the diagram of the piano keyboard, is published in Slikkerveer, near Rotterdam, Holland. (Klavarskribo is the Esperanto word for piano writing. The idea was worked out by C. Pot between 1905 and 1931, and copyrighted on 6 September 1933. A similar method was proposed earlier by Gustave Neuhaus in his book *Zur Einführung in die Neuhaussche Notenschrift Natürliches Notensystem*, published in Nuremberg in 1906. Richard Zeiler published several works in this notation in 1906)

15 MARCH 1933

The Berlin Radio issues an absolute ban on broadcasting of "Negro Jazz."

15 MAY 1934

Nicolas OBOUHOV, Russian expatriate composer and religious mystic, who has adopted the signature "Nicholas l'Illuminé," presents in Paris the first demonstration of the *Croix Sonore*, an electronic musical instrument in the form of a cross, in a program of his works designed to accomplish a theosophic synthesis of divinity by means of demiurgic aggregations of twelve chromatic notes in a non-dodecaphonic order and to achieve instant communication on a telepathic musical wavelength with the extra-terrestrial intelligences of the Spiritus Mundi.

14 SEPTEMBER 1936

The first music typewriter is patented in Berlin under the trade name *Nototyp Rundstatler*, possessing 44 keys in four rows: (1) upper row: clefs, numerals for time signatures, sharps, flats and bar lines (2) second row: notes on the staff up to the third line (3) third row: notes above the middle line (4) lowest row: stems. (Rests, dots, crescendo, diminuendo, etc. are distributed among all four rows)

13 JANUARY 1938

Maurice MARTENOT takes out the patent No. 841,128 for a microtonal keyboard of his electronic instrument ONDES MUSICALES, which can produce 1/12 tones, constructed especially to approximate the intervallic scale of the Hindu *ragas*.

10 MARCH 1940

The first American television broadcast of an operatic work takes place in New York, presenting a condensed version of Leoncavallo's opera *Pagliacci* performed by members of the Metropolitan Opera Company.

1 FEBRUARY 1941

Under the megadollar threat of a lawsuit for the infringement of copyright, Western Union and Postal Telegraph discontinue the use of the song *Happy Birthday to You* in their telephoned "singing telegrams," upon the disconcerting discovery that the tune, with the original words *Good Morning Dear Teacher*, is taken from *Song Stories for the Kindergarten* by the sisters Patty S. and Mildred J. HILL, copyrighted by Clayton F. Summy Publishing Company of Chicago.

1 MARCH 1941

Seth FLINT, the bugler who played the bugle call marking the end of the Civil War, at Appomattox on 9 April 1865, dies at Worcester, New York, at the age of ninety-three.

18 NOVEMBER 1942

A millennium has elapsed since the death of Odo DE CLUGNY, the Benedictine monk who expanded the hexachordal system of the ancients into a continuous diatonic scale from A to G, and formulated the distinction between B-flat (*b rotundum*, so named from its shape, and later developed into the modern flat sign) and B natural (*b quadratum* which evolved into the modern natural sign).

1 JUNE 1943

To circumvent the prohibition by the Nazi authorities in occupied Paris to play music by Darius MILHAUD as a non-Aryan Frenchman making his home in America, Milhaud's *Scaramouche* for two pianos is performed by two Aryan French pianists at the École Normale de Musique in Paris, anagrammatically programmed as Mous-Arechac by Hamid-al-Usurid.

1 MARCH 1944

Hans KRÁSA, 44-year-old Prague-born Jewish composer of finely wrought music sensitized by anguished atonalities, perishes in the Nazi concentration camp at Auschwitz.

8 APRIL 1945

At the approach of the final hour of Nazidämmerung, the Austrian conductor Leopold REICHSWEIN, one of the few musicians who was lured by the opportunities for individual and racial aggrandizement offered by the Nazi doctrine, kills himself in Vienna.

21 MAY 1946

Central Park in the Dark by Charles IVES, written in 1906, is performed for the first time at Columbia University, New York. It is in three-part form, with strings maintaining the dreamy shimmering of the dark, in intervallic columns, first in major thirds (forming whole-tone harmonies), then in quartal structures, then in tritones overlapped by fifths, then in pure quintal harmonies, while the middle section erupts in shrill sounds of the youthful revelry contrasted with the still continuing lyric reverie. (A forgotten performance of the piece was given about 1907. Ives wrote in a hasty note: "*Central Park* was played between the acts in a downtown theater in New York, in 1906 or 1907. The players had a hard time with it—the piano player got mad, stopped in the middle, and kicked in the bass drum. However it would be hardly fair to those old fellers who stood up for a dangerous job to say this was the first performance. The present 1946 performance was the first." An alternative title was *A Contemplation of Nothing Serious, or Central Park in the Dark in the Good Old Summer Time*.)

13 MAY 1948

The Hospital, musico-medical suite for orchestra by Dr. Herman M. PARRIS of Philadelphia, portraying a young woman's appendectomy in ten prophylactic vivisections, introducing a smiling nurse (*Allegro e amabile*), anxious intensive care (*Andantino*), the operating room (*Allegro*, realistically followed by *Molto agitato*) and anesthesia (*Presto*), set to music in an impartially bland idiom, imitative of Handel, Tchaikovsky and Gershwin, is performed for the first time by the Doctors' Orchestral Society in New York.

3 SEPTEMBER 1949

Charles KELLOGG, "California Nature Singer," reputed to be able to reproduce the song of any bird, thanks to his congenitally ornithomorphic syrinx in addition to the normal larynx (his tessitura encompassed $12\frac{1}{2}$ octaves, reaching into the ultrasonic range beyond 14,000 cycles), dies at the age of 80 at Morgan Hill, California. (On 6 September 1926 he broadcast a shrill note over radio station KGO, which extinguished a candle in Hawaii and a chemical flame on the Berkeley campus of the University of California, where the test was made)

8 SEPTEMBER 1950

An organ based on the division of the octave into 31 unequal degrees, originally proposed for acoustical reasons by the celebrated Dutch astronomer Christiaan HUYGENS (1629–1695) in his *Nouveau Cycle Harmonique*, in which the smallest interval is $\frac{1}{5}$ of a tone, a system which permits sounds to be produced in pure Pythagorean intonation as well as in the traditional scales of tempered semitones, is demonstrated for the first time in Rotterdam.

5 APRIL 1961

Len LYE demonstrates at the Museum of Modern Art in New York his tangible motion sculptures creating their own musical compositions through incidental collisions of rods and rings and music-box flanges attached to them.

6 MARCH 1964

The Swedish pianist Karl-Erik Welin wounds himself in the knee with a power saw during the Stockholm performance of an enhanced piano piece by Knut WIGGEN requiring the explosion of a pyrotechnical device purporting to be a charge of dynamite and sawing off the legs of the piano preliminary to working over the keyboard with the intention of demolishing it, too. (Welin's knee injury was not grave, and the prognosis excellent. Because of his failure to operate the power saw properly, the Swedish music critic Sten Broman suggested the incorporation of classes in power saw handling at the Stockholm High School of Music.)

24 APRIL 1964

The Swiss Exposition of Industry opens in Lausanne, architecturally reflecting the modern world in its wall-less Pavillon Échange, with the world première of *Les Échanges* by Rolf LIEBERMANN, scored for 52 machines, including teletypes, cash registers, staplers and copying devices, timed by an electronic computer to last exactly 195 seconds.

17 SEPTEMBER 1966

TIS-MW-2, a metamusical audio-visual spectacle by the 37-year-old Polish modernist Boguslaw SCHÄFFER, to a non-ontological alogical oneirological scenario for an illusory narrator reciting a series of discrete surrealistic fragments of irrationally oriented non-temporal events to the accompaniment of an indeterminate instrumental ensemble, with demoniac illuminations scintillating in sudden silences, anguished outcries, implosive borborigmuses and choreic singultations, is performed for the first time in the course of the 10th International Festival of Contemporary Music in Warsaw ("Warsaw Autumn").

20 NOVEMBER 1967

Smell Piece for Mills College for frying pans and foods by the intransigently radical 30-year-old American avant-garde composer Robert MORAN, originally intended to produce a conflagration sufficiently thermal to burn down the college, is performed for the first time at Mills College in Oakland, California.

1 JUNE 1969

Rosemary BROWN, middle-aged British housewife and amateur pianist, gives the first performance, televised by the British Broadcasting Corporation Television Studio, of a *Moment Musical* for piano by Franz SCHUBERT, composed by him in 1969 and transmitted to her by posthumous telepathy. (A number of piano pieces by BACH, MOZART, BEETHOVEN, CHOPIN, LISZT, BRAHMS, DEBUSSY and RACHMANINOFF were similarly dictated to her at various times, proving that a prolonged state of death fatally affects the sense of elementary harmony even among musicians once known for their unerring skill in composition)

3 FEBRUARY 1972

The Natural Sound Workshop, founded by Kirk NUROCK and dedicated to the artistic exploration of bodily sounds, presents its first public performance in Greenwich Village in New York, with a group of naturally sounding men and women belching, burping, farting, hard breathing, regurgitating, sneezing, talking with mouths full, moaning, groaning, yowling, whistling, erupting in polyglot glossolalia, babbling, gabbling, blowing, singing while inhaling air, audibly stretching limbs and pandiculating, shaking, vibrating, lip-fluttering, tongue-clicking, snapping fingers, clapping hands, slapping exposed flesh, cracking bones, murmuring, mumbling, imitating animal sounds, rolling thighs, profusely salivating in chromatic tremolos, gargling, gurgling, gnashing teeth, making dental glissandos, sibilating, sighing, grunting, coughing, choking, gagging, cackling, giggling, cooing, tittering, yawning, cachinnating, whimpering, whining, shouting, screaming, chanting, bouncing, humping and somersaulting.

9 FEBRUARY 1973

Kyldex I (abbreviation of Kybernetischluminodynamische Experimente) by the prime apostle of concrete music Pierre HENRY, set for five electronically activated erotic sculptures, human dancers, fifteen programmed audiovisual sequences of variable durations determined by audience reaction, nine light-effect complexes, stroboscopic projections and a striptease (da capo ad lib.), extracurricularly accompanied by recorded dog barks and various assorted animal and human eructations, is produced in Hamburg.

21 SEPTEMBER 1975

The Young Penis Symphony (*a.k.a. First Symphonie*) by the Korean composer Nam June PAIK is performed for the first time in San Francisco by a cast of ten young (and not so young) penises protruded through a Japanese rice paper curtain, followed by a female sequel, *La Mamelle* (*The Young Breast Symphony*), composed by Ken FRIEDMAN, and featuring a pair of protruding mammary glands.

24 SEPTEMBER 1975

Lowell CROSS presents in Iowa City the total realization of SCRIABIN's symphonic poem *Prometheus*, including the mystic part for color organ (*luce*) on a specially designed electronic keyboard which coordinates color projections to accompany changes of pitch in the score, with James Dixon conducting the University of Iowa Symphony Orchestra.

24 APRIL 1976

Music for Eighteen Musicians for violin, cello, two clarinets, four pianos, four female voices, three marimbas, two xylophones and a metallaphone by the 39-year-old American composer Steve REICH, who unintentionally became the guru of modern minimalism by extracting a maximum effect from a minimum of musical material, is performed for the first time in New York.

6 MAY 1976

Concerto for Bassoon and Low Strings in five movements by the remarkable 44-year-old Soviet composer Sofia GUBAIDULINA, of ethnic Tatar origin, in which the bassoon indulges in audacious acrobatic feats of atonal saltation with tricky trills, transcendental tremolos, labial glissandos and shrieks and laughter through the tube, accompanied by four cellos and three double-basses in a visuviation of euphonious discords deployed over their entire diapason, is presented for the first time in the Hall of the Union of Soviet Composers in Moscow, with Valery Popov as soloist in a prescribed series of salto mortale virtuosity.

5 AUGUST 1978

At a meeting of citizens of Parowan, Utah, it is resolved to name a local mountain Mt. Messiaen, in honor of the French composer Olivier MESSIAEN, who spent a month in Utah in 1973 and wrote a symphonic work, *Des Canyons aux étoiles*, to glorify the natural beauty of the state.

11 OCTOBER 1990

Sotheby's of New York hosts an auction of the "Property from the Estate of Virgil THOMSON" at which the contents of the composer's ninth-floor apartment at the historic Chelsea Hotel (where he lived for more than half a century) are sold for the benefit of the Virgil Thomson Foundation, Ltd. Among the most covetted items were a fine black silk brocade vest belonging to Gertrude Stein ($18,000) and an art deco ebonized wood and chrome dining table, reputedly "Shanghai-ed" from the basement of the apartment of *Modern Music* magazine pioneer Minna Ledermann and her husband Mell Daniel, which hosted legendary meals for some of the twentieth-century's most illustrious cultural figures ($6,500). Also included in the sale were Thomson's American Rococo Revival walnut bedstead ($1,100), in which much of his post–World War II music was composed, a collection of 43 (many first) edition works by Gertrude Stein ($14,000), some bearing personal inscriptions by the poet, and numerous paintings by the composer's lifetime companion, Maurice Grosser.

20 MARCH 1991

The U.S.S.R. Radio-Television Concert Orchestra gives the first concert in its history of works devoted entirely to a living American composer, the 65-year-old Kirke MECHEM, in a program that includes his overture *The Jayhawk* and *Symphonies Nos. 1* and 2, conducted by the American conductor Corrick Brown and performed in the historic Hall of Columns, simultaneously broadcast throughout the U.S.S.R.

"STAR-SPANGLED STRAVINSKY," FROM *A THING OR TWO ABOUT MUSIC*

This comes from A Thing or Two About Music *(1948), which ought to be reissued as* Slonimsky's Book of Musical Anecdotes.

Few musicians realize that according to law they can be arrested for playing sour notes in *The Star-Spangled Banner*. Stravinsky found that out, much to his discomfiture, when he conducted his own arrangement of the national anthem in a concert with the Boston Symphony Orchestra in January 1944. His arrangement adheres generally to the established tonality, but there are some contrapuntal countersubjects and toward the end a modulatory digression into the subdominant is introduced by means of a passing seventh, commonly known as a blue note. Stravinsky declared: "Searching about for a vehicle through which I might best express my gratitude at becoming an American citizen, I chose to harmonize and orchestrate as a national chorale the beautiful sacred anthem, *The Star-Spangled Banner*. It is a desire to do my bit in these grievous times toward fostering and preserving the spirit of patriotism in this country that inspires me to tender this, my humble work, to the American people."

The American people, however, seemed little appreciative. After the first rendition of the embellished anthem, at least one person among those present made a telephone call to the Boston police. The constables, at first perplexed by the necessity of appearing as a jury on musical matters, dug up a statute in the law books which clearly states:

> Whoever plays, sings, or renders *The Star-Spangled Banner* in any public place, theater, motion picture hall, restaurant or café, or at any public entertainment other than as a whole and separate composition or number, without embellishment or addition in the way of national or other melodies, or whoever plays, sings, or renders *The Star Spangled Banner* or any part thereof as dance music, as an exit march, or as a part of a medley of any kind shall be punished by a fine of not more than one hundred dollars.

On the night of the second concert, with Stravinsky conducting, a squad of twelve policemen, including a captain and a sergeant, joined the symphony audience, all set to arrest Stravinsky in case of any infringement on the statutory harmonies. Before the concert got under way, the captain remarked: "Let him change it just once, and we'll grab him." Fortunately Stravinsky was forewarned, and when he launched into *The Star-Spangled Banner*, the harmonies were all serene. The police did not stay to hear the rest of the program.

"Songs of World War II," from *A Thing or Two About Music*

In contrast with the First World War when the production of warlike songs was a major industry, the Second World War did not lend itself to singing mobilization. There was general skepticism concerning the potential contribution of Tin Pan Alley to the nation's morale. In its issue of December 29, 1941, *Time* magazine dismissed the warlike ditties of Broadway's songsmiths in a sweeping survey under the caption, "Of Thee I Sing, Baby." It reported that 260 titles were submitted to music publishers in the three days after Pearl Harbor, in which the alliterations "nasty Nazis" and the rhymes "sap" and "Jap" were recurring devices. A typical song was *You're a Sap, Mister Jap*, with a cover in red showing Uncle Sam spanking a midget-like Jap with the butt of his rifle. A song entitled *The Japs Won't Have a Chinaman's Chance* went into production but was stopped when someone pointed out that the title was disrespectful to the Chinese. The best rhyme among the anti-Jap titles was *To Be Specific, It's Our Pacific*.

The anti-Nazi songs were weak echoes of the blood-thirsty Kaiser-hanging songs of the First World War. There was the half-hearted *Marching to Berlin and to Tokyo* and *When the Yanks Go Marching In*. There was nothing as masculine as the World War I song, *If He Can Fight Like He Can Love, Then Good Night Germany*. Instead, the soldiers preferred sentimental songs such as *White Christmas* (with the inevitable variation, in the South Pacific, "I'm Dreaming of a White Mistress").

Because of the development of radio broadcasting, World War II witnessed a phenomenon that was highly disturbing to the song industry. Enemy songs were picked up on the radio by Allied soldiers. Such was the case of *Lili Marlene*, a German love song composed by Norbert Schultze to a poem by one Hans Leip. The song was written before the war, in 1938, and was entitled *The Lantern Song*. It was sung in Berlin night clubs by a Swedish singer named Lala Andersen, but attracted little attention. After the Nazi invasion of Yugoslavia, a recording of the song was played repeatedly by the Germans over the Belgrade radio station simply because it happened to be one of the few records available. The broadcast was relayed to Italy and to North Africa, and the song caught on, both with the German and the Allied Armies. Goering's wife sang *Lili Marlene*, and fan mail included a letter from the crew of a German submarine dated "Somewhere off New York Harbor," and stating, "Tonight we tuned in softly in order not to wake up Uncle Sam."

The composer Schultze, encouraged by his sudden leap into popularity, contributed two more songs, *Bomber auf Engelland* and *Panzer rollen in Africa vor*.

Unfortunately for him, the bombers were now heard more often over Germany than over England, and the Panzers were rolling in Africa in the wrong direction.

The British took cognizance of the tremendous appeal of *Lili Marlene* in the British Army and produced a film under the title, *The True Story of Lili Marlene*. In it, the original performer of the song was pictured languishing in a concentration camp, and the song was cleverly represented as being anti-Nazi in spirit.

Norbert Schultze turned up safe and sound in the American zone in Berlin in November 1946, working as a gardener on a community vegetable plot. He was also giving piano lessons to musically inclined American soldiers. Shifting his loyalties, he wrote a Military Police march in collaboration with an American lieutenant-colonel. He explained away the composition of his earlier march, *Bombs over England*, as an unfortunate accident. "I just wrote the music for an Air Force documentary film," he told the Americans, "but Goering liked it so much he took it over for propaganda purposes."

The first anti-Hitler song was written in England before the start of official hostilities. It was an innocent ditty entitled *Even Hitler Had a Mother*. The song was scheduled for performance in London, in a musical revue which was to open on April 20, 1939, but the Lord Chamberlain banned the song as an insult to the head of a foreign nation. When it was allowed for public performance in September 1939, the events were too grim for so mild a production, and the song quickly faded away.

Equally ephemeral was another British war song, *We're Gonna Hang Out the Washing on the Siegfried Line if the Siegfried Line's Still There*. It was written on September 11, 1939, by Jimmy Kennedy and Michael Carr and published four days later. So remote seemed the consummation of its promise in the title that the Nazis sang it in derision in the Paris night clubs after the fall of France. Such was the irony of events that when the Allied Armies did reach the Siegfried Line during the last stages of the war, they did not stop long enough for the laundry to be washed and hung there.

The song that really stirred the hearts of Englishmen during the darkest period of the Battle for Britain was one of general import, *There'll Always Be an England*. It was written in March, 1939, by the thirty-three-year-old Hughie Charles, to the words by Ross Parker. Incidentally, the real name of the lyric writer was Michael Ross. He changed it to Ross Parker in conformity with the rule in the entertainment industry that there should be an "R" in the first and the last names of actors, singers, and musicians.

The only anti-Hitler song produced on this side of the Atlantic that had any popular success was *Der Führer's Face*. It was originally featured in the Walt Disney production, *In Nutsy Land*, in which Donald Duck lampooned the "nutsy" Nazis in heavily Germanized English, in which the letter "v" replaced "w," and "f" was substituted for "v."

The industry was pessimistic about war songs. *Downbeat*, in its issue of February 15, 1942, stated: "Half-baked war songs won't build morale. If we must have war songs let's have good ones." In the February 1, 1943 issue of the same magazine, Glenn Miller, the band leader, wrote: "This war won't produce an *Over There*." A monthly magazine entitled *Hit-Kit*, the organ of the Special Service Division, Services of Supply, published a number of songs, but the favorites were mostly revivals or such curious song phenomena as *Roll out the Barrel*, a polka written by a Bohemian musician before the war, which somehow captured the imagination of the soldiers and was sung by both the Axis and Allied Armies.

Perhaps the only spontaneously inspired war song of World War II was *Praise the Lord and Pass the Ammunition*, composed by the soldier-musician Frank

Loesser. The slogan was supposed to have been originated by Father Maguire, who was fleet chaplain for the Pacific Fleet on December 7, 1941, during the attack on Pearl Harbor. According to the lyrics of the song, he manned a gun himself after the gunner and then the gunner's mate were killed, shouting, "We got one," as he fired.

Father Maguire heard the song for the first time when he returned to the United States late in 1942. He expressed his great annoyance and stated, in an interview published in *PM* of November 1, 1942: "I did not man a gun on December 7 or at any other time in my career in the Navy. I wish to state unreservedly that the quotation, 'We got one' is false." As for the phrase, "Praise the Lord and pass the ammunition," Father Maguire admitted that he might have said it in the din of the battle. "It may have been heard by an altar-boy. I don't want to disillusion people. But in these circumstances I would probably have been more likely to use the expression, 'God help us' than 'Praise the Lord.'"

Furthermore Father Maguire remarked, "Chaplains with the armed forces are not allowed to fight." It was known that fifty-six Catholic chaplains were prisoners of the Japanese, and Father Maguire expressed his apprehension that they might be subjected to reprisals for his alleged violation of the rules of war. The facts as Father Maguire remembered them were these: He was on a pier at Pearl Harbor waiting to go in a launch to conduct Mass on a battleship, when the first Japanese planes dropped their torpedoes at 7:50 A.M. December 7. He went first to a destroyer and then to a battleship and "tried to do my duty in accord with naval regulations and international law." He heard confessions and assisted the wounded.

The first World War had its *Mademoiselle from Armentières* with its many ribald versions. The second World War produced *Dirty Gertie from Bizerte*. It is said that the Gertie song was inspired by a mannequin in a department store in Bizerte, which caught the fancy of the American soldiers during the North African campaign. The original mannequin was even photographed in the arms of the soldier who claimed to have composed the song, Sergeant Paul Reif, an experienced Broadway tunesmith. The correspondent who first broke the news about Gertie warned in his dispatch from the Allied Headquarters in North Africa, dated May 29, 1941: "Sorry folks, I can't give you the words—they might burn out the cables and blow out radio tubes. It's enough to say that it will be one of the most popular songs when the boys of this war begin holding legion meetings after it's all over. But until then, you'll just have to wait."

One of the most curious usages of music in war was the scheme of the British Broadcasting Corporation to popularize the slogan "V for Victory" in the Nazi occupied territories. In Morse Code the letter "V" is represented by three dots and a dash. This is also the rhythm of the opening notes of Beethoven's Fifth Symphony. Erika Mann, the daughter of Thomas Mann, wrote in *PM* of July 14, 1940 (and her article was published with the first two measures of the Fifth Symphony inscribed at the top): "This British 'V' Blitz will drive the enemy mad by weapons he is unable to match or even account for. Nazi concentration camps will hammer 'V' rhythm into minds of their slave drivers, and the first notes of Beethoven's Fifth will be sung by children on their way to Nazi schools, whistled in Nazi-dominated factories, played by orchestras tuning their instruments for the Nazi hymn."

In Norway, the "V" sign was often used in triplicate for the words, "ve vil vinne." Performances of Beethoven's Fifth Symphony were greeted with demonstrative applause. Then the Nazis decided to take over the "V" symbol rather than try to suppress it. Their propagandists dug up an old German word *Viktoria* and broadcast the rhythm of Beethoven's Fifth from their radio stations in occupied

Europe with an explanation by the announcer that it was "'V' for victory, which Germany is winning on all fronts."

This war of musical themes provided a necessary outlet for the population of occupied Europe. They were enabled to tease the Nazis without fear of reprisals. The songs played their role when the fronts were quiescent. But when the grim business of invasion was begun, there were no new songs to sing. The soldiers sang old Broadway hits that reminded them of home. It is by those songs that World War II is remembered in the hearts of its soldiers.

BIOGRAPHIES

The first edition of Theodore Baker's *Biographical Dictionary of Musicians* (1900) became a foundation for subsequent editions. Slonimsky took over in 1949 editing the fifth edition that appeared in 1958, adding entries on new subjects, revising those on historical figures, updating those on contemporaries. By the eighth edition (1991) *Baker's* had assumed a stylistic quality that is largely his. My contention is that nobody writes a biographical sketch that is at once informative and discriminating, concise and witty like Slonimsky. Most of the following sketches, divided into several groups organized alphabetically, comes from this most recent edition, unless otherwise identified. In a few cases, I've included earlier versions of Slonimsky's entries on particular subjects, if only to show evidence of his rethinking and re*writing*.

Entries from *Baker's*

Antheil, George (Georg Johann Carl), remarkable American composer who cut a powerful swath in the world of modern music by composing dissonant and loud pieces glorifying the age of the machine; b. Trenton, N.J., July 8, 1900; d. N.Y., Feb. 12, 1959. He studied music theory with Constantin Sternberg in Philadelphia; then went to N.Y. to take lessons in composition with Ernest Bloch. Defying the norms of flickering musical conservatism, Antheil wrote piano pieces under such provocative titles as *Sonate sauvage, Mechanisms*, and *Airplane Sonata*. In 1922 he went to Europe and gave a number of concerts featuring his own compositions as well as some impressionist music. He spent a year in Berlin and then went to Paris, which was to become his domicile for several years; he was one of the 1st American students of the legendary Nadia Boulanger, who was to be the *nourrice* of a whole generation of modernistically minded Americans. In Paris he also made contact with such great literary figures as James Joyce and Ezra Pound; in the natural course of events, Antheil became the self-styled *enfant terrible* of modern music. Naively infatuated with the new world of the modern machine, he composed a *Ballet mécanique* with the avowed intention to "épater les bourgeois." The culmination of Antheil's Paris period was marked by the performance of an orch. suite from his *Ballet mécanique* (June 19, 1926), with musical material taken from a score he wrote for a film by Fernand Léger. He then returned to America as a sort of conquering hero of modern music, and staged a spectacular production of the *Ballet mécanique* at Carnegie Hall in N.Y. on April 10, 1927, employing a set of airplane propellers, 8 pianos, and a large battery of drums, creating an uproar in the audience and much publicity in the newspapers. A revival of the *Ballet mécanique* took place in N.Y. on Feb. 20, 1954, with a recording of the noise of a jet plane replacing the obsolescent propellers, but the piece was received by the public and press as merely a curiosity of the past.

Abandoning all attempts to shock the public by extravaganza, Antheil turned to composition of operas. His 1st complete opera, *Transatlantic*, to his own libretto, portraying the turmoil attendant on the presidential election, and employing jazz rhythms, was staged on May 25, 1930, in Frankfurt, Germany, arousing a modicum of interest. Another opera, *Mr. Bloom and the Cyclops*, based on James Joyce's novel *Ulysses*, never progressed beyond fragmentary sketches. A 2nd opera, *Helen Retires*, with a libretto by John Erskine, was produced in N.Y. on Feb. 28, 1934. In 1936, Antheil moved to Hollywood, where he wrote some film music and ran a syndicated column of advice to perplexed lovers; another of his whimsical diversions was working on a torpedo device, in collaboration with the motion picture actress Hedy Lamarr; they actually filed a patent, No. 2,292,387, dated June 10, 1941, for an invention relating to a "secret communication system involving the use of carrier waves of different frequencies, especially useful in the remote control of dirigible craft, such as torpedoes." It is not known whether the Antheil-Lamarr device was ever used in naval warfare. He continued to write syms., operas, and other works, but in the spirit of the times, reduced his musical idiom to accessible masses of sound. These works were rarely performed, and in the light of musical history, Antheil remains a herald of the avant-garde of yesterday. He publ. an autobiography, *Bad Boy of Music* (N.Y., 1945). He was married to Elizabeth ("Böski") Markus, a niece of the Austrian dramatist and novelist Arthur Schnitzler; she died in 1978. Antheil was the subject of a monograph by Ezra Pound entitled *Antheil and the Treatise on Harmony, with Supplementary Notes* (Chicago, 1927), which, however, had little bearing on Antheil and even less on harmony.

Armstrong, Louis, famous black American jazz trumpeter, singer, bandleader, and entertainer, familiarly known as "Satchmo" (for "Satchel Mouth," with reference to his spacious and resonant oral cavity); b. New Orleans, probably in 1898 (there is no documentation to substantiate his claim that he was born on July 4, 1900); d. N.Y., July 6, 1971. He grew up in Storyville, New Orleans's brothel district, and in his youth was placed in the Colored Waifs' Home, where he played cornet in its brass band. After his release, he learned to play jazz in blues bands in local honky-tonks; also received pointers on cornet playing from "King" Oliver and played in "Kid" Ory's band (1918–19). In 1922 he went to Chicago to play in Oliver's Creole Jazz Band, with which he made his 1st recordings in 1923; then was a member of Fletcher Henderson's band in N.Y. (1924–25). Returning to Chicago, he organized his own jazz combo, the Hot 5, in 1925; made a series of now historic recordings with it, with the Hot 7, and with other groups he led until 1928. From about 1926 he made the trumpet his principal instrument. In 1929 he went to N.Y. again, where he became notably successful through appearances on Broadway, in films, and on radio. From 1935 to 1947 he led his own big band, and in 1947 organized his All Stars jazz combo. In succeeding years he made innumerable tours of the U.S., and also toured widely abroad. He became enormously successful as an entertainer; made many television appearances and several hit recordings, including his best-selling version of *Hello, Dolly* in 1964. Although he suffered a severe heart attack in 1959, he continued to make appearances until his death. Armstrong was one of the greatest figures in the history of jazz and one of the most popular entertainers of his time. His style of improvisation revolutionized jazz performance in the 1920s. His unique gravelly-voiced renditions of jazz and popular songs became as celebrated as his trumpet virtuosity. He was married 4 times. In 1924 he married his 2nd wife, the jazz pianist Lil(lian) Hardin (b. Memphis, Tenn., Feb. 3, 1898; d. while playing in a memorial concert for Armstrong in Chicago, Aug. 27, 1971), who was the pianist for both Oliver and Armstrong in Chicago; they divorced in 1938. Armstrong publ. *Swing the Music* (N.Y., 1936) and *Satchmo: My Life in New Orleans* (N.Y., 1954).

Bach is the name of the illustrious German family which, during 2 centuries, gave to the world a number of musicians and composers of distinction. History possesses few records of such remarkable examples of hereditary art, which culminated in the genius of Johann Sebastian Bach. In the Bach genealogy, the primal member was Johannes or Hans Bach, who is mentioned in 1561 as a guardian of the municipality of Wechmar, a town near Gotha. Also residing in Wechmar was his relative **Veit Bach**; a baker by trade, he was also skillful in playing on a small cittern. Another relative, **Caspar Bach**, who lived from 1570 to 1640, was a Stadtpfeifer in Gotha who later served as a town musician in Arnstadt. His 5 sons,

Caspar, Johannes, Melchior, Nicolaus, and Heinrich, were all town musicians. Another Bach, **Johann(es Hans) Bach** (1550–1626), was known as "der Spielmann," that is, "minstrel," and thus was definitely described as primarily a musician by vocation. His 3 sons, **Johann(es Hans), Christoph,** and **Heinrich,** were also musicians. J.S. Bach took great interest in his family history, and in 1735 prepared a genealogy under the title *Ursprung der musicalisch-Bachischen Familie. The Bach Reader,* compiled by H. David and A. Mendel (N.Y., 1945; rev. ed., 1966), contains extensive quotations from this compendium. Karl Geiringer's books *The Bach Family: Seven Generations of Creative Genius* (N.Y., 1954) and *Music of the Bach Family: An Anthology* (Cambridge, Mass., 1955) give useful genealogical tables of Bach's family. Bach's father, **Johann Ambrosius,** was a twin brother of Bach's uncle; the twins bore such an extraordinary physical resemblance that, according to the testimony of Carl Philipp Emanuel Bach, their own wives had difficulty telling them apart after dark. To avoid confusion, they had them wear vests of different colors. A vulgar suggestion that because of this similarity Bach may have been begotten by his uncle is too gross to require a refutation.

When the family became numerous and widely dispersed, its members agreed to assemble on a fixed date each year. Erfurt, Eisenach, and Arnstadt were the places chosen for these meetings, which are said to have continued until the middle of the 18th century, as many as 120 persons of the name of Bach then assembling. At these meetings, a cherished pastime was the singing of "quodlibets," comic polyphonic potpourris of popular songs. An amusing example attributed to J.S. Bach is publ. in *Veröffentlichungen der Neuen Bach-Gesellschaft* (vol. XXXII, 2).

Bach, Johann Sebastian, supreme arbiter and lawgiver of music, a master comparable in greatness of stature with Aristotle in philosophy and Leonardo da Vinci in art; b. Eisenach, March 21 (baptized, March 23), 1685; d. Leipzig, July 28, 1750. He was a member of an illustrious family of musicians who were active in various capacities as performing artists, composers, and teachers. That so many Bachs were musicians lends support to the notion that music is a hereditary faculty, that some subliminal cellular unit may be the nucleus of musicality. The word "Bach" itself means "stream" in the German language; the rhetorical phrase that Johann Sebastian Bach was not a mere stream but a whole ocean of music ("Nicht Bach aber Meer haben wir hier") epitomizes Bach's encompassing magnitude. Yet despite the grandeur of the phenomenon of Bach, he was not an isolated figure dwelling in the splendor of his genius apart from the zeitgeist, the spirit of his time. Just as Aristotle was not only an abstract philosopher but also an educator (Alexander the Great was his pupil), just as Leonardo da Vinci was not only a painter of portraits but also a practical man of useful inventions, so Bach was a mentor to young students, a master organist and instructor who spent his life within the confines of his native Thuringia as a teacher and composer of works designed for immediate performance in church and in the schoolroom. Indeed, the text of the dedication of his epoch-making work *Das wohltemperierte Clavier oder Praeludia und Fugen* emphasizes its pedagogical aspect: "The Well-tempered Clavier, or Preludes and Fugues in all tones and semitones, both with the major third of Ut Re Mi, and the minor third of Re Mi Fa, composed and notated for the benefit and exercise of musical young people eager to learn, as well as for a special practice for those who have already achieved proficiency and skill in this study." The MS is dated 1722. Bach's system of "equal temperament" (which is the meaning of "well-tempered" in the title *Well-tempered Clavier*) postulated the division of the octave into 12 equal semitones, making it possible to transpose and to effect a modulation into any key, a process unworkable in the chaotic tuning of keyboard instruments before Bach's time. Bach was not the 1st to attempt the tempered division, however. J.C.F. Fischer anticipated him in his collection

Ariadne musica (with the allusion to the thread of Ariadne that allowed Theseus to find his way out of the Cretan labyrinth); publ. in 1700, it contained 20 preludes and fugues in 19 different keys. Undoubtedly Bach was aware of this ed.; actually, the subjects of several of Bach's preludes and fugues are similar to the point of identity to the themes of Fischer's work. These coincidences do not detract from the significance of Bach's accomplishment, for it is the beauty and totality of development that makes Bach's work vastly superior to those of any of his putative predecessors.

It is interesting to note that Bach shared the belief in numerical symbolism held by many poets and artists of his time. By summing up the cardinal numbers corresponding to the alphabetical order of the letters of his last name, he arrived at the conclusion that the number 14 had a special significance in his life (B = 2, A = 1, C = 3, H = 8; 2 + 1 + 3 + 8 = 14). That the number of buttons on his waistcoat in one of his portraits is 14 may be an indication of the significance he attached to this number. The theme of Bach's chorale *Von deinen Thron tret' ich hiermit*, which he wrote shortly before his death, contains 14 notes, while the notes in the entire melody number 43, comprising the sum total of the alphabetical index of letters in J.S. Bach (10 + 19 + 2 + 1 + 3 + 8 = 43). In Bach's chorale prelude *Wenn wir in höchsten Nöten sein*, the principal melody contains 166 notes, which represents the alphabetical sum of the full name JOHANN SEBASTIAN BACH (10 + 15 + 8 + 1 + 14 + 14 + 19 + 5 + 2 + 1 + 19 + 20 + 9 + 1 + 14 + 2 + 1 + 3 + 8 = 166). The symbolism of melodies and harmonies in Baroque music, expressing various states of mind, joy or sadness, has been accepted as a valid "doctrine of affects" by musical philosophers, among them Albert Schweitzer. Indeed, there seems to be little doubt that a natural connection exists between such a line as "Geh' auf! Geh' auf!" and an ascending major arpeggio in a Bach cantata, or that, generally speaking, major modes represent joy and exhilaration, and minor keys suggest melancholy and sadness. We find numerous instances in the choral works of Baroque composers of the use of a broken diminished-seventh-chord in a precipitous downward movement to depict the fall from grace and regression to Hell. The chromatic weaving around a thematic tone often represents in Bach's cantatas and Passions the thorny crown around the head of Jesus Christ. An ascending scale of several octaves, sung by basses, tenors, altos, and sopranos in succession, is found to accompany the words "We follow you." A hypothesis may be advanced that such tonal patterns were used by Baroque composers to facilitate the comprehension of the meaning of the text by the congregation in church performances. Indeed, such word painting has become an accepted procedure in the last 2 or 3 centuries; composers equated major keys with joy and virtue, and minor keys with melancholy and sin. Similarly, fast tempos and duple time are commonly used by composers to express joy, while slow movements are reserved for scenes of sadness.

The term "Baroque" had a humble origin; it was probably derived from *barroco*, the Portuguese word for a deformed pearl; originally it had a decidedly negative meaning, and was often applied in the 17th century to describe a corrupt style of Renaissance architecture. Through the centuries the word underwent a change of meaning toward lofty excellence. In this elevated sense, "Baroque" came to designate an artistic development between the years 1600 and 1800. The advent of Bach marked the greatest flowering of Baroque music; his name became a synonym for perfection. Max Reger was told by Hugo Riemann that he could be the 2nd Bach, and his skill in composition almost justified his aspiration; Ferruccio Busoni was described by his admirers as the Bach of the modern era; a similar honor was claimed for Hindemith by his disciples. Yet the art of Bach remains unconquerable. Although he wrote most of his contrapuntal works as a didactic exercise, there are in his music extraordinary visions into the remote future; consider, for instance, the A-minor Fugue of the 1st book of the *Well-tempered Clavier*, in which the inversion of the subject seems to violate all the rules of proper voice-leading in its bold leap from the tonic upward to the 7th of the scale and then up a third. The answer to the subject of the F minor Fugue of the 1st book suggests the chromatic usages of later centuries. In the art of variations, Bach was supreme. A superb example is his set of keyboard pieces known as the *Goldberg Variations*, so named because it was commissioned by the Russian diplomat Kayserling through the mediation of Bach's pupil Johann Gottlieb Goldberg, who was in Kayserling's service as a harpsichord player. These variations are listed by Bach as the 4th part of the *Clavier-Übung*; the didactic title of this division is characteristic of Bach's intention to write music for utilitarian purposes, be it for keyboard exercises, for church services, or for chamber music. A different type of Bach's great musical projections is exemplified by his *Concerts à plusieurs instruments*, known popularly as the *Brandenburg Concertos*, for they were dedicated to Christian Ludwig, margrave of Brandenburg. They represent the crowning achievement of the Baroque. Nos. 2, 4, and 5 of the *Brandenburg Concertos* are essentially concerti grossi, in which a group of solo instruments—the concertino—is contrasted with the accompanying string orch. Finally, *Die Kunst der Fuge*, Bach's last composition, which he wrote in 1749, represents an encyclopedia of fugues, canons, and various counterpoints based on the same theme. Here Bach's art of purely technical devices, such as inversion, canon, augmentation, diminution, double fugue, triple fugue, at times appearing in fantastic optical symmetry so that the written music itself forms a balanced design, is calculated to instruct the musical mind as well as delight the aural sense. Of these constructions, the most extraordinary is represented by *Das musikalische Opfer* (The Musical Offering), composed by Bach for Frederick the Great of Prussia. Bach's 2nd son, **Carl Philipp Emanuel**, who served as chamber musician to the court of Prussia, arranged for Bach to visit Frederick's palace in Potsdam; Bach arrived there, accompanied by his son **Wilhelm Friedemann**, on May 7, 1747. The ostensible purpose of Bach's visit was to test the Silbermann pianos installed in the palace. The King, who liked to flaunt his love for the arts and sciences, gave Bach a musical theme of his own invention and asked him to compose a fugue upon it. Bach also presented an organ recital at the Heiliggeistkirche in Potsdam and attended a chamber music concert held by the King; on that occasion he improvised a fugue in 6 parts on a theme of his own. Upon his return to Leipzig, Bach set to work on the King's theme. Gallantly, elegantly, he inscribed the work, in scholastic Latin, "Regis Iussu Cantio et Reliqua Canonica Arte Resoluta" ("At the King's command, the cantus and supplements are in a canonic manner resolved"). The initials of the Latin words form the acronym RICERCAR, a technical term etymologically related to the word "research" and applied to any study that is instructive in nature. The work is subdivided into 13 sections; it includes a puzzle canon in 2 parts, marked "quaerendo invenietis" ("you will find it by seeking"). Bach had the score engraved, and sent it to the King on July 7, 1747. Intellectually independent as Bach was, he never questioned the immanent rights of established authority. He was proud of the title Royal Polish and Electoral Saxon Court Composer to the King of Poland and Elector of Saxony, bestowed upon him in 1736 while he was in the service of Duke Christian of Weissenfels, and he even regarded the position of cantor of the Thomasschule in Leipzig as inferior to it. In his dedications to royal personages he adhered to the customary humble style, which was extended even to the typography of his dedicatory prefaces. In such dedications the name of the exalted commissioner was usually printed in large letters, with conspicuous indentation, while Bach's own signature, preceded by elaborate verbal genuflection, appeared in the smallest type of the typographer's box.

Bach's biography is singularly lacking in dramatic events. He attended the Latin school in Eisenach, and apparently was a good student, as demonstrated by his skill in the Latin language. His mother died in 1694; his father remarried and died soon afterward. Bach's school years were passed at the Lyceum in the town of Ohrdruf; his older brother **Johann Christoph** lived there; he helped Bach in his musical studies; stories that he treated Bach cruelly must be dismissed as melodramatic inventions. Through the good offices of Elias Herda, cantor of the Ohrdruf school, Bach received an opportunity to move, for further education, to Lüneburg; there he was admitted to the Mettenchor of the Michaeliskirche. In March of 1703 he obtained employment as an attendant to Johann Ernst, Duke of Weimar; he was commissioned to make tests on the new organ of the Neukirche in Arnstadt; on Aug. 9, 1703, he was appointed organist there. In Oct. 1705 he obtained a leave of absence to travel to Lübeck to hear the famous organist Dietrich Buxtehude. The physical mode of Bach's travel there leaves much to be explained. The common versions found in most biographies tell that Bach made that journey on foot. But the distance between Arnstadt and Lübeck is 212 miles (335 km) and the route lies through the forbidding Harz Mountain chain, with its legendary peak Brocken, which, according to common superstition, was the site of the midnight gathering of a coven of witches. Assuming that Bach had about a month to spend in Lübeck to attend Buxtehude's concerts (or else the journey would not have been worthwhile), he had about 45 days to cover 424 miles (670 km) for a round trip: he would have had to travel on the average of 20 miles a day. The actual travel time between Arnstadt and Lübeck, considering the absence of good roads, must have been much longer. Not only would it have been exhausting in the extreme, even for a young man of 19 (Bach's age at the time), but it would have necessitated a change of 3 or 4 pairs of heavy boots that would wear out in the generally inclement weather during the months of Nov. and Dec. A query for information from the office of the Oberbürgermeister of Arnstadt elicited the suggestion that Bach (and Handel, who made a similar journey before) must have hired himself out as a valet to a coach passenger, a not uncommon practice among young men of the time. The impetus of Bach's trip was presumably the hope of obtaining Buxtehude's position as organist upon his retirement, but there was a peculiar clause attached to the contract for such a candidate: Buxtehude had 5 unmarried daughters; his successor was expected to marry the eldest of them. Buxtehude himself obtained his post through such an expedient, but Bach apparently was not prepared for matrimony under such circumstances.

On June 15, 1707, Bach became organist at the Blasiuskirche in Mühlhausen. On Oct. 17, 1707, he married his cousin Maria Barbara Bach, who was the daughter of **Johann Michael Bach**. On Feb. 4, 1708, Bach composed his cantata *Gott ist mein König* for the occasion of the installation of a new Mühlhausen town council. This was the 1st work of Bach's that was publ. Although the circumstances of his employment in Mühlhausen were seemingly favorable, Bach resigned his position on June 25, 1708, and accepted the post of court organist to Duke Wilhelm Ernst of Weimar. In Dec. 1713 Bach visited Halle, the birthplace of Handel; despite its proximity to Bach's own place of birth in Eisenach, the 2 great composers never met. On March 2, 1714, Duke Wilhelm Ernst offered Bach the position of Konzertmeister. In Sept. 1717 Bach went to Dresden to hear the famous French organist Louis Marchand, who resided there at the time. It was arranged that Bach and Marchand would hold a contest as virtuosos, but Marchand left Dresden before the scheduled event. This anecdote should not be interpreted frivolously as Marchand's fear of competing; other factors may have intervened to prevent the meeting. Johann Samuel Drese, the Weimar music director, died on Dec. 1, 1716; Bach expected to succeed him in that prestigious position, but the Duke gave the post to Drese's son. Again, this episode should not be interpreted as the Duke's lack of appreciation for Bach's superior abilities; the appointment may have merely followed the custom of letting such administrative posts remain in the family. In 1717 Bach accepted the position of Kapellmeister and music director to Prince Leopold of Anhalt in Cöthen, but a curious contretemps developed when the Duke of Weimar refused to release Bach from his obligation, and even had him held under arrest from Nov. 6 to Dec. 2, 1717, before Bach was finally allowed to proceed to Cöthen. The Cöthen period was one of the most productive in Bach's life; there he wrote his great set of *Brandenburg Concertos*, the *Clavierbüchlein für Wilhelm Friedemann Bach*, and the 1st book of *Das Wohltemperierte Clavier*. In Oct. 1719 Bach was in Halle once more, but again missed meeting Handel, who had already gone to England. In 1720 Bach accompanied Prince Leopold to Karlsbad. A tragedy supervened when Bach's devoted wife was taken ill and died before Bach could be called to her side; she was buried on July 7, 1720, leaving Bach to take care of their 7 children. In 1720 Bach made a long journey to Hamburg, where he met the aged Reinken, who was then 97 years old. It is a part of the Bach legend that Reinken was greatly impressed with Bach's virtuosity and exclaimed, "I believed that the art of organ playing was dead, but it lives in you!" Bach remained a widower for nearly a year and a half before he married his 2nd wife, Anna Magdalena Wilcken, a daughter of a court trumpeter at Weissenfels, on Dec. 3, 1721. They had 13 children during their happy marital life. New avenues were opened to Bach when Johann Kuhnau, the cantor of Leipzig, died, on June 5, 1722. Although Bach applied for his post, the Leipzig authorities offered it 1st to Telemann of Hamburg, and when he declined, to Christoph Graupner of Darmstadt; only when Graupner was unable to obtain a release from his current position was Bach given the post. He traveled to Leipzig on Feb. 7, 1723, for a trial performance, earning a favorable reception. On April 22, 1723, Bach was elected to the post of cantor of the city of Leipzig and was officially installed on May 31, 1723. As director of church music, Bach's duties included the care of musicians for the Thomaskirche, Nicolaikirche, Matthaeikirche, and Petrikirche, and he was also responsible for the provision of the music to be performed at the Thomaskirche and Nicolaikirche. There were more mundane obligations that Bach was expected to discharge, such as gathering firewood for the Thomasschule, about which Bach had recurrent disputes with the rector; eventually he sought the intervention of the Elector of Saxony in the affair. It was in Leipzig that Bach created his greatest sacred works: the *St. John Passion*, the Mass in B minor, and the *Christmas Oratorio*. In 1729 he organized at the Thomasschule the famous Collegium Musicum, composed of professional musicians and univ. students with whom he gave regular weekly concerts; he led this group until 1737, and again from 1739 to 1741. He made several visits to Dresden, where his eldest son, Wilhelm Friedemann, served as organist at the Sophienkirche. In June 1747 Bach joined the Societät der Musikalischen Wissenschaften, a scholarly organization founded by a former member of the Collegium Musicum, Lorenz C. Mizler, a learned musician, Latinist, and mathematician who spent his life confounding his contemporaries and denouncing them as charlatans and ignorant pretenders to knowledge. The rules of the society required an applicant to submit a sample of his works; Bach contributed a triple canon in 6 parts and presented it, along with the canonic variations *Vom Himmel hoch da komm' ich her*. This was one of Bach's last works. He suffered from a cataract that was gradually darkening his vision. A British optician named John Taylor, who plied his trade in Saxony, operated on Bach's eyes in the spring of 1749; the operation, performed with the crude instruments of the time, left Bach almost totally blind. The same specialist operated also on Handel, with no better results. The etiology of Bach's last illness is unclear. It is said that on July 18, 1750, his vision suddenly returned (possibly when the cataract receded spontaneously), but a cerebral hemorrhage supervened, and a few days later Bach was dead. Bach's great contrapuntal work, *Die Kunst der Fuge*, remained unfinished. The final page bears this inscription by C.P.E. Bach: "Upon this Fugue, in which the name B-A-C-H is applied as a countersubject, the author died." Bach's widow, Anna Magdalena, survived him by nearly 10 years; she died on Feb. 27, 1760. In 1895 Wilhelm His, an anatomy prof. at the Univ. of Leipzig, performed an exhumation of Bach's body, made necessary because of the deterioration of the wooden coffin, and took remarkable photographs of Bach's skeleton, which he publ. under the title *J.S. Bach, Forschungen über dessen Grabstätte, Gebeine und Antlitz* (Leipzig, 1895). On July 28, 1949, on the 199th anniversary of Bach's death, his coffin was transferred to the choir room of the Thomaskirche.

Of Bach's 20 children, 10 reached maturity. His sons Wilhelm Friedemann, Carl Philipp Emanuel, **Johann Christoph Friedrich**, and **Johann (John) Christian** (the "London" Bach) made their mark as independent composers. Among Bach's notable pupils were Johann Friedrich Agricola, Johann Christoph Altnikol, Heinrich Nicolaus Gerber, Johann Gottlieb Goldberg, Gottfried August Homilius, Johann Philipp Kirnberger, Johann Christian Kittel, Johann Tobias Krebs, and Johann Ludwig Krebs. It is historically incorrect to maintain that Bach was not appreciated by his contemporaries; Bach's sons Carl Philipp Emanuel and the "London" Bach kept his legacy alive for a generation after Bach's death. True, they parted from Bach's art of contrapuntal writing; Carl Philipp Emanuel turned to the fashionable *style galant*, and wrote keyboard works of purely harmonic content. The 1st important biography of Bach was publ. in 1802, by J.N. Forkel.

Dramatic accounts of music history are often inflated. It is conventional to say that Bach's music was rescued from oblivion by Mendelssohn, who conducted the *St. Matthew Passion* in Berlin in 1829, but Mozart and Beethoven had practiced Bach's preludes and fugues. Bach's genius was never dimmed; he was never a prophet without a world. In 1850 the centennial of Bach's death was observed by the inception of the Leipzig Bach-Gesellschaft, a society founded by Carl Becker, Moritz Hauptmann, Otto Jahn, and Robert Schumann. Concurrently, the publishing firm of Breitkopf & Härtel inaugurated the publication of the complete ed. of Bach's works. A Neue Bach-Gesellschaft was founded in 1900; it supervised the publication of the important *Bach-Jahrbuch*, a scholarly journal begun in 1904. The bicentennial of Bach's death, in 1950, brought about a new series of memorials and celebrations. With the development of recordings, Bach's works were made available to large masses of the public. Modern composers, even those who champion the total abandonment of all conventional methods of composition and the abolition of musical notation, are irresistibly drawn to Bach as a precursor; suffice it to mention Alban Berg's use of Bach's chorale *Es ist genug* in the concluding section of his Violin Concerto dedicated to the memory of Alma Mahler's young daughter. It is interesting to note also that Bach's famous acronym B-A-C-H consists of 4 different notes in a chromatic alternation, thus making it possible to use it as an element of a 12-tone row. Bach's images have been emblazoned on popular T-shirts; postage stamps with his portrait have been issued by a number of nations in Europe, Asia, and Africa. The slogan "Back to Bach," adopted by composers of the early 20th century, seems to hold true for every musical era.

Baker, Theodore, American writer on music, and the compiler of the original edition of the present dictionary bearing his name; b. N.Y., June 3, 1851; d. Dresden, Oct. 13, 1934. As a young man, he was trained for business pursuits; in 1874 he decided to devote himself to musical studies; he went to Leipzig, where he took courses with Oskar Paul; he received his Ph.D. there in 1882 for his dissertation *Über die Musik der nordamerikanischen Wilden*, the 1st serious study of American Indian music. He lived in Germany until 1890; then returned to the U.S., and became literary ed. and translator for the publishing house of G. Schirmer, Inc. (1892); he retired in 1926 and went back to Germany. In 1895 he publ. *A Dictionary of Musical Terms*, which went through more than 25 printings and sold over a million copies; another valuable work was *A Pronouncing Pocket Manual of Musical Terms* (1905). He also issued *The Musician's Calendar and Birthday Book* (1915–17). In 1900 G. Schirmer, Inc., publ. *Baker's Biographical Dictionary of Musicians*, which became Baker's imperishable monument. The 1st ed. included the names of many American musicians not represented in musical reference works at the time; a 2nd ed. was publ. in 1905; the 3rd ed., revised and enl. by Alfred Remy, was issued in 1919; the 4th ed. appeared in 1940 under the general editorship of Carl Engel. A Supplement in 1949 was compiled by Nicolas Slonimsky, who undertook in 1958 a completely revised 5th ed. of the Dictionary and compiled the Supplements of 1965 and 1971. In 1978 Slonimsky edited the 6th ed., in 1984 the 7th ed., and in 1991 the 8th ed.

Bartók, Béla, great Hungarian composer; b. Nagyszentmiklós, March 25, 1881; d. N.Y., Sept. 26, 1945. His father was a school headmaster; his mother was a proficient pianist, and he received his 1st piano lessons from her. He began playing the piano in public at the age of 11. In 1894 the family moved to Pressburg, where he took piano lessons with László Erkel, son of the famous Hungarian opera composer; he also studied harmony with Anton Hyrtl. In 1899 he enrolled at the Royal Academy of Music in Budapest, where he studied piano with István Thomán and composition with Hans Kocsslcr; he graduated in 1903. His earliest compositions reveal the combined influence of Liszt, Brahms, and Richard Strauss; however, he soon became interested in exploring the resources of national folk music, which included not only Hungarian melorhythms but also elements of other ethnic strains in his native Transylvania, including Rumanian and Slovak. He formed a cultural friendship with Zoltán Kodály, and together they traveled through the land collecting folk songs, which they publ. in 1906. In 1907 Bartók succeeded István Thomán as prof. of piano at the Royal Academy of Music. His interest in folk-song research led him to tour North Africa in 1913. In 1919 he served as a member of the musical directorate of the short-lived Hungarian Democratic Republic with Dohnányi and Kodály; was also deputy director of the Academy of Music. Although a brilliant pianist, he limited his concert programs mainly to his own compositions; he also gave concerts playing works for 2 pianos with his 2nd wife, Ditta Pásztory (d. Budapest, Nov. 21, 1982, at the age of 80). In his own compositions he soon began to feel the fascination of tonal colors and impressionistic harmonies as cultivated by Debussy and other modern French composers. The basic texture of his music remained true to tonality, which he expanded to chromatic polymodal structures and unremittingly dissonant chordal combinations; in his piano works he exploited the extreme registers of the keyboard, often in the form of tone clusters to simulate pitchless drumbeats. He made use of strong asymmetrical rhythmic figures suggesting the modalities of Slavic folk music, a usage that imparted a somewhat acrid coloring to his music. The melodic line of his works sometimes veered toward atonality in its chromatic involutions; in some instances he employed melodic figures comprising the 12 different notes of the chromatic scale; however, he never adopted the integral techniques of the 12-tone method.

Bartók toured the U.S. as a pianist from Dec. 1927 to Feb. 1928; also gave concerts in the Soviet Union in 1929. He resigned his position at the Budapest Academy of Music in 1934, but continued his research work in ethnomusicology as a member of the Hungarian Academy of Sciences, where he was engaged in the preparation of the monumental Corpus Musicae Popularis Hungaricae. With the outbreak of World War II, Bartók decided to leave Europe; in the fall of 1940 he went to the U.S., where he remained until his death from polycythemia. In 1940 he received an honorary Ph.D. from Columbia Univ.; he also did folk-song research there as a visiting assistant in music (1941–42). His last completed score, the *Concerto for Orchestra*, commissioned by Koussevitzky, proved to be his most popular work. His 3rd Piano Concerto was virtually completed at the time of his death, except for the last 17 bars, which were arranged and orchestrated by his pupil Tibor Serly.

Throughout his life, and particularly during his last years in the U.S., Bartók experienced constant financial difficulties, and complained bitterly of his inability to support himself and his family. Actually, he was apt to exaggerate his pecuniary troubles, which were largely due to his uncompromising character. He arrived in America in favorable circumstances; his traveling expenses were paid by the American patroness Elizabeth Sprague Coolidge, who also engaged him to play at her festival at the Library of Congress for a generous fee. Bartók was offered the opportunity to give a summer course in composition at a midwestern college on advantageous terms, when he was still well enough to undertake such a task, but he proposed to teach piano instead, and the deal collapsed. Ironically, performances and recordings of his music increased enormously after his death, and the value of his estate reached a great sum of money. Posthumous honors were not lacking: Hungary issued a series of stamps with Bartók's image; a street in Budapest was named Bartók St.; the centenary of his birth (1981) was celebrated throughout the world by concerts and festivals devoted to his works. Forty-three years after his death, his remains were removed from the Ferncliff Cemetery in Hartsdale, N.Y., and taken to Budapest for a state funeral on July 7, 1988.

Far from being a cerebral purveyor of abstract musical designs, Bartók was an ardent student of folkways, seeking the roots of meters, rhythms, and modalities in the spontaneous songs and dances of the people. Indeed, he regarded his analytical studies of popular melodies as his most important contribution to music. Even during the last years of his life, already weakened by illness, he applied himself assiduously to the arrangement of Serbo-Croatian folk melodies of Yugoslavia from recordings placed in his possession. He was similarly interested in the natural musical expression of children; he firmly believed that children are capable of absorbing modalities and asymmetrical rhythmic structures with greater ease than adults trained in the rigid disciplines of established music schools. His remarkable collection of piano pieces entitled, significantly, *Mikrokosmos* was intended as a method to initiate beginners into the world of unfamiliar tonal and rhythmic combinations; in this he provided a parallel means of instruction to the Kodály method of schooling.

Beethoven, Ludwig van, the great German composer whose unsurpassed genius, expressed with supreme mastery in his syms., chamber music, concertos, and piano sonatas, revealing an extraordinary power of invention, marked a historic turn in the art of composition; b. Bonn, Dec. 15 or 16 (baptized, Dec. 17), 1770; d. Vienna, March 26, 1827. (Beethoven himself maintained, against all evidence, that he was born in 1772, and that the 1770 date referred to his older brother, deceased in infancy, whose forename was also Ludwig.) The family was of Dutch extraction (the surname Beethoven meant "beet garden" in Dutch). Beethoven's grandfather, **Ludwig van Beethoven** (b. Malines, Belgium, Jan. 5, 1712; d. Bonn, Dec. 24, 1773), served as choir director of the church of St. Pierre in Louvain in 1731; in 1732 he went to Liège, where he sang bass in the cathedral choir of St. Lambert; in 1733 he became a member of the choir in Bonn; there he married Maria Poll. Prevalent infant mortality took its statistically predictable tribute; the couple's only surviving child was Johann van Beethoven; he married a young widow, Maria Magdalena Leym (née Keverich), daughter of the chief overseer of the kitchen at the palace in Ehrenbreitstein; they were the composer's parents. Beethoven firmly believed that the nobiliary particle "van" in the family name betokened a nobility; in his demeaning litigation with his brother's widow over the guardianship of Beethoven's nephew Karl, he argued before the Vienna magistrate that as a nobleman he should be given preference over his sister-in-law, a commoner, but the court rejected his contention on the ground that "van" lacked the elevated connotation of its German counterpart, "von." Beethoven could never provide a weightier claim of noble descent. In private, he even tolerated without forceful denial the fantastic rumor that he was a natural son of royalty, a love child of Friedrich Wilhelm II, or even of Frederick the Great.

Beethoven's father gave him rudimentary instruction in music; he learned to play both the violin and the piano; Tobias Friedrich Pfeiffer, a local musician, gave him formal piano lessons; the court organist in Bonn, Gilles van Eeden, instructed him in keyboard playing and in music theory; Franz Rovantini gave him violin lessons; another violinist who taught Beethoven was Franz Ries. Beethoven also learned to play the French horn, under the guidance of the professional musician Nikolaus Simrock. Beethoven's academic training was meager; he was, however, briefly enrolled at the Univ. of Bonn in 1789. His 1st important teacher of composition was Christian Gottlob Neefe, a thorough musician who seemed to understand his pupil's great potential even in his early youth. He guided Beethoven in the study of Bach and encouraged him in keyboard improvisation. At the age of 12, in 1782, Beethoven composed 9 *Variations for Piano on a March of Dressler*, his 1st work to be publ. In 1783 he played the cembalo in the Court Orch. in Bonn; in 1784 the Elector Maximilian Franz officially appointed him to the post of deputy court organist, a position he retained until 1792; from 1788 to 1792 Beethoven also served as a violist in theater orchs. In 1787 the Elector sent him to Vienna, where he stayed for a short time; the report that he played for Mozart and that Mozart pronounced him a future great composer seems to be a figment of somebody's eager imagination. After a few weeks in Vienna Beethoven went to Bonn when he received news that his mother was gravely ill; she died on July 17, 1787. He was obliged to provide sustenance for his 2 younger brothers; his father, who took to drink in excess, could not meet his obligations. Beethoven earned some money by giving piano lessons to the children of Helene von Breuning, the widow of a court councillor. He also met important wealthy admirers, among them Count Ferdinand von Waldstein, who was to be immortalized by Beethoven's dedication to him of a piano sonata bearing his name. Beethoven continued to compose; some of his works of the period were written in homage to royalty, as a cantata on the death of the Emperor Joseph II and another on the accession of Emperor Leopold II; other pieces were designed for performance at aristocratic gatherings.

In 1790 an event of importance took place in Beethoven's life when Haydn was honored in Bonn by the Elector on his way to London; it is likely that Beethoven was introduced to him, and that Haydn encouraged him to come to Vienna to study with him. However that might be, Beethoven went to Vienna in Nov. 1792, and began his studies with Haydn. Not very prudently, Beethoven approached the notable teacher Johann Schenk to help him write the mandatory exercises prior to delivering them to Haydn for final appraisal. In the meantime, Haydn had to go to London again, and Beethoven's lessons with him were discontinued. Instead, Beethoven began a formal study of counterpoint with Johann Georg Albrechtsberger, a learned musician and knowledgeable pedagogue; these studies continued for about a year, until 1795. Furthermore, Beethoven took lessons in vocal composition with the illustrious Italian composer Salieri, who served as Imperial Kapellmeister at the Austrian court. Beethoven was fortunate to find a generous benefactor in Prince Karl Lichnowsky, who awarded him, beginning about 1800, an annual stipend of 600 florins; he was amply repaid for this bounty by entering the pantheon of music history through Beethoven's dedication to him of the *Sonate pathétique* and other works, as well as his 1st opus number, a set of 3 piano trios. Among other aristocrats of Vienna who were introduced into the gates of permanence through Beethoven's dedications was Prince Franz Joseph Lobkowitz, whose name adorns the title pages of the 6 String Quartets, op. 18; the *Eroica Symphony* (after Beethoven unsuccessfully tried to dedicate it to Napoleon); the Triple Concerto, op. 56; and (in conjunction with Prince Razumovsky) the 5th and 6th syms.—a glorious florilegium of great music. Prince Razumovsky, the Russian ambassador to Vienna, played an important role in Beethoven's life. From 1808 to 1816 he maintained in his residence a string quartet in which he himself played the 2nd violin (the leader was Beethoven's friend Schuppanzigh). It was to Razumovsky that Beethoven dedicated his 3 string quartets that became known as the Razumovsky quartets, in which Beethoven made use of authentic Russian folk themes. Razumovsky also shared with Lobkowitz the dedications of Beethoven's 5th and 6th syms. Another Russian patron was Prince Golitzyn, for whom Beethoven wrote his great string quartets opp. 127, 130, and 132.

Beethoven made his 1st public appearance in Vienna on March 29, 1795, as soloist in one of his piano concertos (probably the B-flat major Concerto, op. 19). In 1796 he played in Prague, Dresden, Leipzig, and Berlin. He also participated in "competitions," fashionable at the time, with other pianists, which were usually held in aristocratic salons. In 1799 he competed with Joseph Wölffl and in 1800 with Daniel Steibelt. On April 2, 1800, he presented a concert of his works in the Burgtheater in Vienna, at which his 1st Sym., in C major, and the Septet in E-flat major were performed for the 1st time. Other compositions at the threshold of the century were the Piano Sonata in C minor, op. 13, the *Pathétique*; the C-major Piano Concerto, op. 15; "sonata quasi una fantasia" for Piano in C-sharp minor, op. 27, celebrated under the nickname *Moonlight Sonata* (so described by a romantically inclined critic but not specifically accepted by Beethoven); the D-major Piano Sonata known as *Pastoral*; 8 violin sonatas; 3 piano trios; 5 string trios; 6 string quartets; several sets of variations; and a number of songs.

Fétis was the 1st to suggest the division of Beethoven's compositions into 3 stylistic periods. It was left to Wilhelm von Lenz to fully elucidate this view in his *Beethoven et ses trois styles* (2 vols., St. Petersburg, 1852). Despite this arbitrary chronological division, the work became firmly established in Beethoven literature. According to Lenz, the 1st period embraced Beethoven's works from his early years to the end of the 18th century, marked by a style closely related to the formal methods of Haydn. The 2nd period, covering the years 1801–14, was signaled by a more personal, quasi-Romantic mood, beginning with the *Moonlight Sonata*; the last period, extending from 1814 to Beethoven's death in 1827, comprised the most individual, the most unconventional, the most innovative works, such as his last string quartets and the 9th Sym., with its extraordinary choral finale.

Beethoven's early career in Vienna was marked by fine success; he was popular not only as a virtuoso pianist and a composer, but also as a social figure who was welcome in the aristocratic circles of Vienna; Beethoven's students included society ladies and even royal personages, such as Archduke Rudolf of Austria, to whom Beethoven dedicated the so-called Archduke Trio, op. 97. But Beethoven's progress was fatefully affected by a mysteriously growing deafness, which reached a crisis in 1802. On Oct. 8 and 10, 1802, he wrote a poignant document known as the "Heiligenstadt Testament," for it was drawn in the village of Heiligenstadt, where he resided at the time. The document, not discovered until after Beethoven's death, voiced his despair at the realization that the most important sense of his being, the sense of hearing, was inexorably failing. He implored his brothers, in case of his early death, to consult his physician, Dr. Schmidt, who knew the secret of his "lasting malady" contracted 6 years before he wrote the Testament, i.e., in 1796. The etiology of his illness leaves little doubt that the malady was the dreaded "lues," with symptoms including painful intestinal disturbances, enormous enlargement of the pancreas, cirrhosis of the liver, and, most ominously, the porous degeneration of the roof of the cranium, observable in the life mask of 1812 and clearly shown in the photograph of Beethoven's skull taken when his body was exhumed in 1863. However, the impairment of his hearing may have had an independent cause: an otosclerosis, resulting in the shriveling of the auditory nerves and concomitant dilation of the accompanying arteries. Externally, there were signs of tinnitus, a constant buzzing in the ears, about which Beethoven complained. His reverential biographer A.W. Thayer states plainly in a letter dated Oct. 29, 1880, that it was known to several friends of Beethoven that the cause of his combined ailments was syphilis. A full account of Beethoven's illness is found in Dr. Dieter Kerner's book *Krankheiten grosser Musiker* (Stuttgart, 1973; vol. 1, pp. 89–140).

To the end of his life Beethoven hoped to find a remedy for his deafness among the latest "scientific" medications. His Konversationshefte bear a pathetic testimony to these hopes; in one, dated 1819, he notes down the address of a Dr. Mayer, who treated deafness by "sulphur vapor" and a vibration machine. By tragic irony, Beethoven's deafness greatly contributed to the study of his personality, thanks to the existence of the "conversation books" in which his interlocutors wrote down their questions and Beethoven replied, a method of communication which became a rule in his life after 1818. Unfortunately, Beethoven's friend and amanuensis, Anton Schindler, altered or deleted many of these; it seems also likely that he destroyed Beethoven's correspondence with his doctors, as well as the recipes which apparently contained indications of treatment by mercury, the universal medication against venereal and other diseases at the time.

It is remarkable that under these conditions Beethoven was able to continue his creative work with his usual energy; there were few periods of interruption in the chronology of his list of works, and similarly there is no apparent influence of his moods of depression on the content of his music; tragic and joyful musical passages had equal shares in his inexhaustible flow of varied works. On April 5, 1803, Beethoven presented a concert of his compositions in Vienna at which he was soloist in his 3rd Piano Concerto; the program also contained performances of his 2nd Sym. and of the oratorio *Christus am Oelberge*. On May 24, 1803, he played in Vienna the piano part of his Violin Sonata, op. 47, known as the *Kreutzer Sonata*, although Kreutzer himself did not introduce it; in his place the violin part was taken over by the mulatto artist George Bridgetower. During the years 1803 and 1804 Beethoven composed his great Sym. No. 3, in E-flat major, op. 55, the *Eroica*. It has an interesting history. Beethoven's disciple Ferdinand Ries relates that Beethoven tore off the title page of the MS of the score orig. dedicated to Napoleon, after learning of his proclamation as Emperor of France in 1804, and supposedly exclaimed, "So he is a tyrant like all the others after all!" Ries reported this story shortly before his death, some 34 years after the composition of the *Eroica*, which throws great doubt on its credibility. Indeed, in a letter to the publishing firm of Breitkopf & Härtel, dated Aug. 26, 1804, long after Napoleon's proclamation of Empire, Beethoven still refers to the title of the work as "really

Bonaparte." His own copy of the score shows that he crossed out the designation "Inttitulata Bonaparte," but allowed the words written in pencil, in German, "Geschrieben auf Bonaparte" to stand. In Oct. 1806, when the 1st ed. of the orch. parts was publ. in Vienna, the sym. received the title "Sinfonia eroica composta per festeggiare il sovvenire d'un grand' uomo" ("heroic symphony, composed to celebrate the memory of a great man"). But who was the great man whose memory was being celebrated in Beethoven's masterpiece? Napoleon was very much alive and was still leading his Grande Armée to new conquests, so the title would not apply. Yet, the famous funeral march in the score expressed a sense of loss and mourning. The mystery remains. There is evidence that Beethoven continued to have admiration for Napoleon. He once remarked that had he been a military man he could have matched Napoleon's greatness on the battlefield. Beethoven and Napoleon were close contemporaries; Napoleon was a little more than a year older than Beethoven.

In 1803 Emanuel Schikaneder, manager of the Theater an der Wien, asked Beethoven to compose an opera to a libretto he had prepared under the title *Vestas Feuer* (The Vestal Flame), but he soon lost interest in the project and instead began work on another opera, based on J.N. Bouilly's *Léonore, ou L'Amour conjugal*. The completed opera was named *Fidelio*, which was the heroine's assumed name in her successful efforts to save her imprisoned husband. The opera was given at the Theater an der Wien on Nov. 20, 1805, under difficult circumstances, a few days after the French army entered Vienna. There were only 3 performances before the opera was rescheduled for March 29 and April 10, 1806; after another long hiatus a greatly revised version of *Fidelio* was produced on May 23, 1814. Beethoven wrote 3 versions of the Overture for *Léonore*; for another performance, on May 26, 1814, he revised the Overture once more, and this time it was performed under the title *Fidelio Overture*.

An extraordinary profusion of creative masterpieces marked the years 1802–8 in Beethoven's life. During these years he brought out the 3 String Quartets, op. 59, dedicated to Count Razumovsky; the 4th, 5th, and 6th syms.; the Violin Concerto; the 4th Piano Concerto; the Triple Concerto; the *Coriolan* Overture; and a number of piano sonatas, including the D minor, op. 31; No. 2, the *Tempest*; the C major, op. 53, the *Waldstein*; and the F minor, op. 57, the *Appassionata*. On Dec. 22, 1808, his 5th and 6th syms. were heard for the 1st time at a concert in Vienna; the concert lasted some 4 hours. Still, financial difficulties beset Beethoven. The various annuities from patrons were uncertain, and the devaluation of the Austrian currency played havoc with his calculations. In Oct. 1808, King Jerome Bonaparte of Westphalia offered the composer the post of Kapellmeister of Kassel at a substantial salary, but Beethoven decided to remain in Vienna. Between 1809 and 1812, Beethoven wrote his 5th Piano Concerto; the String Quartet in E-flat major, op. 74; the incidental music to Goethe's drama *Egmont*; the 7th and 8th syms.; and his Piano Sonata in E-flat major, op. 81a, whimsically subtitled "Das Lebewohl, Abwesenheit und Wiedersehn," also known by its French subtitle, "Les Adieux, l'absence, et le retour." He also added a specific description to the work, "Sonate caractéristique." This explicit characterization was rare with Beethoven; he usually avoided programmatic descriptions, preferring to have his music stand by itself. Even in his 6th Sym., the *Pastoral*, which bore specific subtitles for each movement and had the famous imitations of birds singing and the realistic portrayal of a storm, Beethoven decided to append a cautionary phrase: "More as an expression of one's feelings than a picture." He specifically denied that the famous introductory call in the 5th Sym. represented the knock of Fate at his door, but the symbolic association was too powerful to be removed from the legend; yet the characteristic iambic tetrameter was anticipated in several of Beethoven's works, among them the *Appassionata* and the 4th Piano Concerto. Czerny, who was close to Beethoven in Vienna, claimed that the theme was derived by Beethoven from the cry of the songbird Emberiza, or Emmerling, a species to which the common European goldfinch belongs, which Beethoven may have heard during his walks in the Vienna woods, a cry that is piercing enough to compensate for Beethoven's loss of aural acuity. However that may be, the 4-note motif became inexorably connected with the voice of doom for enemies and the exultation of the victor in battle. It was used as a victory call by the Allies in World War II; the circumstance that 3 short beats followed by one long beat spelled V for Victory in Morse code reinforced its effectiveness. The Germans could not very well jail people for whistling a Beethoven tune, so they took it over themselves as the 1st letter of the archaic German word "Viktoria," and trumpeted it blithely over their radios. Another famous nicknamed work by Beethoven was the *Emperor Concerto*, a label attached to the 5th Piano Concerto, op. 73. He wrote it in 1809, when Napoleon's star was still high in the European firmament, and some publicist decided that the martial strains of the music, with its sonorous fanfares, must have been a tribute to the Emperor of the French. Patriotic reasons seemed to underlie Beethoven's designation of his Piano Sonata, op. 106, as the *Hammerklavier Sonata*, that is, a work written for a hammer keyboard, or fortepiano, as distinct from harpsichord. But all of Beethoven's piano sonatas were for fortepiano; moreover, he assigned the title *Hammerklavier* to each of the 4 sonatas, namely opp. 101, 106, 109, and 110, using the old German word for fortepiano; by so doing, he desired to express his patriotic consciousness of being a German.

Like many professional musicians, Beethoven was occasionally called upon to write a work glorifying an important event or a famous personage. Pieces of this kind seldom achieve validity, and usually produce bombast. Such a work was Beethoven's *Wellingtons Sieg oder Die Schlacht bei Vittoria*, celebrating the British victory over Joseph Bonaparte, Napoleon's brother who temporarily sat on the Spanish throne. In 1814, Beethoven wrote a cantata entitled *Der glorreiche Augenblick*, intended to mark the "glorious moment" of the fall of his erstwhile idol, Napoleon.

Personal misfortunes, chronic ailments, and intermittent quarrels with friends and relatives preoccupied Beethoven's entire life. He ardently called for peace among men, but he never achieved peace with himself. Yet he could afford to disdain the attacks in the press; on the margin of a critical but justified review of his *Wellington's Victory*, he wrote, addressing the writer: "You wretched scoundrel! What I excrete [he used the vulgar German word *scheisse*] is better than anything you could ever think up!"

Beethoven was overly suspicious; he even accused the faithful Schindler of dishonestly mishandling the receipts from the sale of tickets at the 1st performance of the 9th Sym. He exaggerated his poverty; he possessed some shares and bonds which he kept in a secret drawer. He was untidy in personal habits: he often used preliminary drafts of his compositions to cover the soup and even the chamber pot, leaving telltale circles on the MS. He was strangely naive; he studiously examined the winning numbers of the Austrian government lottery, hoping to find a numerological clue to a fortune for himself. His handwriting was all but indecipherable. An earnest Beethoveniac spent time with a microscope trying to figure out what kind of soap Beethoven wanted his housekeeper to purchase for him; the scholar's efforts were crowned with triumphant success: the indecipherable word was *gelbe*—Beethoven wanted a piece of yellow soap. Q.E.D. The copying of his MSS presented difficulties; not only were the notes smudged, but sometimes Beethoven even failed to mark a crucial accidental. A copyist said that he would rather copy 20 pages of Rossini than a single page of Beethoven. On the other hand, Beethoven's sketchbooks, containing many alternative drafts, are extremely valuable, for they introduce a scholar into the inner sanctum of Beethoven's creative process.

Beethoven had many devoted friends and admirers in Vienna, but he spent most of his life in solitude. Carl Czerny reports in his diary that Beethoven once asked him to let him lodge in his house, but Czerny declined, explaining that his aged parents lived with him and he had no room for Beethoven. Deprived of the pleasures and comforts of family life, Beethoven sought to find a surrogate in his nephew Karl, son of Caspar Carl Beethoven, who died in 1815. Beethoven regarded his sister-in-law as an unfit mother; he went to court to gain sole guardianship over the boy; in his private letters, and even in his legal depositions, he poured torrents of vilification upon the woman, implying even that she was engaged in prostitution. In his letters to Karl he often signed himself as the true father of the boy. In 1826 Karl attempted suicide; it would be unfair to ascribe this act to Beethoven's stifling avuncular affection; Karl later went into the army and enjoyed a normal life.

Gallons of ink have been unnecessarily expended on the crucial question of Beethoven's relationship with women. That Beethoven dreamed of an ideal life companion is clear from his numerous utterances and candid letters to friends, in some of which he asked them to find a suitable bride for him. But there is no inkling that he kept company with any particular woman in Vienna. Beethoven lacked social graces; he could not dance; he was unable to carry on a light conversation about trivia; and behind it all there was the dreadful reality of his deafness. He could speak, but could not always understand when he was spoken to. With close friends he used an unwieldy ear trumpet; but such contrivances were obviously unsuitable in a social gathering. There were several objects of his secret passions, among his pupils or the society ladies to whom he dedicated his works. But somehow he never actually proposed marriage, and they usually married less hesitant suitors. It was inevitable that Beethoven should seek escape in fantasies. The greatest of these fantasies was the famous letter addressed to an "unsterbliche Geliebte," the "Immortal Beloved," couched in exuberant emotional tones characteristic of the sentimental romances of the time, and strangely reminiscent of Goethe's novel *The Sorrows of Young Werther*. The letter was never mailed; it was discovered in the secret compartment of Beethoven's writing desk after his death. The clues to the identity of the object of his passion were maddeningly few. He voiced his fervid anticipation of an impending meeting at some place indicated only by the initial letter "K."; he dated his letter as Monday, the 6th of July, without specifying the year. Eager Beethoveniacs readily established that the most likely year was 1812, when July 6 fell on a Monday. A complete inventory of ladies of Beethoven's acquaintance from 14 to 40 years of age was laid out, and the lengthy charade unfolded, lasting one and a half centuries. The most likely "Immortal Beloved" seemed to be Antoine Brentano, the wife of a merchant. But Beethoven was a frequent visitor at their house; his letters to her (sent by ordinary city post) and her replies expressed mutual devotion, but they could not be stylistically reconciled with the torrid protestation of undying love in the unmailed letter. And if indeed Frau Brentano was the "Immortal Beloved," why could not a tryst have been arranged in Vienna when her husband was away on business? There were other candidates; one researcher established, from consulting the town records of arrivals and departures, that Beethoven and a certain lady of his Vienna circle were in Prague on the same day, and that about 9 months later she bore a child who seemed to bear a remarkable resemblance to Beethoven. Another researcher, exploring the limits of the incredible, concluded that Beethoven had sexual relations with his sister-in-law and that his execration of her stemmed from this relationship. It was asserted also that a certain musician conversant with the lowlife of Vienna supplied Beethoven with *filles de joie* for pay. The nadir of monstrous speculation was reached by a pseudo-Freudian investigator who advanced the notion that Beethoven nurtured incestuous desires toward his nephew and that his demands drove the boy to his suicide attempt.

The so-called 3rd style of Beethoven was assigned by biographers to the last 10 or 15 years of his life. It included the composition of his monumental 9th Sym., completed in 1824 and 1st performed in Vienna on May 7, 1824; the program also included excerpts from the *Missa Solemnis* and *Die Weihe des Hauses* (The Consecration of the House). It was reported that Caroline Unger, the contralto soloist in the *Missa Solemnis*, had to pull Beethoven by the sleeve at the end of the performance so that he would acknowledge the applause he could not hear. With the 9th Sym., Beethoven completed the evolution of the symphonic form as he envisioned it. Its choral finale was his manifesto addressed to the world at large, to the text from Schiller's ode *An die Freude* (To Joy). In it, Beethoven, through Schiller, appealed to all humanity to unite in universal love. Here a musical work, for the 1st time, served a political ideal. Beethoven's last string quartets, opps. 127, 130, 131, and 132, served as counterparts of his last sym. in their striking innovations, dramatic pauses, and novel instrumental tone colors.

In Dec. 1826, on his way back to Vienna from a visit in Gneixendorf, Beethoven was stricken with a fever that developed into a mortal pleurisy; dropsy and jaundice supervened to this condition; surgery to relieve the accumulated fluid in his organism was unsuccessful, and he died on the afternoon of March 26, 1827. It was widely reported that an electric storm struck Vienna as Beethoven lay dying; its occurrence was indeed confirmed by the contemporary records in the Vienna weather bureau, but the story that he raised his clenched fist aloft as a gesture of defiance to an overbearing Heaven must be relegated to fantasy; he was far too feeble either to clench his fist or to raise his arm. The funeral of Beethoven was held in all solemnity.

Beethoven was memorialized in festive observations of the centennial and bicentennial of his birth, and of the centennial and sesquicentennial of his death. The house where he was born in Bonn was declared a museum. Monuments were erected to him in many cities. Commemorative postage stamps bearing his image were issued not only in Germany and Austria, but in Russia and other countries. Streets were named after him in many cities of the civilized world, including even Los Angeles.

Beethoven's music marks a division between the Classical period of the 18th century, exemplified by the great names of Mozart and Haydn, and the new spirit of Romantic music that characterized the entire course of the 19th century. There are certain purely external factors that distinguish these 2 periods of musical evolution; one of them pertains to sartorial matters. Music before Beethoven was *Zopfmusik*, pigtail music. Haydn and Mozart are familiar to us by portraits in which their heads are crowned by elaborate wigs; Beethoven's hair was by contrast luxuriant in its unkempt splendor. The music of the 18th century possessed the magnitude of mass production. The accepted number of Haydn's syms., according to his own count, is 104, but even in his own catalogue Haydn allowed a duplication of one of his symphonic works. Mozart wrote about 40 syms. during his short lifetime. Haydn's syms. were constructed according to an easily defined formal structure; while Mozart's last syms. show greater depth of penetration, they do not depart from the Classical convention. Besides, both Haydn and Mozart wrote instrumental works variously entitled cassations, serenades, divertimentos, and suites, which were basically synonymous with syms.

Beethoven's syms. were few in number and mutually different. The 1st and 2nd syms. may still be classified as *Zopfmusik*, but with the 3rd Sym. he entered a new world of music. No sym. written before had contained a clearly defined funeral march. Although the 5th Sym. had no designated program, it lent itself easily to programmatic interpretation. Wagner attached a bombastic label, "Apotheosis of the Dance," to Beethoven's 7th Sym. The 8th Sym. Beethoven called his "little sym.," and the 9th is usually known as the *Choral* sym. With the advent of Beethoven, the manufacture of syms. en masse had ceased; Schumann, Brahms, Tchaikovsky, and their contemporaries wrote but a few syms. each, and each had a distinctive physiognomy. Beethoven had forever destroyed *Zopfmusik*, and opened the floodgates of the Romantic era. His music was individual; it was emotionally charged; his Kreutzer Sonata served as a symbol for Tolstoy's celebrated moralistic tale of that name, in which the last movement of the sonata leads the woman pianist into the receptive arms of the concupiscent violinist. But technically the sonata is very difficult for amateurs to master, and Tolstoy's sinners were an ordinary couple in old Russia.

Similarly novel were Beethoven's string quartets; a musical abyss separated his last string quartets from his early essays in the same form. Trios, violin sonatas, cello sonatas, and the 32 great piano sonatas also represent evolutionary concepts. Yet Beethoven's melody and harmony did not diverge from the sacrosanct laws of euphony and tonality. The famous dissonant chord introducing the last movement of the 9th Sym. resolves naturally into the tonic, giving only a moment's pause to the ear. Beethoven's favorite device of pairing the melody in the high treble with triadic chords in close harmony in the deep bass was a peculiarity of his style but not necessarily an infringement of the Classical rules. Yet contemporary critics found some of these practices repugnant and described Beethoven as an eccentric bent on creating unconventional sonorities. Equally strange to the untutored ear were pregnant pauses and sudden modulations in his instrumental works. Beethoven was not a contrapuntist by taste or skill. With the exception of his monumental *Grosse Fuge*, composed as the finale of the String Quartet, op. 133, his fugal movements were usually free canonic imitations. There is only a single instance in Beethoven's music of the crab movement, a variation achieved by running the theme in reverse. But he was a master of instrumental variation, deriving extraordinary transformations through melodic and rhythmic alterations of a given theme. His op. 120, 33 variations for piano on a waltz theme by the Viennese publisher Diabelli, represents one of the greatest achievements in the art.

When Hans von Bülow was asked which was his favorite key signature, he replied that it was E-flat major, the tonality of the *Eroica*, for it had 3 flats: one for Bach, one for Beethoven, and one for Brahms. Beethoven became forever the 2nd B in popular music books.

The literature on Beethoven is immense. The basic catalogues are those by G. Kinsky and H. Halm, *Das Werk Beethovens. Thematisch-Bibliographisches Verzeichnis seiner sämtlichen vollendeten Kompositionen*, publ. in Munich and Duisburg in 1955, and by W. Hess, *Verzeichnis der Gesamtausgabe veröffentlichten Werke Ludwig van Beethovens*, publ. in Wiesbaden in 1957. Beethoven attached opus numbers to most of his works, and they are essential in a catalogue of his works.

Berberian, Cathy, versatile American mezzo-soprano; b. Attleboro, Mass., July 4, 1925; d. Rome, March 6, 1983. She was of Armenian parentage; she studied singing, dancing, and the art of pantomime; took courses at Columbia Univ. and N.Y. Univ.; then went to Italy; attracted wide attention in 1958, when she performed the ultrasurrealist. *Fontana Mix* by John Cage, which demanded a fantastic variety of sound effects. Her vocal range extended to 3 octaves, causing one bewildered music critic to remark that she could sing both Tristan and Isolde. Thanks to her uncanny ability to produce ultrahuman (and subhuman) tones, and her willingness to incorporate into her professional vocalization a variety of animal noises, guttural sounds, grunts and growls, squeals, squeaks and squawks, clicks and clucks, shrieks and screeches, hisses, hoots, and hollers, she instantly became the darling of inventive composers of the avant-garde, who eagerly dedicated to her their otherwise unperformable works. She married one of them, **Luciano Berio**, in 1950, but they were separated in 1966 and divorced in 1968. She could also intone classical music, and made a favorable impression with her recording of works by Monteverdi. Shortly before her death she sang her own version of the *Internationale* for an Italian television program commemorating the centennial of the death of Karl Marx (1983). She was an avant-garde composer in her own right; she wrote multimedia works, such as *Stripsody*, an arresting soliloquy of labial and laryngeal sounds, and an eponymously titled piano piece, *Morsicat(h)y*. She resented being regarded as a "circus freak," and insisted that her objective was merely to meet the challenge of the new art of her time.

Berlin, Irving (real name, **Israel Balin**), fabulously popular Russian-born American composer of hundreds of songs that became the musical conscience of the U.S.; b. Mogilev, May 11, 1888; d. N.Y., Sept. 22, 1989, at the incredible age of 101. Fearing anti-Semitic pogroms, his Jewish parents took ship when he was 5 years old and landed in N.Y. His father made a scant living as a synagogue cantor, and Izzy, as he was called, earned pennies as a newsboy. He later got jobs as a busboy, in time graduating to the role of a singing waiter in Chinatown. He learned to improvise on the bar piano and, at the age of 19, wrote the lyrics of a song, *Marie from Sunny Italy*. Because of a printing error, his name on the song appeared as Berlin instead of Balin. He soon acquired the American vernacular and, throughout his career, never tried to experiment with sophisticated language, thus distancing himself from his younger contemporaries, such as Gershwin and Cole Porter. He was married in 1912, but his young bride died of typhoid fever, contracted during their honeymoon in Havana, Cuba. He wrote a lyric ballad in her memory, *When I Lost You*, which sold a million copies. He never learned to read or write music, and composed most of his songs in F-sharp major for the convenience of fingering the black keys of the scale. To modulate into other keys he had a special hand clutch built at the piano keyboard, so that his later songs acquired an air of technical variety. This piano is now installed at the Smithsonian Institution in Washington, D.C. His 1st biographer, Alexander Woollcott, referred to him as a "creative ignoramus," meaning it as a compliment. Victor Herbert specifically discouraged Irving Berlin from learning harmony for fear that he would lose his natural genius for melody, and also encouraged him to join the American Soc. of Composers, Authors, and Publishers (ASCAP) as a charter member, a position that became the source of his fantastically prosperous commercial success.

Berlin was drafted into the U.S. Army in 1917 but did not have to serve in military action. In the army he wrote a musical revue, *Yip, Yip, Yaphank*, which contained one of his most famous tunes, *God Bless America*; it was for some reason omitted in the original show, but returned to glory when songster Kate Smith performed it in 1938. The song, patriotic to the core, became an unofficial American anthem. In 1925, when Berlin was 37 years old, he met Ellin Mackay, the daughter of the millionaire head of the Postal Telegaph Cable Co., and proposed to her. She accepted, but her father threatened to disinherit her if she would consider marrying a Jewish immigrant. Money was not the object, for by that time Berlin was himself a contented millionaire. The yellow press of N.Y. devoted columns upon columns to the romance; the 2 eventually married in a civil ceremony at the

Municipal Building. Ironically, it was the despised groom who helped his rich father-in-law during the financial debacle of the 1920s, for while stocks fell disastrously, Berlin's melodies rose in triumph all over America. The marriage proved to be happy, lasting 62 years, until Ellin's death in July of 1988. Berlin was reclusive in his last years of life; he avoided making a personal appearance when members of ASCAP gathered before his house to serenade him on his 100th birthday.

Berlin was extremely generous with his enormous earnings. According to sales records compiled in 1978, *God Bless America* brought in $673,939.46 in royalties, all of which was donated to the Boy and Girl Scouts of America. Another great song, *White Christmas*, which Berlin wrote for the motion picture *Holiday Inn*, became a sentimental hit among American troops stationed in tropical bases in the Pacific during World War II; 113,067,354 records of this song and 5,566,845 copies of sheet music for it were sold in America between 1942 and 1978. The homesick marines altered the 1st line from "I'm dreaming of a white Christmas" to "I'm dreaming of a white mistress," that particular commodity being scarce in the tropics. In 1954 Berlin received the Congressional Medal of Honor for his patriotic songs. His financial interests were taken care of by his publishing enterprise, Irving Berlin Music, Inc., founded in 1919, and also by ASCAP. According to some records, his income tax amounted to 91% of his total earnings.

Borge, Victor (real name, **Borge Rosenbaum**), variously talented Danish pianist and inborn humorist who, in his American avatar, carved for himself a unique niche as a provider of "comedy in music"; b. Copenhagen, Jan. 3, 1909, of Russian Jewish extraction (his father having left Russia to avoid being drafted into the imperial army). He entertained no ambition to become a 2nd Horowitz, but he developed a remarkable facility and prestidigital velocity on the keys. He escaped being a wunderkind, however, and took some theory courses at the Copenhagen Cons. His next stop after Denmark was Berlin, where he became a pupil of a pupil of Liszt. Later he was a pupil of a pupil of Busoni. He never developed the necessary *Sitzfleisch* for a virtuoso career, but he was sufficiently adept at the piano to arrange for a concert tour in Sweden. In the meantime, the Nazis invaded Denmark and there was nothing for Borge to do but to go to the U.S., where he had connections through his American-born wife. He emigrated in 1940 and became a U.S. citizen in 1948. In America he changed his name to Victor Borge and inaugurated a Broadway show under the logo "Comedy in Music" (1953), giving a total of 849 performances—unprecedented in N.Y. annals for a 1-man show. As a diversion he also started a poultry farm on his rural estate, specializing in Rock Cornish hens. He mastered idiomatic English to such an extent that he could improvise jokes that invariably elicited chuckles. He also developed a sepulchral voice imitating bass singers and an ornithological coloratura à la Jenny Lind. Thus equipped, he made a career on television, continuing his solo appearances well into his 80s.

Boulez Pierre, celebrated French composer and conductor; b. Montbrison, March 26, 1925. He studied composition with Olivier Messiaen at the Paris Cons., graduating in 1945; later took lessons with René Leibowitz, who initiated him into the procedures of serial music. In 1948 he became a theater conductor in Paris; made a tour of the U.S. with a French ballet troupe in 1952. In 1954 he organized in Paris a series of concerts called "Domaine Musical," devoted mainly to avant-garde music. In 1963 he delivered a course of lectures on music at Harvard Univ., and on May 1, 1964, made his American debut as conductor in N.Y. In 1958 he went to Germany, where he gave courses at the International Festivals for New Music in Darmstadt. It was in Germany that he gained experience as conductor of opera; he was one of the few Frenchmen to conduct

Wagner's *Parsifal* in Germany; in 1976 he was engaged to conduct the *Ring* cycle in Bayreuth. The precision of his leadership and his knowledge of the score produced a profound impression on both the audience and the critics. He was engaged to conduct guest appearances with the Cleveland Orch., and in 1971 he was engaged as music director of the N.Y. Phil., a choice that surprised many and delighted many more. From the outset he asserted complete independence from public and managerial tastes, and proceeded to feature on his programs works by Schoenberg, Berg, Webern, Varèse, and other modernists who were reformers of music, giving a relatively small place to Romantic composers. This policy provoked the expected opposition on the part of many subscribers, but the management decided not to oppose Boulez in his position as music director of the orch. The musicians themselves voiced their full appreciation of his remarkable qualities as a professional of high caliber, but they described him derisively as a "French correction," with reference to his extraordinary sense of rhythm, perfect pitch, and memory, but a signal lack of emotional participation in the music. In America, Boulez showed little interest in social amenities and made no effort to ingratiate himself with men and women of power. His departure in 1977 and the accession of the worldly Zubin Mehta as his successor were greeted with a sigh of relief, as an antidote to the stern regimen imposed by Boulez. While attending to his duties at the helm of the N.Y. Phil., he accepted outside obligations; from 1971 to 1975 he served as chief conductor of the London BBC Sym. Orch.; as a perfect Wagnerite he gave exemplary performances of Wagner's operas both in Germany and elsewhere. He established his residence in Paris, where he had founded, in 1974, the Inst. de Recherche & Coordination Acoustique/Musique, a futuristic establishment generously subsidized by the French government; in this post he could freely carry out his experimental programs of electronic techniques with the aid of digital synthesizers and a complex set of computers capable of acoustical feedback. In 1989 he was awarded the Praemium Imperiale prize of Japan for his various contributions to contemporary music. His own music is an embodiment of such futuristic techniques; it is fiendishly difficult to perform and even more difficult to describe in the familiar terms of dissonant counterpoint, free serialism, or indeterminism. He specifically disassociated himself from any particular modern school of music. He even publ. a pamphlet with the shocking title *Schoenberg est mort*, shortly after Schoenberg's actual physical death; he similarly distanced himself from other current trends.

Brahms, Johannes, great German composer; b. Hamburg, May 7, 1833; d. Vienna, April 3, 1897. His father, who played the double bass in the orch. of the Phil. Soc. in Hamburg, taught Brahms the rudiments of music; later he began to study piano with Otto F.W. Cossel, and made his 1st public appearance as a pianist with a chamber music group at the age of 10. Impressed with his progress, Cossel sent Brahms to his own former teacher, the noted pedagogue Eduard Marxsen, who accepted him as a scholarship student, without charging a fee. Soon Brahms was on his own, and had to eke out his meager subsistence by playing piano in taverns, restaurants, and other establishments (but not in brothels, as insinuated by some popular biographers). On Sept. 21, 1848, at the age of 15, Brahms played a solo concert in Hamburg under an assumed name. In 1853 he met the Hungarian violinist Eduard Reményi, with whom he embarked on a successful concert tour. While in Hannover, Brahms formed a friendship with the famous violin virtuoso Joseph Joachim, who gave him an introduction to Liszt in Weimar. Of great significance was his meeting with Schumann in Düsseldorf. In his diary of the time, Schumann noted: "Johannes Brahms, a genius." He reiterated his appraisal of Brahms in his famous article "Neue Bahnen" (New Paths), which appeared in the *Neue Zeitschrift für Musik* on Oct. 28, 1853; in a characteristic display of metaphor, he described young Brahms as having come into life as Minerva sprang in full armor from the brow of Jupiter. Late in 1853, Breitkopf & Härtel publ. his 2 piano sonatas and a set of 6 songs. Brahms also publ., under the pseudonym of G.W. Marks, a collection of 6 pieces for piano, 4-hands, under the title *Souvenir de la Russie* (Brahms never visited Russia). Schumann's death in 1856, after years of agonizing mental illness, deeply affected Brahms. He remained a devoted friend of Schumann's family; his correspondence with Schumann's widow Clara reveals a deep affection and spiritual intimacy, but the speculation about their friendship growing into a romance exists only in the fevered imaginations of psychologizing biographers. Objectively judged, the private life of Brahms was that of a middle-class bourgeois who worked systematically and diligently on his current tasks while maintaining a fairly active social life. He was always ready and willing to help young composers (his earnest efforts on behalf of Dvořák were notable). Brahms was entirely free of professional jealousy; his differences with Wagner were those of style. Wagner was an opera composer, whereas Brahms never wrote for the stage. True, some ardent admirers of Wagner (such as Hugo Wolf) found little of value in the music of Brahms, while admirers of Brahms (such as Hanslick) were sharp critics of Wagner, but Brahms held aloof from such partisan wranglings.

From 1857 to 1859 Brahms was employed in Detmold as court pianist, chamber musician, and choir director. In the meantime he began work on his 1st piano concerto. He played it on Jan. 22, 1859, in Hannover, with Joachim as conductor. Other important works of the period were the 2 serenades for orch. and the 1st string sextet. He expected to be named conductor of the Hamburg Phil. Soc., but the directoriat preferred to engage, in 1863, the singer Julius Stockhausen in that capacity. Instead, Brahms accepted the post of conductor of the Singakademie in Vienna, which he led from 1863 to 1864. In 1869 he decided to make Vienna his permanent home. As early as 1857 he began work on his choral masterpiece, *Ein deutsches Requiem*; he completed the score in 1868, and conducted its 1st performance in the Bremen Cathedral on April 10, 1868, although the 1st 3 movements had been given by Herbeck and the Vienna Phil. on Dec. 1, 1867. In May 1868 he added another movement to the work (the 5th, "Ihr habt nun Traurigkeit") in memory of his mother, who died in 1865; the 1st performance of the final version was given in Leipzig on Feb. 18, 1869. The title of the German Requiem had no nationalistic connotations; it simply stated that the text was in German rather than Latin. His other important vocal scores include *Rinaldo*, a cantata; the *Liebeslieder* waltzes for Vocal Quartet and Piano, 4-hands; the *Alto Rhapsody*; the *Schicksalslied*; and many songs. In 1869 he publ. 2 vols. of *Hungarian Dances* for Piano Duet; these were extremely successful. Among his chamber music works, the Piano Quintet in F minor; the String Sextet No. 2, in G major; the Trio for French Horn, Violin, and Piano; the 2 String Quartets, op. 51; and the String Quartet op. 67 are exemplary works of their kind. In 1872 Brahms was named artistic director of the concerts of Vienna's famed Gesellschaft der Musikfreunde; he held this post until 1875. During this time, he composed the *Variations on a Theme by Joseph Haydn*, op. 56a. The title was a misnomer; the theme occurs in a Feld-partita for Military Band by Haydn, but it was not Haydn's own; it was orig. known as the St. Anthony Chorale, and in pedantic scholarly eds. of Brahms it is called St. Anthony Variations. Otto Dessoff conducted the 1st performance of the work with the Vienna Phil. on Nov. 2, 1873.

For many years friends and admirers of Brahms urged him to write a sym. He clearly had a symphonic mind; his piano concertos were symphonic in outline and thematic development. As early as 1855 he began work on a full-fledged sym.; in

1862 he nearly completed the 1st movement of what was to be his 1st Sym. The famous horn solo in the finale of the 1st Sym. was jotted down by Brahms on a picture postcard to Clara Schumann dated Sept. 12, 1868, from his summer place in the Tyrol; in it Brahms said that he heard the tune played by a shepherd on an Alpine horn; and he set it to a rhymed quatrain of salutation. Yet Brahms was still unsure about his symphonic capacity. (A frivolous suggestion was made by an irresponsible psychomusicologist that it was when Brahms grew his famous luxuriant beard that he finally determined to complete his symphonic essay; such pogonological speculations illustrate the degree to which musical criticism can contribute to its own ridiculosity.) The great C-minor Sym., his 1st, was completed in 1876 and 1st performed at Karlsruhe on Nov. 4, 1876, conducted by Dessoff. Hans von Bülow, the German master of the telling phrase, called it "The 10th," thus placing Brahms on a direct line from Beethoven. It was also Hans von Bülow who cracked a bon mot that became a part of music history, in referring to the 3 B's of music, Bach, Beethoven, and Brahms. The original saying was not merely a vacuous alphabetical generalization; Bülow's phrase was deeper; in answering a question as to what was his favorite key, he said it was E-flat major, the key of Beethoven's *Eroica*, because it had 3 B's in its key signature (in German, B is specifically B-flat, but by extension may signify any flat)—1 for Bach, 1 for Beethoven, and 1 for Brahms. The witty phrase took wing, but its sophisticated connotation was lost at the hands of professional popularizers.

Brahms composed his 2nd Sym. in 1877; it was performed for the 1st time by the Vienna Phil. on Dec. 30, 1877, under the direction of Hans Richter, receiving a fine acclaim. Brahms led a 2nd performance of the work with the Gewandhaus Orch. in Leipzig on Jan. 10, 1878. Also in 1878 Brahms wrote his Violin Concerto; the score was dedicated to Joachim, who gave its premiere with the Gewandhaus Orch. on Jan. 1, 1879. Brahms then composed his 2nd Piano Concerto, in B-flat major, and was soloist in its 1st performance in Budapest, on Nov. 9, 1881. There followed the 3rd Sym., in F major, 1st performed by the Vienna Phil., under the direction of Hans Richter, on Dec. 2, 1883. The 4th Sym., in E minor, followed in quick succession; it had its 1st performance in Meiningen on Oct. 25, 1885. The symphonic cycle was completed in less than a decade; it has been conjectured, without foundation, that the tonalities of the 4 syms. of Brahms—C, D, F, and E—correspond to the fugal subject of Mozart's Jupiter Sym., and that some symbolic meaning was attached to it. All speculations aside, there is an inner symmetry uniting these works. The 4 syms. contain 4 movements each, with a slow movement and a scherzo-like Allegretto in the middle of the corpus. There are fewer departures from the formal scheme than in Beethoven, and there are no extraneous episodes interfering with the grand general line. Brahms wrote music pure in design and eloquent in sonorous projection; he was a true classicist, a quality that endeared him to the critics who were repelled by Wagnerian streams of sound, and by the same token alienated those who sought something more than mere geometry of thematic configurations from a musical composition.

The chamber music of Brahms possesses similar symphonic qualities; when Schoenberg undertook to make an orch. arrangement of the Piano Quartet of Brahms, all he had to do was to expand the sonorities and enhance instrumental tone colors already present in the original. The string quartets of Brahms are edifices of Gothic perfection; his 3 violin sonatas, his 2nd Piano Trio (the 1st was a student work and yet it had a fine quality of harmonious construction), all contribute to a permanent treasure of musical classicism. The piano writing of Brahms is severe in its contrapuntal texture, but pianists for a hundred years included his rhapsodies and intermezzos in their repertoire; and Brahms was able to impart sheer delight in his Hungarian rhapsodies and waltzes; they represented the Viennese side of his character, as contrasted with the profound Germanic quality of his syms. The song cycles of Brahms continued the evolution of the art of the lieder, a natural continuation of the song cycles of Schubert and Schumann.

Brahms was sociable and made friends easily; he traveled to Italy, and liked to spend his summers in the solitude of the Austrian Alps. But he was reluctant to appear as a center of attention; he declined to receive the honorary degree of Mus.D. from Cambridge Univ. in 1876, giving as a reason his fear of seasickness in crossing the English Channel. He was pleased to receive the Gold Medal of the Phil. Soc. of London in 1877. In 1879 the Univ. of Breslau proffered him an honorary degree of Doctor of Philosophy, citing him as "Artis musicae severioris in Germania nunc princeps." As a gesture of appreciation and gratitude he wrote an *Akademische Festouvertüre* for Breslau, and since there was no Channel to cross on the way, he accepted the invitation to conduct its premiere in Breslau on Jan. 4, 1881; its rousing finale using the German student song "Gaudeamus igitur" pleased the academic assembly. In 1887 he was presented with the Prussian Order "Pour le Mérite." In 1889 he received the freedom of his native city of Hamburg; also in 1889, Franz Joseph, the Emperor of Austria, made him a Commander of the Order of Leopold. With success and fame came a sense of self-sufficiency, which found its external expression in the corpulence of his appearance, familiar to all from photographs and drawings of Brahms conducting or playing the piano. Even during his Viennese period Brahms remained a sturdy Prussian; his ideal was to see Germany a dominant force in Europe philosophically and militarily. In his workroom he kept a bronze relief of Bismarck, the "Iron Chancellor," crowned with laurel. He was extremely meticulous in his working habits (his MSS were clean and legible), but he avoided wearing formal dress, preferring a loosely fitting flannel shirt and a detachable white collar, but no cravat. He liked to dine in simple restaurants, and he drank a great deal of beer. He was indifferent to hostile criticism; still, it is amazing to read the outpouring of invective against Brahms by George Bernard Shaw and by American critics; the usual accusations were of dullness and turgidity. When Sym. Hall was opened in Boston in 1900 with the lighted signs "Exit in Case of Fire," someone cracked that they should more appropriately announce "Exit in Case of Brahms." Yet, at the hands of successive German conductors Brahms became a standard symphonist in N.Y., Boston, Philadelphia, and Baltimore. From the perspective of a century, Brahms appears as the greatest master of counterpoint after Bach; one can learn polyphony from a studious analysis of the chamber music and piano works of Brahms; he excelled in variation forms; his piano variations on a theme of Paganini are exemplars of contrapuntal learning, and they are also among the most difficult piano works of the 19th century. Posterity gave him a full measure of recognition; Hamburg celebrated his sesquicentennial in 1983 with great pomp. Brahms had lived a good life, but died a bad death, stricken with cancer of the liver.

*Bryant, Allan**, American composer; b. Detroit, July 12, 1931. He attended Princeton Univ.; then went to Germany, where he worked at the electronic studio in Cologne. Returning to the U.S., he wrote music with multimedia resources designed for theatrical representation. His works include *Quadruple Play* for Amplified Rubber Bands utilizing Contact Microphones and coordinated with an Audio-controlled Lighting System (1966); *Impulses* for a Variety of Percussion, Concussion, and Discussion Sounds (1967); *Bang-Bang* for Loud Instruments, including an Amplified Circular Violin (1967); *X-es Sex*, an intersexual happening, with Boots and Balloons (1967); also political works, e.g. *Liberate Isang Yun* (1967) for a Multimillion-decibel Electronic Sound calculated to reach the ears of the South Korean abductors of the dissident Korean composer Isang Yun from West Berlin (he was liberated in 1969 in response to the tremendous acoustical pressure of the Bryant piece).

Budd, Harold, American composer of extreme avant-garde tendencies; b. Los Angeles, May 24, 1936. He studied composition and acoustics with Gerald Strang and Aurelio de la Vega at Calif. State Univ. at Northridge (B.A., 1963) and with Ingolf Dahl at the Univ. of Southern Calif. (M.Mus., 1966). From 1969 to 1976 he was on the faculty of the Calif. Inst. of the Arts. An exponent of optically impressive music, he judged the quality of a work by its appearance on paper, in the firm conviction that visual excellence is cosubstantial with audible merit. His compositions are mostly designed for mixed media; some of them are modular, capable of being choreographed one into another; some are mere verbalizations of the intended mode of performance, calculated to stultify, confuse, or exasperate the listening beholder. Perhaps the most arresting and bewildering of such misleading works in his catalogue is something called *Intermission Piece*, to be played at random with a "barely audible amplitude spectrum" during intermission, with the audience "physically or conceptually absent," so that the number of performances runs into thousands, including every time an intermission during a concert occurs any place in the world.

WORKS: *Analogies from Rothko* for Orch. (1964); *The 6th This Year* for Orch. (1967); *September Music* (1967); *November* (1967; score displayed as a painting at the Museum of Contemporary Crafts in N.Y.); *Black Flowers*, a "quiet chamber ritual for 4 performers," to be staged in semidarkness on the threshold of visibility and audibility (1968); *Intermission Piece* (1968; 1st heard as musicians tuned their instruments and practiced various passages of the music scheduled to be played, during the intermission, at Hartford, Conn., Jan. 28, 1970); *1 Sound* for String Quartet glissando (1968); *Mangus Colorado* for Amplified Gongs (1969; Buffalo, Feb. 4, 1970); *Lovely Thing* for Piano, telling the player: "Select a chord—if in doubt call me (in lieu of performance) at 231-662-7819 for spiritual advice" (Memphis, Tenn., Oct. 23, 1969); *Lovely Thing* for Strings (1969); *California 99* (1969); *The Candy-Apple Revision* (1970); *Wonder's Edge* for Piano, Electric Guitar, and Electronics (San Francisco, Feb. 26, 1982).

Burgess, Anthony, celebrated British novelist, author of *A Clockwork Orange* and other imaginative novels, who began his career as a professional musician; b. Manchester, Feb. 25, 1917. He played piano in jazz combos in England, at the same time studying classical compositions without a tutor. Despite his great success as a novelist, he continued to write music, and developed a style of composition that, were it not for his literary fame, would have earned him a respectable niche among composers. His music is refreshingly rhythmical and entirely tonal, but not without quirky quartal harmonies and crypto-atonal melodic flights. He publ. *This Man and Music* (London, 1982).

WORKS: 3 syms. (1937; 1956, subtitled *Sinfoni Melayu*, and based on Malaysian themes; 1975); *Sinfonietta* for Jazz Combo (1941); symphonic poem, *Gibraltar* (1944); *Song of a Northern City* for Piano and Orch. (1947); *Partita* for String Orch. (1951); *Ludus Multitonalis* for Recorder Consort (1951); Concertino for Piano and Percussion (1951); *Cantata for Malay College* (1954); Concerto for Flute and Strings (1960); Passacaglia for Orch. (1961); Piano Concerto (1976); Cello Sonata (1944); 2 piano sonatas (1946, 1951); incidental music for various plays; songs.

Bussotti, Sylvano, Italian composer of the avant-garde; b. Florence, Oct. 1, 1931. He studied violin; at the age of 9 was enrolled in the Cherubini Cons. in

Florence, where he studied theory with Roberto Lupi, and also took piano lessons with Luigi Dallapiccola, while continuing his basic violin studies. In 1956 he went to Paris, where he studied privately with Max Deutsch. He became active as a theatrical director; also exhibited his paintings at European galleries. From 1979 to to 1981 he was artistic director of the Teatro La Fenice in Venice; he also taught at the Fiesole School of Music (from 1980). As a composer he adopted an extreme idiom, in which verbalization and pictorial illustrations are combined with aleatory discursions within the framework of multimedia productions. Many of his scores look like abstract expressionist paintings, with fragments of musical notation interspersed with occasional realistic representations of human or animal forms. From 1965 he devoted himself principally to creating works for the musical theater, which he described as BUSSOTTI-OPERABALLET.

WORKS: *Memoria* for Baritone, Chorus, and Orch. (1962); *Fragmentations* for Harp (1962); *La Passion selon Sade*, his crowning achievement, which makes use of theatrical effects, diagrams, drawings, surrealistic illustrations, etc., with thematic content evolving from a dodecaphonic nucleus, allowing great latitude for free interpolations, and set in an open-end form in which fragments of the music are recapitulated at will, until the players are mutually neutralized. The unifying element of the score is the recurrent motive D-Es-A-D-E, spelling the name De Sade, interwoven with that of B-A-C-H. The 1st production of *La Passion selon Sade* took place in Palermo on Sept. 5, 1965. His grand opera *Lorenzaccio*, in 23 scenes, employing a multitude of performers, which required 230 costumes, all designed by Bussotti himself, was produced at the opening of the Venice Festival of Contemporary Music on Sept. 7, 1972. Among Bussotti's other conceits is *5 Pieces for David Tudor* (1959), in which the dedicatee wears thick gloves to avoid hitting single and potentially melodious tones on the keyboard. Among his other works of various descriptions are 3 pieces for puppet theater: *Nottetempolunapark* (1954); *Arlechinbatocieria* (1955); *Tre mascare in gloria* (1956); *7 Fogli* for various instrumental combinations (1959); *Phrase à trois* for String Trio (1960); *Torso* for Voices, Speaker, and Instrumentalists (1960–63); *La Partition ne peut se faire que dans la violence* for Orch. (1962); *I semi di Gramsci* for Quartet and Orch. (1967); *Tableaux vivants* for 2 Pianos (1965); *Rara Requiem* to words in several languages (1969); *Opus Cygne* for Flute and Orch. (Baden-Baden, Oct. 20, 1979).

Cage, John (Milton, Jr.), highly inventive American composer, writer, philosopher, and artist of ultramodern tendencies; b. Los Angeles, Sept. 5, 1912. So important did Cage's work eventually become in music history that even the *Encyclopaedia Britannica* described him as a "composer whose work and revolutionary ideas profoundly influenced mid–20th-century music." His father, John Milton Cage, Sr., was an inventor, his mother active as a clubwoman in California. He studied piano with Fannie Dillon and Richard Buhlig in Los Angeles and with Lazare Lévy in Paris; returning to the U.S., he studied composition in California with Adolph Weiss and Schoenberg, and with Henry Cowell in N.Y. On June 7, 1935, Cage married, in Los Angeles, Xenia Kashevaroff; they were divorced in 1945. In 1938–39 he was employed as a dance accompanist at the Cornish School in Seattle, where he also organized a percussion group. He developed Cowell's piano technique, making use of tone clusters and playing directly on the strings, and initiated a type of procedure to be called "prepared piano," which consists of placing on the piano strings a variety of objects, such as screws, copper coins, and rubber bands, which alter the tone color of individual keys. Eventually the term and procedure gained acceptance among avant-garde composers and was listed as a legitimate method in several music dictionaries. In 1949 Cage was awarded a

Guggenheim fellowship and an award from the National Academy of Arts and Letters for having "extended the boundaries of music."

Cage taught for a season at the School of Design in Chicago (1941–42); he then moved to N.Y., where he began a fruitful association with the dancer Merce Cunningham, with whom he collaborated on a number of works that introduced radical innovations in musical and choreographic composition. He served as musical adviser to the Merce Cunningham Dance Co. until 1987. Another important association was his collaboration with the pianist David Tudor, who was able to reify Cage's exotic inspirations, works in which the performer shares the composer's creative role. In 1952, at Black Mountain College, he presented a theatrical event historically marked as the earliest musical Happening.

With the passing years Cage departed from the pragmatism of precise musical notation and definite ways of performance, electing instead to mark his creative intentions in graphic symbols and pictorial representations. He established the principle of indeterminacy in musical composition, producing works any 2 performances of which can never be identical. In the meantime, he became immersed in an earnest study of mushrooms, acquiring formidable expertise and winning a prize in Italy in competition with professional mycologists. He also became interested in chess, and played demonstration games with Marcel Duchamp, the famous painter turned chessmaster, on a chessboard designed by Lowell Cross to operate on aleatory principles with the aid of a computer and a system of laser rays. In his endeavor to achieve ultimate freedom in musical expression, he produced a piece entitled *4'33"*, in 3 movements, during which no sounds are intentionally produced. It was performed in Woodstock, N.Y., on Aug. 29, 1952, by David Tudor, who sat at the piano playing nothing for the length of time stipulated in the title. This was followed by another "silent" piece, *0'00"*, an idempotent "to be played in any way by anyone," presented for the 1st time in Tokyo, Oct. 24, 1962. Any sounds, noises, coughs, chuckles, groans, and growls produced by the listeners are automatically regarded as integral to the piece itself, so that the wisecrack about the impossibility of arriving at a fair judgment of a silent piece, since one cannot tell what music is not being played, is invalidated by the uniqueness of Cage's art.

Cage is a consummate showman, and his exhibitions invariably attract music-lovers and music-haters alike, expecting to be exhilarated or outraged, as the case may be. In many such public Happenings he departs from musical, unmusical, or even antimusical programs in favor of a free exercise of surrealist imagination, often instructing the audience to participate actively, as for instance going out into the street and bringing in garbage pails needed for percussion effects, with or without garbage. His music is publ. by C.F. Peters Corp. and has been recorded on many labels. In view of the indeterminacy of so many of Cage's works, the catalog publ. by Peters in 1969 can only serve as a list of titles and suggestions of contents. In order to eliminate the subjective element in composition, Cage resorts to a method of selecting the components of his pieces by dice throwing, suggested by the Confucian classic *I Ching*, an ancient Chinese oracle book; the result is a system of total serialism, in which all elements pertaining to acoustical pulses, pitch, noise, duration, relative loudness, tempi, combinatory superpositions, etc., are determined by previously drawn charts. His stage work *Europeras 1 & 2* (1987), which he wrote, designed, staged, and directed, is a sophisticated example, a collage comprised of excerpts from extant operas selected and manipulated by a computer software program, *IC* (short for *I Ching*), designed by Cage's assistant, Andrew Culver. The scheduled opening of *Europeras 1 & 2*, which was to take place on Nov. 15, 1987, was delayed and its location changed due to a fire, reportedly set by a vagrant in search of food, which devastated the Frankfurt Opera House just a few days before the opening.

Cage is also a brilliant writer, much influenced by the manner, grammar, syntax, and glorified illogic of Gertrude Stein. Among his works are *Silence* (1961), *A Year from Monday* (1967), *M* (1973), *Empty Words* (1979), and *X* (1983). He developed a style of poetry called "mesostic," which uses an anchoring string of letters down the center of the page that spell a name, a word, or even a line of text relating to the subject matter of the poem. Mesostic poems are composed by computer, the "source material" pulverized and later enhanced by Cage into a semi-coherent, highly evocative poetic text. He has also collaborated on a number of other projects, most recently *The First Meeting of the Satie Society*, with illustrations by Jasper Johns, Cy Twombly, Robert Rauschenberg, Sol LeWitt, Mell Daniel, Henry David Thoreau, and Cage himself, in preparation by the Limited Editions Club. Since Cage's works are multigenetic, his scores have been exhibited in galleries and museums; he returns annually to Crown Point Press in San Francisco to make etchings. A series of 52 paintings, the *New River Watercolors*, executed in 1987 at the Miles C. Horton Center at the Virginia Polytechnic Inst. and State Univ., has been shown at the Phillips Collection in Washington, D.C. (1990).

Cage was elected to the American Academy and Inst. of Arts and Letters in 1968 and to the American Academy of Arts and Sciences in 1978; he was inducted into the 50-member American Academy of Arts and Letters in 1989. In 1981 he received the Mayor's Award of Honor in N.Y. City. He was named Commander of the Order of Arts and Letters by the French Minister of Culture in 1982, and received an Honorary Doctorate of Performing Arts from the Calif. Inst. of the Arts in 1986. In 1988–89 Cage was Charles Eliot Norton Prof. of Poetry at Harvard Univ., for which he prepared a series of lengthy mesostic poems incorporating the writings of R. Buckminster Fuller, Henry David Thoreau, Marshall McLuhan, and others. In the summer of 1989 he was guest artist at the International Festivals in Leningrad and Moscow, at which he presented works characteristically entitled *Music for* . . . , which he conducted chironomically by pointing out instruments that were to enter. In late 1989 he traveled to Japan to receive the prestigious and lucrative Kyoto Prize.

Callcott, John Wall, English organist and composer; b. London, Nov. 20, 1766; d. Bristol, May 15, 1821. Early in life he developed a particular talent for composing glees and catches; won 3 prize medals at a contest of the Catch Club of London (1785) for his catch *O Beauteous Fair*; a canon, *Blessed Is He*; and a glee, *Dull Repining Sons of Care*. He received his Mus.Bac and Mus.Doc. from Oxford (1785, 1800); was a cofounder of the Glee Club (1787). During Haydn's visit to London in 1791, Callcott took a few lessons with him and wrote a sym. in imitation of his style. His mind gave way from overwork on a projected biographical dictionary of musicians, and he was institutionalized just before he reached the quirky letter Q. He recovered; but not sufficiently to continue his work, and was released in 1812. In addition to numerous glees, catches, and canons, he wrote *A Musical Grammar* (London, 1806), a standard elementary textbook that went through numerous eds. in England and America. A 3-vol. collection of glees, catches, and canons, with a biographical memoir, was publ. posthumously by his son-in-law, William Horsley (London, 1824).

Calloway, Cab(ell), noted black American jazz singer and bandleader; b. Rochester, N.Y., Dec. 25, 1907. After making his way to Chicago, he began his career as a singer and dancer; in 1928–29 he led the Alabamians, and in 1929 took over the leadership of the Missourians, with which he established himself in N.Y. (1930); he subsequently led various other groups. He was a proponent of scat singing, characterized by nonsense syllabification and rapid glossolalia with the melodic line largely submerged under an asymmetric inundation of rhythmic heterophony. He compiled *Hepster's Dictionary*, listing jazz terms (1938), and publ. an informal autobiography, *Of Minnie the Moocher and Me* (N.Y., 1976).

Caruso, Enrico (Errico), celebrated Italian tenor; b. Naples, Feb. 27, 1873; d. there, Aug. 2, 1921. He was the 18th child of a worker's family, his father being a machinist. All 17 children born before him died in infancy; 2 born after him survived. He sang Neapolitan ballads by ear; as a youth he applied for a part in *Mignon* at the Teatro Fondo in Naples, but was unable to follow the orch. at the rehearsal and had to be replaced by another singer. His 1st serious study was with Guglielmo Vergine (1891–94); he continued with Vincenzo Lombardi. His operatic debut took place at the Teatro Nuovo in Naples on Nov. 16, 1894, in *L'Amico Francesco*, by an amateur composer, Mario Morelli. In 1895 he appeared at the Teatro Fondo in *La Traviata, La Favorita*, and *Rigoletto*; during the following few seasons he added *Aida, Faust, Carmen, La Bohème*, and *Tosca* to his repertoire. The decisive turn in his career came when he was chosen to appear as leading tenor in the 1st performance of Giordano's *Fedora* (Teatro Lirico, Milan, Nov. 17, 1898), in which he made a great impression. Several important engagements followed. In 1899 and 1900 he sang in St. Petersburg and Moscow; between 1899 and 1903 he appeared in 4 summer seasons in Buenos Aires. The culmination of these successes was the coveted opportunity to sing at La Scala; he sang there in *La Bohème* (Dec. 26, 1900), and in the 1st performance of Mascagni's *Le Maschere* (Jan. 17, 1901). At the Teatro Lirico in Milan he took part in the 1st performances of Franchetti's *Germania* (March 11, 1902) and Cilea's *Adriana Lecouvreur* (Nov. 6, 1902). In the spring season of 1902 he appeared (with Melba) in Monte Carlo, and was reengaged there for 3 more seasons. He made his London debut as the Duke in *Rigoletto* (Covent Garden, May 14, 1902) and was immediately successful with the British public and press. He gave 25 performances in London until July 28, 1902, appearing with Melba, Nordica, and Calvé. In the season of 1902–3, Caruso sang in Rome and Lisbon; during the summer of 1903 he was in South America. Finally, on Nov. 23, 1903, he made his American debut at the Metropolitan Opera, in *Rigoletto*. After that memorable occasion, Caruso was connected with the Metropolitan to the end of his life. He traveled with various American opera companies from coast to coast; he happened to be performing in San Francisco when the 1906 earthquake nearly destroyed the city. He achieved his most spectacular successes in America, attended by enormous publicity. In 1907 Caruso sang in Germany (Leipzig, Hamburg, Berlin) and in Vienna; he was acclaimed there as enthusiastically as in the Anglo-Saxon and Latin countries. A complete list of his appearances is given in the appendix of his biography by Pierre Key and Bruno Zirato (Boston, 1922). Caruso's fees soared from $2 as a boy in Italy in 1891 to the fabulous sum of $15,000 for a single performance in Mexico City in 1920. He made recordings in the U.S. as early as 1902; his annual income from this source alone netted him $115,000 at the peak of his career. He excelled in realistic Italian operas; his Cavaradossi in *Tosca* and Canio in *Pagliacci* became models which every singer emulated. He sang several French operas; the German repertoire remained completely alien to him; his only appearances in Wagnerian roles were 3 performances of *Lohengrin* in Buenos Aires (1901). His voice possessed such natural warmth and great strength in the middle register that as a youth he was believed to be a baritone. The sustained quality of his bel canto was exceptional and enabled him to give superb interpretations of lyrical parts. For dramatic effect, he often resorted to the "coup de glotte" (which became known as the "Caruso sob"); here the singing gave way to intermittent vocalization without tonal precision. While Caruso was criticized for such usages from the musical standpoint, his characterizations on the stage were overwhelmingly impressive. Although of robust health, he abused it by unceasing activity. He was stricken with a throat hemorrhage during a performance at the Brooklyn Academy of Music (Dec. 11, 1920), but was able to sing in N.Y. one last time, on Dec. 24, 1920. Several surgical operations were performed in an effort to arrest a pleurisy; Caruso was taken to Italy, but succumbed to the illness after several months of remission. He was known as a convivial person and a lover of fine food (a brand of macaroni was named after him). He possessed a gift for caricature; a collection of his drawings was publ. in N.Y. in 1922 (2nd ed., 1951). His private life was turbulent; his liaison (never legalized) with Ada Giachetti, by whom he had 2 sons, was painfully resolved by court proceedings in 1912, creating much disagreeable publicity; there were also suits brought against him by 2 American women. In 1906 the celebrated "monkey-house case" (in which Caruso was accused of improper behavior toward a lady while viewing the animals in Central Park) threatened for a while his continued success in America. On Aug. 20, 1918, he married Dorothy Park Benjamin of N.Y., over the strong opposition of her father, a rich industrialist. Caruso received numerous decorations from European governments, among them the Order of Commendatore of the Crown of Italy; the Légion d'honneur; and the Order of the Crown Eagle of Prussia. A fictional film biography, *The Great Caruso*, was made of his life in 1950.

Cohen, Leonard, Canadian balladeer; b. Montreal, Sept. 21, 1934. One of the few Jews who made it as a pop singer, he went into such highbrow stuff as writing poetry and publishing sentimental novels. At the same time, he strummed his guitar and sang such maudlin romances as *Suzanne* and such alienation tunes as *Stranger Song*, such heart-impinging implorations as *Hey, That's No Way to Say Goodbye*, and such beseeching tunes as *Sisters of Mercy*. He sang at the Newport Folk Festival in 1967 and teamed with Judy Collins in his American tour. Like Bob Dylan and other troubled songsters, Cohen periodically withdrew from public view to meditate about his alienation. His *Songs of Love and Hate* exemplified such psychological quaquaversality. He returned to the world at large and released an album symbolic of his healing graft, *New Skin for the Old Ceremony*.

Cowell, Henry (Dixon), remarkable, innovative American composer; b. Menlo Park, Calif., March 11, 1897; d. Shady, N.Y., Dec. 10, 1965. His father, of Irish birth, was a member of a clergyman's family in Kildare; his mother was an American of progressive persuasion. Cowell studied violin with Henry Holmes in San Francisco; after the earthquake of 1906, his mother took him to N.Y., where they were compelled to seek support from the Soc. for the Improvement of the Condition of the Poor; they returned to Menlo Park, where Cowell was able to save enough money, earned from menial jobs, to buy a piano. He began to experiment with the keyboard by striking the keys with fists and forearms; he named such chords "tone clusters" and at the age of 13 composed a piece called *Adventures in Harmony*, containing such chords. Later he began experimenting in altering the sound of the piano by placing various objects on the strings, and also by playing directly under the lid of the piano *pizzicato* and *glissando*. He first exhibited these startling innovations on March 5, 1914, at the San Francisco Musical Soc. at the St. Francis Hotel, much to the consternation of its members, no doubt. The tone clusters per se were not new; they were used for special sound effects by composers in the 18th century to imitate thunder or cannon fire. The Russian composer Vladimir Rebikov applied them in his piano piece *Hymn to Inca*, and Charles Ives used them in his *Concord Sonata* to be sounded by covering a set of white or black keys with a wooden board. However, Cowell had a priority by systematizing tone clusters as harmonic amplifications of tonal chords, and he devised logical notation for them. The tone clusters eventually acquired legitimacy in the works of many European and American composers. Cowell also extended the sonorities of tone clusters to instrumental combinations and applied them in several of his symphonic works. In the meantime Cowell began taking lessons in composition with E.G. Strickland and Wallace Sabin at the Univ. of Calif. in Berkeley, and later with Frank Damrosch at the Inst. of Musical Art in N.Y., and, privately, with Charles Seeger (1914–16). After brief service in the U.S. Army in 1918, where he was employed first as a cook and later as arranger for the U.S. Army Band, he became engaged professionally to give a series of lectures on new music, illustrated by his playing his own works on the piano. In 1928 he went to Russia, where he attracted considerable attention as the 1st American composer to visit there; some of his pieces were publ. in a Russian ed., the 1st such publications by an American. Upon return to the U.S., he was appointed lecturer on music at The New School in N.Y.

In 1931 he received a Guggenheim fellowship grant, and went to Berlin to study ethnomusicology with Erich von Hornbostel. This was the beginning of his serious study of ethnic musical materials. He had already experimented with some Indian and Chinese devices in some of his works; in his *Ensemble* for Strings (1924) he included Indian thundersticks; the piece naturally aroused considerable curiosity. In 1931 he formed a collaboration with the Russian electrical engineer Leon Theremin, then visiting the U.S.; with his aid he constructed an ingenious instrument which he called the Rhythmicon; it made possible the simultaneous production of 16 different rhythms on 16 different pitch levels of the harmonic series. He demonstrated the Rhythmicon at a lecture-concert in San Francisco on May 15, 1932. He also composed an extensive work entitled *Rhythmicana*, but it did not receive a performance until Dec. 3, 1971, at Stanford Univ., using advanced electronic techniques. In 1927 Cowell founded the *New Music Quarterly* for publication of ultramodern music, mainly by American composers.

Cowell's career was brutally interrupted in 1936, when he was arrested in California on charges of homosexuality (then a heinous offense in California) involving the impairment of the morals of a minor. Lulled by the deceptive promises of a wily district attorney of a brief confinement in a sanatorium, Cowell pleaded guilty to a limited offense, but he was vengefully given a maximum sentence of imprisonment, up to 15 years. Incarcerated at San Quentin, he was assigned to work in a jute mill, but indomitably continued to write music in prison. Thanks to interventions in his behalf by a number of eminent musicians, he was paroled in 1940 to Percy Grainger as a guarantor of his good conduct; he obtained a full pardon on Dec. 9, 1942, from the governor of California, Earl Warren, after it was discovered that the evidence against him was largely contrived. On Sept. 27, 1941, he married Sidney Robertson, a noted ethnomusicologist. He was then able to resume his full activities as ed. and instructor; he held teaching positions at The New School for Social Research in N.Y. (1940–62), the Univ. of Southern Calif., Mills College, and the Peabody Cons. of Music in Baltimore (1951–56); was also appointed adjunct prof. at summer classes at Columbia Univ. (1951–65). In 1951 Cowell was elected a member of the National Academy of Arts and Letters; received an honorary Mus.D. from Wilmington College (1953) and from Monmouth (Ill.) College (1963). In 1956–57 he undertook a world tour with his wife through the Near East, India, and Japan, collecting rich prime materials for his compositions, which by now had acquired a decisive turn toward the use of ethnomusicological melodic and rhythmic materials, without abandoning, however, the experimental devices which were the signposts of most of his works. In addition to his symphonic and chamber music, Cowell publ. in 1930 an important book, *New Musical Resources*. He also ed. a symposium, *American Composers on American Music*; in collaboration with his wife he wrote the basic biography of Charles Ives (1955).

Craft, Robert (Lawson), American conductor and brilliant writer on music; b. Kingston, N.Y., Oct. 20, 1923. He studied at the Juilliard School of Music (B.A., 1946) and the Berkshire Music Center; took courses in conducting with Monteux. During World War II he was in the U.S. Army Medical Corps. In 1947 he conducted the N.Y. Brass and Woodwind Ensemble. He was conductor of the Evenings-on-the-Roof and the Monday Evening Concerts in Los Angeles (1950–68). A decisive turn in his career was his encounter with Stravinsky in 1948, whom he greatly impressed by his precise knowledge of Stravinsky's music; gradually he became Stravinsky's closest associate. He was also instrumental in persuading Stravinsky to adopt the 12-tone method of composition, a momentous turn in Stravinsky's creative path. He collaborated with Stravinsky on 6 vols. of a catechumenical and discursive nature: *Conversations with Igor Stravinsky* (N.Y., 1959); *Memories and Commentaries* (N.Y., 1960); *Expositions and Developments* (N.Y., 1962); *Dialogues and a Diary* (N.Y., 1963); *Themes and Episodes* (N.Y., 1967); *Retrospections and Conclusions* (N.Y., 1969). Resentful of frequent referral to him as a musical Boswell, Craft insists that his collaboration with Stravinsky was more akin to that between the Goncourt brothers, both acting and reacting to an emerging topic of discussion, with Stravinsky evoking his ancient memories in his careful English, or fluent French, spiced with unrestrained discourtesies toward professional colleagues on the American scene, and Craft reifying the material with an analeptic bulimia of quaquaversal literary, psychological, physiological, and culinary references in a flow of finely ordered dialogue. His other publications include *Prejudices in Disguise* (N.Y., 1974); *Stravinsky in Photographs and Documents* (with Vera Stravinsky; London, 1976; N.Y., 1978); *Current Convictions: Views and Reviews* (N. Y., 1977); *Present Perspectives* (N.Y., 1984). He also tr. and ed. *Stravinsky, Selected Correspondence* (2 vols., N.Y., 1982, 1984).

Crawford, Ruth Porter, remarkable American composer; b. East Liverpool, Ohio, July 3, 1901; d. Chevy Chase, Md., Nov. 18, 1953. She studied composition with **Charles Seeger,** whom she later married; her principal piano teacher was Heniot Lévy. She dedicated herself to teaching and to collecting American folk songs; when still very young, she taught at the School of Musical Arts in Jacksonville, Fla. (1918–21); then gave courses at the American Cons. in Chicago (1925–29) and at the Elmhurst College of Music in Illinois (1926–29). In 1930 she received a Guggenheim fellowship. She became known mainly as a compiler of American folk songs; publ. *American Folk Songs for Children* (1948), *Animal Folk Songs for Children* (1950), and *American Folk Songs for Christmas* (1953). Her own compositions, astonishingly bold in their experimental aperçus and insights, often anticipated many techniques of the future avant-grade; while rarely performed during her lifetime, they had a remarkable revival in subsequent decades.

Crumb, George (Henry Jr.), distinguished and innovative American composer; b. Charleston, W.Va., Oct. 24, 1929. He was brought up in a musical environment; his father played the clarinet and his mother was a cellist; he studied music at home; began composing while in school, and had some of his pieces performed by the Charleston Sym. Orch. He then took courses in composition at Mason College in Charleston (B.M., 1950); later enrolled at the Univ. of Illinois (M.M., 1952) and continued his studies in composition with Ross Lee Finney at the Univ. of Michigan (D.M.A., 1959); in 1955 he received a Fulbright fellowship for travel to Germany, where he studied with Boris Blacher at the Berlin Hochschule für Musik. He further received grants from the Rockefeller (1964), Koussevitzky (1965), and Coolidge (1970) foundations; in 1967 held a Guggenheim fellowship, and also was given the National Inst. of Arts and Letters Award. In 1968 he was awarded the Pulitzer Prize in music for his *Echoes of Time and the River*. Parallel to working on his compositions, he was active as a music teacher. From 1959 to 1964 he taught piano and occasional classes in composition at the Univ. of Colorado at Boulder; in 1965 he joined the music dept. of the Univ. of Pa.; in 1983 he was named Annenberg Prof. of the Humanities there. In his music, Crumb is a universalist. Nothing in the realm of sound is alien to him; no method of composition is unsuited to his artistic purposes; accordingly, his music can sing as sweetly as the proverbial nightingale, and it can be as rough, rude, and crude as a primitive man of the mountains. The vocal parts especially demand extraordinary skills of lungs, lips, tongue, and larynx to produce such sound effects as percussive tongue clicks, explosive shrieks, hissing, whistling, whispering, and sudden shouting of verbal irrelevancies, interspersed with portentous syllabification, disparate phonemes, and rhetorical logorrhea. In startling contrast, Crumb injects into his sonorous kaleidoscope citations from popular works, such as the middle section of Chopin's *Fantaisie-Impromptu*, Ravel's *Bolero*, or some other "objet trouvé," a procedure first introduced facetiously by Erik Satie. In his instrumentation, Crumb is no less unconventional. Among the unusual effects in his scores is instructing the percussion player to immerse the loudly sounding gong into a tub of water, having an electric guitar played with glass rods over the frets, or telling wind instrumentalists to blow soundlessly through their tubes. Spatial distribution also plays a role: instrumentalists and singers are assigned their reciprocal locations on the podium or in the hall. All this is, of course, but an illustrative décor; the music is of the essence. Like most composers who began their work around the middle of the 20th century, Crumb adopted the Schoenbergian idiom, seasoned with pointillistic devices. After these preliminaries, he wrote his unmistakably individual *Madrigals*, to words by the martyred poet Federico García Lorca, scored for voice and instrumental groups. There followed the most extraordinary work, *Ancient Voices of Children*, performed for the 1st time at a chamber music festival in Washington, D.C., on Oct. 31, 1970; the text is again by Lorca; a female singer intones into the space under the lid of an amplified grand piano; a boy's voice responds in anguish; the accompaniment is supplied by an orch. group and an assortment of exotic percussion instruments, such as Tibetan prayer stones, Japanese temple bells, a musical saw, and a toy piano. A remarkable group of 4 pieces, entitled *Makrokosmos*, calls for unusual effects; in one of these, the pianist is ordered to shout at specified points of time. Crumb's most grandiose creation is *Star-Child*, representing, in his imaginative scheme, a progression from tenebrous despair to the exaltation of luminous joy. The score calls for a huge orch., which includes 2 children's choruses and 8 percussion players performing on all kinds of utensils, such as pot lids, and also iron chains and metal sheets, as well as ordinary drums; it had its 1st performance under the direction of Pierre Boulez with the N.Y. Phil. on May 5, 1977.

Czerny, Carl, celebrated Austrian pianist, composer, and pedagogue; b. Vienna, Feb. 20, 1791; d. there, July 15, 1857. He was of Czech extraction (*czerny* means "black" in Czech), and his 1st language was Czech. He received his early training from his father, Wenzel Czerny, a stern disciplinarian who never let his son play with other children and insisted on concentrated work. Czerny had the privilege of studying for 3 years with Beethoven, and their association in subsequent years became a close one. Czerny also received advice as a pianist from Hummel and

BIOGRAPHIES

Clementi. He made trips to Leipzig (1836); visited Paris and London (1837) and Italy (1846); with these exceptions, he remained all his life in Vienna. His self-imposed daily schedule for work was a model of diligence; he denied himself any participation in the social life of Vienna and seldom attended opera or concerts. Very early in life he demonstrated great ability as a patient piano teacher; Beethoven entrusted to him the musical education of his favorite nephew. When Czerny himself became a renowned pedagogue, many future piano virtuosos flocked to him for lessons, among them Liszt (whom he taught without a fee), Thalberg, Theodore Kullak, Döhler, Jaëll, and Anna Belleville-Oury. Despite the heavy teaching schedule, Czerny found time to compose a fantastic amount of piano music, 861 opus numbers in all, each containing many individual items; these included not only piano studies and exercises, for which he became celebrated, but also sonatas, concertos, string quartets, masses, and hymns. In addition, he made numerous piano arrangements of classical syms., including all of Beethoven's, and wrote fantasies for piano on the themes from famous operas of the time. So dedicated was he to his chosen work that he renounced all thoughts of marriage (but a secret confession of his Platonic adoration of an unnamed female person was found among his MSS); in this wistful deprivation, Czerny's fate paralleled Beethoven's. For a century there has been a fashion among musical sophisticates to deprecate Czerny as a pathetic purveyor of manufactured musical goods; his contemporary John Field, the originator of the genre of piano nocturnes, described Czerny as a "Tintenfass"—an inkpot. A quip was circulated that Czerny hated children, and that he publ. his voluminous books of piano exercises to inflict pain on young pianists. Of late, however, there has been a change of heart toward Czerny as a worthy composer in his own right. Stravinsky expressed his admiration for Czerny, and modern composers have written, with a half-concealed smile, pieces "à la manière de Czerny." Czerny was unexpectedly revealed to be a musician of imaginative fancy and engaging pedantic humor, as for instance in his Brobdingnagian arrangement of Rossini's Overture to *William Tell* for 16 pianists playing 4-hands on 8 pianos; pieces for 3 pianists playing 6-hands on a single keyboard; etc. Obsessed by an idea of compassing all musical knowledge at once, he publ. an *Umriss der ganzen Musikgeschichte* (Mainz, 1851), and also a vol. in English entitled *Letters to a Young Lady on the Art of Playing the Pianoforte from the Earliest Rudiments to the Highest State of Cultivation* (the young lady in the title was never identified). Of his studies the most famous are *Schule der Geläufigkeit*, op. 299, and *Schule der Fingerfertigkeit*, op. 740; others are *Die Schule des Legato und Staccato*, op. 335; *40 tägliche Studien*, op. 337; *Schule der Verzierungen*, op. 355; *Schule des Virtuosen*, op. 365; *Schule der linken Hand*, op. 399; etc. His Sonata, op. 7, was popular; among his piano transcriptions to be mentioned is *Fantaisie et Variations brillantes* on an aria from Persiani's opera *Ines de Castro*. Czerny's autobiography, *Erinnerungen aus meinem Leben*, was ed. by W. Kolneder (Baden-Baden, 1968; publ. in part in Eng. in the *Musical Quarterly*, July 1956).

Da Ponte, Lorenzo (real name, **Emanuele Conegliano**), famous Italian librettist; b. Ceneda, near Venice, March 10, 1749; d. N.Y., Aug. 17, 1838. He was of a Jewish family; was converted to Christianity at the age of 14, and assumed the name of his patron, Lorenzo da Ponte, Bishop of Ceneda. He then studied at the Ceneda Seminary and at the Portogruaro Seminary, where he taught from 1770 to 1773; in 1774 obtained a post as prof. of rhetoric at Treviso, but was dismissed in 1776 for his beliefs concerning natural laws. He then went to Venice, where he led an adventurous life, and was banished in 1779 for adultery; subsequently lived in Austria and in Dresden; in 1782 he settled in Vienna and became official poet to the Imperial Theater; met Mozart and became his friend and librettist of his most famous operas, *Le nozze di Figaro, Don Giovanni*, and *Così fan tutte*. From 1792 to 1798 he was in London; traveled in Europe; then went to N.Y. in 1805. After disastrous business ventures, with intervals of teaching, he became interested in various operatic enterprises. In his last years he was a teacher of Italian at Columbia College. He publ. *Memorie* (4 vols., N.Y., 1823–27; Eng. tr., London, 1929, and Philadelphia, 1929).

Debussy, (Achille-)Claude, great French composer whose music created new poetry of mutating tonalities and became a perfect counterpart of new painting in France; b. St.-Germain-en-Laye, Aug. 22, 1862; d. Paris, March 25, 1918. Mme. Mauté de Fleurville, the mother-in-law of the poet Verlaine, prepared him for the Paris Cons.; he was admitted at the age of 10 and studied piano with Marmontel (2nd prize, 1877) and solfège with Lavignac (3rd medal, 1874; 2nd, 1875; 1st, 1876). He further took courses in harmony with Emile Durand (1877–80) and practiced score reading under Bazille. In 1880 Marmontel recommended him to Mme. Nadezhda von Meck, Tchaikovsky's patroness. She summoned him to Interlaken, and they subsequently visited Rome, Naples, and Ficsole. During the summers of 1881 and 1882, Debussy stayed with Mme. von Meck's family in Moscow, where he became acquainted with the syms. of Tchaikovsky; however, he failed to appreciate Tchaikovsky's music and became more interested in the idiosyncratic compositions of Mussorgsky. Back in France, he became friendly with Mme. Vasnier, wife of a Paris architect and an amateur singer.

Debussy made his earliest professional appearance as a composer in Paris on May 12, 1882, at a concert given by the violinist Maurice Thieberg. In Dec. 1880 he enrolled in the composition class of Guiraud at the Paris Cons. with the ambition of winning the Grand Prix de Rome; after completing his courses, he won the 2nd Prix de Rome in 1883. Finally, on June 27, 1884, he succeeded in obtaining the Grand Prix de Rome with his cantata *L'Enfant prodigue*, written in a poetic but conservative manner reflecting the trends of French romanticism. During his stay in Rome he wrote a choral work, *Zuleima* (1885–86), after Heine's *Almanzor*, and began work on another cantata, *Diane au bois*. Neither of these 2 incunabulae was preserved. His choral suite with orch., *Printemps* (1887), failed to win formal recognition. He then set to work on another cantata, *La Damoiselle élue* (1887–89), which gained immediate favor among French musicians.

In 1888 Debussy visited Bayreuth, where he heard *Parsifal* and *Die Meistersinger von Nürnberg* for the 1st time, but Wagner's grandiloquence never gained his full devotion. What thoroughly engaged his interest was the oriental music that he heard at the Paris World Exposition in 1889. He was fascinated by the asymmetric rhythms of the thematic content and the new instrumental colors achieved by native players; he also found an inner valence between these oriental modalities and the verses of certain French impressionist poets, including Mallarmé, Verlaine, Baudelaire, and Pierre Louÿs. The combined impressions of exotic music and symbolist French verses were rendered in Debussy's vocal works, such as *Cinq poèmes de Baudelaire* (1887–89), *Ariettes oubliées* (1888), *Trois mélodies* (1891), and *Fêtes galantes* (1892). He also wrote *Proses lyriques* (1892–93) to his own texts. For the piano, he composed *Suite bergamasque* (1890–1905), which includes the famous *Clair de lune*. In 1892 he began work on his instrumental *Prelude à l'après-midi d'un faune*, after Mallarmé, which comprises the quintessence of tonal painting with its free modal sequences under a subtle umbrage of oscillating instrumentation. The work was 1st heard in Paris on Dec. 22, 1894; a program book cautioned the audience that the text contained sensuous elements that might be distracting to young females. It was about that time that Debussy attended a performance of Maeterlinck's drama *Pelléas et Mélisande*, which inspired him to begin work on an opera on that subject. In 1893 there followed *Trois chansons de Bilitis*, after prose poems by Louÿs, marked by exceptional sensuality of the text in a musical context of free modality; a later work, *Les Chansons de Bilitis* for 2 harps, 2 flutes, and celesta, was heard in Paris in 1901 as incidental music to accompany recited and mimed neo-Grecian poetry of Louÿs. Between 1892 and 1899 Debussy worked on *3 Nocturnes* for orch.: *Nuages, Fêtes*, and *Sirènes*.

As the 20th century dawned, Debussy found himself in a tangle of domestic relationships. A tempestuous liaison with Gabrielle Dupont (known as Gaby Lhéry) led to a break, which so distressed Gaby that she took poison. She survived, but Debussy sought more stable attachments; on Oct. 19, 1899, he married Rosalie Texier, with whom he made his 1st attempt to form a legitimate union. But he soon discovered that like Gaby before her, Rosalie failed to satisfy his expectations, and he began to look elsewhere for a true union of souls. This he found in the person of Emma Bardac, the wife of a banker. He bluntly informed Rosalie of his dissatisfaction with their marriage. Like Gaby 7 years before, Rosalie, plunged into despair by Debussy's selfish decision, attempted suicide; she shot herself in the chest but missed her suffering heart. Debussy, now 42 years old, divorced Rosalie on Aug. 2, 1905. Bardac and her husband were divorced on May 4, 1905; Debussy married her on Jan. 20, 1908. They had a daughter, Claude-Emma (known as "Chouchou"), born Oct. 15, 1905; she was the inspiration for Debussy's charming piano suite, *Children's Corner* (the title was in English, for Chouchou had an English governess). She survived her father by barely a year, dying of diphtheria on July 14, 1919.

With his opera *Pelléas et Mélisande*, Debussy assumed a leading place among French composers. It was premiered at the Opéra-Comique in Paris on April 30, 1902, after many difficulties, including the open opposition of Maeterlinck, who objected to having the role of Mélisande sung by the American soprano Mary Garden, whose accent jarred Maeterlinck's sensibilities; he wanted his mistress, Georgette Leblanc, to be the 1st Mélisande. The production of the opera aroused a violent controversy among French musicians and littérateurs. The press was vicious in the extreme: "Rhythm, melody, tonality, these are 3 things unknown to Monsieur Debussy," wrote the doyen of the Paris music critics, Arthur Pougin. "What a pretty series of false relations! What adorable progressions of triads in parallel motion and fifths and octaves which result from it! What a collection of dissonances, sevenths and ninths, ascending with energy! . . . No, decidedly I will never agree with these anarchists of music!" Camille Bellaigue, who was Debussy's classmate at the Paris Cons., conceded that *Pelléas et Mélisande* "makes little noise," but, he remarked, "it is a nasty little noise." The English and American reports were no less vituperative, pejorative, and deprecatory. "Debussy disowns melody and despises harmony with all its resources," opined the critic of the *Monthly Musical Record* of London. Echoing such judgments, the *Musical Courier* of N.Y. compared Debussy's "disharmony" with the sensation of "an involuntary start when the dentist touches the nerve of a sensitive tooth." And the American writer James Gibbons Huneker exceeded all limits of permissible literary mores by attacking Debussy's physical appearance. "I met Debussy at the Café Riche the other night," he wrote in the N.Y. *Sun*, "and was struck by the unique ugliness of the man. . . . [H]e looks more like a Bohemian, a Croat, a Hun, than a Gaul." These utterances were followed by a suggestion that Debussy's music was fit for a procession of head-hunters of Borneo, carrying home "their ghastly spoils of war."

Debussy's next important work was *La Mer*, which he completed during a sojourn in England in 1905. It was 1st performed in Paris, on Oct. 15, 1905. Like his String Quartet, it was conceived monothematically; a single musical idea permeated the entire work despite a great variety of instrumentation. It consists of 3 symphonic sketches: *De l'aube à midi sur la mer* (From Sunrise to Moon); *Jeux de vagues* (Play of the Waves); and *Dialogue du vent et de la mer* (Dialogue of Wind and the Sea). *La Mer* was attacked by critics with even greater displeasure than *Pelléas et Mélisande*. The American critic Louis Elson went so far as to suggest that the original title was actually *Le Mal de mer*, and that the last movement represented a violent seizure of vomiting. To summarize the judgment on Debussy, a vol. entitled *Le Cas Debussy* was publ. in Paris in 1910. It contained a final assessment of Debussy as a "déformateur musical," suffering from a modern nervous disease that affects one's power of discernment.

Meanwhile, Debussy continued to work. To be mentioned is the remarkable orch. triptych, *Images* (1906–12), comprising *Gigues, Ibéria*, and *Rondes de printemps*. In 1908 he conducted a concert of his works in London; he also accepted engagements as conductor in Vienna (1910), Turin (1911), Moscow and St. Petersburg (1913), and Rome, Amsterdam, and The Hague (1914). Among other works of the period are the piano suites, *Douze préludes* (2 books, 1909–10; 1910–13) and *Douze études* (2 books, 1915). *En blanc et noir*, for 2 pianos, dates from 1915. On May 15, 1913, Diaghilev produced Debussy's ballet *Jeux* in Paris. On May 5, 1917, Debussy played the piano part of his Violin Sonata at its premiere in Paris with violinist Gaston Poulet. But his projected tour of the U.S. with the violinist Arthur Hartmann had to be abandoned when it was discovered that Debussy had irreversible cancer of the colon. Surgery was performed in Dec. 1915, but there was little hope of recovery. The protracted 1st World War depressed him; his hatred of the Germans became intense as the military threat to Paris increased. He wrote the lyrics and the accompaniment to a song, *Noël des enfants*, in which he begged Santa Claus not to bring presents to German children whose parents were destroying the French children's Christmas. To underline his national sentiments, he emphatically signed his last works "musicien français." Debussy died on the evening of March 25, 1918, as the great German gun, "Big Bertha," made the last attempt to subdue the city of Paris by long-distance (76 miles) bombardment.

Debussy emphatically rejected the term "impressionism" as applied to his music. But it cannot alter the essential truth that like Mallarmé in poetry, he created a style peculiarly sensitive to musical mezzotint, a palette of half-lit delicate colors. He systematically applied the oriental pentatonic scale for exotic evocations, as well as the whole-tone scale (which he did not invent, however; earlier samples of its use are found in works by Glinka and Liszt). His piece for piano solo, *Voiles*, is written in a whole-tone scale, while its middle section is set entirely in the pentatonic scale. In his music Debussy emancipated discords; he also revived the archaic practice of consecutive perfect intervals (particularly fifths and fourths). In his formal constructions, the themes are shortened and rhythmically sharpened, while in the instrumental treatment the role of individual solo passages is enhanced and the dynamic range made more subtle.

Dragon, Carmen, American conductor, composer, and arranger; b. Antioch, Calif., July 28, 1914; d. Santa Monica, Calif., March 28, 1984. He learned to play piano, double bass, accordion, trumpet, and trombone. He studied music at San Jose State College; then went to San Francisco, where he played the piano in a nightclub. His next move was to Hollywood, where he effloresced as an arranger for movie stars who could not read music. He conducted background music for radio shows. In a higher elevation, he composed a patriotic band piece, *I'm an American*. His concerts supplied pleasurable fare for contented music-lovers. His son **Daryl Dragon** (b. Los Angeles, Aug. 27, 1942) became one-half of the popular music team Captain and Tennille.

Dylan, Bob (real name, **Robert Allen Zimmerman**), American folksinger and songwriter; b. Duluth, Minn., May 24, 1941. He adopted the name Dylan out of admiration for the poet Dylan Thomas. Possessed by wanderlust, he rode freight trains across the country; played guitar and crooned in the coffeehouses of N.Y. He also improvised songs to his own lyrics. His nasalized country-type semi-Western style and his self-haunted soft guitar-strumming captured the imagination not only of untutored adolescents but also of certified cognoscenti in search of convincing authenticity. In 1966 he broke his neck in a motorcycle accident, which forced him to interrupt his charismatic career for 2 years. In 1970 he was awarded an honorary doctorate from Princeton Univ., the 1st such honor given to a popular singer innocent of all academic training. A group of militants in the Students for a Democratic Soc. adopted the name "Weathermen" after a line from Dylan's song *Subterranean Homesick Blues*, "You don't need a weatherman to know which way the wind blows." The Weathermen claimed credit for several bombings in N.Y. City during 1969 and 1970.

Fiedler, Arthur, highly popular American conductor; b. Boston, Dec. 17, 1894; d. Brookline, Mass., July 10, 1979. Of a musical family, he studied violin with his father, Emanuel Fiedler, a member of the Boston Sym. Orch.; his uncle, Benny Fiedler, also played violin in the Boston Sym. Orch. In 1909 he was taken by his father to Berlin, where he studied violin with Willy Hess, and attended a class on chamber music with Ernst von Dohnányi; he also had some instruction in conducting with Arno Kleffel and Rudolf Krasselt. In 1913 he formed the Fiedler Trio with 2 other Fiedlers. In 1915, with the war raging in Europe, he returned to America, and joined the 2nd-violin section of the Boston Sym. Orch. under Karl Muck; later he moved to the viola section; he also doubled on the celesta, when required. In 1924 he organized the Arthur Fiedler Sinfonietta, a professional ensemble of members of the Boston Sym. Orch. In 1929 he started a series of free open-air summer concerts at the Esplanade on the banks of the Charles River in Boston, presenting programs of popular American music intermingled with classical numbers. The series became a feature in Boston's musical life, attracting audiences of many thousands each summer. In 1930 Fiedler was engaged as conductor of the Boston Pops, which he led for nearly half a century. Adroitly combining pieces of popular appeal with classical works and occasional modern selections, he built an eager following, eventually elevating the Boston Pops to the status of a national institution. He was seemingly undisturbed by the clinking of beer steins, the pushing of chairs, the shuffling of feet, and other incidental sound effects not provided for in the score but which were an integral part of audience participation at Pops concerts. For Fiedler was a social man, gregarious, fond of extracurricular activities; one of his favorite pastimes was riding on fire engines; this addiction was rewarded by a number of nominations as honorary chief of the fire depts. of several American cities. He became commercially successful and willingly accepted offers to advertise for whisky or for orange juice; this popularity, however, cost him a degradation to a lower rank of music-makers, so that his cherished ambition to conduct guest engagements in the regular subscription series of the Boston Sym. Orch. never materialized. On Jan. 4, 1977, President Ford bestowed upon him the Medal of Freedom. As a mark of appreciation from the city of Boston, a footbridge near the Esplanade was named after him, with the 1st 2 notes of the Prelude to *Tristan und Isolde*, A and F, marking the initials of Arthur Fiedler's name, engraved on the plaque. His death was mourned by Boston music-lovers in a genuine outpouring of public grief.

Fleischmann, Ernest (Martin), German-born American music administrator; b. Frankfurt am Main, Dec. 7, 1924. His family moved to South Africa, where he studied accounting at the Univ. of the Witwatersrand. He then devoted himself to music studies, obtaining a B.Mus. at the Univ. of Cape Town (1954). He was ambitious and took lessons in conducting with the then-resident British conductor, Albert Coates; also acted as an organizer of musical events, including the Van Riebeeck Festival in Cape Town (1952). Furthermore, he served as director of music and drama for the Johannesburg Festival (1956). In the process he learned Afrikaans, and acquired a literary fluency in English. Seeking ever wider fields of endeavor, he went to London, becoming a naturalized citizen in 1959; he acted as general manager of the London Sym. Orch. until 1967 and also made a number of conducting appearances in England. He finally emigrated to the U.S., which became the main center of his activities; in 1969 he was appointed executive director of the Los Angeles Phil. as well as general manager of the Hollywood Bowl. Ever sure of his direction, he was a powerful promoter of the orch. he headed, so that the Los Angeles Phil. became actively involved in extensive national and international tours, garnering profitable recording contracts in addition to television and radio broadcasts, youth programs, and special festivals. Well-educated and fluent in several European languages, Fleischmann acquired an international reputation as a highly successful entrepreneur; he was repeatedly offered new jobs, which he declined. In personal relationships he was known for his abrasive manners. In this respect he revived the style of musical promotion of yore, as if following European impresarios of the previous century. That he created opposition and sometimes even open enmity was to be expected, but he invariably defeated opposition by assuming a genially patronizing attitude toward all adversaries. Courteous but always effective in the difficult trade of musical politics, he has through the years continued to enhance his reputation and influence.

Fox, Virgil (Keel), famous American organist; b. Princeton, Ill., May 3, 1912; d. West Palm Beach, Fla., Oct. 25, 1980. He studied piano as a child, but soon turned to the organ as his favorite instrument. He played the organ at the 1st Presbyterian Church in his hometown at the age of 10, and gave his 1st public recital in Cincinnati at 14. He then enrolled in the Peabody Cons. in Baltimore, graduating in 1932. To perfect his playing he went to Paris, where he took lessons with Marcel Dupré at St. Sulpice and Louis Vierne at Notre Dame. He returned to the U.S. in 1938 and became head of the organ dept. at the Peabody Cons. From 1946 to 1965 he was organist at the Riverside Church in N.Y., where he played on a 5-manual, 10,561-pipe organ specially designed for him. He then launched a remarkable career as an organ soloist. He was the 1st American to play at the Thomaskirche in Leipzig, and also played at Westminster Abbey in London. As a solo artist, he evolved an idiosyncratic type of performance in which he embellished Baroque music with Romantic extravaganza; he also took to apostrophizing his audiences in a whimsical mixture of lofty sentiment and disarming self-deprecation. This type of personalized art endeared him to the impatient, emancipated musical youth of America, and he became one of the few organists who could fill a concert hall. He also displayed a robust taste for modern music; he often played the ear-stopping, discordant arrangement of *America* by Charles Ives. Wracked by cancer, he gave his last concert in Dallas on Sept. 26, 1980.

Franco (real name, L'Okanga La Ndju Pene Luambo Makiadi), influential African singer, songwriter, guitarist, and bandleader; b. Sona-Bata, Congo, 1938; d. there (Zaire), Oct. 12, 1989. His fame grew to legendary proportions in Zaire both as a guitar virtuoso and as founder (1956) of O.K. Jazz (for the initials of an early sponsor and also Orch. Kinois), later renamed T.P.O.K. Jazz (for Tout

Poussant, "all powerful"), with which Franco made over 100 recordings. The personnel of the group ranged from 10 to 30 members and included in its 30-plus-year life virtually every major performing musician in Zaire; its sound was predominated by horns and guitars, seasoned with extensive vocals and fortified by a variety of percussion instruments. Franco's musical interests and activities followed the political trends of his country; Zaire became independent in 1960, and in 1972 saw a nationwide cultural campaign toward "authentic" expression in an effort to recapture African traditions. While early influences upon the group and upon Franco's compositions came from Cuban music, they later shifted to Congolese traditions; the Cuban rumba became "rumba odemba" (odemba being a bark used to make an aphrodisiac brew), and distinctly Cuban melodies became elongated and sinuous, more akin to the speech-melodies of Lingala, a native tonal language. He was generally supportive of Zaire's nationalism, and his song lyrics (in both Lingala and French) spoke forcefully on issues ranging from AIDS and equal rights to world peace; nonetheless, the social commentary heard in the songs *Helene* and *Jackie* was deemed "immoral" in 1978, causing him to be jailed; he was soon pardoned, however, and subsequently was decorated by President Mobutu; he was later dubbed "Le Grand Maître" of Zairian music, the 2nd native musician (after Kabaselle) to be so honored. T.P.O.K. Jazz made its 1st U.S. tour in 1983, returning in 1989, shortly before Franco's death, to give a sold-out performance in N.Y. In the 1980s he spent much time in Brussels; he established a 2nd band to accompany him in his European performances, and also organized a nightclub/hotel and record label in Zaire. Although Franco remains relatively unknown in the U.S., his stature in his own country grew to phenomenal proportions; the nation of Zaire, by presidential decree, went into a 5-day mourning at his death, during which his music was heard continuously on the radio. Among his most popular albums are *En Colere Vol. 1, 24 Ans d'Âge Vol. 4, Ekaba-Kaba, Le Response de Mario*, and *Live en Hollande*.

Franklin, Benjamin, great American statesman; b. Boston, Jan. 17, 1706; d. Philadelphia, April 17, 1790. An amateur musician, he invented (1762) the "armonica," an instrument consisting of a row of glass discs of different sizes, set in vibration by light pressure. A string quartet mistakenly attributed to him came to light in Paris in 1945, and was publ. there (1946); the parts are arranged in an ingenious "scordatura"; only open strings are used, so that the quartet can be played by rank amateurs. Franklin wrote entertainingly on musical subjects; his letters on Scottish music are found in vol. VI of his collected works.

Freed, Alan, American disc jockey and passionate popularizer of rock 'n' roll; b. Johnstown, Pa., Dec. 15, 1922; d. Palm Springs, Calif., Jan. 20, 1965. His greatest achievement was to desegregate black music by introducing it into white-sponsored radio stations. He was also credited with originating the term rock 'n' roll in 1951, although it had been used long before in a musical about a pleasure-boat cruise. He began broadcasting in Cleveland; then went to N.Y. in 1954 to take command of the radio station WINS, which became one of the most popular purveyors of rock 'n' roll. He also acted in the movie *Rock around the Clock*. He began having trouble when stabbings and riots occurred at some of his public concerts in 1958; he was even accused of encouraging such shenanigans for the sake of publicity. Then, with a horrifying peripeteia fit for a Greek tragedy, he suffered a monumental downfall in 1963, when he was convicted of "payola," accepting bribes from commercial record companies for putting their songs on the air. On top of that, he was charged with income-tax evasion. He quit the oppressive city of N.Y. and fled to the more tolerant, laid-back state of California, but he soon died, ignored by enemies and friends alike, in the vacuous spa of Palm Springs.

Galas, Diamanda (Dimitria Angeliki Elena), remarkable American avant-garde composer and vocalist of Greek extraction; b. San Diego, Aug. 29, 1955. She studied biochemistry, psychology, music, and experimental performance at the Univ. of Calif. at San Diego (1974-79); she also took private vocal lessons. In her scientific studies she and a group of medical students began investigating extreme mental states, using themselves as subjects in a series of bizarre mind-altering experiments; her resultant understanding of psychopathology (notably schizophrenia and psychosis) became an underlying subject in most of her work. After some success as a jazz pianist, she began a vocal career, in which her remarkable precision and advanced technique attracted attention. Although she has performed such demanding works as Xenakis's microtonal *N'Shima* (Brooklyn Phil., Jan. 15, 1981) and Globokar's *Misère* (West German Radio Orch., Cologne, 1980), she is best known for her theatrical performances of her own solo vocal works, given at venues ranging from the Donaueschingen Festival to the N.Y. rock club Danceteria. Her compositions, most of which employ live electronics and/or tape, are improvised according to rigorous, complex "navigation(s) through specified mental states." Her performances have stringent requirements for lighting and sound and possess a shattering intensity. Her brother Philip Dimitri Galas, a playwright whose works were as violent as is his sister's music, died of AIDS in the late 1980s; her increasing emotional and political involvement in what she regards as this "modern plague" led to her 4-part work *Masque of the Red Death* (1986–). She publ. an esthetic statement as "Intravenal Song" in *Perspectives of New Music*, XX (1981).

Garcia, Jerry, American rock musician; b. San Francisco, Aug. 1, 1942. He was a school dropout, and served in the U.S. Army before associating himself with various rock groups, especially those cultivating the new electronic sound. Garcia's most successful creation was a group bearing the puzzling name The Grateful Dead. (One theory is that the name was taken from signs on trucks: "Grateful, for proper passing on the left, and Dead, for illegal passing on the right.") He engaged a harmonica player named **"Pig Pen" McKernan** (b. San Bruno, Calif., Sept. 8, 1945; d. of drug-cum-alcohol ingestion, in Marin County, Calif., March 8, 1973), and also brought in a violinist named **Phil Lesh** (b. Berkeley, Calif., March 15, 1940); another acquisition was a keyboard player who doubled as a vocalist, **Keith Godchaux** (b. San Francisco, July 19, 1948; d. an unnatural death, Ross, Calif., July 23, 1980). The immediate predecessor of The Grateful Dead was a group named the Warlocks. The mortuary connotations of the group continued with such albums as *Workingman's Dead*, but there were also in its repertoire some antonyms, such as *American Beauty*. Garcia's innovative use of electronic amplification established a state of the art for clean, loud, psychedelic rock sound. The Grateful Dead made so much money that they could make a sensational tour to Egypt to play at the foot of the Pyramids for the benefit of the mummified ungrateful dead once buried there, and incidentally contributed funds to the Egyptian Dept. of Antiquities.

Gershwin, George, immensely gifted American composer, brother of **Ira Gershwin**; b. N.Y., Sept. 26, 1898; d. Los Angeles, July 11, 1937. His real name was **Jacob Gershvin**, according to the birth registry; his father was an immigrant from Russia whose original name was Gershovitz. Gershwin's extraordinary career began when he was 16, playing the piano in music stores to demonstrate new popular songs. His studies were desultory; he took piano lessons with Ernest Hutcheson and Charles Hambitzer in N.Y.; studied harmony with Edward Kilenyi and Rubin Goldmark; later on, when he was already a famous composer of popular music, he continued to take private lessons; he studied counterpoint with

Henry Cowell and Wallingford Riegger; during the last years of his life, he applied himself with great earnestness to studying with Joseph Schillinger in an attempt to organize his technique in a scientific manner; some of Schillinger's methods he applied in *Porgy and Bess*. But it was his melodic talent and a genius for rhythmic invention, rather than any studies, that made him a genuinely important American composer. As far as worldly success was concerned, there was no period of struggle in Gershwin's life; one of his earliest songs, *Swanee*, written at the age of 19, became enormously popular (more than a million copies sold; 2,250,000 phonograph records). He also took time to write a lyrical *Lullaby* for String Quartet (1920). Possessing phenomenal energy, he produced musical comedies in close succession, using fashionable jazz formulas in original and ingenious ways. A milestone in his career was *Rhapsody in Blue* for Piano and Jazz Orch., in which he applied the jazz idiom to an essentially classical form. He played the solo part at a special concert conducted by Paul Whiteman at Aeolian Hall in N.Y. on Feb. 12, 1924. The orchestration was by Ferde Grofé, a circumstance that generated rumors of Gershwin's inability to score for instruments; these rumors, however, were quickly refuted by his production of several orch. works, scored by himself in a brilliant fashion. He played the solo part of his Piano Concerto in F, with Walter Damrosch and the N.Y. Sym. Orch. (Dec. 3, 1925); this work had a certain vogue, but its popularity never equaled that of the *Rhapsody in Blue*. Reverting again to a more popular idiom, Gershwin wrote a symphonic work, *An American in Paris* (N.Y. Phil., Dec. 13, 1928, Damrosch conducting). His *Rhapsody No. 2* was performed by Koussevitzky and the Boston Sym. on Jan. 29, 1932, but was unsuccessful; there followed a *Cuban Overture* (N.Y., Aug. 16, 1932) and Variations for Piano and Orch. on his song *I Got Rhythm* (Boston, Jan. 14, 1934, composer soloist). In the meantime, Gershwin became engaged in his most ambitious undertaking: the composition of *Porgy and Bess*, an American opera in a folk manner, for black singers, after the book by Dubose Heyward. It was first staged in Boston on Sept. 30, 1935, and in N.Y. on Oct. 10, 1935. Its reception by the press was not uniformly favorable, but its songs rapidly attained great popularity (*Summertime; I Got Plenty o' Nuthin'; It Ain't Neccessarily So; Bess, You Is My Woman Now*); the opera has been successfully revived in N.Y. and elsewhere; it received international recognition when an American company of black singers toured with it in South America and Europe in 1955. Gershwin's death (of a gliomatous cyst in the right temporal lobe of the brain) at the age of 38 was mourned as a great loss to American music. The 50th anniversary of his death brought forth a number of special tributes in 1987, including a major joint broadcast of his music by the PBS and BBC television networks. His musical comedies include *Our Nell* (1922); *Sweet Little Devil* (1924); *Lady, Be Good!* (1924); *Primrose* (1924); *Tip-Toes* (1925); *Oh Kay!* (1926); *Strike Up the Band* (1927); *Funny Face* (1927); *Rosalie* (1928); *Treasure Girl* (1928); *Show Girl* (1929); *Girl Crazy* (1930); *Of Thee I Sing* (1931; a political satire which was the 1st musical to win a Pulitzer Prize); *Pardon My English* (1933); *Let 'Em Eat Cake* (1933); for motion pictures: *Shall We Dance, A Damsel in Distress*, and *The Goldwyn Follies* (left unfinished at his death; completed by Vernon Duke). A collection of his songs and piano transcriptions, *George Gershwin's Song Book*, was publ. in 1932 and reprinted as *Gershwin Years in Song* (N.Y., 1973).

Getty, Gordon, American composer who bears the unique brunt of being a scion of a billionaire; b. Los Angeles, Dec. 20, 1933. In 1945 he was taken to San Francisco, where he studied English literature at San Francisco State College (graduated, 1956) and took courses at the San Francisco Cons. of Music. From his earliest attempts at composition, he proclaimed faith in the primacy of consonance and a revival of Romantic ideals. His preference lay with vocal music, and he possessed a natural gift for writing a fetching melodic line. For his songs and choruses he selected the poems of Housman, Tennyson, Poe, and Emily Dickinson. He also produced an opera, *Plump Jack*, based on the character of Shakespeare's Falstaff (excerpts only; San Francisco, March 13, 1985). The inevitable headline in one of several newspaper reviews was "Billionaire Has a Hit in *Plump Jack*!" Every music critic writing about Getty must deal with the inescapable suspicion that his music is the accidental outgrowth of his material fortune, and must conquer conscious or subliminal prejudice in favor or disfavor of a work. Getty deserves full credit for braving this test courageously, ignoring bouquets and brickbats and persevering in writing his kind of music. Among his other works are the piano pieces *Homework Suite, 3 Diatonic Waltzes*, and *Tiefer und Tiefer* (all 1986), and a vocal work, *The White Election* for Soprano and Piano, to poems by Emily Dickinson (1986).

Gould, Glenn (Herbert), remarkably individualistic Canadian pianist; b. Toronto, Sept. 25, 1932; d. there, Oct. 4, 1982. His parents were musically gifted and gladly fostered his precocious development; he began to play piano, and even compose, in his single-digit years. At the age of 10, he entered the Royal Cons. of Music in Toronto, where he studied piano with Alberto Guerrero, organ with Frederick C. Silvester, and music theory with Leo Smith; he received his diploma as a graduate at 13, in 1945. He made his debut in Toronto on May 8, 1946. As he began practicing with total concentration on the mechanism of the keyboard, he developed mannerisms that were to become his artistic signature. He reduced the use of the pedal to a minimum in order to avoid a harmonic haze; he cultivated "horizontality" in his piano posture, bringing his head down almost to the level of the keys. He regarded music as a linear art; this naturally led him to an intense examination of Baroque structures; Bach was the subject of his close study rather than Chopin; he also cultivated performances of the early polyphonists Sweelinck, Gibbons, and others. He played Mozart with emphasis on the early pianoforte techniques; he peremptorily omitted the Romantic composers Chopin, Schumann, and Liszt from his repertoire. He found the late sonatas of Beethoven more congenial to his temperament, and, remarkably enough, he played the piano works of the modern Vienna school—Schoenberg, Berg, and Webern—perhaps because of their classical avoidance of purely decorative tonal formations. Following his U.S. debut in Washington, D.C. (Jan. 2, 1955), he evoked unequivocal praise at his concerts, but in 1964 he abruptly terminated his stage career and devoted himself exclusively to recording, which he regarded as a superior art to concertizing. This enabled him to select the best portions of the music he played in the studio, forming a mosaic unblemished by accidental mishaps. A great part of the interest he aroused with the public at large was due to mannerisms that marked his behavior on the stage. He used a 14-inch-high chair that placed his eyes almost at the level of the keyboard; he affected informal dress; he had a rug put under the piano and a glass of distilled water within reach. He was in constant fear of bodily injury; he avoided shaking hands with the conductor after playing a concerto; and he sued the Steinway piano company for a large sum of money when an enthusiastic representative shook his hand too vigorously. But what even his most ardent admirers could not palliate was his unshakable habit of singing along with his performance; he even allowed his voice to be audible on his carefully wrought, lapidary phonograph recordings. Socially, he was a recluse; he found a release from his self-imposed isolation in editing a series of radio documentaries for the CBC. He called 3 of them a "solitude tragedy." Symbolically, they were devoted to the natural isolation of the Canadian Arctic, the insular life of Newfoundland, and the religious hermetism of the Mennonite sect. He also produced a radio documentary on Schoenberg, treating him as a musical hermit. Other activities included conducting a chamber orch. without an audience. Needless to add, Gould never married. See T. Page, ed., *The Glenn Gould Reader* (N.Y., 1985).

Guarneri, famous Italian family of violin makers. The Italian form of the name was **Guarnieri**; Guarneri was derived from the Latin spelling, **Guarnerius**; the labels invariably used the Latin form. **Andrea,** head of the family (b. Cremona, c. 1625; d. there, Dec. 7, 1698), was a pupil of Nicolo Amati; he lived in Amati's house from 1641 to 1646, and again from 1650 to 1654, when, with his wife, he moved to his own house in Cremona and began making his own violins, labeling them as "alumnus" of Amati and, after 1655, "ex alumnis," often with the additional words of "sub titolo Sanctae Theresiae." Andrea's son **Pietro Giovanni,** known as **Peter of Mantua** (b. Cremona, Feb. 18, 1655; d. Mantua, March 26, 1720), worked first at Cremona; then went to Mantua, where he settled; he also used the device "sub titolo Sanctae Theresiae." Another son of Andrea, **Giuseppe Giovanni Battista,** known as **Silius Andreae** (b. Cremona, Nov. 25, 1666; d. there, c.1740), worked in his father's shop, which he eventually inherited; in his own manufactures, he departed from his father's model and followed the models of Stradivarius. Giuseppe's son **Pietro** (b. Cremona, April 14, 1695; d. Venice, April 7, 1762) became known as **Peter of Venice**; he settled in Venice in 1725, and adopted some features of the Venetian masters Montagnana and Serafin. Another son of Giuseppe, **(Bartolomeo) Giuseppe Antonio,** known as **Giuseppe del Gesù,** from the initials IHS often appearing on his labels (b. Cremona, Aug. 21, 1698; d. there, Oct. 17, 1744), became the most celebrated member of the family; some of his instruments bear the label "Joseph Guarnerius Andreae Nepos Cremonae," which establishes his lineage as a grandson of Andrea. His violins are greatly prized, rivaling those of Stradivarius in the perfection of instrumental craftsmanship; he experimented with a variety of wood materials, and also made changes in the shapes of his instruments during different periods of his work. Such great virtuoso violinists as Heifetz, Stern, Szeryng, Grumiaux, and Paganini used his instruments.

Haley, Bill (William John Clifton, Jr.), popular American singer, guitarist, and bandleader; b. Highland Park, Mich., July 6, 1925; d. Harlingen, Texas, Feb. 9, 1981. He began to play guitar as a youth, and at the age of 15 embarked on a tour with country-and-western groups; soon formed his own band, The Saddlemen; in 1952 it was renamed The Comets, to impart a more cosmological beat to the music. Haley precipitated the rock-'n'-roll era with his rendition of *Crazy Man Crazy* in 1953; there followed his hit version of Joe Turner's *Shake, Rattle and Roll*, which combined the elements of the blues, country music, and urban pop. His fame skyrocketed in 1955 with his strident projection of *Rock around the Clock*. Immortalized in the motion picture *Blackboard Jungle*, it became the banner of the rising generation of long-haired, wide-eyed, loose-eared, spaced-out, stoned American youth; 22 million albums of this song were sold. But like so many instinctual musicians of the period, Haley gradually sank into a state of oblivious torpor, and his once-agile style gave way to the irresistible ascent of the more sexually explicit art of Elvis Presley.

Harrison, Lou, inventive American composer and performer; b. Portland, Oreg., May 14, 1917. He studied with Cowell in San Francisco (1934–35) and with Schoenberg at the Univ. of Calif. at Los Angeles (1941). He taught at Mills College in Oakland, Calif. (1937–40; 1980–85), the Univ. of Calif. at Los Angeles (1942), Reed College in Portland, Oreg. (1949–50), Black Mountain College in North Carolina (1951–52), and San Jose State Univ. (from 1967). He also was a music critic for the *New York Herald-Tribune* (1945–48). He held 2 Guggenheim fellowships (1952, 1954). His interests are varied: he invented 2 new principles of clavichord construction; built a Phrygian aulos; developed a process for direct composing on a phonograph disc; in 1938 proposed a theory in interval control, and in 1942 supplemented it by a device for rhythm control; also wrote plays and versified poematically. He was one of the earliest adherents of an initially small group of American musicians who promoted the music of Ives, Ruggles, Varèse, and Cowell; he prepared for publication Ives's 3rd Sym., which he conducted in its 1st performance in 1946. He visited the Orient in 1961, fortifying his immanent belief in the multiform nature of music by studying Japanese and Korean modalities and rhythmic structures. Seeking new sources of sound production, he organized a percussion ensemble of multitudinous drums and such homely sound makers as coffee cans and flowerpots. He also wrote texts in Esperanto for some of his vocal works. He later composed for the Indonesian gamelan; many of these instruments were constructed by his longtime associate and friend William Colvig.

Hauer, Josef Matthias, significant Austrian composer and music theorist; b. Wiener-Neustadt, near Vienna, March 19, 1883; d. Vienna, Sept. 22, 1959. After attending a college for teachers, he became a public-school instructor; at the same time he studied music. An experimenter by nature, with a penchant for mathematical constructions, he developed a system of composition based on "tropes," or patterns, which aggregated to thematic formations of 12 different notes. As early as 1912 he publ. a piano piece, entitled *Nomos* (Law), which contained the germinal principles of 12-tone music; in his theoretical publications he elaborated his system in greater detail. These were *Über die Klangfarbe*, op. 13 (Vienna, 1918; augmented as *Vom Wesen des Musikalischen*, Leipzig and Vienna, 1920; 3rd ed., rev. and augmented, 1966); *Deutung des Melos: Eine Frage an die Künstler und Denker unserer Zeit* (Leipzig, Vienna, and Zürich, 1923); *Vom Melos zur Pauke: Eine Einführung in die Zwölftonmusik* (Vienna, 1925; 2nd ed., 1967); and *Zwölftontechnik: Die Lehre von den Tropen* (Vienna, 1926; 2nd ed., 1953), in which the method of composing in the 12-tone technique was illustrated with practical examples. Hauer vehemently asserted his priority in 12-tone composition; he even used a rubber stamp on his personal stationery proclaiming himself the true founder of the 12-tone method. This claim was countered, with equal vehemence but with more justification, by Schoenberg; indeed, the functional basis of 12-tone composition in which the contrapuntal and harmonic structures are derived from the unifying tone row did not appear until Schoenberg formulated it and put it into practice in 1924. Hauer lived his entire life in Vienna, working as a composer, conductor, and teacher. Despite its forbidding character, his music attracted much attention.

Haydn, (Franz) Joseph, illustrious Austrian composer, brother of **(Johann) Michael Haydn**; b. Rohrau, Lower Austria, probably March 31, 1732 (baptized, April 1, 1732); d. Vienna, May 31, 1809. He was the 2nd of 12 children born to Mathias Haydn, a wheelwright, who served as village sexton, and Anna Maria Koller, daughter of the market inspector and a former cook in the household of Count Harrach, lord of the village. Their 2nd son, Michael, also became a musician. On Sundays and holidays music was performed at home, the father accompanying the voices on the harp, which he had learned to play by ear. When Haydn was a small child his paternal cousin Johann Mathias Franck, a choral director, took him to Hainburg, where he gave him instruction in reading, writing, arithmetic, and instrumental playing. When Haydn was 8 years old, Karl Georg Reutter, Kapellmeister at St. Stephen's Cathedral in Vienna, engaged him as a soprano singer in the chorus. After his voice began to break, he moved to the household of Johann Michael Spangler, a music teacher. He obtained a loan of 150 florins from Anton Buchholz, a friend of his father's, and was able to rent an attic room where he could use a harpsichord. In the same house lived the famous Italian poet and opera librettist Pietro Metastasio, who recommended Haydn to a resident Spanish family as a music tutor. He was also engaged as accompanist to students of Nicolò Porpora, for whom he performed various menial tasks in exchange for composition lessons. He made a diligent study of *Gradus ad Parnassum* by Fux and *Der vollkommen Capellmeister* by Mattheson. Soon he began to compose keyboard music. In 1751 he wrote the singspiel *Der krumme Teufel*. A noblewoman, Countess Thun, engaged him as harpsichordist and singing teacher; he met Karl Joseph von Fürnburg, for whom he wrote his 1st string quartets. In 1759 Haydn was engaged by Count Ferdinand Maximilian von Morzin as Kapellmeister at his estate in Lukaveč. On Nov. 26, 1760, he married Maria Anna Keller, the eldest daughter of his early benefactor, a Viennese wigmaker.

A decided turn in Haydn's life was his meeting with Prince Paul Anton Esterházy. Esterházy had heard one of Haydn's syms. during a visit to Lukaveč, and engaged him to enter his service as 2nd Kapellmeister at his estate in Eisenstadt; Haydn signed his contract with Esterházy on May 1, 1761. Prince Paul Anton died in 1762, and his brother, Prince Nikolaus Esterházy, known as the "Magnificent," succeeded him. He took Haydn to his new palace at Esterháza, where Haydn was to provide 2 weekly operatic performances and 2 formal concerts. Haydn's service at Esterháza was long-lasting, secure, and fruitful; there he composed music of all descriptions, including most of his known string quartets, about 80 of his 104 syms., a number of keyboard works, and nearly all his operas; in 1766 he was elevated to the rank of 1st Kapellmeister. Prince Nikolaus Esterházy was a cultural patron of the arts, but he was also a stern taskmaster in his relationship to his employees. His contract with Haydn stipulated that each commissioned work had to be performed without delay, and that such a work should not be copied for use by others. Haydn was to present himself in the "antichambre" of the palace each morning and afternoon to receive the Prince's orders, and he was obliged to wear formal clothes, with white hose and a powdered wig with a pigtail or a hairbag; he was to have his meals with the other musicians and house servants. In particular, Haydn was obligated to write pieces that could be performed on the baryton, an instrument which the Prince could play; in consequence, Haydn wrote numerous pieces for the baryton. He also wrote 3 sets of 6 string quartets each (opp. 9, 17, and 20), which were brought out in 1771–72. His noteworthy syms. included No. 49, in F minor, *La passione*; No. 44, in E minor, known as the *Trauersinfonie*; No. 45, in F-sharp minor; and the famous *Abschiedsinfonie* (the *Farewell* Sym.), performed by Haydn at Esterháza in 1772. The last movement of the *Farewell* Sym. ends in a long slow section during which one musician after another ceases to play and leaves the stage, until only the conductor and a single violinist remain to complete the work. The traditional explanation is that Haydn used the charade to suggest to the Prince that his musicians deserved a vacation after their arduous labors, but another and much more plausible version, found in *Anedotti piacevoli ed interessanti*, publ. in 1830 by G.G. Ferrari, who personally knew Haydn, is that the Prince had decided to disband the orch. and that Haydn wished to impress on him the sadness of such a decision; the known result was that the orch. was retained. In 1780 Haydn was elected a member of the Modena Phil. Soc.; in 1784 Prince Henry of Prussia sent him a gold medal; in 1785 he was commissioned to write a "passione istrumentale," *The 7 Last Words*, for the Cathedral of Cádiz; in 1787 King Friedrich Wilhelm II gave him a diamond ring; many other distinctions were conferred upon him. During his visits to Vienna he formed a close friendship with Mozart, who was nearly a quarter of a century younger, and for whose genius Haydn had great admiration. If the words of Mozart's father can be taken literally, Haydn told him that Mozart was "the greatest composer known to me either in person or by name." Mozart reciprocated Haydn's regard for him by dedicating to him a set of 6 string quartets. Prince Nikolaus Esterházy died in 1790, and his son Paul Anton (named after his uncle) inherited the estate. After he disbanded the orch., Haydn was granted an annuity of 1,000 florins; nominally he remained in the service of the new Prince as Kapellmeister, but he took up permanent residence in Vienna.

In 1790 Johann Peter Salomon, the enterprising London impresario, visited Haydn and persuaded him to travel to London for a series of concerts. Haydn accepted the offer, arriving in London on Jan. 1, 1791. On March 11 of that year he appeared in his 1st London concert in the Hanover Square Rooms, presiding at the keyboard. Haydn was greatly feted in London by the nobility; the King himself expressed his admiration for Haydn's art. In July 1791 he went to Oxford to receive the honorary degree of Mus.D. For this occasion, he submitted his Sym. No. 92, in G major, which became known as the *Oxford* Sym.; he composed a 3-part canon, *Thy Voice, O Harmony, Is Divine*, as his exercise piece. It was also in England that he wrote his Sym. No. 94, in G major, the *Surprise* Sym. The surprise of the title was provided by the loud drum strokes at the end of the main theme in the slow movement; the story went that Haydn introduced the drum strokes with the sly intention of awakening the London dowagers, who were apt to doze off at a concert. On his journey back to Vienna in the summer of 1792 Haydn stopped in Bonn, where young Beethoven showed him some of his works, and Haydn agreed to accept him later as his student in Vienna. In 1794 Haydn went to London once more. His 1st concert, on Feb. 10, 1794, met with great success. His *London* syms., also known as the *Salomon* syms., because Haydn wrote them at Salomon's request, were 12 in number, and they included No. 99, in E-flat major; No. 100, in G major, known as the *Military* Sym.; No. 101, in D major, nicknamed *The Clock* because of its pendulum-like rhythmic accompanying figure; No. 102, in B-flat major; No. 103, in E-flat major, known as the *Drum Roll* Sym.; and No. 104, in D major. A philatelic note: Haydn sent the MS of his oratorio *The Creation* to Salomon in London for its 1st performance there. The package was delivered on March 23, 1800, by stagecoach and sailboat from Vienna, and the postage was £30 16s. 0d., a sum equal to £650 today, c.$1,000. In 1800, this sum was enough to buy a horse, or to pay the living expenses for a family of 4 for a year.

Returning to Vienna, Haydn resumed his contact with the Esterházy family. In 1794 Prince Paul Anton died and was succeeded by his son Nikolaus; the new Prince revived the orch. at Eisenstadt, with Haydn again as Kapellmeister. Conforming to the new requirements of Prince Nikolaus, Haydn turned to works for the church, including 6 masses. His Mass in C major was entitled *Missa in tempore belli* (1796), for it was composed during Napoleon's drive toward Vienna. The 2nd Mass, in B-flat major, the *Heiligmesse*, also dates from 1796. In 1798 he composed the 3rd Mass, in D minor, which is often called the *Nelsonmesse*, with reference to Lord Nelson's defeat of Napoleon's army at the Battle of the Nile. The 4th Mass, in B-flat major (1799), is called the *Theresienmesse*, in honor of the Austrian Empress Maria Theresa. The 5th Mass, in B-flat major, written in 1801, is known as the *Schöpfungsmesse*, for it contains a theme from the oratorio *Die Schöpfung* (*The Creation*). The 6th Mass, in B-flat major (1802), is referred to as the *Harmoniemesse*, for its extensive use of wind instruments; the word "harmonie" is here used in the French meaning, as the wind instrument section. Between 1796 and 1798 Haydn composed his great oratorio *Die Schöpfung*, which was 1st performed at a private concert for the nobility at the Schwarzenburg Palace in Vienna on April 29, 1798. In 1796 he wrote the

Concerto in E-flat major for Trumpet, which became a standard piece for trumpet players. In 1797 Haydn was instructed by the Court to compose a hymn-tune of a solemn nature that could be used as the national Austrian anthem. He succeeded triumphantly in this task; he made use of this tune as a theme of a set of variations in his String Quartet in C major, op. 76, no. 3, which itself became known as the *Emperor* Quartet. The original text for the hymn, written by Lorenz Leopold Haschka, began "Gott erhalte Franz den Kaiser." This hymn had a curious history: a new set of words was written by August Heinrich Hoffmann during a period of revolutionary disturbances in Germany preceding the general European revolution of 1848; its 1st line, "Deutschland, Deutschland über alles," later assumed the significance of German imperialism; in its original it meant merely, "Germany above all (in our hearts)." Between 1799 and 1801 Haydn completed the oratorio *Die Jahreszeiten*; its text was tr. into German from James Thomson's poem *The Seasons*. It was first performed at the Schwarzenburg Palace in Vienna on April 24, 1801. In 1802, beset by illness, Haydn resigned as Kapellmeister to Prince Nikolaus.

Despite his gradually increasing debility, Haydn preserved the saving grace of his natural humor; in response to the many salutations of his friends, he sent around a quotation from his old song *Der Alte*, confessing his bodily weakness. Another amusing musical jest was Haydn's reply to a society lady who identified herself at a Vienna party as a person to whom Haydn had dedicated a lively tune ascending on the major scale; she sang it for him, and he replied wistfully that the tune was now more appropriate in an inversion. Haydn made his last public appearance at a concert given in his honor in the Great Hall of the Univ. of Vienna on March 27, 1808, with Salieri conducting *Die Schöpfung*. When Vienna capitulated to Napoleon, he ordered a guard of honor to be placed at Haydn's residence. Haydn died on May 31, 1809, and was buried at the Hundsturm Cemetery. In consequence of some fantastic events, his skull became separated from his body before his reinterment at Eisenstadt in 1820; it was actually exhibited under glass in the hall of the Gesellschaft der Musikfreunde in Vienna for a number of years, before being reunited with his body in the Bergkirche in Eisenstadt on June 5, 1954, in a solemn official ceremony.

Haydn was often called "Papa Haydn" by his intimates in appreciation of his invariable good humor and amiable disposition. Ironically, he never became a papa in the actual sense of the word. His marriage was unsuccessful; his wife was a veritable termagant; indeed, Haydn was separated from her for most of his life. Still, he corresponded with her and sent her money, even though, according to a contemporary report, he never opened her letters.

In schoolbooks Haydn is usually described as "father of the symphony," the creator of the classical form of the sym. and string quartet. Historically, this absolute formulation cannot be sustained; the symphonic form was established by Stamitz and his associates at the Mannheim School; the string quartet was of an even earlier provenance. But Haydn's music was not limited to formal novelty; its greatness was revealed in the variety of moods, the excellence of variations, and the contrast among the constituent movements of a sym.; string quartets, as conceived by Haydn, were diminutions of the sym.; both were set in sonata form, consisting in 3 contrasting movements, *Allegro, Andante, Allegro*, with a *Minuet* interpolated between the last 2 movements. It is the quality of invention that places Haydn above his contemporaries and makes his music a model of classical composition. A theory has been put forward that Haydn's themes were derived from the folk melodies of Croatian origin that he had heard in the rural environment of his childhood, but no such adumbrations or similarities can be convincingly proved. Genius is a gift bestowed on a musician or poet without external urgencies.

The intimate *Volkstümlichkeit*, a popular impressiveness of Haydn's music, naturally lent itself to imaginative nicknames of individual compositions. There are among his syms. such appellations as *Der Philosoph* and *Der Schulmeister*; some were titled after animals: *L'Ours* and *La Poule*; others derived their names from the character of the main theme, as in *Die Uhr* (The Clock), the *Paukenschlag* (Surprise), and the *Paukenwirbel* (Drum Roll). Among Haydn's string quartets are *La Chasse*, so named because of the hunting horn fanfares; the *Vogelquartett*, in which one hears an imitation of birdcalls; the *Froschquartett*, which seems to invoke a similarity with frog calls in the finale; and the *Lerchenquartett*, containing a suggestion of a lark call. The famous *Toy* Sym., scored for an ensemble which includes the rattle, the triangle, and instruments imitating the quail, cuckoo, and nightingale, was long attributed to Haydn but is actually a movement of a work by Leopold Mozart.

Haydn played a historic role in the evolution of functional harmony by adopting 4-part writing as a fundamental principle of composition, particularly in his string quartets. This practice has also exercised a profound influence on the teaching of music theory.

Hayes, Roland, distinguished black American tenor; b. Curryville, Ga., June 3, 1887; d. Boston, Jan. 1, 1977. His parents were former slaves. He studied singing with A. Calhoun in Chattanooga, Tenn., and later at Fisk Univ. in Nashville; subsequently continued vocal studies in Boston and in Europe. He made his concert debut in Boston on Nov. 15, 1917, in a program of German lieder and arias by Mozart; then made a successful tour in the U.S. In 1920 he went to London, where he studied the German repertoire with Sir George Henschel. A grand European tour followed, with appearances in Paris, Vienna, Leipzig, Munich, Amsterdam, Madrid, and Copenhagen. In 1924 he gave more than 80 concerts in the U.S., obtaining a veritable triumph for his interpretation of lyrical German and French songs, and most particularly for his poignant rendition of Negro spirituals. In 1925 he was awarded the Spingarn Medal for "most outstanding achievement among colored people," and in 1939 he received the honorary degree of Mus.D. from Wesleyan Univ. in Delaware, Ohio. He publ. expert arrangements of 30 Negro spirituals, *My Songs* (N.Y., 1948).

Hayman, Richard, American composer of the extreme avant-garde; b. Sandia, N.Mex., July 29, 1951. He studied humanities and philosophy at Columbia Univ.; attended classes of Vladimir Ussachevsky in electronic music; also studied flute with Eleanor Laurence at the Manhattan School of Music and had sessions on Indian vocal music with Ravi Shankar; consulted with Philip Corner and John Cage on the problems of ultramodern music; attended Pierre Boulez's conducting seminars at the Juilliard School of Music. He eked out a meager living by intermittent employment as a construction worker, gardener, operating-room assistant in a hospital, and church pipe-organ renovator; earned an occasional few dollars as a subject in sleep-laboratory experiments; as a last resort, boldly peddled earplugs in the N.Y. subway. He arranged exhibitions of his graffiti at the Univ. of Buffalo; organized assemblages of objects and sounds at the Avant-Garde Festival at Shea Stadium in N.Y.; wrote provocatively titled articles. In 1975 he was appointed an ed. of *Ear* magazine. Perhaps his most mind-boggling musical work is *Dali*, composed at the command of Salvador Dali, scored for large orch., and notated on a toothpick, with instructions to "ascend chromatically in slow pulse." It was "performed" on March 23, 1974. Another work is *it is not here*, a light-and-sound piece, realized in Morse code at the Museum of Modern Art in N.Y. on June 14, 1974. Other pieces are *heartwhistle*, with the audience beating their collective pulses and whistling continuous tones (Aug. 3, 1975); *sleep whistle*, with the composer whistling while asleep in a store window during a paid sleep exhibition (Dec. 7, 1975); *roll*, with the composer rolling, lying down, in the street, covered with bells as a token of Hindu devotion (April 9, 1975); *dreamsound*, a sleep event in which the composer makes various sounds for the benefit of slumbering participants (Berkeley, Calif., Feb. 20, 1976); *home* for a Telephone; *Boo Boo* for Piano; *Buff Her Blind* for Musical Toys and Electronic Instruments; *spirits* for Transduced Piano.

Helmholtz, Hermann (Ludwig Ferdinand) von, celebrated German scientist and acoustician; b. Potsdam, Aug. 31, 1821; d. Berlin, Sept. 8, 1894. He studied medicine at the Friedrich Wilhelm Medical Inst. in Berlin (M.D., 1843); also learned to play the piano. He was an assistant at Berlin's Anatomical Museum and prof. extraordinary at the Academy of Fine Arts (1848–49), assistant prof. and director of Königsberg's Physiological Inst. (1849–55), and prof. of anatomy and physiology at the Univ. of Bonn (1855–58) and the Univ. of Heidelberg (1858–71). He became prof. of physics at the Univ. of Berlin in 1871, and from 1888 served as the 1st director of the Physico-Technical Inst. in Berlin. He was ennobled in 1882. His most important work for those interested in music was his *Lehre von den Tonempfindungen als physiologische Grundlage für die Theorie der Musik* (Braunschweig, 1863; Eng. tr. by A. Ellis as *On the Sensations of Tone as a Physiological Basis for the Theory of Music*, London, 1875; new ed., N.Y., 1948), in which he established a sure physical foundation for the phenomena manifested by musical tones, either single or combined. He supplemented and amplified the theories of Rameau, Tartini, Wheatstone, Corti, and others, furnishing impregnable formulae for all classes of consonant and dissonant tone effects, and proving with scientific precision what Hauptmann and his school sought to establish by laborious dialectic processes. His labors resulted primarily in instituting the laws governing the differences in quality of tone (tone color) in different instruments and voices, covering the whole field of harmonic, differential, and summational tones, and those governing the nature and limits of music perception by the human ear.

Hendrix, Jimi (James Marshall), black American rock guitarist, singer, and songwriter; b. Seattle, Nov. 27, 1942; d. as a result of asphyxiation while unconscious after taking an overdose of barbiturates in London, Sept. 18, 1970. Being lefthanded, he taught himself to play the guitar upside down; played in a high school band before dropping out of school during his senior year to join the U.S. Army paratroopers. Following his discharge (1961), he worked with groups in Nashville, Vancouver, and Los Angeles. In 1964 he went to N.Y., where he joined the Isley Brothers and found a ready response for his wild attire and erotic body locomotions; after working with Curtis Knight's group (1964–65), he formed his own outfit, Jimmy James and the Blue Flames. He then went to England, where he organized the Jimi Hendrix Experience (1966) with bass guitarist Noel Redding and drummer Mitch Mitchell. The live Hendrix experience was replete with the most provocative stage manner, which he frequently culminated by setting his guitar on fire. After recording his 1st album, *Are You Experienced?* (1967), he made his 1st appearance in the U.S. with his group at the Monterey (Calif.) Pop Festival that same year. He then recorded the albums *Axis: Bold as Love* (1968) and *Electric Ladyland* (1968), followed by a knockout appearance at the Woodstock Festival (1969). Several of his albums were released posthumously.

Hildegard von Bingen, German composer, poetess, and mystic; b. Bemersheim, near Alzey, 1098; d. Rupertsberg, near Bingen, Sept. 17, 1179. Her noble parents, Hildebert and Mechtild, promised to consecrate her to the Church since she was their 10th child; accordingly, she began her novitiate as a child; joined with the reclusive mystic Jutta of Spanheim, who with her followers occupied a cell of the

Benedictine monastery of Disibodenberg. At 15 Hildegard took the veil, and succeeded Jutta as Mother Superior in 1136. Between 1147 and 1150 she founded a monastery on the Rupertsberg (near Bingen) with 18 sisters; around 1165 she founded another house at Eibingen (near Rüdesheim). She is called "abbess" in letters drawn up by Frederick Barbarossa in 1163. She was known as the "Sybil of the Rhine," and conducted extensive correspondence with popes, emperors, kings, and archbishops. She was thus greatly involved in politics and diplomacy. Several fruitless attempts were made to canonize her, but her name is included in the Roman Martyrology, and her feast is celebrated on Sept. 17. Hildegard is musically important through her monophonic chants, several of which were settings of her lyric and dramatic poetry. She collected her poems in the early 1150s under the title *Symphonia armonie celestium revelationum*. This vol. survives in 2 sources, both in early German neumes; it comprises 70-odd liturgical poems (the exact number varies, depending on classification), all with melismatic music. The poetry is rich with imagery, and it shares the apocalyptic language of her visionary writings. The music is not typical of plainchant, but involves a technique unique to Hildegard; it is made of a number of melodic patterns recurring in different modal positions, which operate as open structures allowing for internal variation in different contexts. She also wrote a morality play in dramatic verse, *Ordo virtutum*, which includes 82 melodies which are similarly structured but distinctly more syllabic in style. She pointed out that her music is written in a range congenial to women's voices, contrasting with the formal Gregorian modes. Hildegard was also known for her literary works, which include prophecy, medical and scientific treatises, and hagiographies, as well as letters.

Honegger, Arthur (Oscar), remarkable French composer; b. Le Havre (of Swiss parents), March 10, 1892; d. Paris, Nov. 27, 1955. He studied violin in Paris with Lucien Capet; then took courses with L. Kempter and F. Hegar at the Zürich Cons. (1909-11). Returning to France in 1912, he entered the Paris Cons., in the classes of Gédalge and Widor; also took lessons with d'Indy. His name 1st attracted attention when he took part in a concert of Les Nouveaux Jeunes in Paris on Jan. 15, 1918. In 1920 the Paris critic Henri Collet publ. an article in *Comoedia* in which he drew a fortuitous parallel between the Russian Five and a group of young French composers whom he designated as Les Six. These Six were Honegger, Milhaud, Poulenc, Auric, Durey, and Tailleferre. The label persisted, even though the 6 composers went their separate ways and rarely gave concerts together. Indeed, only Honegger, Milhaud, and Poulenc became generally known; Auric limited his activities mainly to the theater and the cinema, while Germaine Tailleferre produced some musical plays and concert pieces; as to Durey, he was known more as a dedicated member of the French Communist Party than as a composer. In the early years of his career, Honegger embraced the fashionable type of urban music, with an emphasis on machine-like rhythms and curt, pert melodies. In 1921 he wrote a sport ballet, *Skating Rink*, and a mock-militaristic ballet, *Sousmarine*. In 1923 he composed the most famous of such machine pieces, *Mouvement symphonique No. 1*, subtitled *Pacific 231*. The score was intended to be a realistic tonal portrayal of a powerful American locomotive, bearing the serial number 231. The music progressed in accelerating rhythmic pulses toward a powerful climax, then gradually slackened its pace until the final abrupt stop; there was a simulacrum of a lyrical song in the middle section of the piece. *Pacific 231* enjoyed great popularity and became in the minds of modern-minded listeners a perfect symbol of the machine age. Honegger's 2nd *Mouvement symphonique*, composed in 1928, was a musical rendering of the popular British sport rugby. His *Mouvement symphonique No. 3*, however, bore no identifying subtitle. This abandonment of allusion to urban life coincided chronologically with a general trend away from literal representation and toward absolute music in classical forms, often of historical or religious character. Among his most important works in that genre were *Le Roi David*, to a biblical subject, and *Jeanne d'Arc au bûcher*, glorifying the French patriot saint on the semimillennium of her martyrdom. Honegger's syms. were equally free from contemporary allusions; the first 2 lacked descriptive titles; his 3rd was entitled *Liturgique*, with a clear reference to an ecclesiastical ritual; the 4th was named *Deliciae Basilienses*, because it was written to honor the city of Basel; the somewhat mysterious title of the 5th, *Di tre re*, signified nothing more arcane than the fact that each of its movements ended on the thrice-repeated note D. Honegger spent almost all of his life in France, but he retained his dual Swiss citizenship, a fact that caused some biographers to refer to him as a Swiss composer. In 1926 he married the pianist-composer **Andrée Vaurabourg** (1894–1980), who often played piano parts in his works. In 1929 he paid a visit to the U.S.; he returned in 1947 to teach summer classes at the Berkshire Music Center at Tanglewood, but soon after his arrival was stricken with a heart ailment and was unable to complete his term; he returned to Paris and remained there until his death. He publ. a book, *Je suis compositeur* (Paris, 1951; Eng. tr., London, 1966).

Hovhaness (Chakmakjian), Alan (Vaness Scott), prolific and proficient American composer of Armenian-Scottish descent; b. Somerville, Mass., March 8, 1911. He took piano lessons with Adelaide Proctor and with Heinrich Gebhard in Boston; his academic studies were at Tufts Univ.; in 1932 he enrolled in the New England Cons. of Music in Boston as a student of Frederick Converse; then was a scholarship student of Martinů at the Berkshire Music Center at Tanglewood in 1942. From his earliest attempts at composition, he took great interest in the musical roots of his paternal ancestry, studying the folk songs assembled by the Armenian musician Komitas. He gradually came to believe that music must reflect the natural monody embodied in national songs and ancient church hymns. In his music he adopted modal melodies and triadic harmonies. This *parti pris* had the dual effect of alienating him from the milieu of modern composers while exercising great attraction for the music consumer at large. By dint of ceaseless repetition of melodic patterns and relentless dynamic tension, he succeeded in creating a sui generis type of impressionistic monody, flowing on the shimmering surfaces of euphony, free from the upsetting intrusion of heterogeneous dissonance; an air of mysticism pervades his music, aided by the programmatic titles which he often assigns to his compositions. After completion of his studies, he served on the faculty of the New England Cons. of Music (1948–51); then moved to N.Y. He was awarded 2 Guggenheim fellowships (1954 and 1958). In 1959 he received a Fulbright fellowship and traveled to India and Japan, where he collected native folk songs for future use and presented his own works, as pianist and conductor, receiving acclaim. In 1962 he was engaged as composer-in-residence at the Univ. of Hawaii; then traveled to Korea. He eventually settled in Seattle. A composer of relentless fecundity, he produced over 60 syms.; several operas, quasi-operas, and pseudo-operas; and an enormous amount of choral music. The totality of his output is in excess of 370 opus numbers. In a laudable spirit of self-criticism, he destroyed 7 of his early syms. and began numbering them anew so that his 1st numbered sym. (subtitled *Exile*) was chronologically his 8th. He performed a similar auto-da-fé on other dispensable pieces. Among his more original compositions is a symphonic score *And God Created Great Whales*, in which the voices of humpback whales recorded on tape were used as a solo with the orch.; the work was performed to great effect in the campaign to save the whale from destruction by human (and inhuman) predators.

Ives, Charles (Edward), one of the most remarkable American composers, whose individual genius created music so original, so universal, and yet so deeply national in its sources of inspiration that it profoundly changed the direction of American music; b. Danbury, Conn., Oct. 20, 1874; d. N.Y., May 19, 1954. His father, George Ives, was a bandleader of the 1st Conn. Heavy Artillery during the Civil War, and the early development of Charles Ives was, according to his own testimony, deeply influenced by his father. At the age of 12, he played the drums in the band and also received from his father rudimentary musical training in piano and cornet playing. At the age of 13 he played organ at the Danbury Church; soon he began to improvise freely at the piano, without any dependence on school rules; as a result of his experimentation in melody and harmony, encouraged by his father, he began to combine several keys, partly as a spoof, but eventually as a legitimate alternative to traditional music; at 17 he composed his *Variations on America* for organ in a polytonal setting; still earlier he wrote a band piece, *Holiday Quick Step*, which was performed by the Danbury Band in 1888. He attended the Danbury High School; in 1894 he entered Yale Univ., where he took regular academic courses and studied organ with Dudley Buck and composition with Horatio Parker; from Parker he received a fine classical training; while still in college he composed 2 full-fledged syms., written in an entirely traditional manner demonstrating great skill in formal structure, fluent melodic development, and smooth harmonic modulations. After his graduation in 1898, Ives joined an insurance company; also played organ at the Central Presbyterian Church in N.Y. (1899–1902). In 1907 he formed an insurance partnership with Julian Myrick of N.Y.; he proved himself to be an exceptionally able businessman; the firm of Ives & Myrick prospered, and Ives continued to compose music as an avocation. In 1908 he married Harmony Twichell. In 1918 he suffered a massive heart attack, complicated by a diabetic condition, and was compelled to curtail his work both in business and in music to a minimum because his illness made it difficult to handle a pen. He retired from business in 1930, and by that time had virtually stopped composing. In 1919 Ives publ. at his own expense his great masterpiece, *Concord Sonata*, for piano, inspired by the writings of Emerson, Hawthorne, the Alcotts, and Thoreau. Although written early in the century, its idiom is so extraordinary, and its technical difficulties so formidable, that the work did not receive a performance in its entirety until John Kirkpatrick played it in N.Y. in 1939. In 1922 Ives brought out, also at his expense, a volume of *114 Songs*, written between 1888 and 1921 and marked by great diversity of style, ranging from lyrical Romanticism to powerful and dissonant modern invocations. Both the *Concord Sonata* and the *114 Songs* were distributed gratis by Ives to anyone wishing to receive copies. His orch. masterpiece, *3 Places in New England*, also had to wait nearly 2 decades before its 1st performance; of the monumental 4th Sym., only the 2nd movement was performed in 1927, and its complete performance was given posthumously in 1965. In 1947 Ives received the Pulitzer Prize for his 3rd Sym., written in 1911.

The slow realization of the greatness of Ives and the belated triumphant recognition of his music were phenomena without precedent in music history. Because of his chronic ailment, and also on account of his personal disposition, Ives lived as a recluse, away from the mainstream of American musical life; he never went to concerts and did not own a record player or a radio; while he was well versed in the musical classics, and studied the scores of Beethoven, Schumann, and Brahms, he took little interest in sanctioned works of modern composers; yet he anticipated many technical innovations, such as polytonality, atonality, and even 12-tone formations, as well as polymetric and polyrhythmic configurations, which were prophetic for his time. In the 2nd movement of the *Concord Sonata* he specified the application of a strip of wood on the white and the black keys of the piano to produce an echo-like sonority; in his unfinished *Universe Symphony* he planned an antiphonal representation of the heavens in chordal counterpoint and the earth in contrasting orch. groups. He also composed pieces of quarter-tone piano music. A unique quality of his music was the combination of simple motifs, often derived from American church hymns and popular ballads, with an extremely complex dissonant counterpoint which formed the supporting network for the melodic lines. A curious idiosyncrasy is the frequent quotation of the "fate motive" of Beethoven's 5th Sym. in many of his works. Materials of his instrumental and vocal works often overlap, and the titles are often changed during the process of composition. In his orchestrations he often indicated interchangeable and optional parts, as in the last movement of the *Concord Sonata*, which has a part for flute obbligato; thus he reworked the original score for large orch. of his *3 Places in New England* for a smaller ensemble to fit the requirements of Slonimsky's Chamber Orch. of Boston, which gave its 1st performance, and it was in this version that the work was 1st publ. and widely performed until the restoration of the large score was made in 1974. Ives possessed an uncommon gift for literary expression; his annotations to his works are both trenchant and humorous; he publ. in 1920 *Essays before a Sonata* as a literary companion vol. to the *Concord Sonata*; his *Memos* in the form of a diary, publ. after his death, reveal an extraordinary power of aphoristic utterance. He was acutely conscious of his civic duties as an American, and once circulated a proposal to have federal laws enacted by popular referendum. His centennial in 1974 was celebrated by a series of conferences at his alma mater, Yale Univ.; in N.Y., Miami, and many other American cities; and in Europe, including Russia. While during his lifetime he and a small group of devoted friends and admirers had great difficulties in having his works performed, recorded, or publ., a veritable Ives cult emerged after his death; eminent conductors gave repeated performances of his orch. works, and modern pianists were willing to cope with the forbidding difficulties of his works. In terms of the number of orch. performances, in 1976 Ives stood highest among modern composers on American programs, and the influence of his music on the new generation of composers reached a high mark, so that the adjective "Ivesian" became common in music criticism to describe certain acoustical and coloristic effects characteristic of his music. America's youth expressed especial enthusiasm for Ives, which received its most unusual tribute in the commercial marketing of a T-shirt with Ives's portrait. All of the Ives MSS and his correspondence were deposited by Mrs. Ives at Yale Univ. forming a basic Ives archive. The Charles Ives Soc., in N.Y., promotes research and publications. Letters from Ives to Nicolas Slonimsky are reproduced in the latter's book *Music since 1900* (4th ed., N.Y., 1971). A television movie, "A Good Dissonance Like a Man," produced and directed by Theodor W. Timreck in 1977, with the supervision of Vivian Perlis, depicts the life of Ives with fine dramatic impact. See also *Modern Music . . . Analytical Index*, complied by Wayne Shirley and ed. by William and Carolyn Lichtenwanger (N.Y., 1976).

Jackson, Michael (Joseph), black American rock superstar; b. Gary, Ind., Aug. 29, 1958. He began his career as a rhythm-and-blues singer, then joined his 4 brothers in a group billed as The Jackson Five, which scored immediate success. But Michael Jackson soon outshone his brothers and was accorded superstar status in the field of popular music with his lycanthropic album *Thriller* (1983), also issued on videocassette, in which Jackson turns into a werewolf, scaring his sweet girlfriend out of her wits. The album sold some 30 million copies universe-wide, certified in the *Guinness Book of World Records* in 1984 as the largest sale ever of a single album. According to one enthusiast, Jackson could count on an audience of one-quarter of the entire earth's population (c.2,000,000,000). In 1984 he won a record number of 8 Grammys for his assorted talents. Jackson's androgynous appearance and his penchant for outlandish apparel (he wore a sequined naval commodore's costume at the Grammy show) seem to act like a stream of powerful pheromones on squealing admiring youths of both sexes. Jackson suffered a minor catastrophe when his hair caught fire during the filming of a TV commercial, and he had to be outfitted with an inconspicuous hairpiece to cover the burned spot. In collaboration with Lionel Richie, he penned the song *We Are the World* in support of African famine relief; it won a Grammy Award as best song of 1985. In 1987 he brought out the album *Bad* (which means good), and then launched a major solo tour of the U.S. in 1988. On Sept. 19, 1986, his *Captain EO* opened at the Disneyland Theme Park in Anaheim, Calif., featuring Jackson as a singing and dancing commander of a motley space crew. His autobiography was publ. as *Moonwalk* (N.Y., 1988).

James, Harry (Haag), popular American jazz trumpeter and bandleader; b. Albany, Ga., March 15, 1916; d. Las Vegas, July 5, 1983. His father was a trumpeter and his mother a trapeze artist with the Mighty Haag Circus; he took up the drums at the age of 4 and the trumpet at 8; became leader of a circus band at 12. He worked as a contortionist until going with his family to Texas, where he played trumpet in local dance bands. After playing with Ben Pollack's band (1935–37), he became a featured member of Benny Goodman's orch. (1937–39), being featured in such songs as *One O'Clock Jump, Sing, Sing, Sing,* and *Life Goes to a Party*. His virtuoso technique was striking; he could blow *dolce* and even *dolcissimo*, but when needed he blew with deafening *fortissimo*; could also perform ultra-chromatic glissando. He struck out on his own as a bandleader in 1939, producing a sensation with his trumpet version of *You Made Me Love You* in 1941; subsequently was a leading figure of the big band era, bringing out many hit recordings and touring extensively; one of his hit songs, *Ciribiribin*, became his theme song. Several of his albums, including the self-proclamatorily-titled *Wild about Harry*, sold into the millions, even in wartime, when shellac, from which disks were manufactured, was rationed. In 1943 he married Betty Grable, the pin-up girl of the G.I.s in World War II, famous for the lissome beauty of her nether limbs. She was his 2nd wife, out of a total of 4. They were divorced in 1965. Faithful to the slogan that "the show must go on," James, wracked with the pain of fatal lymphatic cancer, continued to perform; he played his last gig in Los Angeles, on June 26, 1983, nine days before his death. He observed, as he was dying, "Let it just be said that I went up to do a one-nighter with Archangel Gabriel."

Johnson, James Weldon, black American lyricist, librettist, anthologist, and writer on music (also a poet, novelist, newspaper editor, lawyer, and international diplomat); b. Jacksonville, Fla., June 17, 1871; d. in an automobile accident at Wiscasset, Maine, June 26, 1938. He studied literature at Atlanta University; then returned to Jacksonville, becoming a teacher and school principal; after self-study, became a lawyer (1898; the first black to pass the Florida bar examinations). A poem written for school use in 1900 to commemorate Abraham Lincoln's birthday, *Lift Every Voice and Sing*, was set to music by his brother, the composer **J. Rosamond Johnson,** and performed in Jacksonville the same year; though its beginnings were inauspicious, the song gradually acquired popularity, and in 15 years became known as "the Negro National Anthem." In the summer of 1899 the brothers visited N.Y. in an attempt to find a producer for their collaborative Gilbert and Sullivan-styled operetta, *Tolosa, or The Royal Document*; while their effort failed, they became acquainted with Oscar Hammerstein and many figures in the black musical life of N.Y. They returned to N.Y. in subsequent summers, selling some 30 songs to various musical reviews, and moved there permanently in 1902, forming, with Bob Cole, an enormously successful songwriting team of Cole and Johnson Bros.; among their hit songs, mostly in black dialect, were *Under the Bamboo Tree* (1902), which was parodied by T.S. Eliot in "Fragment of the Agon," *Congo Love Song* (1903), and, under the pseudonym **Will Handy**, *Oh, Didn't He Ramble* (1902), which was to become a jazz standard; the team's success was such that they became known as "Those Ebony Offenbachs." In 1906 James Weldon Johnson was consul to Venezuela, and later, to Nicaragua. During this period he wrote his only novel, *The Autobiography of an Ex-Colored Man* (publ. anonymously, as if it were a true confession; Boston, 1912), in which he gives vivid descriptions of the "ragtime" musical life in N.Y. during the first decade of the century; soon afterward, his trans. of Granados's *Goyescas* was used for the Metropolitan Opera's first performance of this work. In 1926 he compiled (with a lengthy and valuable introduction) *The Book of American Negro Spirituals* (N.Y.), with arrangements by his brother, and, in 1927, *The 2nd Book of American Negro Spirituals*; his book *Black Manhattan* (N.Y., 1930), a historical study of blacks in N.Y., also draws together considerable information on black musical life. He also wrote an autobiography, *Along This Way* (1931). His papers are on deposit at Yale Univ.

Jones, "Spike" (Lindley Armstrong), American bandleader; b. Long Beach, Calif., Dec. 14, 1911; d. Los Angeles, May 1, 1965. He played drums as a boy; then led a school band. On July 30, 1942, he made a recording of a satirical song, *Der Führer's Face,* featuring a Bronx-cheer razzer; then toured the U.S. with his band, The City Slickers, which included a wash board, a Smith and Wesson pistol, anti-bug Flit guns in E-flat, doorbells, anvils, hammers to break glass, and a live goat trained to bleat rhythmically. Climactically, he introduced the Latrinophone (a toilet seat strung with catgut). With this ensemble, he launched a Musical Depreciation Revue. He retired in 1963, when the wave of extravaganza that had carried him to the crest of commercial success subsided. In his heyday he was known as the "King of Corn."

Joplin, Janis (Lyn), American rock and blues singer; b. Port Arthur, Texas, Jan. 19, 1943; d. of an overdose of heroin, Los Angeles, Oct. 4, 1970. She spent an unhappy childhood; ran away from home and delved into the bohemian life of San Francisco. After a brief stint in college, she joined the rock group Big Brother and the Holding Company as lead vocalist in 1966, winning acclaim for her rendition of *Love Is Like a Ball and Chain* when she appeared with the group at the Monterey International Pop Festival in 1967. Her passionate wailing in a raspy voice immediately established her as an uninhibited representative of the younger generation. After recording the album *Cheap Thrills* (1967), she left Big Brother and struck out on her own; formed her own backup group, the Full Tilt Boogie Band, in 1968 and then appeared in such esoteric emporia as the Psychedelic Supermarket in Boston, Kinetic Playground in Chicago, Whisky A-Go-Go in Los Angeles, and Fillmore East in N.Y. She produced the albums *I Got Dem Ol' Kozmic Blues Again Mama* and *Pearl* before her early demise. She was arrested in Tampa, Fla., in 1969 for having hurled porcine epithets at a policeman, which further endeared her to her public. On the more positive side, the Southern Comfort Distillery Co. presented her with a fur coat in recognition of the publicity she gave the firm by her habitual consumption of a quart of Southern Comfort at each of her appearances; she injected religious passion into a commercial theme in one of her own songs, *Oh Lord, Won't You Buy Me a Mercedes-Benz?*

Kagel, Mauricio (Maurizio Raúl), remarkable Argentine composer; b. Buenos Aires, Dec. 24, 1931. He studied in Buenos Aires with Juan Carlos Paz and Alfredo Schiuma; also attended courses in philosophy and literature at the Univ.

of Buenos Aires. In 1949 he became associated with the Agrupación Nueva Música. From 1949 to 1956 he was choral director at the Teatro Colón. In 1957 he obtained a stipend of the Academic Cultural Exchange with West Germany and went to Cologne, which he made his permanent home. From 1960 to 1966 he was a guest lecturer at the International Festival Courses for New Music in Darmstadt; in 1961 and 1963 he gave lectures and demonstrations of modern music in the U.S., and in 1964–65 was Slee Prof. of composition at the State Univ. of N.Y. at Buffalo. In 1969 he became director of the Inst. of New Music at the Rheinische Musikschule in Cologne. In 1974 he was made prof. at the Cologne Hochschule für Musik. As a composer, Kagel evolved an extremely complex system in which a fantastically intricate and yet wholly rational serial organization of notes, intervals, and durations is supplemented by aleatory techniques; some of these techniques are derived from linguistic permutations, random patterns of lights and shadows on exposed photographic film, and other seemingly arcane processes. In his hyper-serial constructions, he endeavors to unite all elements of human expression, ultimately aiming at the creation of a universe of theatrical arts in their visual, aural, and societal aspects.

Karajan, Herbert von, preeminent Austrian conductor in the grand Germanic tradition, great-grandson of **Theodor Georg von Karajan**; b. Salzburg, April 5, 1908; d. Anif, near Salzburg, July 16, 1989. He was a scion of a cultured family of Greek-Macedonian extraction whose original name was Karajannis. His father was a medical officer who played the clarinet and his brother was a professional organist. Karajan himself began his musical training as a pianist; he took lessons with Franz Ledwinka at the Salzburg Mozarteum. He further attended the conducting classes of the Mozarteum's director, Bernhard Paumgartner. Eventually he went to Vienna, where he pursued academic training at a technical college and took piano lessons from one J. Hofmann; then entered the Vienna Academy of Music as a conducting student in the classes of Clemens Krauss and Alexander Wunderer. On Dec. 17, 1928, he made his conducting debut with a student orch. at the Vienna Academy of Music; shortly afterward, on Jan. 23, 1929, he made his professional conducting debut with the Salzburg Orch. He then received an engagement as conductor of the Ulm Stadttheater (1929–34). From Ulm he went to Aachen, where he was made conductor of the Stadttheater; he subsequently served as the Generalmusikdirektor there (1935–42). On April 9, 1938, he conducted his 1st performance with the Berlin Phil., the orch. that became the chosen medium of his art. On Sept. 30, 1938, he conducted *Fidelio* at his debut with the Berlin Staatsoper. After his performance of *Tristan und Isolde* there on Oct. 21, 1938, he was hailed by the *Berliner Tageblatt* as "das Wunder Karajan." His capacity of absorbing and interpreting the music at hand and transmitting its essence to the audience became his most signal characteristic; he also conducted all of his scores from memory, including the entire *Ring des Nibelungen*. His burgeoning fame as a master of both opera and sym. led to engagements elsewhere in Europe. In 1938 he conducted opera at La Scala in Milan and also made guest appearances in Belgium, the Netherlands, and Scandinavia. In 1939 he became conductor of the sym. concerts of the Berlin Staatsoper Orch.

There was a dark side to Karajan's character, revealing his lack of human sensitivity and even a failure to act in his own interests. He became fascinated by the ruthless organizing solidity of the National Socialist party; on April 8, 1933, he registered in the Salzburg office of the Austrian Nazi party, where his party number was 1 607 525; barely a month later he joined the German Nazi party in Ulm, as No. 3 430 914. He lived to regret these actions after the collapse of the Nazi empire, but he managed to obtain various posts, and in 1947 he was officially denazified by the Allies' army of occupation. His personal affairs also began to interfere with his career. He married the operetta singer Elmy Holgerloef in 1938, but divorced her in 1942 to marry Anita Gütermann. Trouble came when the suspicious Nazi genealogists discovered that she was one-quarter Jewish and suggested that he divorce her. But World War II was soon to end, and so was Nazi hegemony. He finally divorced Gütermann in 1958 to marry the French fashion model Eliette Mouret.

The irony of Karajan's racial pretensions was the physical inadequacy of his own stature. He stood only 5'8" tall, but he made up for his modest height by cultivating his rich chevelure of graying hair, which harmonized with his romantic podium manner. Greatly successful with the commercial world, he made about 800 sound and video recordings, which sold millions of copies. Karajan was also an avid skier and mountain-climbing enthusiast; he piloted his own plane and drove a fleet of flamboyant and expensive sports cars. He acquired considerable wealth, and kept homes in Switzerland and on the French Riviera. Supplementing his devotion to modern technology, Karajan was also a devotee of assorted physical and spiritual fads. He practiced yoga and aerobics, and for a while embraced Zen Buddhism. Moreover, he was known to believe in the transmigration of souls, and expressed a hope of being reborn as an eagle soaring above the Alps, his favorite mountain range. As an alternative, he investigated the technique of cryogenics, hoping that his body could be thawed a century or so later to enable him to enjoy yet another physical incarnation. None of these endeavors prevented him from being overcome by a sudden heart attack in his home at Anif in the Austrian Alps. A helicopter with a medical staff was quickly summoned to fly him to a hospital, but it arrived too late.

Karajan was characteristically self-assertive and unflinching in his personal relationships and in his numerous conflicts with managers and players. Although he began a close relationship with the Vienna Sym. Orch. in 1948, he left it in 1958. His association as conductor of the Philharmonia Orch. of London from 1948 to 1954 did more than anything to re-establish his career after World War II, but in later years he disdained his relationship with that ensemble. When Wilhelm Furtwängler, the longtime conductor of the Berlin Phil., died in 1954, Karajan was chosen to lead the orch. on its 1st tour of the U.S. However, he insisted that he would lead the tour only on the condition that he be duly elected Furtwängler's successor. Protesters were in evidence for his appearance at N.Y.'s Carnegie Hall with the orch. on March 1, 1955, but his Nazi past did not prevent the musicians of the orch. from electing him their conductor during their visit to Pittsburgh on March 3. After their return to Germany, the West Berlin Senate ratified the musicians' vote on April 5, 1955.

Karajan soon came to dominate the musical life of Europe as no other conductor had ever done. In addition to his prestigious Berlin post, he served as artistic director of the Vienna Staatsoper from 1956 until he resigned in a bitter dispute with its general manager in 1964. He concurrently was artistic director of the Salzburg Festival (1957–60), and thereafter remained closely associated with it. From 1969 to 1971 he held the title of artistic adviser of the Orch. de Paris. In the meantime, he consolidated his positions in Berlin and Salzburg. On Oct. 15, 1963, he conducted the Berlin Phil. in a performance of Beethoven's 9th Sym. at the gala concert inaugurating the orch.'s magnificent new concert hall, the Philharmonie. In 1967 he organized his own Salzburg Easter Festival, which became one of the world's leading musical events. In 1967 he re-negotiated his contract and was named conductor-for-life of the Berlin Phil. He made a belated Metropolitan Opera debut in N.Y. on Nov. 21, 1967, conducting *Die Walküre*. He went on frequent tours of Europe and Japan with the Berlin Phil., and also took the orch. to the Soviet Union (1969) and China (1979).

In 1982 Karajan personally selected the 23-year-old clarinetist Sabine Meyer as a member of the Berlin Phil. (any romantic reasons for his insistence were not apparent). The musicians of the orch. rejected her because of their standing rule to exclude women, but also because the majority of the musicians had less appreciation of Fräulein Meyer as an artist than Karajan himself did. A compromise was reached, however, and in 1983 she was allowed to join the orch. on probation. She resigned in 1984 after a year of uneasy co-existence.

In 1985 Karajan celebrated his 30th anniversary as conductor of the Berlin Phil., and in 1988 his 60th anniversary as a conductor. In 1987 he conducted the New Year's Day Concert of the Vienna Phil., which was televised to millions on both sides of the Atlantic. In Feb. 1989 he made his last appearance in the U.S., conducting the Vienna Phil. at N.Y.'s Carnegie Hall. In April 1989 he announced his retirement from his Berlin post, citing failing health. Shortly before his death, he dictated an autobiographical book to Franz Endler; it was publ. in an English tr. in 1989.

Key, Francis Scott, American lawyer and author of the words of the U.S. national anthem, *The Star-Spangled Banner*; b. Carroll County, Md., Aug. 1, 1779; d. Baltimore, Jan. 11, 1843. He wrote the text of the anthem aboard a British ship (where he was taken as a civilian emissary to intercede for release of a Maryland physician) on the morning of Sept. 14, 1814, setting it to the tune of the popular British drinking song *To Anacreon in Heaven*, written by John Stafford Smith. The text and the tune did not become the official national anthem until March 3, 1931, when the bill establishing it as such was passed by Congress and signed by President Herbert Hoover.

Kleinsinger, George, American composer; b. San Bernardino, Calif., Feb. 13, 1914; d. N.Y., July 28, 1982. He was apprenticed to study dentistry, then turned to music; studied with Philip James at N.Y. Univ. (B.A., 1937) and at the Juilliard Graduate School with Jacobi and Wagenaar (1938–40). From his earliest attempts at composition, he adopted a hedonistic regard toward music as a medium of education and entertainment. In this vein he wrote in 1942 a Broadway musical for children entitled *Tubby the Tuba*, which was highly successful; other works in a similarly whimsical manner were *Pee-Wee the Piccolo* (1946); *Street Corner Concerto* for Harmonica and Orch. (1946); and *Brooklyn Baseball Cantata* (1948). His crowning work was the chamber opera *Archy and Mehitabel*, based on the popular comic strip featuring a garrulous cockroach and an emotional cat; it was first performed in N.Y. on Dec. 6, 1954, and later metamorphosed into a Broadway musical under the title *Shinbone Alley*. Kleinsinger's private life reflected the eccentricity of his musical talents; he inhabited the famous bohemian Hotel Chelsea in N.Y., where he maintained a running waterfall, a turtle, a skunk, an iguana, 40 fish, a dog, a python, and a cat. He used to play the piano with a boa constrictor wrapped around him. How he maintained his menagerie in peace was his guarded secret.

Korngold, Erich Wolfgang, remarkable Austrian-born American composer, son of **Julius Korngold**; b. Brünn, May 29, 1897; d. Los Angeles, Nov. 29, 1957. He received his earliest musical education from his father, then studied with Fuchs, Zemlinsky, and Grädener in Vienna. His progress was astounding; at the age of 12 he composed a Piano Trio, which was soon publ., revealing a competent technique and an ability to write in a style strongly influenced by Richard Strauss. About the same time he wrote (in piano score) a pantomime, *Der Schneemann*; it was orchestrated by Zemlinsky and performed at the Vienna Court Opera (Oct. 4, 1910), creating a sensation. In 1911 Nikisch conducted Korngold's *Schauspiel-Ouvertüre* with the Leipzig Gewandhaus Orch.; that same year the youthful composer gave a concert of his works in Berlin, appearing also as a pianist; his Sinfonietta was conducted by Weingartner and the Vienna Phil. in 1913. Korngold was not quite 19 when his 2 short operas, *Der Ring des Polykrates* and *Violanta*, were produced in Munich. His 1st lasting success came with the simultaneous premiere in Hamburg and Cologne of his opera *Die tote Stadt* (Dec. 4, 1920). In 1929 he began a fruitful collaboration with the director Max Reinhardt; in 1934 he went to Hollywood to arrange Mendelssohn's music for Reinhardt's film version of *A Midsummer Night's Dream*. He taught at the Vienna Academy of Music (1930–34) before settling in Hollywood. He became a naturalized U.S. citizen in 1943.

Korngold's music represents the last breath of the Romantic spirit of Vienna; it is marvelously consistent with the melodic, rhythmic, and harmonic style of the judicious modernity of the nascent 20th century. When Mahler heard him play some of his music as a young boy, he kept repeating: "Ein Genie! Ein Genie!" Korngold never altered his established idiom of composition, and was never tempted to borrow modernistic devices, except for some transitory passages in major seconds or an occasional whole-tone scale. After the early outbursts of incautious enthusiasms on the part of some otherwise circumspect critics nominating Korngold as a new Mozart, his star, his erupting nova, began to sink rapidly, until it became a melancholy consensus to dismiss his operas at their tardy revivals as derivative products of an era that had itself little to exhibit that was worthwhile. Ironically, his film scores, in the form of orchestrated suites, experienced long after his death a spontaneous renascence, particularly on records, and especially among the unprejudiced and unopinionated American musical youth, who found in Korngold's music the stuff of their own new dreams.

Lamothe, Georges, French composer; b. 1837; d. Courbevoie, Oct. 15, 1894. He was a prolific composer of dance music; wrote more than 1,000 opus numbers.

Le Caine, Hugh, Canadian, physicist, acoustician, and innovative creator of prototypical electronic musical instruments; b. Port Arthur, Ontario, May 27, 1914; d. Ottawa, July 3, 1977, of a stroke suffered 364 days after a motorcycle accident en route to Montreal. Although his childhood training combined music and science, he chose to emphasize science in his formal studies; he received a B.S. degree from Queen's Univ. in Kingston, Ontario, in 1938 and an M.S. in 1939, and obtained his Ph.D. in nuclear physics from the Univ. of Birmingham in 1952; he also studied piano briefly at the Royal Cons. of Music of Toronto and privately with Viggo Kihl. His childhood dream was to one day apply scientific techniques to the development and invention of new musical instruments, and he went on to develop ground-breaking electronic musical instruments which ultimately formed the basis of pioneering electronic music studios at the Univ. of Toronto (1959) and McGill Univ. in Montreal (1964). He exhibited electronic-music instruments at Expo '67 in Montreal; contributed numerous articles on his findings in various scholarly journals. While he saw himself as a designer of instruments which assisted others in creative work, he himself realized a number of striking electronic compositions in the course of his development, among them the now-classic *Dripsody* (1959), which used only the sound of a single drop of water falling; other compositions were *Alchemy* (1964) and *Perpetual Motion* for Data Systems Computer (1970). His instruments revolutionized musical composition; his Sackbut synthesizer (1945–48; 1954–60; 1969–73) is today recognized as the 1st voltage-controlled synthesizer; among his other instruments are The Spectrogram (1959–62; designed to facilitate the use of complex sine tones in composition), The Alleatone (c.1962; "a controlled chance device selecting one of 16 channels with weighted probabilities"), Sonde (1968–70; which can generate

200 sine waves simultaneously), and Polyphone (1970; a polyphonic synthesizer operated by a keyboard with touch-sensitive keys).

Lennon, John (Winston), English rock singer, guitarist, poet, and songwriter, member of the celebrated group The Beatles; b. Liverpool, Oct. 9, 1940, during a German air raid on the city; d. N.Y., Dec. 8, 1980, gunned down by a wacko in front of his apartment building. He was educated by an aunt after his parents separated; played the mouth organ as a child; later learned the guitar; was encouraged to become a musician by the conductor of a Liverpool-Edinburgh bus. Emotionally rocked over by Elvis Presley's animal magnetism, he became infatuated with American popular music; formed his 1st pop group, the Quarry Men, in 1957. He was soon joined by 3 other rock-crazed Liverpudlians, **Paul McCartney, George Harrison,** and Stuart Sutcliffe, in a group he first dubbed the Silver Beatles, later to become simply The Beatles. (Inspired by the success of a local group, The Crickets, Lennon hit upon the name The Beatles, which possessed the acoustical ring of the coleopterous insect *beetle* and the rock-associated *beat*.) The Beatles opened at the pseudo-exotic Casbah Club in Liverpool in 1959; soon moved to the more prestigious Cavern Club (1961), where they co-opted Pete Best as drummer. In 1960 they played in Hamburg, scoring a gratifyingly vulgar success with the beer-sodden customers by their loud, electrically amplified sound. Back in England, The Beatles crept on to fame. In 1961 they were taken up by the perspicacious promoter Brian Epstein, who launched an extensive publicity campaign to put them over the footlights. Sutcliffe died of a brain hemorrhage in 1962. Best left the group and was replaced by Richard Starkey, whose "nom-de-beatle" became **Ringo Starr**. The quartet opened at the London Palladium in 1963 and drove the youthful audience to a frenzy, a scene that was to be repeated elsewhere in Europe, in America, in Japan, and in Australia. After a period of shocked recoil, the British establishment acknowledged the beneficial contribution of The Beatles to British art and the Exchequer. In 1965 each Beatle was made a Member of the Order of the British Empire. Although American in origin, the type of popular music plied by Lennon and The Beatles as a group had an indefinably British lilt. The meter was square; the main beat was accentuated; syncopation was at a minimum; the harmony was modal, with a lowered submediant in major keys as a constantly present feature; a propensity for plagal cadences and a proclivity for consecutive triadic progressions created at times a curiously hymnal mood. But professional arrangers employed by The Beatles invested their bland melodies in raucous dissonance; electronic amplification made the music of The Beatles the loudest in the world for their time. The lyrics, most of them written by Lennon and McCartney, were distinguished by suggestive allusions, sensuous but not flagrantly erotic, anarchistic but not destructive, cynical but also humane. There were covert references to psychedelic drugs. The Beatles produced the highly original films *A Hard Day's Night, Help!, Yellow Submarine,* and *Let It Be.* The most successful individual songs in The Beatles' repertoire were *Love Me Do, I Want to Hold Your Hand, Can't Buy Me Love, Ticket to Ride, Day Tripper, All My Loving, I Wanna Be Your Man, And I Love Her, 8 Days a Week, Yesterday, Michelle, Eleanor Rigby, With a Little Help from My Friends, Sergeant Pepper's Lonely Hearts Club Band, Magical Mystery Tour, Lady Madonna, You're Gonna Lose That Girl, Norwegian Wood, Good Day Sunshine, Hey Jude;* also title songs of the films. The Beatles were legally dissolved in 1970. By then Lennon's career had taken a new turn as a result of his relationship with the Japanese-American avant-garde film producer and artist **Yoko Ono;** through her, Lennon's social consciousness was raised, and he subsequently became an outspoken activist for peace. They appeared nude on the cover of their album 2

Virgins and celebrated their honeymoon with a "bed-in" for peace. Lennon withdrew from public life in 1975. He and Ono brought out the album *Imagine* (1971), which contained what would become his best-known song of the period, *Imagine*; they also collaborated on his last album, *Double Fantasy* (1980), which achieved great popularity. The shock waves produced by Lennon's senseless murder reverberated throughout the world; crowds in deep mourning marched in N.Y., Liverpool, and Tokyo; Ono issued a number of declarations urging Lennon's fans not to give way to despair. Not even the death of Elvis Presley generated such outbursts of grief. A photograph taken on the afternoon before his murder, of John in the nude, embracing a fully dressed Ono, was featured on the cover of a special issue of *Rolling Stone* magazine (Jan. 22, 1981). His life was the subject of a touching documentary film, *Imagine*, in 1988.

Lewis, Jerry Lee, gyrating American rock 'n' roll and country-music pianist and singer; b. Ferriday, La., Sept. 29, 1935. He assaulted the piano keys with unusual ferocity as if seeking the rock bottom of the sound, and whenever he had a chance also vocalized in a frenetic seizure of the larynx. He tried every style, including rock, folk, western, and rhythm-and-blues, always hitting hard on mental torment. He never wrote his own songs, but he sure could metamorphosize and transmogrify ready-made tunes such as *Great Balls of Fire* (1957). His rendition of *Whole Lotta Shakin' Going On* (1957) became a rock-'n'-roll classic. His career came to a halt in 1958 during his English tour after it was revealed in lurid headlines that he was traveling with a 13-year-old girl, who he said was his 1st cousin and child wife. Even his records were put on the shelf at radio stations, and he was reduced to playing at village fairs and roadhouses. It was not until 1968 that he was able to return to public favor, with records such as *Another Place, Another Time* and *What's Made Milwaukee Famous (Has Made a Loser Out of Me)*. In 1977 he recorded an autobiographical single, *Middle-Age Crazy*. With his sister Linda Gail Lewis, he brought out the album *Together* (1969); his later albums included *The Session* (1973), *Southern Roots* (1973), *Jerry Lee Lewis Keeps Rockin'* (1978), and *Killer Country* (1980).

Lockwood, Annea (actually, **Anna Ferguson**), New Zealand composer and instrument builder; b. Christchurch, July 29, 1939. She studied at Canterbury Univ. in New Zealand (B.Mus., 1961); then went to London, where she took courses with Peter Racine Fricker and Gottfried M. Koenig at the Royal College of Music (diplomas in piano and composition, 1963); also attended courses in new music in Darmstadt (1961–62), had lessons with Koenig at the Hochschule für Musik in Cologne (1963–64), and studied at the Bilthoven (Netherlands) Electronic Music Center (1963–64); also worked in computer composition at the Electronic Music Studio in Putney, England (1970), and undertook research at the Univ. of Southampton's Inst. for Sound and Vibration Research (1969–72). In 1968 she gave non-lectures at the Anti-Univ. of London; later taught at Hunter College of the City Univ. of N.Y. (1973–78) and Vassar College (1973–83). In 1968, with her then husband, Harvey Matusow, she undertook a series of experiments in total art, including aural, oral, visual, tactile, gustatory, and olfactory demonstrations and sporadic transcendental manifestations; of these, the most remarkable was the summoning (in German) of Beethoven's ghost at a séance held in London on Oct. 3, 1968, with sound recorded on magnetic tape, which in playback revealed some surprisingly dissonant music of apparently metapsychic origin, tending to indicate that Beethoven was a posthumous avant-garde composer. The séance was preceded by the burning of a combustible piano and of an inflammable microphone. Not content with setting the piano afire, she also demonstrated the drowning of an upright piano in a lake in Amarillo, Texas (Dec.

27, 1972). Since the mid-1970s, her concerns have been with aural perception and the utilization of sounds found in nature and the environment in participatory, on-site installations.

WORKS (descriptive materials provided by the composer): Violin Concerto (1962); *À Abélard, Héloïse*, chamber cantata for Mezzo-soprano and 10 Instruments (1963); *Glass Concert* for 2 Performers and Amplified Glass Instruments (1966); *River Archives*, recordings of select world rivers and streams (1966–); *Tiger Balm*, tape collage of sensual and erotic sounds including sonic images of a woman and a tiger making love (1972); *Malaman*, solo chant using very old words for sound from many languages, based upon the belief that these words contain and can release specific, useful acoustic energy (1974); *World Rhythms*, 10-channel live mix of the sounds of such natural phenomena as earthquakes, radio waves from a pulsar star, fire, human breathing, tree frogs, geysers, etc., together with a biorhythm produced by a gong player (1975); *Spirit Songs Unfolding* for Tape and Slides (1977); *Delta Run*, mixed-media work for Tape, Slide Projection, and Movement centered around a dying sculptor's reflections on death (1982); *A Sound Map of the Hudson River*, illustration work tracing the course of the Hudson, by means of recordings of water and ambient sounds made over the course of a year along its banks, from source to ocean (1982–83); *Night and Fog*, settings of texts by Osip Mandelstam and Carolyn Forche for Baritone, Baritone Saxophone, Percussion, and Tape (1987); *The Secret Life* for Amplified Double Bass, using a form of improvisatory ventriloquism with the player initially talking about his or her relationship with the bass, then the point of view shifting to the bass itself, which talks back to the player, all spoken material being transduced through the bass itself (1989); *Amazonia Dreaming* for Snare Drum (1989); *Nautilus* for Didjeridu, Conch Shells, and Percussion (1989).

Lombardo, Guy (actually, **Gaetano Alberto**), popular Canadian-American bandleader; b. London, Ontario (of Italian parents), June 19, 1902; d. Houston, Nov. 5, 1977. With his brother Carmen Lombardo, the saxophone player, he organized a dance band, The Royal Canadians, and took it to the U.S. in 1924; 2 other brothers, Lebert and Victor, were also members of the band. The band rapidly rose to success on the commercial wave of pervasive sentimentality; in 1928 it was publicized as the purveyor of "the sweetest music this side of Heaven"; in 1929 they began playing at the Roosevelt Grill, where they held sway for some 33 years; thereafter they performed at the Waldorf-Astoria Hotel; the band's rendition of *Auld Lang Syne* was a nostalgic feature at each New Year's Eve celebration from 1929, being broadcast live on radio and later on television. In his arrangements, Lombardo cultivated unabashed emotionalism; in his orchestrations, all intervallic interstices were well filled and saxophones were tremulous with vibrato. The result was a velvety, creamy, but not necessarily oleaginous harmoniousness, which possessed an irresistible appeal to the obsolescent members of the superannuated generation of the 1920s. His preferred dynamic was *mezzo-forte*, and his favorite tempo, *andante moderato*; he never allowed the sound of his band to rise to a disturbing *forte* or to descend to a squeaking *pianissimo*. He was a wizard of the golden mean, and his public loved it. With J. Altshul, he publ. the autobiography *Auld Acquaintance* (N.Y., 1975).

Lully, Jean-Baptiste (originally, **Giovanni Battista Lulli**), celebrated Italian-born French composer; b. Florence, Nov. 28, 1632; d. Paris, March 22, 1687. The son of a poor Florentine miller, he learned to play the guitar at an early age. His talent for singing brought him to the attention of Roger de Lorraine, Chevalier de Guise, and he was taken to Paris in 1646 as a page to Mlle. d'Orléans, a young cousin of Louis XIV. He quickly adapted to the manner of the French court;

although he mastered the language, he never lost his Italian accent. There is no truth in the report that he worked in the kitchens, but he did keep company with the domestic servants, and it was while he was serving in Mlle. d'Orléans's court in the Tuileries that he perfected his violin technique. He also had the opportunity to hear the 24 Violons du Roi and was present at performances of Luigi Rossi's *Orfeo* at the Louvre in 1647. When Mlle. d'Orléans suffered political disgrace in 1652 and was forced to leave Paris, Lully was released from her service, and early in 1653 he danced with the young Louis XIV in the ballet *La Nuit*. Shortly thereafter, he was made compositeur de la musique instrumentale du Roi, with joint responsibility for the instrumental music in court ballets. At some time before 1656 he became conductor of Les Petits Violons du Roi, a smaller offshoot of the grand bande. This ensemble was heard for the 1st time in 1656 in *La Galanterie du temps*. Thanks to Lully's strict discipline with regard to organization and interpretation, Les Petits Violons soon came to rival the parent ensemble. The 2 groups were combined in 1664.

Lully became a naturalized French citizen in 1661, the same year in which he was appointed surintendant de la musique et compositeur de la musique de la chambre; he also became maître de la musique de la famille royale in 1662. His association with Molière commenced in 1664; he provided Molière with the music for a series of comédies-ballets, culminating with *Le Bourgeois Gentilhomme* in 1670. Lully acquired the sole right to form an Académie Royale de Musique in 1672, and thus gained the power to forbid performances of stage works by any other composer. From then until his death he produced a series of tragédies lyriques, most of which were composed to texts by the librettist Philippe Quinault. The subject matter for several of these works was suggested by the King, who was extravagantly praised and idealized in their prologues. Lully took great pains in perfecting these texts, but was often content to leave the writing of the inner voices of the music to his pupils. His monopoly of French musical life created much enmity. In 1674 Henri Guichard attempted to establish an Académie Royale des Spectacles, and their ensuring rivalry resulted in Lully accusing Guichard of trying to murder him by mixing arsenic with his snuff. Lully won the court case that followed, but the decision was reversed on appeal. A further setback occurred when Quinault was thought to have slandered the King's mistress in his text of *Isis* (1677) and was compelled to end his partnership with Lully in disgrace for some time. The King continued to support Lully, however, in spite of the fact that the composer's homosexuality had become a public scandal (homosexuality at the time was a capital offense). Lully's acquisition of titles culminated in 1681, when noble rank was conferred upon him with the title Secrétaire du Roi. In his last years he turned increasingly to sacred music. It was while he was conducting his *Te Deum* on Jan. 8, 1687, that he suffered a symbolic accident, striking his foot with a pointed cane used to pound out the beat. Gangrene set in, and he died of blood poisoning 2 months later. Lully's historical importance rests primarily upon his music for the theater. He developed what became known as the French overture, with its 3 contrasting slow-fast-slow movements. He further replaced the Italian recitativo secco style with accompanied French recitative. Thus, through the Italian-born Lully, French opera came of age.

Madonna (born **Madonna Louise Veronica Ciccone**), fantastically popular and audacious American rock singer, improviser, and actress; b. Bay City, Mich., Aug. 16, 1958. She took up acting and dancing while attending junior high school in Pontiac, Mich.; after private dance lessons with Christopher Flynn (1972–76), she studied on a scholarship at the Univ. of Michigan (1976–78). Making her way to N.Y., she eked out a living by modeling and acting in an underground softcore film;

aboveground, she worked with Alvin Ailey's dance group, and studied choreography with Pearl Lang; then studied drums and guitar with Dan Gilroy. After working with the disco star Patrick Hernandez in Paris, she returned to N.Y., appearing as a drummer and singer with Gilroy's Breakfast Club rock outfit. In 1982 she organized her own band, and in 1983 brought out her 1st album, *Madonna*; with her album *Like a Virgin* (1984), she captured the imagination of America's youth, which led to her 1st coast-to-coast tour. In 1985 Madonna pursued her thespian bent by appearing in the critically acclaimed film *Desperately Seeking Susan*; also acted in *Who's That Girl?* (1987). The popular movie *Dick Tracy* (1990) featured Madonna as a slinky, sequined, torch-singer gun moll. Her album *True Blue* (1986) proved a popular success. In 1987 she made a smashingly successful tour of Europe. In 1989, the year of her album *Like a Prayer*, she was listed among *People Magazine*'s "20 Who Defined the Decade"; she also was awarded *Musician Magazine*'s highest editorial distinction, "Artist of the Decade." Her athletic "Blond Ambition" tour of 1990 was criticized for its use of more than 50% canned music. That same year she brought out the sizzling video *Justify My Love*.

Mahler, Gustav, great Austrian composer and conductor; b. Kalischt, Bohemia, July 7, 1860; d. Vienna, May 18, 1911. He attended school in Iglau; in 1875 entered the Vienna Cons., where he studied piano with Julius Epstein, harmony with Robert Fuchs, and composition with Franz Krenn. He also took academic courses in history and philosophy at the Univ. of Vienna (1877–80). In the summer of 1880 he received his 1st engagement as a conductor, at the operetta theater in the town of Hall in Upper Austria; subsequently he held posts as theater conductor at Ljubljana (1881), Olmütz (1882), Vienna (1883), and Kassel (1883–85). In 1885 he served as 2nd Kapellmeister to Anton Seidl at the Prague Opera, where he gave several performances of Wagner's operas. From 1886 to 1888 he was assistant to Arthur Nikisch in Leipzig; in 1888 he received the important appointment of music director of the Royal Opera in Budapest. In 1891 he was engaged as conductor at the Hamburg Opera; during his tenure there, he developed a consummate technique for conducting. In 1897 he received a tentative offer as music director of the Vienna Court Opera, but there was an obstacle to overcome. Mahler was Jewish, and although there was no overt anti-Semitism in the Austrian government, an imperial appointment could not be given to a Jew. Mahler was never orthodox in his religion, and had no difficulty in converting to Catholicism, which was the prevailing faith in Austria. He held this position at the Vienna Court Opera for 10 years; under his guidance, it reached the highest standards of artistic excellence. In 1898 Mahler was engaged to succeed Hans Richter as conductor of the Vienna Phil. Here, as in his direction of opera, he proved a great interpreter, but he also allowed himself considerable freedom in rearranging the orchestration of classical scores when he felt it would redound to greater effect. He also aroused antagonism among the players by his autocratic behavior toward them. He resigned from the Vienna Phil. in 1901; in 1907 he also resigned from the Vienna Court Opera. In the meantime, he became immersed in strenuous work as a composer; he confined himself exclusively to composition of symphonic music, sometimes with vocal parts; because of his busy schedule as conductor, he could compose only in the summer months, in a villa on the Wörthersee in Carinthia. In 1902 he married Alma Schindler; they had 2 daughters. The younger daughter, Anna Mahler, was briefly married to Ernst Krenek; the elder daughter died in infancy. Alma Mahler studied music with Zemlinsky, who was the brother-in-law of Arnold Schoenberg.

Having exhausted his opportunities in Vienna, Mahler accepted the post of principal conductor of the Metropolitan Opera in N.Y. in 1907. He made his

American debut there on Jan. 1, 1908, conducting *Tristan und Isolde*. In 1909 he was appointed conductor of the N.Y. Phil. His performances both at the Metropolitan and with the N.Y. Phil. were enormously successful with the audiences and the N.Y. music critics, but inevitably he had conflicts with the board of trustees in both organizations, which were mostly commanded by rich women. He resigned from the Metropolitan Opera; on Feb. 21, 1911, he conducted his last concert with the N.Y. Phil. and then returned to Vienna; he died there of pneumonia on May 18, 1911, at the age of 50. The N.Y. newspapers publ. lurid accounts of his struggle for artistic command with the regimen of the women of the governing committee. Alma Mahler was quoted as saying that although in Vienna even the Emperor did not dare to order Mahler about, in N.Y. he had to submit to the whims of 10 ignorant women. The newspaper editorials mourned Mahler's death, but sadly noted that his N.Y. tenure was a failure. As to Mahler's own compositions, the N.Y. *Tribune* said bluntly, "We cannot see how any of his music can long survive him." His syms. were sharply condemned in the press as being too long, too loud, and too discordant. It was not until the 2nd half of the 20th century that Mahler became fully recognized as a composer, the last great Romantic symphonist. Mahler's syms. were drawn on the grandest scale, and the technical means employed for the realization of his ideas were correspondingly elaborate. The sources of his inspiration were twofold: the lofty concepts of universal art, akin to those of Bruckner, and ultimately stemming from Wagner; and the simple folk melos of the Austrian countryside, in pastoral moods recalling the intimate episodes in Beethoven's syms. True to his Romantic nature, Mahler attached descriptive titles to his syms.; the 1st was named the *Titan*; the 2nd, *Resurrection*; the 3rd, *Ein Sommermorgentraum*; and the 5th, *The Giant*. The great 8th became known as "sym. of a thousand" because it required about 1,000 instrumentalists, vocalists, and soloists for performance; however, this sobriquet was the inspiration of Mahler's agent, not of Mahler himself. Later in life Mahler tried to disassociate his works from their programmatic titles; he even claimed that he never used them in the 1st place, contradicting the evidence of the MSS, in which the titles appear in Mahler's own handwriting. Mahler was not an innovator in his harmonic writing; rather, he brought the Romantic era to a culmination by virtue of the expansiveness of his emotional expression and the grandiose design of his musical structures. Morbid by nature, he brooded upon the inevitability of death; one of his most poignant compositions was the cycle for voice and orch. *Kindertotenlieder*; he wrote it shortly before the death of his little daughter, and somehow he blamed himself for this seeming anticipation of his personal tragedy. In 1910 he consulted Sigmund Freud in Leiden, Holland, but the treatment was brief and apparently did not help Mahler to resolve his psychological problems. Unquestionably, he suffered from an irrational feeling of guilt. In the 3rd movement of his unfinished 10th Sym., significantly titled *Purgatorio*, he wrote on the margin, "Madness seizes me, annihilates me," and appealed to the Devil to take possession of his soul. But he never was clinically insane. He died of a heart attack brought on by a bacterial infection.

Mahler's importance to the evolution of modern music is very great; the early works of Schoenberg and Berg show the influence of Mahler's concepts. A society was formed in the U.S. in 1941 "to develop in the public an appreciation of the music of Bruckner, Mahler and other moderns." An International Gustav Mahler Soc. was formed in Vienna in 1955, with Bruno Walter as honorary president. On Mahler's centennial, July 7, 1960, the government of Austria issued a memorial postage stamp of 1½ shillings, with Mahler's portrait.

Mamoulian, Rouben, Russian-born director of operas, musicals, and films; b. Tiflis, Oct. 8, 1897; d. Los Angeles, Dec. 4, 1987. He showed an early interest in theater, founding a drama studio in his native city in 1918; in 1920 he toured England with the Russian Repertory Theater. Later he directed several hit plays in London during a 3-year span. In 1923 he emigrated to the U.S. to become director of operas and operettas at the George Eastman Theater in Rochester, N.Y. He was an innovator of both stage and screen, using an imaginative and bold blend of all the components of film with the new dimension of sound. He directed the noted early "talkie" *Applause* in 1929, as well as the film version of Gershwin's *Porgy and Bess* in 1935. He was the 1st director to use a mobile camera in a sound movie, and among the 1st to use a multiple-channel sound track. He directed the film of the Rodgers and Hammerstein musical *Oklahoma!* (1955), which was the 1st musical to utilize songs and dance as an integral part of the dramatic flow of the plot.

Maria Antonia Walpurgis, electress of Saxony, daughter of the elector of Bavaria, later Holy Roman Emperor Charles VII; b. Munich, July 18, 1724; d. Dresden, April 23, 1780. She was not only a generous patroness of the fine arts, but a trained musician, pupil of Hasse and Porpora (1747–52); under the pseudonym E.T.P.A. (Ermelinda Talea Pastorella Arcada, her name as member of the Academy of Arcadians) she produced and publ. 2 Italian operas to her own librettos, and sang in their premieres: *Il trionfo della Fedeltà* (Dresden, 1754) and *Talestri, regina delle Amazoni* (Nymphenburg, near Munich, Feb. 6, 1760); she also wrote texts of oratorios and cantatas for Hasse and Ristori.

Markert, Russell, innovative American choreographer; b. Jersey City, N.J., Aug. 8, 1899; d. Waterbury, Conn., Dec. 8, 1990. He served in the Army Quartermaster Corps in France, where he performed in military shows in his free time. His professional career began on Broadway, where he danced in and later directed the annual revue *Earl Carroll's Vanities*. In 1925 in St. Louis he founded a women's precision dance troupe called the Missouri Rockets; the group was seen and immediately signed to perform by the owner of N.Y.'s Roxy Theater. When Radio City Music Hall opened in 1932, the troupe was invited to be resident there and became the Rockettes. A Rockettes routine usually had its inception in an evocative piece of music; applicants were required to have a background in modern jazz in addition to "exceptionally limber kicks." In the heyday of the Music Hall, Markert trained and rehearsed some 2,500 young women for performances to capacity audiences every day of the year. He retired in 1971. The Juilliard School in N.Y. offers a Russell Markert Dance Scholarship.

Martins, João Carlos, Brazilian pianist; b. São Paulo, June 25, 1940. He studied piano with José Kliass; made his professional debut at Teresopolis in 1954; other concerts followed in Brazilian cities; in 1960 he made his American debut at Carnegie Hall in N.Y., evoking superlatives for his "passionate subjectivity" from the critics; later he made a specialty of performing all of Bach's 48 preludes and fugues in 2 consecutive concerts; he also appeared as a soloist with orchs. in N.Y., Philadelphia, and Boston. But at the height of his successes, in 1969, he was knocked down during a soccer match, and hurt his arm to the point of a painful neuralgia, so that he had to stop playing piano. But in a surprising change of direction, he went into banking, managed a champion prizefighter, started a construction company, and became a multimillionaire in devalued Brazilian currency. An even more surprising development followed when, in 1981, he was appointed to the post of the Brazilian state secretary of culture; in this capacity he exhibited an extraordinary knack for urban recovery in the direction of futuristic Americanization. In the meantime, his neurological ailment subsided, and he returned to his career as a virtuoso pianist.

McFerrin, Bobby (Robert), gifted black American popular vocalist, son of **Robert McFerrin**; b. N.Y., March 11, 1950. He studied music theory from the age of 6 and played piano in high school, forming a quartet that copied the styles of Henry Mancini and Sergio Mendes. In 1970 he heard Miles Davis's fusion album *Bitches Brew* and completely changed his musical direction. He studied music at Sacramento State Univ. and at Cerritos College; then played piano professionally until 1977, when he began to develop his voice; toured in 1980 with jazz vocalist Jon Hendricks, and debuted a solo act in 1982. His recordings include *Bobby McFerrin* (1982), *The Voice* (1984), *Spontaneous Improvisation* (1986), *Simple Pleasures* (1988; includes the song *Don't Worry, Be Happy*, which made him a household name), and *Medicine Music* (1991); also made several music videos and sang with Herbie Hancock, Yo-Yo Ma, Manhattan Transfer, and others. In 1989 he established the 11-voice ensemble Voicestra, with which he created the sound track for *Common Threads*, a 1989 documentary on the AIDS quilt; the group's 1st concert tour, in 1990, received critical acclaim. McFerrin began studying conducting in 1989, making his debut with a performance of Beethoven's Sym. No. 7 with the San Francisco Sym. on March 11, 1990. Technically, McFerrin is a virtuoso, using a remarkable range of voices with sophisticated control and accompanying them with body percussion, breath, and other self-generated sounds. Esthetically, he fuses a number of musical styles, including jazz, rock, and New Age, in a brilliant palette; his solo and ensemble shows are based on various improvisatory structures through which he produces highly polished, expertly burnished works.

McKuen, Rod (Marvin), American minstrel and lyricist; b. Oakland, Calif., April 29, 1933. He ran away from a previously broken home at the age of 11; bummed as a logger and roadman; roped calves and dogged bulls in and out of rodeo shows; became a disc jockey and scriptwriter in a psychological warfare unit during the Korean War. Returning to the U.S., he appeared as a folksy balladeer in San Francisco nightclubs; obtained a music theory book and learned to write tunes; supported himself by playing supporting roles in otherwise unsupportable bit parts in the movies; eked out a posh living by crashing parties and gorging himself on choice comestibles. He became a roving poet, dispensing a plethora of facile country-style songs with monosyllabic assonances for rhymes and a simple appeal of scenes of non-obscene free love against an artificially flavored pastoral landscape. His 1st anthology of verse, *An Autumn Came*, was a failure, but he stumbled into a poetic bonanza with the commercially issued vols. *Stanyan Street* and *Listen to the Warm*. He never indentured himself to an agent, and so was able to reap a lucrative harvest of success, blandly chanting, "I have no special bed, I give myself to those who offer love." He publ. a memoir, *Finding My Father* (N.Y., 1976), in which he stated, "I was born a bastard; some people spend their entire lives becoming one." His putative natural father was a lumberjack who died about 1965.

Mehta, Zubin, exuberant, effulgent, and eloquent Indian conductor, son of **Mehli Mehta**; b. Bombay, April 29, 1936. The family belonged to the historic tribe of Parsi nobles, the fire-worshiping followers of Zarathustra who fled en masse from the turbulence of Persia 13 centuries before Zubin Mehta's birth. He was tutored in music by his father; he learned to play violin and piano; when he was 16 he successfully conducted a rehearsal of the Bombay Sym. Orch. Before deciding on a musical career, he took a course in medicine at St. Xavier College in Bombay; but he turned away from the unesthetic training in dissection, and instead went to Vienna, where he practiced to play the double bass at the Academy of Music and took conducting lessons with Hans Swarowsky. During the summers of 1956 and 1957, he attended conducting classes at the Accademia Chigiana in Siena with Carlo Zecchi and Alceo Galliera. In 1957 he graduated from the Vienna

Academy of Music, and made his professional debut conducting the Tonkünstler Orch. in the Musikverein. In 1958 he married the Canadian singer Carmen Lasky; they had 2 children, but were divorced in 1964; she married Zubin Mehta's brother Zarin in 1966, thus making Zubin an uncle by marriage of his own children. On July 20, 1969, he married the actress Nancy Kovack in a dual ceremony, Methodist and Zoroastrian. In the meantime his career progressed by great strides; he won the competition of the Royal Liverpool Phil. in 1958, and conducted it for a season as an assistant; later he obtained guest engagements in Austria and Yugoslavia. In 1959 he competed in a conducting test in Tanglewood, and won 2nd prize. In 1960 he received a bona fide engagement to conduct the Vienna Sym. Orch.; that same year he also made a highly successful appearance as a guest conductor with the Philadelphia Orch.; later in 1960 he conducted 2 concerts of the Montreal Sym. Orch. and produced such a fine impression that he was appointed its music director. In 1962 Mehta took the Montreal Sym. Orch. to Russia, where he gave 8 concerts; then conducted 2 concerts with it in Paris and 1 in Vienna, where he took 14 bows in response to a vociferous ovation. In the meantime he received a contract to conduct the Los Angeles Phil., becoming its associate conductor in 1961 and its music director in 1962; he was thus the holder of 2 major conducting jobs, a feat he was able to accomplish by commuting on newfangled jet airplanes; he was also the youngest conductor to function in this dual capacity. His career was now assuming the allure of a gallop, aided by his ability, rare among conductors, to maintain his self-control under trying circumstances. He has the reputation of a bon vivant; his joy of life is limitless. Professionally, he maintains an almost infallible reliability; he conducts all of his scores, even the most mind-boggling modern scores, and operas as well, from memory. He is also a polyglot; not only is he eloquent in English and Hindi, but he is fluent in German, French, and Spanish; he even speaks understandable Russian. He made his debut at the Metropolitan Opera in N.Y. on Dec. 29, 1965, conducting *Aida*. His performances of *Carmen* and *Turandot* were highly praised. In 1967 he resigned his post in Montreal; in 1968 he was named music adviser of the Israel Phil.; in 1977 he became its music director. In 1978 he left the Los Angeles Phil. after he received an offer he could not refuse, the musical directorship of the N.Y. Phil.; in 1980 he toured with it in Europe. In 1991 he left his post with the N.Y. Phil. His association with the Israel Phil. was particularly affectionate; he conducted it during the Six-Day War and at the 25th anniversary of Israel's independence; in 1974 he was given an honorary Ph.D. by Tel Aviv Univ. No Jew could be more Israeli than the Parsi Mehta. *Time* glorified him with a cover story in its issue of Jan. 19, 1968.

Melachrino, George (Miltiades), English conductor of popular music; b. London, May 1, 1909; d. there, June 18, 1965. He studied at London's Trinity College of Music; then conducted his own band; subsequently launched the Melachrino Strings (1945), which he imbued with a sort of black-velvet coloration that made the "Melachrino sound" a byword among music-lovers. He could play every instrument except harp and piano. His recording albums bore titles of irresistible sentimentality, e.g., *Music for Two People Alone, Music for a Nostalgic Traveler* (known in Europe under the name of *Reverie*), and *Music for Relaxation*.

Milton, John, amateur English composer and father of the great poet John Milton; b. Stanton St. John, near Oxford, c.1563; d. London (buried), March 15, 1647. He was a chorister at Christ Church, Oxford (1572–77); apparently remained at Oxford for several years, and in 1585 went to London, where he was admitted to the Scriveners' Co. in 1600; in that year he married Sarah Jeffrey. He composed 8 anthems for 4 to 6 Voices; 7 Psalm settings; 2 madrigals for 5 Voices; Motet for 6 Voices; *In Nomine* a 6; 4 fantasias a 5 and a 6 (1 ed. in Musica

Britannica, IX, 1955; 2nd ed., 1962). See G. Arkwright, ed., *John Milton: Six Anthems*, Old English Edition, XXII (1900), and C. Hill, ed., *Sir William Leighton: The Teares or Lamentations of a Sorrowful Soul*, Early English Church Music, XI (1970).

Mitropoulos, Dimitri, celebrated Greek-born American conductor and composer; b. Athens, March 1, 1896; d. after suffering a heart attack while rehearsing Mahler's 3rd Sym. with the orch. of the Teatro alla Scala, Milan, Nov. 2, 1960. He studied piano with Wassenhoven and harmony with A. Marsick at the Odeon Cons. in Athens; wrote an opera after Maeterlinck, *Sœur Béatrice* (1918), performed at the Odeon Cons. (May 20, 1919); in 1920, after graduation from the Cons., he went to Brussels, where he studied composition with Paul Gilson; in 1921 he went to Berlin, where he took piano lessons with Busoni at the Hochschule für Musik (until 1924); concurrently was répétiteur at the Berlin State Opera. He became a conductor of the Odeon Cons. orch. in Athens (1924); was its co-conductor (1927–29) and principal conductor (from 1929); was also prof. of composition there (from 1930). In 1930 he was invited to conduct a concert of the Berlin Phil.; when the soloist Egon Petri became suddenly indisposed, Mitropoulos substituted for him as soloist in Prokofiev's Piano Concerto No. 3, conducting from the keyboard (Feb. 27, 1930). He played the same concerto in Paris in 1932 as a pianist-conductor, and later in the U.S. His Paris debut as a conductor (1932) obtained a spontaneous success; he conducted the most difficult works from memory, which was a novelty at the time; also led rehearsals without a score. He made his American debut with the Boston Sym. Orch. on Jan. 24, 1936, with immediate acclaim; that same year he was engaged as music director of the Minneapolis Sym. Orch.; there he frequently performed modern music, including works by Schoenberg, Berg, and other representatives of the atonal school; the opposition that naturally arose was not sufficient to offset his hold on the public as a conductor of great emotional power. He resigned from the Minneapolis Sym. Orch. in 1949 to accept the post of conductor of the N.Y. Phil.; shared the podium with Stokowski for a few weeks, and in 1950 became music director. In 1956 Leonard Bernstein was engaged as associate conductor with Mitropoulos, and in 1958 succeeded him as music director. With the N.Y. Phil., Mitropoulos continued his policy of bringing out important works by European and American modernists; he also programmed modern operas (*Elektra, Wozzeck*) in concert form. A musician of astounding technical ability, Mitropoulos became very successful with the general public as well as with the musical vanguard whose cause he so boldly espoused. While his time was engaged mainly in the U.S., Mitropoulos continued to appear as guest conductor in Europe; he also appeared on numerous occasions as conductor at the Metropolitan Opera in N.Y. (debut conducting *Salome*, Dec. 15, 1954) and at various European opera theaters. He became an American citizen in 1946. As a composer, Mitropoulos was one of the earliest among Greek composers to write in a distinctly modern idiom.

Mozart, Wolfgang Amadeus (baptismal names, **Johannes Chrysostomus Wolfgangus Theophilus**), supreme Austrian genius of music whose works in every genre are unsurpassed in lyric beauty, rhythmic variety, and effortless melodic invention, son of **(Johann Georg) Leopold**, brother of **Maria Anna**, and father of **Franz Xaver Wolfgang Mozart**; b. Salzburg, Jan. 27, 1756; d. Vienna, Dec. 5, 1791. He and his sister, tenderly nicknamed "Nannerl," were the only 2 among the 7 children of Anna Maria and Leopold Mozart to survive infancy. Mozart's sister was 4½ years older; she took harpsichord lessons from her father, and Mozart as a very young child eagerly absorbed the sounds of music. He soon began playing the harpsichord himself, and later studied the violin. Leopold was an excellent musician, but he also appreciated the theatrical validity of the performances that Wolfgang and Nannerl began giving in Salzburg. On Jan. 17, 1762, he took them to Munich, where they performed before the Elector of Bavaria. In Sept. 1762 they played for Emperor Francis I at his palace in Vienna. The family returned to Salzburg in Jan. 1763, and in June 1763 the children were taken to Frankfurt, where Wolfgang showed his skill in improvising at the keyboard. In Nov. 1763 they arrived in Paris, where they played before Louis XV; it was in Paris that Wolfgang's 1st compositions were printed (4 sonatas for Harpsichord, with Violin ad libitum). In April 1764 they proceeded to London; there Wolfgang played for King George III. In London he was befriended by Bach's son Johann Christian Bach, who gave exhibitions improvising 4-hands at the piano with the child Mozart. By that time Mozart had tried his ability in composing serious works; he wrote 2 syms. for a London performance, and the MS of another very early sym., purportedly written by him in London, was discovered in 1980. Leopold wrote home with undisguised pride: "Our great and mighty Wolfgang seems to know everything at the age of 7 that a man acquires at the age of 40." Knowing the power of publicity, he diminished Wolfgang's age, for at the time the child was fully 9 years old. In July 1765 they journeyed to the Netherlands, then set out for Salzburg, visiting Dijon, Lyons, Geneva, Bern, Zürich, Donaueschingen, and Munich on the way. Arriving in Salzburg in Nov. 1766, Wolfgang applied himself to serious study of counterpoint under the tutelage of his father. In Sept. 1767 the family proceeded to Vienna, where Wolfgang began work on an opera, *La finta semplice*; his 2nd theater work was a singspiel, *Bastien und Bastienne*, which was produced in Vienna at the home of Dr. Franz Mesmer, the protagonist of the famous method of therapy by "animal magnetism," which became known as Mesmerism. On Dec. 7, 1768, Mozart led a performance of his *Missa solemnis* in C minor before the royal family and court at the consecration of the Waisenhauskirche. Upon Mozart's return to Salzburg in Jan. 1769, Archbishop Sigismund von Schrattenbach named him his Konzertmeister; however, the position was without remuneration. Still determined to broaden Mozart's artistic contacts, his father took him on an Italian tour. The announcement for a concert in Mantua on Jan. 16, 1770, just a few days before Mozart's 14th birthday, was typical of the artistic mores of the time: "A Symphony of his own composition; a harpsichord concerto, which will be handed to him, and which he will immediately play *prima vista*; a Sonata handed him in like manner, which he will provide with variations, and afterwards repeat in another key; an Aria, the words for which will be handed to him and which he will immediately set to music and sing himself, accompanying himself on the harpsichord; a Sonata for harpsichord on a subject given him by the leader of the violins; a Strict Fugue on a theme to be selected, which he will improvise on the harpsichord; a Trio in which he will execute a violin part *all'improvviso*; and, finally, the latest Symphony by himself." Legends of Mozart's extraordinary musical ability grew; it was reported, for instance, that he wrote out the entire score of *Miserere* by Allegri, which he had heard in the Sistine Chapel at the Vatican only twice. Young Mozart was subjected to numerous tests by famous Italian musicians, among them Giovanni Sammartini, Piccini, and Padre Martini; he was given a diploma as an elected member of the Accademia Filarmonica in Bologna after he had passed examinations in harmony and counterpoint. On Oct. 10, 1770, the Pope made him a Knight of the Golden Spur. He was commissioned to compose an opera; the result was *Mitridate, rè di Ponto*, which was performed in Milan on Dec. 26, 1770; Mozart himself conducted 3 performances of this opera from the harpsichord; after a short stay in Salzburg, they returned to Milan in 1771, where he composed the serenata *Ascanio in Alba* for the wedding festivities of Archduke Ferdinand (Oct. 17, 1771). He returned to Salzburg late in 1771; his patron, Archbishop Schrattenbach, died about that time, and his successor, Archbishop Hieronymus Colloredo, seemed to be indifferent to Mozart as a musician. Once more Mozart went to Italy, where his newest opera, *Lucio Silla*, was performed in Milan on Dec. 26, 1772. He returned to Salzburg in March 1773, but in July of that year he went to Vienna, where he became acquainted with the music of Haydn, who greatly influenced his instrumental style. Returning to Salzburg once more, he supervised the production of his opera *Il Rè pastore*, which was performed on April 23, 1775.

In March 1778 Mozart visited Paris again for a performance of his "Paris" Sym. at a Concert Spirituel. His mother died in Paris on July 3, 1778. Returning to Salzburg in Jan. 1779, he resumed his duties as Konzertmeister and also obtained the position of court organist at a salary of 450 gulden. In 1780 the Elector of Bavaria commissioned from him an opera seria, *Idomeneo*, which was successfully produced in Munich on Jan. 29, 1781. In May 1781 Mozart lost his position with the Archbishop in Salzburg and decided to move to Vienna, which became his permanent home. There he produced the operatic masterpiece *Die Entführung aus dem Serail*, staged at the Burgtheater on July 16, 1782, with excellent success. On August 4, 1782, he married Constanze Weber, the sister of Aloysia Weber, with whom he had previously been infatuated. Two of his finest syms.—No. 35 in D major, "Haffner," written for the Haffner family of Salzburg, and No. 36 in C major, the "Linz"—date from 1782 and 1783, respectively. From this point forward Mozart's productivity reached extraordinary dimensions, but despite the abundance of commissions and concert appearances, he was unable to earn enough to sustain his growing family. Still, melodramatic stories of Mozart's abject poverty are gross exaggerations. He apparently felt no scruples in asking prosperous friends for financial assistance. Periodically he wrote to Michael Puchberg, a banker and a brother Freemason (Mozart joined the Masonic Order in 1784), with requests for loans (which he never repaid); invariably Puchberg obliged, but usually granting smaller amounts than Mozart requested. (The market price of Mozart autographs has grown exponentially; a begging letter to Puchberg would fetch, some 2 centuries after it was written, a hundred times the sum requested.) In 1785 Mozart completed a set of 6 string quartets which he dedicated to Haydn; unquestionably the structure of these quartets owed much to Haydn's contrapuntal art. Haydn himself paid a tribute to Mozart's genius; Mozart's father quoted him as saying, "Before God and as an honest man I tell you that your son is the greatest composer known to me either in person or by name." On May 1, 1786, Mozart's great opera buffa, *Le nozze di Figaro*, was produced in Vienna, obtaining a triumph with the audience; it was performed in Prague early in 1787 with Mozart in attendance. It was during that visit that Mozart wrote his 38th Sym., in D major, known as the "Prague" Sym.; it was in Prague, also, that his operatic masterpiece *Don Giovanni* was produced, on Oct. 29, 1787. It is interesting to note that at its Vienna performance the opera was staged under the title *Die sprechende Statue*, unquestionably with the intention of sensationalizing the story; the dramatic appearance of the statue of the Commendatore, introduced by the ominous sound of trombones, was a shuddering climax to the work. In Nov. 1787 Mozart was appointed Kammermusicus in Vienna as a successor to Gluck, albeit at a smaller salary: he received 800 gulden per annum as against Gluck's salary of 2,000 gulden. The year 1788 was a glorious one for Mozart and for music history; it was the year when he composed his last 3 syms.: No. 39 in E-flat major; No. 40 in G minor; and No. 41 in C major, known under the name "Jupiter" (the Jovian designation was apparently attached to the work for the 1st time in British concert programs; its earliest use was in the program of the Edinburgh Festival in Oct. 1819). In the spring of 1789 Mozart went to Berlin; on the way he appeared as soloist in one of his piano concertos before the Elector of Saxony in Dresden, and also played the organ at the Thomaskirche in Leipzig. His visits in Potsdam and Berlin were marked by his private concerts at the court of Friedrich Wilhelm II; the King commissioned from him a set of 6 string quartets and a set of 6 piano sonatas, but Mozart died before completing these commissions. Returning to Vienna, he began work on his opera buffa *Così fan tutte* (an untranslatable sentence because *tutte* is the feminine plural, so that the full title would be "Thus do all women"). The opera was 1st performed in Vienna on Jan. 26, 1790. In Oct. 1790 Mozart went to Frankfurt for the coronation of Emperor Leopold II. Returning to Vienna, he saw Haydn, who was about to depart for London. In 1791, during his last year of life, he completed the score of *Die Zauberflöte*, with a German libretto by Emanuel Schikaneder. It was performed for the 1st time on Sept. 30, 1791, in Vienna. There followed a mysterious episode in Mozart's life; a stranger called on him with a request to compose a Requiem; the caller was an employee of Count Franz von Walsegg, who intended to have the work performed as his own in memory of his wife. Mozart was unable to finish the score, which was completed by his pupil Süssmayr, and by Eybler.

The immediate cause of Mozart's death at the age of 35 has been the subject of much speculation. A detailed examination of his medical history is found in P. Davies, "Mozart's Illnesses and Death—1: The Illnesses, 1756–90" and "2: The Last Year and the Fatal Illness," *Musical Times* (Aug. and Oct. 1984). Almost immediately after the sad event, myths and fantasies appeared in the press; the most persistent of them all was that Mozart had been poisoned by Salieri out of professional jealousy; this particularly morbid piece of invention gained circulation in European journals; the story was further elaborated upon by a report that Salieri confessed his unspeakable crime on his deathbed in 1825. Pushkin used the tale in his drama *Mozart and Salieri*, which Rimsky-Korsakov set to music in his opera of the same title; a fanciful dramatization of the Mozart-Salieri rivalry was made into a successful play, *Amadeus*, by Peter Shaffer, which was produced in London in 1979 and in N.Y. in 1980; it subsequently gained wider currency through its award-winning film version of 1984. The notion of Mozart's murder also appealed to the Nazis; in the ingenious version propagated by some German writers of the Hitlerian persuasion, Mozart was a victim of a double conspiracy of Masons and Jews who were determined to suppress the flowering of racial Germanic greatness; the Masons, in this interpretation, were outraged by his revealing of their secret rites in *Die Zauberflöte*, and allied themselves with plutocratic Jews to prevent further spread of his dangerous revelations. Another myth related to Mozart's death that found its way into the majority of Mozart biographies and even into respectable reference works was that a blizzard raged during his funeral and that none of his friends could follow his body to the cemetery; this story is easily refuted by the records of the Vienna weather bureau for the day (see N. Slonimsky, "The Weather at Mozart's Funeral," *Musical Quarterly*, Jan. 1960). It is also untrue that Mozart was buried in a pauper's grave; his body was removed from its original individual location because the family neglected to pay the mandatory dues.

The universal recognition of Mozart's genius during the 2 centuries since his death has never wavered among professional musicians, amateurs, and the general public. In his music, smiling simplicity was combined with somber drama; lofty inspiration was contrasted with playful diversion; profound meditation alternated with capricious moodiness; religious concentration was permeated with human tenderness. Devoted as Mozart was to his art and respectful as he was of the rules of composition, he was also capable of mocking the professional establishment. A delightful example of this persiflage is his little piece *Ein musikalischer Spass*, sub-titled "Dorf Musikanten," a "musical joke" at the expense of "village musicians," in which Mozart all but anticipated developments of modern music, 2 centuries in the future; he deliberately used the forbidden consecutive fifths, allowed the violin to escape upward in a whole-tone scale, and finished the entire work in a welter of polytonal triads. Mozart is also the only great composer to have a town named after him—the town of Mozart, in the province of Saskatchewan, Canada, lying between Synyard and Elfros on a CPR main line that skirts the south end of Big Quill Lake. It consists of 2 elevators, a covered curling rink, a Centennial hall, a co-op store, and a handful of well-kept homes. A local recounts that the town was named in the early 1900s by one Mrs. Lunch, the wife of the station-master, who was reportedly a talented musician and very well thought of in the community. She not only named the town Mozart but also brought about the naming of the streets after other, equally famous musicians: Chopin, Wagner, and Liszt.

The variety of technical development in Mozart's works is all the more remarkable considering the limitations of instrumental means in his time; the top-most note on his keyboard was F above the 3rd ledger line, so that in the recapitulation in the 1st movement of his famous C major Piano Sonata, the subject had to be dropped an octave lower to accommodate the modulation. The vocal technique displayed in his operas is amazing in its perfection; to be sure, the human voice has not changed since Mozart's time, but he knew how to exploit vocal resources to the utmost. This adaptability of his genius to all available means of sound production is the secret of the eternal validity of his music, and the explanation of the present popularity of mini-festivals, such as the N.Y. concert series advertised as "Mostly Mozart."

Nancarrow, Conlon, remarkable American-born Mexican composer, innovator in the technique of recording notes on a player-piano roll; b. Texarkana, Ark., Oct. 27, 1912. He played the trumpet in jazz orchs.; then took courses at the Cincinnati College-Cons. of Music (1929–32); subsequently traveled to Boston, where he became a private student of Nicolas Slonimsky, Walter Piston, and Roger Sessions. In 1937 he joined the Abraham Lincoln Brigade and went to Spain to fight in the ranks of the Republican Loyalists against the brutal assault of General Franco's armies. Classified as a premature anti-Fascist after the Republican defeat in Spain, he was refused a U.S. passport and moved to Mexico City, where he remained for 40 years, eventually obtaining Mexican citizenship (1956). In 1981, with political pressures defused in the U.S., Nancarrow was able to revisit his native land and to participate in the New American Music Festival in San Francisco. In 1982 he was a composer-in-residence at the Cabrillo Music Festival in Aptos, Calif.; also traveled to Europe, where he participated at festivals in Austria, Germany, and France. An extraordinary event occurred in his life in 1982, when he was awarded the "genius grant" of $300,000 by the MacArthur Foundation of Chicago, enabling him to continue his work without any concerns about finances. The unique quality of Nancarrow's compositions is that they can be notated only by perforating player-piano rolls to mark the notes and rhythms, and can be performed only by activating such piano rolls. This method of composition gives him total freedom in conjuring up the most complex contrapuntal, harmonic, and rhythmic combinations that no human pianist or number of human pianists could possibly perform. The method itself is extremely laborious; a bar containing a few dozen notes might require an hour to stamp out on the piano roll. Some of his studies were publ. in normal notation in Cowell's *New*

Music Quarterly. Copland, Ligeti, and other contemporary composers expressed their appreciation of Nancarrow's originality in high terms of praise. On Jan. 30, 1984, Nancarrow gave a concert of his works in Los Angeles, in a program including his *Prelude and Blues for Acoustic Piano* and several of his studies. An audiovisual documentary on Nancarrow was presented on slides by Eva Soltes. A number of Nancarrow's *Studies for Player Piano* that could be adequately notated were publ. in *Soundings 4* (1977), accompanied with critical commentaries by Gordon Mumma, Charles Amirkhanian, John Cage, Roger Reynolds, and James Tenney. On Oct. 15, 1988, his 3rd String Quartet was given its premiere performance in Cologne by the London-based Arditti Quartet, perhaps the only ensemble in the world capable of realizing Nancarrow's exceedingly complex score.

Newton, Wayne, American singer of popular music; b. Roanoke, Va., April 3, 1942. He began his career on television as a pop singer; was then propelled to commercial greatness at the neon-lighted casinos of Las Vegas and other artistically repugnant but monetarily attractive haunts; he also shrewdly invested his lucre in real-estate ventures; his recordings sold into the millions. An additional plus was his loud proclamation of the American virtues of legitimate motherhood, honest capitalism, and right-wing Republicanism.

Nikolais, Alwin (Theodore), American choreographer, stage director, and composer; b. Southington, Conn., Nov. 25, 1912. He studied piano; played in movie houses for the silent films. In 1929 he began to study dance with a pupil of Mary Wigman; became director of the Hartford (Conn.) Parks Marionette Theater and later chairman of the dance dept. of the Hartt School of Music there. From 1942 to 1946 he served in military counterintelligence in Europe; then studied with Hanya Holm in N.Y. He became director of the Henry Street Settlement Playhouse (1948), where he organized the Alwin Nikolais Dance Theatre. He wrote music for many of his dance productions, including works in the electronic medium. His principal choreographic innovation is the technique of body extension by tubular projections and disks attached to the head and upper and nether limbs, so that a biped dancer becomes a stereogeometrical figure; often in his productions clusters of dancers form primitivistic ziggurats.

Nyiregyházi, Erwin, remarkable but eccentric Hungarian-American pianist; b. Budapest, Jan. 19, 1903; d. Los Angeles, April 13, 1987. He absorbed music by a kind of domestic osmosis, from his father, a professional tenor, and his mother, an amateur pianist. An exceptionally gifted *wunderkind*, he had perfect pitch and a well-nigh phonographic memory as a very small child; played a Haydn sonata and pieces by Grieg, Chopin, and himself at a concert in Fiume at the age of 6. In 1910 he entered the Budapest Academy of Music, studying theory with Albert Siklós and Leo Weiner, and piano with István Thomán. In 1914 the family moved to Berlin, where he became a piano student of Ernst von Dohnányi. He made his debut in Germany playing Beethoven's 3rd Piano Concerto with the Berlin Phil. (Oct. 14, 1915). In 1916 he began studying with Frederic Lamond, a pupil of Liszt, who was instrumental in encouraging Nyiregyházi to study Liszt's music, which was to become the most important part of his concert repertoire. In 1920 he went to the U.S.; his American debut (Carnegie Hall, N.Y., Oct. 18, 1920) was sensationally successful; the word "genius" was freely applied to him by critics usually restrained in their verbal effusions. Inexplicably, his American career suffered a series of setbacks; he became involved in a lawsuit with his manager; he married his next manager, a Mrs. Mary Kelen, in 1926, but divorced her a year later. He then went to California, where he became gainfully employed as a studio pianist in Hollywood; in 1930 he made a European tour; then lived in N.Y.

and in Los Angeles. Beset by personal problems, he fell into a state of abject poverty, but resolutely refused to resume his concert career; he did not even own a piano. He married frequently, and as frequently divorced his successive wives. In 1972 he married his 9th wife, a lady 10 years his senior; she died shortly afterward. Attempts were made in vain by friends and admirers in Calif. to induce him to play in public; a semi-private recital was arranged for him in San Francisco in 1974; a recording of his playing of Liszt was issued in 1977; it was greeted with enthusiastic reviews, all expressing regret for his disappearance from the concert stage. Nyiregyházi composed several hundred works, mostly for piano; they remain in MS. As a child, Nyiregyházi was the object of a "scientific" study by Géza Révész, director of the Psychological Laboratory in Amsterdam, who made tests of his memory, sense of pitch, ability to transpose into different keys at sight, etc.; these findings were publ. in German as *Psychologische Analyse eines musikalisch hervorragenden Kindes* (Leipzig, 1916) and in Eng. as *The Psychology of a Musical Prodigy* (London, 1925), but the examples given and the tests detailed in the book proved to be no more unusual than the capacities of thousands of similarly gifted young musicians.

Ohlsson, Garrick (Olof), talented American pianist; b. Bronxville, N.Y., April 3, 1948. He entered the preparatory division of the Juilliard School of Music in 1961 as a student of Sascha Gorodnitzki and later of Rosina Lhévinne (B.Mus., 1971); also studied privately with Olga Barabini and Irma Wolpe. He won the Busoni (1966) and Montreal (1968) competitions; then made his N.Y. recital debut on Jan. 5, 1970; later that year he gained international recognition when he became the 1st American pianist to win the prestigious quinquennial Chopin Competition in Warsaw. A Polish writer described Ohlsson as a "bear-butterfly" for his ability to traverse the entire spectrum of 18 dynamic degrees discernible on the modern piano, from the thundering fortississimo to the finest pianississimo, with reference also to his height (6 foot, 4 inches), weight (225 lbs.), and stretch of hands (an octave and a fifth in the left hand and an octave and a fourth in the right hand). His interpretations are marked by a distinctive Americanism, technically flawless and free of Romantic mannerisms.

A succession of entries on the composer Pauline Oliveros appears here, if only to show how biographies have been revised, in this case from the Sixth Baker's *into the Seventh and finally the Eighth, eliminating a reference to SCUM that, as the composer wrote me recently, was "specious, spurious and untrue."*

Oliveros, Pauline, American avant-garde composer; b. Houston, May 30, 1932. She received the rudiments of musical education from her mother and grandmother; studied composition at the Univ. of Houston (1949–52), at San Francisco State College (1954–56), and privately with Robert Erickson. In 1967 she joined the faculty of the Univ. of California at San Diego. She cultivates total music in mixed media.

WORKS: *Trio* for flute, piano and page turner (1961); *Outline* for flute, percussion and string bass (1963); *Duo* for accordion and bandoneon with optional mynah bird obbligato, see-saw version (1964); *Variation for Sextet* (1964); *Pieces of Eight* for wind octet, cash register and magnetic tape (1965); *Rock Symphony* for electronic tape (1965); *Seven Sets of Mnemonics* for multimedia (1965); *Bye Bye Butterfly* for oscillators, amplifiers, and assorted tapes (1965); *Participle Dangling in Honor of Gertrude Stein* for tape, mobile and work crew (1966); *Engineer's Delight* for piccolo and 7 conductors (1967); *Evidence for Computing Bimolecular and Termolecular Mechanism in the Hydrochlorination of Cyclohexene,* for inter-media (1968); *Double-Basses at 20 Paces* (1968); *The Dying*

Alchemist for multimedia (1968); *Night Jar* for viola d'amore (1968); *The Wheel of Fortune*, improvisation suggested by the trump cards of the Tarot deck (1969); *One Sound* for string quartet, an invariant quadritone monody; *Apple Box Orchestra with Bottle Chorus* (1970). In her later avatar she embraced Tibetan Buddhism and adopted a static type of composition with no perceptible tonal variation; typical of this style is her *Rose Mountain* for vocal monotone and accordion (1977; renamed *Horse Sings From Cloud*, after a dream about flying horses). She is a member of the militant feminist group SCUM (acronym for "Society for Cutting Up Men").

Oliveros, Pauline, American composer; b. Houston, Texas, May 30, 1932. She was of a musical family; her mother and grandmother were piano teachers from whom she learned the rudiments of music; she also took violin lessons with William Sydler and studied accordion playing with Marjorie Harrigan. From her earliest days she became sensitive to pleasing animal sounds, and was able aurally to suppress the rude noise of motorcars in her environment. She added to her practical musical knowledge by studying the French horn with J.M. Brandsetter. From 1949 to 1952 she studied composition with Paul Koepke at the Univ. of Houston; in 1954 she enrolled at San Francisco State College (B.A., 1958); also studied privately with Robert Erickson (1954–60), who initiated her into modern harmony, the art of asymmetrical rhythms, group improvisation, and acoustical sonorism. Gradually, she expanded her receptivity into the range of subliminal sounds, derived from the overtone series, differential tones, and sonic abstractions. In 1960 she composed a piano sextet which explored a variety of such elusive tonal elements; it received the Pacifica Foundation National Prize. Advancing further into the domain of new sonorities, she wrote a choral work, *Sound Patterns*, to wordless voices (1962), which received a prize in the Netherlands. With Morton Subotnick and others she organized the San Francisco Tape Music Center, and experimented with the resources of magnetic tape. On July 22, 1967, she presented in San Francisco a 12-hour marathon of recorded electronic music of her own composition. In 1967 she joined the music faculty of the Univ. of Calif. at San Diego, where she remained until 1981. There she was able to develop her ideas further afield. Taking advantage of her skill as a gardener, she arrayed garden hoses and lawn sprinklers as part of a musical ensemble accompanied by the sounds of alarm clocks and various domestic utensils. Occasionally, a musician was instructed to bark. To this enriched artistic vocabulary was soon added a physical and psychosomatic element; performers had to act the parts of a magician, a juggler, and a fortune-teller. Page turners, piano movers, and floor sweepers were listed as performing artists. In her later works she reduced such kinetic activities and gradually began to compose ceremonial works of sonic meditation, sotto voce murmuration, lingual lallation, and joyful ululation, with the purpose of inducing an altered state of consciousness or unconsciousness; sometimes an exotic but usually digestible meal was served at leisurely intervals. Pauline Oliveros often presided over such sessions, singing and playing her faithful accordion; sometimes this music was left to be unheard by ordinary ears, but it could be perceived mystically. In 1979 she took part in the Berlin Festival of Metamusic, to audible acclaim. In 1977 she obtained first prize from the city of Bonn for a work commemorating the sesquicentennial of Beethoven's death; the piece was verbally notated with the intention to subvert perception of the entire city so that it would become a perceptual theater. As she moved higher into the realm of cosmic consciousness, Pauline Oliveros introduced the psychic element into her works; in 1970 she drew an equation for an indefinite integral of the differential *psi* (for psychic unit), to create the state of Oneness. Apart from her metamusical activities, she became a karate expert, the holder of the third Kyu black belt in Shotokan-style karate.

Oliveros, Pauline, American composer; b. Houston, May 30, 1932. Her mother and grandmother, both piano teachers, taught her the rudiments of music; received instruction in violin from William Sydler, accordion from Marjorie Harrigan, and horn from J.M. Brandsetter; studied composition with Paul Koepke and accordian with William Palmer at the Univ. of Houston (1949–52); continued her studies at San Francisco State College (B.A., 1957) and privately with Robert Erickson (1954–60). She was co-director of the San Francisco Tape Music Center (1961–65); after it became the Mills Tape Music Center, she was its director (1966–67); then caught at the Univ. of Calif. at San Diego (1967–81); held a Guggenheim fellowship (1973–74). She publ. *Pauline's Proverbs* (1976) and *Software for People: Collected Writings 1963–80* (1984). Initiated into modern harmony, the art of asymmetrical rhythms, group improvisation, and acoustical sonorism by Robert Erickson, she gradually expanded her receptivity into the range of subliminal sounds derived from the overtone series, differential tones, and sonic abstractions. In 1960 she composed a Piano Sextet which explored a variety of such elusive tonal elements; it received the Pacifica Foundation National Prize. Advancing further into the domain of new sonorities, she wrote a choral work, *Sound Patterns*, to wordless voices (1962), which received a prize in the Netherlands. While in San Diego, she was able to develop her ideas still further. Taking advantage of her skill as a gardener, she arrayed garden hoses and lawn sprinklers as part of a musical ensemble accompanied by the sounds of alarm clocks and various domestic utensils. Occasionally, a musician was instructed to bark. To this enriched artistic vocabulary was soon added a physical and psychosomatic element; performers acted the parts of a magician, a juggler, and a fortune-teller. Page turners, piano movers, and floor sweepers were listed as performing artists. In her later works she reduced such kinetic activities and gradually began to compose ceremonial works of sonic meditation, sotto voce murmuration, lingual lallation, and joyful ululation, with the purpose of inducing an altered state of consciousness; sometimes an exotic but usually digestible meal was served at leisurely intervals. She often presided over such sessions, singing and playing her faithful accordian; sometimes this music was left to be unheard by ordinary ears, but it could be perceived musically. In 1977 she obtained 1st prize from the city of Bonn for a work commemorating the sesquicentennial of Beethoven's death; the piece was verbally notated with the intention to subvert perception of the entire city so that it would become a perceptual theater. As she moved higher into the realm of cosmic consciousness, she introduced the psychic-element into her works; in 1970 she drew an equation for an indefinite integral of the differential *psi* (for psychic unit), to create the state of Oneness.

WORKS: *Variation for Sextet* for Flute, Clarinet, Trumpet, Horn, Cello, and Piano (1960); *Sound Patterns* for Chorus (1961); Trio for Trumpet, Piano, and Page Turner (1961); Trio for Trumpet, Accordina, and Double Bass (1961); *7 Passages* for 2-channel Tape, Mobile, and Dancer (1963); *Five* for Trumpet and Dancer (1964); *Duo* for Accordion and Bandoneon, with possible Mynah Bird Obbligato (1964); *Apple Box Orchestra* for 10 Performers, Amplified Apple Boxes, etc. (1964); *Pieces of Eight* for Wind Octet and a number of Props, including Cash Register (1965); *7 Sets of Mnemonics*, multimedia piece (1965); *George Washington Slept Here* for Amplified Violin, Film Projections, and Tape (1965); *Bye Bye Butterfly* for Oscillators, Amplifiers, and Tapes (1965); *Winter Light* for Tape, Mobile, and Figure (1965); *Participle Dangling in Honor of Gertrude Stein* for Tape, Mobile, and Work Crew (1966); *Theater Piece for Trombone Player* for Garden Hose, Instruments, and Tape (1966); *Night Jar* for Viola d'Amore (1968); *Festival House* for

Orch., Mimes, Light, and Film Projections (1968); *Double Basses at Twenty Paces* for 2 Double Basses, Tape, and Projections (1968); *The Dying Alchemist* for Narrator, Violinist, Trumpet, Piccolo, Percussion, and Slides (1969); *The Wheel of Fortune*, suggested by the trump cards of the tarot deck, for Clarinet (1969); *Aeolian Partitions* for Flute, Clarinet, Violin, Cello, and Piano (1969); *To Valerie Solanis and Marilyn Monroe, in Recognition of Their Desperation*, verbally notated score (1970; Solanis, the founder of SCUM, i.e., the Society to Cut Up Men, tried unsuccessfully to shoot the pop artist Andy Warhol; Monroe committed suicide); *Meditation on the Points of the Compass* for Chorus and Percussion (1970); *Bonn Feier*, intended to convert the city of Bonn into an imagined total theater (1971); *Post Card Theater*, multimedia event with an Exotic Potluck Dinner (1972); *1000 Aces* for String Quartet (1972); *Sonic Images*, subliminal audience fantasy (1972); *Crow Two*, ceremonial opera (1974); *Bear Mountain Slow Runner* for Voice and Accordion (1975; renamed *Horse Sings from Cloud*, inspired by a dream image of a horse being lifted to a cloud by birds); *Willow Brook Generations and Reflections* for Wind Instruments and Vocalists (1976); *The Yellow River Map*, ceremonial meditation for a lot of people (1977); *King Kong Sings Along* for Chorus (1977); *Rose Moon*, ceremonial for Chorus and Percussion (1977); *The Witness* for Virtuoso Instrumentalists (1978); *El relicario de los animales* for Soprano and 20 Instruments (1979); *Carol Plantamura* for Voice and 20 Instruments (1979); *Gone with The Wind, 1980* for Assorted Ensembles (1980); *Wheel of Times*, for String Quartet and Electonics (1982); *The Mandala* for 4 Clarinetists, 8 Crystal Glasses, Bass Drum, and Finger Cymbals (timeless date of composition).

Pachmann, Vladimir de, eccentric Russian-born Italian pianist; b. Odessa, July 27, 1848; d. Rome, Jan. 6, 1933. He received his primary music education at home from his father, an Austrian lawyer and amateur musician; his mother was Turkish. He then was a pupil of J. Dachs at the Vienna Cons. (1866–68), graduating with the Gold Medal. He began his concert career with a tour of Russia in 1869; he was 40 years old before he made a decisive impact on the international scene; his 1st American tour, in 1891, was sensationally successful, and it was in America that he began exhibiting his curious eccentricities, some of them undoubtedly calculated to produce shock effect: he made grimaces when he did not like his own playing and shouted "Bravo!" when he played a number to his satisfaction; even more bizarre was his crawling under the grand piano after the concert, claiming that he was looking for the wrong notes he had accidentally hit; all this could be explained as idiosyncratic behavior; but he also allowed himself to mutilate the music itself, by inserting arpeggios between phrases and extra chords at the end of a piece. Most American critics were outraged by his shenanigans, but some, notably Philip Hale, found mitigation in the poetic quality of his interpretations. Pachmann was particularly emotional in playing Chopin, when his facial contortions became quite obnoxious; James Huneker dubbed him "Chopinzee." Pachmann did not lack official honors; in 1885, on his tour of Denmark, he was made a Knight of the Order of Danebrog; in 1916 the Royal Phil. Society of London awarded him its Gold Medal. He made his last tour of the U.S. in 1925; spent his last years in Italy, becoming a naturalized Italian citizen in 1928. His personal life was turbulent; he married frequently (the exact number of his wives is in dispute). His 1st wife was his pupil, the Australian Maggie Oakey (1864–1952), who toured as Marguerite de Pachmann from the time of their marriage (1884) until their divorce (1895); she later married a French lawyer, becoming known as Marguerite de Pachmann-Labori. Pachmann and his 1st wife had a son, Adrian de Pachmann (c.1893–1937), who also became a pianist.

Paderewski, Ignacy (Jan), celebrated Polish pianist and composer; b. Kurylowka, Podolia (Russian Poland), Nov. 18, 1860; d. N.Y., June 29, 1941. His father was an administrator of country estates; his mother died soon after his birth. From early childhood, Paderewski was attracted to piano music; he received some musical instruction from Peter Sowinski, who taught him 4-hand arrangements of operas. His 1st public appearance was in a charity concert at the age of 11, when he played piano with his sister. His playing aroused interest among wealthy patrons, who took him to Kiev. He was then sent to Warsaw, where he entered the Cons., learned to play trombone, and joined the school band. He also continued serious studies of piano playing; his teachers at the Warsaw Cons. were Schlözer, Strobl, and Janotha. In 1875 and 1877 he toured in provincial Russian towns with the Polish violinist Cielewicz; in the interim periods he took courses in composition at the Warsaw Cons., and upon graduation in 1878 he was engaged as a member of the piano faculty there. In 1880 he married a young music student named Antonina Korsak, but she died 9 days after giving birth to a child, on Oct. 10, 1880. In 1882 he went to Berlin to study composition with Kiel; there he met Anton Rubinstein, who gave him encouraging advice and urged him to compose piano music. He resigned from his teaching job at the Warsaw Cons. and began to study orchestration in Berlin with Heinrich Urban. While on a vacation in the Tatra Mountains (which inspired his *Tatra Album* for piano) he met the celebrated Polish actress Modjeska, who proposed to finance his further piano studies with Leschetizky in Vienna. Paderewski followed this advice and spent several years as a Leschetizky student. He continued his career as a concert pianist. On March 3, 1888, he gave his 1st Paris recital, and on Nov. 10, 1888, played a concert in Vienna, both with excellent success. He also began receiving recognition as a composer. Anna Essipoff (who was married to Leschetizky) played his piano concerto in Vienna under the direction of Hans Richter. Paderewski made his London debut on May 9, 1890. On Nov. 17, 1891, he played for the 1st time in N.Y., and was acclaimed with an adulation rare for pianists; by some counts he gave 107 concerts in 117 days in N.Y. and other American cities and attended 86 dinner parties; his wit, already fully developed, made him a social lion in wealthy American salons. At one party, it was reported, the hostess confused him with a famous polo player who was also expected to be a guest, and greeted him effusively. "No," Paderewski is supposed to have replied, "he is a rich soul who plays polo, and I am a poor Pole who plays solo." American spinsters beseeched him for a lock of his luxurious mane of hair; he invariably obliged, and when his valet observed that at this rate he would soon be bald, he said, "Not I, my dog." There is even a story related by a gullible biographer that Paderewski could charm beasts by his art and that a spider used to come down from the ceiling in Paderewski's lodging in Vienna and sit at the piano every time Paderewski played a certain Chopin étude. Paderewski eclipsed even Caruso as an idol of the masses. In 1890 he made a concert tour in Germany; also toured South America, South Africa, and Australia. In 1898 he purchased a beautiful home, the Villa Riond-Bosson on Lake Geneva, Switzerland; in 1899 he married Helena Gorska, Baroness von Rosen. In 1900, by a deed of trust, Paderewski established a fund of $10,000 (the original trustees were William Steinway, Major H.L. Higginson, and Dr. William Mason), the interest from which was to be used for triennial prizes given "to composers of American birth without distinction as to age or religion" for works in the following categories: syms., concertos, and chamber music. In 1910, on the occasion of the centennial of Chopin's birth, Paderewski donated $60,000 for the construction of the Chopin Memorial Hall in Warsaw; in the same year he contributed $100,000 for the erection of the statue of King Jagiello in Warsaw, on the quinquecentennial of his victory over the Teutonic Knights in 1410. In 1913 he purchased a ranch in Paso Robles in Calif.

Although cosmopolitan in his culture, Paderewski remained a great Polish patriot. During the First World War he donated the entire proceeds from his concerts to a fund for the Polish people caught in the war between Russia and Germany. After the establishment of the independent Polish state, Paderewski served as its representative in Washington; in 1919 he was named prime minister of the Polish Republic, the 1st musician to occupy such a post in any country at any period. He took part in the Versailles Treaty conference; it was then that Prime Minister Clemenceau of France welcomed Paderewski with the famous, if possibly apocryphal, remark: "You, a famous pianist, a prime minister! What a comedown!" Paderewski resigned his post on Dec. 10, 1919. He reentered politics in 1920 in the wake of the Russian invasion of Poland that year, when he became a delegate to the League of Nations; he resigned on May 7, 1921, and resumed his musical career. On Nov. 22, 1922, he gave his 1st concert after a hiatus of many years at Carnegie Hall in N.Y. In 1939 he made his last American tour. Once more during his lifetime Poland was invaded, this time by both Germany and Russia. Once more Paderewski was driven to political action. He joined the Polish government-in-exile in France and was named president of its parliament on Jan. 23, 1940. He returned to the U.S. on Nov. 6, 1940, a few months before his death. At the order of President Roosevelt, his body was given state burial in Arlington National Cemetery, pending the return of his remains to Free Poland. Paderewski received many honors. He held the following degrees: Ph.D. from the Univ. of Lemberg (1912); D.Mus. from Yale Univ. (1917); Ph.D. from the Univ. of Krakow (1919); D.C.L. from Oxford Univ. (1920); LL.D. from Columbia Univ. (1922); Ph.D. from the Univ. of Southern Calif. (1923); Ph.D. from the Univ. of Poznan (1924); and Ph.D. from the Univ. of Glasgow (1925). He also held the Grand Cross of the French Legion of Honor (1922). A postage stamp with his picture was issued in Poland in 1919, and 2 postage stamps honoring him in the series "Men of Liberty" were issued in the U.S. in 1960.

As an artist, Paderewski was a faithful follower of the Romantic school, which allowed free, well-nigh improvisatory declensions from the written notes, tempi, and dynamics; judged by 20th-century standards of precise rendering of the text, Paderewski's interpretations appear surprisingly free, but this very personal freedom of performance moved contemporary audiences to ecstasies of admiration. Also, Paderewski's virtuoso technique, which astonished his listeners, has been easily matched by any number of pianists of succeeding generations. Yet his position in the world of the performing arts remains undiminished by the later achievements of younger men and women pianists. As a composer, Paderewski also belongs to the Romantic school. At least one of his piano pieces, the *Menuet in G* (which is a movement of his set of *6 Humoresques* for piano), achieved enormous popularity. His other compositions, however, never sustained a power of renewal and were eventually relegated to the archives of unperformed music. His opera *Manru* (1897–1900), dealing with folk life in the Tatra Mountains, was produced in Dresden on May 29, 1901, and was also performed by the Metropolitan Opera in N.Y. on Feb. 14, 1902. Another major work, a Sym. in B minor, was first performed by the Boston Sym. Orch. on Feb. 12, 1909. His other works included a Piano Concerto in A minor (1888); *Fantaisie polonaise* for Piano and Orch. (1893); Violin Sonata (1880); songs; and the following compositions for piano solo: *Prelude and Capriccio; 3 Pieces* (Gavotte, Mélodie, Valse mélancholique); *Krakowiak; Elégie; 3 Polish Dances; Introduction and Toccata; Chants du voyageur* (5 pieces); *6 Polish Dances; Album de mai* (5 pieces), *Variations and Fugue; Tatra Album* (also arr. for Piano, 4-hands); *6 Humoresques de concert* (which includes the famous *Menuet in G*); *Dans le désert; Miscellanea* (7 pieces); *Légende; Sonata in E-flat minor* (1903). A complete list of Paderewski's works was publ. in the *Bolletino bibliografico musicale* (Milan, 1932).

Paik, Nam June, Korean-American avant-garde composer and experimenter in the visual arts; b. Seoul, July 20, 1932. He studied first at the Univ. of Tokyo; then took courses in music theory with Thrasybulos Georgiades in Munich and with Wolfgang Fortner in Freiburg im Breisgau. Turning toward electronics, he did experimental work at the Electronic Music Studio in Cologne (1958–60); attended the summer seminars for new music at Darmstadt (1957–61). In his showings he pursues the objective of total art as the sum of integrated synesthetic experiences, involving all sorts of actions: walking, talking, dressing, undressing, drinking, smoking, moving furniture, engaging in quaquaversal commotion intended to demonstrate that any human or inhuman action becomes an artistic event through the power of volitional concentration of an ontological imperative. Paik attracted attention at his duo recitals with the topless cellist Charlotte Moorman, at which he acted as a surrogate cello, with his denuded spinal column serving as the fingerboard for Moorman's cello bow, while his bare skin provided an area for intermittent pizzicati. About 1963 Paik began experimenting with videotape as a medium for sounds and images; his initial experiment in this field was *Global Groove*, a high-velocity collage of intermingled television bits, which included instantaneous commercials, fragments from news telecasts, and subliminal extracts from regular programs, subjected to topological alterations. His list of works (some of them consisting solely of categorical imperatives) includes *Ommaggio a Cage* for piano demolition, breakage of raw eggs, spray painting of hands in jet black, etc. (Düsseldorf, Nov. 13, 1959); *Symphony for 20 Rooms* (1961); *Variations on a Theme of Saint-Saëns* for Cello and Piano, with the pianist playing *Le Cygne* while the cellist dives into an oil drum filled with water (N.Y., Aug. 25, 1965, composer at the keyboard, cellist Moorman in the oil drum); *Performable Music*, wherein the performer is ordered to make with a razor an incision of no less than 10 centimeters on his left forearm (Los Angeles, Dec. 2, 1965); *Opéra sextronique* (1967); *Opéra électronique* (1968); *Creep into the Vagina of a Whale* (c.1969); *Young Penis Symphony*, a protrusion of 10 erectile phalluses through a paper curtain (c.1970; first perf. at "La Mamelle," San Francisco, Sept. 21, 1975, under the direction of Ken Friedman, who also acted as one of the 10 performers). Of uncertain attribution is a sym. designated as No. 3, which Paik delegated to Friedman, who worked on it in Saugus, Calif., the epicenter of the earthquake of Feb. 9, 1971, and of which the earthquake itself constituted the finale.

Penderecki, Krzysztof, celebrated Polish composer; b. Debica, Nov. 23, 1933. (His name is pronounced Kzhýshtov Penderétskee, not Penderekee.) He was educated in Krakow, where he took courses at the Jagellonian Univ.; after private composition studies with F. Skolyszewski, he received instruction in theory from A. Malawski and S. Wiechowicz at the State Higher School of Music (1955–58); was a lecturer in composition there (1958–66), remaining with it when it became the Academy of Music as rector (1972–87) and as prof. (from 1972); also was prof. of composition at the Essen Folkwang Hochschule für Musik (1966–68) and at Yale Univ. (from 1973). He rapidly acquired a reputation as one of the most original composers of his time, receiving numerous honors: received honorary memberships in the Royal Academy of Music in London (1975), the Akademie der Künste of the German Democratic Republic (1975), the Royal Academy of Music in Stockholm (1975), etc.; was awarded the Herder Prize of the Federal Republic of Germany (1977), the Grand Medal of Paris (1982), the Sibelius Prize of Finland (1983), the Premio Lorenzo il Magnifico of Italy (1985), etc.; received honorary doctorates from several univs. After a few works of an academic nature, he developed a hyper-modern technique of composition in a highly individual style, in which no demarcation line is drawn between consonances and dissonances, tonal or atonal melody, traditional or innovative instrumentation; an egalitarian attitude prevails toward all available resources of sound. While his idiom is naturally complex, he does not disdain tonality, even in its overt triadic forms. In his creative evolution, he has bypassed orthodox serial procedures; his music follows an athematic course, in constantly varying metrical and rhythmic patterns. He utilizes an entire spectrum of modern sonorities, expanding the domain of tone to unpitched elements, making use of such effects as shouting, hissing, and verbal ejaculations in vocal parts, at times reaching a climax of aleatory glossolalia; tapping, rubbing, or snapping the fingers against the body of an instrument; striking the piano strings by mallets, etc. For this he designed an optical notation, with symbolic ideograms indicating the desired sound; thus a black isosceles triangle denotes the highest possible pitch; an inverted isosceles triangle, the lowest possible pitch; a black rectangle for a sonic complex of white noise within a given interval; vertical lines tied over by an arc for arpeggios below the bridge of a string instrument; wavy lines of varying amplitudes for extensive vibrato; curvilinear figures for aleatory passages; dots and dashes for repetitions of a pattern; sinusoidal oscillations for quaquaversal glissandos; etc. He applies these modern devices to religious music, including masses in the orthodox Roman Catholic ritual. Penderecki's most impressive and most frequently perf. work is his *Tren pamieci ofiarom Hiroszimy* (Threnody in Memory of Victims of Hiroshima) for 52 String Instruments (1959–60), rich in dynamic contrasts and ending on a tone cluster of 2 octavefuls of icositetraphonic harmony.

Petrucci, Ottaviano dei, Italian music publisher; b. Fossombrone, June 18, 1466; d. Venice, May 7, 1539. He was the descendant of an impoverished family of the nobility. He went to Venice about 1490; petitioned in 1498 for the exclusive privilege of printing "canto figurato" and "intabolature d'organo e de liuto" in the Venetian dominions for a period of 20 years; the privilege was granted on May 25, 1498. His 1st vol., *Harmonice musices odhecaton A*, was issued on May 15, 1501; it contained 96 works, mostly French chansons for 3 and 4 Voices. It was followed by *Canti B* (1501) and *Canti C* (1503), which contained 49 and 137 works, respectively. In 1507 he became the 1st printer to publ. lute tablature. When the war of the League of Cambrai against the Venetian Republic made further work impossible, he returned to Fossombrone (1511), leaving his associates Amedeo Scotto and Nicolò da Rafael to oversee his affairs in Venice. He was active as a publisher in Fossombrone until about 1521, bringing out eds. of both musical and non-musical works. He received a 15-year privilege from Pope Leo X in 1513 for printing mensural music and organ tablature (the privilege to publ. keyboard music was revoked in 1516); also received a 5-year extension of his Venetian privilege in 1514; ceased publishing from 1516 to 1519, again most likely due to the unsettled times. In 1520 he built a paper mill in Acqua Santa, near Fossombrone; was recalled to Venice by the senate in 1536 to supervise the publication of Latin and Italian classical texts. His eds., printed with great neatness, are rare and highly prized specimens of early presswork. In Venice he brought out eds. of works by leading composers of the Netherlands school, as well as by Italian composers. His publications in Fossombrone continued to highlight Italian music, with the French school displacing the Netherlands masters. Modern eds. of his publications include the following: K. Jeppesen, ed., *Die mehrstimmige italienische Laude um 1500: Das 2. Laudenbuch des O. d.P.* (1507) (Leipzig and Copenhagen, 1935); R. Schwartz, ed., *O. P.: Frottole, Buch I und IV*, Publikationen Älterer Musik, VIII (Leipzig, 1935); H. Hewitt, ed., *Harmonice Musices Odhecaton A* (Cambridge, Mass., 1942; 2nd ed., rev., 1946); G. Cesari, R. Monterosso, and B. Disertori, eds., *Le frottole nell' edizione principe di O. P., I: Libri, I, II, e III*, Istituta et Monumenta, i/1 (1954); B. Disertori, ed., *Le frottole* *per canto e liuto intabulate da Franciscus Bossinensis*, Istituzioni e Monumenti dell'arte Musicale Italiana, new series, iii (1964); H. Hewitt, ed., *O. P.: Canti B numero cinquante* (*Venice, 1502*), Monuments of Renaissance Music, II (1967).

Pound, Ezra (Loomis), greatly significant American man of letters and amateur composer; b. Hailey, Idaho, Oct. 30, 1885; d. Venice, Nov. 1, 1972. He was educated at Hamilton College (Ph.B., 1905) and the Univ. of Pa. (M.A., 1906). He went to England, where he established himself as a leading experimental poet and influential critic. He also pursued a great interest in early music, especially that of the troubadours, which led him to try his hand at composing. With the assistance of George Antheil, he composed the opera *Le Testament*, after poems by François Villon (1923; Paris, June 19, 1926); it was followed by a 2nd opera, *Calvacanti* (1932), and a 3rd, left unfinished, based on the poetry of Catullus. In 1924 he settled in Rapallo. Although married to Dorothy Shakespear, daughter of one of Yeats's friends, he became intimate with the American violinist Olga Rudge; Rudge bore him a daughter in 1925 and his wife bore him a son in 1926. Through the influence of Rudge, his interest in music continued, and he became a fervent champion of Vivaldi; he also worked as a music reviewer and ran a concert series with Rudge, Inverno Musicale. A growing interest in economic history and an inordinate admiration for the Fascist dictator Benito Mussolini led Pound down the road of political obscurantism. During World War II, he made many broadcasts over Rome Radio on topics ranging from literature to politics. His condemnation of Jewish banking circles in America and the American effort to defeat Fascism led to his arrest by the Allies after the collapse of Il Duce's regime. In 1945 he was sent to a prison camp in Pisa. In 1946 he was sent to the U.S. to stand trial for treason, but was declared insane and confined to St. Elizabeth's Hospital in Washington, D.C. Finally, in 1958, he was released and allowed to return to Italy, where he died. Among his writings on music is his *Antheil and the Treatise on Harmony* (1924). He also composed several works for solo violin for Rudge, including *Fiddle Music* (1924) and *Al poco giorno* (Berkeley, March 23, 1983); he also arranged Gaucelm Faidit's *Plainte pour la mort du roi Richart Coeur de Lion*. The uncatalogued collection of Pound's musical MSS at Yale Univ. includes various musical experiments, including rhythmic and melodic realizations of his poem *Sestina: Altaforte*. Among the composers who have set his poems to music are Copland, Luytens, and Berio.

Pringsheim, Klaus, German conductor and composer; b. Feldafing, near Munich, July 24, 1883; d. Tokyo, Dec. 7, 1972. A scion of a highly cultured family, he studied mathematics with his father, a prof. at Munich Univ., and physics with Röntgen, the discoverer of X-rays. His twin sister, Katherine, was married to Thomas Mann. In Munich, Pringsheim took piano lessons with Bernhard Stavenhagen and composition with Ludwig Thuille. In 1906 he went to Vienna and was engaged as assistant conductor of the Court Opera, under the tutelage of Gustav Mahler, who took him as a pupil in conducting and composition, a relationship that developed into profound friendship. Mahler recommended him to the management of the German Opera in Prague; Pringsheim conducted there from 1909 to 1914; then was engaged as conductor and stage director at the Bremen Opera (1915–18) and music director of the Max Reinhardt theaters in Berlin (1918–25). In 1923–24 he conducted in Berlin a Mahler cycle of 8 concerts, featuring all of Mahler's syms. and songs with orch. In 1927 he became the music critic of the socialist newspaper *Vorwärts*. A turning point in Pringsheim's life came in 1931 with an invitation to teach music at the Imperial Academy of Music in Tokyo, where he taught until 1937; several of his Japanese students became prominent composers. From 1937 to 1939 Pringsheim served as music adviser to the Royal Dept. of Fine Arts in Bangkok, Thailand. In 1939 he returned to Japan; was briefly interned in 1944 as an opponent of the Axis policies. In 1946 he went to California; after some intermittent activities, he returned to Japan in 1951; was appointed director of the Musashino Academy of Music in Tokyo; continued to conduct; also wrote music reviews for English-language Tokyo newspapers. As a composer, Pringsheim followed the neo-Romantic trends, deeply influenced by Mahler. His compositions include a Concerto for Orch. (Tokyo, Oct. 13, 1935); Japanese radio opera, *Yamada Nagasama* (1953); Concertino for Xylophone and Orch. (1962); *Theme, Variations, and Fugue* for Wind Orch. (his last composition, 1971–72); and a curious album of 36 2-part canons for Piano (1959). A chapter from his theoretical work *Pythagoras, die Atonalität und wir* was publ. in *Schweizerische Musikzeitung* (1957). His reminiscences, "Mahler, My Friend," were publ. posthumously in the periodical *Composer* (1973–74). Pringsheim was a signatory of a letter of protest by surviving friends of Mahler against the motion picture *Death in Venice*, after a novelette of Thomas Mann, in which the central character, a famous writer who suffers a homosexual crisis, was made to resemble Mahler.

Prokofiev (Prokofieff), Sergei (Sergeievich), great Russian composer of modern times, creator of new and original formulas of rhythmic, melodic, and harmonic combinations that became the recognized style of his music; b. Sontsovka, near Ekaterinoslav, April 27, 1891; d. Moscow, March 5, 1953. His mother was born a serf in 1859, 2 years before the emancipation of Russian serfdom, and she assumed (as was the custom) the name of the estate where she was born, Sontsov. Prokofiev was born on that estate on April 27, 1891, although he himself erroneously believed that the date was April 23; the correct date was established with the discovery of his birth certificate. He received his 1st piano lessons from his mother, who was an amateur pianist; he improvised several pieces, and then composed a children's opera, *The Giant* (1900), which was performed in a domestic version. Following his bent for the theater, he put together 2 other operas, *On Desert Islands* (1902) and *Ondine* (1904–7); fantastic subjects obviously possessed his childish imagination. He was 11 years old when he met the great Russian master, Taneyev, who arranged for him to take systematic private lessons with Reinhold Glière, who became his tutor at Sontsovka during the summers of 1903 and 1904 and by correspondence during the intervening winter. Under Glière's knowledgeable guidance in theory and harmony, Prokofiev composed a sym. in piano version and still another opera, *Plague*, based upon a poem by Pushkin. Finally, in 1904, at the age of 13, he enrolled in the St. Petersburg Cons., where he studied composition with Liadov and piano with Alexander Winkler; later he was accepted by no less a master than Rimsky-Korsakov, who instructed him in orchestration. He also studied conducting with Nikolai Tcherepnin, and form with Wihtol. Further, he entered the piano class of Anna Essipova. During the summers, he returned to Sontsovka or traveled in the Caucasus and continued to compose, already in quite an advanced style; the Moscow publisher Jurgenson accepted his 1st work, a piano sonata, for publication; it was premiered in Moscow on March 6, 1910. It was then that Prokofiev made his 1st visit to Paris, London, and Switzerland (1913); in 1914 he graduated from the St. Petersburg Cons., receiving the Anton Rubinstein Prize (a grand piano) as a pianist-composer with his Piano Concerto No. 1, which he performed publicly at the graduation concert. Because of audacious innovations in his piano music (he wrote one piece in which the right and left hands played in different keys), he was described in the press as a "futurist," and because of his addiction to dissonant and powerful harmonic combinations, some critics dismissed his works as "football music." This idiom was explicitly demonstrated in his *Sarcasms* and *Visions fugitives*, percussive and sharp, yet not lacking in lyric charm. Grotesquerie and irony animated his early works; he also developed a strong attraction toward subjects of primitive character. His important orch. work, the *Scythian Suite* (arr. from music written for a ballet, *Ala and Lolly*, 1915), draws upon a legend of ancient Russian sun-worship rituals. While a parallel with Stravinsky's *Le Sacre du printemps* may exist, there is no similarity between the styles of the 2 works. The original performance of the *Scythian Suite*, scheduled at a Koussevitzky concert in Moscow, was canceled on account of the disruption caused by war, which did not prevent the otherwise intelligent Russian music critic Sabaneyev, blissfully unaware that the announced premiere had been canceled, from delivering a blast of the work as a farrago of atrocious noises. (Sabaneyev was forced to resign his position after this episode.) Another Prokofiev score, primitivistic in its inspiration, was the cantata *Seven, They Are Seven*, based upon incantations from an old Sumerian religious ritual. During the same period, Prokofiev wrote his famous *Classical Symphony* (1916–17), in which he adopted with remarkable acuity the formal style of Haydn's music. While the structure of the work was indeed classical, the sudden modulatory shifts and subtle elements of grotesquerie revealed decisively a new modern art.

After conducting the premiere of his *Classical Symphony* in Petrograd on April 21, 1918, Prokofiev left Russia by way of Siberia and Japan for the U.S. (the continuing war in Europe prevented him from traveling westward). He gave concerts of his music in Japan and later in the U.S., playing his 1st solo concert in N.Y. on Oct. 29, 1918. Some American critics greeted his appearance as the reflection of the chaotic events of Russia in revolution, and Prokofiev himself was described as a "ribald and Bolshevist innovator and musical agitator." "Every rule in the realm of traditional music writing was broken by Prokofiev," one N.Y. writer complained. "Dissonance followed dissonance in a fashion inconceivable to ears accustomed to melody and harmonic laws." Prokofiev's genteel *Classical Symphony* struck some critics as "an orgy of dissonant sound, an exposition of the unhappy state of chaos from which Russia suffers." A N.Y. critic indulged in the following: "Crashing Siberians, volcano hell, Krakatoa, sea-bottom crawlers. Incomprehensible? So is Prokofiev." But another critic issued a word of caution, suggesting that "Prokofiev might be the legitimate successor of Borodin, Mussorgsky, and Rimsky-Korsakov." The critic was unintentionally right; Prokofiev is firmly enthroned in the pantheon of Russian music.

In 1920 Prokofiev settled in Paris, where he established an association with Diaghilev's Ballets Russes, which produced his ballets *Chout* (a French transliteration of the Russian word for buffoon), *Le Pas d'acier* (descriptive of the industrial development in Soviet Russia), and *L'Enfant prodigue*. In 1921 Prokofiev again visited the U.S. for the production of the opera commissioned by the Chicago Opera Co., *The Love of Three Oranges*. In 1927 he was invited to be the pianist for a series of his own works in Russia. He gave a number of concerts in Russia again in 1929, and eventually decided to remain there. In Russia he wrote some of his most popular works, including the symphonic fairy tale *Peter and the Wolf*, staged by a children's theater in Moscow, the historical cantata *Alexander Nevsky*, the ballet *Romeo and Juliet*, and the opera *War and Peace*.

Unexpectedly, Prokofiev became the target of the so-called proletarian group of Soviet musicians who accused him of decadence, a major sin in Soviet Russia at the time. His name was included in the official denunciation of modern Soviet composers issued by reactionary Soviet politicians. He meekly confessed that he had been occasionally interested in atonal and polytonal devices during his stay in Paris, but insisted that he had never abandoned the ideals of classical Russian music. Indeed, when he composed his 7th Sym., he described it specifically as a youth sym., reflecting the energy and ideals of new Russia. There were also significant changes in his personal life. He separated from his Spanish-born wife, the singer Lina Llubera, the mother of his 2 sons, and established a companionship with Myra Mendelson, a member of the Young Communist League. She was a writer and assisted him on the libretto of *War and Peace*. He made one final attempt to gain favor with the Soviet establishment by writing an opera based on a heroic exploit of a Soviet pilot during the war against the Nazis. But this, too, was damned by the servile Communist press as lacking in true patriotic spirit, and the opera was quickly removed from the repertory. Prokofiev died suddenly of heart failure on March 5, 1953, a few hours before the death of Stalin. Curiously enough, the anniversary of Prokofiev's death is duly commemorated, while that of his once powerful nemesis is officially allowed to be forgotten.

Riley, Terry (Mitchell), American composer and performer of the extreme experimental left; b. Colfax, Calif., June 24, 1935. He studied piano with Duane Hampton at San Francisco State College (1955–57) and composition with Seymour Shifrin and William Denny at the Univ. of Calif. at Berkeley (M.A., 1961); went to Europe and played piano and saxophone in cabarets in Paris and in Scandinavia. In 1970 he was initiated in San Francisco as a disciple of Pandit Pran Nath, the North Indian singer, and followed him to India. He was a creative associate at the Center for Creative and Performing Arts at the State Univ. of N.Y. at Buffalo (1967); from 1971 to 1980 he was associate prof. at Mills College in Oakland, Calif. In 1979 he held a Guggenheim fellowship. In his music, Riley explores the extremes of complexity and gymnosophistical simplicity. His astrological signs are Sun in Cancer (euphemistically known in southern California as Moon Children so as to exorcise middle-aged fear of malignancy), Scorpio Rising, and Aries Moon.

Rinuccini, Ottavio, great Italian poet and librettist; b. Florence, Jan. 20, 1562; d. there, March 28, 1621. He was born into a family of the nobility and became a prominent courtier; commenced writing verses for court entertainments about 1579; was also active in the Accademia Fiorentina and the Accademia degli Alterati, taking the name "Il Sonnacchioso" ("the somnolent one"). He collaborated with Bardi in preparing intermedi for the wedding of the Grand Duke Ferdinando I (1589); Corsi and Peri then set his pastoral *Dafne* to music, which work is generally recognized as the 1st opera in the monodic style (Florence, 1598). Rinuccini's *Euridice*, with music by Peri, was performed in 1600; another setting, by Caccini, in 1602. He also wrote the libretto of Monteverdi's *Arianna* (1608). These texts were republ. by A. Solerti in vol. II of *Gli albori del melodramma* (Milan, 1905) and by A. Della Corte, *Drammi per musica dal Rinuccini allo Zeno* (Turin, 1958).

Robbins, Marty (real name, **Martin David Robinson**), American country-western singer; b. Glendale, Ariz., Sept. 26, 1925; d. Nashville, Tenn., Dec. 8, 1982. He enlisted in the navy in 1944, and was stationed in the Pacific; after the end of the war, he worked as a ditchdigger in Phoenix, Ariz., and began to play the guitar and sing songs of his own invention; his unassuming, happy-go-lucky way of singing country songs soon won him a following; he took part in the broadcasts from the Grand Ole Opry in Nashville, Tenn., and in 1953 produced his 1st hit, *Singin' the Blues*. Other hits followed: *El Paso, Tonight Carmen, Devil Woman, Teen-age Dream, A White Sport Coat and a Pink Carnation, Up to My Shoulders in a Headache*, etc. He became a successful country-music balladeer. In 1970 he was elected to the Nashville Songwriters' Hall of Fame. In 1979 the National Cowboy Hall of Fame gave him its Golden Trustee Award for his gunfighter ballads. He was also inducted into the Country Music Hall of Fame (1982). A passionate stock-car racer, he providentially survived a number of theoretically fatal accidents. He used to say that he was in the song business because he despised honest labor. His songs extolled the beauty of a loving heart, but when his own heart had to undergo quadruple coronary bypass surgery, he died.

Rubinstein, Arthur (actually **Artur**), celebrated Polish-born American pianist; b. Lodz, Jan. 28, 1887; d. Geneva, Dec. 20, 1982. He was a product of a merchant family with many children, of whom he alone exhibited musical propensities. He became emotionally attached to the piano as soon as he saw and heard the instrument; at the age of 7, on Dec. 14, 1894, he played pieces by Mozart, Schubert, and Mendelssohn at a charity concert in Lodz. His 1st regular piano teacher was one Adolf Prechner. He was later taken to Warsaw, where he had piano lessons with Alexander Rózycki; then went to Berlin in 1897 to study with Heinrich Barth; also received instruction in theory from Robert Kahn and Max Bruch. In 1900 he appeared as soloist in Mozart's A major Concerto, K.488, in Potsdam; he repeated his success that same year when he played the work again in Berlin under Joachim's direction; then toured in Germany and Poland. After further studies with Paderewski in Switzerland (1903), he went to Paris, where he played with the Lamoureux Orch. and met Ravel, Dukas, and Thibaud. He also played the G minor Piano Concerto by Saint-Saëns in the presence of the composer, who commended him. The ultimate plum of artistic success came when Rubinstein received an American contract. He made his debut at Carnegie Hall in N.Y. on Jan. 8, 1906, as soloist with the Philadelphia Orch. in his favorite Saint-Saëns concerto. His American tour was not altogether successful, and he returned to Europe for further study. In 1915 he appeared as soloist with the London Sym. Orch. During the season 1916–17, he gave numerous recitals in Spain, a country in which he was to become extremely successful; from Spain he went to South America, where he also became a great favorite; he developed a flair for Spanish and Latin American music, and his renditions of the piano works of Albéniz and Manuel de Falla were models of authentic Hispanic modality. Villa-Lobos dedicated to Rubinstein his *Rudepoema*, regarded as one of the most difficult piano pieces ever written. Symbolic of his cosmopolitan career was the fact that he maintained apartments in N.Y., Beverly Hills, Paris, and Geneva. He was married to Aniela Mlynarska in 1932. Of his 4 children, 1 was born in Buenos Aires, 1 in Warsaw, and 2 in the U.S. In 1946 he became an American citizen. On June 11, 1958, Rubinstein gave his 1st postwar concert in Poland; in 1964 he played in Moscow, Leningrad, and Kiev. In Poland and in Russia he was received with tremendous emotional acclaim. But he forswore any appearances in Germany as a result of the Nazi extermination of the members of his family during World War II. On April 30, 1976, at the age of 89, he gave his farewell recital in London.

Rubinstein was one of the finest interpreters of Chopin's music, to which his fiery temperament and poetic lyricism were particularly congenial. His style of playing tended toward bravura in Classical compositions, but he rarely indulged in mannerisms; his performances of Mozart, Beethoven, Schumann, and Brahms were particularly inspiring. In his characteristic spirit of robust humor, he made jokes about the multitude of notes he claimed to have dropped, but asserted that a worse transgression against music would be pedantic inflexibility in tempo and dynamics. He was a bon vivant, an indefatigable host at parties, and a fluent, though not always grammatical, speaker in most European languages, including Russian and his native Polish. In Hollywood, he played on the sound tracks for the motion pictures *I've Always Loved You* (1946), *Song of Love* (1947), and *Night Song* (1947). He also appeared as a pianist, representing himself, in the films *Carnegie Hall* (1947) and *Of Men and Music* (1951). A film documentary entitled *Artur Rubinstein, Love of Life* was produced in 1975; a 90-minute television special, *Rubinstein at 90*, was broadcast to mark his entry into that nonagenarian age in 1977; he spoke philosophically about the inevitability of dying. He was the recipient of numerous international honors: a membership in the French Académie des Beaux Arts and the Légion d'Honneur, and the Order of Polonia Restituta of Poland; he held the Gold Medal of the Royal Phil. Soc. of London and several honorary doctorates from American institutions of learning. He was a passionate supporter of Israel, which he visited several times. In 1974 an international piano competition bearing his name was inaugurated in Jerusalem. On April 1, 1976, he received the U.S. Medal of Freedom, presented by President Ford. During the last years of his life, he was afflicted with retinitis pigmentosa, which led to his total blindness; but even then he never lost his joie de vivre. He once said that the slogan "wine, women, and song" as applied to him was 80% women and only 20% wine and song. And in a widely publicized interview he gave at the age of 95 he declared his ardent love for Annabelle Whitestone, the Englishwoman who was assigned by his publisher to help him organize and edit his autobiography, which appeared as *My Young Years* (N.Y., 1973) and *My Many Years* (N.Y., 1980). He slid gently into death in his Geneva apartment, as in a pianissimo ending of a Chopin nocturne, ritardando, morendo . . . Rubinstein had expressed a wish to be buried in Israel; his body was cremated in Switzerland; the ashes were flown to Jerusalem to be interred in a separate emplacement at the cemetery, since the Jewish law does not permit cremation.

Rudhyar, Dane (real name, **Daniel Chennevière**), French-born American composer, painter, and renowned mystical philosopher; b. Paris, March 23, 1895; d. San Francisco, Sept. 13, 1985. He changed his name in 1917 to Rudhyar, derived from an old Sanskrit root conveying the sense of dynamic action and the color red, astrologically related to the zodiacal sign of his birth and the planet Mars. He studied philosophy at the Sorbonne in Paris (baccalauréat, 1911), and took music courses at the Paris Cons. In composition he was largely self-taught; he also achieved a certain degree of proficiency as a pianist; developed a technique which he called "orchestral pianism." In 1913 the publisher Durand commissioned him to write a short book on Debussy, with whom he briefly corresponded. At the same time he joined the modern artistic circles in Paris. In 1916 he went to America; became a naturalized American citizen in 1926. His "dance poems" for Orch., *Poèmes ironiques* and *Vision végétale*, were performed at the Metropolitan Opera in N.Y. (April 4, 1917). In 1918 he visited Canada; in Montreal he met the pianist Alfred Laliberté, who was closely associated with Scriabin, and through him Rudhyar became acquainted with Scriabin's theosophic ideas. In Canada he also publ. a collection of French poems, *Rapsodies* (Toronto, 1918). In 1920 he went to Hollywood to write scenic music for *Pilgrimage Play, The Life of Christ*, and also acted the part of Christ in the prologue of the silent film version of *The Ten Commandments* produced by Cecil B. DeMille. In Hollywood he initiated the project of "Introfilms," depicting inner psychological states on the screen through a series of images, but it failed to receive support and was abandoned. Between 1922 and 1930 he lived in Holywood and N.Y.; was one of the founding members of the International Composers Guild in N.Y. In 1922 his orch. tone poem *Soul Fire* won the $1,000 prize of the Los Angeles Phil.; in 1928 his book *The Rebirth of Hindu Music* was publ. in Madras, India. After 1930 Rudhyar devoted most of his time to astrology. His 1st book on the subject, *The Astrology of Personality* (1936), became a standard text in the field; it was described by Paul Clancy, the pioneer in the publication of popular astrological magazines, as "the greatest step forward in astrology since the time of Ptolemy." A new development in Rudhyar's creative activities took place in 1938 when he began to paint, along nonrepresentational symbolistic lines; the titles of his paintings (*Mystic Tiara, Cosmic Seeds, Soul and Ego, Avatar*, etc.) reflect theosophic themes. His preoccupations with astrology left him little time for music; about 1965 he undertook a radical revision of some early compositions, and wrote several new ones; was also active as a lecturer.

The natural medium for Rudhyar's musical expression was the piano; his few symphonic works were mostly orchestrations of original piano compositions. In his writing for piano he built sonorous chordal formations supported by resonant pedal points, occasionally verging on polytonality; a kinship with Scriabin's piano music was clearly felt, but Rudhyar's harmonic idiom was free from Scriabin's Wagnerian antecedents. Despite his study of oriental religions and music, Rudhyar did not attempt to make use of Eastern modalities in his own music. He lived his last years in Palo Alto, Calif., and kept active connections with the world of theosophy; he also orchestrated his early piano works. Before his death his wife asked him whom he expected to meet beyond the mortal frame; he replied, "Myself."

Russolo, Luigi, Italian inventor, painter, and futurist composer; b. Portogruaro, April 30, 1885; d. Cerro di Laveno, Varese, Feb. 4, 1947. In 1909 he joined the futurist movement of Marinetti; formulated the principles of "art of noises" in his book, *L'arte dei rumori* (Milan, 1916); constructed a battery of noise-making instruments ("intonarumori"), with which he gave concerts in Milan (April 21, 1914) and Paris (June 18, 1921), creating such a commotion in the concert hall that on one occasion a group of outraged concertgoers mounted the stage and physically attacked Russolo and his fellow noisemakers. The titles of his works sing the glory of the machine and of urban living: *Convegno dell'automobili e dell'aeroplani, Il Risveglio di una città, Si pranza sulla terrazza dell'Hotel.* In his "futurist manifesto" of 1913 the noises are divided into 6 categories, including shrieks, groans, clashes, explosions, etc. In 1929 he constructed a noise instrument which he called "Russolophone." Soon the novelty of machine music wore out, the erstwhile marvels of automobiles and airplanes became commonplace, and the future of the futurists turned into a yawning past; Russolo gradually retreated from cultivation of noise and devoted himself to the most silent of all arts, painting. His pictures, influenced by the modern French school, and remarkable for their vivid colors, had several successful exhibitions in Paris and N.Y. The text of Russolo's manifesto is reproduced, in an Eng. tr., in N. Slonimsky's *Music since 1900.*

Sadra, I Wayan, significant Indonesian composer, performer, and writer on music; b. Denpasar, Bali, Aug. 1, 1953. He attended the local high school cons., Konservatori Karawitan (KOKAR; graduated, 1972), where he specialized in traditional Balinese music, particularly *gender wayang* (music for the Balinese shadow play). In 1973–74 he worked with the well-known experimental Indonesian choreographer Sardono W. Kusumo; after touring with his group in Europe and the Middle East, Sadra settled in Jakarta, where he studied painting and taught Balinese gamelan at Institut Kesenian Jakarta (IKJ, Jakarta Fine Arts Inst.; 1975–78); also taught Balinese music at the Indonesian Univ. (1978–80), and experimental composition, Balinese gamelan, and music criticism at Sekolah Tinggi Seni Indonesia Surakarta (STSI, National College of the Arts; from 1983), where he earned a degree in composition (1988); concurrently wrote new-music criticism for various Indonesian newspapers, including *Suara Karya* and *Bali Post.* He appeared widely as a performer with traditional Indonesian ensembles; performed throughout Indonesia and Europe, and in Singapore, Japan, Hong Kong, Australia, and Seoul. In 1988 he was keynote speaker at the national Pekan Komponis (Composers' Festival) in Jakarta; in 1989, appeared in California at the

Pacific Rim Festival; in 1990, was a featured participant at Composer-to-Composer in Telluride, Colo. Concurrent with the development of Indonesia's national identity has come an increase of national new-music festivals, increased interaction among artists from different regions, and the greater degree of individual freedom to create autonomous music; all have contributed to the emergence of a distinct Indonesian esthetic and a contemporary art music. Sadra is one of the outstanding young composers to emerge from this period, and his works have contributed much to the development of "musik kontemporer," "komposisi," and "kreasi baru" ("new creations"). He is also concerned with the social context of performance, considering audience development as important as the development of new works. His compositions are often scored for unusual combinations of instruments. In an experimental piece performed at the Telluride Inst., raw eggs were thrown at a heated black panel; as the eggs cooked and sizzled, they provided both a visual and sonic element for the closing of the piece. He also proposed to the mayor of Solo, Central Java, a new work entitled *Sebuah Kota Yang Bermain Musik* (A City That Plays Music), wherein the entire population of the city would make sounds together for a specified 5 minutes; the proposal was not accepted, but Sadra hopes for its realization in the future.

Satie, Erik (Alfred-Leslie), celebrated French composer who elevated his eccentricities and verbal virtuosity to the plane of high art; b. Honfleur, May 17, 1866; d. Paris, July 1, 1925. He received his early musical training from a local organist, Vinot, who was a pupil of Niedermeyer; at 13 he went to Paris, where his father was a music publisher, and received instruction in harmony from Taudou and in piano from Mathias; however, his attendance at the Cons. was only sporadic between 1879 and 1886. He played in various cabarets in Montmartre; in 1884 he publ. a piano piece which he numbered, with malice aforethought, op. 62. His whimsical ways and Bohemian manner of life attracted many artists and musicians; he met Debussy in 1891; joined the Rosicrucian Society in Paris in 1892 and began to produce short piano pieces with eccentric titles intended to ridicule modernistic fancies and Classical pedantries alike. Debussy thought highly enough of him to orchestrate 2 numbers from his piano suite *Gymnopédies* (1888). Satie was almost 40 when he decided to pursue serious studies at the Paris Schola Cantorum, taking courses in counterpoint, fugue, and orchestration with d'Indy and Roussel (1905–8). In 1898 he had moved to Arcueil, a suburb of Paris; there he held court for poets, singers, dancers, and musicians, among whom he had ardent admirers. Milhaud, Sauguet, and Desormière organized a group, which they called only half-facetiously "École d'Arcueil," in honor of Satie as master and leader. But Satie's eccentricities were not merely those of a Parisian poseur; rather, they were adjuncts to his esthetic creed, which he enunciated with boldness and total disregard for professional amenities (he was once brought to court for sending an insulting letter to a music critic). Interestingly enough, he attacked modernistic aberrations just as assiduously as reactionary pedantry, publishing "manifestos" in prose and poetry. Although he was dismissed by most serious musicians as an uneducated person who tried to conceal his ignorance of music with persiflage, he exercised a profound influence on the young French composers of the 1st quarter of the 20th century; moreover, his stature as an innovator in the modern idiom grew after his death, so that the avant-garde musicians of the later day accepted him as inspiration for their own experiments; thus "space music" could be traced back to Satie's *musique d'ameublement*, in which players were stationed at different parts of a hall playing different pieces in different tempi. The instruction in his piano piece *Vexations*, to play it 840 times in succession, was carried out literally in N.Y. on Sept. 9, 1963, by a group of 5 pianists working in relays overnight, thus setting a world's record for duration of any musical composition. When critics accused Satie of having no idea of form, he publ. *Trois Morceaux en forme de poire*, the eponymous pear being reproduced in color on the cover; other pieces bore self-contradictory titles, such as *Heures séculaires et instantanées* and *Crépuscule matinal de midi*; other titles were *Pièces froides, Embryons desséchés, Prélude en tapisserie, Préludes flasques (pour un chien), Descriptions automatiques*, etc. In his ballets he introduced jazz for the 1st time in Paris; at the performance of his ballet *Relâche* (Nov. 29, 1924), the curtain bore the legend "Erik Satie is the greatest musician in the world; whoever disagrees with this notion will please leave the hall." He publ. a facetious autobiographical notice as *Mémoires d'un amnésique* (1912); N. Wilkins tr. and ed. *The Writings of Erik Satie* (London, 1980).

Scelsi, Giacinto (actually, **Conte Giacinto Scelsi di Valva**), remarkable Italian composer; b. La Spezia, Jan. 8, 1905; d. Rome, Aug. 9, 1988. He was descended from a family of the nobility. He received some guidance in harmony from Giacinto Sallustio; after studies with Egon Koehler in Geneva, he completed his formal training with Walter Klein in Vienna (1935–36), where he became interested in the Schoenbergian method of writing music outside the bounds of traditional tonality; at the same time, he became deeply immersed in the study of the musical philosophy of the East, in which the scales and rhythms are perceived as functional elements of the human psyche. As a result of these multifarious absorptions of ostensibly incompatible ingredients, Scelsi formulated a style of composition that is synthetic in its sources and pragmatic in its artistic materialization. His works began to have a considerable number of performances in Italy and elsewhere, most particularly in the U.S. A curious polemical development arose after his death, when an Italian musician named Vieri Tosatti publ. a sensational article in the *Giornale della Musica*, declaring "I was Giacinto Scelsi." He claimed that Scelsi used to send him thematic sections of unfinished compositions, usually in the 12-tone system, for development and completion, using him as a ghostwriter. So many of such "improvisations" did Scelsi send to Tosatti that the latter had 2 other musicians to serve as secondary "ghosts," who, in turn, confirmed their participation in this peculiar transaction. The matter finally got to the court of public opinion, where it was decided that the works were genuine compositions by Scelsi, who improvised them on his electric piano, and merely ed. for better effect by secondary arrangers.

Schaeffer, Boguslaw (Julien), outstanding Polish composer, pedagogue, writer on music, and playwright; b. Lwow, June 6, 1929. He studied violin in Opole; then went to Krakow, where he took courses in composition with Malawski at the State High School of Music and in musicology with Jachimecki at the Jagiello Univ. (1949–53); later received instruction in advanced techniques from Nono (1959). In 1963 he became prof. of composition at the Krakow Cons.; served as prof. of composition at the Salzburg Mozarteum (from 1986). In 1967 he founded the periodical *Forum Musicum*, devoted to new music; in addition to his writings on music, he was active as a playwright from 1979; he was the most widely performed playwright in Poland during the 1987–88 season, winning an award at the Wroclaw Festival of Contemporary plays in 1987. As a composer, he received many awards, and numerous concerts of his works were presented in Poland and abroad. He is married to **Mieczyslawa Janina Hanuszewska-Schaeffer.** Their son, **Piotr (Mikolaj) Schaeffer** (b. Krakow, Oct. 1, 1958), is a music journalist. Schaeffer's earliest compositions (*19 Mazurkas* for Piano, 1949) were inspired by the melorhythms of Polish folk songs, but he made a decisive turn in 1953 with his *Music for Strings: Nocturne*, which became the 1st serial work by a

Polish composer; he devised a graphic and polychromatic optical notation indicating intensity of sound, proportional lengths of duration, and position of notes in melodic and contrapuntal lines, with the components arranged in binary code; he also wrote music in the "third stream" style, combining jazz with classical procedures. In 1960 he invented topophonical music in a tone-color passacaglia form in his *Topofonica* for 40 Instruments. In 1967 he introduced his own rhythmic system, built on metric-tempo proportions. In 1970 he began using synthesizers and computers. Many of his chamber scores, such as *Quartet 2+2*, utilize indeterminacy. In his music for and with actors, he uses mixed-media procedures. With his *Missa elettronica* (1975), he charted a bold course in sacred music. Schaeffer is regarded as one of the foremost composers of microtonal scores. *Three Short Pieces* for Orch. (1951) and *Music* for String Quartet (1954) are notable examples of his early microtonal works in which he uses a 24-tone row with 23 different microtonal intervals. In 1979 he introduced a new kind of instrumentation in which the disposition of instruments totally changes many times, thus utilizing various changing orchs.; in his Organ Concerto the disposition of instruments changes 53 times. Each of his orch. works and concertos follows this new disposition, sometimes very specifically, as in his *Musica ipsa*.

Schenker, Heinrich, outstanding Austrian music theorist; b. Wisniowczyki, Galicia, June 19, 1868; d. Vienna, Jan. 13, 1935. He studied jurisprudence at the Univ. of Vienna (Dr.Jur., 1890); concurrently took courses with Bruckner at the Vienna Cons. He composed some songs and piano pieces; Brahms liked them sufficiently to recommend Schenker to his publisher Simrock. For a while Schenker served as accompanist of the baritone Johannes Messchaert; then returned to Vienna and devoted himself entirely to the development of his theoretical research; gathered around himself a group of enthusiastic disciples who accepted his novel theories, among them Otto Vrieslander, Hermann Roth, Hans Weisse, Anthony van Hoboken, Oswald Jonas, Felix Salzer, and John Petrie Dunn. He endeavored to derive the basic laws of musical composition from a thoroughgoing analysis of the standard masterworks. The result was the contention that each composition represents a horizontal integration, through various stages, of differential triadic units derived from the overtone series. By a dialectical manipulation of the thematic elements and linear progressions of a given work, Schenker succeeded in preparing a formidable system in which the melody is the "Urlinie" (basic line), the bass is "Grundbrechung" (broken ground), and the ultimate formation is the "Ursatz" (background). The result seems as self-consistent as the Ptolemaic planetary theory of epicycles. Arbitrary as the Schenker system is, it proved remarkably durable in academia; some theorists even attempted to apply it to modern works lacking in the triadic content essential to Schenker's theories.

Schoenberg (originally, **Schönberg), Arnold (Franz Walter),** great Austrian-born American composer whose new method of musical organization in 12 different tones related only to one another profoundly influenced the entire development of modern techniques of composition; b. Vienna, Sept. 13, 1874; d. Los Angeles, July 13, 1951. He studied at the Realschule in Vienna; learned to play the cello, and also became proficient on the violin. His father died when Schoenberg was 16; he took a job as a bank clerk to earn a living; an additional source of income was arranging popular songs and orchestrating operetta scores. Schoenberg's 1st original work was a group of 3 piano pieces, which he wrote in 1894; it was also about that time that he began to take lessons in counterpoint from Alexander Zemlinsky, whose sister he married in 1901. He also played cello in Zemlinsky's instrumental group, Polyhymnia. In 1897 Schoenberg wrote his 1st String Quartet, in D major, which achieved public performance in Vienna on March 17, 1898. About the same time he wrote 2 songs with piano accompaniment which he designated as op. 1. In 1899 he wrote his 1st true masterpiece, *Verklärte Nacht*, set for string sextet, which was first performed in Vienna by the Rosé Quartet and members of the Vienna Phil. on March 18, 1902. It is a fine work, deeply imbued with the spirit of Romantic poetry, with its harmonic idiom stemming from Wagner's modulatory procedures; it remains Schoenberg's most frequently performed composition, known principally through its arrangement for string orch. About 1900 he was engaged as conductor of several amateur choral groups in Vienna and its suburbs; this increased his interest in vocal music. He then began work on a choral composition, *Gurre-Lieder*, of monumental proportions, to the translated text of a poem by the Danish writer Jens Peter Jacobsen. For grandeur and opulence of orchestral sonority, it surpassed even the most formidable creations of Mahler or Richard Strauss; it calls for 5 solo voices, a speaker, 3 male choruses, an 8-part mixed chorus, and a very large orch. Special music paper of 48 staves had to be ordered for the MS. He completed the 1st 2 parts of *Gurre-Lieder* in the spring of 1901, but the composition of the remaining section was delayed by 10 years; it was not until Feb. 23, 1913, that Franz Schreker was able to arrange its complete performance with the Vienna Phil. and its choral forces.

In 1901 Schoenberg moved to Berlin, where he joined E. von Wolzogen, F. Wedekind, and O. Bierbaum in launching an artistic cabaret, which they called Überbrettl. He composed a theme song for it with trumpet obbligato, and conducted several shows. He met Richard Strauss, who helped him to obtain the Liszt Stipendium and a position as a teacher at the Stern Cons. He returned to Vienna in 1903 and formed friendly relations with Gustav Mahler, who became a sincere supporter of his activities; Mahler's power in Vienna was then at its height, and he was able to help him in his career as a composer. In March 1904 Schoenberg organized with Alexander Zemlinsky the Vereinigung Schaffender Tonkünstler for the purpose of encouraging performances of new music. Under its auspices he conducted on Jan. 26, 1905, the 1st performance of his symphonic poem *Pelleas und Melisande*; in this score occurs the 1st use of a trombone glissando. There followed a performance on Feb. 8, 1907, of Schoenberg's *Kammersymphonie*, op. 9, with the participation of the Rosé Quartet and the wind instrumentalists of the Vienna Phil.; the work produced much consternation in the audience and among critics because of its departure from traditional tonal harmony, with chords built on fourths and nominal dissonances used without immediate resolution. About the same time, he turned to painting, which became his principal avocation. In his art, as in his music, he adopted the tenets of Expressionism, that is, freedom of personal expression within a self-defined program. Schoenberg's reputation as an independent musical thinker attracted to him such progressive-minded young musicians as Alban Berg, Anton von Webern, and Egon Wellesz, who followed Schoenberg in their own development. His 2nd String Quartet, composed in 1908, which included a soprano solo, was his last work that carried a definite key signature, if exception is made for his *Suite* for Strings, ostentatiously marked as in G major, which he wrote for school use in America in 1934. On Feb. 19, 1909, Schoenberg completed his piano piece op. 11, no. 1, which became the 1st musical composition to dispense with all reference to tonality. In 1910 he was appointed to the faculty of the Vienna Academy of Music; in 1911 he completed his important theory book *Harmonielehre*, dedicated to the memory of Mahler; it comprises a traditional exposition of chords and progressions, but also offers illuminating indications of possible new musical developments, including fractional tones and melodies formed by the change of timbre on the same note. In 1911 he went again to Berlin, where he became an instructor at the Stern Cons. and taught composition privately. In 1912 he brought out a work that attracted a great deal of attention: *5 Orchesterstücke*, which was performed for the 1st time not in Germany, not in Austria, but in London, under the direction of Sir Henry Wood, who conducted it there on Sept. 3, 1912; the critical reception was that of incomprehension, with a considerable measure of curiosity. The score was indeed revolutionary in nature, each movement representing an experiment in musical organization. In the same year Schoenberg produced another innovative work, a cycle of 21 songs with instrumental accompaniment, entitled *Pierrot Lunaire,* and consisting of 21 "melodramas," to German texts translated from verses by the Belgian poet Albert Giraud. Here he made systematic use of *Sprechstimme,* with a gliding speech-song replacing precise pitch (not an entire innovation, for Engelbert Humperdinck had applied it in his incidental music to Rosmer's play *Königskinder* in 1897). The work was given, after some 40 rehearsals, in Berlin on Oct. 16, 1912, and the reaction was startling, the purblind critics drawing upon the strongest invective in their vocabulary to condemn the music.

Meanwhile, Schoenberg made appearances as conductor of his works in various European cities (Amsterdam, 1911; St. Petersburg, 1912; London, 1914). During World War I he was sporadically enlisted in military service; after the Armistice, he settled in Mödling, near Vienna. Discouraged by his inability to secure performances for himself and his associates in the new music movement, he organized in Vienna, in Nov. 1918, the Verein für Musikalische Privataufführungen (Society for Private Musical Performances), from which critics were demonstratively excluded, and which ruled out any vocal expression of approval or disapproval. The organization disbanded in 1922. About that time, Schoenberg began work on his *Suite* for Piano, op. 25, which was to be the 1st true 12-tone piece consciously composed in that idiom. In 1925 he was appointed prof. of a master class at the Prussian Academy of Arts in Berlin. With the advent of the beastly Nazi regime, the German Ministry of Education dismissed him from his post as a Jew. As a matter of record, Schoenberg had abandoned his Jewish faith in Vienna on March 21, 1898, and in a spirit of political accommodation converted to Catholicism, which was the principal faith in Austria; 35 years later, horrified by the hideous persecution of Jews at the hands of the Nazis, he was moved to return to his ancestral faith and was reconverted to Judaism in Paris on July 24, 1933. With the rebirth of his hereditary consciousness, he turned to specific Jewish themes in works such as *Survivor from Warsaw* and *Moses und Aron.* Although Schoenberg was well known in the musical world, he had difficulty obtaining a teaching position; he finally accepted the invitation of Joseph Malkin, founder of the Malkin Cons. of Boston, to join its faculty. He arrived in the U.S. on Oct. 31, 1933. After teaching in Boston for a season, he moved to Hollywood. In 1935 he became a prof. of music at the Univ. of Southern Calif., and in 1936 accepted a similar position at the Univ. of Calif. in Los Angeles, where he taught until 1944, when he reached the mandatory retirement age of 70. On April 11, 1941, he became a naturalized American citizen. In 1947 he received the Award of Merit for Distinguished Achievements from the National Inst. of Arts and Letters. In the U.S. he changed the original spelling of his name from Schönberg to Schoenberg.

In 1924 Schoenberg's creative evolution reached the all-important point at which he found it necessary to establish a new governing principle of tonal relationship, which he called the "method of composing with 12 different notes related entirely to one another." This method was adumbrated in his music as early as 1914, and is used partially in his *5 Klavierstücke*, op. 23, and in his *Serenade*, op. 24; it was employed for the 1st time in its integral form in the piano *Suite*, op. 25 (1924); in it, the thematic material is based on a group of 12 different notes arrayed in a certain pre-arranged order; such a tone row was henceforth Schoenberg's mainspring of thematic invention; development was provided by the devices of inversion, retrograde, and retrograde inversion of the basic series; allowing for transposition, 48 forms were obtainable in all, with counterpoint and harmony, as well as melody, derived from the basic tone row. Immediate repetition of thematic notes was admitted; the realm of rhythm remained free. As with most historic innovations, the 12-tone technique was not the creation of Schoenberg alone but was, rather, a logical development of many currents of musical thought. Josef Matthias Hauer rather unconvincingly claimed priority in laying the foundations of the 12-tone method; among others who had elaborated similar ideas at about the same time with Schoenberg was Jef Golyscheff, a Russian émigré who expounded his theory in a publication entitled "12 Tondauer-Musik." Instances of themes consisting of 12 different notes are found in the *Faust Symphony* of Liszt and in the tone poem *Also sprach Zarathustra* of Richard Strauss in the section on Science. Schoenberg's great achievement was the establishment of the basic 12-tone row and its changing forms as foundations of a new musical language; using this idiom, he was able to write music of great expressive power. In general usage, the 12-tone method is often termed "dodecaphony," from Greek *dodeca,* "12," and *phone,* "sound." The tonal composition of the basic row is devoid of tonality; an analysis of Schoenberg's works shows that he avoided using major triads in any of their inversions, and allowed the use of only the 2nd inversion of a minor triad. He deprecated the term "atonality" that was commonly applied to his music. He suggested, only half in jest, the term "atonicality," i.e., absence of the dominating tonic. The most explicit work of Schoenberg couched in the 12-tone idiom was his *Klavierstück,* op. 33a, written in 1928–29, which exemplifies the clearest use of the tone row in chordal combinations. Other works that present a classical use of dodecaphony are *Begleitungsmusik zu einer Lichtspielszene,* op. 34 (1929–30); Violin Concerto (1934–36); and Piano Concerto (1942). Schoenberg's disciples Berg and Webern followed his 12-tone method in general outlines but with some personal deviations; thus, Berg accepted the occasional use of triadic harmonies, and Webern built tone rows in symmetric groups. Other composers who made systematic use of the 12-tone method were Egon Wellesz, Ernst Krenek, René Leibowitz, Roberto Gerhard, Humphrey Searle, and Luigi Dallapiccola. As time went on, dodecaphony became a lingua franca of universal currency; even in Russia, where Schoenberg's theories were for many years unacceptable on ideological grounds, several composers, including Shostakovich in his last works, made use of 12-tone themes, albeit without integral development. Ernest Bloch used 12-tone subjects in his last string quartets, but he refrained from applying inversions and retrograde forms of his tone rows. Stravinsky, in his old age, turned to the 12-tone method of composition in its total form, with retrograde, inversion, and retrograde inversion; his conversion was the greatest artistic vindication for Schoenberg, who regarded Stravinsky as his most powerful antagonist, but Schoenberg was dead when Stravinsky saw the light of dodecaphony.

Schoenberg's personality was both heroic and egocentric; he made great sacrifices to sustain his artistic convictions, but he was also capable of engaging in bitter polemics when he felt that his integrity was under attack. He strongly opposed the claims of Hauer and others for the priority of the 12-tone method of composition, and he vehemently criticized in the public press the implication he saw in Thomas Mann's novel *Doktor Faustus,* in which the protagonist was described as the inventor of the 12-tone method of composition; future historians, Schoenberg argued, might confuse fiction with facts, and credit the figment of Mann's imagination with Schoenberg's own discovery. He was also subject to superstition in the form of triskaidecaphobia, the fear of the number 13; he seriously believed that there was something fateful in the circumstance of his birth on the 13th of the month. Noticing that the title of his work *Moses und Aaron* contained 13 letters, he crossed out the 2nd "a" in Aaron to make it 12. When he turned 76 and someone remarked facetiously that the sum of the digits of his age was 13, he seemed genuinely upset, and during his last illness in July 1951, he expressed his fear of not surviving July 13; indeed, he died on that date. Schoenberg placed his MSS in the Music Division of the Library of Congress in Washington, D.C.; the remaining materials were deposited after his death at the Schoenberg Inst. at the Univ. of Southern Calif. in Los Angeles. Schoenberg's centennial in 1974 was commemorated worldwide. A *Journal of the Schoenberg Institute* began publ. in 1976, under the editorship of Leonard Stein.

Schoenberg's personality, which combined elements of decisive affirmation and profound self-negation, still awaits a thorough analysis. When he was drafted into the Austrian armed forces during World War I (he never served in action, however) and was asked by the examiner whether he was the "notorious" modernist composer, he answered "someone had to be, and I was the one." He could not understand why his works were not widely performed. He asked a former secretary to Serge Koussevitzky why the Boston Sym. Orch. programs never included any of his advanced works; when the secretary said that Koussevitzky simply could not understand them, Schoenberg was genuinely perplexed. "Aber, er spielt doch Brahms!" he said. To Schoenberg, his works were the natural continuation of German classical music. Schoenberg lived in Los Angeles for several years during the period when Stravinsky was also there, but the two never made artistic contact. Indeed, they met only once, in a downtown food market, where they greeted each other, in English, with a formal handshake. Schoenberg wrote a satirical canon, *Herr Modernsky,* obviously aimed at Stravinsky, whose neo-Classical works ("ganz wie Papa Bach") Schoenberg lampooned. But when Schoenberg was dead, Stravinsky said he forgave him in appreciation of his expertise in canonic writing.

In his private life, Schoenberg had many interests; he was a fairly good tennis player, and also liked to play chess. In his early years in Vienna, he launched several theoretical inventions to augment his income, but none of them ever went into practice; he also designed a set of playing cards. The MSS of arrangements of Viennese operettas and waltzes he had made in Vienna to augment his meager income were eventually sold for large sums of money after his death. That Schoenberg needed money but was not offered any by an official musical benefactor was a shame. After Schoenberg relocated to Los Angeles, which was to be his final destination, he obtained successful appointments as a prof. at the Univ. of Southern Calif. and eventually at the Univ. of Calif., Los Angeles. But there awaited him the peculiar rule of age limitation for teachers, and he was mandatorily retired when he reached his seventieth year. His pension from the Univ. of Calif., Los Angeles, amounted to $38 a month. His difficulty in supporting a family with growing children became acute and eventually reached the press. He applied for a grant from the munificent Guggenheim Foundation, pointing out that since several of his own students had received such awards, he was now applying for similar consideration, but the rule of age limitation defeated him there as well. It was only after the Schoenberg case and its repercussions in the music world that the Guggenheim Foundation cancelled its offensive rule. Schoenberg managed to square his finances with the aid of his publishing income, however, and, in the meantime, his children grew up. His son Ronald (an anagram of Arnold) eventually became a city judge, an extraordinary development for a Schoenberg!

Schubert, Franz (Peter), great Austrian composer, a supreme melodist and an inspired master of lieder, brother of **Ferdinand (Lukas) Schubert;** b. Himmelpfortgrund (then a suburb of Vienna and now a part of that city), Jan. 31, 1797; d. Vienna, Nov. 19, 1828. He studied violin with his father, a schoolmaster, and received instruction on the piano from his brother Ignaz; in addition, he took lessons in piano, organ, singing, and theory with Holzer, the choirmaster. In 1808 he became a member of the Vienna Imperial Court chapel choir, and also entered the Stadtkonvict, a training school for court singers, where he studied music with the Imperial Court organist Wenzel Ruzicka and with the famous court composer Salieri. He played violin in the school orch. and conducted it whenever an occasion called for it. He began composing in school; wrote a *Fantasie* for Piano, 4-hands, several chamber music works, orch. overtures, and the unfinished singspiel *Der Spiegelritter*. His 1st song, *Hagars Klage*, is dated March 30, 1811. In 1813 he left the Stadtkonvict, but Salieri, evidently impressed by his talent, continued to give him instruction. He further attended a training college for teachers in Vienna, and then became an instructor at his father's school. Although very young, he began writing works in large forms; between 1813 and 1816 he composed 5 syms., 4 masses, several string quartets, and also some stage music. He also wrote his 1st opera, *Des Teufels Lustschloss*. It was then that he wrote some of his most famous lieder. He was only 17 when he wrote *Gretchen am Spinnrade*, and only 18 when he composed the overpowering dramatic song *Erlkönig*. The prodigious facility that Schubert displayed is without equal; during the year 1815 he composed about 140 songs; on a single day, Oct. 15, he wrote 8 lieder. From his sketches, it is possible to follow his method of composition; he would write the melody 1st, indicate the harmony, and then write out the song in full; often he subjected the finished work to several revisions. He became friendly with the poets Johann Mayrhofer and Franz von Schober, and set a number of their poems to music. In 1817 he lodged with Schober and his widowed mother, arranging to pay for his keep from his meager resources. It was then that he met the noted baritone Johann Michael Vogl, who put many of Schubert's songs on his concert programs. Outstanding lieder from this period include the *3 Harfenspieler, Der Wanderer, Der Tod und das Mädchen, Ganymed, An die Musik*, and *Die Forelle*. During the summer of 1818, he served as music tutor to the family of Count Esterházy at Zélesz in Hungary. On March 1, 1818, his Overture in C major, "in the Italian style," became his 1st orch. work to be accorded a public performance in Vienna. On June 14, 1820, his singspiel *Die Zwillingsbrüder* was performed at the Kärnthnertortheater in Vienna. On Aug. 19, 1820, a score of his incidental music for the play *Die Zauberharfe* was heard at the Theater an der Wien; this score contains an overture that became subsequently popular in concert performances under the name *Rosamunde Overture*, although it was not composed for the score to the play *Rosamunde, Fürstin von Zypern*, which was produced at the Theater an der Wien more than 3 years later, on Dec. 20, 1823. Although Schubert still had difficulties in earning a living, he formed a circle of influential friends in Vienna, and appeared as a pianist at private gatherings; sometimes he sang his songs, accompanying himself at the keyboard; he was also able to publ. some of his songs. A mystery is attached to his most famous work, begun in 1822, the Sym. in B minor, known popularly as the "Unfinished" Sym. Only 2 movements are known to exist; portions of the 3rd movement, a Scherzo, remain in sketches. What prevented him from finishing it? Speculations are as rife as they are worthless, particularly since he was usually careful in completing a work before embarking on another composition. A hundred years after Schubert's death, an enterprising phonograph company arranged a contest for the completion of the "Unfinished" Sym.; prizes were given, but the products delivered, even some signed by well-known composers, were spectacularly poor. In 1823 he completed his masterly song cycle *Die schöne Müllerin*; in 1824 he once again spent the summer as a private tutor in Count Esterházy's employ in

Zélesz. In 1827 he wrote another remarkable song cycle, *Die Winterreise*. On March 26, 1828, he presented in Vienna a public concert of his works. From that year, which proved to be his last, date such masterpieces as the piano sonatas in C minor, A major, and B-flat major; the String Quintet in C major; and the 2 books of songs collectively known as the *Schwanengesang*. His health was frail, and he moved to the lodgings of his brother Ferdinand. On the afternoon of Nov. 19, 1828, Schubert died, at the age of 31. For a thorough account of his illness, see E. Sams's "Schubert's Illness Reexamined," *Musical Times* (Jan. 1980). There is no incontrovertible evidence that Schubert died of syphilis; from all accounts of his daily life, he was never promiscuous, and was not known to engage in unseemly liaisons.

Schubert is often described as the creator of the genre of strophic lieder; this summary description is chronologically untenable; Zelter wrote strophic lieder a generation before him. Goethe, whose poems were set to music by Zelter, Beethoven, and Schubert, favored Zelter's settings. What Schubert truly created was an incomparably beautiful florilegium of lieder typifying the era of German Romantic sentiment and conveying deeply felt emotions, ranging from peaceful joy to enlightened melancholy, from philosophic meditation to throbbing drama; the poems he selected for his settings were expressive of such passing moods. He set to music 72 poems by Goethe, 47 by Mayrhofer, 46 by Schiller, 44 by Wilhelm Müller, 28 by Matthison, 23 by Hölty, 22 by Kosegarten, 13 by Körtner, 12 by Schober, and 6 by Heine.

In a sense, Schubert's *Moments musicaux, Impromptus*, and other piano works are songs without texts; on several occasions he used musical material from his songs for instrumental works, as in the great *Wanderer Fantasia* for Piano, based on his song *Der Wanderer*, and the "Forellen" Piano Quintet, in which the 4th movement is a set of variations on the song *Die Forelle*. His String Quartet in D minor includes a set of variations on his song *Der Tod und das Mädchen* in its 2nd movement. But Schubert was not given to large theater works and oratorios. Even his extended works in sonata form are not conceived on a grand scale but, rather, are constructed according to the symmetry of recapitulations; his music captivates the listeners not by recurring variety but by the recalled felicities; time and again in his MSS, he simply indicates the repetition of a group of bars by number. Therein lies the immense difference between Schubert and Schumann, both Romantic poets of music: where Schubert was satisfied with reminding the listener of a passage already heard, Schumann variegates. Schubert was indeed the most symmetrical composer in the era of free-flowing musical prose and musical poetry.

Much confusion exists in the numbering of Schubert's syms., the last being listed in most catalogues as No. 9; the missing uncounted sym. is No. 7, which exists as a full draft, in 4 movements, of which the 1st 110 bars are fully scored; several "completions" exist, the 1st by John Francis Barnett, made in 1883; the 2nd by Felix Weingartner, manufactured in 1934; and the 3rd, and perhaps the most Schubertomorphic, constructed with artful imitation of Schubert's ways and means, by Brian Newbould, in 1977. The "Unfinished" Sym. is then No. 8. There remains the "Gmunden" or "Gastein" Sym., so named because Schubert was supposed to have written it in Gastein, in the Tirol, in 1825. It was long regarded as irretrievably lost, but was eventually identified with No. 9, the great C major Sym. Incredibly, as late as 1978 there came to light in a somehow overlooked pile of music in the archives of the Vienna Stadtsbibliothek a sketch of still another Schubert sym., composed during the last months of his life; this insubstantial but magically tempting waft of Schubert's genius was completed by Brian Newbould; it is numbered as his 10th.

The recognition of Schubert's greatness was astonishingly slow. Fully 40 years elapsed before the discovery of the MS of the "Unfinished" Sym. Posthumous performances were the rule for his sym. premieres, and the publication of his syms. was exceedingly tardy. Schumann, ever sensitive to great talent, was eager to salute the kindred genius in Schubert's syms., about whose "Heavenly length" he so admiringly complained. But it took half a century for Schubert to become firmly established in music history as one of the great Sch's (with Chopin phonetically counted in).

Schumann, Clara (Josephine) (née **Wieck**), famous German pianist, teacher, and composer, daughter of **Friedrich Wieck** and wife of **Robert (Alexander) Schumann**; b. Leipzig, Sept. 13, 1819; d. Frankfurt am Main, May 20, 1896. She was only 5 when she began musical training with her father; made her debut at the Leipzig Gewandhaus on Oct. 20, 1828, where she gave her 1st complete recital on Nov. 8, 1830; her father then took her on her 1st major concert tour in 1831–32, which included a visit to Paris. Upon her return to Leipzig, she pursued additional piano training as well as studies in voice, violin, instrumentation, score reading, counterpoint, and composition; she also publ. several works for piano. In 1838 she was named kk. Kammervirtuosin to the Austrian court. Schumann entered Clara's life in 1830 when he became a lodger in the Wieck home; in 1837 he asked her to marry him, a request which set off a contentious battle between the couple and Clara's father; the issue was only settled after the couple went to court, and they were finally married on Sept. 12, 1840. They went to Dresden, and then to Düsseldorf (1850). In spite of her responsibilities in rearing a large family, she continued to pursue a concert career. She also became active as a teacher, serving on the faculty of the Leipzig Cons. and teaching privately. After her husband's death in 1856, she went to Berlin in 1857; after a sojourn in Baden-Baden (1863–73), she lived intermittently in Berlin (1873–78). Throughout these years, she toured widely as a pianist; made regular appearances in England from 1856; toured Russia in 1864. In 1878 she settled in Frankfurt as a teacher at the Hoch Cons., a position she retained with distinction until 1892. She made her last public appearance as a pianist in 1891. As a pianist, she was a masterly and authoritative interpreter of Schumann's compositions; later she became an equally admirable interpreter of Brahms, her lifelong friend. She was completely free of all mannerisms, and impressed her audiences chiefly by the earnestness of her regard for the music she played. A remarkable teacher, she attracted students from many countries. As a composer, she revealed a genuine talent especially in her numerous character pieces for piano. She wrote a Piano Concerto (1836), a Piano Trio (1847), a Piano Concertino (1847), *Drei Romanzen* for Violin and Piano (1853), and some songs. Schumann made use of her melodies in several of his works. She wrote cadenzas to Beethoven's concertos in C minor and G major; ed. the Breitkopf & Hartel edition of Schumann's works, and some of his early correspondence; also ed. finger exercises from Czerny's piano method.

Scriabin, Alexander (Nikolaievich), remarkable Russian composer whose solitary genius had no predecessors and left no disciples, father of **Marina Scriabine**; b. Moscow, Jan. 6, 1872; d. there, April 27, 1915. His father was a lawyer; his mother, Lyubov Petrovna (née Shchetinina), was a talented pianist who had studied with Leschetizky at the St. Petersburg Cons.; his mother died of tuberculosis when he was an infant, and his father remarried and spent the rest of his life in the diplomatic service abroad. Scriabin was reared by an aunt, who gave him initial instruction in music, including piano; at 11 he began regular piano lessons with Georgi Conus, and at 16 became a pupil of Zverev; in 1885 he commenced the study of theory with Taneyev. When he entered the Moscow Cons. in 1888, he continued his studies with Taneyev, and also received instruction in piano with

Safonov. He practiced assiduously, but never became a virtuoso pianist; at his piano recitals, he performed mostly his own works. Graduating with a gold medal from Safonov's class, Scriabin remained at the Moscow Cons. to study fugue with Arensky, but failed to pass the required test and never received a diploma for composition. Upon leaving the Cons. in 1892, he launched a career as a concert pianist. By that time he had already written several piano pieces in the manner of Chopin; the publisher Jurgenson brought out his opp. 1, 2, 3, 5, and 7 in 1893. In 1894 Belaieff became his publisher and champion, financing his 1st European tour in 1895; on Jan. 15, 1896, Scriabin gave a concert of his own music in Paris. Returning to Russia, he completed his 1st major work, a Piano Concerto, and was soloist in its 1st performance on Oct. 23, 1897, in Odessa. In the same year, he married the pianist Vera Isakovich. They spent some time abroad; on Jan. 31, 1898, they gave a joint recital in Paris in a program of Scriabin's works. From 1898 to 1903 Scriabin taught piano at the Moscow Cons. His 1st orch. work, *Rêverie*, was conducted in Moscow by Safonov on March 24, 1899; he also conducted the 1st performance of Scriabin's 1st Sym. (March 29, 1901). Scriabin's 2nd Sym. was brought out by Liadov in St. Petersburg (Jan. 25, 1902). After the death of Belaieff in 1904, Scriabin received an annual grant of 2,400 rubles from the wealthy Moscow merchant Morosov, and went to Switzerland, where he began work on his 3rd Sym., *Le Poème divin*; it had its 1st performance in Paris on May 29, 1905, under the direction of Arthur Nikisch. At that time Scriabin separated from Vera Isakovich and established a household with Tatiana Schloezer, sister of the music critic Boris de Schloezer, who subsequently became Scriabin's close friend and biographer. In Dec. 1906 he appeared as a soloist with Modest Altschuler and the Russian Sym. Society in N.Y.; also gave recitals of his works there and in other U.S. music centers. Tatiana Schloezer joined him in N.Y. in Jan. 1907, but they were warned by friends familiar with American mores of the time that charges of moral turpitude might be brought against them, since Scriabin had never obtained a legal divorce from his 1st wife and Tatiana Schloezer was his common-law wife. There was no evidence that such charges were actually contemplated, but to safeguard themselves against such a contretemps, they went to Paris in March 1907. Altschuler continued to champion Scriabin's music, and on Dec. 10, 1908, gave the world premiere with his Russian Sym. Orch. of Scriabin's great work *Le poème de l'extase*; the 1st Russian performance followed in St. Petersburg (Feb. 1, 1909). In the spring of 1908, Scriabin met Serge Koussevitzky, who became one of his most ardent supporters, both as a conductor and as a publisher. He gave Scriabin a 5-year contract with his newly established publishing firm Editions Russes, with a generous guarantee of 5,000 rubles annually. In the summer of 1910, Koussevitzky engaged Scriabin as soloist on a tour in a chartered steamer down the Volga River, with stopovers and concerts at all cities and towns of any size along the route. Scriabin wrote for Koussevitzky his most ambitious work, *Promethée*, or *Poème du feu*, with an important piano part, which featured the composer as soloist at its premiere in Moscow (March 15, 1911). The score also included a color keyboard (*clavier à lumière* or, in Italian, *luce*) intended to project changing colors according to the scale of the spectrum, which Scriabin devised (for at that time he was deeply immersed in the speculation about parallelism of all arts in their visual and auditory aspects). The construction of such a color organ was, however, entirely unfeasible at the time, and the premiere of the work was given without *luce*. A performance with colored lights thrown on a screen was attempted by Altschuler at Carnegie Hall in N.Y. on March 20, 1915, but it was a total failure. Another attempt was made in Moscow by Safonov after Scriabin's death, but that, too, was completely unsuccessful. The crux of the problem was that the actual notes written on a special staff in the score had to be translated into a color spectrum according to Scriabin's visualization of corresponding colors and keys (C major was red, F-sharp major was bright blue, etc.). Perhaps the nearest approximation to Scriabin's scheme was the performance of *Promethée* by the Univ. of Iowa Sym. Orch. on Sept. 24, 1975, under the direction of James Dixon, with a laser apparatus constructed by Lowell Cross; previously, the American pianist Hilde Somer made use of the laser to accompany her solo piano recitals of Scriabin's works, without attempting to follow the parallelism of sounds and colors envisioned by Scriabin, but nonetheless conveying the idea underlying the scheme. The unique collaboration between Scriabin and Koussevitzky came to an unfortunate end soon after the production of *Promethée*; Scriabin regarded Koussevitzky as the chief apostle of his messianic epiphany, while Koussevitzky believed that it was due principally to his promotion that Scriabin reached the heights in musical celebrity; to this collision of 2 mighty egotisms was added a trivial disagreement about financial matters. Scriabin left Koussevitzky's publishing firm, and in 1912 signed a contract with Jurgenson, who guaranteed him 6,000 rubles annually. In 1914 Scriabin visited London and was soloist in his Piano Concerto and in *Prometheus* at a concert led by Sir Henry Wood (March 14, 1914); he also gave a recital of his own works there (March 20, 1914). His last public appearance was in a recital in Petrograd on April 15, 1915; upon his return to Moscow, an abscess developed in his lip, leading to blood poisoning; he died after a few days' illness. His 3 children (of the union with Tatiana Schloezer) were legitimized at his death. His son Julian, an exceptionally gifted boy, was accidentally drowned at the age of 11 in the Dnieper River at Kiev (June 22, 1919); Julian's 2 piano preludes, written in the style of the last works of his father, were publ. in a Scriabin memorial vol. (Moscow, 1940).

Scriabin was a genuine innovator in harmony. After an early period of strongly felt influences (Chopin, Liszt, and Wagner), he gradually evolved in his own melodic and harmonic style, marked by extreme chromaticism; in his piano piece *Désir*, op. 57 (1908), the threshold of polytonality and atonality is reached; the key signature is dispensed with in his subsequent works; chromatic alterations and compound appoggiaturas create a harmonic web of such complexity that all distinction between consonance and dissonance vanishes. Building chords by fourths rather than by thirds, Scriabin constructed his "mystic chord" of 6 notes (C, F-sharp, B-flat, E, A, and D), which is the harmonic foundation of *Promethée*. In his 7th Piano Sonata (1913) appears a chordal structure of 25 notes (D-flat, F-flat, G, A, and C, repeated in 5 octaves), which was dubbed "a 5-story chord." These harmonic extensions were associated in Scriabin's mind with theosophic doctrines; he aspired to a universal art in which the impressions of the senses were to unite with religious experience. He made plans for the writing of a "Mysterium," which was to accomplish such a synthesis, but only the text of a preliminary poem (*L'Acte préalable*) was completed at his death. Scriabin dreamed of having the "Mysterium" performed as a sacred action in the Himalayas, and actually made plans for going to India; the outbreak of World War I in 1914 put an end to such a project. Scriabin's fragmentary sketches for *L'Acte préalable* were arranged in 1973 by the Russian musician Alexander Nemtin, who supplemented this material with excerpts from Scriabin's 8th Piano Sonata, *Guirlandes*, and Piano Preludes, op. 74; the resulting synthetic score was performed in Moscow on March 16, 1973, under the title *Universe*; a species of color keyboard was used at the performance, projecting colors according to Scriabin's musical spectrum.

Seeger, Charles (Louis), eminent American musicologist, ethnomusicologist, teacher, and composer; b. Mexico City (of American parents), Dec. 14, 1886; d. Bridgewater, Conn., Feb. 7, 1979. He was educated at Harvard Univ. (graduated,

1908); after conducting at the Cologne Opera (1910–11), he returned to the U.S. as chairman of the music dept. of the Univ. of Calif. at Berkeley (1912–19), where he gave the 1st classes in musicology in the U.S. (1916); then taught at N.Y.'s Inst. of Musical Art (1921–33) and the New School for Social Research (1931–35); at the latter, he gave the 1st classes (with Henry Cowell) in ethnomusicology in the U.S. (1932); was also active in contemporary music circles, as a composer and a music critic. He served as a technical adviser on music to the Resettlement Administration (1935–38), as deputy director of the Federal Music Project of the Works Progress Administration (1938–41), and as chief of the music division of the Pan-American Union (1941–53) in Washington, D.C.; was also a visiting prof. at Yale Univ. (1949–50). He subsequently was a research musicologist at the Inst. of Ethnomusicology at the Univ. of Calif. in Los Angeles (1960–70), and then taught at Harvard Univ. (from 1972). He was a founder and chairman (1930–34) of the N.Y. Musicological Soc., which he helped to reorganize as the American Musicological Soc. in 1934; was its president (1945–46) and also president of the American Soc. for Comparative Musicology (1935) and the Soc. for Ethnomusicology (1960–61; honorary president from 1972). Seeger also was instrumental (with Cowell and Joseph Schafer) in the formation of the N.Y. Composers' Collective (1932); since he was profoundly interested in proletarian music throughout the 1930s, he wrote on the need for a revolutionary spirit in music for such publications as *The Daily Worker*; he also contributed songs under the name Carl Sands to *The Workers Song Books* (1934 and 1935). Two of his essays are of especial historical interest: "On Proletarian Music" (*Modern Music*, XI/3 [1934]), which lamented the dearth of folk songs in the work of professional musicians, and "Grassroots for American Composers" (*Modern Music*, XVI [1938–40]), which, by shedding earlier Marxist rhetoric, had wide influence on the folk movement in the 1950s. Since many of his compositions were destroyed by fire at Berkeley in 1926, his extraordinary contribution to American music rests upon his work as a scholar whose uniquely universalist vision for the unification of the field of musicology as a whole continues to challenge the various, sometimes contentious contributing factions: musicology, ethnomusicology, and comparative musicology. He was also a noted teacher; one of his most gifted students, **Ruth (Porter) Crawford**, became his 2nd wife. In addition to his son **Pete(r) Seeger**, 2 other of his children became musicians: **Mike (Michael) Seeger** (b. N.Y., Aug. 15, 1933) was a folksinger and instrumentalist; after learning to play various folk instruments on his own, he became active in promoting the cause of authentic folk music of the American Southeast; became widely known for his expertise as a banjo player; with John Cohen and Tom Paley, he organized the New Lost City Ramblers in 1958; then founded the Strange Creek Singers in 1968. **Peggy** (actually, **Margaret**) Seeger (b. N.Y., June 17, 1935) was a folksinger, songwriter, and song collector; studied both classical and folk music; after further training at Radcliffe College, she became active as a performer; settled in England in 1956, becoming a naturalized subject in 1959; became a leading figure in the folk-music revival.

Shostakovich, Dmitri (Dmitrievich), preeminent Russian composer of the Soviet generation, whose style and idiom of composition largely defined the nature of new Russian music, father of **Maxim Shostakovich**; b. St. Petersburg, Sept. 25, 1906; d. Moscow, Aug. 9, 1975. He was a member of a cultured Russian family; his father was an engineer employed in the government office of weights and measures; his mother was a professional pianist. Shostakovich grew up during the most difficult period of Russian revolutionary history, when famine and disease decimated the population of Petrograd. Of frail physique, he suffered from malnutrition; Glazunov, the director of the Petrograd Cons., appealed personally to the Commissar of Education, Lunacharsky, to grant an increased food ration for Shostakovich, essential for his physical survival. At the age of 9, he commenced piano lessons with his mother; in 1919 he entered the Petrograd Cons., where he studied piano with Nikolayev and composition with Steinberg; graduated in piano in 1923, and in composition in 1925. As a graduation piece, he submitted his 1st Sym., written at the age of 18; it was 1st performed by the Leningrad Phil. on May 12, 1926, under the direction of Malko, and subsequently became one of Shostakovich's most popular works. He pursued postgraduate work in composition until 1930. His 2nd Sym., composed for the 10th anniversary of the Soviet Revolution in 1927, bearing the subtitle *Dedication to October* and ending with a rousing choral finale, was less successful despite its revolutionary sentiment. He then wrote a satirical opera, *The Nose*, after Gogol's whimsical story about the sudden disappearance of the nose from the face of a government functionary; here Shostakovich revealed his flair for musical satire; the score featured a variety of modernistic devices and included an interlude written for percussion instruments only. *The Nose* was produced in Leningrad on Jan. 12, 1930, with considerable popular acclaim, but was attacked by officious theater critics as a product of "bourgeois decadence," and quickly withdrawn from the stage. Somewhat in the same satirical style was his ballet *The Golden Age* (1930), which included a celebrated dissonant *Polka*, satirizing the current disarmament conference in Geneva. There followed the 3rd Sym., subtitled *May First* (Leningrad, Jan. 21, 1930), with a choral finale saluting the International Workers' Day. Despite its explicit revolutionary content, it failed to earn the approbation of Soviet spokesmen, who dismissed the work as nothing more than a formal gesture of proletarian solidarity. Shostakovich's next work was to precipitate a crisis in his career, as well as in Soviet music in general; it was an opera to the libretto drawn from a short story by the 19th-century Russian writer Leskov, entitled *Lady Macbeth of the District of Mtzensk*, and depicting adultery, murder, and suicide in a merchant home under the Czars. It was produced in Leningrad on Jan. 22, 1934, and was hailed by most Soviet musicians as a significant work comparable to the best productions of Western modern opera. But both the staging and the music ran counter to growing Soviet puritanism; a symphonic interlude portraying a scene of adultery behind the bedroom curtain, orchestrated with suggestive passages on the slide trombones, shocked the Soviet officials present at the performance by its bold naturalism. After the Moscow production of the opera, *Pravda*, the official organ of the Communist party, publ. an unsigned (and therefore all the more authoritative) article accusing Shostakovich of creating a "bedlam of noise." The brutality of this assault dismayed Shostakovich; he readily admitted his faults in both content and treatment of the subject, and declared his solemn determination to write music according to the then-emerging formula of "socialist realism." His next stage production was a ballet, *The Limpid Brook*, portraying the pastoral scenes on a Soviet collective farm. In this work he tempered his dissonant idiom, and the subject seemed eminently fitting for the Soviet theater; but it, too, was condemned in *Pravda*, this time for an insufficiently dignified treatment of Soviet life. Having been rebuked twice for 2 radically different theater works, Shostakovich abandoned all attempts to write for the stage, and returned to purely instrumental composition. But as though pursued by vengeful fate, he again suffered a painful reverse. His 4th Sym. (1935–36) was placed in rehearsal by the Leningrad Phil., but withdrawn before the performance when representatives of the musical officialdom and even the orch. musicians themselves sharply criticized the piece. Shostakovich's rehabilitation finally came with the production of his 5th Sym. (Leningrad, Nov. 21, 1937), a work of rhapsodic grandeur, culminating in a powerful climax; it was hailed, as though by spontaneous consensus, as a model of true Soviet art, classical in formal design, lucid in its harmonic idiom, and optimistic in its philosophical connotations. The height of his rise to recognition was achieved in his 7th Sym. He began its composition during the siege of Leningrad by the Nazis in the autumn of 1941; he served in the fire brigade during the air raids; then flew from Leningrad to the temporary Soviet capital in Kuibishev, on the Volga, where he completed the score, which was performed there on March 1, 1942. Its symphonic development is realistic in the extreme, with the theme of the Nazis, in mechanical march time, rising to monstrous loudness, only to be overcome and reduced to a pathetic drum dribble by a victorious Russian song. The work became a musical symbol of the Russian struggle against the overwhelmingly superior Nazi war machine; it was given the subtitle *Leningrad Symphony*, and was performed during the war by virtually every orch. in the Allied countries. After the tremendous emotional appeal of the *Leningrad Symphony*, the 8th Sym., written in 1943, had a lesser impact; the 9th, 10th, and 11th syms. followed (1945, 1953, 1957) without attracting much comment; the 12th Sym. (1960–61), dedicated to the memory of Lenin, aroused a little more interest. But it was left for his 13th Sym. (Leningrad, Dec. 18, 1962) to create a controversy which seemed to be Shostakovich's peculiar destiny; its vocal 1st movement for solo bass and male chorus, to words by the Soviet poet Evtushenko, expressing the horror of the massacre of Jews by the Nazis during their occupation of the city of Kiev, and containing a warning against residual anti-Semitism in Soviet Russia, met with unexpected criticism by the chairman of the Communist party, Nikita Khrushchev, who complained about the exclusive attention in Evtushenko's poem to Jewish victims, and his failure to mention the Ukrainians and other nationals who were also slaughtered. The text of the poem was altered to meet these objections, but the 13th Sym. never gained wide acceptance. There followed the remarkable 14th Sym. (1969), in 11 sections, scored for voices and orch., to words by Federico García Lorca, Apollinaire, Rilke, and the Russian poet Küchelbecker. Shostakovich's 15th Sym., his last (perf. in Moscow under the direction of his son **Maxim** on Jan. 8, 1972), demonstrated his undying spirit of innovation; the score is set in the key of C major, but it contains a dodecaphonic passage and literal allusions to motives from Rossini's *William Tell Overture* and the Fate Motif from Wagner's *Die Walküre*. Shostakovich's adoption, however limited, of themes built on 12 different notes, a procedure that he had himself condemned as anti-musical, is interesting both from the psychological and sociological standpoint; he experimented with these techniques in several other works; his 1st explicit use of a 12-tone subject occurred in his 12th String Quartet (1968). Equally illuminating is his use in some of his scores of a personal monogram, D.S.C.H. (for D, Es, C, H in German notation, i.e., D, E-flat, C, B). One by one, his early works, originally condemned as unacceptable to Soviet reality, were returned to the stage and the concert hall; the objectionable 4th and 13th syms. were publ. and recorded; the operas *The Nose* and *Lady Macbeth of the District of Mtzensk* (renamed *Katerina Izmailova*, after the name of the heroine) had several successful revivals.

Shostakovich excelled in instrumental music. Besides the 15 syms., he wrote 15 string quartets, a String Octet, Piano Quintet, 2 piano trios, Cello Sonata, Violin Sonata, Viola Sonata, 2 violin concertos, 2 piano concertos, 2 cello concertos, 24 preludes for Piano, 24 preludes and fugues for Piano, 2 piano sonatas, and several short piano pieces; also choral works and song cycles.

What is remarkable about Shostakovich is the unfailing consistency of his style of composition. His entire oeuvre, from his 1st work to the last (147 opus numbers in all), proclaims a personal article of faith. His idiom is unmistakably of the 20th century, making free use of dissonant harmonies and intricate contrapuntal designs, yet never abandoning inherent tonality; his music is teleological, leading invariably to a tonal climax, often in a triumphal triadic declaration. Most of his works carry key signatures; his metrical structure is governed by a unifying rhythmic pulse. Shostakovich is equally eloquent in dramatic and lyric utterance; he has no fear of prolonging his slow movements in relentless dynamic rise and fall; the cumulative power of his kinetic drive in rapid movements is overwhelming. Through all the peripeties of his career, he never changed his musical language in its fundamental modalities. When the flow of his music met obstacles, whether technical or external, he obviated them without changing the main direction. In a special announcement issued after Shostakovich's death, the government of the U.S.S.R. summarized his work as a "remarkable example of fidelity to the traditions of musical classicism, and above all, to the Russian traditions, finding his inspiration in the reality of Soviet life, reasserting and developing in his creative innovations the art of socialist realism, and in so doing, contributing to universal progressive musical culture." His honors, both domestic and foreign, were many: the Order of Lenin (1946, 1956, 1966), People's Artist of the U.S.S.R. (1954), Hero of Socialist Labor (1966), Order of the October Revolution (1971), honorary membership in the American Inst. of the Arts (1943), honorary Doctor of Oxford Univ. (1958), Laureate of the International Sibelius Prize (1958), and Doctor of Fine Arts from Northwestern Univ. (1973). He visited the U.S. as a delegate to the World Peace Conference in 1949, as a member of a group of Soviet musicians in 1959, and to receive the degree of D.F.A. from Northwestern Univ. in 1973. A postage stamp of 6 kopecks, bearing his photograph and an excerpt from the *Leningrad Symphony*, was issued by the Soviet Post Office in 1976 to commemorate his 70th birthday. A collected edition of his works was publ. in Moscow (42 vols., 1980–).

Sinatra, Frank (Francis Albert), popular American singer and actor; b. Hoboken, N.J., Dec. 12, 1915, of immigrant Italian parents. He had no training as a singer and could not read music; after singing in a school glee club and on amateur radio shows, he appeared on N.Y. radio shows. In 1939 he became a singer with Harry James, and then gained fame as a vocalist with Tommy Dorsey (1940–42). Inspired by the tone production of Dorsey's trombone playing, he evolved, by convex inhalation from a corner of the mouth, a sui generis "mal canto" in *sotto voce* delivery, employing a Caruso-like *coup-de-glotte* at climactic points. This mode of singing, combined with an engagingly slender physique, stirred the young females of the World War II era to fainting frenzy at his performances. Sinatra's press agents were quick to exploit the phenomenon, dubbing him "Swoonlight Sinatra." He eventually overcame his anesthetic appeal and became a successful baritone crooner. In 1952 he revealed an unexpected dramatic talent as a movie actor, eliciting praise from astonished cinema critics and an Academy Award for his appearance in *From Here to Eternity*. Other successful films followed, and his singing career gained momentum as he toured throughout the globe. He also made numerous recordings and television appearances. A fixture on the nightclub circuit, the Univ. of Nevada at Las Vegas conferred on him the honorary degree of Literarum Humanitarum Doctor, in appreciation of his many highly successful appearances in the hotels and gambling casinos of Las Vegas (1976). President Reagan was so moved to present him with the U.S. Presidential Medal of Freedom in 1985.

Slonimsky, Sergei (Mikhailovich), greatly talented Russian composer, nephew of **Nicolas (Nikolai Leonidovich) Slonimsky;** b. Leningrad, Aug. 12, 1932. A member of a highly intellectual family (his father was a well-known Soviet author; his paternal grandfather, an economist, the author of the 1st book on Karl Marx in the Russian language; his father's maternal uncle was a celebrated Russian ed. and literary critic; his father's maternal aunt was the noted piano teacher Isabelle Vengerova), he studied at the Leningrad Cons., taking composition with Boris Arapov and Orest Evlakhov (graduated, 1955) and piano with Vladimir Nilsen (graduated, 1956); he also took courses in musicology with F. Rubtzov (folk music) and N. Uspensky (polyphonic analysis). While a student, he wrote a fairy-tale suite, *Frog-Princess*, and in 1951 composed a string quartet on Russian folk motifs. In 1959 he was appointed to the faculty of the Leningrad Cons. For further study of folk music he traveled into the countryside, in the rural regions of Pskov and Novgorod. Concurrently, he explored the technical modalities of new music, in the tradition of Soviet modernism, evolving a considerable complexity of texture in a framework of dissonant counterpoint, while safeguarding the tonal foundation in triadic progressions. Some of his works, such as his opera *Virineya*, represent a contemporary evolution of the Russian national school of composition, broadly diatonic and spaciously songful; his other works tend toward ultra-modern practices, including polytonality, microtonality, dodecaphony, tone-clusters, amplified sound, prepared piano, electronic sonorism, aleatory proceedings, and spatial placement of instruments. His Concerto for Orch. employs electronically amplified guitars and solo instruments; even more advanced is his *Antiphones* for String Quartet, employing non-tempered tuning and an "ambulatory" setting, in which the players are placed in different parts of the hall and then walk, while playing, en route to the podium; the piece is especially popular at modern music festivals. A prolific composer, he has written 9 syms. and a remarkably varied catalogue of chamber music pieces which he produces with a facility worthy of Rossini. He also has an easy hand with choral works. Although his natural impulse tends towards the newest sound elements, he proves remarkably successful in gathering and transforming folk motifs and rhythms, as in his *Novgorod* choruses, composed for the American Festival of Soviet Music of 1988. The most unusual subject, for a Soviet composer, was an opera based on the life and death of the Catholic Queen of Scotland, Mary Stuart. *Mary Stuart* was 1st produced in Kuibyshev on Oct. 1, 1983, and then subsequently performed in Leningrad and in Leipzig (1984). It was then selected for a gala production at the Edinburgh Festival in Scotland, where it was given on Aug. 22, 1986, by the Leningrad Opera in a performance in the Russian language. The score utilizes authentic Scottish folk songs, suitably arranged in modern harmonies, as well as original themes in the pentatonic scale. The opera received the prestigious Glinka Prize in 1983. Slonimsky encountered considerable difficulties in producing his chamber opera, *The Master and Margarita*, after a novel by Bulgakov, because the subject had to do with mystical religious events. The Soviet authorities delayed its production for nearly 15 years. Finally, with a liberal change in the political climate, the opera was produced, 1st in East Germany, and, eventually and to considerable acclaim, in Leningrad, on Dec. 1, 1989. Practically all of his music, including the operas, has been publ. Apart from his work as a composer and teacher, Slonimsky contributes music criticism to Soviet magazines; he also publ. a valuable analytic survey, *The Symphonies of Prokofiev* (Leningrad, 1976).

Sorabji, Kaikhosru Shapurji (actually, **Leon Dudley**), remarkable English pianist, writer on music, and composer of unique gifts; b. Chingford, Aug. 14, 1892; d. Wareham, Dorset, Oct. 14, 1988. His father was a Parsi, his mother of Spanish-Sicilian extraction. He was largely self-taught in music; after appearing with notable success as a pianist in London, Paris, Vienna (1921–22), Glasgow, and Bombay, he gave up the concert platform and began writing on music. Through sheer perseverance and an almost mystical belief in his demiurgic powers, he developed an idiom of composition of extraordinary complexity, embodying within the European framework of harmonies the Eastern types of melodic lines and asymmetrical rhythmic patterns, and creating an enormously intricate but architectonically stable edifice of sound. His most arresting work is his magisterial *Opus Clavicembalisticum*, completed in 1930, taking about 5 hours to play and comprising 3 parts with 12 subdivisions, including a theme with 49 variations and a passacaglia with 81 variations; characteristically, the score is dedicated to "the everlasting glory of those few men blessed and sanctified in the curses and execrations of those many whose praise is eternal damnation." Sorabji gave its premiere in Glasgow under the auspices of the Active Society for the Propagation of Contemporary Music on Dec. 1, 1930. Wrathful at the lack of interest in his music, Sorabji issued in 1936 a declaration forbidding any performance of his works by anyone anywhere; since this prohibition could not be sustained for works actually publ., there must have been furtive performances of his piano works in England and the U.S. by fearless pianists. Sorabji eventually mitigated his ban, and in 1975 allowed the American pianist Michael Habermann to perform some of his music; in 1976 he also gave his blessing to the English pianist Yonty Solomon, who included Sorabji's works in a London concert on Dec. 7, 1976; on June 16, 1977, Solomon gave in London the 1st performance of Sorabji's 3rd Piano Sonata. Gradually, Sorabji's music became the cynosure and the lodestone of titanically endowed pianists. Of these, the most Brobdingnagian was the Australian pianist Geoffrey Madge, who gave the second complete performance in history of *Opus Clavicembalisticum* at the 1982 Holland Festival in Utrecht; he repeated this feat at the 1st American performance of the work at the Univ. of Chicago on April 24, 1983; 2 weeks later he played it in Bonn. True to his estrangement from the human multitudes and music officials, Sorabji took refuge far from the madding crowd in a castle he owned in England; a notice at the gate proclaims: Visitors Unwelcome. Yet as he approached his 90th birthday, he received at least 2 American musicians who came to declare their admiration, and allowed them to photocopy some of his MSS.

Stokowski, Leopold (Anthony), celebrated, spectacularly endowed, and magically communicative English-born American conductor; b. London (of a Polish father and an Irish mother), April 18, 1882; d. Nether Wallop, Hampshire, Sept. 13, 1977. He attended Queen's College, Oxford, and the Royal College of Music in London, where he studied organ with Stevenson Hoyte, music theory with Walford Davies, and composition with Sir Charles Stanford. At the age of 18 he obtained the post of organist at St. James, Piccadilly. In 1905 he went to America and served as organist and choirmaster at St. Bartholomew's in N.Y.; became a U.S. citizen in 1915. In 1909 he was engaged to conduct the Cincinnati Sym. Orch.; although his contract was for 5 years, he obtained a release in 1912 in order to accept an offer from the Philadelphia Orch. This was the beginning of a long and spectacular career as a sym. conductor; he led the Philadelphia Orch. for 24 years as its sole conductor, bringing it to a degree of brilliance that rivaled the greatest orchs. in the world. In 1931 he was officially designated by the board of directors of the Philadelphia Orch. as music director, which gave him control over the choice of guest conductors and soloists. He conducted most of the repertoire by heart, an impressive accomplishment at the time; he changed the seating of the orch., placing violins to the left and cellos to the right. After some years of leading the orch. with a baton, he finally dispensed with it and shaped the music with the 10 fingers of his hands. He emphasized the colorful elements in the music; he was the creator of the famous "Philadelphia sound" in the strings, achieving a well-nigh *bel canto* quality. Tall and slender, with an aureole of blond hair, his figure presented a striking contrast with his stocky, mustachioed German predecessors; he was the 1st conductor to attain the status of a star comparable to that of a motion picture actor. Abandoning the proverbial ivory tower in which most conductors dwelt, he actually made an appearance as a movie actor in the film *One Hundred Men and a Girl*. In 1940 he agreed to participate in the production of Walt Disney's celebrated film *Fantasia*, which featured both live performers and animated characters; Stokowski conducted the music and in one sequence engaged in a bantering colloquy with Mickey Mouse. He was lionized by the Philadelphians; in 1922 he received the Edward Bok Award of $10,000 as "the person who has done the most for Philadelphia." He was praised in superlative terms in the press, but not all music critics approved of his cavalier treatment of sacrosanct masterpieces, for he allowed himself to alter the orchestration; he doubled some solo passages in the brass, and occasionally introduced percussion instruments not provided in the score; he even cut out individual bars that seemed to him devoid of musical action. Furthermore, Stokowski's own orch. arrangements of Bach raised the pedantic eyebrows of professional musicologists; yet there is no denying the effectiveness of the sonority and the subtlety of color that he succeeded in creating by such means. Many great musicians hailed Stokowski's new orch. sound; Rachmaninoff regarded the Philadelphia Orch. under Stokowski, and later under Ormandy, as the greatest with which he had performed. Stokowski boldly risked his popularity with the Philadelphia audiences by introducing modern works. He conducted Schoenberg's music, culminating in the introduction of his formidable score *Gurre-Lieder* on April 8, 1932. An even greater gesture of defiance of popular tastes was his world premiere of *Amériques* by Varèse on April 9, 1926, a score that opens with a siren and thrives on dissonance. Stokowski made history by joining the forces of the Philadelphia Orch. with the Philadelphia Grand Opera Co. in the 1st American performance of Berg's masterpiece *Wozzeck* (March 31, 1931). The opposition of some listeners was now vocal; when the audible commotion in the audience erupted during his performance of Webern's Sym., he abruptly stopped conducting, walked off the stage, then returned only to begin the work all over again. From his earliest years with the Philadelphia Orch., Stokowski adopted the habit of addressing the audience, to caution them to keep their peace during the performance of a modernistic score, or reprimanding them for their lack of progressive views; once he even took to task the prim Philadelphia ladies for bringing their knitting to the concert. In 1933 the board of directors took an unusual step in announcing that there would be no more "debatable music" performed by the orch.; Stokowski refused to heed this proclamation. Another eruption of discontent ensued when he programmed some Soviet music at a youth concert and trained the children to sing the Internationale. Stokowski was always interested in new electronic sound; he was the 1st to make use of the Theremin in the orch. in order to enhance the sonorities of the bass section. He was instrumental in introducing electrical recordings. In 1936 he resigned as music director of the Philadelphia Orch.; he was succeeded by Eugene Ormandy, but continued to conduct concerts as co-conductor of the orch. until 1938. From 1940 to 1942 he took a newly organized All-American Youth Orch. on a tour in the U.S. and in South America. During the season 1942–43 he was associate conductor, with Toscanini, of the NBC Sym. Orch.; he shared the season of 1949–50 with Mitropoulos as conductor of the N.Y. Phil.; from 1955 to 1960 he conducted the Houston Sym. Orch. In 1962 he organized in N.Y. the American Sym. Orch. and led it until 1972; on April 26, 1965, at the age of 83, he conducted the orch. in the 1st complete performance of the 4th Sym. of Charles Ives. In 1973 he went to London, where he continued to make recordings and conduct occasional concerts; he also appeared in television interviews. He died in his sleep at the age of 95; rumor had it that he had a contract signed for a gala performance on his 100th birthday in 1982. Stokowski was married 3 times: his 1st wife was the pianist **Olga Samaroff**, whom he married in 1911; they were divorced in 1923; his 2nd wife was Evangeline Brewster Johnson, heiress to the Johnson and Johnson drug fortune; they were married in 1926 and divorced in 1937; his 3rd marriage, to Gloria Vanderbilt, produced a ripple of prurient newspaper publicity because of the disparity in their ages; he was 63, she was 21; they were married in 1945 and divorced in 1955. Stokowski publ. *Music for All of Us* (N.Y., 1943), which was translated into the Russian, Italian, and Czech languages.

Stravinsky, Igor (Feodorovich), great Russian-born French, later American composer, one of the supreme masters of 20th-century music, whose works exercised the most profound influence on the evolution of music through the emancipation of rhythm, melody, and harmony, son of **Feodor (Ignatievich)** and father of **Sviatoslav Soulima Stravinsky**; b. Oranienbaum, near St. Petersburg, June 17, 1882; d. N.Y., April 6, 1971 (his body was flown to Venice and buried in the Russian corner of the cemetery island of San Michele). He was brought up in an artistic atmosphere; he often went to opera rehearsals when his father sang, and acquired an early love for the musical theater. He took piano lessons with Alexandra Snetkova, and later with Leokadia Kashperova, who was a pupil of Anton Rubinstein; but it was not until much later that he began to study music theory, 1st with Akimenko and then with Kalafati (1900–1903). His progress in composition was remarkably slow; he never entered a music school or a cons., and never earned an academic degree in music. In 1901 he enrolled in the faculty of jurisprudence at St. Petersburg Univ., and took courses there for 8 semesters, without graduating; a fellow student was Vladimir Rimsky-Korsakov, a son of the composer. In the summer of 1902 Stravinsky traveled in Germany, where he met another son of Rimsky-Korsakov, Andrei, who was a student at the Univ. of Heidelberg; Stravinsky became his friend. He was introduced to Rimsky-Korsakov, and became a regular guest at the latter's periodic gatherings in St. Petersburg. In 1903–4 he wrote a piano sonata for the Russian pianist Nicolai Richter, who performed it at Rimsky-Korsakov's home. In 1905 he began taking regular lessons in orchestration with Rimsky-Korsakov, who taught him free of charge; under his tutelage Stravinsky composed a Sym. in E-flat major; the 2nd and 3rd movements from it were performed on April 27, 1907, by the Court Orch. in St. Petersburg, and a complete performance of it was given by the same orch. on Feb. 4, 1908. The work, dedicated to Rimsky-Korsakov, had some singularities and angularities that showed a deficiency of technique; there was little in this work that presaged Stravinsky's ultimate development as a master of form and orchestration. At the same concert, his *Le Faune et la bergère* for Voice and Orch. had its 1st performance; this score revealed a certain influence of French Impressionism. To celebrate the marriage of Rimsky-Korsakov's daughter Nadezhda to the composer Maximilian Steinberg on June 17, 1908, Stravinsky wrote an orch. fantasy entitled *Fireworks*. Rimsky-Korsakov died a few days after the wedding; Stravinsky deeply mourned his beloved teacher and wrote a funeral song for Wind Instruments in his memory; it was 1st performed in St. Petersburg on Jan. 30, 1909. There followed a *Scherzo fantastique* for Orch., inspired by Maeterlinck's book *La Vie des abeilles*. As revealed in his correspondence with Rimsky-Korsakov, Stravinsky had at 1st planned a literal program of composition, illustrating events in the life of a beehive by a series of descriptive sections; some years later, however, he gratuitously denied all connection of the work with Maeterlinck's book.

A signal change in Stravinsky's fortunes came when the famous impresario Diaghilev commissioned him to write a work for the Paris season of his company, the Ballets Russes. The result was the production of his 1st ballet masterpiece, *The*

Firebird, staged by Diaghilev in Paris on June 25, 1910. Here he created music of extraordinary brilliance, steeped in the colors of Russian fairy tales. There are numerous striking effects in the score, such as a glissando of harmonics in the string instruments; the rhythmic drive is exhilarating, and the use of asymmetrical time signatures is extremely effective; the harmonies are opulent; the orchestration is coruscating. He drew 2 orch. suites from the work; in 1919 he reorchestrated the music to conform to his new beliefs in musical economy; in effect he plucked the luminous feathers off the magical firebird, but the original scoring remained a favorite with conductors and orchs. Stravinsky's association with Diaghilev demanded his presence in Paris, which he made his home beginning in 1911, with frequent travels to Switzerland. His 2nd ballet for Diaghilev was *Pétrouchka*, produced in Paris on June 13, 1911, with triumphant success. Not only was the ballet remarkably effective on the stage, but the score itself, arranged in 2 orch. suites, was so new and original that it marked a turning point in 20th-century music; the spasmodically explosive rhythms, the novel instrumental sonorities, with the use of the piano as an integral part of the orch., the bold harmonic innovations in employing 2 different keys simultaneously (C major and F-sharp major, the "Pétrouchka Chord") became a potent influence on modern European composers. Debussy voiced his enchantment with the score, and young Stravinsky, still in his 20s, became a Paris celebrity. Two years later, he brought out a work of even greater revolutionary import, the ballet *Le Sacre du printemps* (Rite of Spring; Russian title, *Vesna sviashchennaya*, literally Spring the Sacred); its subtitle was "Scenes of Pagan Russia." It was produced by Diaghilev with his Ballets Russes in Paris on May 29, 1913, with the choreography by Nijinsky. The score marked a departure from all conventions of musical composition; while in *Pétrouchka* the harmonies, though innovative and dissonant, could still be placed in the context of modern music, the score of *Le Sacre du printemps* contained such corrosive dissonances as scales played at the intervals of major sevenths and superpositions of minor upon major triads with the common tonic, chords treated as unified blocks of sound, and rapid metrical changes that seemingly defied performance. The score still stands as one of the most daring creations of the modern musical mind; its impact was tremendous; to some of the audience at its 1st performance in Paris, Stravinsky's "barbaric" music was beyond endurance; the Paris critics exercised their verbal ingenuity in indignant vituperation; one of them proposed that *Le Sacre du printemps* should be more appropriately described as *Le Massacre du printemps*. On May 26, 1914, Diaghilev produced Stravinsky's lyric fairy tale *Le Rossignol*, after Hans Christian Andersen. It too abounded in corrosive discords, but here it could be explained as "Chinese" music illustrative of the exotic subject. From 1914 to 1918 he worked on his ballet *Les Noces* (Russian title, *Svadebka*; literally, Little Wedding), evoking Russian peasant folk modalities; it was scored for an unusual ensemble of chorus, soloists, 4 pianos, and 17 percussion instruments.

The devastation of World War I led Stravinsky to conclude that the era of grandiose Romantic music had become obsolete, and that a new spirit of musical economy was imperative in an impoverished world. As an illustration of such economy, he wrote the musical stage play *L'Histoire du soldat*, scored for only 7 players, with a narrator. About the same time he wrote a work for 11 instruments entitled *Ragtime*, inspired by the new American dance music. He continued his association with Diaghilev's Ballets Russes in writing the ballet *Pulcinella*, based on themes by Pergolesi and other 18th-century Italian composers. He also wrote for Diaghilev 2 short operas, *Renard*, to a Russian fairy tale (Paris, May 18, 1922), and *Mavra*, after Pushkin (Paris, June 3, 1922). These 2 works were the last in which he used Russian subjects, with the sole exception of an orch. *Scherzo à la russe*, written in 1944. Stravinsky had now entered the period usually designated as neo-Classical. The most significant works of this stage of his development were his Octet for Wind Instruments and the Piano Concerto commissioned by Koussevitzky. In these works, he abandoned the luxuriant instrumentation of his ballets and their aggressively dissonant harmonies; instead, he used pandiatonic structures, firmly tonal but starkly dissonant in their superposition of tonalities within the same principal key. His reversion to old forms, however, was not an act of ascetic renunciation but, rather, a grand experiment in reviving Baroque practices, which had fallen into desuetude. The Piano Concerto provided him with an opportunity to appear as soloist; Stravinsky was never a virtuoso pianist, but he was able to acquit himself satisfactorily in such works as the Piano Concerto; he played it with Koussevitzky in Paris on May 22, 1924, and during his 1st American tour with the Boston Sym. Orch., also under Koussevitzky, on Jan. 23, 1925. The Elizabeth Sprague Coolidge Foundation commissioned him to write a pantomime for string orch.; the result was *Apollon Musagète*, given at the Library of Congress in Washington, D.C., on April 27, 1928. This score, serene and emotionally restrained, evokes the manner of Lully's court ballets. He continued to explore the resources of neo-Baroque writing in his *Capriccio* for Piano and Orch., which he performed as soloist, with Ansermet conducting, in Paris, on Dec. 6, 1929; this score is impressed by a spirit of hedonistic entertainment, harking back to the *style galant* of the 18th century; yet it is unmistakably modern in its polyrhythmic collisions of pandiatonic harmonies. Stravinsky's growing disillusionment with the external brilliance of modern music led him to seek eternal verities of music in ancient modalities. His well-nigh monastic renunciation of the grandiose edifice of glorious sound to which he himself had so abundantly contributed found expression in his operaoratorio *Oedipus Rex*; in order to emphasize its detachment from temporal aspects, he commissioned a Latin text for the work, even though the subject was derived from a Greek play; its music is deliberately hollow and its dramatic points are emphasized by ominous repetitive passages. Yet this very austerity of idiom makes *Oedipus Rex* a profoundly moving play. It had its 1st performance on May 30, 1927; its stage premiere took place in Vienna on Feb. 23, 1928. A turn to religious writing found its utterance in Stravinsky's *Symphony of Psalms*, written for the 50th anniversary of the Boston Sym. and dedicated "to the glory of God." The work is scored for chorus and orch., omitting the violins and violas, thus emphasizing the lower instrumental registers and creating an austere sonority suitable to its solemn subject. Owing to a delay of the Boston performance, the world premiere of the *Symphony of Psalms* took place in Brussels on Dec. 13, 1930. In 1931 he wrote a Violin Concerto commissioned by the violinist Samuel Dushkin, and performed by him in Berlin on Oct. 23, 1931. On a commission from the ballerina Ida Rubinstein, he composed the ballet *Perséphone*; here again he exercised his mastery of simplicity in formal design, melodic patterns, and contrapuntal structure. For his American tour he wrote *Jeu de cartes*, a "ballet in 3 deals" to his own scenario depicting an imaginary game of poker (of which he was a devotee). He conducted its 1st performance at the Metropolitan Opera in N.Y. on April 27, 1937. His concerto for 16 instruments entitled *Dumbarton Oaks*, named after the Washington, D.C., estate of Mr. and Mrs. Robert Woods Bliss, who commissioned the work, was 1st performed in Washington, on May 8, 1938; in Europe it was played under the noncommittal title *Concerto in E-flat*; its style is hermetically neo-Baroque. It is germane to note that in his neo-Classical works Stravinsky began to indicate the key in the title, e.g., Concerto in D for Violin and Orch. (1931), Concerto in E-flat (*Dumbarton Oaks*, 1938), Sym. in C (1938), Concerto in D for String Orch. (1946), and Serenade in A for Piano (1925).

With World War II engulfing Europe, Stravinsky decided to seek permanent residence in America. He had acquired French citizenship on June 10, 1934; in 1939 he applied for American citizenship; he became an American citizen on Dec. 28, 1945. To celebrate this event he made an arrangement of the *Star-Spangled Banner*, which contained a curious modulation into the subdominant in the coda. He conducted it with the Boston Sym. on Jan. 14, 1944, but because of legal injunctions existing in the state of Massachusetts against intentional alteration, or any mutilation, of the national anthem, he was advised not to conduct his version at the 2nd pair of concerts, and the standard version was substituted. In 1939–40 Stravinsky was named Charles Eliot Norton lecturer at Harvard Univ.; about the same time he accepted several private students, a pedagogical role he had never exercised before. His American years form a curious panoply of subjects and manners of composition. He accepted a commission from the Ringling Bros. to write a *Circus Polka* "for a young elephant." In 1946 he wrote *Ebony Concerto* for a swing band. In 1951 he completed his opera *The Rake's Progress*, inspired by Hogarth's famous series of engravings, to a libretto by W.H. Auden and C. Kallman. He conducted its world premiere in Venice, on Sept. 11, 1951, as part of the International Festival of Contemporary Music there. The opera is a striking example of Stravinsky's protean capacity for adopting different styles and idioms of composition to serve his artistic purposes; *The Rake's Progress* is an ingenious conglomeration of disparate elements, ranging from 18th-century British ballads to cosmopolitan burlesque. But whatever transmutations his music underwent during his long and productive career, he remained a man of the theater at heart. In America he became associated with the brilliant Russian choreographer Balanchine, who produced a number of ballets to Stravinsky's music, among them his *Apollon Musagète*, Violin Concerto, Sym. in 3 movements, *Scherzo à la russe*, *Pulcinella*, and *Agon*. It was in his score of *Agon* that he essayed for the 1st time to adopt the method of composition with 12 tones as promulgated by Schoenberg; *Agon* (the word means "competition" in Greek) bears the subtitle "ballet for 12 tones," perhaps in allusion to the dodecaphonic technique used in the score. Yet the 12-tone method had been the very antithesis of his previous tenets. In fact, an irreconcilable polarity existed between Stravinsky and Schoenberg even in personal relations. Although both resided in Los Angeles for several years, they never met socially; Schoenberg once wrote a canon in which he ridiculed Stravinsky as Herr Modernsky, who put on a wig to look like "Papa Bach." After Schoenberg's death, Stravinsky became interested in examining the essence of the method of composition with 12 tones, which was introduced to him by his faithful musical factotum Robert Craft; Stravinsky adopted dodecaphonic writing in its aspect of canonic counterpoint as developed by Webern. In this manner he wrote his *Canticum sacrum ad honorem Sancti Marci nominis*, which he conducted at San Marco in Venice on Sept. 13, 1956. Other works of the period were also written in a modified 12-tone technique, among them *The Flood*, for Narrator, Mime, Singers, and Dancers, presented in a CBS-TV broadcast in N.Y. on June 14, 1962; its 1st stage performance was given in Hamburg on April 30, 1963.

Stravinsky was married twice; his 1st wife, Catherine Nosenko, whom he married on Jan. 24, 1906, and who bore him 3 children, died in 1939; on March 9, 1940, Stravinsky married his longtime mistress, Vera, who was formerly married to the Russian painter Serge Sudeikin. She was born Vera de Bosset in St. Petersburg, on Dec. 25, 1888, and died in N.Y. on Sept. 17, 1982, at the age of 93. An ugly litigation for the rights to the Stravinsky estate continued for several years between his children and their stepmother; after Vera Stravinsky's death, it was finally settled in a compromise, according to which 2/9 of the estate went to each of his 3 children and a grandchild and 1/9 to Robert Craft. The value of the

Stravinsky legacy was spectacularly demonstrated on Nov. 11, 1982, when his working draft of *Le Sacre du printemps* was sold at an auction in London for the fantastic sum of $548,000, higher than any MS by any composer. The purchaser was Paul Sacher, the Swiss conductor and philanthropist. Even more fantastic was the subsequent sale of the entire Stravinsky archive, consisting of 116 boxes of personal letters and 225 drawers containing MSS, some of them unpubl. Enormous bids were made for it by the N.Y. Public Library and the Morgan Library, but they were all outbid by Sacher, who offered the overwhelming purse of $5,250,000, which removed all competition. The materials were to be assembled in a specially constructed 7-story Sacher Foundation building in Basel, to be eventually opened to scholars for study.

In tribute to Stravinsky as a naturalized American citizen, the U.S. Postal Service issued a 2-cent stamp bearing his image to mark his centennial in 1982, an honor theretofore never granted to a foreign-born composer (the possible exception being Victor Herbert, but his entire career was made in America).

Few composers escaped the powerful impact of Stravinsky's music; ironically, it was his own country that had rejected him, partly because of the opposition of Soviet ideologues to modern music in general, and partly because of Stravinsky's open criticism of Soviet ways in art. But in 1962 he returned to Russia for a visit, and was welcomed as a prodigal son; as if by magic, his works began to appear on Russian concert programs, and Soviet music critics issued a number of laudatory studies of his works. Yet it is Stravinsky's early masterpieces, set in an attractive colorful style, that continue to enjoy favor with audiences and performers, while his more abstract and recursive scores are appreciated mainly by specialists.

Sumac, Yma (real name **Emperatriz Chavarri**), Peruvian-born American singer of a phenomenal diapason, whose origin is veiled in mystical mist; b. Ichocan, Sept. 10, 1927. She was reared in the Andes; it is credible that she developed her phenomenal voice of 5 octaves in range because her lungs were inflated by the necessity of breathing enough oxygen at the high altitude. However that might be, she married Moises Vivanco, who was an arranger for Capitol Records and who launched her on a flamboyant career as a concert singer; with him and their cousin, Cholito Rivero, she toured South America as the Inca Taky Trio (1942–46); then settled in the U.S. and became a naturalized citizen in 1955. She was billed by unscrupulous promoters as an Inca princess, a direct descendant of Atahualpa, the last emperor of the Incas, a Golden Virgin of the Sun God worshiped by the Quechua Indians. On the other hand, some columnists spread the scurrilous rumor that she was in actuality a Jewish girl from Brooklyn whose real name was Amy (retrograde of Yma) Camus (retrograde of Sumac). But Sumac never spoke with a Brooklyn accent. She exercised a mesmeric appeal to her audiences, from South America to Russia, from California to Central Europe; expressions such as "miraculous" and "amazing" were used by Soviet reviewers during her tour of Russia in 1962; "supersonic vocal skill" was a term applied by an American critic. Her capacity did not diminish with age; during her California appearances in 1984 and again in 1988 she still impressed her audiences with the expressive power of her voice.

Tatum, Art(hur), noted black American jazz pianist; b. Toledo, Ohio, Oct. 13, 1910; d. Los Angeles, Nov. 5, 1956. He was blind in one eye and had limited vision in the other; he attended a school for the blind in Columbus, Ohio, and learned to read Braille music notation; at the age of 16, began to play in nightclubs. In 1932 he went to N.Y. and became successful on the radio. In 1938 he made a spectacular tour of England; then pursued his career in N.Y. and Los Angeles; organized his own trio in 1943. In 1947 he appeared in the film *The*

Fabulous Dorseys. His art as a jazz improviser was captured on more than 600 recordings. He brought "stride" piano playing to a point of perfection, scorning such academic niceties as proper fingering, but achieving small miracles with ornamental figurations in the melody while throwing effortless cascades of notes across the keyboard; he also had a knack of improvising variations on popular pieces by defenseless deceased classical composers; his audiences adored Art's art, while professional musicians knitted their brows in wild surmise.

Tenducci, Giusto Ferdinando, celebrated Italian castrato soprano, nicknamed "Triorchis" (triple-testicled); b. Siena, c.1735; d. Genoa, Jan. 25, 1790. He made appearances in Venice and Naples before going to London in 1758; there he sang at the King's Theatre until 1760; after a stay in a debtor's prison, he resumed his career and secured a notable success as Arbaces in the premiere of Arne's *Artaxerxes* in 1762; was again active at the King's Theatre (1763–66). He then went to Ireland, where he contracted a marriage with his 16-year-old pupil Dora Maunsell in Cork; outraged members of her family had him jailed and his new bride spirited away; shortly afterward, however, the 2 were reunited and allegedly produced 2 children. After a sojourn in Edinburgh, he returned to England in 1770 and sang at the Worcester Three Choirs Festival; then was a featured artist in the Bach-Abel Concerts in London. By 1778 he was in Paris; sang again in London in 1785. He adapted 4 operas for the Dublin stage, and also wrote English, French, and Italian songs. His wife is reputed to have been the author of the book *A True Genuine Narrative of Mr and Mrs Tenducci* (1768).

Tchaikovsky, Piotr Ilyich, famous Russian composer, brother of **Modest Tchaikovsky**; b. Votkinsk, Viatka district, May 7, 1840; d. St. Petersburg, Nov. 6, 1893. The son of a mining inspector at a plant in the Urals, he was given a good education; had a French governess and a music teacher. When he was 10, the family moved to St. Petersburg and he was sent to a school of jurisprudence, from which he graduated at 19, becoming a government clerk; while at school he studied music with Lomakin, but did not display conspicuous talent as either a pianist or composer. At the age of 21 he was accepted in a musical inst., newly established by Anton Rubinstein, which was to become the St. Petersburg Cons. He studied with Zaremba (harmony and counterpoint) and Rubinstein (composition); graduated in 1865, winning a silver medal for his cantata to Schiller's *Hymn to Joy*. In 1866 he became prof. of harmony at the Moscow Cons. As if to compensate for a late beginning in his profession, he began to compose with great application. His early works (a programmatic sym. subtitled *Winter Dreams*, some overtures and small pieces for string quartet) reveal little individuality. With his symphonic poem *Fatum* (1868) came the 1st formulation of his style, highly subjective, preferring minor modes, permeated with nostalgic longing and alive with keen rhythms. In 1869 he undertook the composition of his overture-fantasy *Romeo and Juliet*; not content with what he had written, he profited by the advice of Balakirev, whom he met in St. Petersburg, and revised the work in 1870; but this version proved equally unsatisfactory; Tchaikovsky laid the composition aside, and did not complete it until 1880; in its final form it became one of his most successful works. The Belgian soprano, Désirée Artôt, a member of an opera troupe visiting St. Petersburg in 1868, took great interest in Tchaikovsky, and he was moved by her attentions; for a few months he seriously contemplated marriage, and so notified his father (his mother had died of cholera when he was 14 years old). But this proved to be a passing infatuation on her part, for soon she married the Spanish singer Padilla; Tchaikovsky reacted to this event with a casual philosophical remark about the inconstancy of human attachments. Throughout his career Tchaikovsky never allowed his psychological turmoil to interfere with his work. Besides teaching and composing, he contributed music criticism to Moscow newspapers for several years (1868–74), made altogether 26 trips abroad (to Paris, Berlin, Vienna, N.Y.), and visited the 1st Bayreuth Festival in 1876, reporting his impressions for the Moscow daily *Russkyie Vedomosti*. His closest friends were members of his own family, his brothers (particularly Modest, his future biographer), and his married sister Alexandra Davidov, at whose estate, Kamenka, he spent most of his summers. The correspondence with them, all of which was preserved and eventually publ., throws a true light on Tchaikovsky's character and his life. His other close friends were his publisher, Jurgenson, Nikolai Rubinstein, and several other musicians. The most extraordinary of his friendships was the epistolary association with Nadezhda von Meck, a wealthy widow whom he never met but who was to play an important role in his life. Through the violinist Kotek she learned about Tchaikovsky's financial difficulties, and commissioned him to write some compositions, at large fees; then arranged to pay him an annuity of 6,000 rubles. For more than 13 years they corresponded voluminously, even when they lived in the same city (Moscow, Florence); on several occasions she hinted that she would not be averse to a personal meeting, but Tchaikovsky invariably declined such a suggestion, under the pretext that one should not see one's guardian angel in the flesh. On Tchaikovsky's part, this correspondence had to remain within the circumscribed domain of art, personal philosophy, and reporting of daily events, without touching on the basic problems of his existence. On July 18, 1877, he contracted marriage with a conservatory student, Antonina Milyukova, who had declared her love for him. This was an act of defiance of his own nature; Tchaikovsky was a homosexual, and made no secret of it in the correspondence with his brother Modest, who was also a homosexual. He thought that by flaunting a wife he could prevent the already rife rumors about his sexual preference from spreading further. The result was disastrous, and Tchaikovsky fled from his wife in horror. He attempted suicide by walking into the Moskva River in order to catch pneumonia, but suffered nothing more severe than simple discomfort. He then went to St. Petersburg to seek the advice of his brother Anatol, a lawyer, who made suitable arrangements with Tchaikovsky's wife for a separation. (They were never divorced; she died in an insane asylum in 1917). Von Meck, to whom Tchaikovsky wrote candidly of the hopeless failure of his marriage (without revealing the true cause of that failure), made at once an offer of further financial assistance, which he gratefully accepted. He spent several months during 1877–78 in Italy, Switzerland, Paris, and Vienna. During these months he completed one of his greatest works, the 4th Sym., dedicated to von Meck. It was performed for the 1st time in Moscow on Feb. 22, 1878, but Tchaikovsky did not cut short his sojourn abroad to attend the performance. He resigned from the Moscow Cons. in the autumn of 1878, and from that time dedicated himself entirely to composition. The continued subsidy from von Meck allowed him to forget money matters. Early in 1878 he completed his most successful opera, *Evgeny Onegin* ("lyric scenes," after Pushkin); it was 1st produced in Moscow by a cons. ensemble, on March 29, 1879, and gained success only gradually; the 1st performance at the Imperial Opera in St. Petersburg did not take place until Oct. 31, 1884. A morbid depression was still Tchaikovsky's natural state of mind, but every new work sustained his faith in his destiny as a composer, despite many disheartening reversals. His Piano Concerto No. 1, rejected by Nikolai Rubinstein as unplayable, was given its world premiere (somewhat incongruously) in Boston, on Oct. 25, 1875, played by Hans von Bülow, and afterward was performed all over the world by famous pianists, including Nikolai Rubinstein. The Violin Concerto, criticized by Leopold Auer (to whom the score was originally dedicated) and attacked by Hanslick with sarcasm and virulence at its world premiere by Brodsky in Vienna (1881), survived all its detractors to become one of the most celebrated pieces in the violin repertoire. The 5th Sym. (1888) was successful from the very first. Early in 1890 Tchaikovsky wrote his 2nd important opera, *The Queen of Spades*, which was produced at the Imperial Opera in St. Petersburg in that year. His ballets *Swan Lake* (1876) and *The Sleeping Beauty* (1889) became famous on Russian stages. But at the peak of his career, Tchaikovsky suffered a severe psychological blow; von Meck notified him of the discontinuance of her subsidy, and with this announcement she abruptly terminated their correspondence. He could now well afford the loss of the money, but his pride was deeply hurt by the manner in which von Meck had acted. It is indicative of Tchaikovsky's inner strength that even this desertion of one whom he regarded as his staunchest friend did not affect his ability to work. In 1891 he undertook his only voyage to America. He was received with honors as a celebrated composer; he led 4 concerts of his works in N.Y. and one each in Baltimore and Philadelphia. He did not linger in the U.S., however, and returned to St. Petersburg in a few weeks. Early in 1892 he made a concert tour as a conductor in Russia, and then proceeded to Warsaw and Germany. In the meantime he had purchased a house in the town of Klin, not far from Moscow, where he wrote his last sym., the *Pathétique*. Despite the perfection of his technique, he did not arrive at the desired form and substance of this work at once, and discarded his original sketch. The title *Pathétique* was suggested to him by his brother Modest; the score was dedicated to his nephew, Vladimir Davidov. Its music is the final testament of Tchaikovsky's life, and an epitome of his philosophy of fatalism. In the 1st movement, the trombones are given the theme of the Russian service for the dead. Remarkably, the score of one of his gayest works, the ballet *The Nutcracker*, was composed simultaneously with the early sketches for the *Pathétique*. Tchaikovsky was in good spirits when he went to St. Petersburg to conduct the premiere of the *Pathétique*, on Oct. 28, 1893 (which was but moderately successful). A cholera epidemic was then raging in St. Petersburg, and the population was specifically warned against drinking unboiled water, but apparently he carelessly did exactly that. He showed the symptoms of cholera soon afterward, and nothing could be done to save him. The melodramatic hypothesis that the fatal drink of water was a defiance of death, in perfect knowledge of the danger, since he must have remembered his mother's death of the same dread infection, is untenable in the light of publ. private letters between the attendant physician and Modest Tchaikovsky at the time. Tchaikovsky's fatalism alone would amply account for his lack of precaution. Almost immediately after his death a rumor spread that he had committed suicide, and reports to that effect were publ. in respectable European newspapers (but not in Russian publications), and repeated even in some biographical dictionaries (particularly in Britain). After the grim fantasy seemed definitely refuted, a ludicrous paper by an émigré Russian woman was publ., claiming private knowledge of a homosexual scandal involving a Russian nobleman's nephew (in another version a member of the Romanov imperial family) which led to a "trial" of Tchaikovsky by a jury of his former school classmates, who offered Tchaikovsky a choice between honorable suicide or disgrace and possible exile to Siberia; a family council, with Tchaikovsky's own participation, advised the former solution, and Tchaikovsky was supplied with arsenic; the family doctor was supposed to be a part of the conspiracy, as were Tchaikovsky's own brothers. Amazingly enough, this outrageous fabrication was accepted as historical fact by some biographers, and even found its way into the pages of *The New Grove Dictionary of Music and Musicians* (1980). In Russia, the truth of Tchaikovsky's homosexuality was totally suppressed, and any references to it in his diary and letters were expunged.

As a composer, Tchaikovsky stands apart from the militant national movement of the "Mighty Five." The Russian element is, of course, very strong in his music, and upon occasion he made use of Russian folk songs in his works, but this national spirit is instinctive rather than consciously cultivated. His personal relationship with the St. Petersburg group of nationalists was friendly without being close; his correspondence with Rimsky-Korsakov, Balakirev, and others was mostly concerned with professional matters. Tchaikovsky's music was frankly sentimental; his supreme gift of melody, which none of his Russian contemporaries could match, secured for him a lasting popularity among performers and audiences. His influence was profound on the Moscow group of musicians, of whom Arensky and Rachmaninoff were the most talented. He wrote in every genre, and was successful in each; besides his stage works, syms., chamber music, and piano compositions, he composed a great number of lyric songs that are the most poignant creations of his genius. By a historical paradox, Tchaikovsky became the most popular Russian composer under the Soviet regime. His subjectivism, his fatalism, his emphasis on melancholy moods, even his reactionary political views (which included a brand of amateurish anti-Semitism), failed to detract from his stature in the new society. In fact, official spokesmen of Soviet Russia repeatedly urged Soviet composers to follow in the path of Tchaikovsky's aesthetics. His popularity is also very strong in Anglo-Saxon countries, particularly in America; much less so in France and Italy; in Germany his influence in insignificant.

Turner, Tina (real name, **Anna Mae Bullock**), pulsating black American soul and rock singer and actress; b. Brownsville, Tenn., Nov. 26, 1939. She joined Ike Turner and his band, the Kings of Rhythm, in St. Louis in 1956; the 2 were married in 1958, and toured the chitlin' circuit as the Ike and Tina Turner Revue, accompanied by a female dance-and-vocal trio named the Ikettes. Their 1st successful recording was *A Fool in Love* (1960); she made an explosive impact as a sexually provocative singer, belting out such numbers as *I've Been Lovin' You Too Long* and *River Deep, Mountain High* (1966). A 1969 tour of the U.S. with the Rolling Stones catapulted the Revue onto center stage; they won a Grammy Award for their recording of *Proud Mary* in 1971. While continuing to make appearances with her husband, she also made the solo albums *Let Me Touch Your Hand* (1972) and *Tina Turns the Country On* (1974). In 1975 she appeared as the Acid Queen in the rock-opera film *Tommy*, and that same year brought out the album *Acid Queen*. Having loved her husband too long, she left him in 1976 and obtained a divorce in 1978. She then pursued a solo career as a raunch-and-roll songstress, producing the tremendously successful album *Private Dancer* in 1984; that same year she won 4 Grammy Awards, with *What's Love Got to Do with It?* being honored as best song and best record of the year. In 1985 she starred in the film *Mad Max beyond Thunderdome*. With K. Loder, she publ. the book *I, Tina: My Life Story* (N.Y., 1986).

Varèse, Edgard (Victor Achille Charles), remarkable French-born American composer, who introduced a totally original principle of organizing the materials and forms of sound, profoundly influencing the direction of new music; b. Paris, Dec. 22, 1883; d. N.Y., Nov. 6, 1965. The original spelling of his first Christian name was Edgard, but most of his works were first publ. under the name **Edgar**; about 1940 he chose to return to the legal spelling. He spent his early childhood in Paris and in Burgundy, and began to compose early in life. In 1892 his parents went to Turin; his paternal grandfather was Italian; his other grandparents were French. He took private lessons in composition with Giovanni Bolzoni, who taught him gratis. Varèse gained some performing experience by playing percussion in the school orch. He stayed there until 1903; then went to Paris. In 1904 he entered the Schola Cantorum, where he studied composition, counterpoint, and fugue with Albert Roussel, preclassical music with Charles Bordes, and conducting with Vincent d'Indy; then entered the composition class of Charles-Marie Widor at the Cons. in 1905. In 1907 he received the "bourse artistique" offered by the City of Paris; at that time he founded and conducted the chorus of the Université Populaire and organized concerts at the Château du Peuple. He became associated with musicians and artists of the avant-garde; also met Debussy, who showed interest in his career. In 1907 he married a young actress, Suzanne Bing; they had a daughter. Together they went to Berlin, at that time the center of new music that offered opportunities to Varèse. The marriage was not successful, and they separated in 1913. Romain Rolland gave to Varèse a letter of recommendation for Richard Strauss, who in turn showed interest in Varèse's music. He was also instrumental in arranging a performance of Varèse's symphonic poem *Bourgogne*, which was performed in Berlin on Dec. 15, 1910. But the greatest experience for Varèse in Berlin was his meeting and friendship with Busoni. Varèse greatly admired Busoni's book on new music esthetics, and was profoundly influenced by Busoni's views. He composed industriously, mostly for orch.; the most ambitious of these works was a symphonic poem, *Gargantua*, but it was never completed. Other works were *Souvenirs, Prélude à la fin d'un jour, Cycles du Nord*, and an incomplete opera, *Oedipus und die Sphinx*, to the text by Hofmannsthal. All these works, in manuscript, were lost under somewhat mysterious circumstances, and Varèse himself destroyed the score of *Bourgogne* later in life. A hostile reception that he encountered from Berlin critics for *Bourgogne* upset Varèse, who expressed his unhappiness in a letter to Debussy. However, Debussy responded with a friendly letter of encouragement, advising Varèse not to pay too much attention to critics. As early as 1913, Varèse began an earnest quest for new musical resources; upon his return to Paris, he worked on related problems with the Italian musical futurist Luigi Russolo, although he disapproved of the attempt to find a way to new music through the medium of instrumental noises. He was briefly called to the French army at the outbreak of the First World War, but was discharged because of a chronic lung ailment. In 1915 he went to N.Y. There he met the young American writer Louise Norton; they set up a household together; in 1921, when she obtained her own divorce from a previous marriage, they were married. As in Paris and Berlin, Varèse had chronic financial difficulties in America; the royalties from his few publ. works were minimal; in order to supplement his earnings he accepted a job as a piano salesman, which was repulsive to him. He also appeared in a minor role in a John Barrymore silent film in 1918. Some welcome aid came from the wealthy artist Gertrude Vanderbilt, who sent him monthly allowances for a certain length of time. Varèse also had an opportunity to appear as a conductor. As the U.S. neared the entrance into war against Germany, there was a demand for French conductors to replace the German music directors who had held the monopoly on American orchs. On April 1, 1917, Varèse conducted in N.Y. the Requiem Mass of Berlioz. On March 17, 1918, he conducted a concert of the Cincinnati Sym. Orch. in a program of French and Russian music; he also included an excerpt from *Lohengrin*, thus defying the general ban on German music. However, he apparently lacked that indefinable quality that makes a conductor, and he was forced to cancel further concerts with the Cincinnati Sym. Orch. Eager to promote the cause of modern music, he organized a sym. orch. in N.Y. with the specific purpose of giving performances of new and unusual music; it presented its first concert on April 11, 1919. In 1922 he organized with Carlos Salzedo the International Composers' Guild, which gave its inaugural concert in N.Y. on Dec. 17, 1922. In 1926 he founded, in association with a few progressive musicians, the Pan American Society, dedicated to the promotion of music of the Americas. He intensified his study of the nature of sound, working with the acoustician Harvey Fletcher (1926–36), and with the Russian electrical engineer Leon Theremin, then resident in the U.S. These studies led him to the formulation of the concept of "organized sound," in which the sonorous elements in themselves determined the progress of composition; this process eliminated conventional thematic development; yet the firm cohesion of musical ideas made Varèse's music all the more solid, while the distinction between consonances and dissonances became no longer of basic validity. The resulting product was unique in modern music; characteristically, Varèse attached to his works titles from the field of mathematics or physics, such as *Intégrales, Hyperprism* (a projection of a prism into the 4th dimension), *Ionisation, Density 21.5* (the specific weight of platinum), etc., while the score of his large orch. work *Arcana* derived its inspiration from the cosmology of Paracelsus. An important development was Varèse's application of electronic music in his *Déserts* and, much more extensively, in his *Poème électronique*, commissioned for the Brussels World Exposition in 1958. He wrote relatively few works in small forms, and none for piano solo. The unfamiliarity of Varèse's idiom and the tremendous difficulty of his orch. works militated against frequent performances. Among conductors, only Leopold Stokowski was bold enough to put Varèse's formidable scores *Amériques* and *Arcana* on his programs with the Philadelphia Orch.; they evoked yelps of derision and outbursts of righteous indignation from the public and the press. Ironically, it was left to a mere beginner, Nicolas Slonimsky, to be the 1st to perform and record Varèse's unique masterpiece, *Ionisation*. An extraordinary reversal of attitudes toward Varèse's music, owing perhaps to the general advance of musical intelligence and the emergence of young music critics, took place within Varèse's lifetime, resulting in a spectacular increase of interest in his works and the number of their performances; also, musicians themselves learned to overcome the rhythmic difficulties presented in Varèse's scores. Thus Varèse lived to witness this long-delayed recognition of his music as a major stimulus of modern art; his name joined those of Stravinsky, Ives, Schoenberg, and Webern among the great masters of 20th-century music. Recognition came also from an unexpected field when scientists working on the atom bomb at Oak Ridge in 1940 played Slonimsky's recording of *Ionisation* for relaxation and stimulation in their work. In 1955 he was elected to membership in the National Inst. of Arts and Letters and in 1962 in the Royal Swedish Academy. He became a naturalized U.S. citizen in 1926. Like Schoenberg, Varèse refused to regard himself as a revolutionary in music; indeed, he professed great admiration for his remote predecessors, particularly those of the Notre Dame school, representing the flowering of the Arts Antiqua. On the centennial of his birth in 1983, festivals of his music were staged in Strasbourg, Paris, Rome, Washington, D.C., N.Y., and Los Angeles. In 1981, Frank Zappa, the leader of the modern school of rock music and a sincere admirer of Varèse's music, staged in N.Y. at his own expense a concert of Varèse's works; he presented a similar concert in San Francisco in 1982.

Wagner, (Wilhelm) Richard, great German composer whose operas, written to his own librettos, have radically transformed the concept of stage music, postulating the inherent equality of drama and symphonic accompaniment, and establishing the uninterrupted continuity of the action; b. Leipzig, May 22, 1813; d. Venice, Feb. 13, 1883. The antecedents of his family, and his own origin, are open to controversy. His father was a police registrar in Leipzig who died when Wagner was only 6 months old; his mother, Johanna (Rosine), née Pätz, was the daughter of a baker in Weissenfels; it is possible also that she was an illegitimate offspring of Prince Friedrich Ferdinand Constantin of Weimar. Eight months after her husband's death, Johanna Wagner married, on Aug. 28, 1814, the actor Ludwig Geyer. This hasty marriage generated speculation that Geyer may have been Wagner's real father; Wagner himself entertained this possibility, pointing out the similarity of his and Geyer's prominent noses; in the end he abandoned this surmise. The problem of Wagner's origin arose with renewed force after the triumph of the Nazi party in Germany, as Hitler's adoration of Wagner was put in jeopardy by suspicions that Geyer might have been Jewish and that if Wagner was indeed his natural son then he himself was tainted by Semitic blood. The phantom of Wagner's possible contamination with Jewish hemoglobin struck horror into the hearts of good Nazi biologists and archivists; they delved anxiously into Geyer's own ancestry, and much to the relief of Goebbels and other Nazi intellectuals, it was found that Geyer, like Wagner's nominal father, was the purest of Aryans; Wagner's possible illegitimate birth was of no concern to the racial tenets of the Nazi *Weltanschauung*.

Geyer was a member of the Court Theater in Dresden, and the family moved there in 1814. Geyer died on Sept. 30, 1821; in 1822 Wagner entered the Dresden Kreuzschule, where he remained a pupil until 1827. Carl Maria von Weber often visited the Geyer home; these visits exercised a beneficial influence on him in his formative years. In 1825 he began to take piano lessons from a local musician named Humann, and also studied violin with Robert Sipp. Wagner showed strong literary inclinations, and under the spell of Shakespeare, wrote a tragedy, *Leubald*. In 1827 he moved with his mother back to Leipzig, where his uncle Adolf Wagner gave him guidance in his classical reading. In 1828 he was enrolled in the Nikolaischule; while in school, he had lessons in harmony with Christian Gottlieb Müller, a violinist in the theater orch. In June 1830 he entered the Thomasschule, where he began to compose; he wrote a String Quartet and some piano music; his *Overture* in B-flat major was performed at the Leipzig Theater on Dec. 24, 1830, under the direction of the famous musician Heinrich Dorn. Now determined to dedicate himself entirely to music, he became a student of Theodor Weinlig, cantor of the Thomaskirche, from whom he received a thorough training in counterpoint and composition. His 1st publ. work was a Piano Sonata in B-flat major, to which he assigned the opus number 1; it was brought out by the prestigious publishing house of Breitkopf & Härtel in 1832. He then wrote an overture to *König Enzio*, which was performed at the Leipzig Theater on Feb. 17, 1832; it was followed by an Overture in C major, which was presented at a Gewandhaus concert on April 30, 1832. Wagner's 1st major orch. work, a Sym. in C major, was performed at a Prague Cons. concert in Nov. 1832; on Jan. 10, 1833, it was played by the Gewandhaus Orch. in Leipzig; he was 19 years old at the time. In 1832 he wrote an opera, *Die Hochzeit*, after J.G. Büsching's *Ritterzeit und Ritterwesen*; an introduction, a septet, and a chorus from this work are extant. Early in 1833 he began work on *Die Feen*, to a libretto after Carlo Gozzi's *La Donna serpente*. Upon completion of *Die Feen* in Jan. 1834, he offered the score to the Leipzig Theater, but it was rejected. In June 1834 he began to sketch out a new opera, *Das Liebesverbot*, after Shakespeare's play *Measure for Measure*. In July 1834 he obtained the position of music director with Heinrich Bethmann's theater company, based in Magdeburg; he made his debut in Bad Lauschstadt, conducting Mozart's *Don Giovanni*. On March 29, 1836, he led in Magdeburg the premiere of his opera *Das Liebesverbot*, presented under the title *Die Novize von Palermo*. Bethmann's company soon went out of business; Wagner, who was by that time deeply involved with Christine Wilhelmine ("Minna") Planer, an actress with the company, followed her to Königsberg, where they were married on Nov. 24, 1836. In Königsberg he composed the overture *Rule Britannia*; on April 1, 1837, he was appointed music director of the

Königsberg town theater. His marital affairs suffered a setback when Minna left him for a rich businessman by the name of Dietrich. In Aug. 1837 he went to Riga as music director of the theater there; coincidentally, Minna's sister was engaged as a singer at the same theater; Minna soon joined her, and became reconciled with Wagner. In Riga Wagner worked on his new opera, *Rienzi, der letzte der Tribunen*, after a popular novel by Bulwer-Lytton.

In March 1839 he lost his position in Riga; he and Minna, burdened by debts, left town to seek their fortune elsewhere. In their passage by sea from Pillau they encountered a fierce storm, and the ship was forced to drop anchor in the Norwegian fjord of Sandwike. They made their way to London, and then set out for Boulogne; there Wagner met Meyerbeer, who gave him a letter of recommendation to the director of the Paris Opéra. He arrived in Paris with Minna in Sept. 1839, and remained there until 1842. He was forced to eke out a meager subsistence by making piano arrangements of operas and writing occasional articles for the *Gazette Musicale*. In Jan. 1840 he completed his Overture to *Faust* (later rev. as *Eine Faust-Ouvertüre*). Soon he found himself in dire financial straits; he owed money that he could not repay, and on Oct. 28, 1840, he was confined in debtors' prison; he was released on Nov. 17, 1840. The conditions of his containment were light, and he was able to leave prison on certain days. In the meantime he had completed the libretto for *Der fliegende Holländer*; he submitted it to the director of the Paris Opéra, but the director had already asked Paul Foucher to prepare a libretto on the same subject. The director was willing, however, to buy Wagner's scenario for 500 French francs; Wagner accepted the offer (July 2, 1841). Louis Dietsch brought out his treatment of the subject in his opera *Le Vaisseau fantôme* (Paris Opéra, Nov. 9, 1842).

In 1842 Wagner received the welcome news from Dresden that his opera *Rienzi* had been accepted for production; it was staged there on Oct. 20, 1842, with considerable success. *Der fliegende Holländer* was also accepted by Dresden, and Wagner conducted its first performance there on Jan. 2, 1843. On Feb. 2 of that year, he was named 2nd Hofkapellmeister in Dresden, where he conducted a large repertoire of Classical operas, among them *Don Giovanni, Le nozze di Figaro, Die Zauberflöte, Fidelio*, and *Der Freischütz*. In 1846 he conducted a memorable performance in Dresden of Beethoven's 9th Sym. In Dresden he led the prestigious choral society Liedertafel, for which he wrote several works, including the "biblical scene" *Das Liebesmahl der Apostel*. He was also preoccupied during those years in working on the score and music for *Tannhäuser*, completing it on April 13, 1845. He conducted its first performance in Dresden on Oct. 19, 1845. He subsequently revised the score, which was staged to better advantage there on Aug. 1, 1847. Concurrently, he began work on *Lohengrin*, which he completed on April 28, 1848. Wagner's efforts to have his works publ. failed, leaving him again in debt. Without waiting for further performances of his operas that had already been presented to the public, he drew up the first prose outline of *Der Nibelungen-Mythus als Entwurf zu einem Drama*, the prototype of the epic *Ring* cycle; in Nov. 1848 he began work on the poem for *Siegfrieds Tod*. At that time he joined the revolutionary Vaterlandsverein, and was drawn into active participation in the movement, culminating in an open uprising in May 1849. An order was issued for his arrest, and he had to leave Dresden; he made his way to Weimar, where he found a cordial reception from Liszt; he then proceeded to Vienna, where a Prof. Widmann lent him his own passport so that Wagner could cross the border of Saxony on his way to Zürich; there he made his home in July 1849; Minna joined him there a few months later. Shortly before leaving Dresden he had sketched 2 dramas, *Jesus von Nazareth* and *Achilleus*; both remained unfinished. In Zürich he wrote a number of essays expounding his philosophy of art: *Die Kunst und die Revolution* (1849), *Das Kunstwerk der Zukunft* (1849), *Kunst und Klima* (1850), *Oper und Drama* (1851; rev. 1868), and *Eine Mitteilung an meine Freunde* (1851). The ideas expressed in *Das Kunstwerk der Zukunft* gave rise to the description of Wagner's operas as "music of the future" by his opponents; they were also described as *Gesamtkunstwerk*, "total artwork," by his admirers. He rejected both descriptions as distortions of his real views. He was equally opposed to the term "music drama," which nevertheless became an accepted definition for all of his operas.

In Feb. 1850 Wagner was again in Paris; there he fell in love with Jessie Laussot, the wife of a wine merchant; however, she eventually left Wagner, and he returned to Minna in Zürich. On Aug. 28, 1850, Liszt conducted the successful premiere of *Lohengrin* in Weimar. In 1851 he wrote the verse text of *Der junge Siegfried*, and prose sketches for *Das Rheingold* and *Die Walküre*. In June 1852 he finished the text of *Die Walküre* and of *Das Rheingold*; he completed the entire libretto of *Der Ring des Nibelungen* on Dec. 15, 1852, and it was privately printed in 1853. In Nov. 1853 he began composition of the music for *Das Rheingold*, completing the full score on Sept. 26, 1854. In June 1854 he commenced work on the music of *Die Walküre*, which he finished on March 20, 1856. In 1854 he became friendly with a wealthy Zürich merchant, Otto Wesendonck, and his wife, Mathilde. Wesendonck was willing to give Wagner a substantial loan, to be repaid out of his performance rights. The situation became complicated when Wagner developed an affection for Mathilde, which in all probability remained Platonic. But he set to music 5 lyric poems written by Mathilde herself; the album was publ. as the *Wesendonk-Lieder* in 1857. In 1855 he conducted a series of 8 concerts with the Phil. Society of London (March 12–June 25). His performances were greatly praised by English musicians, and he had the honor of meeting Queen Victoria, who invited him to her loge at the intermission of his 7th concert. In June 1856 he made substantial revisions in the last dramas of *Der Ring des Nibelungen*, changing their titles to *Siegfried* and *Götterdämmerung*. Throughout these years he was preoccupied with writing a new opera, *Tristan und Isolde*, permeated with the dual feelings of love and death. In April 1857 he prepared the first sketch of *Parzival* (later titled *Parsifal*). In 1858 he moved to Venice, where he completed the full score of the 2nd act of *Tristan und Isolde*. The Dresden authorities, acting through their Austrian confederates and still determined to bring Wagner to trial as a revolutionary, pressured Venice to expel him from its territory. Once more Wagner took refuge in Switzerland; he decided to stay in Lucerne; while there he completed the score of *Tristan und Isolde*, on Aug. 6, 1859.

In Sept. 1859 he moved to Paris, where Minna joined him. In 1860 he conducted 3 concerts of his music at the Théâtre-Italien. Napoleon III became interested in his work, and in March 1860 ordered the director of the Paris Opéra to produce Wagner's opera *Tannhäuser*; after considerable work, revisions, and a tr. into French, it was given at the Opéra on March 13, 1861. It proved to be a fiasco, and Wagner withdrew the opera after 3 performances. For some reason the Jockey Club of Paris led a vehement protest against him; the critics also joined in this opposition, mainly because the French audiences were not accustomed to the mystically romantic, heavily Germanic operatic music. Invectives hurled against him by the Paris press make extraordinary reading; the comparison of Wagner's music with the sound produced by a domestic cat walking down the keyboard of the piano was one of the favorite critical devices. The French caricaturists exercised their wit by picturing him in the act of hammering a poor listener's ear. A Wagner "Schimpflexikon" was compiled by Wilhelm Tappert and publ. in 1877 in the hope of putting Wagner's detractors to shame, but they would not be pacified; the amount of black bile poured on him even after he had attained the stature of celebrity is incredible for its grossness and vulgarity. Hanslick used his great literary gift and a flair for a striking simile to damn him as a purveyor of cacophony. Oscar Wilde added his measure of wit. "I like Wagner's music better than anybody's," he remarked in *The Picture of Dorian Gray*. "It is so loud that one can talk the whole time without people hearing what one says." In an amazing turnabout, Nietzsche, a worshipful admirer of Wagner, publ. a venomous denunciation of his erstwhile idol in *Der Fall Wagner*, in which he vesuviated in a sulfuric eruption of righteous wrath; Wagner made music itself sick, he proclaimed; but at the time Nietzsche himself was already on the borderline of madness.

Politically, Wagner's prospects began to improve; on July 22, 1860, he was informed of a partial amnesty by the Saxon authorities. In Aug. 1860 he visited Baden-Baden, in his 1st visit to Germany in 11 years. Finally, on March 18, 1862, he was granted a total amnesty, which allowed him access to Saxony. In Nov. 1861 Wesendonck had invited Wagner to Venice; free from political persecution, he could now go there without fear. While in Venice he returned to a scenario he had prepared in Marienbad in 1845 for a comic opera, *Die Meistersinger von Nürnberg*. In Feb. 1862 he moved to Biebrich, where he began composing the score for *Die Meistersinger*. Minna, after a brief period of reconciliation with Wagner, left him, settling in Dresden, where she died in 1866. In order to repair his financial situation, he accepted a number of concert appearances, traveling as an orch. conductor to Vienna, Prague, St. Petersburg, Moscow, and other cities (1862–63). In 1862 he gave in Vienna a private reading of *Die Meistersinger*. It is said that the formidable Vienna critic Hanslick was angered when he found out that Wagner had caricatured him in the part of Beckmesser in *Die Meistersinger* (the original name of the character was Hans Lick), and he let out his discomfiture in further attacks on Wagner.

Wagner's fortunes changed spectacularly in 1864 when young King Ludwig II of Bavaria ascended the throne and invited him to Munich with the promise of unlimited help in carrying out his various projects. In return, Wagner composed the *Huldigungsmarsch*, which he dedicated to his royal patron. The publ. correspondence between Wagner and the King is extraordinary in its display of mutual admiration, gratitude, and affection; still, difficulties soon developed when the Bavarian Cabinet told Ludwig that his lavish support of Wagner's projects threatened the Bavarian economy. Ludwig was forced to advise him to leave Munich. Wagner took this advice as an order, and late in 1865 he went to Switzerland. A very serious difficulty arose also in Wagner's emotional life, when he became intimately involved with Liszt's daughter Cosima, wife of Hans von Bülow, the famous conductor and an impassioned proponent of Wagner's music. On April 10, 1865, Cosima Bülow gave birth to Wagner's daughter, whom he named Isolde after the heroine of his opera that Bülow was preparing for performance in Munich. Its premiere took place with great acclaim on June 10, 1865, 2 months after the birth of Isolde, with Bülow conducting. During the summer of 1865 he prepared the prose sketch of *Parzival*, and began to dictate his autobiography, *Mein Leben*, to Cosima. In Jan. 1866 he resumed the composition of *Die Meistersinger*; he settled in a villa in Tribschen, on Lake Lucerne, where Cosima joined him permanently in Nov. 1868. He completed the full score of *Die Meistersinger* on Oct. 24, 1867. On June 21, 1868, Bülow conducted its premiere in Munich in the presence of King Ludwig, who sat in the royal box with Wagner. A son, significantly named Siegfried, was born to Cosima and Wagner on June 6, 1869. On Sept. 22, 1869, *Das Rheingold* was produced in Munich. On June 26, 1870, *Die Walküre* was staged there. On July 18, 1870, Cosima and Bülow were divorced, and on Aug. 25, 1870, Wagner and Cosima were married in Lucerne. In Dec. 1870 Wagner wrote the *Siegfried Idyll*, based on the themes from his opera; it was performed in their villa in Bayreuth on Christmas morning, the day after Cosima's birthday, as a surprise for her. In 1871 he wrote the *Kaisermarsch* to mark the victorious conclusion of the Franco-German War; he conducted it in the presence of Kaiser Wilhelm I at a concert in the Royal Opera House in Berlin on May 5, 1871.

On May 12 of that year, while in Leipzig, Wagner made public his plans for realizing his cherished dream of building his own theater in Bayreuth for the production of the entire cycle of *Der Ring des Nibelungen*. In Dec. 1871 the Bayreuth town council offered him a site for a proposed Festspielhaus; on May 22, 1872, the cornerstone was laid; Wagner commemorated the event by conducting a performance of Beethoven's 9th Sym. (this was his 59th birthday). In 1873 Wagner began to build his own home in Bayreuth, which he called "Wahnfried," i.e., "Free from Delusion." In order to complete the building of the Festspielhaus, he appealed to King Ludwig for additional funds. Ludwig gave him 100,000 talers for this purpose. Now the dream of Wagner's life was realized. Between June and Aug. 1876 *Der Ring des Nibelungen* went through 3 rehearsals; King Ludwig attended the final dress rehearsals; the official premiere of the cycle took place on Aug. 13, 14, 16, and 17, 1876, under the direction of Hans Richter. Kaiser Wilhelm I made a special journey from Berlin to attend the performances of *Das Rheingold* and *Die Walküre*. In all, 3 complete productions of the *Ring* cycle were given between Aug. 13 and Aug. 30, 1876. Ludwig was faithful to the end to Wagner, whom he called "my divine friend." In his castle Neuschwanstein he installed architectural representations of scenes from Wagner's operas. Soon Ludwig's mental deterioration became obvious to everyone, and he was committed to an asylum. There, on June 13, 1883, he overpowered the psychiatrist escorting him on a walk and dragged him to his death in the Starnberg Lake, drowning himself as well. Ludwig survived Wagner by 4 months.

The spectacles in Bayreuth attracted music-lovers and notables from all over the world. Even those who were not partial to Wagner's ideas or appreciative of his music went to Bayreuth out of curiosity. Tchaikovsky was one such skeptical visitor. Despite world success and fame, Wagner still labored under financial difficulties. He even addressed a letter to an American dentist practicing in Dresden (who also treated Wagner's teeth) in which he tried to interest him in arranging Wagner's permanent transfer to the U.S. He voiced disillusionment in his future prospects in Germany, and said he would be willing to settle in America provided a sum of $1 million would be guaranteed to him by American bankers, and a comfortable estate for him and his family could be found in a climatically clement part of the country. Nothing came of this particular proposal. He did establish an American connection when he wrote, for a fee of $5,000, a *Grosser Festmarsch* for the observance of the U.S. centennial in 1876, dedicated to the "beautiful young ladies of America." In the middle of all this, Wagner became infatuated with Judith Gautier; their affair lasted for about 2 years (1876–78). He completed the full score of *Parsifal* (as it was now called) on Jan. 13, 1882, in Palermo. It was performed for the 1st time at the Bayreuth Festival on July 26, 1882, followed by 15 subsequent performances. At the final performance, on Aug. 29, 1882, Wagner stepped to the podium in the last act and conducted the work to its close; this was his last appearance as a conductor. He went to Venice in Sept. 1882 for a period of rest (he had angina pectoris). Early in the afternoon of Feb. 13, 1883, he suffered a massive heart attack, and died in Cosima's presence. His body was interred in a vault in the garden of his Wahnfried villa in Bayreuth.

Wagner's role in music history is immense. Not only did he create works of great beauty and tremendous brilliance, but he generated an entirely new concept of the art of music, exercising an influence on generations of composers all over the globe. Richard Strauss extended Wagner's grandiose vision to symphonic music, fashioning the form of a tone poem that uses leading motifs and vivid pro-grammatic description of the scenes portrayed in his music. Even Rimsky-Korsakov, far as he stood from Wagner's ideas of musical composition, reflected the spirit of *Parsifal* in his own religious opera, *The Legend of the City of Kitezh*. Schoenberg's 1st significant work, *Verklärte Nacht*, is Wagnerian in its color. Lesser composers, unable to escape Wagner's magic domination, attempted to follow him literally by writing trilogies and tetralogies on a parallel plan with his *Ring*; a pathetic example is the career of August Bungert, who wrote 2 operatic cycles using Homer's epics as the source of his libretti. Wagner's reform of opera was incomparably more far-reaching in aim, import, and effect than that of Gluck, whose main purpose was to counteract the arbitrary predominance of the singers; this goal Wagner accomplished through insistence upon the dramatic truth of his music. When he rejected traditional opera, he did so in the conviction that such an artificial form could not serve as a basis for true dramatic expression. In its place he gave the world a new form and new techniques. So revolutionary was Wagner's art that conductors and singers had to undergo special training in the new style of interpretation in order to perform his works. Thus he became the founder of interpretative conducting and of a new school of dramatic singing, so that such terms as "Wagnerian tenor" and "Wagnerian soprano" became a part of the musical vocabulary.

In his many essays and declarations Wagner condemns the illogical plan of Italian opera and French grand opera. To quote his own words, "The mistake in the art-form of the opera consists in this, that a means of expression (music) was made the end, and the end to be expressed (the drama) was made a means." The choice of subjects assumes utmost importance in Wagner's esthetics. He wrote: "The subject treated by the word-tone poet [*Worttondichter*] is entirely human, freed from all convention and from everything historically formal." The new art-work creates its own artistic form; continuous thematic development of basic motifs becomes a fundamental procedure for the logical cohesion of the drama; these highly individualized generating motifs, appearing singly, in bold relief, or subtly varied and intertwined with other motifs, present the everchanging soul states of the characters of the drama, and form the connecting links for the dra-matic situations of the total artwork, in a form of musical declamation that Wagner described as "Sprechsingen." Characters in Wagner's stage works become themselves symbols of such soul states, so that even mythical gods, magic-workers, heroic horses, and speaking birds become expressions of eternal verities, illuminating the human behavior. It is for this reason that Wagner selected in most of his operas figures that reflect philosophical ideas. Yet, this very solemnity of Wagner's great images on the stage bore the seeds of their own destruction in a world governed by different esthetic principles. Thus it came to pass that the Wagnerian domination of the musical stage suddenly lost its power with changes in human society and esthetic codes. Spectators and listeners were no longer interested in solving artistic puzzles on the stage. A demand for human simplicity arose against Wagnerian heroic complexity. The public at large found greater enjoyment in the realistic nonsense of Verdi's romantic operas than in the unre-ality of symbolic truth in Wagner's operas. By the 2nd quarter of the 20th cen-tury, few if any composers tried to imitate Wagner; all at once his grandeur and animation became an unnatural and asphyxiating constraint.

In the domain of melody, harmony, and orchestration, Wagner's art was as revo-lutionary as was his total artwork on the stage. He introduced the idea of an end-less melody, a continuous flow of diatonic and chromatic tones; the tonality became fluid and uncertain, producing an impression of unattainability, so that the listener accustomed to Classical modulatory schemes could not easily feel the direction toward the tonic; the Prelude to *Tristan und Isolde* is a classic example of such fluidity of harmonic elements. The use of long unresolved dominant-ninth-chords and the dramatic tremolos of diminished-seventh-chords contributed to this state of musical uncertainty, which disturbed the critics and the audiences alike. But Wagnerian harmony also became the foundation of the new method of composition that adopted a free flow of modulatory progressions. Without Wagner the chromatic idioms of the 20th century could not exist. In orchestration, too, Wagner introduced great innovations; he created new instruments, such as the so-called "Wagner tuba," and he increased his demands on the virtuosity of individual orch. players. The vertiginous flight of the bassoon to the high E in the Overture to *Tannhäuser* could not have been attempted before the advent of Wagner.

Wagner became the target of political contention during World War I when audiences in the Allied countries associated his sonorous works with German imperialism. An even greater obstacle to further performances of Wagner's music arose with the rise of Hitler. Hitler ordered the slaughter of millions of Jews; he was an enthusiastic admirer of Wagner, who himself entertained anti-Semitic notions; *ergo*, Wagner was guilty by association of mass murder. Can art be separated from politics, particularly when politics become murderous? Jewish musicians in Tel Aviv refused to play the Prelude to *Tristan und Isolde* when it was put on the program of a sym. concert under Zubin Mehta, and booed him for his intention to inflict Wagner on Wagner's philosophical victims.

Several periodicals dealing with Wagner were publ. in Germany and elsewhere; Wagner himself began issuing *Bayreuther Blätter* in 1878 as an aid to understanding his operas; this journal continued publication until 1938. Remarkably enough, a French periodical, *Revue Wagnérienne*, began appearing in 1885, at a time when French composers realized the tremendous power of Wagnerian esthetics; it was publ. sporadically for a number of years. A Wagner Society in London publ., from 1888 to 1895, a quarterly journal entitled, significantly, *The Meister*.

Welk, Lawrence, popular American bandleader and accordionist; b. Strasburg, N.Dak., March 11, 1903. He began playing accordion in German-speaking areas of his native state as a youth; then performed with his own combos, gaining success as a self-described purveyor of "champagne music"; after touring and making numerous radio appearances, he launched his own television program in Los Angeles in 1951; it subsequently was featured on network television (1955–71). He owed his popularity to his skillful selection of programs containing a varied mixture of semi-classical pieces, western American ballads, and Slavic folk-dance tunes. His use of an accordion section in his arrangements, steadfast rhythmic beat, and sentimentalized tempi imparted to his renditions a rudimentary sound quality that made him a favorite with undiscriminating audiences. He publ. (with some outside help) an autobiography, *Wunnerful, Wunnerful!* (N.Y., 1971), radiating euphoria, and a sequel: *Ah-one, ah-two: Life with My Musical Family* (N.Y., 1974).

Whitney, John, American experimental filmmaker, computer-graphics artist, and Pythagorean-inspired speculative theorist of the analogies between musical and visual arts; b. Pasadena, Calif., April 8, 1917. He is a pioneer in 20th-century motion graphics, having invented cinema techniques in the 1940s that became an established part of the repertoire of special effects later used in film titles and television. His interest in the complementarity of visual and aural arts began with a series of experimental films made with his brother James, including the silent *24 Variations* (1939–40) and the series of *5 Film Exercises* (1943–44), which made use of synthesized pendulum music. With the development of computer graphics, he produced a number of what are now classic pieces, utilizing the music of a variety of composers; these include *Permutations* (1968; re-ed., 1979; with Indian tabla music by Balachandra), *Matrix I* (1971; with music adapted from sonatas by Antonio Soler) and *III* (1972; with music from Terry Riley's *Rainbow in Curved Air*), and *Arabesque* (1975; with improvised music by Manoocheher Sadeghi). In the 1980s, advanced computer technology enabled him to compose both music and graphics; he produced a number of compositions inspired by Native American subjects, including *Hopi, Navajo, Chaco, Mimbres Star* (inspired by 1 of literally thousands of 8th- through 10th-century plates discovered in 1989 in Mimbres, N.Mex.), and *Black Elk*. These and many other computer-generated aural/visual compositions exemplify his ideas about the inherent complementarity of music and visual art, with the harmonic motion evident in tonal music made visible in the charge and release of tensional visual forces. His work has been supported by IBM; he also received NEA grants and a Guggenheim fellowship (1947–48). After retiring from his teaching position in the art dept. of the Univ. of Calif. at Los Angeles in 1986, he devoted himself to producing aural/visual compositions in his studio in Pacific Palisades, Calif. He publ. *Digital Harmony: On the Complementarity of Music and Visual Art* (Peterborough, N.H., 1980); see also his "Writing on Water—Action Painting with Music," *Media Arts Journal* (Spring–Summer 1990).

Wilson, Jackie, top-seeded black American rock-and-roll singer; b. Detroit, June 9, 1934; d. Mount Holly, N.J., Jan. 21, 1984. He was trained as a boxer but, yielding to his mother's pleas, he turned to the relatively less hazardous pursuit of rock singing. In 1953 he joined Billy Ward and the Dominoes, a rhythm-and-blues group, as its lead singer. In 1957 he launched a successful solo career. He made discs for the Motown Record Co. in Detroit; his recording of *Lonely Teardrops* topped the popularity charts in its category in 1959, selling more than a million copies. Among his other hits were *Am I the Man* and *Higher and Higher*. A bit of scandal touched him in 1961 when he was shot in a N.Y. hotel by a scorned female groupie; he was not badly hurt. As a performer, Wilson exercised a mesmeric force over his audience; his voice was almost operatic in its range; he emulated coloratura effects with his explosions of blues chromatics. All this was abruptly ended when he suffered a massive heart attack on stage on Sept. 29, 1975, in Cherry Hill, N.J., resulting in an irreversible coma. He lingered for several years while a court battle for his estate raged between his estranged wife and a son by a previous marriage. The wife won the litigation.

Zappa, Frank (Francis Vincent), seeded American rock artist; b. Baltimore, Dec. 21, 1940, of Italian descent (Zappa means "hoe" in Italian). The family moved to California. From his school days he played guitar and organized groups with weird names such as The Omens and Captain Glasspack and His Magic Mufflers. In 1960 he composed the sound track for the film *The World's Greatest Sinner*, and in 1963 he wrote another sound track, *Run Home Slow*. In 1965 he joined the rhythm-and-blues band The Soul Giants; he soon took it under his own aegis and thought up for it the surrealist logo *The Mothers of Invention*. His recording of it, and another album, *Freak Out!*, became underground hits; along with *We're Only in It for the Money* and *Cruising with Ruben and The Jets*, these works constituted the earliest "concept" albums, touching every nerve in a gradually decivilized California life-style—rebellious, anarchistic, incomprehensible, and yet tantalizing. The band became a mixed-media celebration of total artistic, political, and social opposition to the Establishment, the ingredients of their final album, *Mothermania*. Moving farther afield, Zappa produced a video-movie, *200 Motels*, glorifying itinerant sex activities. He became a cult figure, and as such suffered the penalty of violent adulation. Playing in London in 1971, he was painfully injured when a besotted fan pushed him off the stage. Similar assaults forced Zappa to hire an athletic bodyguard for protection. In 1982 his planned appearance in Palermo, Sicily, the birthplace of his parents, had to be cancelled because the mob rioted in anticipation of the event. He deliberately confronted the most cherished social and emotional sentiments by putting on such songs as *Broken Hearts Are for Assholes*, and his release *Jewish Princess* offended, mistakenly, the sensitivity of American Jews. His production *Joe's Garage* contained Zappa's favorite scatological materials, and he went on analyzing and ridiculing urinary functions in such numbers as *Why Does It Hurt When I Pee*. He managed to upset the members of his own faith in the number titled *Catholic Girls*. His *Hot Rats*, a jazz-rock release, included the famous *Willie the Pimp*, and exploited the natural revulsion to unclean animals. In 1980 he produced the film *Baby Snakes*, which shocked even the most impervious senses. He declared in an interview that classical music is only "for old ladies and faggots." But he astounded the musical community when he proclaimed his total adoration of the music of Edgar Varèse and gave a lecture on Varèse in N.Y. Somehow, without formal study, he managed to absorb the essence of Varèse's difficult music. This process led Zappa to produce truly astonishing full orch. scores reveling in artful dissonant counterpoint, *Bob in Dacron and Sad Jane* and *Mo' 'n Herb's Vacation*, and the cataclysmic *Penis Dimension* for chorus, soloists, and orch., with a text so anatomically precise that it could not be performed for any English-speaking audience.

An accounting of Zappa's scatological and sexological proclivities stands in remarkable contrast to his unimpeachable private life and total abstention from alcohol and narcotic drugs. An unexpected reflection of Zappa's own popularity was the emergence of his adolescent daughter, curiously named Moon Unit, as a voice-over speaker on his hit *Valley Girls*, in which she used the vocabulary of growing womanhood of the San Fernando Valley near Los Angeles, with such locutions as "Grody to the Max" (repellent) and "Barfs Me Out" (disgusting). His son, Dweezil Zappa, is also a musician; his 1st album, *Havin' a Bad Day*, was modestly successful. In 1985 Zappa became an outspoken opponent of the activities of the PMRC (Parents Music Resource Center), an organization comprised largely of wives of U.S. Senators who accused the recording industry of exposing the youth of America to "sex, violence, and the glorification of drugs and alcohol." Their demands to the RIAA (Recording Industry Association of America) included the labeling of record albums to indicate lyric content. Zappa voiced his opinions in no uncertain terms, first in an open letter published in *Cashbox*, and then in one direct to President Reagan; finally, on Sept. 19, 1985, he appeared at the 1st of a series of highly publicized hearings involving the Senate Commerce, Technology and Transportation Committee, the PMRC, and the RIAA, where he delivered a statement to Congress which began "The PMRC proposal is an ill-conceived piece of nonsense which fails to deliver any real benefits to children, infringes the civil liberties of people who are not children and promises to keep the courts busy for years, dealing with the interpretational and enforcemental problems inherent in the proposal's design." Audio excerpts from these hearings can be heard, in original and Synclavier-manipulated forms, on his album *Zappa Meets The Mothers of Prevention*. Other recent recordings which make extensive use of the Synclavier include *Francesco Zappa* and *Jazz From Hell*. With P. Occhiogrosso, he publ. an unrestrained autobiographical vol., *The Real Frank Zappa Book* (N.Y., London, Toronto, Sydney, and Tokyo, 1988), rich in undeleted scatalogical expletives.

CONCEPTS

As a monumentally concise writer, Slonimsky has authored several dictionaries of musical whatevers, including a full-length book, *Lectionary of Music* (1989). My own favorite Slonimsky dictionary appeared initially as an eighty-page appendix to the Third Edition of *Music Since 1900* (1971), which mixes familiar terms with those less familiar, including a few wholly of his own invention, which have never been used by anyone since. To this text, reprinted in its entirety, I've inserted alphabetically definitions drawn from three other sources: his *Lectionary*, identified as LM; an appendix to his *Thesaurus of Scales and Melodic Patterns* (1947), identified as TSMP; and the *Pocket Manual of Musical Terms* (Fourth Edition, 1978), identified hereafter as PMMT.

DEFINITIONS
(MOSTLY FROM *MUSIC SINCE 1900*)

Absolute Pitch. Ability to name instantly and without fail any note struck on the piano keyboard or played on an instrument. This is an innate faculty, which appears in a musical child at a very early age, distinct from relative pitch, common among all musicians, in which an interval is named in relation to a previously played note. Absolute pitch is rare, even among professional musicians and is not a sure indication of great musical talent. Wagner and Tchaikovsky lacked it, but many obscure musicians possess it to an astonishing degree, being able to name the most complicated dissonant chords. Absolute pitch is also known as PERFECT PITCH. PMMT

Absolute Music. The term ABSOLUTE MUSIC is applied to music that is free from programmatic designs, psychological affiliations or illustrative associations; its Latin etymology connotes independence. In its function ABSOLUTE MUSIC is parasynonymous with ABSTRACT MUSIC, but the two terms are differentiated in their temporal points of reference. ABSOLUTE MUSIC is of ancient heritage, while ABSTRACT MUSIC is a relatively recent phenomenon, marked by structural athematism in an atonal context.

Abstract Music. Abstraction in music implies a separation of sonic structures from representational images, whether pictorial or psychological. ABSTRACT MUSIC is the antonym of all musical styles that are concrete or naturalistic; abstract works are usually short, athematic and rhythmically asymmetric. Intellectual fantasy, rather than sensual excitation, is the generating impulse of ABSTRACT MUSIC; its titles are derived from constructivistic and scientific concepts: Structures, Projections, Extensions, Frequencies, Sound. The German composer Boris Blacher has developed a successful form of ABSTRACT OPERA, in which concrete action takes place in a swarm of discrete sonic particles, disjected words in several languages and isolated melodic fragments. ABSTRACT EXPRESSIONISM, a term applied to non-objective painting, is sometimes used to describe musical works of abstract quality with expressionistic connotations. A subsidiary genre of ABSTRACT MUSIC is ALEATORY MUSIC, in which the process of musical cerebration is replaced by a random interplay of sounds and rhythms.

Absurd Music. The vocable *surd*, cognate with *sourdine*, implies a muted sound; *Absurd* suggests a becalmed truth, but not necessarily nonsense. There are mathematical equations that seem to contradict common sense; in fact, square roots that cannot be resolved precisely, are called irrational numbers, or by the now obsolete

307

term surd, a cousin of ABSURD. The inner validity of absurd logic was enunciated by Tertullian when he said: "Credo quia absurdum est." Oxymoronic pairs, such as "passionate indifference," or "glacial fire," are intrinsically absurd, and yet eloquent in their self-contradiction. ABSURD MUSIC cultivates analogous incompatibilities. It is particularly effective in modern opera, where a scene of horror may be illustrated by a frivolous waltz, or a festive celebration by the somber strains of a funereal march. The modern techniques of POLYTONALITY and ATONALITY represent MUSIC OF THE ABSURD to the withered sensitivity of an old-fashioned ear.

Accompaniment. In modern music, ACCOMPANIMENT transcends its traditional ancillary function and becomes an integral part of the entire composition. The simplest form of modern ACCOMPANIMENT is that of POLYTONALITY, in which the melody is set in one key and the harmony in another. Rhythmically, the modern ACCOMPANIMENT rarely follows the inflections of the melody; deliberate oxymoronic usages are enhanced by translocated accents.

Acoustics. By definition, acoustical phenomena are fundamental to all music. The overtone series, which is the generator of the basic major triad, is also the source of nominal dissonances. The tritone, deprecated as "diabolus in musica" by medieval scholiasts, is the foundation stone of ATONALITY, POLYTONALITY and other modern techniques. Acoustically, it is the 45th overtone at the distance of $6\frac{1}{2}$ octaves from the fundamental note, with which it forms a concord. Scriabin, theorizing ex post facto, regarded his MYSTIC CHORD as a consonance, because its constituents approximate the high overtones. An interesting practical application of the acoustical properties of the overtone series is found in Ravel's *Boléro*, where at one point the melody is accompanied by a group of flutes and piccolos constituting the 6th, 8th, 10th and 12th overtones progressing in parallel formations. In the score Ravel marks the gradually decreasing dynamics of these high notes, corresponding to a natural tapering of the strength of overtones in higher elevations. This calculated enhancement of natural overtones affects the timbre of the solo instrument. If performed correctly with the dynamics scrupulously observed, the solo player will find to his dismay that his instrument has undergone a curious change in its tone color. With the aid of electronic means of tone production, this effect can be produced artificially, generating hybrid sonorities such as a half-bassoon and a half-trombone, or a timbre which is a third-oboe, a third-clarinet and a third-violin.

Rhythms can be combined in special proportions with the overtone series. In 1932 Henry Cowell, in collaboration with Leon Theremin, constructed the *Rhythmicon*, an instrument which generates a series of rhythmic beats in an overtone series, the number of beats being proportional to the position of each overtone, so that the octave has two beats per time unit, the interval of the 12th, three beats, the major third over two octaves, five beats, etc. This arrangement makes it possible to devise polyrhythmic counterpoint of great variety and unique sonority. Acoustical innovations and improvements in the purity of intonation are not without musical perils, however. Perfect tuning in orchestral performance would generate differential tones and make a sonic jungle out of a classical symphony. The desire of modern architects to attain acoustical perfection often leads to orchestral pollution in the concert hall. Old-fashioned rococo architecture, with its ornate brocades and heavy curtains, contributed the necessary dampening of sounds and echoes that secured harmonious euphony. Modern acousticians eliminated the decorations, removed the tasselled seat covers and cushioned surfaces, replacing them by plywood and plastic, and added an array of mobiles suspended from the ceiling to eliminate microsonic impurities. But these elaborations resulted in some unwelcome side-effects. Parasitical noises were neutralized, but a variety of unsuspected musical micro-organisms, overtones and differential tones, rose from the instruments themselves, flooding the hall in a harmonious plasma that all but destroyed the natural equilibrium of tonal imperfections and mutual reverberations that were responsible for the rich resonance intuitively achieved by the musical architects of the past. The consequences of such modernization were painfully evident in the scientifically designed Philharmonic Hall at Lincoln Center in New York. The resulting acoustical anarchy was fortunately corrected by an ingenious rearrangement of the physical properties of the auditorium and the stage, so that the natural heterogeneity of sonic euphony was restored.

Additive Composition. As the term implies, ADDITIVE COMPOSITION is effectuated by a series of successive additions to an initial thematic statement. The connection is mechanistic by definition, but if by chance, or subliminal design, a dominant melorhythmic figure emerges, a paradoxical rondo is the result.

Aerostatic Suspension. In Impressionistic scores, the shimmering interference of euphonious dissonances generates a sonic inversion which forces the lighter elements to ascend into the upper harmonic regions. At some point an equilibrium of overtones and differential tones is established. This euphony, with ethereal sonorities wafted by the winds of flutes, oboes, clarinets and flageolet-like upper strings, suggests a physical convection which may be described as AEROSTATIC SUSPENSION.

Aleatory Music. The word ALEATORY is derived from the Latin "alea," that is, a die. (Julius Caesar exclaimed after crossing the Rubicon, "Alea jacta est.") ALEATORY MUSIC in the literal sense is not a new invention. "Dice music" was a popular parlor game in the 18th century. A celebrated example is in *Musikalisches Würfelspiel*, attributed to Mozart. In the second half of the 20th century, composers of the AVANT-GARDE introduced true ALEATORY methods. A pioneer work was *Music of Changes* by John Cage, derived from chance operations found in the ancient Chinese book of oracles *I-Ching*, in which random numbers are obtained by throwing sticks. By drawing an arbitrary table of correspondences between numbers and musical parameters (pitch, note-value, rests) it is possible to derive a number of desirable melorhythmic curves. Human or animal phenomena may also serve as primary data. Configurations of fly specks on paper, pigeon droppings on a park bench, the design of crushed mosquitoes on wallpaper, the parabolic curve of an expectoration directed towards a spittoon, dissection of birds as practiced in ancient Rome, etc. are all excellent materials for ALEATORY MUSIC. At a HAPPENING in an American mid-western university, the anal discharge of a pig, which was administered a clyster, was used as an Aleatory datum. Mauricio Kagel has made use of partially exposed photographic film for ALEATORY composition. The composer-engineer Iannis Xenakis organizes ALEATORY MUSIC in STOCHASTIC terms, which possess the teleological quality absent in pure ALEATORY pursuits. Among affiliated subjects of ALEATORY MUSIC are PROBABILITY, INFORMATION THEORY, STOCHASTIC COMPOSITION, CYBERNETICS, EXPERIMENTAL MUSIC, COMPUTER MUSIC, EMPIRICAL MUSIC and INDETERMINACY.

Algorithm. In mathematical usage, an ALGORITHM is an operator devised for the solution of problems arising in the theory of numbers. Directions given in puzzle canons to indicate the time and the interval of entry are ALGORITHMS. The most ubiquitous ALGORITHM in modern music is the TRITONE. It compasses a chord containing 11 different intervals, for the sum of the first 11 numbers equals 66, which corresponds in semitone units to $5\frac{1}{2}$ octaves, the tritone being half an octave. The TRITONE is also the the operating ALGORITHM in the problem of distributing 12 different notes of the chromatic scale into four mutually exclusive triads. Here the modus operandi is to build two major triads separated by a tritone, and two minor triads a whole tone higher whose tonics are also at a distance of a tritone (e.g., C major, F-sharp major, D minor, G-sharp minor). Magical properties emerge from such operations. It is remarkable, for instance, that four mutually exclusive triads can be arranged only by using a pair of major triads and a pair of minor triads, and that no other distribution is possible. But it is also possible to split the chromatic scale into a group of diminished, minor, major and augmented triads, one of each, a symmetric and elegant solution, suggesting similarly elegant formulas in mathematics. Algorithmic composition is a virgin field for experimentation in modern techniques.

Allusive Quotation. Folk songs, contrapuntal elaborations on a given cantus firmus, quotations from the doom-laden chant *Dies irae*, have been for centuries a favorite resource of ALLUSIVE QUOTATIONS. Richard Strauss inserted the theme of the funeral march from Beethoven's *Eroica* in the score of his *Metamorphosen*, a dirge on the death of Germany, written during the last weeks of World War II. Alban Berg quoted Bach's chorale *Es ist genug* at the conclusion of his *Violin Concerto* as a memorial for Manon Gropius, daughter of Mahler's widow by a second marriage, who died young. Quotations from a composer's own scores are not rare; a notorious modern example is the egocentric series of quotations used by Strauss in the score of his tone poem *Ein Heldenleben*. But perhaps the most extraordinary assembly of assorted thematic memos, memories and mementos is found in *Sinfonia* by Luciano Berio, in which he quotes metamorphosed fragments from works of Mahler, Debussy, Ravel and others.

Alphabetical Monograms. The origin of musical notation is alphabetical or syllabic. The names of the notes of the initial hexachord of the major scale were taken by Guido d'Arezzo from the first syllables of a Latin hymn, and this syllabic nomenclature is still in use in the Latin countries and in Russia. In German, the musical notes are designated by letters from A to H; thanks to this alphabetic denomination, it is possible to contrive musical themes out of words and names comprising these letters, the most illustrious example being the theme B-A-C-H. That such an artificial method of thematic invention does not hamper a composer of genius, is proved by Schumann's *Carnaval*, which is based on the spelling of the name of the town of ASCH (in German nomenclature either A-flat, C, B or A, E-flat, C, B). Dmitri Shostakovich based the main themes of his *Tenth Symphony* and the *Eighth String Quartet* on his ALPHABETICAL MONOGRAM, in German nomenclature, D.SCH. Mario Castelnuovo-Tedesco extended his system of ALPHABETICAL MONOGRAMS to 25 letters of the Italian alphabet, arranging the notes chromatically and filling two full octaves from A to Z.

Ambulation. AMBULATORY activities by performers during a concert in the process of playing is a particular case of SPATIAL DISTRIBUTION, in which the position of the players in physical space is treated as an independent parameter. AMBULATION is also related to VECTORIALISM; in both the direction of the source of sound depends on the placement, stationary or kinetic, of the performers. In an AMBULATORY composition, the players are usually instructed to make their entrances on the stage while playing the initial bars upon their instruments which they carry with them. Some avant-garde composers even demanded the pushing of a grand piano on the stage while performing a one-arm composition on the keyboard. Rational AMBULATION is practiced in *Antiphones* for string quartet by the Soviet composer Sergei Slonimsky. In the opening of the work the cello player, originally seated in the middle of the last row of the concert hall, is instructed to walk with his instrument to the stage, while playing passages in a non-tempered scale; the other players are engaged in walking movements one after another, in a manner of an ambulatory fugato.

Anagrams. By analogy with literal ANAGRAMS, in which words and sentences are derived from a given matrix (e.g., "Flit on, cheering angel" from Florence Nightingale), notes of a musical subject can be rearranged in order to generate plausible thematic variations. The 12 notes of the chromatic scale yield 479,001,600 possible permutations suitable for dodecaphonic usages. Polyanagrams, formed by linear (melodic), vertical (harmonic) and oblique (fugal) parameters, are comprised in the generic term COMBINATORIALITY, introduced by Milton Babbitt. Perhaps the most intricate Polyanagram is *Anagrama* by the Argentine-born avant-garde composer Mauricio Kagel, scored for speaking chorus, 4 vocalists and instruments, to the text derived from Dante's *Divina Commedia*, subject to a number of permutations forming plausible sentences in different languages.

Anarchy and Autarchy. Innovating composers since the time of Wagner have been accused of promoting musical ANARCHY. An educated French music critic wrote after attending the first performance of Debussy's *Pelléas et Mélisande*, "No, I will never have anything to do with these anarchists of music!" But when Schoenberg enunciated his method of composition with 12 tones related only to one another, the outcries against atonal ANARCHY changed to charges of esthetic AUTARCHY. To refute such accusations, Schoenberg wrote, in a letter from Hollywood dated 3 June 1937, and addressed to Nicolas Slonimsky: "What I did was neither revolution nor anarchy. I possessed from my very first start a thoroughly developed sense of form and a strong aversion for exaggeration. There is no falling into order, because there was never disorder. There is no falling at all, but on the contrary, there is an ascending to a higher and better order."

Animal and Human Noises. The introduction of parts for animals into musical composition is an old and cherished fantasy. Imitations of bird songs have been part of music since the Middle Ages; but an actual sound of a bird occurs for the first time in Ottorino Respighi's *Pines of Rome* which includes a phonograph recording of a Roman nightingale. When a dog incidentally barked during a recording of Walter Piston's ballet suite *The Incredible Flutist*, the conductor decided to keep it in the final recording. A part for cat's meow appears in the score of Nicolas Slonimsky's piece *Anatomy of Melancholy*, to be enacted by a real cat whose tail is pulled during the performance. Electronic transcriptions provide an opportunity to supply recorded or synthetic animal noises. The tape recording of the cetacean song of a humpback whale has been incorporated into the symphonic poem *And God Created Great Whales* by the American composer Alan Hovhaness. Human noises—whistling, shrieking, grunting—were cultivated by the Italian Futurists and further propagated by the cosmopolitan AVANT-GARDE.

Andante (It., ăhn-dähn′tĕh). "Going," "moving"; a tempo mark indicating a moderately slow, easily flowing movement between *adagio* and *allegretto*.— *Andante affettuoso*, rather slowly and pathetic . . . *A. cantabile*, flowingly, in a singing style . . . *A. con moto, A. mosso, A. un poco allegretto*, a flowing and rather more animated movement . . . *A. non troppo*, easily flowing, but not too fast . . . *A. maestoso*, a flowing and stately movement . . . *A. pastorale*, flowing with tranquil simplicity . . . *A. sostenuto*, rather slow, flowing smoothly . . . *Meno andante*, slower. PMMT

Anti-Music. ANTI-MUSIC is a concept formulated by analogy with the hypothetical phenomenon of Anti-Matter, in which the electrical charges of subatomic particles are reversed, so that the physical encounter between matter and Anti-Matter would result in mutual annihilation. ANTI-MUSIC reverses the acoustical charges of consonances and dissonances. The valences in the series of overtones are similarly reversed, so that the diminishing intervals in the upper part of the harmonic series are regarded as increasingly euphonious concords, and those close to the fundamental tone as discords, requiring a resolution. A manual of ANTI-MUSIC is yet to be written. Triadic formations, tonal sequences, symmetric periods and harmonious cadences would be ruled out in such a textbook. ANTI-MUSIC of this nature would then be taught in elementary schools along with the physical principles of anti-matter. But old music would not be entirely excluded. In special seminars, courses will be given in ANTI-ANTI-MUSIC, in which consonances will regain their respected status, while dissonances will once more be relegated to a dependency. It is even possible that in the fantastic world of ANTI-MUSIC, tolerance will be granted to such teratological practices as those of Bach, Beethoven, Brahms, Debussy and Schoenberg.

Asomatous Variations. Etymologically, the adjective ASOMATOUS signifies incorporeality, the lack of a soma, a material body. In composition, ASOMATOUS VARIATIONS are metamorphoses of an absent theme. Often a theme is cumulative, building up part by part, a practice as frequent among classical composers as in ultra-modern music. In DODECAPHONIC MUSIC, the principal series is sometimes evolved by such a cumulative thematic accretion. ASOMATOUS VARIATIONS serve a descriptive purpose in Vincent d'Indy's *Istar Variations*. In this work, portraying the passage of the Babylonian goddess Istar through seven gates, at each of which she deposits a part of her garments, the theme does not appear in its totality until the final gate is reached. Elgar's *Enigma Variations* are based on a clearly outlined subject, but Elgar repeatedly hinted that this visible theme is but a counterpoint to a prime motive, which remains ASOMATOUS. Composers of the AVANT-GARDE cultivate the art of ASOMATOUS VARIATIONS with such determination that, in some ultra-modern works, an accidental repetition of a motive automatically marks the end of performance.

Athematic Composition. ATHEMATIC COMPOSITION is the product of a deliberate effort to separate the melodic line into segregated groups of phrases and motives bearing no relation to one another. ATHEMATIC MUSIC does not adhere to any formal organization; a work without connected themes can therefore start and end at any point. Karlheinz Stockhausen arranges some of his works in segments which can be played in any order whatsoever, with this stipulation that when a performer, accidentally or intentionally, arrives at the same segment, it marks the ending. ATHEMATIC COMPOSITION tends towards atonal designs, in which the principle of non-repetition of melodic material is paramount. An athematic work need not be incoherent or inchoate; successive melodic statements may be related by a preferential use of a certain interval or a certain rhythmic configuration. In this sense, it may be said that an ATHEMATIC COMPOSITION has either zero or an indefinitely large number of themes.

Atonality. Etymologically, ATONALITY is a negative concept which connotes the absence of tonality. The term was first applied by hostile critics as a derisive description of a type of modern composition in which tonality was almost entirely disfranchised and integral chromaticism served as the guiding principle of melodic writing. Atonal composers avoid the repetition of a particular tone in order to preclude the appearance of an adventitious tonic. By natural predisposition such melodies invited a dissonant harmonization. Under such circumstances the key signature becomes superfluous. The desire to obviate the tonic-dominant relationship in atonal writing has led to the replacement of the perfect fifth by the tritone and of the octave by a major seventh. One of the most frequently occurring chordal formations in ATONAL MUSIC is a contraction of the four-part major triad, with the octave reduced to a major seventh, the fifth to a tritone and the major third to a sesquitone: C-E-G-C→C-D-sharp-F-sharp-B. The same chord can be obtained by raising the lowest note a semitone and leaving the upper three notes unaltered: C-E-G-C→C-sharp-E-G-C. This chord may also be analyzed as a diminished-seventh chord with an unresolved appoggiatura. Consecutive blocks of such chords at a distance of a minor third are favorite devices of IMPRESSIONIST composers.

The gradual atrophy of tonality has resulted in the non-repetition of essential melodic notes, culminating in the organization of melodic writing making use of all 12 different tones. Tertian melodies and harmonies, affiliated with triadic structures, gave way to quartal and quintal progressions. Ascending or descending melodic fourths became the hallmark of atonal writing, gradually approaching the asymptote of integral dodecaphony in a cumulative PANDIATESSARON, an edifice of perfect fourths comprising all 12 tonics of the cycle of scales in the counterclockwise direction. Atonal structures guided by the principle of non-repetition are found in many works by 20th-century composers. An interesting example is an ornamental passage in Stravinsky's opera *Le Rossignol*, introducing the song of the Chinese nightingale. It traverses two ascending perfect fifths, a descending minor sixth, an ascending major seventh, an ascending minor third, a descending major third and an ascending major seventh. Not a single note is repeated, and the characteristic atonal interval of a major seventh occurs twice.

Tonal scales and modes derive their individuality from asymmetry of the pattern of tones and semitones. Atonal progressions are formed by the division of the octave into equal parts: two tritones, or three major thirds, four minor thirds, six major seconds, or 12 semitones. An augmented triad consisting of two major thirds is regarded as a dissonance in traditional harmony. When in 1903 the Russian composer Vladimir Rebikov used an augmented triad as the concluding chord of his opera *The Christmas Tree*, his daring was decried by academic critics. The diminished-seventh chord, consisting of minor thirds, is also an atonal dissonance, requiring a resolution into a triad. An atonal scale of 8 notes, obtained by the interpolation of symmetrically placed major or minor seconds in the sesquitone scale, is a frequently used coloristic device. It is described in Russian music dictionaries as Rimsky-Korsakov's scale. The WHOLE-TONE SCALE, representing the division of the octave into six equal parts, is a progression of a distinctly atonal nature, for it lacks the tonic-dominant complex and the leading tone.

The musical notation of ATONAL MUSIC, which in the larval phase of chromatic harmony bristled with double-sharps and double-flats, has been functionally simplified. When the fiction of a phantom tonality could no longer be maintained, double-sharps, double-flats and such vestigial tonal symbols as E-sharp and B-sharp, F-flat and C-flat were replaced by their enharmonic equivalents.

The cradle of ATONALITY is Central Europe, the birthplace of Freud's psychoanalysis, Kafka's existential Angst, the asymmetrical imagery of Kandinsky and the relativistic universe of Einstein. It seems fitting that these artistic and scientific developments occurred at about the same time. The controlled hesitancy, directed anxiety and Hesychastic omphaloskepsis of the period could be musically expressed with congenial intimacy only by atonal constructions. The circumstance that the TRITONE, the "diabolus in musica" of the medieval theorists, became the cornerstone of ATONALITY is a most significant reversal of musicosophical concepts of good and evil. It is also interesting to note that the tritone, being half an octave, is a neutral interval. On the psychological level this neuter quality suggests sexlessness. In his *Harmonielehre* Schoenberg remarks that "angels, our higher nature, are also sexless." In this assertion Schoenberg contradicts St. Thomas Aquinas who argued that angels must be of the masculine gender because Jacob wrestled with one and he would not have wrestled either with a woman or with a neuter hermaphrodite.

ATONAL melodies cultivate wide intervallic leaps, in order to avoid the monotony of consecutive small intervals. Although individual phrases in ATONAL MUSIC are usually short, the cumulative melodic curve appears long and sustained. Moreover, there is a singular sense of equilibrium inherent in a good atonal melody, in which the incidence of high notes is balanced by a countervailing group of low notes, with the solid central range representing a majority of essential notes. The computation of the relative frequency of individual notes in an ATONAL MELODY reveals the characteristics of the bell-shaped probability curve of Gauss. Since the duration of an individual note affects the general equilibrium of a melody, the sum of the products of duration in arbitrary units multiplied by the distance in semitones from the center of the melodic range must be zero, if the intervals below the central line are to be counted with a minus sign.

Several systems of atonal notation have been proposed in which accidentals are replaced by special symbols. Joseph Matthias Hauer suggested a multilineal staff. Jefim Golyscheff, a Russian who was active in Germany after World War I as composer and painter, and who eventually settled in Brazil, notated sharps with a cross inside a white circle and designated note values by stems. A similar notation was adopted by the Russian composer Nicolas Obouhov. He gave a demonstration of it at a concert of his works in Petrograd on 3 February 1916; he called his system "Absolute Harmony."

Herbert Eimert gives the following description of the essence of ATONALITY in his *Atonale Musiklehre* (1924): "Atonality, as the word itself implies, lack modes, major and minor keys, and eliminates the entire harmonic apparatus of tonal music—cadences, leading tones, anticipations, resolutions, enharmonism, altered tones, etc.—as well as the concept of consonance and dissonance in their technical harmonic, but not psychological, aspects. The 12 mutually unrelated and independent tones of the tempered scale form the material of ATONAL MUSIC. The foundation of atonal material is therefore not a scale, or a progression of tones, but a group of tones, a complex, and specifically the only possible number of different tones, namely 12 tones." Hauer has this to say about ATONALITY: "In atonal music there are no tonic, dominant, subdominant, degrees, resolutions, consonances, dissonances, but only the 12 intervals of equal temperament; its scales consist therefore of 12 tempered semitones. In an ATONAL MELODY all purely physical, sensual, as well as trivial and sentimental elements, are eliminated, and its law, its *nomos*, is only that the 12 tones of the tempered scale must be played again and again."

Schoenberg and Alban Berg deprecated the use of the term ATONALITY. Berg concluded his talk on the subject, broadcast over the Vienna Radio on 8 June 1936, with these words: "Antichrist himself could not have thought up a more diabolical appellation than ATONAL!"

Aud Music. Optical art has given rise to a concentrated type of visual craft known as Op Art. By analogy, auditory art in its intense modern organization may be termed Aud Music. Op Art makes its impact felt by a direct assault on the visual nerve. Aud Music directs its onslaught against the auditory nerve. If *trompe l'oeil* in Op Art deceives the eye by rotating spirals, three-dimensional palimpsests, etc., the technique of *trompe l'oreille* in Aud Music confuses the ear by an unnerving succession of explosive musical fragments and sudden silences. Op Art and Aud Music freely combine in Audio-Visual syndromes. Fascinated by the optically concentric grooves of a phonograph disc, the painter Picabia called it Optophone.

To paraphrase Apollinaire, AUD MUSIC explores "a rational use of non-similitudinarianism." It makes music out of elements that are non-musical. Op Art tends to become music; modern artists often depict musical objects, such as a realistic metronome with an eye on the pendulum by Man Ray, which he entitled *Object of Destruction*, or a burning tuba by René Magritte. AUD MUSIC makes use of sound producing objects that are not musical instruments, as exemplified by the symphonic poem for 100 metronomes of György Ligeti. Other examples of Aud and Op Art acting in concert are Sculptures Sonores, sound-producing sculptures. Engineering applications of Aud Music are illustrated by the *Rhythmicon*, constructed by Theremin and Henry Cowell and the *Sonotron*, an acoustical accelerator built by Iannis Xenakis on the model of the Cyclotron and designed to synthesize sonic particles into a sound mass.

Jean Cocteau spoke of "oreilles myopes," referring to those suffering from auditory astigmatism. White light, analyzed by the spectroscope into primary colors, has inspired Op Art; by analogy, a linear evolution of a sonic complex generates AUD MUSIC.

Autogenetic Composition. AUTOGENETIC COMPOSITION, especially in modern music, is the function of melodic invention that makes the development of the basic idea seem inevitable. Bach anticipated the process in his riddle canons; modern composers, proceeding from premises entirely different from those of Bach, apply the method in advanced techniques. AUTOGENETIC COMPOSITION is an intelligent evaluation of the potentialities of an original invention.

Automatic Composition. True AUTOMATIC COMPOSITION can become a reality only with a considerable advance of electronic music. A photoelectric cell may be used to trigger selected groups of notes and to imprint them on a rotating roll of paper. A coordinating device can be constructed to dictate rhythms. An automatic musical typewriter can recapitulate whole sections of a composition. AUTOMATIC MUSIC should not be confused with automatic writing as employed by spiritualists. A British housewife appeared on television in the summer of 1969 and claimed that her diluted imitations of works by Schubert and Liszt were dictated to her by them, and that she wrote them down automatically. Her claims were never subjected to controlled examination, but if substantiated they would prove that a prolonged state of death fatally affects the ability to compose even among celebrated musicians.

Baroque Music. The type of contrapuntal music developed within the historical period of about 1600–1750. Bach and Handel belonged to this era. Although the word "Baroque" originally implied a bizarre and even crude quality, it has acquired the opposite meaning of dignity and precise craftsmanship. PMMT

Bebop. BEBOP, Rebop, or simply BOP, is one of the many onomatopoeic vocables descriptive of jazz techniques. The most striking characteristic of BEBOP is its maximal velocity, sometimes reaching 20 notes a second in clear articulation, with a strong off-beat stress. The invention of the term and the technique is generally attributed to the American Negro jazz player Dizzy Gillespie. BEBOP is marked by irregular syncopation, a widely ranging melody of quasi-atonal configurations and, most importantly, by an accompaniment in rapidly changing modernistic harmonies, making use of unresolved dissonances and polytonal combinations. The verbalization of BEBOP can be traced to a counting jingle *Four or Five Times*, a disc issued by the Victor Company in 1928, in which the following line occurs, "BEBOP one, BEBOP two, BEBOP three." BOP as a verb was used in the comic strips in the 1920's, meaning to hit or to clobber. An erudite discussion of BOP is found in an article by Peter Tamony in the Spring, 1959, issue of the San Francisco periodical *Jazz*.

Bitonality. As the term indicates, BITONALITY is the simultaneous use of two different keys. The most effective type of BITONALITY is the combination of two polarized major triads whose tonics lie on the diametrically opposite points in the cycle of scales, and form the interval of a tritone. The sum of the absolute values of sharps or flats in the key signatures of such triads is always six (e.g. C major and F-sharp major, with zero sharps and six sharps respectively, or A-flat major and D major with key signatures of 4 flats and 2 sharps). The most frequently employed type of BITONALITY is the complex of C major and F-sharp major triads, which forms the harmonic foundation of Stravinsky's *Pétrouchka*, and is often called "Pétrouchka Chord." It is also known as "Parisian Chord," on account of the vogue that it subsequently acquired among Paris composers. The chord is of a clearly pianistic origin, with the white keys of C major contrasted with the black keys of F-sharp major; indeed, Stravinsky had originally planned to use these bitonal materials in a *Konzertstück* for piano and orchestra, and this accounts for the important piano part in the score of *Pétrouchka*. Acoustically, the most advantageous position of these two chords is the spacing of one in open harmony, in root position in the low register, and of the other in close harmony in the first inversion of the triad (e.g. C, G, E, A-sharp, C-sharp, F-sharp). In this disposition, the outer voices, the middle voices and the inner voices are all in the relationship of a tritone. It is of importance to note that the major hexachords based on such polarized scales aggregate to 12 different notes. BITONALITY of minor triads is encountered more seldom owing to poor acoustical balance of such combinations. In NEO-CLASSICAL music, a modal type of BITONALITY has come into existence, as exemplified by such complexes as C major and D major, in the Lydian mode. Such cases of BITONALITY are also part of PANDIATONICISM. Another type of BITONALITY is a combination of two major or minor triads with a tone in common, for instance C major combined with E major or E-flat major, favored particularly by composers of ethnic associations, among them Vaughan Williams and Roy Harris. It is interesting that a decreasing progression of intervals, beginning with 9 semitones and ending with 3 semitones, will form a bitonal major chord consisting of triads in second inversions (e.g. G, E, C, G, C-sharp, F-sharp, A-sharp, C-sharp) and that an increasing progression from 3 semitones to 9 semitones will form a bitonal combination of two minor triads in root positions (e.g., D, F, A, D, G-sharp, D-sharp, B, G-sharp). All these types of BITONALITY pursue the aims of euphony, either by polarization or by Pandiatonic approximation. A very important non-euphonious type of BITONALITY is homonymous BITONALITY of major and minor triads in close harmony (e.g., C, E, G, C, E-flat, G), with a friction point at a semitone between the major and the minor third of the same triad. It was cultivated assiduously by Stravinsky from his earliest period. In its linear devolution, it offers a stimulating quasi-atonal melodic design.

In his variations on the tune of *America*, written in 1891, Charles Ives combines F major with A-flat major. In order to bring out the bitonal resonance, he marks one of the tonalities *pianississimo* and the other *fortissimo*.

Blues. The word Blue is an old American colloquialism expressing melancholy. The BLUES, in plural, is an American ballad form, marked by leisurely syncopation, in 4/4 time, in slow tempo. In its melancholy lilt, the BLUES forms the counterpart of the Elegy, the Bohemian Dumka or the Brazilian Modinha. Its distinctive characteristic is the "blue note" of the flatted seventh in major keys; the third is often flatted too. The sentiment of the BLUES reflects the long history of the suffering of the Negro people in the South; some elements in the Negro Spirituals and in Stephen Foster's songs are direct progenitors of the BLUES. The first composer of the BLUES in the modern sense was W. C. Handy; his songs, *The Memphis Blues* (1911) and *The St. Louis Blues* (1914), established the genre. On 17 May 1969 the United States Post Office issued a commemorative 6-cent stamp showing W. C. Handy playing the trumpet, with the legend "Father of the Blues." Ravel has a BLUES movement in his *Violin Sonata*. The most famous concert piece in the BLUES idiom is Gershwin's *Rhapsody in Blue*.

In its classic form, BLUES consists of a series of 12-bar strophes, with the following harmonic progression: 4 bars of tonic, 2 bars of subdominant, 2 bars of tonic, 1 bar of dominant, 1 bar of subdominant and 2 bars of tonic; the plagal cadence is *de rigueur*. As in all jazz, there are infinite variations on this harmonic succession, with atonal protuberances in the melody and pandiatonic excrescences in the accompaniment.

Boogie-Woogie. Like most terms of JAZZ music, BOOGIE-WOOGIE is an onomatopoeic alliterative word suggesting a certain type of rhythmic beat. BOOGIE-WOOGIE invaded the public arena at a concert of popular American music given in Carnegie Hall in New York on 23 December 1938. It is the only JAZZ form that has adopted an explicit classical model, of the type of passacaglia and chaconne, with the principal theme given in the bass and thus determining the harmonic scheme. The pattern of BOOGIE-WOOGIE is remarkably regular. It consists of a 12-bar period: 4 bars of tonic harmony, 2 bars of subdominant harmony, 2 bars of tonic harmony, 2 bars of dominant harmony and again 2 bars of tonic harmony. As in all JAZZ forms, the meter is in 4/4 time, but the rhythmic pattern is set in rapid motion, most often with dotted-eighth notes followed by sixteenth-notes. The bass is usually written in even eight-notes, in broken octaves, and is sometimes described as "walking bass." The persistent eighth-notes, rhythm is suggested by the title of an early BOOGIE-WOOGIE song, Beat Me Daddy, Eight to the Bar.

Bruitism. BRUITISM is a genre of musical composition consisting of noises. The pioneer work of BRUITISM was *Arte dei Rumori* by the Italian Futurist Luigi Russolo, in which he codified the noises of friction, attrition, sibilation, percussion and concussion. Edgar Varèse elevated the inchoate BRUITISTIC scheme to a purely musical form in his epoch-making work *Ionization*.

Circuitry. Modern scores for MIXED MEDIA performances often have the appearance of blueprints for the electric circuits in scientific instruments and digital computers. An early example of musical CIRCUITRY is the part marked *Luce* in Scriabin's *Prometheus*, intended to fill the concert hall with changing colors corresponding to fluctuations in instrumental timbre. The detailed directions as to lighting given by Schoenberg in his monodrama *Erwartung* are in the same category. The Russian composer Nicolas Obouhov, who called himself "Nicolas l'Illuminé," designed an electronic instrument in the form of a cross, called *Croix Sonore*. In the CIRCUITRY of some ultra-modern scores the SPATIAL DISTRIBUTION of instruments becomes a musical parameter. Elliott Carter, Lukas Foss, Krzysztof Penderecki, Jani Christou, Sylvano Bussoti, Iannis Xenakis, John Cage and others, wrote works stipulating the position of each instrument in relation to the rest of the ensemble.

Collective Nouns. The following are suggestions for COLLECTIVE NOUNS to designate groups of musical instruments: a fluviality of flutes, an exhalation of piccolos, a conviviality of clarinets, a scabrosity of bassoons, a promiscuity of saxophones, an oriflamme of French horns, a plangency of oboes, an ambrosia of harps, a flourish of trumpets, a pomposity of trombones, a phlogiston of tubas, a circumspection of pianos, an enfilade of violins, a reticence of violas, an elegance of cellos, a teratology of double-basses, a titillation of triangles, and the Brobdingnagian borborygmuses of bass drums.

Combinatoriality. In general topology the concept of COMBINATORIALITY applies to the functional congruence of geometrical figures of the same order of continuity. Thus a square can be brought into topological congruence with a circle because all the points of the former are in an enumerable correspondence of the other. On the other hand, the geometry of figure 8 cannot be made congruent with a square or a circle without cutting. The American composer and theorist Milton Babbitt extended the term COMBINATORIALITY to serial techniques. The parameter of continuity in dodecaphonic writing is the order of succession of the 12 thematic notes in their four forms, basic, retrograde, inversion and inverted retrograde, all of which are combinatorially congruent. Furthermore, the tone-row can be functionally divided into two potentially congruent groups of six notes each, or three groups of four notes each, or four groups of three notes each, with each such group becoming a generating serial nucleus possessing a degree of subsidiary COMBINATORIALITY. Extending the concept of COMBINATORIALITY to other parameters of serial music, a state of total SERIALISM is attained, in which not only the actual notes of a series, but also meter, rhythm, intervalic configurations, dynamics and instrumental timbres are organized in sets and subsets. The subsets in turn are organized as combinatorial derivations, possessing their own order of continuity and congruence. Of these, the most fruitful is the principle of rotation, in which each successive set is obtained by the transposition of the first note of the series to the end of a derived set. Thus the first set, 1, 2, 3, . . . 12, appears after rotation as subset 2, 3, 4, 5, . . . 12, 1, or as 3, 4, 5, 6, . . . 12, 1, 2, etc. Inversion, retrograde and inverted retrograde can be subjected to a similar type of rotation. The additive Fibonacci series, in which each number equals the sum of the two preceding numbers, as in 1, 1, 2, 3, 5, 8, 13, 21, is another fertile resource for the formation of sets, subsets and other derivations. The Fibonacci numbers can be used for building non-dodecaphonic tone-rows, in which case the numbers will indicate the distance from the central tone in semitones, modulo 12, so that 13 becomes functionally identical with 1, 21 with 9, etc. The numerical field of COMBINATORIALITY is circumscribed by 12 different notes. But experiments have been conducted, notably by Ernst Krenek, with artificial scales of 13 equal degrees, obtained with the aid of electronic instruments. Potential uses of COMBINATORIALITY operating with sets of more than 12 notes in an octave are limitless.

Controlled Improvisation. An arrangement of available thematic elements, following a definite formal design and confined within a specified period of time, has been described as CONTROLLED IMPROVISATION. Accordingly, the performer selects attractive or significant motives and phrases of an otherwise non-integrated work, as though drawing pre-set lines from a printer's tray, resetting them at will, duplicated, fragmented, or upside-down. Karlheinz Stockhausen, Lukas Foss, Earle Brown, and others have availed themselves of this manner of composition.

Country Music. As it is practiced in the American South, COUNTRY MUSIC is deeply imbued with sentimental balladry, with curiously oblique cadences that impart an archaic flavor to the melody. The syncopated beat, characteristic of RAGTIME and JAZZ, is practically absent in these bland songs.

C-sharp Minor. This key, to judge from its use by composers, particularly in piano pieces, has a meditative, somewhat somber nature. Typical in this regard is the first movement of Beethoven's *Moonlight* Sonata, which suggested to an imaginative critic the surface of a moonlit lake in Switzerland. The famous Prelude in C-sharp minor by Rachmaninoff is an example of the use of this key for solemn evocation of old Russia, with bells ringing over the resonant harmonies. Schumann's *Études symphoniques*, also in C-sharp minor, fit into the description of meditative recollection. There is an evocative Tchaikovsky Nocturne in C-sharp minor. This tonality is rarely encountered as the principal key of a symphonic work. The most outstanding example is Mahler's Symphony No. 5, which begins with the funereal measures of doom, but modulations are frequent in the score. Prokofiev set his last symphony, No. 7, in C-sharp minor; he called the work a *Youth Symphony*, glorifying the spirit of the young Soviet generation. The finale is in the major tonic of the key, enharmonically notated as D-flat major. What is most intriguing in this work is that its opus number is 131, which is the opus number also of one of Beethoven's last string quartets, also in C-sharp minor. Prokofiev, ever alert to numerical parallels and contrived coincidences, could not have been unaware of this double identity of key and opus number, but apparently he decided to enjoy the joke in private. Not one of the usually alert Soviet analysts of Prokofiev's works has noted this similarity. LM

Cubism. The musical counterpart of CUBISM in art is the erection of massive sonorous complexes moving *en bloc* at different speeds and angular motion. Such harmonic boulders produce the best effect in POLYTRIADIC STRUCTURES. CUBISTIC music must be static, with a low potential. There should be no intermediate melodic or harmonic shifts between CUBISTIC complexes, but tremolo effects within each unit may contribute to resonant power congruent with massive sonic structures.

Cyrenaic Hedonism. Hedonistic traits in modern music developed as a natural psychological reaction to the cataclysm of World War I. Composers and the public sought relaxation in hedonistic dalliance, Cyrenaic in its complete orgiastic abandon and Sybaritic in its quest for mindless comforts. The center of this cult of music for pleasure was France; it enjoyed a particular vogue between 1920 and 1935, when the slogan of NEW SIMPLICITY was launched as an antidote to post-Romantic solipsism. In form and content this new music cultivated the elegant conceits of the French rococo period, with an emphasis on Epicurean qualities designed to please the palate. Historically, it was the long-delayed fruition of the musical cuisine of Rossini, with occasional polyharmonies and asymmetric rhythms used for modern seasoning.

Dadaism. The word DADAISM was invented by Tristan Tzara of 8 February 1916 at a congenial gathering of friends in a Zürich café. According to one of the many versions, the word Dada owes its origin to French infantiloquy as a sort of dental lallation. Esthetically, DADAISM was the product of the frustrations endured during the First World War. Its philosophy was entirely negative. Derived from the vociferously proclaimed detestation of all art, music and poetry, DADAISM stood close to FUTURISM in its furious onslaught on all established values, but failed to offer a new art to replace the old. Despite its violently negative code, DADAISM prepared a well-manured ground for the flowering of such fertile stylistic vegetation as SURREALISM. DADAISM also cast its proleptic shadow on the AVANT-GARDE of the 1960's and the improvisatory art of the HAPPENINGS.

Demolition. Public DEMOLITION of musical instruments as part of new techniques of the American and British AVANT-GARDE came into vogue shortly after the conclusion of World War II, possibly as a sado-masochistic exercise of aggressive tendencies, frustrated by the unconditional surrender of the ex-enemies. Contests in the swiftness of destroying upright pianos have been held in clubs and colleges. According to the established rules of the game, a piano had to be reduced to comminuted fragments that could be passed through an aperture of specified dimensions (usually a circle 6 inches in diameter.) In Stockholm, Sweden, a young pianist concluded his recital by igniting a dynamite charge previously secreted inside the piano, blowing it up. An exploding splinter wounded him in the leg. The American AVANT-GARDE composer La Monte Young set a violin on fire at one of his exhibits.

Bakunin, the scientific anarchist, said, "Die Lust der Zerstörung ist eine schaffende Lust." This "creative impulse of destruction" has received its full vindication in the anti-piano activities of the modern times.

Demotic Music. DEMOTIC MUSIC is a generic category that comprises all genres of popular music—rural, urban, pop, country, folk, western, jazz, tin-pan alley, commercial jingles. Modern applications of the resources of DEMOTIC MUSIC are obtained by diatonic translocation, atonal dismemberment and rhythmic compression. Hexachordal diatonic melodies may be metamorphosed into complex melorhythmic progressions without losing their DEMOTIC morphology. ABECEDARIAN MUSIC for children is a fruitful source of such topological transformation. Not all simple music is necessarily DEMOTIC, unless the folk quality is expressed in a composed work with utmost fidelity. Some obscure composers have succeeded in producing tunes that seem to be authentically DEMOTIC. The universally popular tune, *Dark Eyes*, regarded by many as an autochthonous Russian Gypsy song, is actually a violin piece, entitled *Valse-hommage* composed by a German band leader active in Russia in the 1880's. The Neapolitan ballad *Funiculi-Funicula*, mistaken by many for a genuine folk tune, was written by an Italian vocal teacher resident in London.

Dilapidation of Tonality. The disappearance of explicit key signatures from the notation of modern composition was the first symptom of the DILAPIDATION OF TONALITY and deterioration of traditional harmony. The key signature has a reason for existence in NEO-CLASSICAL works in which the tonic-dominant relationship is still extant and triadic modulations strong. But the dormant chromaticism erupts all the more viciously against tonal restraints, and the key signature, if it is set down at all, exists only to be denied. The chromaticization of the modern idiom during the last decades of the 19th-century resulted in an enormous proliferation of double-sharps and double-flats. As enharmonic modulation reared its multicolored head, the antinomy between the tonality symbolized by the key signature and the florid panchromatic display reached the point of arithmetical incompatibility. Seven notes of the diatonic scale represented by seven positions on the music staff and seven letters of the alphabet were to provide notation for the 12 different notes of the chromatic scale. Academic musicians, eager to preserve the fiction of eminent tonality, and being unable to find a common denominator between 7 and 12, erected a fantastic network of accidentals; triple sharps and triple flats pollulate in the *Canons and Fugues* of Wilhelm Middelschulte. A whole section, acoustically equivalent to C major, masquerades in intervalic enharmonies as B-sharp and D-double-flat major in the piano part of Ravel's *Trio*.

Debussy was similarly involved in exotic structures of double-flats and double-sharps in a triadic passage of his *Feuilles mortes*.

Even in the 19th century, tonality was often nominal and the key signature an armature without a function. *Intermezzo No. 4,* op. 76, by Brahms is ostensibly in B-flat major, but the tonic triad is not reached until the final two bars. This type of tonal convention may be described as teleological tonality in which the tonic is the goal rather than the point of departure. The language of ATONALITY arose from the products of the decay of tonal relationships. Genuinely atonal melodies lack the homing instinct; they meander and maunder without the beacon of a tonic in sight. The attraction of the tonic does not exist in atonal writing; the members of an atonal melody are weightless. This atonal assembly deprived of tonal gravity, came to be organized by Arnold Schoenberg in a mutually gravitating dodecaphonic complex. Key signatures are obviously superfluous in atonal and dodecaphonic music, but not in POLYTONALITY where different key signatures are used simultaneously.

The supremacy of tonality demanded that each composition should end in the same key, or in a related key, in which it began. How strong the prerequisite of this tonal uniformity was felt by composers of the 19th century is illustrated by a whimsical annotation of Richard Strauss in his song entitled *Wenn*, published in 1897. In the original version, the principal key is D-flat major, but the final seven bars and the concluding chord are in D major. Strauss supplied an alternative coda in which the transition was made to the original key, with the following footnote: "Vocalists who may perform this song before the end of the 19th century are advised by the composer to transpose the last seven bars a semitone lower so as to arrive at the end of the song in the same key in which it began."

Displaced Tonality. A modernistic resource in tonal techniques which has been successfully applied by composers who are reluctant to abandon tonality altogether, is a DISPLACEMENT of the tonic by an instant modulation a semitone higher or a semitone lower. Translocation by larger intervals is not effective. Major scales are more suitable for such translocation because of the greater intervalic strength within a major tetrachord, while minor tetrachords are often ambiguous. Transposition of the initial three notes of a major scale a semitone higher or lower forms a group of six different notes; a similar translocation in a minor key will entail a duplication of one member of the series. Examples of melodic translocations are found in many works of Prokofiev and Shostakovich.

Dissonant Counterpoint. The term DISSONANT COUNTERPOINT came into usage in the 1920's as a sort of apologetic declaration by proponents of ATONAL MUSIC. It emphasized the functional equality of dissonance and consonance in all types of contrapuntal techniques. In fugal writing, in particular, a strong tendency was evinced to use the tritone as the interval of entry, instead of the traditional perfect fifth of the tonic-dominant complex. DISSONANT COUNTERPOINT does not exclude consonances but puts them on probation. However, the perfect octave, as a cadential interval, is generally shunned by the theoreticians of DISSONANT COUNTERPOINT, and is usually replaced by a major seventh.

Dodecaphonic Music. In historical perspective, DODECAPHONIC MUSIC is the product of a luxuriant development of chromatic melody and harmony. A conscious avoidance of all tonal centers led to the abolition of key signature and a decline of triadic harmony. The type of composition in which all tonal points of reference have been eliminated became known as ATONALITY. It was from this paludous atmosphere of inchoate ATONALITY that the positive and important technical idiom of dodecaphonic composition was gradually evolved and eventually formulated by Arnold Schoenberg as the "method of composing with 12 tones related only to one another." Schoenberg's first explicit use of his method occurs in his *Serenade*, op. 24, written in 1924. Five fundamental ideas underlie Schoenberg's method: (1) Dodecaphonic monothematism in which the entire work is derived from a 12-tone row (*Tonreihe*) which comprises 12 different notes of the chromatic scale. (2) The tone-row is utilized in four conjugate forms: the original, retrograde, inversion, and retrograde inversion. (3) Although the order of the notes in the tone-row is rigidly observed, the individual members of the series can be placed in any octave position, a peculiar feature of dodecaphonic music which results in the wide distribution of the thematic ingredients over the entire vocal or instrumental range of a single part or over sections of different parts. (4) Since each of the 4 forms of the basic 12-tone series can be transposed to any starting point of the chromatic scale, the total of all available forms is 48. (5) Melody, harmony and counterpoint are functions of the tone-row, which may appear in all its avatars, horizontally as melody, vertically as harmony and diagonally as canonic counterpoint. It may also be distributed partly in melodic progressions, partly in harmonic or contrapuntal structures, creating DODECAPHONIC MELOHARMONY or MELOCOUNTERPOINT. Because of the providential divisibility of number 12, the 12-tone row can be arranged in 6 groups in 2-part counterpoint, 4 groups in 3-part counterpoint (or harmony), 3 groups in 4-part harmony or 2 groups in 6-part harmony.

In a communication sent to Nicolas Slonimsky in 1939, Ernst Krenek describes the relationship between ATONALITY and the method of composing with 12 tones as follows: "ATONALITY is a state of the musical material brought about through a general historical development. The 12-tone technique is a method of writing music within the realm of ATONALITY. The sense of key has been destroyed by ATONALITY. The method of composing with 12 tones was worked out in order to replace the old organization of the material by certain new devices."

Schoenberg was not alone in his dodecaphonic illumination. Several musicians, mostly in Austria and Germany, evolved similar systems of organizing the resources of the chromatic scale in a logical and self-contained system of composition. Jef Golyscheff, Russian composer and painter who lived in Germany and eventually settled in Brazil, worked on the problem as early as 1914, and in 1924 published a collection which he called *12 Tondauer Musik*, making use of 12 different tones in thematic structures. At about the same time Nicolas Obouhov invented a system which he called "Absolute Harmony" and which involved the use of all 12 chromatic tones without doubling; he played his piano pieces written in this system at a concert in Petrograd on 3 February 1916.

Passages containing 12 different notes in succession, apart from the simple chromatic scale, are found even in classical works. There is a highly chromaticized passage in Mozart's *G Minor Symphony* derived from three mutually exclusive diminished-seventh chords, aggregating to 12 different notes. The main subject in the section "Of Science" in the score of *Also sprach Zarathustra* by Richard Strauss contains all 12 different notes of the chromatic scale, but they remain uninverted, untergiversated and otherwise unmetamorphosed, and thus cannot be regarded as a sampler of dodecaphonic writing.

Liszt's *Faust Symphony* opens with a theme consisting of four successive augmented triads descending by semitones comprising all 12 different tones, but it cannot be meaningfully described as an anticipation of the dodecaphonic method. Charles Ives has a 12-tone series of different chromatic notes in his instrumental piece *Tone Road No. 3*, which he wrote in 1915. This intuitive invention is important not only as an illustration of his prophetic genius, but also as another indication that dodecaphonic ideas appeared in the minds of musicians working in different parts of the world, completely independent of each other.

Among scattered examples of 12-tone composition of the pre-dodecaphonic years is *L'adieu à la vie* for piano by Alfredo Casella, which ends on a chord of 12 different notes. An amusing example of dodecaphonic prevision is the *Hymn to Futurism* by César Cui, written in 1917, when the last surviving member of the Russian Mighty Five was 82 years old. Intended as a spoof, the piece contains a passage of three mutually exclusive diminished-seventh chords in arpeggio adding up to 12 different notes, and another passage comprising two mutually exclusive augmented triads with a complementary scale of whole tones passing through the unoccupied six spaces, forming another series of 12 different notes. The fact that Cui had two dodecaphonic series in his short composition demonstrates that even in a musical satire the thematic use of 12 different notes was a logical outcome of the process of tonal decay, serving as a fertilizer for the germination of dodecaphonic organisms.

Schoenberg was intensely conscious of the imperative need of asserting his priority in the invention of the method of composition with 12 tones. Among contenders for the honor was Fritz Klein, the author of an extremely ingenious composition for orchestra, *Die Maschine*, subtitled "eine extonale Selbstsatire," published in 1921 under the characteristic pseudonym "Heautontimorumenos" (i.e., Self-Tormentor). This pseudonym Klein took from the title of a play by Terence, which contains the famous aphorism: "Homo sum; humani nil a me alienum puto." Klein's score contains a remarkable array of inventions: a "Mutterakkord" containing 12 different notes and 11 different intervals, a "Pyramidakkord," patterns of rhythmically repeated 12 notes, etc., all presaging the future developments of integral serialism. When queried by Nicolas Slonimsky regarding Klein's role in the history of Dodecaphonic composition, Schoenberg replied (in English): "Although I saw Klein's 12-tone compositions about 1919, 1920 or 1921, I am not an imitator of him. I wrote the melody for *Scherzo* composed of 12 tones in 1915. In the first edition of my *Harmonielehre* (1911), there is a description of the new harmonies and their application which has probably influenced all these men who now want to become my models."

A much more formidable challenge to Schoenberg's dodecaphonic priority was made by Joseph Matthias Hauer of Vienna, who had experimented with 12-tone composition independently from Schoenberg. But his method differed from Schoenberg's in essential aspects. He built 12-tone subjects from 6-tone "tropes," and allowed free permutation of each trope, a concept that was entirely alien to Schoenberg's fundamental doctrine of thematic ordering of the tone-row. Still, Schoenberg regarded Hauer's theories as sufficiently close to his own method to take notice of them. Schoenberg described the dodecaphonic situation in Vienna in a retrospective note published in the program book of a concert of his chamber music given in New York in 1950: "In 1921 I showed my former pupil Erwin Stein the means I had invented to provide profoundly for a musical organization granting logic, coherence and unity. I then asked him to keep this a secret and to consider it as my private method with which to do the best for my artistic purposes." (The arcane character of this report calls to mind a Latin cryptogram in which the astronomer Huygens encoded his discovery of the rings of Saturn to insure the priority of his observations.) "If I were to escape the danger of being his imitator," Schoenberg continued, "I had to unveil my secret. I called a meeting of friends and pupils, to which I also invited Hauer, and gave a lecture on my new method, illustrating it by examples of some finished compositions of mine. Everybody recognized that my method was quite different from that of others." Hauer refused to surrender his own claims as the spiritual protagonist of 12-tone music. A man of an irrepressible polemical temper, he even had a rubber stamp made, which he used in his private correspondence, and which carried the following legend: "Josef Matthias Hauer, der geistiger Urhaber und trotz vielen schlechten Nachahmern immer noch der einziger Kenner und Könner der Zwöftonmusik."

Although Schoenberg's title to the formulation and practical application of the method of composing with 12 tones was finally recognized, in 1948 he came into an unexpected collision with a fictional claimant, Adrian Leverkühn, the hero of Thomas Mann's novel *Doktor Faustus*, described as the inventor of the 12-tone method of composition. In an indignant letter to the editors of the *Saturday Review of Literature* Schoenberg protested against this misappropriation of his invention. The idea that Leverkühn might be considered as a fictional portrait of Schoenberg himself infuriated him. "Leverkühn is depicted," Schoenberg wrote, "from beginning to end, as a lunatic. I am seventy-four and I am not yet insane, and I have never acquired the disease from which this insanity stems. I consider this an insult."

John Stuart Mill once expressed fears that musical invention might soon exhaust its resources, considering the limited number of melodies that could be derived from the eight degrees of the major or the minor scale. He reckoned without the eventual proliferation of chromatic melodies. There are 479,001,600 permutations of 12 units, and as many possible melodies consisting of 12 different notes each. In the dodecaphonic firmament, the melodic horizon is practically unlimited.

The properties of 12-tone composition are truly magical. A priori, it would seem impossible that the 12 notes of the chromatic scale could be arranged in four mutually exclusive triads, considering that its organization was the product of negation of tonality. Yet it has been found empirically that there are two basic solutions of this problem, each capable of three transpositions. But there is a limiting condition: two of these triads must be major and two minor. On the basis of C, these solutions are: (1) C major, D minor, F-sharp major, G-sharp minor; (2) C major, B-flat major, G-sharp minor and F-sharp minor. The ever-present tritone is the interval between the tonics of each pair in the first solution, and between the tonics of the first and last triad in the second solution. It is also possible to distribute the 12 chromatic tones in a group containing a diminished triad, a minor triad, a major triad and an augmented triad. Furthermore it is possible to arrange four mutually exclusive triads in a continuous chain of major and minor thirds, forming a chord of the minor 23rd, e.g. F-sharp major, E major, D minor, C minor in an ascending series. This is the unique solution of this particular problem. The symmetry of these arrangements is extraordinary. These findings were first published in 1947 in Nicolas Slonimsky's *Thesaurus of Scales and Melodic Patterns*, and have been since verified by a digital computer without adding any new solutions.

Far from being sterile excogitations, the theory of mutually exclusive triads has had its practical application long before it was explicitly formulated. A passage including four mutually exclusive triads occurs in the concluding section of Debussy's *Prélude à l'Après-midi d'un Faune* (E major, C minor, D major, B-flat minor, with the melody descending chromatically from G-sharp down to F.)

The method of composing with 12 tones related only to one another did not remain a rigid dogma. Its greatest protagonists, besides Schoenberg himself, were his disciples Alban Berg and Anton von Webern. Somewhat frivolously, they have been described as the Vienna Trinity, with Schoenberg the Father, Berg the Son, and Webern the Holy Ghost. Both Berg and Webern introduced considerable innovations into the Schoenbergian practice. While Schoenberg studiously avoided triadic constructions, Alban Berg used the conjunct series of alternating minor and major triads capped by three whole tones as the principal subject of his last work, the *Violin Concerto* (1935). Schoenberg practically excluded symmetric intervallic constructions and sequences, but Alban Berg inserted, in his opera *Lulu*, a dodecaphonic episode built on two mutually exclusive whole-tone scales. Anton von Webern dissected the 12-tone series into autonomous sections of 6, 4 or 3 units in a group, and related them individually to one another by inversion, retrograde and inverted retrograde. This fragmentation enabled him to make use of canonic imitation much more freely than would have been possible according to the strict Schoenbergian doctrine.

The commonly used term for DODECAPHONIC MUSIC in German is *Zwölf-tonmusik*. In American usage it was translated literally as 12-tone music, but English music theorists strenuously object to this terminology, pointing out that a tone is an acoustical phenomenon and that DODECAPHONY deals with the arrangement of written notes, and that it should be consequently called 12-note music. In Italy the method became known as *Dodecafonia* or *Musica dodecafonica*. Incidentally, the term *Dodecafonia* was first used by the Italian music scholar Domenico Alaleona in his article *L'armonia modernissima* published in *Rivista Musicale* in 1911 but it was applied there in the sense of total chromaticism as an extension of Wagnerian harmony.

The proliferation of dodecaphony in Italy was as potent as it was unexpected, considering the differences between Germanic and Latin cultures, the one introspective and speculative, the other humanistic and practical. Luigi Dallapiccola was one of the earliest adepts, but he liberalized Schoenberg's method and admitted tonal elements. In his opera *Il Prigioniero*, written in 1944, he made use of four mutually exclusive triads.

The greatest conquest of Schoenberg's method was the totally unexpected conversion of Igor Stravinsky whose entire esthetic code had seemed to stand in opposition to any predetermined scheme of composition; yet he adopted it when he was already in his seventies. Many other composers of world renown turned to dodecaphonic devices as a thematic expedient without full utilization of the four basic forms of the tone-row. Béla Bartók made use of a 12-tone melody in his *Second Violin Concerto*, but he modified its structure by inner permutations within the second statement of the tone-row. Ernest Bloch, a composer for whom the constrictions of modern techniques had little attraction, made use of 12-tone subjects in his *Sinfonia Breve* and in his last string quartets. English composers who have adopted the technique of 12-tone composition with various degrees of consistency are Michael Tippett, Lennox Berkeley, Benjamin Frankel, Humphrey Searle, and Richard Rodney Bennett. William Walton makes use of a 12-tone subject in the fugal finale of his *Second Symphony*. Benjamin Britten joined the dodecaphonic community by way of tonality. In his expressionist opera *The Turn of the Screw*, he adopts a motto of alternating perfect fifths and minor thirds (or their respective inversions), aggregating to a series of 12 different notes. The Spanish composer Roberto Gerhard, who settled in England, wrote in a fairly strict dodecaphonic idiom. In France the leader of the dodecaphonic school is René Leibowitz, who also wrote several books on the theory of 12-tone composition. Wladimir Vogel, a Russian-born composer of German parentage, making his home in Switzerland, has adopted Schoenberg's method in almost all of his works. The Swiss composer Frank Martin has extended the principles of dodecaphonic writing to include a number of tonal and modal ramifications.

In America Schoenberg's method has found a fertile ground, not only among his students but also among composers who had pursued different roads. Roger

Sessions, Virgil Thomson, and David Diamond have followed Schoenberg's method with varying degrees of fidelity. Aaron Copland used the dodecaphonic technique in some of his chamber music works; in the orchestral compositions entitled *Connotations* commissioned for the opening concert of Lincoln Center, New York, in 1962, he applied the totality of DODECAPHONY to characterize the modern era of music. Walter Piston interpolated a transitional 12-tone passage in his ballet suite *The Incredible Flutist*. He resisted integral dodecaphony until his septuagenarian calendae, when in his *Eighth Symphony* he adopted Schoenberg's method in all its orthodoxy. Leonard Bernstein inserted a 12-tone series in the score of his *Age of Anxiety* to express inner agitation and anguished expectancy of the music. Samuel Barber made an excursion into the dodecaphonic field in a movement of his *Piano Sonata*. Gian Carlo Menotti turned dodecaphony into parody in his opera *The Last Savage* to illustrate the decadence of modern civilization into which the hero was unexpectedly catapulted from his primitivistic habitat.

In Soviet Russia dodecaphony still remains officially unacceptable as a "formalistic" device. (In a speech delivered in Moscow on 8 March 1963, Nikita Khrushchev, then Prime Minister of the Soviet Union, observed: "They call it dodecaphony, but we call it cacophony.") Nevertheless, some blithe spirits of the young Soviet generation, among them Andrei Volkonsky, Valentin Silvestrov and Sergei Slonimsky, have written and published works in the 12-tone idiom.

The following is a summation of theoretical postulates, subsidiary lemmata and practical usages of dodecaphonic techniques.

(1) The generating dodecaphonic series must be constructed in such a way as to establish a strong mutual valence of the component members, relating them only to one another in accordance with Schoenberg's prescription, and avoiding any suggestion of chordal derivation, particularly that of a triadic nature.

(2) Intervals most suitable for the construction of a viable series are those that carry no tonal affiliation, with particular preference for the major seventh, the minor ninth, and the tritone. Since the intervallic difference between the major seventh and the tritone is a perfect fourth and the difference between the minor ninth and the tritone is a perfect fifth, these differential intervals have acquired a peculiar structural importance in DODECAPHONIC MUSIC, provided they do not appear poised strategically in the potential relationship of the tonic and dominant, or tonic and subdominant. Melodic successions of perfect fourths or perfect fifths are favored since they tend towards atonal asymptotes. Historically, such quartal and quintal progressions led to the distinctive evolution of atonal patterns preceding the formation of strictly dodecaphonic conformations.

(3) Identical intervals between successive pairs of thematic tones are to be used with circumspection so as not to impair the individuality of members of the tone-row and prevent their degeneration and entropic coalescence into chromatic or diatonic scales or into easily decipherable chordal combinations.

(4) Although the original tone-row must be stated in full in the exposition, immediate repetition of a single tone in the series is not to be regarded as a disruptive factor, for such repetition may be simply a synonym for a rhythmic prolongation.

(5) Since the concept of tonality is irrelevant to DODECAPHONIC MUSIC, the key signature is automatically eliminated. For the same reason chromatic alterations pertinent to tonal usages and modulation are reduced to their simplest enharmonic equivalents; double sharps and double flats are completely eliminated. Some dodecaphonic composers insist on prefixing every note with a sharp, flat or natural, but this type of notation is visually distracting and wasteful.

(6) Functional and operative equivalence of melody, harmony and counterpoint is of fundamental importance to the Dodecaphonic techniques and constitutes its most innovative feature; thus the 12 tones of the series may be distributed either horizontally in melodic lines, vertically in harmonic columns, or diagonally in contrapuntal formations becoming different dimensions of a unified dodecaphonic space.

(7) Triadic chordal formations are unacceptable in vertical constructions as well as in horizontal melodies. Major triads, particularly in root positions, are inadmissible; their inversions are to be avoided in conspicuous positions. Only slightly less objectionable are minor triads in root positions, but inversions of minor triads in an atonal context are often tolerated. Explicit dominant-seventh chords, implying as they do the presence of the leading tone, are incompatible with the atonal essence of dodecaphony. Similarly obnoxious are diminished-seventh chords because of their connotations as leading-tone harmonies and also because of their uniform intervallic structure.

(8) PANDIATONICISM and POLYTONALITY have no place in the dodecaphonic vocabulary on account of their tonal derivation. Generally speaking, acoustical euphony, inflated sonorities and facile fluidity of harmonic progressions are contrary to dodecaphonic esthetics; any external effects of a melodious or harmonious nature are in conflict with the austere spirit and philosophical severity of the serial designs.

(9) Although the fundamental series and its derivations are available in 12 transpositions, such exhaustive utilization of serial materials is rarely found in actual works. Paradoxically, the most favored transpositions, particularly in sections corresponding to recapitulation in classical forms, stand in a quartal-quintal relationship, demonstrating once more the strength of the classical legacy in dodecaphonic composition. One would expect frequent transpositions at a tritone, but such is not the case, because the tritone is apt to be of strategic use in the original series, and would duplicate itself in such a transposition.

(10) The formal structure of works written in the 12-tone idiom is remarkably conservative, following the classical models of variations, passacaglia, prelude, suite, or serenade. The most striking instance of this classical consciousness is the organization of Alban Berg's expressionistic opera *Lulu*, a definitely serial work, which nevertheless contains individual sections bearing titles of Baroque forms. Variations are especially congenial to dodecaphonic organization, with the 12-tone row representing the theme and the retrograde, inversion and inverted retrograde being the three basic variations.

(11) Large forms, such as sonatas and symphonies, are not suited to dodecaphonic treatment owing to the essentially tonal thematic relationship between the exposition, the development and the recapitulation. For similar reasons, dodecaphonic treatment cannot be applied to fugal forms. Canonic imitation is possible when the 12-tone row is fragmented into subdivisions of 3, 4, or 6 notes each, as in some works by Anton von Webern, where such infradodecaphonic segments stand in a structural symmetric relationship of inverted and retrograde correspondence to one another.

(12) Polymetric and polyrhythmic developments are but rarely encountered in DODECAPHONIC compositions. Binary and ternary time signatures of the classical type are prevalent, while compound meters are rare. Triplets, quintuplets and other groups of prime divisions of note values are virtually absent because of the difficulty of fitting such groups into the serial melodic-harmonic scheme. Certain rhythmic predilections may be noted, especially the "Schoenberg Sigh," consisting of a short note on the strong beat immediately followed by an unstressed long note.

(13) In orchestration, traditional scoring prevails. There is no inclination to introduce exotic or unusual instruments; the flexaton in the score of Schoenberg's *Variations for Orchestra* is an exception. Special percussion effects are alien to the spirit of DODECAPHONIC MUSIC. On the other hand, there is a great variety of sound-color (*Klangfarbe*), with a fine gradation of dynamic elements.

(14) Historically, esthetically and structurally, 12-tone music is an evolutionary product of the ultra-chromatic modalities of the post-Wagnerian school of composition. The algorithms of chromatic convergence and divergence in DODECAPHONIC harmony are common. An experimental proof of this evolutionary origin of DODECAPHONIC melody and harmony may be provided by a calculated cancellation of a minimal number of sharps or flats, never exceeding a shift of a semitone, with the resulting product being an essentially diatonic composition with functional chromatic passing notes. Conversely, a simple diatonic melody may be metamorphosed into a DODECAPHONIC series provided that invariance of the vectorial factor is observed, so that the directional intervalic design remains unaltered. Repeated notes in the original diatonic melody can be replaced by their immediate neighbors. Operating according to these procedures, the Viennese melody *Ach du lieber Augustin*, the initial refrain of which happens to contain 12 notes if the last repeated note is omitted, can be transmuted dodecaphonically according to the following formula, in which the capital letters represent the notes of the original tune, ascending intervals are designated by the plus sign, descending intervals by the minus sign, and the numbers are semitone units: G, A, G + 1, F + 1, E + 1, C + 2, C + 1, D + 2, G + 4, G + 3, E - 1, C. It is to be observed that in this case a conscious effort has been made to retain the first and last notes of the original melody, thus preserving an explicit dominant-tonic relationship.

(15) The hereditary characteristics of the DODECAPHONIC techniques strongly point to their ultimate classical origins. The very foundation of the thematic arrangements in inversions and retrograde forms is an old classical and even pre-classical method of varying a thematic subject. Furthermore, there seems to be a tendency in the works of Schoenberg, Berg and Anton von Webern to extend the field of classical devices, particularly in the use of ostinati composed of a segment of the 12-tone row. Thus the tolerance of an immediate repetition of a thematic tone is extended to the repetition of a thematic fragment.

In view of the possibility of such DODECAPHONIC self-pollination, there is no reason to fear that DODECAPHONIC COMPOSITION would degenerate into an endless permutation of the available 479,001,600 combinations resulting from the factorial algorithm (12!). The second and the third generations of composers of 12-tone music have devised other methods of serial construction, the most interesting of them being a sort of DODECAPHONIC amputation, which reduces the 12-tone row to a hendecaphonic or decaphonic group of thematic notes. An attractive resource is to leave the amputated member of the series completely out of the account until the very end of a composition, when it would suddenly appear like a *tonus ex machina* and, suspended in a protracted fermata, would assert itself as a triumphantly recessive prodigal tonic.

Electronic Music. ELECTRONIC MUSIC was revealed to the world on 5 August 1920 when the Russian engineer and cello player Leon Theremin gave a demonstration of his *Thereminovox* at the Moscow Technological Institute. The apparatus consisted of a set of cathode tubes, a vertical antenna and a metal arc; the sound was produced heterodynamically by the movement of the right hand which changed the electric potential in the area, creating a differential tone which determined the height of pitch. The left hand manipulated the field in the vicinity of the metal arc, regulating the power and the timbre of the sound. In constructing this instrument Theremin seemed to carry out Lenin's dictum that "socialism is proletarian dictatorship plus electrification." Theremin's invention was followed by a number of electronic instruments, among which the most successful was *Les Ondes Martenot*, a keyboard instrument for which a number of modern French composers wrote special works. In Germany, Joerg Mager constructed an electronic instrument which he called *Sphärophon*, and later developed other models, *Partiturophon* and *Kaleidophon*. A more practical and a more successful electronic instrument was *Trautonium* manufactured by Friedrich Trautwein; Hindemith wrote some music for it. Oscar Sala introduced some innovations into the *Trautonium* in an electronic organ which he called *Mixtur-Trautonium*.

Unlimited musical horizons opened to ELECTRONIC MUSIC with the introduction of the so-called *Synthesizers*, capable of producing any frequency with the utmost precision and distribute the relative strength of the overtones so as to create any desired instrumental timbre. With the aid of *Synthesizers* it becomes possible to construct scales of any number of equal degrees. Ernst Krenek wrote a piece of music containing 13 equal parts of the octave. Among the capacities of the modern *Synthesizer* is the reproduction of a recorded composition at any speed without altering the pitch. No problem of articulation arises, for the generation of the sound is electronic, completely independent of all mechanical elements. In 1969 the American engineer, providentially named Moog, perfected a portable synthesizer which advanced the techniques of ELECTRONIC MUSIC still further. The *Moog*, as it came to be called, may well become the house instrument of the second half of the 20th century.

ELECTRONIC MUSIC requires special notation. One of the earliest attempts at a practical system was made in 1937 by Percy Grainger in his *Free Music* for 4 electronic instruments constructed by Theremin, indicating pitch and dynamic intensities in a four-part score on graph paper.

Epigonism. The original meaning of the word *epigones* is "those who were born later." In Greek mythology and history, it was applied to descendants of the seven heroic warriors who conquered the city of Thebes. In modern usage, epigonism has acquired derogatory connotations; an epigone is seen as a mediocrity in the following of greatness. An example of musical epigonism is illustrated in the career of Siegfried Wagner, the "little son of a great father." He wrote operas tantalizingly Wagnerian in their libretti and in their music but totally lacking the greatness that Wagner infused into his music dramas. When Hans von Bülow called Richard Strauss "Richard the Second," it was not, however, with the purpose of derogation but with the intention of elevating him to the great legacy of Richard the First, Wagner. Even though Richard Strauss himself adopted many Wagnerian dramatic devices, he created works so powerful and so individual that it would be wrong to apply the term *epigone* to him. A typical Wagnerian epigone was August Bungert, who wrote two operatic cycles built on the model of the *Ring*, to libretti drawn from Homer's epics; his efforts are pathetic examples of infertile futility. The adoption of a certain method of composition first established by a great master is not necessarily the mark of an epigone. Many contemporary composers have adopted Schoenberg's method of composing with 12 tones, among them such superb musicians as Anton von Webern and Alban Berg, and they certainly cannot be described as epigones. Nor does a return to the technique of composers of a much earlier era constitute epigonism. Stravinsky adopted the techniques of the Baroque, but it would be a mistake to regard his neo-Classical works as the products of an epigone. However, the imitators of Stravinsky's emulation of the Baroque are typical epigones, or rather epigones of the second remove. To justify the introduction of a historical or aesthetic category such as epigonism, it is necessary to establish a direct line of succession from a great master to his less significant followers. Furthermore, a great master must also be a great innovator in order to generate a line of epigones. Debussy was such a great master, and his epigones are legion. Mere imitators are not epigones in the historical sense of significant succession. Thousands of composers in the second half of the 18th century imitated Handel without creating a distinct movement of epigonism. Thousands of composers intitated Mendelssohn in the second half of the 19th century, but they could not be called Mendelssohn's epigones in the aesthetic sense. Boccherini was derisively described as "the wife of Haydn" because of the close kinship of his musical idiom to that of Haydn, but again it would be misleading to call him an epigone of Haydn.

To conclude: Epigonism, a historical phenomenon in the arts, is characterized by the emergence of artists, writers, or musicians who consciously or unconsciously adopt a mode of formal composition that constitutes a logical continuation of the artistic accomplishments of a master who inspired them. Such a group, furthermore, must create a certain aesthetic atmosphere in which they can breathe freely and contribute signally to the formation of a school possessing distinct stylistic features. It would not be difficult to compile a suggestive list of composers during the past century who were true epigones of a great master. Such a classification would be more enlightening and conducive to the proper understanding of stylistic evolution than the commonly used practice of relegating such *di minores* of the arts to the rubric of "other contemporary composers." Max Reger was an epigone of the Romantic movement. Arensky and Kalinnikov were epigones of Tchaikovsky's Russian Romanticism. But it would be misleading to describe Rachmaninoff and Glazunov as epigones, because they elevated themselves above pure imitation of their predecessors and created their own distinguished style of composition. LM

Ethnic Resources. National musical cultures have developed from two distinct resources: the ethnic legacy and universally adopted techniques of composition. When Villa-Lobos was asked "What is folklore?" he replied, "I am folklore!" By this declaration he meant to say that in his original melodic inventions he gave expression to the artistic consciousness of the Brazilian people. In his *Bachianas brasileiras*, Bachian counterpoint gives ancillary service to ethnic Brazilianism. Charles Ives created single-handedly a modern American idiom that employs ETHNIC RESOURCES in a perfect SYNCRETISM of substance and technique. In Russia, the primacy of ETHNIC RESOURCES is maintained partly by the national spirit of the people and partly by the ideological principles of SOCIALIST REALISM which prescribes the realistic style of music within the framework of national modalities.

Ethnic musical materials are not necessarily incompatible with modern techniques. It is possible to arrange a popular tune dodecaphonically by applying various intervalic extensions and compressions, while retaining the vectorial parameters of the original melody. Perhaps the most congenial modern technique in making use of ETHNIC RESOURCES is PANDIATONICISM, in which the tonal functions are preserved and enhanced.

Etiology. The study of causation, or ETIOLOGY, is of importance not only in medicine and physics, but also in the fine arts. Particularly informing is the ETIOLOGY of ultra-modern music which is often likened by hostile observers to a symptom of mass dyscrasia. But to its adepts new music is the revelation of a superior psyche. Dostoyevsky, who suffered from epilepsy, advances the daring notion that during an epileptic *grand mal* the mind penetrates the ultimate mysteries of life and death. Similarly, the manifestations of the musical AVANT-GARDE, whether in the popular or technically complex field, are to their participants the proleptic vistas of the new universal art. Schoenberg, more than any other composer, endured endless abuse on the part of uncomprehending critics, but he never doubted the correctness of his chosen path. Edgar Varèse, who was similarly abused, wrote in a personal letter in 1931: "I know where I am going, and what will follow. My plan is clearly drawn, its development logical, its result assured." In the perspective of history, both Schoenberg and Varèse proved right. The ETIOLOGY of their genius is a lesson for the future.

Euphony. Etymologically, EUPHONY implies a happy sound, but it is not necessarily synonymous with consonant harmony. A succession of dissonances, if they follow a natural tonal sequence, may sound entirely euphonious to the ear, while a progression of disembodied open fifths or disemboweled multiple octaves could register as uneuphonious and unsettling. Psychological apperception is the determining factor in this aural impression. Generally speaking, soft dissonances are tolerated better than loud consonances. Even more decisive is the factor of linear EUPHONY. A single line of an atonal melody impresses an untutored ear as an unacceptable dissonance, even though no simultaneous complex of sounds is involved. If an atonal melody were to be performed at a very slow tempo with long silences between the individual notes, no linear disharmony could then result. But the faster the tempo, the more disruptive to the peace of mind does an atonal melody become. It should be remembered that the word *harmonia* meant a melody in ancient Greek music. A rapid succession of tones unconnected by a uniform tonality will appear as a meaningless jumble of notes to an inexperienced listener. On the other hand, a musician trained in the art of listening to serial music will accept atonal melodies as legitimate expressions of a musical sentiment. The linearity of melody depends exclusively on the instant dampening of a sound in the cochlea without a tinnitus, but the memory of the previous sound persists, much in the manner that the retina of the eye retains the static images of a cinematographic film. It would be interesting to speculate on the possible course of music as an art if the cochlea, too, possessed the ability to retain sounds for a fraction of a second. Suffice it to say that all music, vocal, instrumental or percussive, would then become polyphonic.

Expressionism. EXPRESSIONISM stands in a reciprocal relationship to IMPRESSIONISM, as its functional and psychological counterpart. IMPRESSIONISM derives its source of inspiration from external sources, whereas EXPRESSIONISM conjures up its images in the inner world of the human psyche and exteriorizes its states as an intimate subjective report. IMPRESSIONISM tends to be pictorial and exotic; EXPRESSIONISM is introspective and metaphysical. Impressionistic literature, art and music are easily projected outside; EXPRESSIONISM is an arcane medium, born in the deepest recesses of the psychic complex and cannot easily be translated into the common language of the arts. The receiver of colorful images of Impressionist art or music has the means of comparing the precise reality with the artist's impressions of it. No such scale of comparison is available to an outside recipient of Expressionist art, for it is a product of the artist's dream in which the dreamer experiences shock and surprise despite the fact that he is both the author and the victim of his own dreams. Because of this duality of the Expressionistic process, the art of EXPRESSIONISM itself suffers from the trauma of illogic; it is characterized by the breakdown of illation and by the disruption of the consequential processes of psychic transmission. The unreality of EXPRESSIONIST drama, poetry, painting and music, is the greatest obstacle for general comprehension. But once the curtain is removed and the secret images of a dreamer reach the observer in the form of poetry, art or music, EXPRESSIONISM becomes a universal medium of mass communication and the greatest multiplier of artistic emotion.

It is natural that because of the basic antimony between the sources of IMPRESSIONISM and EXPRESSIONISM, each should generate a distinctive musical language. IMPRESSIONISM thrives on equilibrated euphony of harmonious dissonances, while EXPRESSIONISM prefers the harsh syntax of ATONALITY. The coloristic opulence of Impressionist music is obtained through the expansion of tonal materials into the spacious structures of resonant harmonies and exotic scales. EXPRESSIONISM, on the other hand, communicates its deep-seated anxieties through chromatic congestion and atonal dispersion. IMPRESSIONISM builds its thematic contents on fluctuating modality, block harmonies and parallel progressions of triadic formations. EXPRESSIONISM rejects modality, tonality and all diatonic textures. Its melodies are constructed parabolically, away from a putative tonic. In its evocation of the classical past, IMPRESSIONISM integrates the diatonic materials into the enhanced edifices of PANDIATONICISM. The harmonic idiom of EXPRESSIONISM is formed by the superposition of fourths and fifths. Progressions of consecutive perfect fourths or fifths result in the formation of 12 different notes in a panchromatic complex, preparing the foundation of the method of composing with 12 tones related only to one another, as formulated by Schoenberg.

There are profound differences in the historic, cultural and geographic factors in the development of IMPRESSIONISM and EXPRESSIONISM. IMPRESSIONISM is Gallic, EXPRESSIONISM Germanic. The French syllabification of IMPRESSIONISTIC poetry is a paradigm of euphonious instrumentation, with the vowels acquiring specific weights and distinctive colors. The German texts of EXPRESSIONIST songs offer no sonorous gratification of resonant vocables, but in their guttural strength they seem to deepen the penetration of the philosophical and often mystical notions underlying the words.

Though IMPRESSIONISM in music is a close counterpart of pictorial art, no Impressionist composer of any stature has ever tried his hand at painting pictures. EXPRESSIONISM is basically a psychic development with no esthetic contact with painting, and yet composers of the Expressionist school, notably Schoenberg and Berg, possessed a striking talent for painting in the EXPRESSIONIST style. Jef Golyscheff, the composer of early atonal music, emigrated to Brazil and became an Expressionist painter. Carl Ruggles, an American composer who developed a sui generis EXPRESSIONIST style in an atonal idiom, abandoned composition entirely and devoted himself to abstract painting.

Fetishes and Taboos. In the inexorable course of history and of the arts, FETISHES of yesterday become TABOOS of tomorrow. The following modernistic FETISHES of the recent musical past have become TABOOS: (1) The diminished-seventh chord, once favored by Italian opera composers, the *Accorde di Stupefazione*, used to melodramatize the high points in operatic action. Verdi, who was responsible for some of the most effective applications of this "Chord of Stupefaction," often in parallel chromatic progressions, in his own operas, issued a stern warning to young composers not to abuse it. No self-respecting composer of today would resort to such unsophisticated practices, except for musical persiflage. (2) Tonal sequences, particularly those rising or descending by degrees, known as *Rosalias*, after an old popular Italian ballad, "Rosalia, mia cara." Indeed, sequences of any kind have virtually disappeared from 20th-century music. (3) The WHOLE-TONE SCALE, once a FETISH of IMPRESSIONISM, has now sunk into noxious desuetude as a cinematic effect used to portray strutting Nazis, mad scientists or schizoid females on the sound track. (4) Parallel progressions of major-ninth chords and consecutive formations of second inversions of major triads at intervals of minor thirds, one of the most prized formulas of IMPRESSIONISM. (5) The *Pétrouchka Chord*, known also as *Parisian Chord*, consisting of two major triads at the distance of a tritone. This early instance of BITONALITY, which became a FETISH of modern French music in the second quarter of the 20th century has been disfranchised and relegated to the category of FRAUDULENT MODERNISM. There are even signs and tokens on the firmament that the sacrosanct FETISH of the 20th century, the DODECAPHONIC method of composition, is on the point of deciduous decay, losing its dodecuple integrity and degenerating into the lipogrammatic hendecaphonic or decaphonic series.

Formalism. The term FORMALISM has acquired a specific pejorative meaning in Soviet esthetics, as a method inimical to the essence of desirable art. The *Encyclopedic Music Dictionary*, published in Moscow in 1966, defines FORMALISM as follows: "FORMALISM represents an artificial separation of form from content, and the attribution to formal elements of self-sufficient primary values to the detriment of musical content. . . . In contemporary esthetics, FORMALISM becomes a method of art hostile to realism and cultivated especially by the adepts of MODERNISM. FORMALISM is based on the theory of art for art's sake, counterposing the artist to society and art itself to life, seeking to create an artistic form detached from objective reality. The governing precepts of FORMALISM are the negation of ideological and realistic content of a work of art, a construction of arbitrary new forms, combined with the denial of national cultural heritage. In the final analysis, FORMALISM results in the abolition of artistic imagery and disintegration of formal coherence. In musical practice, FORMALISM rejects the ideational and emotional musical values and denies the capacity of a musical work to reflect reality. Proponents of FORMALISM attempt to justify their fallacious doctrine by pointing out the specific nature of music as an art lacking the external connection with the world of real objects, such as is present in painting or sculpture, and intrinsically incapable of conveying a concrete narrative characteristic of literature. The esthetic teaching of Marxism refutes FORMALISM by a scientific approach to music as a special form of social ideology. The reactionary theories of FORMALISM are assiduously cultivated in books and articles by the apologists of musical MODERNISM. The struggle for the correct formulation of SOCIALIST REALISM leads to the removal of FORMALISM from its pedestal. One should not confuse FORMALISM, however, with genuine individual originality or with true innovation in the field of musical forms and in the inner substance of a composition, which constitute an unalienable part of authentic realistic art."

Furniture Music. In his sustained effort to degrade music and to reduce it to a menial level, Erik Satie was prompted to inaugurate a demonstration of *Musique d'ameublement*, which he defined as "new music played during intermission at theatrical events or at a concert, designed to create a certain ambience." At an actual performance at the Paris Art Gallery, Satie placed his musicians in separate groups, and urged the public to treat them as functional objects, to speak loudly and not to listen with professional attention. The performers were free to play anything they wished regardless of the repertoire selected by their confrères.

Futurism. FUTURISM is a modern movement in the arts that emerged in Italy early in the 20th century, under the aegis of the Italian poet Marinetti. Its musical credo was formulated by Balilla Pratella in his *Manifesto of Futurist Musicians* issued in Milan on 11 October 1910 and supplemented by a *Technical Manifesto of Futurist Music* of 11 March 1911. On 11 March 1913 Luigi Russolo published his own *Futurist Manifesto*. In these declarations the Italian FUTURISTS proclaimed their complete disassociation from classical, romantic and IMPRESSIONIST music and announced their aim to build an entirely new music inspired by the reality of life in the new century, with the machine as the source of inspiration. And since modern machines were most conspicuous by the noise they made, Pratella and Russolo created a new art of noises, *Arte dei Rumori*. Russolo designed special noise instruments and subdivided them into six categories. His instruments were rudimentary and crude, with amplification obtained by megaphones, but there is no denying that the Futurists provided a prophetic vision of the electronic future of fifty years later. It is interesting to note that most Futurist musicians and poets were also painters. Their pictures, notably those of Luigi Russolo, emphasized color rather than machine-like abstractions, and generally approximated the manner of Abstract EXPRESSIONISM. In the music by Pratella and others we find a profusion of modern devices of their Futurist day, with a foremost place given to the WHOLE-TONE SCALE. The Futurists gave monody preference over polyphony, and steady rhythm to asymmetry. The future of the Futurists appears passé, but they opened the gates to the experimenters of the actual chronological future, which none of them lived to witness.

Game Music. Games of musical compositions, in which cards, each containing a musical phrase, are put together according to special rules, are of considerable antiquity. One such game, *Musikalisches Würfelspiel*, was put on the market in London in 1806 and was announced as "Mozart's musical game, enclosed in an elegant box instructing in a system of easy composition by mechanical means of an unlimited number of waltzes, rondos, hornpipes, reels and minuets." The attribution to Mozart is spurious, but the game itself has a certain ingenuity. The players were to throw a pair of dice, and the number indicated the particular card containing a musical phrase. Since the sequence was arranged so that each card was interchangeable with other cards containing melodies in approximately the same range set in similar harmonies, there was obviously no danger of running into difficulties. A much more modern conceit was suggested by an English musician William Hayes in his book entitled *The Art of Composing Music by a Method Entirely New, Suited to the Meanest Capacity*, published in 1751, in which the author, with a rather crude satirical intent, explained the principle of the game: "Take a brush with stiff bristles (like a toothbrush), dip it into an inkwell, and, by scraping the bristles with the finger, spatter with one sweep a whole composition onto the staff paper. You have only to add stems, bar lines, slurs, etc., to make the opus ready for immediate performance. Whole and half-notes are entirely absent, but who cares for sustained tones anyway!" This is indeed a proleptic anticipation of methods of composition used by the AVANT-GARDE 200 years after the publication of this lively manual.

An interesting modern game can be devised using several sets of dodecaphonic cards, each set containing all 12 notes of the chromatic scale. The deck is shuffled and distributed among players. One after another, the players put down duplicates in their hands and collect a missing note of the next dodecaphonic series from the cards put down by other players. The winner is the player who first assembles all 12 different notes.

The most ambitious musical game of the modern era is *Stratégie* by Iannis Xenakis, first performed at the Venice Festival on 23 April 1963. In it, two conductors lead two different orchestras in two uncoordinated works. The audience declares the winner, taking into consideration the excellence of each orchestral group, marking points on the scoreboard for most striking rhythms, best color effects and finest instrumental solos.

Modern scores descriptive of games are numerous. Arthur Honegger wrote a symphonic movement *Rugby*, Arthur Bliss composed a ballet entitled *Checkmate*, Paul Reif selected *Philidor's Defense* as the title of a work for a chamber orchestra, inspired by a chess game played in 1858. Stravinsky portrayed a poker game in his *Jeu de Cartes*, a ballet in three deals in which the joker is defeated by a royal flush in hearts. A more abstract score by Stravinsky, entitled *Agon*, also portrays a game. Debussy's ballet score *Jeux* depicts an allegorical game of tennis.

Gauche Dexterity. Satire and burlesque depend for their effect on a deliberate violation of traditional rules of melodic structure, rhythmic symmetry and harmonic euphony. A sophisticated imitation of such semi-literate gaucherie often becomes an art in itself. Examples are many: Stravinsky reproduces the heterogeneous harmony of the barrel organ in *Pétrouchka*; Darius Milhaud tonalizes the natural cacophony of a barroom in the score of *Le Boeuf sur le toit*. Erik Satie elevated the dexterity of his gaucherie into a high art of musical persiflage; he was helped in it by his lack of an academic technique of composition; it was easier for him than for real masters to imitate ineptitude.

Gebrauchsmusik. The term GEBRAUCHSMUSIK, or Utilitarian Music, came into vogue shortly after the end of World War I; its earliest mention is found in the German magazine *Signale für die Musikalische Welt* of December 1918. GEBRAUCHSMUSIK promoted the utilization of new mechanical instruments, the radio, the phonograph and music for the films. A variety of GEBRAUCHSMUSIK was GEMEINSCHAFTSMUSIK, Community music, which cultivated choral singing. The term GEMEINSCHAFTSMUSIK was later changed to Sing- und Spielmusik, in the generic category of HAUSMUSIK. Probably the first work written specially for such groups by a modern composer was *Das neue Werk* by Paul Hindemith. Stylistically, GEBRAUCHSMUSIK has developed a type of modern melody, rhythm, harmony and orchestration making free use of utilitarian dissonance, polytonal combinations and polymetric arrangements. An innovation in GEBRAUCHSMUSIK is spoken rhythmic song, a variant of SPRECHSTIMME. In opera, the librettos were usually satirical and political, with a radical bent, especially PROLETARIAN MUSIC. From Germany, operatic GEBRAUCHSMUSIK was transplanted to America, where economic impoverishment contributed to its popularity. GEBRAUCHSMUSIK had little success in Russia, France or Italy, countries with a rich operatic culture, in which there was no necessity of reducing operatic productions to miniature dimensions. HAUSMUSIK, and GEBRAUCHSMUSIK in general, relied on the participation of the audience. Children's music is a natural product of GEBRAUCHSMUSIK. Hindemith wrote the first piece of GEBRAUCHSMUSIK designed specially for singing and acting by children, *Wir bauen eine Stadt*.

Gestalt. GESTALT is a fashionable psychological term which, in an attractively misapprehended scientific German nomenclature, connotes an ensemble of apperceptions produced by a series of sensory stimuli. The word, which can be literally translated as form, figure or appearance, indicates a psychological interaction between the physical nature of a given phenomenon and the inner interpretation of it by a receptive mind. The shape of a white vase against a uniformly black background, may be perceived as two human figures facing each other if the symmetric sides of the vase are drawn to resemble silhouettes. In music, GESTALT is capable of many interpretations, of which the most literal is enharmonic ambivalence, as for instance the perception of a triad as a dissonance in the context of alien harmonies. Thus, if a C major triad is sounded immediately after an unrelated dominant-seventh chord based on E-flat, the ear would demand its resolution into the dissonant syndrome of the preceding dominant-seventh chord. Generally speaking, GESTALT is apprehended as an entire ensemble of musical parameters, comprising form, proportional distribution of consonances and dissonances, diatonic or chromatic tropism, symmetry or asymmetry of melorhythmic figurations, etc.

Grandmother Chord. Chord, invented by Nicolas Slonimsky on February 13, 1938, containing all 12 different tones and different intervals symmetrically invertible in relation to the central interval, the tritone, which is the inversion of itself; the intervallic structure being a row of alternatingly odd and even intervals (counted in semitones), the odd-numbered series forming a diminishing arithmetical progression, and the even-numbered series an increasing progression. TSMP

Graphic Notation. Ever since 1000 A.D. when Guido d'Arezzo drew a line to mark the arbitrary height of pitch, musical notation has been geometric in its symbolism. The horizontal coordinate of the music staff still represents the temporal succession of melodic notes, and the vertical axis indicates the simultaneous use of two or more notes in a chord. Duration values have, through the centuries of evolution, been indicated by the color and shape of notes and stems to which they were attached. The composers of the AVANT-GARDE, eager to reestablish the mathematical correlation between the coordinates of the musical axes have written scores in which the duration was indicated by proportional distance between the notes. Undoubtedly such geometrical precision contributes to the audiovisual clarity of notation, but it is impractical in actual usage. A passage in whole-notes or half-notes followed by a section in rapid rhythms would be more difficult to read than the imprecise notation inherited from the past. In orchestral scores, there is an increasing tendency to cut off the inactive instrumental parts in the middle of the page rather than to strew such vacuums with a rash of rests. A graphic system of tablature notation was launched in Holland under the name *Klavarskribo*, an Esperanto word meaning keyboard writing. It has been adopted in many schools in Holland.

New sounds demanded new notational symbols. Henry Cowell, who invented tone-clusters, notated them by drawing thick vertical lines attached to a stem. Similar notation was used for similar effects by the Russian composer Vladimir Rebikov. In his book, *New Musical Resources*, Cowell tackled the problem of non-binary rhythmic division and outlined a plausible system that would satisfy this need by using square, triangular and rhomboid shapes of notes. Alois Hába of Czechoslovakia, a pioneer in microtonal music, devised special notation for quarter-tones, third-tones and sixth-tones.

As long as the elements of pitch, duration, intervalic extension and polyphonic simultaneity remain in force, the musical staff can accommodate these elements more or less adequately. Then noises were introduced by the Italian Futurists into their works. In his compositions, the Futurist Luigi Russolo drew a network of curves, thick lines and zigzags to represent each particular noise. But still the measure and the proportional lengths of duration retained their validity. The situation changed dramatically with the introduction of ALEATORY processes and the notion of indeterminacy of musical elements. The visual appearance of aleatory scores assumes the aspect of ideograms. John Cage, in particular, remodeled the old musical notation so as to give improvisatory latitude to the performer. The score of his *Variations I* suggests the track of cosmic rays in a cloud chamber. His *Cartridge Music* looks like an exploding supernova, and his *Fontana Mix* is a projection of irregular curves upon a strip of graph paper. The Polish Avant-Garde composer Krzysztof Penderecki uses various graphic symbols to designate such effects as the highest possible sound on a given instrument, free improvisation within a certain limited range of chromatic notes, or icositetraphonic tone-clusters.

In music for MIXED MEDIA, notation ceases to function per se, giving way to pictorial representation of the actions or psychological factors involved. Indeed, the modern Greek composer Jani Christou introduces the Greek letter *psi* to indicate the psychology of the musical action, with geometric ideograms and masks symbolizing changing mental states ranging from complete passivity to panic. The score of *Passion According to Marquis de Sade* by Sylvano Bussotti looks like a surrealistic painting with musical notes strewn across its path. The British Avant-Garde composer Cornelius Cardew draws black and white circles, triangles and rectangles to indicate musical action. Iannis Xenakis prefers to use numbers and letters indicating the specific tape recordings to be used in his musical structures. Some composers abandon the problem of notation entirely, recording their inspirations on tape.

The attractiveness of a visual pattern is a decisive factor. The American avant-garde composer Earle Brown draws linear abstractions of singular geometric excellence. Karlheinz Stockhausen often supplements his analytical charts by elucidatory (or tantalizingly obscurative) annotations.

The chess grandmaster Tarrasch said of a problematical chess move: "If it is ugly, it is bad." *Mutatis mutandis*, the same criterion applies to a composer's musical graph.

Gymnosophistical Homophony. The description Gymnosophist is applied to an Indian sect that flourished about 1,000 A.D. who preached abstinence from carnal delights, refused to wear clothes and limited themselves to the simplest modes of communication. Etymologically, the word is derived from the Greek roots for "naked" and "wisdom." Archaizing usages and affectation of utmost simplicity in musical composition may well be called GYMNOSOPHISTICAL; naked fifths, in particular, when applied ostentatiously in modern works, creating the impression of luxurious abstemiousness, are GYMNOSOPHISTICAL. Erik Satie, in his sophisticated practice of GYMNOSOPHISTICAL harmonies in such works as *Gymnopédies*, provides a perfect example of the style, deliberately bleak in its renunciation of harmonious carnality and yet thoroughly modern in its invocation of secret rites and suggested aberrations. For different reasons, Stravinsky adopted GYMNOSOPHISTICAL modalities in his neo-Grecian works, as a reaction against the proliferation of colorful sonorities in instrumental music, including his own. GYMNOSOPHISTICAL HOMOPHONY is a natural medium also for neo-ecclesiastical composition in quintal or quartal gemination.

Harmony. 1. A musical combination of tones or chords.—2. A chord, either consonant or dissonant.—3. The harmonic texture of a piece; as 2-part, 3-part harmony . . . *Chromatic harmony* has chromatic tones and modulations . . . *Close harmony* (in 4-part writing) has the 3 highest parts within the compass of an octave . . . *Compound harmony* has 2 or more essential chord-tones doubled . . . *Dispersed, Extended harmony*, see OPEN HARMONY . . . *Essential harmony*, (a) the fundamental triads of a key; (b) the harmonic frame of a composition minus all figuration and ornaments . . . *False harmony*, (a) the inharmonic relation; (b) discord produced by imperfect preparation or resolution; (c) discord produced by wrong notes or chords . . . *Figured harmony* varies the simple chords by figuration of all kinds . . . *Open harmony* (in 4-part writing) spreads the 3 highest parts beyond the compass of an octave . . . *Pure harmony*, music performed with pure (not tempered) intonation, as by a string quartet, or unaccompanied chorus . . . *Spread harmony*, open harmony . . . *Strict harmony*, composition according to strict rules for the preparation and resolution of dissonances . . . *Tempered harmony*, music performed with tempered intonation, as on the organ or piano. PMMT

Hausmusik. After a long period of alienation from the masses, modern composers in Germany came to the conviction that music should cease to be a hermetic art for select audiences and should be returned to its source, the home. HAUSMUSIK, as such "home music" became known, was a development parallel to

GEBRAUCHSMUSIK. Dissonant harmony and asymmetric rhythms were not excluded, as long as the performance did not present technical difficulties. Usually HAUS-MUSIK was written for voices or SPRECHSTIMME, with piano accompaniment and obbligato parts for instruments easy to play, such as recorders, clarinets and violins.

Hendecaphonic Serialism. With the gradual relaxation of dodecaphonic stric-tures in the orthodox Schoenbergian doctrine, serial composers have begun to resort to a lipogrammatic device of omitting a member of a 12-tone subject, reducing the series to a HENDECAPHONIC form, containing only 11 tones. The missing tone, conspicuous by its absence, may be introduced in the coda with a panache suggesting the apparition of an actual tonic.

Hirsute Chromaticism. A judicious mixture of chromatic and diatonic modes in a serial work is entirely valid as a mode, idiom or a style. What cannot be tolerated in a modern composition of any pretensions to self-consistency is the hairy growth of chromatics upon a diatonic or pandiatonic melodic and harmonic surface, with membranous pellicles obscuring the melorhythmic lines without protecting them. When instances of such HIRSUTE CHROMATICISM occur inadvertently, a depilatory agent should be applied in order to restore the basic musical design. At the same time, care should be taken not to fall into the extremes of unesthetic alopecia.

Homonymity. In music, as in verbal communication, identical sounds often acquire different connotations according to the context. For example, *mental process* in anatomy refers not to the state of mind but to the bony promontory that forms the chin, the key word being derived from *mentum*, chin, not from *mens*, mind, while the word *process* comes from proceed in the sense of out-growth. A C-major chord, if written with an F-flat instead of E, loses its white immaculacy and becomes a dissonant suspension over the A-flat major triad. HOMONYMITY plays a particularly significant role in DODECAPHONIC MUSIC. A seg-ment of a 12-tone series may prove to be homonymous with another segment of another form of the same series. This fragmentary replication is of great structural importance in the theory and practice of COMBINATORIALITY.

Icositetraphony. As the etymology of the term indicates, ICOSITETRAPHONY deals with music using 24 equal intervals in an octave (icosi = 20; tetra = 4; phone = sound), i.e., in quarter-tones. A tone-row composed of 24 different notes in quar-ter-tones is an icositetraphonic series. In modern works ICOSITETRAPHONY usually occurs in conglomerates, as in the coda of Krzysztof Penderecki's *Threnody for the Victims of Hiroshima* and in Sergei Slonimsky's *Concerto Buffo*.

Immaculacy. The irresistible attraction that C major exercises on many modern composers is a curious phenomenon. Scriabin ends his *Poème de l'Extase* with a protracted coda of IMMACULATE C major in a veritable sunburst of white-hot flame on the waves of the luminiferous ether. C major was also the favorite key of Prokofiev, a composer whose esthetic precepts were diametrically opposed to Scriabin's; to him C major was simply a pianistic convenience lying naturally under the fingers. Pianistically, C major is associated with whiteness, but on many old keyboard instruments the keys of diatonic C major were black. Also pianistic in origin is PANDIATONICISM; a great many pandiatonic constructions in piano works are examples of C-major IMMACULACY. Even Schoenberg, for all of his anti-triadic teachings, succumbed to the temptation: his *Piano Concerto* ends on an enhanced C-major chord.

Impressionism. The term IMPRESSIONISM was first used in an article by Louis Leroy published in the Paris journal *Charivari* in its issue of 25 April 1874, to characterize the type of painting cultivated by French artists who exhibited at the Paris Salon des Refusés, with specific reference to *Sunrise* by Claude Monet, subtitled "an impression." This painting was Impressionistic in the sense that it brought out the subjective impact of the landscape on the artist, as it registered in his inner eye. Far from being offended by the irony implied in the word IMPRESSIONISM, the French modernists of the time accepted it as an honorable title. It was not the first time in cultural and political history that a sobriquet intended as a pejorative appellation was elevated to the dignity of a dictionary definition. When the French aristocrats dismissed the Paris revolutionaries as sans-culottes, because they did not wear the culottes, the knee breeches, the expression was adopted triumphantly by the populace. When the German Kaiser described the British expeditionary force in World War I as "a contemptible little army," the English gleefully accepted this depreciative nomination, turning its sharp point against the Germans themselves as their vaunted superiority began to crumble. A group of American realistic painters, active in the first decade of the 20th century was described as Ashcan School by reactionary critics, and it was under that name that the group had proudly entered the annals of American art. The term Baroque originally meant uncouth, ungainly or bizarre, but it has risen in its semantical evolution to represent the noblest period in the history of fine arts.

Only slightly less derisive than IMPRESSIONISM was the term Symbolism, applied to modern French poets whose imagery dealt with symbols rather than with realities. The word Symbolism appeared for the first time in print in the Paris daily *Le Figaro* of 18 September 1886. As IMPRESSIONISM in art, Symbolism was the product of a reaction against the hegemony of academic realism. The painter Courbet said, "Le réalisme c'est la négation de l'idéal." To poets and to painters alike, music was the supreme medium of artistic expression. Paul Verlaine formulated this belief in the famous line, "De la musique avant toute chose." He insisted that words themselves should be selected for the quality of their sound: "Les mots seront choisis en tant que sonores." Gauguin declared that he sought to achieve a musical expression in his exotic paintings: "Je cherche plus la suggestion que la description, comme le fait la musique." Conversely, the spectrum of light appears as a determining factor of musical expression to composers of the Impressionist school. Debussy spoke of "lumière sonore," such as is produced by an analytical diffraction of tones. The constant interchange of auditory and visual aspects in music and in art is illustrated by the titles both of Impressionist paintings and musical compositions. Whistler gave musical captions to his paintings— Symphonies, Nocturnes—while titles of Debussy's works are often taken from painting—Esquisses, Images. Poets were apt to speak of music that can be seen and of paintings that can be heard. After hearing Debussy's *Prélude à l'Après-midi d'un Faune*, Stéphane Mallarmé, whose poem inspired the work, inscribed the book to Debussy, with a quatrain, which equates word, light and sound in one sensation: "Sylvain d'haleine première/ Si ta flûte a réussi/ Ouïs toute la lumière/ Qu'y soufflera Debussy!" In a modern tale of fantasy a scientist transplants the optical nerve to the ear and the auditory nerve to the eye, so that the human subjects on whom he performed this experiment heard colors and saw tones.

In *Les Fleurs du Mal*, Baudelaire said: "J'aime avec fureur les choses où le son se mêle à la lumière."

The interpenetrability of all senses, including the olfactory and the gustatory, was the dream of poets, artists and musicians. Baudelaire wrote: "Les parfums, les couleurs et les sons se répondent." In his essays *À rebours*, Huysmans conjures up an organ of liqueurs. As the organist pulls out the stops, each discharges a drop of wine accompanied by the sound of corresponding instrumental color. The clarinet gives the taste of curaçao sec; the oboe serves kummel; for the flute there is anisette; for the trombone gin and whiskey, while the tuba filters strong vodka.

The flight from nominalism among poets, painters and musicians of France a hundred years ago had a touch of mystical taboo which forbade the naming of the deity in primitive religions. Mallarmé wrote: "To name an object is to suppress three quarters of the enjoyment of a poem; to divine gradually, to suggest, that is the dream." In order to be effective, art had to be a matrix of uncertainties. The French poet Charles Brugnot wrote the lines which Ravel selected as an epigraph for his piano suite *Gaspard de la nuit*: "Je croyais entendre/ une vague harmonie enchanter mon sommeil/ et près de moi s'épandre un murmure pareil/ aux chants entrecoupés d'une voix triste et tendre."

Above all, IMPRESSIONISM should not serve a utilitarian purpose or perform a function. Henri de Regnier spoke of "le plaisir délicieux et toujours nouveau d'une occupation inutile." Ravel put these words in the score of his *Valses nobles et sentimentales*.

If the aim of IMPRESSIONISM is to suggest uncertain images, then such images must be clothed in uncertain sounds; in music such sounds are dissonances. The yearning desire for dissonant harmonies can be traced back to Horace's pithy oxymoron, "Concordia discors," and to Keats, who said that "discords make the sweetest airs." Verlaine was explicit when he spoke poetically of "accords harmonieusement dissonants." Dissonances are indeed harmonious in Impressionist music as discordant tones are suspended in airy equilibrium above the sustained basses that support columns of natural overtones.

Walter Pater said: "Impressionism is a vivid personal reflection of a fugitive effect." Spectral evanescence lies in the nature of Impressionist art and music. Sounds that suggest perfumes are ephemeral; they shimmer, they waver, and they vanish. Impressionist melodies are transparencies of a magic lantern; the images succeed each other without organic cohesion. There is no thematic development; the progress of the music depends on contrasts of contiguous thematic statements and colorful juxtapositions of sound. IMPRESSIONISM shuns the grandiosity of epic arts and the emotionalism of romance. No human passions invest the scores of Impressionist music, and the sonorities are never overwhelming. It is characteristic of Impressionist composers that in the selection of their subjects they favor the moon over the sun. Verlaine's poem *Clair de Lune* inspired Debussy's famous piano piece. Schoenberg, in his *Pierrot lunaire*, a work that possesses distinct Impressionistic qualities, selected a group of poems focused on a moonstruck lover with the pale disk of the moon projected on the back of his garment.

A suggestion of sensuality is often more forceful than a realistic description of carnality. Whispered words are more enervating than raucous outcries. Distant rhythms of throbbing drums, brief effervescences of quickly extinguished melodic phrases, muted instrumental colors, all this suggests faint mementos of passionate events. Debussy's most dyspeptic critic Camille Bellaigue (who was Debussy's classmate at the Paris Conservatoire) grudgingly admitted that Debussy's music "fait peu de bruit," but, he added malevolently, it makes "un vilain petit bruit." John Ruskin exploded in righteous indignation against modern French music: "Musicians, like painters, are almost virulently determined in their efforts to abolish the laws of sincerity and purity, and to invent, each for his own glory, new modes of dissolute and lascivious sound." When Debussy's *Prélude à l'après-midi d'un Faune* was first performed in Paris in 1894, a cautionary notice was inserted in the program: "The poem of Mallarmé, which inspired Debussy, is so sadistic that the management decided not to print it in the program book, because young girls attend these concerts." The great romanticist of French music Gounod, addressing students at the Paris Académie des Beaux Arts on 20 October 1883, warned them: "Do not be seduced by those hollow words, Realism, Idealism, Impressionism. They belong to the nihilist vocabulary, which now constitutes modern art."

Paul Verlaine described IMPRESSIONISM in a line of singular intimacy as "la chanson grise où l'Indécis au Précis se joint." And he summarized the esthetic code of Symbolist poetry and Impressionist art in a challenging invitation, "Pas la Couleur, rien que la Nuance!" The formula fits the music of French IMPRESSIONISM to perfection: in it the indecisiveness of the design is mitigated by the precision of execution. Bright colors are relinquished in favor of infinitesimally subtle nuances. Just as the eye is trained to differentiate between light and shadow in Impressionist art, so the ear is disciplined to discriminate between the measured quanta of sonic impulses in Impressionist music.

IMPRESSIONISM is the differential calculus of music, in which the infinitesimal particles of coloristic sound are integrated into a potent musical factor. Debussy himself insisted that he was a realistic composer and he deprecated the term IMPRESSIONISM. He wrote to his publisher Durand, in March 1908: "I am trying to create musical reality, the kind that some imbeciles call IMPRESSIONISM, a term which I consider most unfitting."

IMPRESSIONISM has created its own tonal vocabulary and harmonic syntax. Its inspiration came from remote antiquity in time and far distances in space. When the Paris Exposition of 1889 presented Oriental dancers from Indochina with their strange bell-like musical instruments, Debussy and his friends found new resources in the polychromatic monody of the exotic modes from the East, free from contrapuntal and harmonic artificiality of western music. At the same time manufactured products from Japan began to arrive at the Paris markets, wrapped in Japanese rice paper with the symbolic prints by unknown masters. It was this wrapping paper, rather than the goods it enveloped, that provided pictorial resources to many French painters. Debussy selected a Japanese drawing of a typhoon wave for the cover of his score of *La Mer*. James Gibbons Huneker was not far wrong in his horrified contemplation of Debussy as a revenant from the East. "If the western world ever adopted eastern tonalities," he wrote, "Claude Debussy would be the one composer who would manage its system. I see his curious asymmetrical face, the pointed fawn ears, the projecting cheekbones. The man is a wraith from the East. His music was heard long ago in the hill temples of Borneo; was made as a symphony to welcome the head-hunters with their ghastly spoils of war!"

The innovations introduced by Impressionist techniques are as significant in the negation of old formulas as in the affirmation of the novelties. They may be summarized in the following categories:

MELODY: (1) Extreme brevity of substantive thematic statements. (2) Cultivation of monothematism and the elimination of all auxiliary notes, ornaments, melodic excrescences and rhythmic protuberances. (3) Introduction of simulacra of old Grecian and ecclesiastical modes calculated to evoke the spirit of serene antiquity in stately motion of rhythmic units. (4) Thematic employment of pentatonic scales to conjure up imitative sonorities and tintinnisonant Orientalistic effects. (5) Coloristic use of the scale of whole tones for exotic ambience. (6) Rapid iteration of single notes to simulate the rhythms of primitive drums.

HARMONY: (1) Extension of tertian chord formations into chords of the eleventh, or raised eleventh, and chords of the thirteenth. (2) Modulatory schemes in root progressions of intervals derived from the equal division of the octave into 2,3,4,6 and 12 parts in preference to the traditional modulations following the order of the cycle of fourths and fifths. (3) Motion by block harmonies without transitions. (4) Preferential use of plagal cadences either in triadic harmonies or extended chordal formations. (5) Quartal harmonies used as harmonic entities which move in parallel formations. (6) Modal harmonization in root positions of perfect triads within a given mode, with the intervalic relationships between the melody notes and the bass following the formula 8, 3, 5, 8, etc. when harmonizing an ascending scale or mode, and the reverse numerical progression 8, 5, 3, 8, etc. in harmonizing a descending scale or mode, excluding the incidence of the diminished fifth between the melody and the bass; the reverse numerical progression, 8, 5, 3, 8, 5, etc. for an ascending scale results in a common harmonization in tonic, dominant and subdominant triads in root position; the same common harmonization results when the formula 8, 3, 5, 8, 3, etc. is applied to the harmonization of a descending scale; this reciprocal relationship between a modal and a tonal harmonization is indeed magical in its precise numerical formula. (7) Intertonal harmonization in major triads, in which no more than two successive chords belong to any given tonality, with the melody moving in contrary motion to the bass; since only root positions of major triads are used, the intervals between the melody and the bass can be only a major third, a perfect fifth and an octave. In harmonizing an ascending scale, whether diatonic, chromatic or partly chromatic, the formula is limited to the numerical intervalic progression 3, 5, 8, 3, 5, etc., and the reverse in harmonizing a descending scale, i.e., 8, 5, 3, 8, 5, 3, etc. Cadential formulas of pre-Baroque music are often intertonal in their exclusive application of major triads in root positions. A remarkable instance of the literal application of the formula of intertonal harmonization is found in the scene of Gregory's prophetic vision in Mussorgsky's opera *Boris Godunov*, in which the ascending melodic progression, itself intertonal in its peculiar modality, B, C-sharp, E, F-sharp, G, is harmonized successively in the major triads in root positions, E major, C-sharp major, A major, F-sharp major, E-flat major. Another instance of intertonal harmonization occurs in the second act of Puccini's opera *Tosca*, in which the motto of the chief of police, a descending whole-tone scale in the bass, is harmonized in ascending major triads in root positions, in contrary motion; the intervalic relationship between the melody and the bass follows the formula 8, 3, 5, 8, 3, 5, 8,. (8) Parallel progressions of inversions of triads, particularly second inversions of major triads, with the root progression ascending or descending in minor thirds, so that the basses outline a diminished-seventh chord. (9) Parallel progressions of major ninth-chords, also with a bass moving by minor thirds. (10) Parallel progressions of inverted dominant-seventh chords, particularly 6/5/3 chords. (11) Free use of unattached and unresolved dissonant chords, particularly suspensions of major sevenths over diminished-seventh chords. (12) Cadential formulas with the added major sixth over major triads in close harmony.

COUNTERPOINT: (1) A virtual abandonment of Baroque procedures; abolition of tonal sequences and of strict canonic imitation. (2) Reduction of fugal processes to adumbrative thematic echoes, memos and mementos. (3) Cultivation of parallel motion of voices, particularly consecutive fourths and organum-like perfect fifths.

FORM: (1) Desuetude of sectional symphonies of the classical or romantic type, and their replacement by coloristic tone poems of a rhapsodic genre. (2) Virtual disappearance of thematic development with its function being taken over by dynamic elements. (3) Cessation in the practice of traditional variations, discontinuance of auxiliary embellishments, melodic and harmonic figurations whether above, below or around the thematic notes and the concomitant cultivation of instrumental variations in which the alteration of tone color becomes the means of variegation. A theme may be subjected to augmentation or diminution and in some cases to topological dislocations of the intervalic parameters. Thus the tonal theme of Debussy's *La Mer* is extended in the climax into a series of whole tones. (4) Homeological imitation of melorhythmic formulas of old dance forms, often with pandiatonic amplification of the harmony. (5) A general tendency towards miniaturization of nominally classical forms, such as sonata or prelude.

INSTRUMENTATION: (1) Coloristic employment of unusual instrumental combinations. (2) Predilection for attenuated sonorities, with muted strings and muted brass, and considerable expansion of the role of woodwind instruments and of the decorative sonorities of the harp and the celesta. (3) Projection of evocative but brief solos, often in unusual registers. (4) The planting of deep pedal points over which the strings and the woodwinds are suspended in aerostatic equilibrium, often with a muted horn, trumpet or trombone, penetrating the euphonious mist. (5) Careful cultivation of multiple divided strings. (6) Periodic sonic expansions and compressions, massive heavings and sudden recessions. (7) Fluctuation of dynamic rhythms and constant oscillation of thematic particles. (8) Fragmentation of melodic patterns and pulverization of ingredients in tremolos. (9) Heterogeneous instrumental combinations tending to alter the natural tone color of an individual instrument. (10) Frequent application of dynamic antiphony of homogeneous or heterogeneous instrumental groupings.

Inaudible Music. Since electronic instruments are capable of generating any frequency, it is possible to reproduce sounds below and above the audible range. The first work for such infrasonic and ultrasonic wavelengths was the INAUDIBLE symphony entitled *Symphonie Humaine* by the French composer Michel Magne, conducted by him in Paris on 26 May 1955. Its movements were entitled *Epileptic Dance, Thanatological Berceuse* and *Interior View of an Assassin*. The INAUDIBLE version was unheard first, followed by a hearing of an audible transcription. The mystical Russian composer Nicolas Obouhov devised in 1918 an INAUDIBLE instrument which he named Ether, theoretically capable of producing infrasonic and ultrasonic sounds ranging from five octaves below the lowest audible tone to five octaves above the highest audible tone. But Obouhov's instrument was never constructed. Avant-garde composers working in mixed media often compose visual music, which can be seen but not heard. A poetic example is the act of releasing a jar full of butterflies "composed" by La Monte Young. Imagination plays a crucial part in the appreciation of INAUDIBLE MUSIC. An interviewer on a broadcast of the British Broadcasting Corporation was sent a defective copy of John and Yoko's Wedding Album (John Lennon was a member of a Liverpudlian vocal quartet, since fallen into innocuous desuetude, known as The Beatles) in which two sides were blank except for an engineer's line-up tone. The broadcaster gave it a warmly favorable review, noting that the pitches differed only by microtones, and that "this oscillation produces an almost subliminal uneven beat which maintains interest on a more basic level," and further observing that the listener could improvise an Indian raga, plainsong or Gaelic mouth music against the drone. John and his Japanese bride Yoko sent him a congratulatory telegram, announcing their intention to release the blank sides for their next album. "Heard melodies are sweet, but those unheard are sweeter."

Indeterminacy. In nuclear physics, the principle of INDETERMINACY states that it is inherently impossible to determine both the position and velocity of any subatomic particle beyond the liminal degree of accuracy. This notion has impressed some modern composers and moved them to apply the INDETERMINACY principle to composition with aleatory or stochastic elements. If the position of a note is indicated precisely, then the rhythm must be optional, and vice-versa. The performing musicians are free to improvise either the actual notes in the nucleus considered indeterminate, or its rhythm, but not both.

Information Theory. In relevant application to modern music, INFORMATION THEORY touches on the problems of GRAPHIC NOTATION, semantics of certain melorhythmic figures, dynamic levels of various parts of a musical work and instrumental color, etc. A composer must be able to convey a maximum amount of information with optimum efficiency. Composers of complicated music have without exception insisted that the knowledge of their modus operandi is unnecessary for the complete comprehension of the musical message. The quality of performance cannot elevate a poorly constructed musical composition to a higher degree of excellence; nor can an indifferent execution of a great masterpiece impair its inherent validity. Musical information can be conveyed with considerable impact by playing a four-hand arrangement of a Beethoven symphony, but would fail to register even in a virtuoso performance of a work lacking in power of communication.

Infra-Modern Music. If Ultra-Modern Music transcends the outer limits of modernism, INFRA-MODERN MUSIC fails to reach even its lowest boundaries, and dwells in the penumbra of pretentious self-inflation. Composers of INFRA-MODERN MUSIC make frequent incursions into the alluring land of dissonant harmonies, but they seldom succeed in manufacturing even a similitudinarian counterfeit. Their attempts to inject atonal or polytonal elements in the effete body of their productions remain as sterile as their imaginations are impotent.

Integration. Harmonic INTEGRATION of a linear progression in dodecaphonic works is an essential factor in Schoenberg's method of composition with 12 tones related only to one another. Melody and harmony become two dimensions of dodecaphonic space, thus contributing to a higher unity of the compositional design. True, melody and harmony are intimately associated in classical music theory in conformity with the laws of chordal relationship, but the great difference between the two concepts lies in the fact that in classical harmony the chordal accompaniment performs the function of melodic tonality, while in serial music it is an integral part of the entire meloharmonic scheme.

Interval. The difference in pitch between two tones. Intervals are regularly measured from the lower tone to the higher. *An interval is:—Augmented*, when wider by a chromatic semitone than major or perfect . . . *Chromatic*, when augmented or diminished (except augm. fourth, and dim. fifth and seventh) . . . *Compound*, when wider than an octave . . . *Consonant*, when not requiring resolution . . . *Diatonic*, when occurring between 2 tones belonging to the same key (except the augmented second and fifth of the harmonic minor scale) . . . *Diminished*, when a chromatic semitone narrower than major or perfect . . . *Dissonant*, when requiring resolution . . . *Enharmonic*, see ENHARMONIC TONES . . . *Extended*, or *Extreme*, when augmented . . . *Flat*, when diminished . . . *Harmonic*, when both tones are sounded together . . . *Imperfect*, when diminished . . . *Inverted*, when the higher tone is lowered, or the lower tone raised, by an octave . . . *Major*, when equal to the standard second, third, sixth, and seventh of the major scale . . . *Melodic*, when the two tones are sounded in succession . . . *Minor*, when a chromatic semitone narrower than major or perfect . . . *Parallel* (with an interval preceding), when its two tones progress in the same direction and at the same interval . . . *Perfect* (or *Perfect major*), when equal to the standard prime, fourth, fifth, and octave of the major scale . . . *Redundant*, when augmented . . . *Simple*, when not wider than an octave . . . *Standard*, when measured upward from the keynote . . . *Superfluous*, when augmented. PMMT

Intervallic Symbolism. Symbolical associations between intervals and ideas are rooted in scholastic theories. An anonymous medieval tract explains the acoustical perfection of the octave by the circumstance that "octavo die Abraha circumcisus erat." The tritone was "diabolus in musica." Bach had correlated certain intervals to specific subjects with considerable precision. Since words could not always be heard, an intervallic equation contributed to the clarity of the meaning. The ascent to heaven was depicted by a rising diatonic scale. Torment was expressed by involuted chromatic passages. The descent into hell was intervallically related to the falling diminished-seventh. Essentially, Wagner's system of leading motives is a species of INTERVALLIC SYMBOLISM. Some modern composers have revived a medieval symbolism of intervals. In Luigi Nono's spectacle for MIXED MEDIA, *Intolleranza*, the characters are associated with specific intervals: the woman with minor seconds and their inversions, major sevenths; the refugee with the tritone and perfect fourths; and his friend with perfect fourths and major seconds. As in Bach's day such associations help to follow the leading motives of the score.

Invariants. With the growing fascination shown by modern composers for the theory of sets, the term INVARIANTS has acquired a certain practical validity. Its relevance is obvious. The 12 tones of the dodecaphonic series are INVARIANTS within a certain set; the derivatives of the tone-row are variables. Number 4 is the INVARIANT in a set of instruments of a string quartet. A flute part interchangeable with that of the piccolo is a variable. Besides the advantage of scientific jargon, the system of musical INVARIANTS clarifies some processes of serial composition. Particularly frequent is the use of the term for segments of different forms of a tone-row, for instance, the basic series and its retrograde, transposed, which happen to have several notes in common, by accident or structural serendipity.

Jazz. The word JAZZ appeared for the first time in print in the sports column in *The Bulletin* of San Francisco in its issue of 6 March 1913. Describing the arrival of a baseball team, the writer "Scoop" Gleeson reported: "Everybody has come back to the old town, full of the old 'jazz' and they promise to knock the fans off their feet with their playing." Gleeson then asks himself a rhetorical question: "What is this jazz? Why, it's a little of that 'old life,' the 'gin-i-ker,' the 'pep,' otherwise known as the enthusiasalum." Reminiscing about the occasion in an article published in the same San Francisco newspaper in its issue of 3 September 1938, "Scoop" Gleeson volunteered the information that the expression "jazz" had been picked up by the Sports editor during a crap game. According to Gleeson, it was first applied to music when a bandleader named Art Hickman launched his dance band, but there is no evidence of such use in any published source. The next verified appearance of the word JAZZ was in *Variety* of 27 October 1916 in a brief communication from Chicago, reporting a concert of JAZZ music, with the word spelled *jass*. Another item in *Variety* followed on 5 January 1917 when it was spelled *Jaz*. An engagement of the Dixie Jass Band of New Orleans in a Chicago cabaret was noted in *Variety* of 16 January 1917. A week later JAZZ reached New York, and it was spelled with two z's in a report in *Variety*. An item in the Victor Record Review of 7 March 1917 reads: "Spell it *Jass, Jas, Jaz*, or JAZZ—nothing can spoil a *Jass* band . . . It has sufficient power and penetration to inject new life into a mummy, and will keep ordinary human dancers on their feet till breakfast time . . ." It was about the same time that the Victor Co. issued the first recording bearing the word *Jass—Dixieland Jass One-Step*.

A number of writers have attempted to connect the word JAZZ with old slang. The word *Jasm* is found in an American novel published in 1860, and a claim has been made without support that its colloquial meaning was male sperm. Other equally unfounded guesses were that the word came from the French slang expression current in New Orleans in the 19th century, and that its verbal form meant to copulate. The determination to track the word down to some kind of sexual meaning has been the motivation of many imaginative but unsupported etymologies. Some have tried to trace it to native African languages. However, considering the specific, clear and plausible description of the word JAZZ as it appeared in print for the first time in 1913, there is no reason to doubt that it was a spontaneous colloquialism generated around San Francisco. The entire history of the word JAZZ is thoroughly covered in the pioneer article by Peter Tamony in an ephemeral periodical *Jazz*, a quarterly of American music, in its issue of October 1958. Analytically, JAZZ may be described as a modern development of the counterpoint of the fourth species. Its rhythmic formula is related to the medieval *Hocketus*, in which the singing line is freely transferred from one voice to another in syncopated singultation. (The word *hocketus* itself is an etymological cognate of hiccups.) Another historical antecedent of JAZZ is the *Quodlibet*, a freely improvised interlude within a definite metrical framework. As practiced by untutored performers, JAZZ produces the collective impact of glossolalia, tonolalia or rhythmolalia.

The paradoxical nature of JAZZ is its combination of unlimited variety of rhythmic patterns with a metric and modal uniformity. JAZZ melodies, almost without exception, are set in major keys, in 4/4 time. But the major tonality is modified by the use of "blue" notes, the lowered seventh and the lowered third in the melody. Some theorists speculate that the systematic incidence of the "blue" seventh is an approximation of the seventh overtone, and is therefore a natural consonance. The lowered third, however, cannot be explained on acoustical grounds. It may well represent a true case of harmonic equivocation, in which the melodic minor third is projected on the major complex in some sort of polytriadic superfetation. It is significant that this major-minor SUPERFETATION is the constant resource of Stravinsky's tonal harmonies.

The basic characteristics of JAZZ are the symmetrical divisions of binary meters and the strong tonality in major keys. Within this framework, the melody, of a syncopated nature, often departs widely from its harmonic connotations.

Historically JAZZ evolved from RAGTIME, a syncopated type of American music that flourished in the last decade of the 19th century and during the first years of the new century. A parallel development is BLUES, a distinctively American ballad form, suffused with nostalgia and redolent of the remembered sufferings of the Negro race, as expressed in the Negro spirituals. Semantically, the term is connected with the colloquialism "to have the blues." The "blue note," that is the flatted seventh in a major key, remains a paramount feature in the BLUES. The acknowledged creator of the genre was W.C. Handy whose song *The Memphis Blues*, published in 1911, was the first of its type.

In the meantime, the temperature of JAZZ music kept rising, and soon acquired the sobriquet HOT JAZZ, as contrasted with the more leisurely type of SWEET JAZZ. HOT JAZZ gave way to COOL JAZZ, which was actually a hotter product, as though the hot water and cold water faucets became switched around in the process of transition.

A new era of JAZZ music dawned in 1935 with a riotous explosion of SWING, which signalized a certain rhythmic manner of performance rather than a definable structural form.

JAZZ, SWING and other types of popular American music of the 1930's coalesced into a general category of JIVE, a generic form that describes the playing style in the 1940's. SWING and JIVE were largely improvisatory in nature; a novel way of organizing popular forms emerged in 1938 with BOOGIE-WOOGIE, based on an orderly harmonic progression in the bass, relating it to the classical formulas of the passacaglia and the chaconne.

A lateral form, BEBOP, Rebop or simply Bop, appeared in the 1940's; in it the main emphasis was on the strong off-beat. With its raucous sound and crude assault on the musical sensorium, SWING music had no room for such poetic refinements as the "blue notes" which vanished from the Swing horizon.

For more than half a century, JAZZ in its various forms was separated from folk music. JAZZ was an urban product; folk music, or country music, remained stagnant in its rural recesses. The instrumentation of JAZZ was based on the trumpet, the saxophone, the banjo, the piano and the drums, with the clarinet emerging as its flamboyant chanticleer in SWING. Country music replaced the piano by the guitar and the trumpet by the rustic fiddle. When country music invaded the radio airwaves, the television channels and the sound movies, it gradually developed into a horrendously successful creation that became known as ROCK 'N' ROLL. Marked by an unrelenting, unremitting beat, ROCK 'N' ROLL reduced the rhythmic wealth of early syncopated music to a two-dimensional construction of bland uniformity. Its cumulative impact is apt to be as powerful as the rhythmic tramp of a regiment of soldiers which can bring down a suspension bridge by generating pendulum-like vibrations of increasing amplitude.

Throughout the history of American popular music, systematic incursions were made into the stylistically distant territory of classical and romantic music, carrying away loot and booty from the uncopyrighted remains of Chopin, Tchaikovsky and Rachmaninoff. Some products of these predatory forays, such as *Russian Rag*, fashioned from Rachmaninoff's defenseless C-sharp minor *Prelude*, are not devoid of inventive cleverness. Indignant outcries arose from the classical-minded musicians against such barbarous practices, but eventually this musical cannibalism subsided of its own accord.

A reconciliation between popular and serious music was effected with taste and vitality in a movement known as the THIRD STREAM, making it possible to introduce JAZZ into serious music.

Kaleidophonia. By analogy with kaleidoscopic images, the term KALEIDOPHONIA may be used to describe a musical composition derived from multiple mirror-like reflections of a central subject. By selecting a code of parameters determining intervals and durations, a Kaleidophonic structure can be designed as a harmonic complex composed of contrapuntal lines in quaquaversal rhythmic dispersion. Joseph Schillinger published in 1940 a volume of musical patterns which he entitled *Kaleidophone*.

Kitsch. The German patois word KITSCH denotes a pretentiously manufactured object, an unimaginative arrangement of artifacts or a heterogeneous collection which is more tasteless than artless. Christmas cards with rhymed doggerel and tinctured flowers, religious gypsum figurines with a clock in the center of the torso, a motion picture representing muscular men lifting rubber weights, chrome gargoyles, dinner plates with reproductions of members of the presidential family and all sorts of tinsel and fustian, are examples of middle-class KITSCH. In music, KITSCH is represented by so-called semi-classical compositions made up of harmonic detritus and melodic debris from the mutilated remains of Rachmaninoff's *Second Piano Concerto*, or Beethoven's *Moonlight Sonata*, or from a mixture of both. KITSCH products are usually given colorful titles such as "Purple Piano" or "Sentimental Violin," and favor for some unfathomable reason the keys of D-flat major or C minor. KITSCH is the degenerate descendant of the German Biedermeier movement. At the distance of a century, the Biedermeier products

348   CONCEPTS

possess a certain charm of old-fashioned sentiment and the musical compositions of the period were invariably correct from the technical standpoint. Modern KITSCH is usually devoid of the most elementary type of technical proficiency and appeals to the lowest classes of commercially conditioned eyes, noses and ears.

Klangfarbe. In its present semantical usage, KLANGFARBE is a special dimension of the musical sound. "It must be possible," Schoenberg states in his *Harmonielehre*, "to form a succession of KLANGFARBEN possessing a mutual relationship of a logical type equivalent to that of the melody formed by a succession of different tones." This melody of tone colors is exemplified in Schoenberg's movement originally entitled *The Changing Chord* in his *Five Orchestral Pieces*. Anton von Webern developed the idea in the direction of serialism of KLANGFARBEN, almost reaching the ultimate dodecaphonic order, in which the fundamental KLANGFARBE series is formed by the successive sounding of 12 different notes by 12 different instruments.

Machine Music. The modern machine became an object of artistic inspiration early in the 20th century. The Italian Futurists made a cult of automobiles and airplanes. George Antheil's *Ballet mécanique* shocked concert audiences by its bruitism. Max Brand produced the first machine opera in *Machinist Hopkins*. Honegger made a declaration of love for powerful American locomotives in his symphonic movement *Pacific 231*. Frederick S. Converse glorified the Ford car in his automobilistic musicorama *Flivver 10,000,000*. But locomotives, automobiles and airplanes soon lost their glamor and became public nuisances. By mid-century the machine as an artistic object became obsolete. It is ironic that no composer was moved to extol in lofty tones the greatest machine adventure of all ages, the landing on the moon.

Major-Minor Syndrome. It was a traditional convention in Baroque music to end a work in a minor key on a major triad; a major third that replaced a minor third in the final triad acquired the name *Tierce de Picardie*. The preference for the major third in final chords is explained by its privileged position as the fifth partial note of the harmonic series, whereas a minor third of the fundamental tone does not occur acoustically. In the practice of modern composers, a major third is often superimposed on a minor third. Scriabin employed such a MAJOR-MINOR SYNDROME in his last opus numbers, but he spread the harmony widely, so that the frictional dissonance of a semitone was avoided. It was Stravinsky who cultivated a true MAJOR-MINOR SYNDROME in placing both the minor and the major third within a triad. He made use of it as a motto in his early choral work *Zvezdoliky*. It occurs also in *Le Sacre du Printemps*. Most importantly, Stravinsky uses it as a melodic palimpsest, breaking up the combined chord, with both the major and the minor third assuming a thematic significance.

Melosomatic Effect. The neologism MELOSOMATIC suggests an interaction between Melos and the physical Soma. It may be traumatic when loud music is played without relief. But a more insidious psychological lesion is produced by personal associations. In his short story, *The Black Monk*, Anton Chekhov, who was a professional physician, describes the deadly effect produced on a young intellectual by the playing of *Angel's Serenade* by Gaetano Braga, resulting in a fatal cerebral hemorrhage when the piece is played again after a long interval of time. Autosuggestion may have been responsible for the death of the Hungarian composer Rezsö Seress, author of the pessimistic popular song *Gloomy Sunday* (it was banned in various localities after numerous suicides were purportedly engendered by it.) By a delayed reaction, forty years after writing this song, the composer himself jumped out of a window. The Russian pianist Alexander Kelberine took a lethal dose of barbiturates after his last concert on January 27, 1940 in Town Hall in New York, for which he arranged a funereal program, consisting entirely of works in minor keys, the last number being Liszt's *Totentanz*. Sexual stimulation is highly melosomatic, as amply demonstrated by the reactions of the young to concerts of popular music, particularly ROCK 'N' ROLL. Tolstoy, who turned against sex after a lifetime of indulgence and sixteen illegitimate children, presented a philosophical study of musical sexuality in his novel *The Kreutzer Sonata*, wherein he tells how the last movement of Beethoven's work, with its propulsive syncopation, overwhelms the natural restraints of the performers, a middle-class married Russian woman pianist and a male violinist, hurling them into a frenzy of illicit passion. It may be questioned that amateurs could ever master the technical difficulties of that diabolically intricate last movement, let alone create enough excitement to carry them away. (There is a famous painting illustrating the climactic scene of the novel, showing the mustachioed violinist implanting a passionate kiss on the lips of a lady pianist while holding both the violin and the bow in his left hand, suggesting that he had the presence of mind to switch the bow from the right hand to the left, but leaving it unexplained as to why he did not deposit the instrument on the lid of the piano in that crucial moment. The painting is widely used as an advertisement for a brand of perfume with a sexy name.)

Melosomatic associations were responsible for the extraordinary vogue of the piano piece *A Maiden's Prayer* by a Polish composeress named Thekla Badarzewska, a wishfulfilling favorite of several generations of unmarried females. In 1937 Stravinsky instituted in Paris a suit against Warner Brothers for the production of a film entitled *The Firebird*, in which a submissive young girl is so unnerved by the phonograph playing of the *Pagan Dance* from Stravinsky's *Firebird* that she wanders into the flat of a professional seducer, who had the piece played continually with malice aforethought, and yields to his infamous desires. The judge failed to appreciate Stravinsky's attitude, since the seductive power of music is supposed to be the composer's greatest pride, and adjudicated the case by granting Stravinsky a token sum of one French franc in compensation for the offense.

Metamusic. Metaphysical visions have obsessed composers through the ages. They dreamed of a METAMUSICAL symphony in which all mankind would participate as a responsive reverberating assembly of congenial souls. Shortly before he died, Scriabin wrote an outline of a METAMUSICAL Mysterium that would embrace all senses in a pantheistic mystical action. Much more earthbound, but musically fascinating, was the project of a *Universe Symphony* by Charles Ives, a work that he hoped to see performed by several orchestras stationed on hilltops overlooking a valley. The Russian mystical composer Nicolas Obouhov envisioned a METAMUSICAL union of all religions. He completed a major part of this work which bore the title *Le Livre de Vie*. He kept the manuscript on a self-made altar under an ikon, in a corner of his small room in Paris. Since this was to be the book of his own life, body and soul, he made all annotations in the original scores in his own blood. He tried to interest American music lovers to have this work produced in a specially built temple in Hollywood, but died with his dream unfulfilled.

Composers of the AVANT-GARDE have at their disposal the means of producing METAMUSICAL scores with the aid of electronic synthesizers. They may even plan to hitch their METAMUSICAL chariot if not to the stars then at least to the planets. There is nothing mystical in the term METAMUSIC. It simply means an art transcending traditional music, by analogy with Aristotle's Metaphysics, which indicates the position of a chapter dealing with philosophy, directly after a discussion of physics in his *Organon*.

Meter, Metre. 1. In music, the symmetrical grouping of musical rhythms.—2. In verse, the division into symmetrical lines. The metre of English hymns is classified according to the kind of feet used, as iambic, trochaic, or dactylic; the figures show the number of syllables in each line:

IAMBIC METRES: *Common metre* (C.M.), 8 6 8 6; *Long metre* (L.M.), 8 8 8 8; *Short metre* (S.M.), 6 6 8 6. These have regularly 4 lines to each stanza; when doubled to 8 lines they are called *Common metre double* (C.M.D.), *Long metre double* (L.M.D.), and *Short metre double* (S.M.D.). They may also have 6 lines in each stanza and are then named *Common particular metre* (C.P.M.), 8 8 6 8 8 6; *Long particular metre* (L.P.M.), or *Long metre 6 lines*, 8 8 8 8 8 8; and *Short particular metre* (S.P.M.), 6 6 8 6 6 8. Besides the above, there are *Sevens and Sixes*, 7 6 7 6; *Tens*, 10 10 10 10; *Hallelujah metre*, 6 6 6 6 8 8 (or 6 6 6 6 4 4 4 4), etc.

TROCHAIC METRES: *Sixes*, 6 6 6 6; *Sixes and Fives*, 6 5 6 5; *Sevens*, 7 7 7 7; *Eights and Sevens*, 8 7 8 7, etc.

DACTYLIC METRES: *Elevens*, 11 11 11 11; *Elevens and Tens*, 11 10 11 10, etc. These are most of the metres in general use. PMMT

Metric Modulation. In a general sense of the word, METRIC MODULATION is a change of time signature. In special modern usage, proleptically applied by Charles Ives and systematically cultivated by Elliott Carter, METRIC MODULATION is a technique in which a rhythmic pattern is superposed on another, heterometrically, and then supersedes it and becomes the basic meter. Usually, such time signatures are mutually prime, e.g., 4/4 and 3/8, and so have no common divisors. Thus the change of the basic meter decisively alters the numerical content of the beat, but the minimal denominator (1/8 when 4/4 changes to 3/8; 1/16 when, e.g., 5/8 changes to 7/16, etc.) remains constant in duration.

Microtonality. Intervals smaller than semitones were used in ancient Greece, but were abandoned in western music with the establishment of the ecclesiastical modes. When greater sensitivity towards tonal elements developed in modern times, composers and theorists began investigating the acoustical, coloristic and affective aspects of intervals smaller than a semitone, particularly quarter-tones. The Mexican composer Julián Carrillo experimented with microtonal intervals as early as 1895, when he published his *Sonido 13* (*13th Sound*); the title referred to the tonal resources beyond the 12 notes of the chromatic scale. Later he organized an international society for the exploration of MICROTONALITY under the grandiose name "Cruzada Intercontinental Sonido 13." He devised special instruments for performance of microtonal intervals and proposed a numerical notation of 96 divisions of the octave, which enabled him to designate precise intervalic values for 1/3-tones, 1/4-tones, 1/6-tones, 1/8-tones and 1/16-tones. As an exercise in MICROTONALITY he arranged Beethoven's *Fifth Symphony* in quarter-tones by dividing each interval into two, so that the octave became a tritone, and the entire range of the work shrank to about three octaves, like some monstrous simulacrum of a physical universe in which the sensorium of auditory frequencies undergoes an extraction of the square root.

The English musician John Foulds experimented with quarter-tones in 1898. He writes in his book *From Music Today* (1934): "In the year 1898 I had tentatively experimented in a string quartet with smaller divisions than usual of the intervals of our scale, quarter-tones. Having proved in performance their practicability and their capability of expressing certain psychological states in a manner incommunicable by any other means known to musicians, I definitely adopted them as an item in my composing technique. . . . Facetious friends may assert roundly that they have heard quarter-tones all their lives, from the fiddle strings and larynxes of their mutual friends, who produced them without any difficulty."

The most systematic investigation of the theory and practice of quarter-tones was undertaken by Alois Hába in Czechoslovakia. "As a boy of 12," he writes, "I played with my three older brothers in my father's village band. We were poor; there were ten children in the family, and I had to contribute to household expenses. When we played for village festivals it often happened that folk singers used intervals different from the tempered scale, and they were annoyed that we could not accompany them properly. This gave me the idea to practice at home playing non-tempered scales on my violin in intervals smaller than a semitone. This was my first 'conservatory' for music in quarter-tones and in sixth-notes."

Probably the first entirely self-consistent work in quarter-tones was the string quartet written by Hába in 1919. He also compiled the first manual containing detailed instructions on composing in quarter-tones, third-tones and sixth-tones, which he published under the fitting title *Neue Harmonielehre* in 1928. Under Hába's supervision the August Foerster piano manufacturing company of Czechoslovakia constructed the first model of a quarter-tone piano which was patented on 18 March 1924. At the same time Hába established the first seminars of MICROTONAL MUSIC at the Prague Conservatory. He and his students published a number of works in quarter-tones, in Hába's special notation containing symbols for half a sharp, a sharp and a half, half a flat, and a flat and a half. A quarter-tone upright piano was constructed by Willi Möllendorf even before Foerster's, but it was only an ordinary piano tuned in quarter-tones and not a specially built instrument. It is now placed in the Deutsches Museum in Munich as a historical relic. The same museum also possesses a quarter-tone Harmonium built by Foerster and a harmonium of 19 divisions of the octave designed by Melchior Sachs.

In 1917 the Russian composer Ivan Wyschnegradsky devised a system of quarter-tones with a motto, inspired by Heraclitus, "Everything flows." In 1924, then living in Paris, he formulated the concept of "pansonority," which in his nomenclature meant a discrete continuum of quarter-tones. To produce fairly accurate quarter-tones he used two pianos or two pairs of pianos tuned a quarter-tone apart. On 10 November 1945 he conducted in Paris an entire program of his works, including a symphonic poem for four pianos entitled *Cosmos*.

In Russia itself quarter-tone music had a brief period of success in the early 1920's, cultivated by the Quarter-Tone Society of Leningrad, founded by Rimsky-Korsakov's grandson Georg.

Charles Ives, whose universal genius touched on many aspects of modern composition, contributed some pieces written in quarter-tones. He tells us that he became aware of the new resources of MICROTONAL MUSIC when his father, a band leader in the Union Army during the Civil War, experimented in tuning band instruments a quarter-tone apart.

Probably the earliest published composition containing quarter-tones was a group of two pieces for cello and piano by Richard H. Stein, composed in 1906, but quarter-tone passages in them were used only as occasional ultra-chromatic interludes. Ernest Bloch inserted quarter-tones in his first piano quintet mainly for their affective value in coloristic appoggiaturas.

American composers David Zeikel and William Harold Halberstadt investigated the potentialities of quarter-tones in the 1940's and wrote special works, mostly for the violin, in quarter-tones. For the sake of completeness it may be mentioned that Nicolas Slonimsky composed an overture for strings, trumpet and percussion in the Phrygian Greek mode using as his theme an extant version of an ancient Greek tune from the accompaniment to the tragedy *Orestes* produced in Athens in 400 B.C.; he conducted this arrangement at the Hollywood Bowl on 13 July 1933. In order to produce the needed two quarter-tones, the open upper strings of the violins, violas and cellos were tuned a quarter-tone up, with the rest of the string instruments preserving the ordinary pitch.

The first quarter-tone piano manufactured in the United States was patented by Hans Barth on 21 July 1931. His instrument had two keyboards of 88 notes each. The upper keyboard was tuned at the regular international pitch and had the usual five black keys and seven white keys. The lower keyboard was tuned a quarter-tone down, and its keys were blue and red.

James Paul White, a Boston musician, constructed in 1883 a microtonal keyboard which he called *Harmon*, and used a notation in which deviations from regular pitch were indicated by plus and minus signs. He theorized that 612 equal divisions of an octave would provide the most practical approximation to pure intonation. His instrument is preserved at the New England Conservatory of Music.

Perhaps the most ambitious project in MICROTONAL MUSIC has been undertaken by the American composer Harry Partch who devised a scale of 43 intervals in an octave, and constructed a number of special instruments, among them a microtonal cello, a reed organ with 43 registrations, and a modern version of the Greek kithara.

Musicologists have made numerous attempts to reconcile the tempered scale with Pythagorean intonation. Perhaps the most complete research in this direction was done by Joseph Yasser in his book *A Theory of Evolving Tonality*, published in New York in 1932, in which he proposed a system of "supra-tonality," with accidentals designated by special symbols for supra-sharp, supra-flat and supra-natural of the synthetic scale.

Quarter-tones were used by composers to suggest the Greek enharmonic mode through the centuries. Halévy incorporated a few quarter-tones in his symphonic poem *Promethée enchaîné*, and Berlioz wrote an interesting account of its first performance in *Revue et Gazette Musicale de Paris* of 25 March 1849: "The employment of quarter-tones in Halévy's work is episodic and very short, and produces a species of groaning sound in the strings, but its strangeness seems perfectly justified here and enhances considerably the wistful prosody of the music."

The Rumanian composer Georges Enesco inserted a transitional passage in quarter-tones in his opera *Oedipe* produced in Paris in 1936. In this case, too, the composer's intention was to evoke the effect of the ancient Greek enharmonic scale.

It must be said that in actual performance on instruments manipulated by humans, quarter-tones and other microtonal divisions are only rough approximations of their true acoustical value. With the advent of electronic instruments, it became possible to reproduce microtonal intervals with absolute precision. Ernst Krenek experimented with a scale of 13 equal intervals in an octave. But despite the extraordinary resources offered by electronic instruments, composers of the Avant-Garde remained singularly indifferent to microtones. The Polish modernist Krzysztof Penderecki has used quarter-tones in massive multi-octave tone-clusters, creating sonorous complexes in icositetraphonic harmony.

A curious disquisition on quarter-tones and other fractional intervals as a logical extension of Chopin's sensitive use of chromatic harmony is contained in a pamphlet by Johanna Kinkel, *Acht Briefe an eine Freundin über Clavier-Unterricht*, published in Stuttgart in 1852: "As we wonder what it is that grips us and fills us with foreboding and delight in Chopin's music, we are apt to find a solution that might appear to many as pure fantasy, namely that Chopin's intention was to release upon us a cloud of quarter-tones, which now appear only as phantom doppelgänger in the shadowy realm within the intervals produced by enharmonic change. Once the quarter-tones are emancipated, an entirely new world of tones will open to us. But since we have been accustomed to the long established divisions into semitones, these new sounds will seem weird, suggesting a splash of discordant waves. Yet the children of the next generation, or the one after next, will suck in these strange sounds with mother's milk, and may find in them a more stimulating and doubly rich art. Chopin seems to push at these mysterious portals; his melodies stream in colliding currents through the semitones as if groping for finer and more spiritual nuances than those that were available for his purposes. And when this door is finally sprung open, we will stand a step nearer to the eternal domain of natural sounds. As it is, we can only give a weak imitation of the Aeolian harp, of the rustle of the forest, of the magical ripple of the waters, unable to render them in their true impressions, because our so-called scales made up of whole tones and semitones are too coarse and have too many gaps, while Nature possesses not only quarter-tones and eighth-tones but an infinite scale of split atoms of sound!"

Mode. 1. A generic term applied to ancient Greek melodic progressions and to church scales established in the Middle Ages and codified in the system of Gregorian chant. The intervals of the Greek modes were counted downwards, and those of the medieval modes were counted upwards, so the intervallic contents were different between the Greek and the church systems. However, the church modes retained the Greek names of the modes. If played on the white keys of the piano, the church modes are: from C to C, Ionian; from D to D, Dorian; from E to E, Phrygian; from F to F, Lydian; from G to G, Mixolydian; from A to A, Aeolian; and from B to B, Locrian. The modes continued to underlie all western music through the 17th century, then gradually gave way to the common major and minor keys.—2. The distinction between a major key (mode) and minor key (mode).—3. Any scalar pattern of intervals, either traditional to a culture (Indian, Japanese, etc.) or invented.—4. A system of rhythmic notation used in the 13th century. PMMT

Modern Music. In the card catalogue of the British Museum, works written after 1800 are included in a section marked MODERN MUSIC. In American usage, MODERN MUSIC is a colloquialism for dance tunes, and popular songs. Medieval manuscripts dealing with musical theory often open with the phrase, "Brevitate gaudent moderni." The moderns that relished brevity were, in the opinion of the anonymous authors of these treatises, the adherents to Ars Nova. In present usage, MODERN MUSIC refers to that written since 1900. The variants are 20th-century music, New Music, Music of Our Time, Music of Today and Contemporary Music.

Monodrama. MONODRAMA is a stage work in which only one actor, speaker, or singer acts, recites or sings. Schoenberg introduced a type of singing recitation, SPRECHSTIMME, in which the actor enunciates his lines in an inflected manner following the melorhythmic design of the music, a technique that came to its full fruition in his *Pierrot Lunaire*. The classical example of a staged MONODRAMA is Schoenberg's *Erwartung*. The Russian composer Vladimir Rebikov evolved a novel type of MONODRAMA which he described as Psychodrama; in it an actor recites his state of mind with a musical accompaniment. In Schoenberg's *Die glückliche Hand*, the central character sings and mimes the story, and a chorus comments on the action in SPRECHSTIMME.

Monte Carlo Method. Statistical laws govern games of chance as well as the parameters of ALEATORY MUSIC. The MONTE CARLO METHOD is the most convenient of all gambling devices for easy musical application. The numbers from 1 to 36 of roulette, of the type used in the casino of Monte Carlo, can be equalized to the 36 chromatic tones of three octaves and notated accordingly as the roulette ball finds its niche, with zero corresponding to the lowest note of an arbitrarily selected progression. Rhythmic figures can be derived from a similar process by equalizing the 36 numbers to 36 different note values; if a smaller number of different rhythms is needed, then a dozen or a half-dozen sets on the roulette table can be selected as primary units. In the MONTE CARLO METHOD the probability of occurrence of a certain number depends on the frequency of previous incidences; thus certain notes may accumulate greater statistical probability of incidence and determine the tonal tropism. Harmonization and contrapuntal lines can be obtained by combining the single melorhythmic lines determined by individual Monte Carlo runs. Normally, atonal melodies and dissonant harmonies would result, but a spontaneous appearance of a dodecaphonic series is as unlikely as picking 12 different cards from a pack at random.

Musique Concrète. MUSIQUE CONCRÈTE was discovered and named on 15 April 1948 in Paris by Pierre Schaeffer, a French radio engineer. Experimenting with the newly invented magnetic tape, he found that a heterogeneous collection of songs, noises, conversations, radio commercials, etc. recorded on tape, presented a realistic phonomontage which may serve for actual composition by superimposing fragments of tape recordings in a polyphony of random sounds, splicing the tape in various ways, running it at different speeds, or backwards, etc. The raw materials of "concrete music" are susceptible to all kinds of treatment and are therefore capable of unlimited transformations. The technique of double and triple recording on the same length of tape makes it possible to create a polyphony of concrete music of great complexity. In fact it is possible to recompose a classical symphony from a recording of a single note, which can subsequently be changed in pitch and arranged in the requisite rhythmic order, superimposed on other tones derived from the original note, altered in tone color by additional electronic manipulation, until a whole work is reconstructed from these constituent tonal dynamic and instrumental elements. The Polish composer Wlodzimierz Kotoński composed an *Etude concrète* for orchestra using as his material a single stroke of the cymbal electronically altered and transposed. The American experimenter Richard Maxfield collected 30 seconds of coughs at a modern ballet recital and expanded these bronchial sonorities into a five-minute orchestral work entitled *Cough Music*.

Mystic Chord. In conformity with his mystical beliefs, Scriabin described the basic chord of *Prometheus*, C, F-sharp, B-flat, E, A, D, as the MYSTIC CHORD. Ex post facto, he regarded these components, seriatim, as 8th, 9th, 10th, 11th, 13th, and 14th overtones. Analytically, the MYSTIC CHORD belongs to the category of the dominant-ninth in a major key with two suspensions, as is made clear by resolving F-sharp to G and A to B-flat.

Narcolepsy. Symphony concerts are notoriously conducive to NARCOLEPSY, and their attendance is sometimes recommended by psychologists as an effective cure of insomnia. Statistical surveys indicate that the narcogenic factors are mainly the pendulum-like rhythmic beats in classical music, particularly when there is no change in dynamics. An unexpected sforzando will wake up even the most inveterate narcoleptic, as illustrated by the story of Haydn's *Surprise Symphony* with its famous chord in the slow movement that was supposed to arouse the somnolent London concert goers from their middle-aged slumber. On the other hand, modern works rarely put people to sleep because of the constant changes in rhythm and dynamics. NARCOLEPSY is also an inevitable outcome of lectures on musicology; according to observations conducted by a trained psychologist at a session of the International Musicological Congress in New York, a deep coma overtook practically the entire audience during the first twenty seconds of a reading from manuscript of a paper by an eminent Dutch musicologist. At the same occasion, attention was suddenly increased by the appearance on the podium of the inventor of a double-bass flute and an ultra-sonic piccolo. He could never succeed in blowing through the long tube of the big flute, which met with sympathy in the audience. The hyper-piccolo could not be heard by humans, but a terrier dog who strayed into the hall showed agitation at the ultra-sonics that canines can hear easily. Both the dog and the inventor were rewarded by hearty applause.

Negative Music. NEGATIVE MUSIC is synonymous with ANTI-MUSIC, but there is a scintilla of a difference between the two terms. ANTI-MUSIC stresses its opposition to any musical actions, whereas NEGATIVE MUSIC operates on the supposition that there may exist negative frequencies as mathematical abstractions, related to audible music as a negative to the positive in photography. NEGATIVE MUSIC would reverse dynamic values; a vocal text containing tender sentiments would be harmonized by loud dissonant noises; conversely, a symphonic poem on the subject of the nuclear war would be depicted by the minutest distillation of monodically concentrated tones. The field for experimentation in NEGATIVE MUSIC is limitless, precisely because it is impossible to speculate about its nature.

Neo-Classicism. When the luxuriance of IMPRESSIONISM reached its point of saturation, it became clear to many composers that further amplification of coloristic devices was no longer stimulating or novel. The Weber-Fechner law postulates that the force of physical impact must be increased exponentially in order to produce an arithmetical increase in the sensory impression, so that a hundredfold magnification of sound is needed to provide a tenfold increase in the physiological effect. It was to be expected that composers and audiences alike would rebound from such sonic inundation. This reaction coincided with the economic collapse following World War I so that it became financially impossible to engage large orchestras or grandiose operatic companies. The cry went all over Europe, "Back to Bach!" To this was added the slogan of NEW SIMPLICITY. Since it was no longer feasible to move forward, musical tastes with the aid of intellectual rationalization made a 180° turn towards the past. But the past could not be recaptured in its literal form, and the new retrograde movement was launched under the name of NEO-CLASSICISM. It was characterized by the following traits: (1) Rehabilitation of diatonicism as the dominant idiom, enhanced by pandiatonic constructions, in which all seven degrees of the diatonic scale are functionally equal (2) Elimination of all programmatic and romantic associations either in the titles or the tonal content of individual works (3) A demonstrative revival of the Baroque forms of Sonata, Serenade, Scherzo, Passacaglia, Toccata and the florid type of variations (4) Demotion of chromatic elements of the scale to their traditional role as passing notes (5) Restrained use of massive sonorities and renunciation of all external and purely decorative effects, such as non-thematic melismas and non-essential harmonic figurations (6) Cultivation of compact forms, such as symphonies and sonatas having a single movement and operas without a chorus and with a reduced orchestral contingent (usually containing 13 instruments), with an important piano part performing the function of the cembalo in Baroque music (7) Reconstruction of old Baroque instruments, particularly the harpsichord and their employment in modernized classical techniques (8) Exploration of canonic and fugal writing without adherence to strict rules of classical polyphony (9) Radical curtailment of the development section in Baroque forms with a purely nominal recapitulation, and a concise coda free from redundant repetition of final tonic chords.

Neo-Mysticism. The words "Laus Deo" which Haydn used to append to every manuscript upon its completion were simply the expression of his piety and did not imply a claim of direct communication with the Deity. Mystical composers of the 20th century, on the other hand, believed that they were oracles of higher powers. Mahler thought he was possessed by Beelzebub. He scrawled appeals to Satan in the manuscript of his unfinished *Tenth Symphony*; he believed in the mystical magic of all of his music. But it was left to Scriabin to formalize his mystical consciousness in musical terms. His symphony *Prometheus* is based on a six-note chord which he called MYSTIC CHORD. Shortly before his death he sketched out the text for a Mysterium, which he envisioned as a synaesthetic action which would comprise all human senses as receiving organs. A large ensemble of bells was an instrumental feature of this eschatological creation, to be performed high over the Himalayan Mountains.

New Music. Newness is a recurring motive in musical nomenclature. The emergence of rhythmic modalities in the 14th century became historically known as Ars Nova. The monodic type of composition used by the Florentine initiators of opera was published under the name *Nouve musiche*. In painting, *Art Nouveau* was the description given the French art that flourished in the 1890's. The term NEW MUSIC became current about 1920; it denoted a type of modern music marked by a dissonant counterpoint, ATONALITY and brevity of expression. Later, NEW MUSIC became synonymous with ULTRA-MODERN MUSIC.

Non-Toxic Dissonances. DISSONANCES can be said to be NON-TOXIC or non-corrosive if they are embanked within a tonal sequence, or if their candential illation corresponds to traditional modalities. It is the harmonic context that determines the toxicity of a dissonance for an untutored ear. Among the most corrosive dissonances are atonal combinations in which intervals of a high degree of discordance, such as major sevenths, minor seconds and the tritone, are combined with acoustically euphonious intervals of a perfect fifth and a perfect fourth. The absence of thirds, whether major or minor, is the distinctive feature of corrosive harmony, but toxic sonic effects result also from the simultaneous use of two homonymous major and minor triads on account of the interference between the major and minor thirds. Changes in bio-chemical balance and nervous reactions to the impact of toxic dissonances can be measured on a neurograph, providing a scientific clue to the apperception of modern music.

Numbers. The Latin word *Numeri* had a second meaning, music, for it was governed by the law of proportions between two different sounds. In Shakespearean English, NUMBERS refer to musical composition. St. Augustine drew a distinction between *Numeri sonantes*, the actual musical tone that is perceived by the senses, and *Numeri recordabiles*, music that is remembered. In St. Augustine's concept, a melody was formed by a single sound instantaneously perceived and memorably associated with several preceding sounds. Long before St. Augustine, Aristoxenus likened the musical tones of a melody to letters in a language. So intimate was the connection felt between NUMBERS and music that in medieval universities music was taught as part of the Quadrivium of exact sciences, along with arithmetic, geometry and astronomy. This association with NUMBERS was lost in classical and romantic music. Not until the 20th century did the numerical element in music regain its status. Mathematical parameters lie at the foundation of serial music. The calculus of sets is an important tool in rhythmic serialization. Some composers have applied the Fibonacci NUMBERS, in which each term is the sum of its two predecessors, to metrical, rhythmic and intervalic parameters. Simple arithmetical progressions also yield material for rhythmic arrangements. The application of NUMBERS to composition is limitless; the difficulty is to select numerical sets that would provide material for purely musical structures.

Objets Trouvés. Ready-made objects are often incorporated by modern artists as part of a sculpture or a montage. Ultra-modern composers sometimes insert passages from works by other composers as a token of homage and partly as an experiment in construction. Such OBJETS TROUVÉS need not harmonize with their environment which may be completely alien to the nature of the implant. An early example is the sudden appearance of the tune *Ach du lieber Augustin* in Schoenberg's *Second String Quartet*.

Open Form Composition. Works based on CONTROLLED IMPROVISATION, in which materials are selected from available resources, have a venerable ancestry; classical composers supplied alternative versions for transitions and endings as a matter of course. In its modern avatar, OPEN FORM COMPOSITION often delegates the ordering of component parts to the performer. Chronological priority in developing such techniques belongs to the American composer Earle Brown whose *Folio*, written in 1952, affords great latitude in the arranging of given materials. Karlheinz Stockhausen further developed this technique in his *Klavierstücke*, consisting of separate sections which can be performed in any order.

Opera. A form of drama, of Italian origin, in which vocal and instrumental music are essential and predominant. The several acts, usually preceded by instrumental introductions, consist of vocal scenes, recitatives, songs, arias, duets, trios, choruses, etc. accompanied by the orchestra. This is the *Grand* or *Heroic opera*; a *Comedy opera* is a versified comedy set to music; a *Comic opera* has spoken interludes. PMMT

Organized Sound. Sound is an acoustical phenomenon, which all by itself does not make music. Composition begins at the point when two sounds are connected in linear succession or vertical superposition. But the nature of these links is not circumscribed by any rules of melody and harmony. With the emancipation of dissonances in the 20th century, the vertical combinations became free from restraints imposed on them by tradition. Linear progressions, once bound within the framework of modes and scales, are developed in atonal designs. Schoenberg replaced diatonic melody and consonant harmony by the new dodecaphonic discipline. Edgar Varèse advanced the concept of ORGANIZED SOUND, as a complex of successive acoustical phenomena unrelated to one another except by considerations of sonic equilibrium. Dissonant combinations are preferred because they constitute a probabilistic majority and therefore are entitled to greater representation in ORGANIZED SOUND. For the same statistical reasons, successions of melodic notes are apt to generate atonal configurations. The form of works written according to the doctrine of ORGANIZED SOUND is athematic, and the rhythms are usually asymmetric. The valence between successive units, in melody, harmony and rhythm, under such conditions, is an idempotent.

Palimpsest. In musical semantics, the term PALIMPSEST may be used as a substitution for an intentionally erased composition. This erasure may be complete or partial, with some elements of the original idea left under the sonic surface. The hidden design may be discovered by intervalic analysis, comparable to the use of ultra-violet rays in detecting the old text in a parchment covered by a newer piece of writing.

Palindrome. Palindromic words and sentences do not change when they are read backwards. Max Reger, whose last name is a PALINDROME, replied wittily to an admirer who complained that he could see only his back while he conducted a concert: "I am no different front or back." Musical PALINDROMES are synonymous with retrograde movements. In a PALINDROMIC section in Alban Berg's opera *Lulu*, the music revolves backwards to depict the story of Lulu's incarceration and escape. Samplers of PALINDROMIC canons are found in Nicolas Slonimsky's *Thesaurus of Scales and Melodic Patterns*.

Palingenesis. The meaning of the word PALINGENESIS is rebirth, and it is parasynonymous with METEMPSYCHOSIS. In modern musical usage PALINGENESIS corresponds to a reprise, with the important difference that the original material is not recapitulated literally but appears metempsychotically in a form as dissimilar from its progenitor as a reincarnated cat is from its former human avatar. PALINGENESIS is a particularly convenient term to designate an electronically altered sonic substance, or a topologically metamorphosed thematic idea.

Pandiatonicism. The term PANDIATONICISM was coined by Nicolas Slonimsky and was first used in the first edition of his book *Music Since 1900* published in 1937. It is a technique in which all seven degrees of the diatonic scale are used freely in democratic equality. The functional importance of the primary triads, however, remains undiminished in PANDIATONIC harmony. PANDIATONICISM possesses both tonal and modal aspects, with the distinct preference for major keys. The earliest PANDIATONIC extension was the added major sixth over the tonic major triad. A cadential chord of the tonic major seventh is also of frequent occurrence. Independently from the development of PANDIATONICISM in serious music, American JAZZ players adopted it as a practical device. Concluding chords in piano improvisations in JAZZ are usually PANDIATONIC, containing the tonic, dominant, mediant, submediant and supertonic, with the triad in open harmony in the bass topped by a series of perfect fourths. In C major, such chords would be, from the bass up, C, G, E, A, D, G. It is significant that all the components of this Pandiatonic complex are members of the natural harmonic series. With C as the fundamental generator, G is the third partial, E the fifth partial, D the 9th, B the 15th and A the 27th. The perfect fourth is excluded both theoretically and practically, for it is not a member of the harmonic series, an interesting concordance of actual practice and acoustical considerations. With the dominant in the bass, a complete succession of fourths, one of them an augmented fourth, can be built: G, C, F, B, E, A, D, G, producing a satisfying Pandiatonic complex. When the subdominant is in the bass, the most euphonious result is obtained by a major triad in open harmony, F, C, A, in the low register, and E, B, D, G in the upper register. Polytriadic combinations are natural resources of Pandiatonicism, with the dominant combined with the tonic, e.g. C, G, E, D, G, B, making allowance for a common tone; dominant over the subdominant, as in the complex, F, C, A, D, G, B, etc. True Polytonality cannot be used in Pandiatonicism, since all the notes are in the same mode. Pedal points are particularly congenial to the spirit of Pandiatonicism, always following the natural spacing of the component notes, using large intervals in the bass register and smaller intervals in the treble. The esthetic function of Pandiatonicism is to enhance the resources of triadic harmony; that is the reason why the superposition of triads, including those in minor, are always productive of a resonant diatonic bitonality. Although Pandiatonicism has evolved from tertian foundations, it lends itself to quartal and quintal constructions with satisfactory results. Pandiatonicism is a logical medium for the techniques of NEO-CLASSICISM. Many sonorous usages of PANDIATONICISM can be found in the works of Debussy, Ravel, Stravinsky, Casella, Malipiero, Vaughan Williams, Aaron Copland and Roy Harris. The key of C major is particularly favored in piano music, thanks to the "white" quality of the keyboard. Indeed, Pandiatonic piano music developed empirically from free improvisation on the white keys. Small children promenading their little fingers over the piano keyboard at the head level produce Pandiatonic melodies and Pandiatonic harmonies of excellent quality and quite at random.

Pantonality. The term PANTONALITY denotes the use of all major and minor keys with complete freedom and without preference for any particular tonality. PANTONALITY is almost synonymous with OMNITONALITY, the only difference being that PANTONALITY includes atonal melodic progressions and uninhibited dissonant textures, while OMNITONALITY tends to enhance the basic sense of tonality.

Planarianism. A musical composition which can be dissected into two or more parts, with each growing out into a separate independent body may be called PLANARIAN, by analogy with the flatworm of that name that possesses a trifid intestine and is capable of regenerating each of its severed parts into new flatworms. The structure of a work in the style of PLANARIANISM may reach great complexity. Karlheinz Stockhausen has written autogenetic works that can be cut up, with each musical PLANARIAN becoming a self-sufficient sonic organism. This process of vermiculation and its concomitant divisibility has been further advanced by John Cage; at his hands each musical platyhelminth becomes a unique and irreproducible species.

Pointillism. In the nomenclature of modern art, POINTILLISM is a method of applying colored dots to the canvas, forming a cumulative design. In modern music, the term is descriptive of atonal and athematic idioms, in which separate notes are distributed individually rather than as parts of an integral melorhythmic curve. The maximal dispersion of members of a dodecaphonic series in different octave positions is an example of serial POINTILLISM.

Political Symbolism. In the affective usages of the Renaissance, major keys symbolized joy and minor keys sadness. Such correspondence of emotional states and sounds has an acoustical foundation, for the major third is the fifth overtone of the fundamental tone, while the minor third is not a member of the harmonic series and produces interference. This natural preference for major keys as acoustically superior to minor tonalities was the subject of an interesting philosophical exposition of POLITICAL SYMBOLISM given by Anatoly Lunacharsky, Soviet Commissar of Education in an introductory speech at a Moscow concert on 10 December 1919: "Major keys lift the sound; they raise it a semitone up, and its power grows. By analogy with laughter, with its exultant feeling of joy, major keys elevate the mood and cheer us up. Minor keys, on the other hand, droop, leading to a compromise, to a surrender of positions; the sound is lowered, and its power diminishes. Allow me, as an old Bolshevik, to put it this way: major tonality is Bolshevik music; but a minor key is a deeply rooted inner Menshevik. Cultural history chose to call major and minor two different species of modes in the world of sound. Bolsheviks and Mensheviks are the two parties which have not only determined the fate of Russia in the greatest years of her life, but became a world phenomenon, and brought out, along with reactionary and bourgeois slogans, the two most important banners around which all humanity gathers."

Pollution. Harmonic POLLUTION is characterized by indiscriminate disposal of chromatic refuse in a diatonic landscape. The process is vividly illustrated by a fetid organ arrangement of Chopin's *Nocturne* in E-flat major, in which the initial ascending interval of a major sixth, from B-flat to G, is infested by noxious chromatic runs. A polluted version of Prokofiev's *Peter and the Wolf* has been published in America in the absence of a copyright agreement with the Soviet Union; it is characterized by vulgar insertion of auxiliary material in every available melodic or harmonic vacancy. Orchestral POLLUTION manifests itself in a general sonic flatulence and an infarction of supernumerary thirds and sixths. The rhythmic line, too, is an easy victim of POLLUTION. In the remarkable compound rhythmic design in Gershwin's song *I Got Rhythm*, the original asymmetric line is often grossly mutilated, reducing it to Abecedarian syncopation. Erudite arrangements of works of Bach and other classics, made by musicians of intelligence and taste, cannot be cited as examples of musical POLLUTION. Even hyperchromatic pullulation found in some transcriptions by Max Reger, possesses validity, although they should be labelled "artificially flavored with chromatic additives." Some morphological transformations and homeological modifications are legitimate means of modernization. Examples of such artistic enhancement are *Symphonic Metamorphoses on Themes of Carl Maria von Weber* by Hindemith and the ballet *Le Baiser de la Fée* by Stravinsky, imaginatively deformed from themes of Tchaikovsky.

Polymetry. In a linear application, POLYMETRY is a succession of changing meters; polyphonically, POLYMETRY is the simultaneous use of several different meters. POLYMETRY dates back to the Renaissance, exemplified in the double time signature of Spanish dance music, 3/4 against 6/8. In operatic usage, POLYMETRY is encountered in scenes descriptive of simultaneous uncoordinated action, known under the name Imbroglio (literally, entanglement). The concluding section of Stravinsky's *Le Sacre du Printemps*, with its constantly changing time signatures, represents linear POLYMETRY at its greatest complexity. (It is characteristic of changing fashions that in 1940 Stravinsky rearranged this section in more uniform time signatures.) The unequal division of binary and ternary meters, which is a species of linear POLYMETRY, is found in Rimsky-Korsakov's opera *The Legend of the City of Kitezh*, in which the invading Mongols are characterized by the irregularly divided measures of $2/8 + 2/8 + 2/8 + 3/8 = 9/8$ and $3/8 + 2/8 + 3/8 = 8/8$. Linear POLYMETRY of this type is also characteristic of Balkan popular dances. Modern composers, fascinated by purely numerical properties of fractions representing traditional time signatures, often follow a pre-determined arithmetical formula to establish a desired metrical progression. Boris Blacher makes use of the series of numerators 1, 2, 3, 4, 5, 4, 3, 2, 1, in his orchestral *Ornaments*. Elliott Carter employs "metric modulation" by changing meter and tempo in polyphonic writing. The Welsh composer Daniel Jones has developed a system of complex time signatures based on repeated numerical patterns, some of them of extraordinary length, e.g. 32322322232323323332332/4 and 9864323468/8, both used in his *Sonata for Three Kettledrums*. He also has elaborated the techniques of augmentation, diminution and retrograde in changing time signatures, designated by such arithmetical ALGORITHMS as 6432/8 and 3464/8. The numerators in all these examples represent the succession of repeated or changing numbers of beats in a bar.

Perhaps the most remarkable instance of contrapuntal POLYMETRY is found in the second movement of *Three Places in New England* by Charles Ives, illustrating the meeting of two marching bands, with similar marching tunes played simultaneously at different tempi, in the ratio 4/3, so that four bars of the faster march equal three bars of the slower tempo. In his original manuscript Ives coordinated these different tempi within the uniform measures in 4/4 time, marking cross-accents wherever they occurred. At the suggestion made by Nicolas Slonimsky,

Ives agreed to incorporate in the published score an alternative arrangement with non-coincidental barlines, in clear polymetric notation. In his performances of the work, Nicolas Slonimsky conducted three bars in 4/4 time with his right hand and four bars in *alla breve* time with his left hand. In this polymetric coordination, the downbeat of the left hand coincides successively with the downbeat of the right hand, then with the fourth beat of the right hand, with the third beat, with the second beat and again with the downbeat of the right hand. In the first bar the upbeat of the left hand falls between the second and the third beats of the right hand; in the next bar the upbeat of the left hand occurs between the downbeat and the second beat of the right hand, and so on. Those in the orchestra who had parts with the faster march were to follow the conductor's left hand and the rest his right hand. (A critic remarked that Slonimsky's performance was evangelical, for his right hand knew not what his left hand was doing.)

Polyrhythmy. As the etymology of the word indicates, POLYRHYTHMY is the simultaneous occurrence of several different rhythms. POLYRHYTHMY differs from POLYMETRY in that the former indicates a combination of two rhythmic groups, usually consisting of mutually prime numbers of notes or irregular groups of non-coincident patterns, while the latter merely indicates the superposition, or a palimpsest, of two different meters usually having the same note values as their common denominator. If two measures of different time signatures are isochronous, then the effect is both polymetric and polyrhythmic. The problems of the poly-rhythmic notation have been solved by composers of the AVANT-GARDE who prefer to indicate the duration of individual notes or rhythmic groups in seconds rather than note values. Another possible solution of polyrhythmic notation would be to introduce time signatures with denominators not limited to the powers of two. A time signature of 2/3 or 4/7 would replace triplets or septuplets in binary meters, but attempts to introduce such numerical innovations have been unsuccessful.

Polytetrachord. Progression of 12 tetrachords passing through all 12 keys conjunctly (with the last tone of one tetrachord coinciding with the first tone of the next), or disjunctly (with the terminal tone of the first tetrachord separated by a diatonic degree from the initial tone of the next). TSMP

Polytonality. POLYTONALITY is the simultaneous use of several keys. In actual practice, it is difficult to sustain the acoustical separation of more than two different keys, thus reducing POLYTONALITY to BITONALITY. Four mutually exclusive triads are workable in linear arpeggios (e.g., C major, F-sharp major, D minor, G-sharp minor, distributed in ascending quadritonal passages), but the same four keys in columnar superposition could be made effective only by careful differentiation of instrumental groups (e.g., C major in the strings, F-sharp major in muted horns, D minor in clarinets and oboes and G-sharp minor in flutes and piccolos, with optional support of the strings by the bassoons and double-bassoons.)

Simultaneous linear progressions of two or more different tonalities are in the category of POLYTONALITY. Bitonal scales with their tonics at a distance of major or minor thirds or sixths are entirely consonant, even though they run along different tonalities. But even scales in parallel major sevenths, if played at sufficiently large distances, become technically consonant. Theoretically, C major scale played in the lowest available register of the piano and B major scale at a distance of four, five or six octaves, minus a semitone, will form consonant harmony, because B in relation to the low C at such distances constitutes the 15th, 30th and 60th partial of the harmonic series. The coda of *Also sprach Zarathustra* of Richard Strauss contains a B major triad in the high treble with a double-bass playing a low C, an instance often referred to as the first explicit use of POLYTONALITY.

Actually, the members of the B major triad in the treble represent the 60th, 75th and 90th partials of the harmonic series, generated by the low C, and are therefore consonant combinations. Genuine, acoustically pure polytonal combinations can be provided by playing the triads of D major, E major, G major and others against C major in the deep bass without falling into dissonance. Beyond the audible range, even F-sharp major, the farthest key in the cycle of scales from C major, can be brought into the harmonic series. Most polytonal combinations, however, are not even theoretically consonant. An amusing example of POLYTONALITY is Mozart's *Ein musikalischer Spass*, where he makes the horns play in different keys from the rest of the orchestra. But Mozart's professed intention in this "musical joke" was to ridicule the ignorance of village musicians. He could not have anticipated the time when such musical jokes would become a new technique.

Polytriads. POLYTRIADIC harmony may be regarded as a special case of POLYTONALITY, with mobile parts containing complete triads. If the triads move along a single scale or a mode, the resulting technique is POLYMODALITY. Homonymous triads, major and minor, encased within the compass of a perfect fifth (e.g. C, E-flat, E-natural, G), are often found in modern works. Such POLYTRIADS are *e duobus unum*, giving rise to modes possessing the characteristics of both major and minor keys.

Pop Music. The colloquial abbreviation of the term Popular Music into POP MUSIC corresponds to the depreciation and devaluation of materials and resources of the original product. POP MUSIC is a counterpart of Pop Art, with its appeal directed mainly towards the heterogeneous musical, unmusical and antimusical masses. Its effects are achieved by the application of raucous and blatant sound amplified by electronics. POP MUSIC annexes numerous forms from the vast arsenal of sentimental ballads and country music and it manages to instill a tremendous amount of kinetic energy into its public manifestations. While POP MUSIC belongs in the category of DEMOTIC MUSIC, it tends to be more cosmopolitan in its appeal and capable of attracting miscellaneous groups of people without requiring special adaptation to the changing tastes of the audiences.

Pornographic Music. It was Eduard Hanslick who said that the last movement of Tchaikovsky's *Violin Concerto* suggested to him the hideous notion that music can actually stink to the ear. The literal depiction of an episode in *Symphonia Domestica* by Richard Strauss, which illustrates his retirement to the bed chamber with Frau Strauss, to the suggestive accompaniment of two conjugated trumpets, impressed some listeners at its first performance as indecent. In a symphonic interlude in Shostakovich's opera *Lady Macbeth of the District of Mzensk*, with the marital bed occupying the center of the stage, the trombone glissandi seem to give an onomatopoeic representation of sexual intercourse. Graphic notation offers excellent opportunities for suggestive pictorial pornography. The tetraphallic score *Mooga Pook* by the American composer Charles Amirkhanian is a fine example.

Potential Techniques. The number of POTENTIAL TECHNIQUES of musical composition is unlimited, as is the number of mathematical sets or matrices. The best-known numerical set in music is the method of composition with 12 tones, or DODECAPHONIC MUSIC. But it is possible to devise a hendecaphonic method, or decaphonic method, generated respectively by eleven or ten tones in a series. Any technique of composition is valid provided it is self-consistent. It is entirely justified to postulate a system in which only dissonant intervals are used. It is also conceivable to devise a method of composing only with nominal consonances (such a system was applied by Nicolas Slonimsky in his piano suite *Studies in*

Black and White, in which only consonant intervals are used in a scheme of mutually exclusive counterpoint of pandiatonic sets in the right hand played on the white keys and panpentatonic figurations in the left hand played on the black keys). Any number of deficient or lipogrammatic systems of composition can be constructed by stipulating the omission of a note or a group of notes. Some modern poets experimented with omitting certain vowels or consonants in order to achieve a special effect. An American writer tied down the E key on his typewriter and wrote a whole novel without ever using that most frequent letter of the English alphabet, thus dispensing with the definite article, most personal pronouns, etc. The following techniques may be tabulated as possessing a workable rationale and some attractive coloristic features which might give them statistical chances of survival:

(1) Exclusive use of a limited number of notes in a scale, exemplified by the five-note scale, or Pentatonic scale and the Whole-Tone scale of six notes, the so-called Rimsky-Korsakov scale of alternating whole tones and semitones, a scale of nine notes consisting of three disjunct minor thirds with passing notes within the interval of each minor third, etc. (2) Various lipogrammatic or lipographic scales, including the hendecaphonic scale and decaphonic scale, often used by serial composers who do not wish to be restricted to the orthodox dodecaphonic method (3) Residual scales, in which the notes left over in a lipogrammatic composition are used as a matrix in a coda or a cadential codicil. In a hendecaphonic composition, such a codicil would contain a single note repeated in unison, in octave duplications, or in triplicate, quadruplicate, quintuplicate, sextuplicate and septuplicate, using all available octave points. Residual scales are legitimate devices in the building of dodecaphonic series. Thus the seven notes of the C major scale joined by the five notes of the pentatonic scale of the black keys would form a 12-tone matrix. Such a complex may also be called a conjugated diatonic-pentatonic complex (4) Intervallic lipographs, in which certain intervals are deliberately avoided in a serial set. Thirds and sixths, being most intimately associated with classical harmony, may be peremptorily excluded in favor of the seconds and sevenths in order to secure a prevalence of dissonant intervals. Emphatic use of naked fourths and fifths, to the exclusion of all other intervals, is a lipographic device to conjure up an archaic effect. A growing fashion in modern music is the selective assignment of a certain interval to a specific instrument. Béla Bartók made such a selective distribution of intervals in the second movement, *Game of the Couples*, of his *Concerto for Orchestra*, in which five pairs of wind instruments are each given a distinct interval to cultivate. Several modern composers apply such intervalic lipographs to instruments in chamber music (5) Derivative sets, made available as functions of a certain melodic figure differentiated by a given intervalic modulus. Let us differentiate a descending whole-tone scale in the bass by an ascending set of the following intervals: octave, major tenth, perfect 12th, two octaves, etc. Its derivative function will be the ascending melodic line of the following intervals: whole tone, semitone, sesquitone, whole tone, etc. This is a very important progression governing the harmonization in major triads in root position in contrary motion, which is found in Liszt's symphonic poem *Divine Comedy* and in the second act of Puccini's opera *Tosca*, announcing the entrance of the Chief of Police. Let us now harmonize the ascending whole-tone scale in the melody using the same function, that is harmonization by major triads in root position in contrary motion following the intervalic distances between the melody and the bass at a perfect octave, a major tenth, a perfect 12th, a double octave, etc. The function in the bass will be a descending pattern of the following intervals: whole tone, semitone, sesquitone, whole tone, whole tone. This is the

inversion of the melodic function obtained by differentiating by the same modulus the descending whole-tone scale in the bass. We find then that the whole-tone scale differentiated either in a descending bass or in an ascending melodic line will result in an identical function, inverted, and will thus constitute a reciprocal function, or an idempotent. Most interesting of all such reciprocal sets are those in which the principal equation is tonal and the derivative is atonal. A good example is an ascending diatonic scale in the melody arranged in two-part counterpoint with the stipulation that the derivative function should be a descending set seeking the nearest available nominal consonance. Under such conditions the differentiated ascending C major scale in the melody will result in a quasi-chromatic descending derivative set in the bass: C, B, A, A-flat, G, F-sharp, E and E-flat. But an ascending C major scale in the bass, under similar conditions will produce a different descending derivative in the melody, C, B, G-sharp, F, E, C-sharp, B, A. The different results are explained by the fact that while a perfect fifth is a consonance, its inversion, a perfect fourth, is not. Using consonant intervals as the functional operator is of interest because of the possibility of arranging atonally shaped melodies in triadic harmonies. There is a fertile field for experimentation along these lines, for instance harmonizing the ascending chromatic scale in the melody using only members of a single major triad in the bass. (Beginning with C in the melody, it is possible to harmonize the ascending chromatic scale up to A by using only members of the F major triad in the bass, descending and ascending without producing any dissonant intervals, e.g., C, A, F, C, A, F, A, C, F, A.) Such exercises in consonant counterpoint provide unexpected illumination on the nature of diatonic and chromatic scales in their relationship to triadic tonality (6) Intervallic progressions using only consonant intervals with certain specifications can provide a fresh resource for new contrapuntal techniques. A very fertile set of conditions is this: select two consonant intervals and use them in an unbroken series of alternations, with this proviso, that one of the voices must move by degrees, that is a major or a minor second up or down, the other voice adjusting itself accordingly to form the next interval. Let us take the octave E-E and the fifth as the next interval. We now move the upper E to F; since the next interval must be a perfect fifth, the lower voice must move to B-flat. Now let us move the upper note back to E, and since the next interval is again an octave, then the lower voice must go down to E as well. It is now the turn of the lower voice to move up and down gradually. It moves up to F; since the next interval must be a perfect fifth, the upper voice must come down from E to C. The F in the lower voice now returns to E, and since the next interval must be an octave, then the upper voice ascends from C to E. Now the lower voice goes down to D; the next interval is a perfect fifth, so the upper voice comes down from E to A. Trying again, while observing the same conditions of gradual progression vs. free intervallic leaps, the upper voice may go a major second up to F-sharp; in this case the lower voice must respond by moving up to B, forming a perfect fifth with F-sharp; after a return to the octave on E, the upper voice may descend to D-sharp, which will be seconded by the lower voice going up to G-sharp. Then both voices return to their respective E's, and the lower voice will take over the role of the *cantus firmus*. It will move, as the upper voice did before, to F-sharp, forcing the upper voice to move to C-sharp, and after passing through the octave, will descend to D-sharp, necessitating the lowering of the upper voice to A-sharp. The final interval will again be the octave. What is remarkable in this little exercise is that every note of the chromatic scale will be covered, and nine minor triads will be outlined by their tonics and dominants. By adding the missing mediants for each one of these chords in different octaves, one would obtain a third voice of surprising melodiousness. The next experiment may be conducted with a dissonant interval alternating with a consonant interval and finally with two dissonant intervals. The addition of supplemental contrapuntal voices will supply a further resource. (7) Homeological variations, obtained by extensions or compressions of thematic intervals provide a novel method of structural variations. The simplest case is exemplified by a uniform duplication of all intervals. Such an operation would convert Bach's *Chromatic Fugue* into an impressionistic piece of music, because all its semitones would be replaced by progressions of exotic sounding whole-tone scales. If the intervals of the same fugue are halved, the outcome will be a complex of icositetraphonic harmony.

Prepared Piano. PREPARED PIANO is an instrumental technique, which alters the sound by placing various small objects, such as bolts, nuts, metal clips, coins, on the piano strings. The idea may be traced to the old schoolboy trick of putting a piece of paper on the piano strings to produce a tinkling, harpsichord-like sound. The first modern composer to experiment scientifically with such devices was Henry Cowell, who initiated the technique of playing directly on the piano strings, mostly glissando, and developed an extraordinary skill in stopping the strings so as to change their pitch, enabling him to play an ascending scale on the keyboard which, because of the alteration of the length of strings, resulted in a descending scale in actual sound. His disciple John Cage explored further possibilities along these lines, and gave the name to the altered instrument of PREPARED PIANO.

Prolepsis. Schlegel said: "Der Historiker ist ein rückwärts gekehrter Prophet." The notion that a historian might be a prophet of the past is most provocative. The modern cultivation of some of the recessive traits of the musical past represents such a prophecy turned backwards. Consecutive fifths were the rule before the advent of tertian counterpoint; they were strictly forbidden in classical music, but returned early in the 20th century in the guise of neo-archaic usages, and were further reinforced in the practice of consecutive triadic harmonies. The dissonant heterophony of ancient modalities was incorporated as a novelty in NEO-PRIMITIVISM. The "Wicked Bible" became a collector's item because of a negative particle inadvertently omitted from the commandment forbidding adultery. Erik Satie drew a table of anti-commandments in his *Catéchisme du Conservatoire* in which he ridiculed the elevation of once forbidden practices to the status of harmonic laws: "Avec grand soin tu violeras/ Des règles du vieux rudiment./ Quintes de suite tu feras/ Et octaves pareillement./ Au grand jamais ne résoudras/ De dissonance aucunement./ Aucun morceau ne finiras/ Jamais par accord consonnant." The exclusion of major triads in the Schoenbergian table of commandments is the most striking instance of PROLEPSIS. Indeed, every determined violation of the academic rules becomes a case for PROLEPSIS if such a violation becomes itself a rule.

Proletarian Music. The ideological upheaval that accompanied the Soviet revolution of 1917 posed an immediate problem of creating arts that would be consonant with the aims and ideals of socialist society. Since the political structure of the Soviet government was that of the dictatorship of the proletariat, it was imperative to postulate a special type of literature, drama, art and music, that would be proletarian in substance and therefore accessible to the popular masses. Some Soviet theoreticians proposed to wipe off the slate of the arts the entire cultural structure that preceded the revolution and to create a *tabula rasa* on which to build a new proletarian edifice. Among suggestions seriously offered by some musicians in the early days of the Soviet revolution was the confiscation of all musical instruments in order to abolish the tempered scale and to construct new instruments based on the acoustically pure intervals. A more appropriate suggestion was made to compose music which included sounds familiar to a proletarian worker. A symphony of the factory was actually staged in an experimental demonstration, with singers and players placed on rooftops. Shostakovich included a factory whistle in the score of his *May First Symphony*. Alexander Mossolov wrote a ballet called *Iron Foundry*, in which a large sheet of steel was shaken to imitate the sound of the forge. Unsuccessful attempts were made to proletarianize the librettos of old operas. In one production, Puccini's opera *Tosca* was advanced from the Napoleonic times to those of the Paris Commune. Tosca kills not the chief of the Roman police but the anti-Communard general Gallifet, disregarding the fact that the actual general Gallifet died in bed long after the fall of the Commune. Meyerbeer's opera *The Huguenots* was renamed *The Decembrists* and the action transferred to December 1825 to celebrate the rebellion of a group of progressive-minded aristocrats against the accession to the throne of the Czar Nicholas I. The notorious Russian Association of Proletarian Musicians (RAPM) was founded in 1924 to pass judgment on the fitness and unfitness of all music for proletarian consumption. It stipulated an arbitrary code of desirable musical attributes, among them unrelenting optimism, militant socialism, proletarian class consciousness, representational programmaticism and the preferential use of major keys. Beethoven was commended by the RAPM for his rebellious spirit; among Russian composers Mussorgsky was singled out as a creator of realistic art. A difficult problem was posed by Tchaikovsky. His profound pessimism and fatalism, his reactionary political views and particularly his homosexuality seemed an insurmountable barrier for the RAPM theoreticians to overcome. But Tchaikovsky was a favorite composer not only of the popular masses but also of the entire Presidium of the Soviet of People's Commissars. Even from the purely musical standpoint Tchaikovsky was theoretically unacceptable. His preference for minor keys and for melancholy moods in his operas and symphonies were the very antinomy of all that the new society of Soviet Russia stood for. In their attempt to rationalize the popularity of the *Pathétique Symphony*, the RAPM reached the acme of casuistry. In this work, so the argument went, Tchaikovsky delivered a magnificent funeral oration on the tomb of the bourgeoisie, and the superb artistic quality of this lamentation could not fail to please proletarian listeners. But soon the dialectical self-contradictions became evident even to the most obdurate members of the RAPM and factional strife pulled their ideology apart. There were also signs of repugnance against the vicious attacks led by the RAPM against the surviving composers of the pre-revolutionary times, greatly esteemed Conservatory professors and any others who dared to oppose its untenable ideology. The entire controversy was suddenly resolved when the Soviet government summarily disbanded the RAPM. As one composer expressed the nearly unanimous satisfaction at this action, "We could once again dare to write music in 3/4 time," alluding to the RAPM's ridiculous insistence that proletarian music ought to be written in march time.

The valid residue of PROLETARIAN MUSIC found its way to Germany and to America assuming special national idioms. Simplicity of form, utilization of popular dance rhythms and, in theatrical music, a selection of subjects from Revolutionary history or class warfare, were the main characteristics of music for the Proletariat. In America, Proletarian opera flourished briefly in the 1930's with Marc Blitzstein as its chief proponent. In Germany, Kurt Weill, working in close collaboration with the dramatist Bertolt Brecht, created a type of music drama that in its social consciousness had a strong affinity with PROLETARIAN MUSIC. In Russia itself, after the disbandment of the RAPM, viable ideas of PROLETARIAN MUSIC were absorbed in the doctrine of SOCIALIST REALISM.

Prolixity. Brevity is not necessarily an ideal; PROLIXITY is not always a fault. In classical music, PROLIXITY was ingrained in the forms of sonata and court dances, with the required repetitions of complete sections. Only the impatience of modern performers impels them to disregard such redundancies. "Brevitate gaudent moderni," to quote a recurring *incipit* of medieval musical treatises. Beethoven's *Eroica* concludes with the tonic chord repeated 28 times. By contrast, Prokofiev's *March* from *Love for Three Oranges*, ends abruptly on a single C major triad. The natural aversion of modern musicians to restatement and overstatement extends also to tonal sequences with their predictable turns. This homologophobia led finally to the collapse of the tonal system itself, and inspired Schoenberg to promulgate the principle of non-repetition of thematic notes and the formulation of his method of composition with twelve tones related only to one another.

Pseudo-Exoticism. To an imaginative composer, the attraction of exotic lands is in inverse ratio to available information about such lands and in direct ratio to the square of the distance from the non-beholder. "Turkish" music, which had nothing in common with real Turkish modalities, enjoyed a great vogue in the 18th century and was used as a PSEUDO-EXOTIC resource by Mozart. When dancers from Indochina came to perform at the Paris Exposition of 1889, French musicians were fascinated by the unfamiliar sounds of resonant bells and muffled drums in the percussion group that accompanied the dancers. The emergence of IMPRESSIONISM in France owes much to this dance music from the Orient as refracted through the "auricular sites" of a European. The legends of the East provided poetic materials for song texts and operatic librettos. These tenuous impressions were transmuted into a *musique nouvelle*, vibrant with voluptuous *frissons*. Oriental scales were represented in the works of Debussy, Ravel and their imitators by the pentatonic scale which could be conveniently played on the black keys of the piano keyboard. Great composers were able to create a new art derived, however inaccurately, from Oriental sonorities; in fact, several composers, natives of Asia, who studied music in Paris, began to mold their own authentic modes in the Impressionistic manner. When the novelty began to fade, the pentatonic scale, the tinkling bells and other paraphernalia of Oriental music, found their way into the commercial factories of vulgar musicians plying their trade with much profit in the semi-classical division of "modern" music, in Broadway shows and on the soundtrack of exotic movie spectaculars. The proliferation of this PSEUDO-EXOTICISM resulted in the contamination of the genuine product, so that Orientalistic music eventually disappeared from decent practice.

Ragtime. RAGTIME is the earliest manifestation of American syncopated music, which was soon to rise to glory in JAZZ. It was RAGTIME that gave prominence to the piano in popular music. Its rhythmic formula approximates that of the Toccata, with rapid motion and cross-accents. Henry F. Gilbert and Charles Ives cultivated RAGTIME rhythms early in the century. Debussy made use of RAGTIME rhythms in his *Golliwog's Cake Walk* in the piano suite *Children's Corner*. The proliferation of RAGTIME must have been pervasive, considering the outcries of shock and indignation in the music periodicals in the dying days of the old century. An editorial writer fulminated in an article entitled "Degenerate Music," published in *The Musical Courier* of 13 September 1899: "A wave of vulgar, filthy, and suggestive music has inundated the land. The pabulum of theater and summer hotel orchestras is 'coon music.' Nothing but RAGTIME prevails, and the cake-walk with its obscene posturings, its lewd gestures. . . . One reads with amazement and disgust of the historical and aristocratic names joining in this sex dance. Our children, our young men and women, are continually exposed to the contiguity, to the monotonous attrition of this vulgarizing music. It is artistically and morally depressing, and should be suppressed by press and pulpit." In 1901 the American Federation of Musicians adopted a resolution that its members "shall henceforth make every effort to suppress and discourage the playing and publishing of such musical trash by substituting the works of recognized and competent composers, thereby teaching the general public to appreciate a wholesome, decent, and intellectual class of music." When the famous prima donna Nordica included a song by the American composer Ethelbert Nevin in her Chicago recital in 1901, the Chicago *Tribune* deplored her "sense of the fitness of things" in singing a "coon song" alongside a group of German lieder. The monthly *Journal of the International Music Society*, in its issue of June 1905, described RAGTIME in the following words: "It suggests the gait of a hurried mule among anthills; there is a cross-rhythm, with a kind of halting contrapuntal ornamentation in the accompaniment which sometimes brings a stress onto the fourth beat of the bar. The phrases being no longer presented with regular and recurrent pulsations, give rise to a sense of disorder, which, combined with the emotional expression of the music, suggests an irresponsibility and a sense of careless jollity agreeable to the tired or vacuous brain."

As late as 1916, RAGTIME was still a phenomenon to be abhorred, to judge by a letter to the editor from the writer Ivan Narodny published in the New York *Evening Sun*: "The rhythm of RAGTIME suggests the odor of the saloon, the smell of backyards and subways. Its style is decadent. It is music meant for the tired and materially bored minds. It is essentially obvious, vulgar, and yet shockingly strong for the reason that it ends fortissimo." But there were also some philosophically analytic voices in the press. Rupert Hughes wrote soberly in the *Musical Record* of Boston of 1 April 1899: "If RAGTIME were called *tempo di raga* or *rague-temps*, it might win honors more speedily. If the word could be allied to the harmonic *ragas* of the East Indians, it would be more acceptable. The Negroes call their clog-dancing 'ragging' and the dance a 'rag.' There is a Spanish verb *raer* (to scrape), and a French naval term, *ragué* (scraped), both doubtless from the Latin *rado*. RAGTIME will find its way gradually into the works of some great genius and will thereafter be canonized, and the day will come when the decadents of the next, the 20th century, will revolt against it and will call it 'a hidebound, sapless, scholastic form, dead as its contemporaries, canon and fugue.' Meanwhile, it is young and unhackneyed, and throbbing with life. And it is racial."

Redundancy. In electronics guidance systems, REDUNDANCY is a safety factor in the proper functioning of the machine. If a part fails, its redundant replacement immediately goes into action; and if that one fails, still another part is activated to perform the same function. In music, REDUNDANCY is represented by an ostentatious repetition of a thematic motive. It has its application in serial complexes of intervalic, rhythmic and coloristic parameters. By assigning a certain interval for a redundant use by an instrument, an associative equation is established, so that the interval becomes the identifying motto of the instrument itself. Some serial composers assign a single note to an instrument, so that the instrument and the note become inalienably bound. This evokes the memories and practices of serf orchestras in Tsarist Russia, consisting of wind instruments, of which each could produce but a single note, so that each serf playing that instrument often became known under the nickname of E-flat, F-sharp, etc. (When several serfs escaped from the estate of a music-loving Russian landlord, he put out an official notice asking the police to be on the lookout for the fugitives, giving their musical names as identification.)

Retardation. The device of RETARDATION, melodic, harmonic or contrapuntal, consists of holding over a certain note or a harmonic complex while other parts of the musical fabric are shifted. In modern music RETARDATION is not developed in accord with the moving elements but continues indefinitely in order to create a sustained discord. In pandiatonic techniques, this procedure results in a chain of superpositions of the principal triadic harmonies.

Rock 'n' Roll. American popular music has evolved from the dual resources of urban and rural folksongs. Urban popular music found its primary inspiration in the unique modalities of the Negro Spirituals, with their lowered third and seventh, which constitute the foundation of the BLUES. RAGTIME, JAZZ, SWING and such lateral developments as BEBOP and BOOGIE-WOOGIE, all preserve the character of city music. Quite different was the type of popular music cultivated in the rural regions of the country, which represented mostly the tradition of European, and particularly English, folksongs. This country music was marked by a leisurely pace devoid of the nervous excitement and syncopated beat peculiar to the popular productions of city life. With the advent of the electronic age, the barriers between urban and rural music were brought down. In the ensuing implosion and fusion of both genres, a new art was born, which found its fullest expression in the phenomenon of ROCK 'N' ROLL.

The combination of the words ROCK and ROLL appears for the first time on a Columbia phonograph record issued in the early 1930's; the rhythm of this specimen was that of a barcarolle, and the words Rock and Roll obviously referred to the gentle swaying of a boat on the river. This rural serenade was gradually transformed into a much more aggressive type of popular music, ROCK 'N' ROLL, or simply ROCK. Its cradle was in the radio broadcasting studios of Tennessee about 1950. In it, the weaker rhythms of country music overflowed the syncopation of classical JAZZ and reduced the aggressive asymmetry of the urban product to the monotony of an even beat in square time. In ROCK 'N' ROLL the pendulum-like rhythmic motion produces a tremendous accumulation of KINETIC ENERGY, leading to a state of catatonic stupefaction among the listeners and the players themselves. The effect of this constant rhythmic drive is similar to that of the sinusoid wave with a steadily increasing amplitude created by the march of a regiment of soldiers across a suspension bridge, which can break the strongest steel. Thanks to the electronic amplification, ROCK 'N' ROLL became the loudest music ever heard. Otologists have warned that its addicts may lose the sensitivity to the higher harmonics of the human voice and become partially deaf. Ralph Nader, the American Cassandra of urban civilization, has cautioned the public against the danger of sonic pollution by ROCK 'N' ROLL in a letter addressed to a member of the Congress of the United States.

The protagonist of ROCK 'N' ROLL was Elvis Presley, who developed the pelvic technique of rhythmic swing. (He became known as Elvis the Pelvis.) Four Liverpudlians, who became celebrated under the cognomen The Beatles (a palimpsest of Beat and Beetles), joined the ROCK 'N' ROLL movement but evolved a distinctive style of their own, with some characteristics of the English ballad.

The remarkable feature of ROCK 'N' ROLL is the revival of archaic modality with its characteristic plagal cadences, the Dorian mode being a favorite. In harmony, the submediant is lowered in major keys and becomes the minor third of the minor subdominant triad. Parallel triadic progressions, adopted by ROCK 'N' ROLL, also impart an archaic modal quality to the music. It may well be that the fusion of old modes and modern rhythms will create a new type of SYNCRETISM of musical folkways.

Time magazine commented on ROCK 'N' ROLL in its issue of 18 June 1956: "An unrelenting, socking syncopation that sounds like a bull whip; a choleric saxophone honking mating-call sounds; an electric guitar turned up so loud that its sound shatters and splits; a vocal group that shudders and exercises violently to the beat while roughly chanting either a near-nonsense phrase or a moronic lyric in hillbilly idiom."

The Canadian underground newspaper, grandly named *Logos*, gave in 1969 this description of ROCK 'N' ROLL as a social force: "Rock is mysticism, revolution, communion, salvation, poetry, catharsis, eroticism, satori, total communication, the most vibrant art form in the world today. Rock is a global link, as young people everywhere plug into it and add to the form. What this new music suggested was raising your level of consciousness away from the fragmented, intellectual, goal-oriented time and material world to a unified sensual direction in a timeless spiritual environment."

The greatest mass demonstration of ROCK 'N' ROLL, and perhaps the greatest manifestation of the attractive power of music in all history, was the Woodstock, N.Y., Festival in August 1969, when an enormous crowd of young people, estimated at quarter of a million heads, congregated in a farmland to hear their favorite Rock groups. The happening had a profound sociological significance as well, for the audience consisting of youthful non-conformists, popularly known as hippies, seemed to be infused with the spirit of mutual accommodation, altruism and love of peace. ROCK 'N' ROLL music, at least on that occasion, proved that it has indeed the power to soothe a savage breast.

Rotation. In post-Schoenbergian developments of DODECAPHONIC MUSIC the 12-tone series is often modified by ROTATION. As the term implies, the series is shifted a space, so that at its next occurrence, it begins with the second note, and ends with the first; in the subsequent incidence, it starts on the third note, and ends on the second, etc. ROTATION in its various further developments is a fertile device of dodecaphonic techniques.

Scales. The American pedagogue Percy Goetschius used to play the C major scale for his students and ask them a rhetorical question, "Who invented this scale?" and answer it himself, "God!" Then he would play the WHOLE-TONE SCALE and ask again, "Who invented this scale?" And he would announce disdainfully, "Monsieur Debussy!"

Debussy did not invent the WHOLE-TONE SCALE, but he made ample use of it. Other scales, built on quaquaversal intervalic progressions, engaged the attention of composers: the so-called Hungarian Gypsy scale, the pentatonic scale suitable for orientalistic melismas, and the scale of alternating whole tones and semitones, which is classified in Russian encyclopedias as Rimsky-Korsakov's scale. The modern Dutch composer Willem Pijper made prolix use of it, and his disciples, believing that it was his own invention called it Pijper's Scale. In fact, this scale, formed by the insertion of passing notes in the melodically spaced diminished seventh chord, was used by Liszt, Tchaikovsky and many other composers. Scriabin derived a scale of six notes from his MYSTIC CHORD, composed of three whole tones, a minor third, a semitone and a whole tone. Alexander Tcherepnin has devised a scale of nine notes consisting of a whole tone, a semitone, a semitone, a whole tone, a semitone, a semitone, a whole tone, a semitone, a semitone. The Spanish composer Oscar Esplá wrote music based on the scale of the following intervals: semitone, whole tone, semitone, semitone, semitone, whole tone, whole tone, whole tone.

Verdi was impressed by an exotic scale which he found in an Italian music journal, where it was described as "Scala enigmatica." It consists of a semitone, a minor third, three consecutive whole tones, and two consecutive semitones. At the age of 85 Verdi wrote a choral piece based on this "enigmatic" scale.

Ferruccio Busoni experimented with possible scales of seven notes and stated that he had invented 113 different scales of various intervalic structures. The first theorist to examine and classify scales based on the symmetrical division of the octave was Alois Hába, in his book *Neue Harmonielehre*. Joseph Schillinger undertook a thorough codification of all possible scales having any number of notes from two to twelve, working on the problem mathematically. In his *Thesaurus of Scales and Melodic Patterns*, Nicolas Slonimsky has tabulated some two thousand scales within the multiple octave range, including such progressions as the Polytetrachord, bitonal scales of eight notes, scales of three disjunct major or minor pentachords aggregating to two octaves, etc.

Progressions of large intervals, thirds, fourths or fifths, cannot be properly described as scales, without contradicting the etymology of the word derived from scala, a ladder. But helix-like constructions, involving spiraling chromatics may well be called scales. Quarter-tone scales and other microtonal progressions also belong in this category.

Score. A systematic arrangement of the vocal or instrumental parts of a composition on separate staves one above the other . . . *Close* or *compressed score*, a Short score . . . *Full* or *orchestral score*, one in which each vocal and instrumental part has a separate staff . . . *Pianoforte score*, a piano arrangement of an orchestral score, the words of any leading vocal parts being inserted *above* the music without their notes . . . *Open score*, a Full score . . . *Organ score*, like Pianoforte score, sometimes with a third staff for pedal bass . . . *Short score*, any abridged arrangement or skeleton transcript; also, a 4-part vocal score on 2 staves . . . *Supplementary score*, one appended to the body of the score when all parts cannot be written on one page . . . *Vocal score*, that of an *a cappella* composition; also, the vocal parts written out in full, usually on separate staves, the piano accompaniment being arranged or compressed (from the full instrumental score) on 2 staves below the rest. PMMT

Sensory Impact. The quantitative expansion of technical devices in modern music led to a corresponding SENSORY IMPACT on the listeners, often reaching the threshold of physical pain. Incessant playing of modern dance music, electronically amplified beyond the endurance of an average person, may well produce a positive conditioned reflex among the young. Professional music critics have for a century complained about the loudness of modern music, beginning with that of Wagner, but in their case the SENSORY IMPACT is measured not so much by the overwhelming volume of sound as by the unfamiliarity of the idiom. The epithets such as "barbaric" were applied with a fine impartiality to Wagner, Tchaikovsky, Berlioz and Prokofiev, while Debussy, Strauss and Mahler were often described as "cacophonous." It is the relative modernity that makes the SENSORY IMPACT intolerable to a music critic. "This elaborate work is as difficult for popular comprehension as the name of the composer," wrote the Boston *Evening Transcript* in its review of Tchaikovsky's *First Piano Concerto*. An index of vituperative, pejorative and deprecatory words and phrases, the Invecticon appended to Nicolas Slonimsky's *Lexicon of Musical Invective*, demonstrates the extraordinary consistency of the critical reaction to unfamiliar music. Even the gentle Chopin did not escape contumely; he was described in a daily London newspaper as a purveyor of "ranting hyperbole and excruciating cacophony."

Serialism. SERIALISM is a method of composition in which thematic units are arranged in an ordered set. Tonal SERIALISM was promulgated by Schoenberg in 1924, as the culmination of a long period of experiments with atonal chromatic patterns; in retrospect, Schoenberg's method may be regarded as a special case of integral SERIALISM, much as the special theory of relativity is a subset of general relativity. Schoenberg's method deals with the 12 different notes of the chromatic scale; integral SERIALISM organizes different intervals, different rhythmic values, dynamics, etc. in autonomous sets. Fritz Klein expanded the serial concept of dodecaphonic sets to different rhythmic and intervalic values. In his score, *Die Maschine*, published in 1921, he employs sets of 12 identical notes in irregular rhythms, "Pyramid Chords" consisting of intervals arranged in a decreasing arithmetical progression of semitones, and a harmonic complex consisting of 12 different notes and 11 different intervals, the *Mutterakkord*. The mathematical term "set," for a tone-row, was introduced by the American composer Milton Babbitt in 1946. He experimented with techniques of tonal, rhythmic and intervalic sets. George Perle proposed the term "set-complex" to designate 48 different forms generated by a fundamental dodecaphonic series. In all these sets the magic number 12 plays a preponderant role. In the general concept of SERIALISM, sets may contain any number of pitches, in any scale, including non-tempered intervals.

A summary of serial parameters comprises the following: (1) Twelve different pitches as developed by using the method of composition with 12 tones, including apocopated sets, hendecaphonic, decaphonic, enneaphonic, octophonic, heptaphonic, hexaphonic, pentaphonic, tetraphonic, triphonic, diphonic, monophonic and zerophonic. (2) Organization of melody containing 12 different intervals, from a semitone to the octave and the concomitant chords containing 12 different notes and 11 different intervals. (3) Twelve different rhythmic values, which may contain a simple additive set of consecutive integers, a geometrical progression, a set of Fibonacci numbers, etc. (4) Twelve different KLANGFARBEN, in which a melody consists of a succession of disparate notes played by 12 different instruments either in succession, in contrapuntal conjugation, or harmonic coagulation. (5) Spatial SERIALISM, in which 12 different instruments are placed in quaquaversal positions, with no instruments in close proximity. (6) Vectorial SERIALISM, in which the sound generators are distributed at 12 different points of the compass, according to 12 hour marks on the face of a clock, or else arranged spatially on the ceiling, on the floor, in the corners of the auditorium. (7) Dynamic SERIALISM, with 12 different dynamic values ranging from pianississississimo to fortissississississimo, including the intermediate shadings of mezzo-piano and mezzo-forte. (8) Ambulatory SERIALISM, in which 12 musicians make their entrances and exits one by one, in contrapuntal groups, in stretto, or in the fugue, the latter being understood in the literal sense of running. (9) Expressionistic SERIALISM, in which actors and singers assume definite facial expressions marking their psychological identity. (10) SERIALISM of 12 different sound generators, including steamrollers, motor lawn mowers, steam pipes, radiators, ambulance sirens, etc. (11) SERIALISM of 12 visually different mobiles, each producing a distinctive noise. (12) SERIALISM of 12 teratological borborygmuses and sonic simulacra of various physiological functions.

Sesquipedalian Macropolysyllabification. Quaquaversal lucubration about pervicacious torosity and diverticular prosiliency in diatonic formication and chromatic papulation, engendering carotic carmination and decubital nyctalopia, causing borborygmic susurration, teratological urticulation, macroptic dysmimia, bregmatic obstipation, crassamental quisquiliousness, hircinous olophonia and unflexanimous luxation, often produce volmerine cacumination and mitotic ramuliferousness leading to operculate onagerosity and testaceous favillousness, as well as faucal obsonation, parallelepipedal psellismus, pigritudinous mysophia, cimicidal conspurcation, mollitious deglutition and cephalotripsical stultitiousness, resulting despite Hesychastic omphaloskepsis, in epenetic opistography, boustrophedonic malacology, lampadodromic evagination, chartulary cadastration, merognostic heautotimerousness, favaginous moliminosity, fatiscent operosity, temulencious libration and otological oscininity, aggravated by tardigrade inturgescence, nucamentacious oliguria, emunctory sternutation, veneficial pediculation, fremescent dyskinesia, hispidinous cynanthropy, torminal opitulation, crapulous vellication, hippuric rhinodynia, dyspneic nimiety and favillous erethism, and culminating in opisthographic inconcinnity, scotophiliac lipothimia, banaustic rhinorrhea, dehiscent fasciculation, oncological vomiturition, nevoid paludality, exomphalic invultuation, mysophiliac excrementatiousness, flagitious dysphoria, lipogrammatic bradygraphy, orectic aprosexia, parataxic parorexia, lucubicidal nutation, permutational paranomasia, rhoncial fremitus, specular subsaltation, crapulous crepitation, ithyphallic acervation, procephalic dyscrasia, volitional volitation, piscine dermatology, proleptic pistology, verrucous alopecia, hendecaphonic combinatoriality, microaerophilic pandiculation and quasi-hemidemisemibreviate illation.

Sesquitone Scales. Sesquitone is an interval of three semitones. The SESQUITONE SCALE is a progression of minor thirds, or augmented seconds, depending on notation, and is identical with the arpeggiated diminished-seventh chord. Attractive ornamental effects can be obtained by infrapolation, interpolation and ultrapolation, or a combination of these processes. An infra-inter-ultrapolation of the SESQUITONE SCALE produces a chromatically inflected melodic pattern of an orientalistic type. The interpolation of a single note between the successive degrees of the SESQUITONE SCALE forms a scale of alternating whole tones and semitones, widely used by many composers, beginning with Liszt and Tchaikovsky. In Russian reference books it is described as Rimsky-Korsakov's Scale.

Silence. Poets often spoke of the eloquent and the harmonious quality of SILENCE. The lines in Félicien David's *Symphonic Ode* are appropriate: "Ineffables accords de l'éternel silence!/ Chaque grain de sable/ a sa voix/ Dans l'ether onduleux le/ concert se balance:/ Je le sens, je le vois!" The longest SILENCE explicitly written out is the five-bar rest in the score of *L'apprenti Sorcier* by Paul Dukas. György Ligeti composed a work consisting of a quarternote rest. The most ambitious composition utilizing the effect of total silence is *4' 33"* by John Cage, scored for any combination of instruments, *tacet*, and subdivided into three movements during which no intentional sounds are produced. It was unheard for the first time at Woodstock, New York, on 29 August 1952, with David Tudor at the silent piano.

Sonic Exuviation. The effectiveness of a modernistic climax depends on an astute interplay of contrasts. One of the most effective dynamic devices is SONIC EXUVIATION, the shedding of old skin of instrumental sonority, a return to a state of primordial nakedness and a new dressing-up of musical materials and a gradual building of another climax, a cut-off of sonic matter, leaving a soft exposed bodily shape. Such a dramatic EXUVIATION occurs at the end of the last movement of *Three Places in New England* by Charles Ives, where a tremendously powerful heterogeneous complex of sound suddenly crumbles, and a residual gentle chorale is heard in the quiet air.

Spatial Distribution. The placement of musicians on the stage, long a matter of tradition, has assumed an unexpected significance in modern times in the guise of musical vectorialism. Elliott Carter specifies the exact position of the players in his string quartets. Lukas Foss, in his *Elytres* for 12 instruments, places the musicians at maximum distances available on the stage. The use of directional loudspeakers in performances of ultra-modern works is an electronic counterpart of

SPATIAL DISTRIBUTION. In German broadcasting studios experiments have been
made in distributing a 12-tone row in serial works among 12 electronic amplifiers
placed in a clock-like circle, with each amplifier being assigned an individual note
of the series. Empirical applications of the principle of SPATIAL DISTRIBUTION have
been made by various composers early in the century, notably by Erik Satie in his
Musique d'ameublement.

Specular Reflection. The mirror image in Baroque counterpoint is applied to
mutually conjugated melodic inversions, in which the ascending intervals are
reflected by descending intervals, and vice versa. It is theoretically possible to
construct an infinite SPECULAR REFLECTION, in which the intervallic distance
between the two mirrors recedes, so that intervals are inverted in the outer
regions of the instrumental range, extending even into the inaudible spectrum of
ultra-sonic and infra-sonic sounds. In some modern works written specially for
dog audiences, ultra-sonics can achieve considerable effectiveness. Beyond the
canine auditory range, a gap occurs until the frequency of light waves is reached.
Mystically inclined composers may find pantheistic inspiration in these notions of
passing from men through dogs to infinity.

Sprechstimme. SPRECHSTIMME—literally a speech-voice—is a term popularized
in its expressive use by Schoenberg in *Pierrot Lunaire* and later works. It is an
inflected speech, notated on the regular music staff by special symbols indicating
the approximate height of the note. The method was used systematically for the
first time in 1897 in the operatic melodrama *Königskinder* by Engelbert
Humperdinck.

Stochastic Composition. The term STOCHASTIC was introduced into music by
the Greek engineer and composer Iannis Xenakis, to designate an aleatory projection in which the sonic trajectory is circumscribed by the structural parameters of
the initial thematic statement. (The word itself comes from the Greek root meaning "the aim of an arrow.") STOCHASTIC procedures are in actual practice equivalent to controlled improvisation.

Stop. 1. That part of the organ mechanism which admits and "stops" the flow
of wind to the grooves beneath the pipes.—2. A set or row of organ pipes of like
character, arranged in graduated succession. These are called *speaking* or *sounding* stops; they are classed as *Flue work* (having flue pipes), and *Reed work* (having
reed pipes); the Flue work has 3 subclasses, (*a*) *Principal work*, having cylindrical
flue pipes of diapason quality, (*b*) *Gedackt work*, having stopped pipes, and (*c*)
Flute work, including all flue stops of a scale too broad or too narrow to produce
diapason-tone, together with such stopped pipes as have chimneys, and all 3- or
4-sided wooden pipes . . . *Auxiliary stop*, one to be drawn with some other stop
or stops, to reinforce the tone of the latter . . . *Complete stop*, one having at least
one pipe for each key of the manual to which it belongs . . . *Compound stop*, see
MIXTURE STOP . . . *Divided stop*, one the lower half of whose register is controlled
by a different stop-knob from the upper, and bears a different name . . . *Flue stop*,
one composed of flue pipes . . . *Foundation stop*, one of normal 8' pitch . . . *Half
stop, incomplete* or *imperfect stop*, one producing (about) half the tones of the
full scale of its manual . . . *Mechanical stop*, one not having a set of pipes, but
governing some mechanical device; such are the couplers, tremulant, bell signal,
etc. . . . *Mixture stop*, one with 2 or more ranks of pipes, thus producing 2 or more
tones for each key (as the Mixture, Carillon, Cornet, Cymbal) . . . *Mutation stop*,
one producing tones a major third or perfect fifth (or a higher octave of either)
above the 8' stops (as the Tierce, Twelfth, Quint) . . . *Partial stop*, a HALF STOP . . .

Pedal stop, a stop on the pedal . . . *Reed stop*, one composed of reed pipes . . . *Solo stop*, one adapted for the production of characteristic melodic effects, whether on the solo organ or not . . . *Sounding* or *speaking stop*, one having pipes and producing musical tones.—3. (*a*) On the violin, etc., the pressure of a finger on a string, to vary the latter's pitch; a *double stop* is when 2 or more strings are so pressed and sounded simultaneously; (*b*) on wind instruments with finger-holes, the closing of a hole by finger or key to alter the pitch; (*c*) on wind instruments of the trumpet family, the partial closing of the bell by inserting the hand. PMMT

Surrealism. The word SURREALISM was coined in 1903 by the French poet Guillaume Apollinaire in his fantastic play *Les Mamelles de Tirésias*, in which he treated the problem of a transsexual transplantation of mammary glands, and which he subtitled "drame surréaliste." SURREALISM became a fashionable movement when André Breton published a surrealist manifesto in 1924. In it, he described SURREALISM as "psychic automatism," anti-rationalistic in essence and completely spontaneous in its creative process. Fantasy and free association were the normative factors of Surrealistic literature and art. Apollinaire described SURREALISM as the rational technique of the improbable. Jean Cocteau equated it with the essence of poetry; in his film *Le Sang du Poéte* he proposed to give a "realistic account of unreal phenomena." The famous French handbook, *Nouveau Petit Larousse*, defines SURREALISM tersely as "tendance d'une école à négliger toute préoccupation logique." Surrealism is oxymoronic in essence, thriving on the incompatibility of the opposites, exemplified by such images as cold flame, thunderous silence, painstaking idleness, quiet desperation. Names of persons often have a surrealistic ring. A Boston dentist, Dr. Toothacher, a Chicago gangster Alturo Indelicato, a Canadian insurance salesman John Death, were living examples of SURREALISM. The furlined cup and saucer, created by the 23-year-old artist Megret Oppenheim in 1936, is a typical surrealistic artifact. Surrealistic incongruity was exemplified also in a piece called Bagel Jewelry, a composition by a New York artist, in which a real bagel was encased in a jewelry box, with a pricetag of $100.

In a modern production of *Hamlet*, the King's line, "We shall call up our friends," acquired a surrealistic twist because of a telephone receiver placed on the table. The Renaissance paintings representing Biblical scenes in which musicians perform on the lute and the theorbo, are both anachronistic and surrealistic in their effect. SURREALISM possesses an oneiristic quality, in which dreams become more real than life. The etymology of the word implies a higher degree of realism, penetrating into the subliminal human psyche.

Surrealist artists are fascinated by musical subjects. Salvador Dali humanized musical instruments. In one of his paintings, a faceless cellist plays on the spinal column of a human cello mounted on a pin. On its buttocks there are the familiar resonators in the forms of symmetric gothic F's. (Life imitates art. At an avant-garde concert in New York a lady cellist performed a solo on the spine of a fellow musician, using a regular bow and applying occasional pizzicatti to his epidermis.) Another musical painting by Dali, bearing the surrealistic title *Six Apparitions of Lenin on a Piano*, represents several heads of Lenin crowned with aureoles strewn across the keyboard. The Belgian surrealist René Magritte painted a burning bass tuba. In the art work *Object for Destruction* by the American surrealist Man Ray, a print of a human eye was attached to the pendulum of a metronome. Real metronomes are the instruments in the score by the Hungarian modernist György Ligeti, containing 100 metronomes all ticking at different speeds. In his vision of socialist music of the future, the Soviet poet Vladimir Mayakovsky conjured up a symphony with rain conduits for flutes. The American band leader Spike Jones introduced a latrinophone, a surrealistic lyre made of a toilet seat strung with violin strings.

Apollinaire urged artists, poets and musicians to cultivate "the insane verities of art." No one has followed his advice more ardently than Erik Satie. He incarnated the spirit of inversion. He entitled his utterly surrealistic score *Parade* "ballet réaliste." Jean Cocteau wrote: "Satie's *Parade* removes the sauce. The result is a completely naked object which scandalizes by its very nakedness. In the theater everything must be false in order to appear true." Satie was very much in earnest when he wrote, "J'emmerde l'art—c'est un métier de con." The titles of his piano pieces are typical of surrealistic self-contradiction: *Crépuscule matinal de midi, Heures séculaires et instantanées, Tyrolienne turque, Sonatine bureaucratique, Fantaisie musculaire, Trois morceaux en forme de poire* (the latter, printed under a cover representing a pear, was a defiant response to criticism that his music was formless).

Swing. Among the many ephemeral terms descriptive of varieties of JAZZ, SWING has gained a permanent historical position. It is not a new slang expression. The word SWING appears in the titles of old American dance tunes: Society Swing of 1908, Foxtrot Swing of 1923, Charleston Swing of 1925. In 1932 Duke Ellington wrote a song with the incipit, "It Don't Mean a Thing if It Ain't Got That Swing." SWING music achieved its first great boom in 1935, largely through the agency of the jazz clarinet player Benny Goodman, introduced to the public as the King of Swing. The American magazine *Downbeat* described SWING in its issue of January 1935 as "a musician's term for perfect rhythm." The November 1935 issue of the magazine carried a glossary of "Swing terms that cats use," in which SWING was defined as "laying it in the groove." This metaphor, borrowed from the phonograph industry, gave rise to the once popular adjective "groovy," in the sense of neat, perk and pert.

SWING music must have exercised a hypnotic effect on the youth of the 1930's. The New York *Times* of 30 May 1938 ran the banner headline, "Swing Band Puts 23,400 in Frenzy. . . . Jitterbugs Cavort as 25 Orchestras Blare in Carnival." Self-appointed guardians of public morals lamented the new craze: "Pastor Scores Swing as Debasing Youth, Declares it Shows an Obvious Degeneracy in our Culture and Frothiness of Age," the New York *Times* headlined. Stravinsky, then a recent American citizen, endorsed Swing. *Time* Magazine quoted him as saying in January, 1941: "I love swings. It is to the Harlem I go. It is so sympathetic to watch the Negro boys and girls dancing and to watch them eating the long, what is it you call them, frankfurters, no—hot dogs—in the long rolls. It is so sympathetic. I love all kinds of swings."

Symbolic Analysis. An overwhelming compulsion on the part of many modern composers to return the art of music to its source, mathematics, is behind many manifestations of the Avant-Garde. Yet no attempt has been made to apply symbolic logic to the stylistic and technical analysis of modern music. A simple statistical survey can determine the ratio between unresolved dissonances and consonant structures in modern works as compared to those of the past. Such an analysis would indicate in mathematical terms the process of the emancipation of dissonances. The next step would be to tabulate certain characteristics of a given modern school of composition and note their presence in another category, which would help to measure the extent of its influence. The Whole-Tone Scale, for instance, was cultivated particularly by the French Impressionists, but it can be found in works of composers who do not subscribe to impressionist esthetics. Progressions of second inversions of major triads in parallel formation, moving by sesquitones, are typical of IMPRESSIONISM. But the same formations can be encountered in the music of non-impressionists. Ravel concludes his string quartet with such triadic progressions, and so does Gustav Holst in his suite *The Planets*, but they are never found in the works of Hindemith, a paragon of Neo-Classicism, or in those of Prokofiev. The index of tonality is very strong, amidst dissonances, in Stravinsky, but is totally absent in Schoenberg. All these styles, idioms and techniques can be designated by a system of symbols; intervals would be numbered in semitones; upward motion would be symbolized by the plus sign, and downward motion by the minus sign. In this scheme the whole-tone scale would be shown by the formula 6 (2), denoting six degrees of two semitones each, with a plus or minus sign indicating the direction of the movement. A bitonal chord such as formed by C major and F sharp major, can be indicated by the symbol, MT for major triad and the number 6 for the tritone. The synchronization of these triads can be indicated by brackets: (MT) (MT + 6). More importantly, symbolic formulas can describe a style. The music of Hindemith, which lacks the Impressionistic element entirely, can be formulated as 50% NC (for Neo-Classical) + 50% NR (Neo-Romantic), with dissonant content and strength of tonal centers indicated by additional symbols or subscripts. Stravinsky's early music could be circumscribed by symbols ED for Ethnic Dissonance. Dodecaphonic method could be indicated by the coefficient 12. Other symbols would denominate metric and rhythmic symmetry or asymmetry. In the SYMBOLIC ANALYSIS of an eclectic composer such as Delius, with basic romanticism modified by a considerable influx of impressionistic harmonies and colors, the following formula would be satisfactory, with R for Romanticism, C for Classicism, E for Ethnic quality and I for Impressionism: 40% R + 20% C + 30% E + 10% I. A table of styles, idioms and techniques, may be drawn in the manner of the periodical table of elements. Just as vacant spaces in Mendeleyev's schematic representation indicated unknown elements which were actually discovered at a later time, so new techniques of modern composition may well come into being by searching application of SYMBOLIC ANALYSIS.

Synaesthesia. Color associations with certain sounds or tonalities are common subjective phenomena. It is said that Newton chose to divide the visible spectrum into seven distinct colors by analogy with the seven degrees of the diatonic scale. Individual musicians differed greatly in associating a sound with a certain color. The most ambitious attempt to incorporate light into a musical composition was the inclusion of a projected color organ in Scriabin's score *Prometheus*, in which the changes of instrumental coloration were to be accompanied by changing lighting in the concert hall. The most common association between tonality and color is that of C major and whiteness. It is particularly strong for pianists for the obvious reason that the C major scale is played on white keys. However, Scriabin who had a very strong feeling for color associations correlated C major with red. By all conjecture F-sharp major should be associated with black, for it comprises all five different black keys of the piano keyboard, but Scriabin associated it with bright blue and Rimsky-Korsakov with dull green. Any attempt to objectivize color associations is doomed to failure if for no other reason than the arbitrary assignment of a certain frequency to a given note. The height of pitch rose nearly a semitone in the last century, so that the color of C would now be associated with C-sharp in relation to the old standards. Some composers dreamed of a total SYNAESTHESIA in which not only audio-visual but tactile, gustatory and olfactory associations would be brought into a sensual synthesis. Baudelaire said: "Les parfums, les couleurs et les sons se répondent." J.K. Huysmans conjured up an organ of liqueurs. He describes it in Chapter IV of his book *A Rebours*: "Interior symphonies were played as one drank a drop of this or that liqueur creating the sensations in the throat analogous to those that music pours into the ear. In this organ of liqueurs,

Curaçao sec corresponded to the clarinet with its somewhat astringent but velvety sound; Kummel suggested the oboe with its nasal quality; Menthe and Anisette were like the flute, with its combination of sugar and pepper, petulance and sweetness; Kirsch recalled the fury of the trumpet; Gin and Whiskey struck the palate with the strident explosions of cornets and trombones; Vodka fulminated with deafening noise of tubas, while raki and mastic hurled thunderclaps of the cymbal and of the bass drum with full force." Huysmans continued by suggesting a string ensemble functioning in the mouth cavity, with the violin representing vodka, the viola tasting like rum, the cello caressing the gustatory rods with exotic liqueurs, and the double-bass contributing its share of bitters.

Composers in mixed media, anxious to embrace an entire universe of senses, are seeking ultimate SYNAESTHESIA by intuitive approximation, subjective objectivization and mystical adumbrations. Schoenberg was extremely sensitive to the correspondences between light and sound. In the score of his monodrama *Die glückliche Hand* he indicates a "crescendo of illumination" with the dark violet light in one of the two grottos quickly turning to brownish red, blue green and then to orange yellow.

Synchrony. Metric or rhythmic SYNCHRONY is an inclusive term of which POLYMETRY AND POLYRHYTHMY are specific instances. Synchronization demands absolutely precise simultaneity of sets of mutually primary numbers of notes within a given unit of time, e.g. 3:2, 5:3, 11:4, etc. Triplets and quintuplets are of course common in free cadenzas since Chopin's time. (There is a consistent use of 4 beats against 3 in Chopin's *Fantaisie-Impromptu*.) But arithmetical precision in synchronizing larger mutually primary numbers of notes cannot be obtained by a human performer no matter how skillful, or by several performers playing different rhythms at once. Such SYNCHRONY becomes feasible with the aid of electronic machines. In 1931, Henry Cowell, working in collaboration with the Russian electric engineer, Leon Theremin, constructed a device, in the form of concentric wheels, which he called Rhythmicon. By manipulating a rheostat with a rudimentary crank, the performer automatically produced precise synchronization of the harmonic series, the number of beats per time unit being equal to the position in the series, so that the fundamental tone had one beat per second, or any other time unit, the second partial note had 2 beats, the third, 3 beats, etc. up to 32 beats produced by the rim of the Rhythmicon. The result was an arithmetically accurate SYNCHRONY score of 32 different time pulses. Since only the mutually non-primary numbers of beats coincided in the process, the collateral effect of rotating the machine was the production of an eerie scale of upper overtones, slower in its initial notes, faster as the position of the overtone was higher. The speed of rotation of the Rhythmicon wheel could be regulated at will, so as to create any desired alteration in tempo or pitch. The initial chord of each main division contains, necessarily so, the entire spectrum of overtones, and their simultaneous impact is of tremendous power, a perfect concord of multitonal consistency in non-tempered intonation.

An entirely novel idea of producing SYNCHRONY with mathematical precision was initiated by Conlon Nancarrow, an American composer living in Mexico City. He worked with a player-piano roll, punching holes at distances proportional to the desired rhythms. He wrote a series of etudes and canons, which could be performed only on the player piano, and which achieved the synchronization of different tempi that could not be attained by living instrumentalists. In his works he was free to select numbers with a fairly low common denominator, in which case there were occasional coincidences between the constituent parts. But the majority of his chosen proportions of the pulse tempi are such that the common denominator was not attained until the end of the piece, if at all. He also wrote a composition in which the relationship of the tempi was 2 to 2, and since the latter is an irrational number (which Nancarrow approximated to 3 decimal points) the contrapuntal parts could, at least theoretically, never meet.

Synergy. SYNERGY is defined by the American architect Buckminster Fuller, the discoverer of new principles of spherical stability in designing structures, as the "behavior of a whole system unpredicted by the behavior of any of its separate parts, or the subassemblies of its parts." SYNERGY in music is a technique whereby the last note of a segment of several thematic notes is the first note of the second segment. These segments can be separated, in which case the conjunctive note is repeated. The method is of considerable value in building serial chains, in which the concatenations of adjacent links may be freely dissolved. With this separation of links, the function of the connecting tone becomes ambiguous, serving as the imaginary tonic of the first segment or an imaginary dominant of the second segment. The specification "imaginary" is important because of the esthetic differences created by such a split of the chain.

Temperament. A system of tuning in which tones of very nearly the same pitch, like C sharp and D flat, are made to sound alike by slightly "tempering" them (that is, slightly raising or lowering them). When applied to all the tones of an instrument (as the piano), this system is called "equal temperament"; when only the keys most used are tuned (as was done formerly), the temperament is "unequal." PMMT

Temporal Parameters. The conjectural duration of a musical composition is a factor of importance per se, a TEMPORAL PARAMETER which has a decisive bearing on the cohesion and relative stability of the constituent parts of the entire work. The 20th century cultivated a type of Brobdingnagian grandiosity which seemed to equate quantity with quality. Among relatively well known symphonic works, the *Alpine Symphony* by Richard Strauss held the record for absolute length, but it was eclipsed by the *Gothic Symphony* of the English composer Havergal Brian, containing 529 pages of full score. The longest piano work of the century is *Opus Clavicembalisticum* by the English-born Parsi composer Kaikhosru Sorabji, which he played for the first and last time in Glasgow on 1 December 1930. The work consists of 12 movements in the form of a theme with 44 variations and a passacaglia with 81 variations. Characteristically, it is dedicated "to the everlasting glory of those few men blessed and sanctified in the curses and execrations of those many whose praise is eternal damnation."

While some composers kept expanding the duration of their individual works, their contemporaries followed the opposite trend towards extreme brevity of musical utterance. The pioneer of this modern concision was Anton von Webern; one of his pieces written in 1911 for several instruments lasts only 19 seconds. The Hungarian composer György Ligeti wrote a movement consisting of a single quarter-tone rest. The ultimate in the infinitesimally small musical forms was achieved by John Cage in his *0' 00"*, "to be performed in any way by anyone," and first presented in this ambiguous form in Tokyo on 24 October 1962.

Teratological Borborygmus. Modern works of the first quarter of the 20th century systematically increased the amount of massive sonorities as though their intention was to produce an otological ACOUSMA, or some other tonitruant Brobdingnagian TERATOLOGICAL BORBORYGMUS, a huge and monstrous intestinal rumbling issuing from the mouthpieces of brass instruments, shrill flageolets of the piccolos and high harmonics in the strings. It was inevitable that a reaction against this loss of all moderation should have set in among composers of the avant-garde. This reaction was made necessary because of the catastrophe of World War I, when it was no longer feasible to place huge orchestral apparatus at the service of composers of macrosonic works. The era of TERATOLOGICAL BORBORYGMUS seemed to end without a hope of recurrence, but the emergence of electrically amplified popular music of the ROCK 'N' ROLL type generated an electronic circus that promised to eclipse the deafening potentialities of the past.

Third Stream. THIRD STREAM denominates a combined art of popular music and modern techniques of composition. The term itself was used for the first by Gunther Schuller at his lecture at the Berkshire Music Center in Tanglewood, given on 17 August 1957. If the first stream is classical, and the second stream is JAZZ, THIRD STREAM is their Hegelian synthesis, which unites and reconciles the classical thesis with the popular antithesis. Instances of such synthetic usages are found in a number of modern works. The Third Stream flows in *Golliwog's Cake Walk* from Debussy's *Children's Corner*, where bits of syncopated ragtime animate the music. Gershwin's *Rhapsody in Blue* is the most important precursor of THIRD STREAM. In constructive application of THIRD STREAM, ultra-modern techniques, including serialistic procedures, can be amalgamated with popular rhythmic resources.

Tinnitus. A sustained pressure on the auditory nerve causes a condition known as TINNITUS, a persistent tintinnabulation in the cochlea in the inner ear. Schumann experienced it during the final stages of his mental illness; he heard a relentless drone on high A-flat. Smetana suffered a similar aural disturbance, but the note he heard was a high E, and he too eventually went insane. He introduced this high E in the violin part at the end of his string quartet, significantly entitled *From My Life*.

Some clinically sane composers active in the last third of the 20th century, who never suffered from a pathological TINNITUS, experimentally created an artificial one. Morton Feldman wrote a violin part with an interminable F-sharp calculated to generate a psychic TINNITUS in the outer and inner ears of performers and listeners alike. La Monte Young devised a TINNITUS of a perfect fifth with a notation, "to be held for a long time." Other ways of affecting the listener is a tape recording of a dripping faucet, or a simulacrum of "white noise" prolonged without a prospect of ever ending. Physical action may be added to a TINNITUS, such as measured drops of lukewarm water on the occipital bone of the head held down by clamps, a device helpful to keep in subjection a particularly recalcitrant listener to a piece of avant-garde music. This method was widely practiced to subdue difficult patients in the 18th-century insane asylums.

Tonal Aura. Aura is a medical term used to describe a premonitive sensation before an epileptic seizure. TONAL AURA is a useful metaphor for a coloristic hypertension created in modern technical innovations, such as playing below the bridge of stringed instruments, fluttertongue on the flute, glissando in the French horn, or a particularly unsettling borborygmus in the bass trombone. Schoenberg's score *Begleitungsmusik zu einer Lichtspielscene*, written for an unrealized abstract motion picture, contains striking instances of Musical Aura, beginning with the sections marked *Threatening Danger* and *Fear* and culminating in the finale, *Catastrophe*.

Tone Clusters. The technique of TONE CLUSTERS was demonstrated for the first time in public by Henry Cowell at the San Francisco Music Club on 12 March 1912, on the day after his fifteenth birthday. It consists of striking a pandiatonic complex of two octaves on white keys using one's forearm or a panpentatonic set of black keys, as well as groups of 3 or 4 notes struck with the fists or the elbow. Cowell notated the TONE CLUSTERS by a thick black line on a stem for rapid notes or a white-note rod attached to a stem for half-notes. By a remarkable coincidence, the Russian composer Vladimir Rebikov made use of the same device, with an identical notation, at about the same time, in a piano piece entitled *Hymn to Inca*. Still earlier, Charles Ives made use of tone clusters in his *Concord Sonata*, to be played with a wood plank to depress the keys. Béla Bartók used TONE CLUSTERS to be played by the palm of the hand in his *Second Piano Concerto*, a device that he borrowed expressly from Cowell, by permission.

Tonolalia. Glossolalia is a preternaturally inspired manifestation of spontaneous and simultaneous multilingual intercourse. TONOLALIA is an analogous verbal neologism, in black different instruments and voices disport themselves in a modernistic quodlibet. Particularly effective are antiphonal uses of TONOLALIA in which an improvised interlude is echoed by another instrument or a group of instruments.

Tritone. The medieval theorists described the TRITONE as "diabolus in musica" and ejected melodic progressions involving the TRITONE from the body of church music as the work of the devil, encompassing as it did the discordant interval of the augmented fourth unfit for a proper tetrachord. In German schools in Bach's time a music student who inadvertently made use of the augmented fourth was punished in class by a rattan blow on the knuckles of the hand.

The earliest suggestion that the use of the TRITONE may not be a *peccatum mortale* was made by Ramos de Pareja in *Musica Practica* published in 1482, but his leniency received little approbation. It was in the natural course of events that the stone rejected by the medieval builders should become the cornerstone of modern music, in all its principal aspects, POLYTONALITY, ATONALITY, DODECAPHONY. The importance of the TRITONE is derived from the very quality that disenfranchised it before, namely its incompatibility with the tonic-dominant complex. Two major triads at the distance of a tritone formed the bitonal "Parisian chord" so popular in the first quarter of the century; complementary hexachords in major keys with tonics distanced by a tritone redound to the formation of a symmetrical 12-tone row; a series of intervals diminishing by a semitone beginning with a major sixth and ending with its inversion, the minor third, forms a bitonal major chord with tonics at a tritone's distance; a chord containing all eleven different intervals is encompassed by five octaves and a tritone from the lowest to the highest note.

Ultra-Modern Music. In the early 1920's it became evident to composers using advanced techniques that the term MODERN MUSIC was no longer sufficiently strong to describe the new trends. In search of further emphasis, they chose the term ULTRA-MODERN MUSIC, that is music beyond the limits of traditional modernism. In announcing the publication of *New Music* magazine, Henry Cowell, its founder and editor, declared that only works in the Ultra-Modern idiom would be acceptable for publication. Some decades later, it was realized that ULTRA-MODERN Music, too, began to show unmistakable signs of obsolescence. Still, certain attributes of ULTRA-MODERN MUSIC have retained their validity: dissonant counterpoint, atonal melodic designs, polymetric and polyrhythmic combinations and novel instrumental sonorities.

Unpremeditated Music. Strictly speaking, no piece of music can be composed with an absolute lack of premeditation. Great improvisers of the past always had a proleptic image, in definite sounds, of what they were going to play. However, the composers of ALEATORY MUSIC in the second half of the 20th century have made serious attempts to create music without a shadow of melody aforethought, or harmony prepense. The absence of premeditation in such cases becomes as essential as in capital crime.

Urbanism. URBANISM is the music of the modern city. It derives its inspiration from urban phenomena, governed by the cult of the machine, and comprising the art of the motion pictures, automobile traffic, newspapers and magazines. Inter-urban machines (locomotives, airplanes) also enter the general concept of URBANISM. Among the most durable works of Urbanist music was Honegger's symphonic movement, *Pacific 231*, glorifying the locomotive. Luigi Russolo wrote a suite for noise instruments, subtitled "a demonstration of automobiles and airplanes," in 1913; it was the first work which contains a reference to airplanes in the title. The American composer Emerson Whithorne composed the earliest piece of airplane music for orchestra, entitled *The Aeroplane*, in 1926. Sports (prize fights, football, rugby) also attracted composers by their new urbanistic romanticism. "Machine" music received its greatest expansion in the 1920's; its typical products were the opera *Jonny Spielt Auf* by Ernst Krenek, *Machinist Hopkins* by Max Brand, and *Lindbergh's Flight* by Kurt Weill. In Russia musical URBANISM coalesced with the development of PROLETARIAN MUSIC, in which the machine was the hero of the production; an example is *The Iron Foundry* by Alexander Mossolov. *Technical Symphony* by the Hungarian composer Eugen Zador and *Poderes de Caballo*, ballet by Carlos Chávez are examples of urbanist symphonic and ballet music. Prokofiev's ballet *Le Pas d'acier*, representing the life in a Soviet factory, is also urbanist in its subject matter. The ostentatious realism of urbanist music fell out of fashion after World War II, but as late as 1964 Aaron Copland wrote a symphonic suite, entitled *Music for a Great City*, descriptive of the sounds of New York City.

Verbalization. Karlheinz Stockhausen was the first to introduce the concept of VERBALIZATION in lieu of musical notation. One of his pieces represents a parabolic curve with the following inscription: "Sound a note. Continue sounding it as long as you please. It is your prerogative." John Cage has elevated VERBALIZATION to the degree of eloquent diction. Earle Brown and Morton Feldman are inventive verbalizationists. La Monte Young tells the player: "Push the piano to the wall. Push it through the wall. Keep pushing." Nam June Paik dictates: "Cut your left arm very slowly with a razor (more than 10 centimeters)." Philip Corner limits himself to a simple command: "One anti-personnel type CBU (Cluster Bomb Unit) will be thrown into the audience."

Verismo. The term VERISMO became popular in the 1890's when it was used to describe the type of operatic naturalism exemplified by Mascagni's opera *Cavalleria Rusticana* and Leoncavallo's *Pagliacci*. The obvious etymological derivation of VERISMO is from vero, true, with reference to the realistic quality of the libretto. Soon the vogue spread into France with the production of *Louise*, a "musical romance" by Gustave Charpentier. In Germany VERISMO assumed satirical and sociological rather than naturalistic forms; in England, Benjamin Britten's *Peter Grimes* may be described as veristic in its subject and execution. VERISMO had no followers in Russia, where nationalistic themes preoccupied the interests of opera composers.

Vibration. Rapid oscillations of a sounding body, such as a string, or a column of air in wind instruments, which result in the production of definite tones. The human ear is capable of perceiving vibrations from about 16 per second to several thousand per second. The lowest *A* on the piano keyboard has 27½ vibrations per second, and the high *C* on the keyboard vibrates at 4224 per second. PMMT

Vigesimosecular Music. A Latinized form of a common word often imparts precision lacking in its vernacular counterpart. The neologism VIGESIMOSECULAR compounds the Latin ordinal numeral 20 with the word for century. By the very ponderosity of its SESQUIPEDALIAN MACROPOLYSYLLABIFICATION, the term evokes deep erudition and concentrated anfractuosity of elucubration. It is therefore reserved for advanced theories and practices of 20th-century music.

Wagneromorphism. An obsessive idolatry of Wagner, common among composers around the turn of the century, a mass genuflection and humicubation before the unquestionable genius of Wagner, produced the phenomenon of WAGNEROMORPHISM. It is characterized by a total absorption of all familiar traits of Wagner's melody and harmony, particularly chromatic suspensions, triadic fanfares, modulatory sequences and dynamic explosions followed by protracted recessions.

Wagneromanticism. This is a telescoped word to describe a style of composition much in vogue late in the 19th century, in which romantic program music is invested in Wagnerian harmonies.

White Sound. By analogy with the complementary colors of the visual spectrum, WHITE SOUND can be described as a sonic continuum containing all available tones within a certain auditory range, or a complex consisting of prescribed intervals, a pandiatonic or panpentatonic TONE CLUSTER, a dodecaphonic or icositetraphonic cumulus, etc. WHITE SOUND can be prismatically analyzed into a linear progression forming a scale of discrete tones.

Whole-Tone Scales. The WHOLE-TONE SCALE gained ephemeral popularity early in the 20th century as an exotic resource cultivated by the IMPRESSIONIST school of composers. If major tonality is masculine, and minor is feminine, then the WHOLE-TONE SCALE is of the neuter gender. It lacks modality; the intervalic progression in the WHOLE-TONE SCALE remains the same in melodic rotation. The perfect fifth and the perfect fourth, the cornerstones of tonality, are absent in the WHOLE-TONE SCALE; there is no dominant or subdominant, and no leading tone. Analytically, the WHOLE-TONE SCALE is atonal. It can also be regarded as the linear function of two mutually exclusive augmented triads. The TRITONE, the "diabolus in musica" of the medieval scholiasts is fundamental to the WHOLE-TONE SCALE, which can be built as the intussusception of three mutually exclusive tritones at the distance of a whole-tone from one another. Because of this association, the WHOLE-TONE SCALE itself became a favorite device of early modernism to portray diabolical forces, menacing apparitions and ineffable mysteries.

The earliest mention of an intentional employment of the WHOLE-TONE SCALE occurs in Mozart's comical divertimento *Die Dorfmusikanten*, subtitled "a musical joke." But Mozart used the WHOLE-TONE SCALE here not to illustrate a malevolent agency, but to ridicule the incompetence of village musicians and their inability to play in tune. The WHOLE-TONE SCALE came into its own as an ominous symbol in Glinka's opera *Ruslan and Ludmila*, in which it is used as a motto of the magician Chernomor. Rossini made use of the WHOLE-TONE SCALE in a song written in 1864 entitled *L'Amour à Pékin*, in which it was described as "gamme chinoise." The possible reason for this reference is that an ancient Chinese panpipe contains two mutually exclusive WHOLE-TONE SCALES in symmetrically disposed tubes. Liszt was fascinated with the WHOLE-TONE SCALE, and was greatly impressed by the *Fantastic Overture* which the Russian amateur composer Baron Vietinghoff-Scheel sent him, and in which WHOLE-TONE SCALES were profusely employed. In his comment on the work, Liszt described the effect as "terrifying to all long and protruding ears." Liszt himself made use of the WHOLE-TONE SCALE in his symphonic poem *Divina Commedia*, illustrating the Inferno; and he used it systematically in his posthumously published organ pieces.

The problem of harmonizing the WHOLE-TONE SCALE tonally was solved by Glinka in a sequence of modulations. Liszt harmonized a descending WHOLE-TONE SCALE which occurs in the bass, by a series of divergent major triads in root positions. It is doubtful whether Puccini was aware of Liszt's application of this harmony, but he used a precisely identical triadic harmonization of the descending WHOLE-TONE SCALE in his opera *Tosca*, as an introduction to the appearance of the sinister Roman chief of Police.

The Russian composer Vladimir Rebikov was probably the first to have written an entire composition derived exclusively from the WHOLE-TONE SCALE and its concomitant series of augmented triads, in his *Les Démons s'amusent* for piano; its title suggests that Rebikov was fully aware of the demoniac association of the WHOLE-TONE SCALE. But it was Debussy who elevated the WHOLE-TONE SCALE from a mere exotic device to a poetic and expressive medium. Its Protean capacity for change and adaptability greatly attracted Debussy and his followers, as an alternative variation of a diatonic scale. A very interesting application of the WHOLE-TONE SCALE occurs in *La Mer*; the principal theme of the first movement is in the Aeolian mode; in the third movement it appears isorhythmically as a progression of whole-tones. The first and the last sections of Debussy's *Voiles* for piano consist of whole tones with the middle section providing a contrast in the pentatonic scale.

A whole catalogue can be compiled of incidental usages of the WHOLE-TONE SCALE. Even Tchaikovsky, not usually given to modern inventions, made use of the WHOLE-TONE SCALE in a modulatory sequence illustrating the appearance of the ghost of the old Countess in his opera *The Queen of Spades*. Rimsky-Korsakov filled the second act of his opera *Le Coq d'or* with WHOLE-TONE SCALES and augmented triads to convey the impression of death and devastation of the battlefield. The entrance of Herod in *Salomé* of Richard Strauss is announced by a leading motive composed of whole-tones. Gustav Holst characterized Saturn in his symphonic suite *The Planets* by a series of whole-tone passages to evoke the mystery of Saturn's rings. Apart from astronomy, the whole-tone scale serves pure fantasy. In his symphonic fairy tale *Kikimora* Liadov paints the mischievous sprite in whole-tones. Paul Dukas introduces the hapless amateur magician in his *L'Apprenti Sorcier* in a series of whole-tones. The English composer Edward Maryon assigns the WHOLE-TONE SCALE to the changelings in his opera *Werewolf*, reserving the diatonic scale for normal children. Another English composer, Havergal Brian, has a chorus singing in WHOLE-TONE SCALES in his opera *The Tigers*, to illustrate the aerial bombardment of London by the Zeppelins during World War I. There are bits of whole-tone figures in Gian Carlo Menotti's children's opera *Help, Help, the Globolinks!* to describe the creatures from outer space. The earthlings in the opera overcome the invading globolinks in victorious C major.

The symbolism of the WHOLE-TONE SCALE is strong in Soviet music. In the opera *Battleship Potemkin* by Oles Tchisko, the Tsarist officers proclaim their authority in whole-tones. In the *Anti-Fascist Symphony* by Boris Mokrousov, the Fascists march in whole-tone steps.

A remarkable demonstration of the perdurability of the whole-tone scale as a symbol of evil is provided by Stravinsky's *Elegy for J. F. K.*, which contains within a 12-tone row two intervallically congruous groups of whole tones, each embanked in a tritone, itself a symbol of deviltry.

With the gradual decline of pictorial and sensorial programmaticism in contemporary music, the WHOLE-TONE SCALE sank into innocuous desuetude. It found its temporary outlet and a stylistic rehabilitation in dodecaphonic usages in the form of two mutually exclusive hexachords. Eventually it joined the subculture of film music. The Nazis advance on the screen to the sound of WHOLE-TONE SCALES in the trombones. Mad scientists hatch their murderous schemes to blow up the world in mighty progressions of whole-tones. Mentally disturbed maidens pluck WHOLE-TONE SCALES on the harp. When Jean Harlow, in her screen biography, climbs up the ladder in the studio before her final collapse, she is accompanied by delicate whole-tone pizzicati. The WHOLE-TONE SCALE is also used, wittily so, in satirical comment on pompous personages in animated cartoons.

Zen. The philosophy of ZEN is at once an infinitely complex and fantastically simple doctrine that accepts irrelevance of response as a legitimate and even elevating part of human discourse. This paradoxical liberating trait exercises a compelling attraction for composers of the Avant-Garde, eager to achieve a total freedom of self-expression combined with the precision of indeterminacy. The verbal and psychological techniques of ZEN can be translated into music through a variety of means which may range from white noise of (theoretically) infinite duration to (theoretically) instantaneous silences. In the field of MIXED MEDIA, in particular, ZEN provides a rich vocabulary of gestures, facial expressions, inarticulate verbalization, ambulatory exercises, performance of physiological functions, etc. In the composition of instrumental music, ZEN expands perception of the minutest quantities of sonic material and imparts eloquence to moments of total impassivity, in which the audible tones become interlopers between areas of inaudibility. Imagination and fantasy in the mind of a practitioner of ZEN may subjectively become more expressive than the realization of the creative impulse in written musical symbols.

TRANSLATIONS

In addition to writing in his adopted language, Slonimsky has produced distinguished English translations, not only of a *Scriabin* biography, whose preface was quoted at the beginning of this book, but of Futurist texts, originally in French and Italian, that are reprinted here not only for the grace of his English but because, as far as I can tell, they have not appeared elsewhere and, indeed, are rarely acknowledged in books about Italian Futurism.

DOWN WITH THE TANGO
AND PARSIFAL!

Futurist Circular Letter to Certain Cosmopolitan Friends who
Arrange Tango Tea Parties and Parsifalize

A year ago, responding to a questionnaire, I denounced the debilitating poison of
the tango. This epidemic swinging gradually invades the whole world. It threatens
to corrupt all races by gelatinizing them. We must therefore inveigh with full force
against the imbecility of this fad and turn back the sheepish current of snobbism.

The ponderous English and German tangos are mechanized lusts and spasms of
people wearing formal attire who are unable to exteriorize their sensibilities, and
plagiarize Parisian and Italian tangos. They are copulated mollusks, who stupidly
alter, morphinize and pulverize the felinity and savagery of Argentina.

To possess a woman one does not rub against her but penetrates her! A knee
between the buttocks? It should be mutual! You will say, this is barbarism! All
right then, let us be barbarians! Down with the tango and its languid thrills! Do
you believe that it is exciting to look into each other's mouth and ecstatically relish
each other's teeth like a couple of hallucinating dentists? Do you find it amusing
to uncork one another to get a spasm out of your partner without ever achieving
it yourself, or maneuver the pointed toes of your shoes like a hypnotized cobbler?
It is like Tristan and Isolde who delay their *frissons* to excite King Mark. It is a
medicinal dropper of passion, a miniature of sexual anguish, a sugared pastry of
desire, lust in open air, delirium tremens, hands and feet of alcoholics, coitus
mimed for the cinema, a masturbation waltz! Fie on this skin diplomacy! Hail the
savagery of brusque possession and the fury of muscular, exalting and fortifying
dance! Tangos are slow and patient funeral processions of sex that is dead! In the
name of health, force, will power and virility we split on the tango and its superannuated enervations!

If the tango is bad, *Parsifal* is worse, because it inoculates an incurable neurasthenia with its floods and inundations of mystical lachrimosity. *Parsifal* is a systematic depreciation of life, a cooperative factory of gloom and desperation, an
unmelodious discharge of squeamish stomachs, indigestion and heavy breath of
virgins at forty, complaints of queasy and constipated old priests, sales in bulk and
retail of remorse and elegant ennui for snobs. It is an insufficiency of blood, kidney weakness, hysteria, anemia and chlorosis! It is a brutalization of man in ludicrous progressions of vanquished and wounded notes, snorting of drunken

organs, wallowing in the vomit of bitter leitmotives, tears and false pearls of Mary Magdalene sitting in décolletage at Maxim's, polyphonic purulence of the wound of Amfortas, lachrymose somnolence of the Knights of the Holy Grail and preposterous satanism of Kundry. Away with all that obsolete offal!

Mesdames et Messieurs, Queens and Kings of Snobbism, you owe absolute obedience to us, the Futurists, the living innovators. Surrender to the enthusiastic putrefaction of the crowds the corpse of Wagner, this innovator of fifty years ago, whose music, surpassed today by Debussy, by Strauss, and by our own great Futurist Pratella, no longer means anything. We will teach you to love the living, oh dear slaves and sheep of snobbism! And here is the most persuasive argument: It is no longer fashionable to love Wagner and *Parsifal*, played everywhere, even in the provinces, or to give tango tea parties like all the good petits bourgeois. So quit the mollifying dances and rumbling organ sounds. We have something more elegant to offer you! Tango and *Parsifal* are no longer chic!

F. T. Marinetti
Milan, 11 January 1914

(Translated from the French by Nicolas Slonimsky)

FUTURIST MANIFESTO OF AEROMUSIC

Synthetic, Geometric, Curative

Our futurist temperament, accelerated by the dynamic quality of mechanical civilization, has attained a hypersensitivity thirsting after essence, speed, and trenchant decision.

Long declamations, hesitating analyses and endless trains of words-lamentations-and-bells die in boredom for the ears of those who are swiftly rising in the air.

The futurist movement, created by a synthesis of Italian innovators inspired with originality and speed, has taught and continues to teach the religion of speed, that is, the attempt to synthesize the world from above.

For, beyond all prosody, beyond free verse and outside the bonds of syntax, we have been able to obtain the synthesis and the synoptic simultaneity of unconstrained tables of words of a new poetry. Furthermore, we shall create a new futurist aeromusic whose law is synthesis—brevity beyond all music.

Music, by its very nature sensuous, enveloping, penetrating and persisting in the nerves after the fashion of a vapor or a perfume, tends towards analysis, while showing itself apt at summing up all the infinity of sensations in a stirring moment—thanks to its harmonic densities.

As futurist poets and musicians

a) We condemn music for music's sake which borders fatally on the fetishism of a set form, on virtuosity or technicism. Virtuosity and technicism have alienated Bach, Beethoven and Chopin from synthesis, and they have confined their genius in a maniacal pursuit of musical architecture and of music for music's sake, scattering and chilling the stirring ardor, the themes and the "finds" in the midst of tiresome development and depressing repetitions.

b) We condemn the custom of setting to music obsolete poems and subjects, the kind that composers, with their usual incompetence, are fatally bound to choose.

Only synthesis of free words can enable music to fuse with poetry.

c) We condemn imitation of classical music. In art, every return is a defeat, or disguised impotence. We must invent, that is to say, extract a personal musical emotion from life.

d) We condemn the use of popular songs, which has led spirits as perspicacious and cultivated as Stravinsky and most inspired talents, as Pratella and Malipiero, away from synthesis in an artificial and monotonous primitivism.

e) We condemn imitations of jazz and negro music, killed by rhythmic uniformity and the absence of inspired composers, long Pucciniesque lamentation asthmatically interrupted by slaps and by the syncopated tom-tom of railway trains.

Futurist music, a synthetic expression of great economic, erotic, heroic, aviational, mechanical dynamism, will be a curative music.

We shall have the following types of syntheses, which will enable us to live sanely in speed, to fly, and to win in the greatest war of tomorrow.

Sonorous block of feelings. Decisive crash. Spatial harmony. Howling interrogation. Decision framed by notes. The regularity of the air motor. The caprice of the air motor. Interpenetration of joyful notes. Triangle of songs suspended at a thousand metres. Musical ascension. Fresh fan of notes over the sea. Aerial simultaneity of harmonies. Anti-human and anti-impressionist expression of the forces of nature. Coupling of echoes.

Italian musicians, be futurists, rejuvenate the souls of your listeners by swift musical syntheses (not exceeding a minute), thunderously arousing the optimistic and active pride of living in the great Italy of Mussolini, which will henceforth be at the head of the Machine Age!

F. T. MARINETTI
MAESTRO GIUNTINI

(From the Italian monthly magazine, *Stile futurista*, August 1934)